Frequently Used Symbols*

C consumption
c marginal propensity to consume
D deposits
D_A demand for Item A
e excess reserve ratio
G government expenditures
I investment
ℓ currency ratio
k Cambridge k, ratio of money holdings to income
L measure of liquidity of wealth
M money
M_D demand for money
M_S supply of money
P price level
P_A price of Item A
p inflation rate
q rate of productivity increase
R reserves
r nominal interest rate
r_r real interest rate
rr reserve requirements on checkable deposits
rr_t reserve requirements on time deposits
r^{at} real after-tax interest rate
T taxes
u unemployment rate
V velocity
W wealth
w rate of wage increases
X exports
Y real income
YP nominal income
Y' personal disposable income
Z tastes

*When the superscript "e" is used in the text with any symbol, it denotes "expected." This list does not include variables used as coefficients in an equation.

MONEY, BANKING, AND THE ECONOMY

Sixth Edition

ALSO AVAILABLE:

Study Guide to Accompany Money, Banking, and the Economy

Sixth Edition

by Steven Beckman, *University of Colorado, Denver,*
and Janet Wolcutt Dimmen, *Wichita State University*

MONEY, BANKING, AND THE ECONOMY

SIXTH EDITION

Thomas Mayer, *University of California, Davis*

James S. Duesenberry, *Harvard University*

Robert Z. Aliber, *University of Chicago*

W. W. Norton & Company
New York • London

The text of this book is composed in Baskerville
with the display set in Optima
Composition by ComCom
Manufacturing by Haddon Craftsmen

Library of Congress Cataloging-in-Publication Data

Mayer, Thomas, 1927–
    Money, banking, and the economy / Thomas Mayer, James S.
Duesenberry, Robert Z. Aliber.—6th ed.
      p. cm.
    Includes bibliographical references and index.
    1. Money—United States. 2. Banks and banking—United States.
3. Monetary policy—United States. I. Duesenberry, James Stemble,
1918– . II. Aliber, Robert Z. III. Title.
HG540.M39 1995
332.1'0973—dc20   95-13313
ISBN 0-393-96848-0

W. W. Norton & Company, Inc., 500 Fifth Avenue, New York, N.Y. 10110
W. W. Norton & Company Ltd., 10 Coptic Street, London WC1A 1PU
  2 3 4 5 6 7 8 9 0

Contents

PART THREE: MONEY, NATIONAL INCOME, AND THE PRICE LEVEL

Preface

When we set out to write this text, we could only hope that its success might carry it to this Sixth Edition. Our goal then was to give students a balanced perspective on a complex subject, rather than to push one aspect of the course at the expense of others. While much has changed in each edition, our goal of a balanced perspective has remained the same, and we continue to be guided by the three major ideas that informed the First Edition.

First, the study of financial institutions need not be a boring recital of facts that students forget right after the final. To be sure, learning about institutions does involve memorizing many new terms; students must learn, for example, what a yield curve is and what the FOMC does. But a serious study of financial institutions consists of more than just memorizing a set of definitions. It also means understanding some of the most recalcitrant economic problems that our nation faces and appreciating the strengths and limitations of contending arguments about their solution. We believe that if students are introduced to these problems and their proposed solutions, it enlivens what would otherwise be mere fodder for memorization. Hence, in this (as in every) edition of our book not only do we discuss these problems as we come to them in various chapters but, in addition, we include a whole chapter on institutional reforms.

Second, the major disputes about monetary theory and policy are not such complex technical issues that they can only be understood by specialists. Although students in an introductory money and banking class certainly cannot follow the typical paper in the *Journal of Monetary Economics,* the basic issues of monetary theory and policy can be explained in language that undergraduates can understand. Hence, in this edition (as before) we take care to explain the debate between Keynesians, monetarists, and the new classicals.

Third, and now commonplace, the U.S. economy does not exist in isolation; a thorough discussion of international finance is a necessary component of a modern money and banking course. This has always been our view, and in this edition it is reflected in two ways. One is by devoting an entire part, Part Five, to international finance. The other is by including in Parts One through Four discussions of international finance wherever they are relevant. Thus, when dealing with financial institutions, we devote an entire chapter to international banking. When discussing central banking, we talk about the Bank of England, the Bundesbank, and the Bank of Japan and take up the attempt to create a European central bank. In explaining how interest rates are determined, we allow an important role for capital inflows and outflows. And in our explanation of how monetary policy affects aggregate expenditures, we give a prominent place to the exchange-rate channel.

Many changes appear in this new, Sixth Edition. Foremost among them is the increased attention to financial topics, an initiative we began in the Fifth Edition. Part One, the "finance" part of the book, now constitutes a greater portion of the book. Part of Chapter 4, "Asset Markets," is new. We have added sections dealing with changes in the relative shares of various financial institutions, the CAPM model, derivatives, the behavioral theory of finance, the concept of duration, and the principal-agent problem. In Chapter 5, "Interest Rates," the term structure of interest rates is now explained in much greater detail.

We have also introduced contemporary ideas and subjects that have matured to the point where they may usefully be imported into the classroom from the confines of professional discourse. For example, we now deal with the credit channel of monetary policy in some detail and discuss the insight it provides into the course of the Great Depression (see Chapters 24 and 27). We have reorganized Chapter 28 so that it now focuses on feedback rules for monetary policy instead of on the stable monetary growth rule. Our discussion of central banking in Chapter 11 now takes up the empirical evidence on the relation between central-bank independence and economic outcomes, as well as the partisan theory of central banking. We have supplemented our discussion of new classical theory (in Chapter 21) by taking up the new Keynesian theory. To make room for such additions, we have eliminated some now less relevant material, such as the burden of a restrictive monetary policy, which had previously been discussed in Chapter 22. All these changes are described in detail in the *Instructor's Manual*.

A number of changes have improved the book pedagogically. We now feature a revised discussion of the Modigliani-Miller theorem in Chapter 3 and a detailed discussion of the meaning of bank capital (a topic that frequently confuses students) in Chapter 6. We have also rewritten and condensed the discussion in Chapter 13 of money as endogenous. Much of Chapter 24, on monetary policy targets and instruments, has been rewritten with an eye toward simplification, and it may now be understood by students who are not familiar with the *IS-LM* mechanism. A new glossary and an appendix with answers to selected end-of-chapter questions are included to aid the study process. Also, we have provided many new boxed inserts addressing current controversies and practical applications; such inserts in the previous edition proved to promote student interest. Among the new boxed inserts are discussions of the financial problems of Orange County, California, whether banks should be required to advance social or material objectives, and currency boards.

The book is organized to permit flexible use in the classroom. To help address the time constraints that instructors face, we have shifted some of the material from chapters to chapter appendices, and thus provided greater flexibility for the selection of topics. In general, we have tried to write chapters so that they will stand independently. For example, some instructors may want to take up the tools of monetary policy along with Part One or shift the chapter on Fed organization from Part One to Part Three. Some instructors may prefer to skip most of Chapter 26, dealing with the history of Fed policy.

A *Study Guide* by Steven Beckman of the University of Colorado at Denver and Janet Wolcutt Dimmen of Wichita State University contains highlights, exercises, and problems for each chapter. We authors have written an *Instructor's Manual*, which contains brief discussions of the chapters as well as answers to the questions at the back of each chapter and more than 1,000 multiple-choice test questions. The test questions, for which we are indebted to Mary H. Acker of Iona College, are also available on computer diskette.

In preparing this Sixth Edition we were fortunate to have the assistance of Marilyn Hirsch, who helped in the revisions of Part Five and Chapters 4 and 5. We have also benefited at various stages from the insights of many colleagues, reviewers, and users of the book: Christine Amsler, Michigan State University; Robert T. Averitt, Smith College; Steve Beckman, University of Colorado at Denver; George Benston, Emory University; William Brainard, Yale University; Philip Brock, Duke University; the late Karl Brunner; Steven A. Cobb, Xavier University (Cincinnati); Eleanor Craig, University of Delaware; Tom E. Davis, Cornell University; Jonathon Eaton, Princeton University; Wilfred J. Ethier, University of Pennsylvania; Andrew Feltenstein, University of Kansas; Peter Frevert, University of Kansas; Milton Friedman, Stanford University; Jack Gelfand, State University of New York at Albany; Beverly Hadaway, University of Texas at Austin; Richard C. Harmstone, Pennsylvania State University at Worthington-Scranton; Thomas Havrilesky, Duke University; Arnold Heggestad, University of Florida at Gainesville; Robert S. Holbrook, University of Michigan; Walter Johnson, University of Missouri at Columbia; David Laidler, University of Western Ontario; Joseph Lo, University of California at Los Angeles; Robert M. Mulligan, Providence College; Peter Olsheski, Pennsylvania State University at Worthington-Scranton; Edmund S. Phelps, Columbia University; James L. Pierce, University of California at Berkeley; William Poole, Brown University; Uri M. Possen, Cornell University; Kevin L. Reffett, Florida State University; John Rutledge, Claremont Men's College; John F. Scoggins, University of Alabama; R.A. Springer, Rensselaer Polytechnic Institute; and Scot Stradley, University of North Dakota.

Donald Lamm, Drake McFeely, and Ed Parsons, all of W. W. Norton and Company, did much more for this book than any author has a right to ask of any editor. Dan Saffer, also of Norton, provided valuable editorial assistance. We are also indebted to Carol Loomis for careful manuscript editing. Finally, we owe a debt to Marguerite Crown and to Ann Frischia for excellent secretarial services on the First Edition, in the dark age before the desktop computer.

T. M., Davis, California
J. S. D., Cambridge, Massachusetts
R. Z. A., Chicago, Illinois
January 1996

ONE

FINANCE— INSTITUTIONS AND THEORY

Money

1

After you have read this chapter, you will be able to:

- Define money and understand the relationship between money, near-monies, and liquidity.
- Discuss the nature of money and its functions.
- Understand what credit money is and why it has value.

We begin with the monetary and financial systems: why they are important and how to study them. We quickly encounter the subtle but essential concept of money, which has tripped up many a student of monetary economics. We'll learn, first, to distinguish between money, on the one hand, and currency, income, and wealth on the other; second, that the value of money depends on its general acceptability; and third, that there is no sharp line of demarcation between those items that are included in the definition of money and several more or less similar items that are excluded.

IMPORTANCE OF THE MONETARY SYSTEM

Why do we create and use money? Basically, we satisfy our needs by producing goods and services, by planting crops, tightening bolts on automobiles, frying hamburgers, or lecturing on relativity theory. The printing of pieces of paper called money carries no direct benefit. If we double the output of our farms, factories, and offices we are better off, but doubling the output of money does not make us better off. In this narrow sense, money is utterly unimportant. Yet in another way money and the financial institutions associated with money are of overwhelming importance. Money makes the exchange of goods much simpler by eliminating the trouble and cost of barter. If the monetary system were to break down, so would our exchange mechanism, and since we rely on a division of labor, without an effective exchange mechanism our productive capacity would be crippled. During the Great Depression, for example, massive bank failures caused a sharp reduction in the quantity of money that severely hindered our exchange mechanism. The result was massive unemployment. There was poverty among potential plenty; people lacked basic necessities, while at the same time there were idle workers and idle factories. The means of payment needed to put them to work were lacking. Another example of a monetary system malfunctioning is unexpected inflation. After both world wars some countries experienced massive inflation, with the value of money dropping practically to zero. Conservative investors who had put their trust in government bonds and other securities denominated in fixed amounts of money were wiped out. In our own country we have not experienced anything nearly as bad since the Revolutionary War, but even so, if you had bought a $1,000 bond in 1953 and had redeemed it 40 years later in 1993, you would have got back in terms of purchasing power only $185. Figure 1.1 shows the consumer price index since 1800. The index changed little until the 1960s, but then took off. The endpaper (see inside back cover) shows the annual inflation rate since 1960.

One can argue about the relative importance of various factors in causing inflation, but it is clear that, at the very least, inflation is a monetary phenomenon in the sense that it measures changes in the value of money. Moreover, regardless of what is the underlying cause of the great inflation since the mid-1960s, it is clear that prices could not have risen nearly as much as they did if the supply of money had not increased.

How well the monetary system functions has much to do with our welfare, both national and individual. We study it for its impact on unemployment

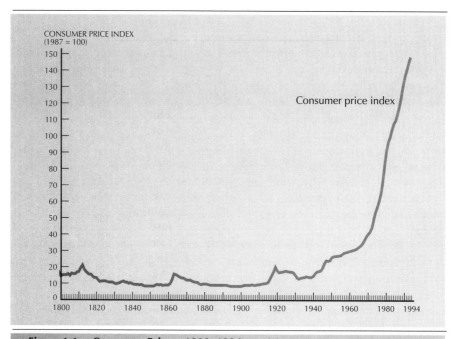

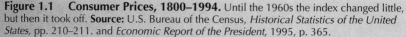

Figure 1.1   Consumer Prices, 1800–1994. Until the 1960s the index changed little, but then it took off. **Source:** U.S. Bureau of the Census, *Historical Statistics of the United States,* pp. 210–211. and *Economic Report of the President,* 1995, p. 365.

and the inflation rate, but also because in mastering the workings of the monetary system, we learn how banks and other financial institutions operate, why interest rates change, and how international exchange affects domestic policy, among other important concerns. On an individual level, understanding the financial system helps you to decide how to invest. It provides the grounding you need to understand the material you are likely to read on investment. On a more mundane level, the interest you pay when you take out a car loan depends in part on monetary factors, such as the Federal Reserve's current policy, and on the inflation rate.

OUTLINE OF THE BOOK

This book explains how the monetary and financial systems function. The first part describes the institutions that create and administer money and other financial assets. Part Two discusses the measurement and creation of money and bank reserves. The third part develops monetary and macroeconomic theory and uses it to explain how the quantity of money and other macroeconomic variables affect national income, employment rates, and price levels. Part Four deals with monetary policy. It should help you to understand what is going on when you read in the newspaper that the Federal Reserve has raised the discount rate or used other tools of monetary policy. The final part of the book focuses on how our monetary system interacts with those of other countries. Our trade deficit of recent years has provided dramatic evidence of what should have been an obvious fact all along—our country does not live in isolation. What happens to the relative values of U.S. and foreign money is a major determinant of whether or not unemployment rates rise here in the United States.

WHAT IS MONEY?

Before going any further we have to settle on a definition of money. As we will see in the following paragraphs, the common uses of the word *money* are simply too vague for economists to use in their studies. In everyday conversation the term *money* is used to mean many different things. One of these is just currency, as when you ask "Do you have any money with you?" But in economics money is never defined solely as currency, because currency and checking deposits do the same thing: they pay for goods and services. In fact, only a small proportion of the dollar value of all purchases, probably around 1 percent or so, is paid for with currency. Hence, if we were to define money as just currency, we would have great difficulty in relating money to the bulk of all purchases that are made. And it is the very fact that money is related to total purchases that makes changes in the supply or demand for money so important for our economy. Since currency and deposits on which checks can be written do the same thing and since we are interested in what money does, we must include checkable deposits along with currency in the definition of money.

One obvious objection to treating deposits as money, just like currency, is that one cannot make some small payments, such as a bus fare, by check, and that even for larger payments checks are sometimes not accepted. This is perfectly true. But it is also true that if someone buying, say, $10 million of securities tried to pay by currency, the deal would look suspicious and probably fall through. Besides, if one were to exclude checking deposits from the definition of money because checks are not accepted for small payments, one should also exclude some currency notes, such as $100 bills.

In fact, it helps to think of money as essentially deposits and of currency as the small change of the system. Although peasants like us use currency for a large proportion of our payments, this is not so for large transactors. They mainly use wire transfers, that is, telex messages or telegrams to transfer money, to avoid losing interest for the time that a check would spend in the mail. By contrast, families in 1984 used currency for 36 percent of their expenditures, checks for 57 percent, and credit cards for 6 percent.

While the popular definition of money as currency is too narrow to be useful in economics, there is another popular definition of money that is too broad. This definition treats money as a synonym for wealth. Saying "she has a lot of money" means that she is wealthy, not necessarily that she holds a lot of currency and deposits. If this particular usage were followed in economics, thus merging money with real estate, stocks, bonds, and all other types of wealth, we would be ignoring the distinctive features of money.

A third popular definition of money is income, by asking, for example, "How much money does he earn?" But defining money as income can be most confusing if we want to discuss, as we later will, whether changes in the money supply bring about changes in income. Your money holdings can increase without your income going up, as occurs, for example, if you sell some shares of stock. Likewise, your income can go up without your money holdings increasing, as happens if you allocate your salary increase to your company's stock purchase program.

Instead of defining money either so narrowly as just currency or so broadly as to include all wealth, economists define money by its functions. Anything that functions as a *medium of exchange,* as a *standard of value,* as a *standard of deferred payment,* or as an extremely liquid *store of wealth* is considered **money.** The first two of these functions are unique to money. We'll take up each of the four in turn.

Medium of Exchange

The medium-of-exchange function of money is obvious. We exchange goods and services for money, and then exchange this money for those goods and services we want to acquire. Such a roundabout system of exchange avoids the great disadvantage of barter, the need for a so-called **double coincidence of wants.** What this rather stuffy phrase means is that to undertake barter, we have to find someone who wants to obtain the goods and services we have to offer *and,* at the same time, can provide the goods and services we want to obtain in exchange.

In a primitive society with little division of labor, such a person may not be so hard to find, since only a few types of goods are being exchanged and, in any case, much of the trading is ceremonial and governed by tradition. But in an advanced society with a myriad of commodities it is a different matter. A seller of steel who wishes to exchange it for, say, vanilla ice cream would have to look around a long time before finding someone who has extra vanilla ice cream and, at the same time, wants steel. By contrast, in an economy with money this exchange process is broken into two parts. Our steel producer first locates someone who wants steel and then someone who has ice cream to sell. It is much easier to locate two such people than to locate a person who just happens to combine both of these characteristics. Another problem with barter is the indivisibility of many goods. For example, a manufacturer of TV sets could hardly give a farmer, say, one-hundredth of a TV set in exchange for a pound of butter.

The inefficiency of *direct* barter then leads to the possibility of replacing it with *indirect* barter, that is, with a system in which some people exchange their goods not directly for the goods they desire, but for the goods they believe are wanted by those who have the goods they want. The more a product is employed for indirect barter, the more useful it becomes as a *trade good* to those who receive it, and hence the greater is the willingness of people to accept it. Even if someone has no use for a piece of bronze, she will be willing to accept it in exchange for her goods, if she expects that those who have the goods she wants will be willing to barter them for bronze. Ultimately it may be used primarily to effect exchange and thus become money.

Despite the great advantage of money over simple barter we do find simple barter used occasionally in a modern economy. Barter may reappear to some extent when the monetary system breaks down during a gigantic inflation, when prices may double every day. In this case money is such a poor store of value that even the very short period of time that must elapse between receiving and spending money is too long to hold it, so that some, though not all, transactions are best conducted by barter.

A more common reason for barter is that prices are not allowed to adjust to equilibrium. Governments may impose controls to set maximum prices, and demand may substantially exceed supply at the controlled prices, as in the Russian case discussed on page 8.

Another situation in which barter is sometimes used is where there are laws setting a minimum price or where sellers with market power can keep their prices from falling when supply exceeds demand. For example, a country may set a minimum price for an agricultural commodity it exports, but then find that it cannot sell all its output at that price. One solution is to barter this commodity with another country that is in a similar fix. Then neither country has to admit that its commodity is worth less than the price asked for it.

Barter also occurs to a limited extent under more normal circumstances, for example, in trading one car for another. Apparently barter arrangements have also become significant in countries with very high tax rates, such as Sweden, as a way of evading taxes.[1]

---

[1] There are "barter clubs" in the United States that allow members to swap goods and services. However, most of this activity involves the use of script as a medium of exchange, and dollars are, of course, used as a standard of value. Hence, these transactions are not really barter trans-

Reversion to Barter

"Necessity for Bartering Helps Explain Why Committee Moved to Seize Power," so ran a headline of a *Wall Street Journal* article on the Soviet Union, following the abortive coup that tried to overthrow President Mikhail Gorbachev.* Barter is an extremely inefficient system, so why would anyone want to revert to it? The article explained it by quoting a manager of a Russian company selling industrial fire alarms: "Since money no longer has value, we've created a barter system. Customers must pay with industrial materials or spare parts that the plant needs to keep going."

As the Soviet Union's trouble worsened, the government printed more rubles to meet the large gap between its receipts and its expenditures. In a market economy such printing of money would lead to inflation. But inflations, however great, generally do not result in a widespread reversion to barter. Instead, people try to minimize the loss of purchasing power of their money by spending it as soon as they receive it and by using foreign currencies as their standard of value. In Israel in the 1970s, for example, prices were stated in dollars, though customers would pay in the local currency, shekels.

But in the Soviet economy at the time prices in the dominant government sector were not allowed to rise. Hence, people had plenty of money to buy all the available goods and then some, yet the stores were running out of merchandise. People found their money almost worthless because there was so little they could buy with it; producers were unwilling to give up valuable goods in exchange for money that was no longer functioning as an adequate medium of exchange. So why not trade your valuable goods for someone else's valuable goods instead? Clumsy and inefficient, yes, but better than getting money that you cannot do much with.

This reversion to barter would not have occurred had prices been allowed to rise. Then, Soviet citizens would have been able to buy goods and services with their rubles and would therefore have reacted to inflation like people in other countries by spending their money more rapidly and by using foreign currencies as a standard of value.

*Elizabeth Tucker, August 20, 1991.

Standard of Value and Deferred Payment

The second function of money is to act as a standard of value; this simply means that we use money as a way of comparing the relative values of various items. We think of, and express, the values of goods and services in terms of money, so that money is the measuring rod of value in the same way that a mile is a measure of distance. Obviously, a modern economy requires continual comparisons of values; buyers have to compare the offers of numerous sellers, and this would be hard to do if different sellers denominated their prices in different goods. For example, if one store demands two pounds of butter for

actions but are merely transactions in an informal currency. Presumably, a major advantage of this arrangement is that it facilitates income-tax evasion.

a pound of beef, and another store demands ten pencils for a pound of beef, which store is cheaper? A similar problem would arise in deciding whether to buy, say, beef or fish if the price of beef is expressed in terms of butter and the price of fish in terms of typewriter ribbons. To make rational decisions, we would have to know the ratios at which any one good exchanges for all the others.

Suppose that we have a very simple economy with only five commodities, A, B, C, D, and E. If there is no standard of value and we want to know the exchange ratios of these five commodities in terms of each other, we have to learn and remember ten different exchange ratios (A:B, A:C, A:D, A:E, B:C, B:D, B:E, C:D, C:E, D:E). But if we use one of these five commodities, say A, as our standard of value, we can express the prices of the other four goods in terms of it, and thus we have to learn only four exchange rates (A:B, A:C, A:D, A:E).

In general, with N commodities, if there is no standard of value, we have to learn $(N-1)N/2$ exchange rates between them. The first part of the expression is $N-1$ because the exchange rate of a commodity with itself is obviously unity, so that we have to discover the exchange rates of only $N-1$ commodities. For each of these commodities we have to know its exchange rate with every other one, so we have $(N-1)N$ exchange rates. But if we know the exchange rate of A with B we already know the exchange rate of B with A and for this reason we divide by 2. Life becomes much simpler if we use one of these commodities as the standard of value. Now, there are only $N-1$ ratios. Hence, a standard of value allows us to achieve an immense economy of effort. Assume, for example, that someone is concerned with 200 items, hardly an outlandish number. Given a standard of value he or she has to ascertain only 199 prices in terms of this standard of value. But in the absence of a standard of value, there are 19,900 exchange ratios to be learned.

Another great advantage of a standard of value is that it simplifies bookkeeping. Imagine trying to manage an accounting system in which the entries in the books consist of the physical quantities of thousands of commodities. Trying to ascertain whether you made a profit or loss would be frightfully time-consuming and quite likely impossible.

One particular function of a standard of value is to act as a standard of deferred payment, that is, a standard in which future payments are expressed. A debt is usually stated as a certain number of dollars. This use of a standard of value creates serious problems because, as unfortunately we have all found out, the value of money varies over time; the dollar you lent last year will not buy as much when you receive it back this year. In this respect, money is a poor standard of value.

Store of Wealth

The final function of money is to serve as a store of wealth. Money has several peculiarities as a store of wealth. One is that it has no, or only trivial, **transactions costs.** Transactions costs are the extra expenses—in both money and time—required to exchange one thing for another. People who decide to hold any other asset as a store of wealth must take the money they receive as income and buy this asset. Later on, when they want to obtain goods or other assets in place of this asset, they have to exchange it for money. Both of these transactions, from money into this asset and, later on, from this asset back into money, involve a cost. For example, suppose that someone saves $10,000 to buy a car next year and decides to put the $10,000 into common stock in the meantime. He now has to take the time and trouble to decide which stock to buy, call a broker, and pay a brokerage fee as well. Then, next year he has again to call the broker and pay another brokerage fee. In contrast, by holding the $10,000 as a bank deposit instead, he could have avoided both the brokerage costs and the implicit costs represented by the time and trouble required to buy the stock. This is a unique characteristic of money, and in this respect money is superior to all other assets.

A second characteristic of money as a store of wealth is that, quite obviously, its value in terms of money is fixed. This is important because debts are normally stated in money terms. Hence money has a fixed value relative to debts and other commitments, such as rental payments. Those who want an asset that will allow them to pay off a debt have a definite incentive to hold money. To be sure, money is not the only asset that has this convenient characteristic; a bond that matures when the debt is due has it too, but buying and selling a bond involve transactions costs.

The absence of significant transactions costs and the fixity of its value in terms of debts are the two basic characteristics of money as a store of wealth. There are two other characteristics that we should consider. First, the value of money changes relative to goods and services. Hence, if someone wants an asset that will have stable purchasing power over goods and services rather than over debts, money is certainly not the ideal one. Since most of us use money primarily to buy goods and services, it may seem that money is not as effective a store of wealth as is a good, even though the money price of the good will vary. While there is certainly some truth to this contention, it is subject to a major qualification. The prices of various goods and services do not fluctuate in unison. Hence, people who hold, say, a certain good or some asset such as stock may find that, despite inflation, they are even worse off than they would have been had they held money instead. Certainly, despite the inflation since 1970, someone who bought seemingly sound Penn Central stock that year, just before the company went bankrupt, would have lost more purchasing power than someone who held money instead. Unfortunately, a really good inflation hedge does not exist. Second, we should bear in mind that some types of money (most notably, currency) have no explicit yield. When you hold, say, $100 of currency you don't earn any interest, as you would were you to hold a bond instead.

Interaction of the Functions of Money

In the United States a single monetary unit, the dollar, fulfills all four functions of money. A dollar bill, for example, is a medium of exchange and a store of wealth, while prices and debts are stated in dollars. But it is not always the case that all functions of money are fulfilled by the same monetary unit. For example, in colonial America many merchants used the British pound as the standard of value in which they kept their books, but Spanish coins were a more common medium of exchange since there were more of them around. Similarly, in Britain, until fairly recently, prices of certain high-status goods, for example, expensive clothes, were stated in terms of guineas; a guinea equals one pound plus one shilling. But guineas were no longer in circulation and the customer paid for these goods with the medium of exchange, pounds and shillings.[2]

   Usually the same unit performs all the functions of money. This is so because it would be inconvenient to use different units as the medium of exchange and the standard of value. For example, suppose that the medium of exchange consists of silver coins, but that the standard of value in which prices are stated is a gold coin. Then at every purchase one would have to do a bit of mental arithmetic to calculate how many silver coins to give the merchant to meet the price set in terms of gold coins. And, as we just pointed out, as a store of wealth the advantage of money is precisely that it is the same unit as the medium of exchange (thus avoiding transactions costs) and as the standard of value (thus having a fixed value in terms of debts). And this requires that all functions be fulfilled by the same monetary unit.

MEASURING THE MONEY SUPPLY

The standard-of-value function does not permit one to measure the money supply, because the standard of value is an abstract unit of measurement. It makes no sense to say, for example, that the standard of value was $400 billion a few years ago, but is $500 billion now. Our standard of value is a dollar—period. Alternatively, we could rely entirely on the medium-of-exchange function, and measure those items used as media of exchange. In fact, this is one measure used commonly by economists. It consists of only two items, currency (plus traveler's checks) and checkable deposits. Money defined this way is called *M-1*, or "narrow money." (Credit card balances are not included, in part because credit cards are merely a way of deferring payment. When you pay by credit card you are getting credit, that is, incurring a debt that you will have to settle later on by handing over a check or currency.) Many economists believe that in determining what money is, one should stress the store-of-wealth function. They therefore prefer to include one other very liquid type of asset in the definition: savings and time deposits of $100,000 or less. This enhanced measure of money, sometimes called "broad money," is known as *M-2*. In this book, unless otherwise specified, we will use "money" to mean *M-2*.

---

[2] The guinea was originally a gold coin while the pound was a silver coin. Dealing in gold rather than silver coinage indicates superior social status, hence the use of guineas for prices of prestigious goods. There is an extensive history of the use of different types of money by various social classes. The lower classes were sometimes paid in copper while the aristocracy dealt in gold. In ancient Greece, for example, the use of gold by the common people was prohibited at one time because gold could be used to bribe the gods, and this was not something the lower classes were supposed to do. Currently we still have one remnant of this tradition of "high" and "low" money—one should not leave pennies as part of a tip.

TYPES OF MONEY

In addition to describing money by its functions, one can also describe it by its types. One type is **full-bodied commodity money** (or just **commodity money**). This is money *that has a value as a commodity fully equal to its value as a medium of exchange.* Suppose you have a gold coin that you can melt down to extract the gold. If you can sell this gold for as much as the face value of the coin, then this coin is a commodity money. Throughout history, most money that has been used has been commodity money, gold and silver for large coins and a base metal, such as copper, for small change. Traditionally countries have been on a silver standard or a gold standard in which the value of money depended on the value of the metals out of which the coins were made.

A variant of commodity money is **representative full-bodied money.** This is a type of money that usually has almost no intrinsic value, but can be redeemed in full-bodied commodity money. It is just a certificate entitling its owner to receive a certain amount of commodity money. It is at times more convenient to carry such a piece of paper than to carry a mass of heavy gold coins.

Then there is **credit money.** This is money *that does not have a value as a commodity fully equal to its monetary value and cannot be redeemed in such full-bodied money.* All U.S. money is credit money; you cannot go to the Treasury and obtain gold or silver coin in exchange for your paper money.

Our currency is **legal tender,** or **fiat money.** This means that it *has to be accepted in payment of a debt* unless the debt instrument itself specifically provides for another form of payment, such as the delivery of commodities. A deposit, on the other hand, is not legal tender. A creditor does not *have* to accept a check and can demand to be paid in currency instead. However, whether or not something is legal tender is *not* the criterion of whether it is money. As long as it is generally accepted in exchange or used as a standard of value, we call it "money."

Nature of Credit Money

An advantage of credit money over other forms of money is that it economizes on scarce resources. Instead of using gold or silver, items with a high cost of production, we use items with trivial production costs, entries on a bank's books (for deposits), paper (for currency notes), or, in the case of coins, some base metals. Money is a token entitling the bearer to draw on the economy's goods and services, and what makes each of us willing to accept it is that we know that *other people* are willing to accept it in exchange for their goods and services. It does not need to have any value as a commodity in its own right any more than the admission ticket to a concert has to be capable of producing music.

This is not to foreclose the issue of whether full-bodied money, such as gold coins, or representative full-bodied money is preferable to credit money. While the quantity of a commodity money is governed by the availability of the commodity, the government controls the quantity of credit money. Opinions

Trade in Colonial America

As an example of how misleading the story of a simple linear evolution from barter to commodity money and eventually to credit can be consider the situation in colonial America. As the historian Gordon Wood tells us, in those days there were often no banks, and in some cases not even a circulating medium. But trading took place. Mostly it was between people who knew each other. Although both barter and money were sometimes used, more often credit was used.

A farmer hired out his children or rented his boat to a neighbor for a fee of, say, 2s 6d; at the same time he used another neighbor's mill or bought a pair of shoes at the local store at a cost of, say, 3s 4d. In the absence of much specie, these fees and costs were usually not paid in cash but were instead entered in each person's account book. Through these numerous exchanges farmers built up in their localities incredibly complicated webs of credits and debts, "book accounts" among neighbors that ran for years at a time.*

Complicated as such credit arrangements were, they were preferable to barter because, as Governor William Bull of South Carolina noted in 1770, unless people knew each other intimately, barter was "extremely troublesome and unpleasant"; they were compelled to spend "near half their Time in Bargains of the most trivial as well as material Consequences."†

*Gordon Wood, *Radicalism in the American Revolution* (New York: Vintage Books, 1993), pp. 67–68.

†Cited in *ibid.,* p. 141.

can reasonably differ on whether it is better to have the quantity of money controlled by accidents, such as the discovery of new gold deposits, or by the government.[3] Some believe that governments, unrestrained by a gold standard or some other rule, tend to increase the quantity of money too fast, so that we get inflation. They do this because in the short run raising the quantity of money rapidly has a very pleasant result: unemployment falls.

The Composition of Money. Many items have been used as money at some time in some place, including whale teeth (Fiji), butter (Norway), rum (Australia), and leather (France). At one time it was usual for textbooks, such as this, to list the characteristics that make a particular substance a convenient form of money. One obvious characteristic is durability. Some others are storability, recognizability, and divisibility. But reality does not always respect what is "obvious." All sorts of items that do not have these characteristics have been used,

[3] Thus Houston McCulloch has responded to the argument that a commodity standard wastes resources with the following analogy: "A similar argument could be made for bicycle locks and chains. If metal locks could be replaced with symbolic paper locks, resources would be released that could be used productively elsewhere. As long as thieves honor paper locks as they would metal locks, your bike will be perfectly secure. Surely hardened steel and phosphor bronze shackles are evidence of irrationality on the part of those who insist on them" (Houston McCulloch, *Money and Inflation* [New York: Academic Press, 1975], p. 78).

including dead rats. In the Western world we tend to think of gold as the "natural" material for money. But while the developed world was on a gold standard for a fairly long time, it was on a silver standard for much longer.

By and large, credit money is a relatively recent innovation because it requires considerable sophistication; people have to grasp the idea that something is valuable if other people will treat it as valuable, despite the fact that it has no value in direct use as a commodity. While there had been previous episodes of credit money, most of the developed countries were on a gold standard as recently as 1930. In general, as one would expect, the evolution of money has been from concrete objects to abstract symbols, that is, from precious metals traded by weight, through coins made of precious metals, to paper money redeemable in precious coins, and to irredeemable paper money and bank deposits. But evolution has not followed a straight line. For example, goldsmiths' deposits, which were essentially checks, were used as a means of payment in seventeenth-century England at a time when paper money was not yet acceptable. Similarly, in the Pacific Island of Yap the monetary system was, in a way, more abstract than ours. The natives used large stones as money. If a canoe carrying a large stone sank, the stone could still be used as money, and transferred from one person's account to another's, even though it could not be recovered. By contrast, if a plane carrying gold between, say New York and London, crashes into the ocean we treat this gold as lost to our monetary system.

ELECTRONIC TRANSFERS: TOWARD A CASHLESS SOCIETY?

In recent years, we have experienced a further evolution of the monetary system with the spread of electronics. Not only are large payments generally made by wire transfer rather than by putting a check in the mail, but almost one in three employees in the United States has his or her salary deposited electronically by the employer. Some retailers have point-of-sale terminals, so that customers can pay by having their accounts debited automatically. More and more corporations are paying each other electronically as well. And there are plans afoot for so-called electronic purses, that is, prepaid cards that can be used to transfer money from a buyer of a good to a seller. Such cards are already used by some transit systems and telephone companies.

One can think of such electronic devices as being essentially similar to checks, but they have two advantages. One is that while strangers will not always accept your check, they will accept your electronic payment. Second, the cost of clearing electronic payments is much less than the cost of clearing checks; paper shuffling is expensive.

One can allow one's imagination to roam beyond such relatively mundane devices and imagine a completely automated payments system. All incomes and other receipts would be credited automatically to a person's account by computer. When making purchases, the buyer's account number would be punched into a computer terminal. The payment would thus be automatically transferred to the seller's account. Recurrent payments, such as mortgage payments and utility bills, would be automatically subtracted from the payer's account, as is already done in some cases. Computer enthusiasts are already developing ways of making payments on the Internet.

MONEY, NEAR-MONIES, AND LIQUIDITY

Since monetary systems change over time, the assets that are considered money change too. As a result, the distinction between money and "other things" is not clear-cut. At any particular time there may be some items that are just midway in the process of becoming money. The line of demarcation between money and nonmoney is therefore blurry. Where to draw this line depends, in part, on what our purpose is, that is, what particular function of money is the most relevant for the problem at hand. For example, if we focus on the medium-of-exchange function, we want to define money as just those items that generally function as media of exchange.

But suppose that we stress the store-of-wealth function instead. If so, we want to include in the definition of money those assets that are extremely liquid, that is, readily spendable, since it is its liquidity that differentiates money from other stores of wealth.

The liquidity of an asset depends on (1) how easily it can be bought or sold, (2) the transactions cost of buying or selling it, and (3) how stable and predictable its price is. Narrow money, at one end of the scale, has perfect liquidity. Since it already is money, there is no cost and trouble in selling it, that is, in turning it into money, and the price of a dollar is constant at one dollar. Toward the other end of the scale there are items like real estate, which may take quite some time to sell, involve a substantial brokerage cost, and may have to be sold at less than the anticipated price. We can rank all items by their liquidity, that is, by their degree of *moneyness*. This raises the question of where along this spectrum of liquidity and moneyness one should draw the line between money and nonmoney.

Liquidity is not a clear-cut concept because its three components can send different messages. Suppose that Asset A is easily sold, but at a significant transactions cost. Asset B takes longer to sell, but has almost no transactions cost. Asset C can be sold rapidly at a low transactions cost, but its price is hard to predict. It is difficult to decide which of these assets is the most liquid, and which the least liquid. Illiquidity is therefore a more subtle thing than not being able to sell an asset quickly. We generally think of a house as an illiquid asset. But you can sell your house very quickly if you offer it at, say, half its true value.

Moreover, the liquidity of an asset can vary over time in a hard-to-determine way. Suppose that you buy some stock at $100 a share and it now rises to $200. In one way this stock has become less liquid; its transactions cost has gone up because if you sell it, you have to pay a tax on your capital gain. This should make you unwilling to sell it. On the other hand, you may feel tempted to realize your capital gain, and therefore be more willing to sell it despite the tax. In this way it has become more liquid. Conversely, when stock prices fall, you can save on taxes by realizing a capital loss, but you may feel reluctant to take the loss and admit you made a mistake when you bought the stock. Liquidity therefore has a psychological element.

But if we ignore these nasty complications, we can draw up a spectrum of liquidity with *M-1* at one extreme and, say, a hoped-for inheritance at the other. Suppose now that one wants to define money in a broader way than just *M-1*. Where should one draw the line? There is no point at which one can draw an obvious and clear-cut line. Regardless of how broadly or narrowly one defines money, there are always some assets that, while excluded from the definition of money, are very close to the borderline. Moneyness is a continuum. We therefore call *items that are excluded from the definition of money but are quite similar to some items that are included* **near-monies.**

These near-monies are items that are highly liquid, but not *quite* as liquid as money. Admittedly, this is rather vague, and it is not clear exactly what items should be included. While stock in corporations is definitely not a near-money, it is not clear whether, say, a government security that matures within two years should be considered a near-money.

SUMMARY

1 The term *money* should not be confused with currency, income, or wealth.

2 The bulk of all payments (measured in dollar terms) is made by wire transfers. Currency accounts for only a trivial proportion of the value of transactions.

3 Money functions as a medium of exchange, as a standard of value, as a standard of deferred payment, and as a store of wealth. As a medium of exchange money avoids the double coincidence of wants required under simple barter. As a standard of value money simplifies the comparison of values and facilitates bookkeeping. As a store of wealth, money is characterized by the virtual absence of transactions costs and by the fixity of its value in terms of most debts. Usually the same unit serves all the functions of money.

4 In terms of measurable quantities the term *money* is used in this book to mean *M-2*.

5 All U.S. money is credit money. The value of credit money is based on the fact that it is generally accepted.

6 Some people envision a cashless society in which most transfers are by electronic book entries. But there are still many advantages to using checks and currency.

7 Near-monies are items that are not quite as liquid as money, but are highly liquid. Moneyness is a matter of degree.

KEY TERMS

money	legal tender
medium of exchange	fiat money
double coincidence of wants	full-bodied money
indirect barter	credit money
standard of value	liquidity
standard of deferred payment	near-monies
transactions costs	point-of-sale terminals

QUESTIONS AND EXERCISES

1 Define and distinguish between the following:
   a. currency
   b. money

c. income

d. wealth

*2 Are your average money holdings greater than, roughly equal to, or less than your income, or is this a meaningless question?

3 Explain why checkable deposits are included in the definition of money.

4 Explain how a medium of exchange economizes on effort. Do so also for a standard of value.

*5 What characteristics distinguish money from other stores of wealth?

6 Explain the meaning of the following terms and state how they differ:

a. full-bodied commodity money

b. representative full-bodied commodity money

c. credit money

*7 Explain why credit money has value.

8 Discuss the meaning of the term *near-monies*. What items are included?

9 Discuss what is meant by liquidity. How would you describe the liquidity of the following:

a. corporate stock

b. an expected inheritance

c. a house

d. a deposit in a savings and loan association

*10 Rather cynically one may describe the exchange of gifts at Christmas as barter. Why do people use barter at that time instead of giving each other money when money is a much better medium of exchange?

FURTHER READING

ALCHIAN, ARMEN. "Why Money?" *Journal of Money, Credit and Banking*, 9 (February 1977), part 2, 133–41. An excellent discussion of the medium-of-exchange role.

AVERY, ROBERT, et al. "The Uses of Cash and Transactions Accounts by American Families," *Federal Reserve Bulletin*, 72 (February 1986), 87–108. The results of a comprehensive survey of family payment habits.

BRUNNER, KARL, and ALLAN MELTZER. "The Uses of Money: Money in the Theory of an Exchange Economy," *American Economic Review*, 61 (December 1971), 784–806. An excellent discussion of the medium-of-exchange function of money, but one that assumes some knowledge of economic theory.

FRANKEL, S. HERBERT. *Two Philosophies of Money*. London: St. Martin's Press, 1977. A short book that asks some basic questions about the government's right to manipulate money.

MELITZ, JACQUES. *Primitive Money*. Reading, Mass.: Addison-Wesley, 1974. An informative discussion of the anthropology of money.

——— "The Polanyi School of Anthropology on Money: An Economist's View," *American Anthropologist*, 72 (October 1970), 1020–40. An interesting survey.

REDISH, ANGELA. "Anchors Aweigh: The Transition from Commodity Money to Fiat Money in Western Economies," *Canadian Journal of Economics*, 26 (November 1993), 777–95. A brief history of the move to fiat money.

SELGIN, GEORGE. "On Ensuring the Acceptability of a New Fiat Money," *Journal of Money, Credit and Banking*, 26 (November 1994), 808–27. An interesting discussion of whether the government can determine what is money.

*Answers to questions preceded by an asterisk are found in the Appendix at the end of the book.

Stocks, Bonds, and Financial Institutions

After you have read this chapter, you will be able to:

- Understand the distinction between stocks, bonds, and hybrid securities.
- Explain why bond prices decline when interest rates rise.
- Identify where the supplies of funds and the demands for them come from.
- List the main types of financial intermediaries and discuss what they do.
- Appreciate why the government regulates financial institutions.

It is only in primitive economies that money is the single or even the dominant financial asset. In all developed economies and even in most less-developed economies, money is only one of many financial assets. In this chapter we look at the reasons for this and at the broad array of financial instruments, such as stocks, bonds, and other securities, that join money in our financial system.

We also take up the institutions through which money and the other financial instruments flow. These financial institutions do not exist for accidental reasons. Instead, they are the result of individuals and institutions making mutually beneficial arrangements. There is, therefore, a certain logic to these financial instruments and institutions. They fill a perceived need, and, presumably, for any perceived need that can be met at a reasonable cost there is a financial institution or a financial instrument that meets it. Hence, we can think about the various financial instruments and institutions as ways in which people cooperate to maximize their welfare.

THE FINANCIAL SYSTEM

A **financial system** consists of the arrangements used to create and exchange **monetary claims,** that is, rights to receive money or other assets. An immense volume of financial transactions in claims and in titles to ownership exists in our economy, and a large and growing industry services it. The financial industry (including insurance) accounts for 15 percent of national income (seven times as much as agriculture, forestry, and fisheries combined) and employs about 6 percent of the U.S. labor force. Why do so many people, some of them extremely well paid, spend their time manipulating claims? Isn't this an awful waste of resources? Well, let's see.

Imagine an economy without a financial industry. In this economy people would still want to defer consumption, that is, to save, perhaps because they expect their income to dwindle or their needs to rise or perhaps because they want to leave an inheritance or to hold productive assets. Similarly, some people would want to borrow, perhaps because their incomes have fallen temporarily and they want to maintain their consumption or perhaps because a loan would let them obtain resources that they could employ profitably.

Suppose that such an economy had only one financial asset—currency—and no IOUs, so that there would be no borrowing and no lending. It would be extremely inefficient. All that savers could do would be to accumulate either currency or physical assets, such as houses or cans of food. Since it takes much expertise to buy productive physical assets (for other than one's own use), many savers would have to settle for a zero rate of return by holding currency. For those who want to invest because they see a profitable way to use resources, such as building a factory, the situation would be bleak too. The only way they could invest would be to save the necessary funds themselves. But who would be able to save enough to build, say, a steel mill?

Obviously, such an economy would be more productive if potential suppliers of funds and potential demanders of funds could get together. They would then benefit from the division of labor. The same way that it makes sense to spend one's time doing what one does best and have someone else grow the food one eats, it makes sense to have others save the funds one will invest in, say, a building or else to have someone invest the funds one has saved.

But the division of labor requires devotion of effort to the exchange of various products. In a complex economy these exchanges will be carried out by specialists. Thus we find specialized financial institutions, such as savings and loans, that bring borrowers and lenders together. One reason this task is so important is that transactions in promises to make payments are hard to evaluate. The buyer of a promise to pay (that is, the lender) is not given an actual good that he or she can evaluate in the way, say, that a buyer of bread can judge the quality of a proffered loaf. Promises are harder to evaluate than most actual goods.

A second reason is that borrowers and lenders do not want to trade in the same types of promises. The type of promise that a lender wishes to obtain when handing over his or her money is usually different from the type of promise that the borrower wants to make. To see why, one has to consider the characteristics of various types of financial assets; we will start with the distinction between equity and debt.

EQUITY VERSUS DEBT

Those who want to obtain funds can often do so in one of two ways: by selling equity (that is, direct ownership of an asset) or by selling debt (IOUs). Since we do not allow people to sell themselves, they can only borrow against their own earning power: they cannot sell equity, such as stock, in it. But for those who own nonhuman capital (that is, income-earning assets other than their own earning power), there is a choice. They can borrow using their assets as collateral, or they can sell equity in them.

Equity

Equity means ownership of some property, whether by a single individual or by a group of individuals. The advantages of ownership are straightforward: if the asset goes up in value the owner benefits directly, as, for instance, when a homeowner discovers that his house has gone up in value. The countervailing disadvantage is that the value of the property may fall.

To understand what equity is, consider first some asset, say a store, owned by a single person. The owner can make an agreement with someone that, in exchange for, say, $100,000, she will take him on as a partner and give him one-quarter of the equity in the store. He is now entitled to one-quarter of the earnings and usually to some say in how the store is run. But suppose the store earns nothing. The partner is then not entitled to any payments. He is a part-owner, not a creditor. Worse still, if the store makes a loss, then the new partner bears part of it. If the store goes bankrupt, he would even be liable for its outstanding debts, and may be forced into personal bankruptcy. (So-called limited partnerships can protect partners against this.)

Partnerships are therefore risky and people usually become partners only in enterprises about which they know a great deal and over which they can exercise some control. Reliance on single proprietorships and partnerships alone would make it virtually impossible to collect the large sums needed in many branches of industry.

Hence another form of ownership was developed—the **corporation.** A corporation differs from a partnership primarily in that the owners of the corporation are not liable for its debts. If you buy stock for $1,000 in a corporation and it fails, your loss can be no more than the $1,000 that you ventured. Apart from this a stockholder is essentially like a partner. He or she is entitled to a proportionate share of the net earnings and, through voting on the directors of the firm, has a say (though usually a trivial one) in the management of the business.

The stockholder is not a creditor, and the difference is important. While a corporation is legally obligated to pay the agreed-on interest to creditors, it is not obligated to make any payments at all to its stockholders. If it makes a loss or if it wants to plow all its earnings back into its business, it can decide not to pay a dividend. If the firm cannot repay a loan when it is due, the creditors can go to court, have it declared bankrupt, and sell off its assets to recoup their loans. By contrast, the corporation is not required to make any payments to its stockholders. Stockholders are **residual claimants.** They get whatever is left over after the firm has paid off its suppliers and employees and after it has met its interest payments. The downside for stockholders is that they are first in line to take a hit if the company incurs a loss; their stock is then worth less. The upside for them is that if the firm earns much more than it needs to pay its interest, the surplus all belongs to them.

When a firm obtains funds by borrowing it has to pay interest, but what is the corresponding cost of equity? It is giving the buyers of the new equity a share in the firm's future earnings and control, just as a partnership does when it takes on a new partner. Suppose, for example, that a company is worth $100 million, has 10 million shares outstanding, and earns $12 million. Each share therefore earns $1.20, which will usually be partly paid out as dividends and partly plowed back into the business. Assume that this company now sells an additional 10 million shares for $10 each. It is now a $200 million company, but each of the former shareholders (unless he bought some of the new stock) now owns only half as big a piece of the company as he did before. Whether this raises or lowers his income depends on whether the company earns on the new capital more or less than the 12 percent it earned on its previous capital.

Debt

Those who want to obtain funds can also borrow them, or, more formally, sell debt. One form of debt, a **bond,** is a promise by the borrower to pay a certain sum by a certain date (called its **maturity**) and to pay a set rate of interest, called the **coupon rate** or just **coupon,** until then. This coupon rate is stated on the bond and does not change unless the company that issues the bond goes bankrupt. Usually, the borrower reserves the right to repay sooner, and thus to escape the obligation to continue making interest payments. However, most corporate bonds limit the right of early repayment by a clause called a **call protection,** saying that if the bond is redeemed before a certain date, the holder will be paid a specific amount in excess of the bond's face value. (The **face value** is the value at which the bond was initially issued.)

The buyer of a bond does not have the option of redeeming it before the due date. To be sure, she can sell it before that date. However, the price she gets for it then is determined by the supply and demand for such bonds, and thus may exceed or fall short of its face value. Several factors determine the price of a bond. For now we will look at only one of them. This is the interest rate that prevails on newly issued bonds of similar maturity and risk of default. Suppose that you own a $1,000 bond that has ten years to run until maturity. It pays 5 percent interest. Corporations are currently selling new ten-year bonds that yield 10 percent, and have the same degree of risk as your bond. Would anyone offer you $1,000 for your bond? Of course not. By investing

$1,000 in a new bond, they would receive $100 a year interest, while by buying your bond, they would only get $50 a year in interest. To find a buyer, you would have to offer your bond for less than $1,000.

But how much less? To get a simple, intuitive answer let's simplify the problem by getting rid of the ten-year maturity. Assume instead that the bond has an infinite life, that it will pay interest every year, but will never be paid off. Consider now the bond buyer's choice. He can buy a new bond for $1,000, and assure himself of $100 of interest in perpetuity, or he can buy your bond and obtain $50 in perpetuity. He will offer you only $500 for your bond, since it pays him only half as much as a new $1,000 bond. Conversely, suppose that interest rates fall to 2½ percent. Your bond would then be worth $2,000, because someone paying $2,000 for it would get the same income stream from it as someone who buys two new $1,000 bonds that earn 2½ percent. Table 2.1 illustrates this principle. The second column, which shows the yield an investor receives on a $1,000 investment, is what drives the bond prices shown in the third column. Investors must receive the same return on the old and new bonds; otherwise, they would switch from the lower-yielding bond to the higher-yielding one. And since the coupon rates on the bonds differ, the only way the yields can be equal is for the price of the old bonds to adjust.

We therefore have the following rule: *for a perpetual bond the price varies strictly inversely to the change in the interest rate on new bonds.*

This strictly inverse rule holds only for perpetual bonds. To see why, ask yourself if you would be willing to pay $2,000 for a $1,000 bond with five years to maturity and with a 10 percent coupon when the prevailing interest rate on new five-year bonds is 5 percent—surely not. Suppose you did pay $2,000 for it.

Table 2.1   Yields and Prices of Bonds

	Coupon rate (percent)	Annual yield per $1,000 invested	Price of each bond with $1,000 face value	Amount earned per $1,000 invested
Interest rate on new bonds is 5 percent:				
New bond	5%	$ 50	$1,000	$ 50
Old bond	5	50	1,000	50
Interest rate on new bonds is 10 percent:				
New bond	10	100	1,000	100
Old bond	5	50	500	100
Interest rate on new bonds is 2 ½ percent:				
New bond	2 ½	25	1,000	25
Old bond	5	50	2,000	25

For five years you would be no worse off than had you bought two new 5 percent bonds for $1,000 each. In either case you would get $100 interest each year on your $2,000 investment. But after five years, when the corporation that issued the bonds redeems them, they will pay only $1,000 regardless of what you paid for the bond. If you had bought the old 10 percent bond for $2,000 you would have a $1,000 capital loss. You will therefore not be willing to pay $2,000 for the bond. Instead you will pay for the bond an amount that gives you exactly the same after-tax yield as you would earn on a 5 percent bond. You will obviously not pay any more for it, and you will not be able to buy it for any less because there are many other potential buyers who would be glad to snap it up at a lower price. Calculating the exact price you would pay is not simple because you have to discount all the interest streams and the final repayment you receive at maturity to calculate the bond's value right now. Fortunately, there are computer programs and financial tables that do the calculations for you.

The longer it takes you to get your money back, the greater is the importance of a security's future interest payments relative to its redemption value. Hence, the prices of short-term securities change less when the interest rate changes than the prices of long-term securities do. For example, at the interest rates prevailing on March 18, 1994, a 1 percent rise in interest rates would have reduced the price of a 5-year government security by 4.2 percent, the price of a 10-year government security by 7.1 percent, and the price of a 30-year government security by 11.6 percent.

Duration

The time it takes to get your money back is measured only roughly by the maturity of the security. A more accurate measure is called **duration.** The reason why a bond's maturity is only a rough measure of how long it takes to get your money back is that you get some of your money back in the form of interest payments prior to maturity. Compare two cases. In one the interest rate on a two-year $1,000 security is 2 percent, and in the other the interest rate is 20 percent. Assume that interest is paid only once a year. In the first case your total receipts will be $1,040. You receive $20 after one year and 98 percent of these $1,040 two years from now when you get your $1,000 back plus $20 interest for the second year. In contrast, in the second case your total receipts will be $1,400. You receive $200 after the first year and only 86 percent (1,200/1,400) of your total receipts at the end of the second year. To dramatize the distinction between maturity and duration, consider a bizarre case in which the interest rate is 100,000 percent. In that case you would be almost indifferent about when you got your principal back; what would matter would be when you get the interest.

Hybrid Securities

It may seem as though the distinction between stocks and bonds, and the parallel distinction between equity and debt is clear-cut: one represents ownership and, hence, "a piece of the action," while the other is a loan. But in as sophisticated a financial system as ours, there are financial instruments that possess some of the characteristics of debt and some of the characteristics of equity. Consider, for example, a bond that is very risky and hence has a high yield. Despite this high risk it is legally a debt, just as a low-risk bond is. But in its economic characteristics it bears some similarity to stock. As far as the investor is concerned, a major distinction between stocks and bonds is that the yield on a typical bond is much more certain than the yield on stock is: unless the corporation goes bankrupt, the bondholder knows what she will earn on the bond. But with a risky bond the proviso "unless the corporation goes bankrupt" is important. Bankruptcy may very well occur. Hence the holder of a risky bond is in a position similar to that of the stockholder. Both have to worry a great deal about what will happen to the corporation.

Among other instruments that blur the economic distinction between stocks and bonds are **preferred stock** and **convertible bonds.** Preferred stock is stock on which the corporation has to pay a minimum dividend before it is allowed to pay a dividend to the holders of its common stock. The income on preferred stock is therefore more assured than the income from common stock is. In exchange for this greater safety preferred stockholders give up the opportunity for greatly enhanced earnings because, regardless of how much the corporation earns, there is a maximum dividend that it has to pay on the preferred stock.

Convertible bonds are bonds that at the owner's discretion can, at a future date, be exchanged for stock at a fixed price. Suppose, for example, that you buy a bond that is convertible in January 1999 into the corporation's common stock at a price of, say, $50 a share. If at that date the stock sells for, say, $100, you make a very nice capital gain, but if the stock sells for only, say, $49 dollars, your right to acquire it at $50 is worthless. Hence, even though you are a bondholder, you stand to benefit if the corporation's stock goes up. Since convertible bonds pay a lower interest rate than do equivalent regular bonds, you also lose something when you buy the convertible bond of a corporation whose stock does not go up sufficiently to make your conversion privilege worth something.

IDENTIFYING THE SUPPLIERS AND DEMANDERS

Having looked at the two basic types of financial assets, stocks and bonds, we now consider who supplies and demands these assets. There are four major sectors of our economy: households, businesses, government, and foreigners. In all four there are some who supply funds and others who demand them. While, on the whole, households are net lenders, some households borrow so that they can consume more than their incomes or buy physical assets such as a house. Businesses borrow from households, but also lend both to each other and to households. Both businesses and households lend to governments by buying government securities. The federal government is the biggest net borrower, but it is also a lender. Some agencies of the federal government, such as the Small Business Administration, make loans to particular types of borrowers; similarly, some state and local government retirement funds lend to businesses by buying their bonds. Foreigners provide funds when they buy IOUs, such as bonds, and demand funds in the United States.

THE SUPPLY OF FUNDS

Suppliers of funds obviously desire as high a yield on their loans as possible. But they also want to minimize the risk they take. Lenders generally prefer a security that pays an assured 5 percent to another security that has a 50 percent chance of paying 30 percent, and a 50 percent chance of paying −20 percent, so that what is called the **mathematical value** of its payment is also 5 percent ($50\% \times 30\% + 50\% \times -20\%$). One reason is that evaluating securities is a difficult and time-consuming job, and buying risky securities requires more evaluation than does buying safe ones. Second, for most people the utility of an additional dollar of income is less to them if their incomes are already high than if their incomes are low. Hence people are better off with a middling income than with a gamble that gives them a chance of receiving either a very high or a very low income and has a mathematical value equal to the middling income. Third, it seems plausible that people dislike uncertainty.

THOSE WHO DEMAND

All the major sectors of the economy contribute to the demand for funds. For households and governments (both foreign and domestic), debt is the only option when funds are needed. The business sector faces the interesting choice between raising funds through debt or raising funds through issuing more equity.

Households

Like other borrowers households want to minimize both the cost of debt and the risk to which debt exposes them. The riskiness of a debt is related to its maturity. The longer the household has to accumulate the funds needed to pay off the debt, the less the chance is that it will be unable to do so and will go bankrupt. For example, few families would feel comfortable with a mortgage that is due every 90 days and that would have to be refinanced four times a year.

The riskiness of a debt also depends on whether the debt, for example, a mortgage, carries a fixed rate of interest or an interest rate that varies. Many mortgage loans, virtually all home-equity loans, and an increasing number of other loans are now made at variable rates. The interest rate on these loans is adjusted periodically to match some measure of current rates.

Which is riskier, a fixed-rate loan or a variable-rate loan? At first glance it may seem that a variable-rate loan is always riskier since the borrower does not know what her payments will be. But this is wrong. What matters is the riskiness of the whole portfolio, not the risk on any individual asset or debt. Consider, for example, someone who owns $100,000 of short-term securities and has a $100,000 mortgage outstanding. If she has a variable-rate mortgage and interest rates rise, she pays more on her mortgage, but earns more on her securities. And if interest rates fall, her loss of income is balanced by her lower mortgage costs. Hence, for her, a variable-rate mortgage is a good hedge, while a fixed-rate mortgage is risky. Moreover, as we will explain later, one major determinant of interest rates is the inflation rate. Inflation raises not only the interest rate, but also most people's nominal incomes. Hence, many people may feel more secure with a variable-rate mortgage than with a fixed-rate mortgage. If inflation raises the interest rate that they have to pay, their income rises too, so that they can afford to pay the higher rate.

Governments

In recent years the federal government has borrowed extensively. It is in a special position as a borrower because its securities are treated as riskless. This is due in part to its ability to create money and to raise taxes and in part to a belief that if the federal government were ever to renege on its debts, the whole financial system would collapse and all other financial assets would be worthless too.[1] State and local governments do not have the power to create money, and their bankruptcy would not wreck the entire financial system. Hence, their securities are not treated as riskless.

As Table 2.2 shows, the federal government borrows both short term and long term. Short-term borrowing has the disadvantage that it forces the Treasury to come to the market frequently to sell new securities to pay off the maturing ones. On the other hand, long-term borrowing is probably somewhat more costly than short-term borrowing.

Businesses

Unlike households and the government, a corporation can raise funds either by borrowing or by selling equity. It can also reinvest its earnings instead of paying them out as dividends. This is equivalent in some ways to selling additional stock to the existing stockholders because the value of stock held by the stockholders goes up by the amount of the reinvested earnings. Which one of these three ways of raising funds should it use?

The simpleminded answer is that the firm's decision whether to issue (that is, sell) new stock or to borrow should depend on whether the interest rate it would have to pay if it would borrow is greater or less than the yield it would have to provide to induce people to buy its stock. This yield consists not only of the dividend, but also of letting the new owners share in any capital gains that accrue on this stock. Since for most companies the interest rate at which they borrow is less than the yield they would have to provide to new stockholders, the simple—but wrong—answer is that they should usually borrow.

---

[1] The government can create money by selling securities to the public, with the Fed then buying an equivalent amount of securities from the public. As the Fed buys securities and pays for them, it creates reserves for depository institutions, which these institutions then use to create money. All this may sound mysterious now, but it will be explained in detail in Chapters 13 and 14.

Table 2.2 Maturity Distribution of the Federal Debt, December 1994	
Debt due with (years):	Percentage of total
1	33.1%
1–5	41.2
5–10	10.5
10–20	3.1
20 and over	12.0
Total	100.0
Memorandum items:	
Average maturity	5 yrs, 6 mo
Total debt (millions of $)	$2,737,789

Note: Covers only marketable, interest-bearing debt held by private investors.
Source: *Economic Report of the President,* 1995, p. 377.

This answer is wrong because it ignores the effect that additional borrowing has on the risks faced by previous lenders and also by the stockholders. As already discussed, creditor claims take precedence over stockholder claims. The firm's equity capital therefore serves as a cushion of safety for lenders. If a firm finances itself, say, 40 percent by borrowing and 60 percent by issuing stock, then this firm can lose 60 percent of its value, and still have enough left to pay off its creditors. By contrast, suppose it had financed itself 75 percent by borrowing and only 25 percent by issuing stock. Then, if it lost more than 25 percent of its value, it would not have enough left to pay off its debts.

Another way of seeing the risk created by borrowing is to look at the flow of payments the firm has to make. Consider a firm that earns $10 million, of which $8 million goes to pay wages and the cost of materials, $1 million is used to pay interest, and $1 million is profit. If this firm's earnings fall to $9 million, it no longer has a profit, but it can still pay the interest that it is legally required to pay. Suppose that this firm had issued less stock and had borrowed more, so that it had to pay, say, $1.5 million in interest. Then, if its earnings fell to $9 million, it would not earn enough to pay all the interest it owed, and unless it could borrow more, sell off some of its assets, or sell additional stock, it would go bankrupt.

Hence, regardless of whether one looks at it in terms of the net worth of the firm or in terms of the flow of payments the firm has to make, the more a firm borrows relative to its equity capital, the riskier it becomes. One consequence of assuming additional risk is that stockholders will demand a higher yield on their stock. If the firm's earnings do not go up sufficiently to compensate stockholders for the additional risk, the price of the firm's stock will fall.

In addition, the more a firm has borrowed relative to its capital, the greater the risk assumed by anyone who lends to it. Hence, if it refinances its prior borrowing, for example, by renewing a bank loan, or if it borrows more, it will then have to pay a higher rate of interest. Thus, *when a firm borrows, its interest costs rise by more than just the interest it is paying on the new loan.* To be sure, old loans carry a previously set interest rate, and hence it may take quite some time until the day of reckoning arrives, but when it does, the firm will have to pay a higher interest rate when it renews or refinances previous loans. Creditors sometimes protect themselves against this delay by a clause in the loan agreement that limits how much the firm can borrow in the future.

The Interaction of Supply and Demand. Figure 2.1 shows the intersection of supply and demand curves for a bond. The supply curve slopes upward. If a borrower can sell his promise to pay, say, $1,000 in ten years plus 8 percent interest until then, for, say $1,100, he will be inclined to sell more such promises than if he can sell them for only $900. The demand curve shows that the lower the market price of a bond is, the greater the demand for bonds will be because the greater will be the earnings of the bond. Someone who buys a $1,000 bond for $500 earns twice as much interest as someone who buys it at $1,000. At p_1 the supply of bonds exceeds the demand, driving bond prices down, while the opposite happens at p_2. Only at p_0 is the market in equilibrium.

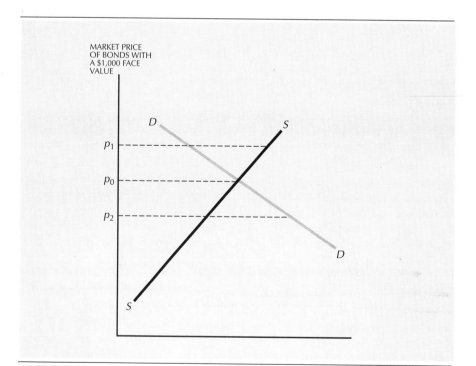

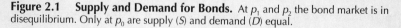

Figure 2.1   Supply and Demand for Bonds. At p_1 and p_2 the bond market is in disequilibrium. Only at p_0 are supply (S) and demand (D) equal.

FINANCIAL MARKETS AND FINANCIAL SERVICES

Having looked at the financing decisions of suppliers and demanders of funds, we now turn to the markets and institutions that bring suppliers and demanders together. Before turning to the specific institutions that operate in these markets, however, we first look at the various financial markets.

Types of Private Financial Institutions

Financial institutions earn their keep by bridging the gap between borrowers and lenders. Table 2.3 lists the major types of financial institutions and their functions, and Table 2.4 shows the size of some of these institutions. They are classified as agents, retailers, depository institutions, and insurers. Some of them fall into several of these classes. By "agents," we mean institutions that undertake certain tasks for borrowers or lenders, such as providing them with advice or buying or selling securities for them. By "retailers," we mean firms, such as Merrill Lynch, that deal with households. Everyone is familiar with the services that insurers provide. But the services of financial intermediaries need more discussion.

Financial intermediaries are firms, like banks, that operate as the middlemen of the financial system. They issue claims on themselves (such as the deposits that savings and loans issue) and use the funds they obtain in exchange for these claims to make loans to others, that is, they intermediate. Why is this a useful activity? There are three benefits to financial intermedia-

---

Table 2.3   Selected Types of Private Financial Institutions

	Function			
	Agents	Retailers	Depository Institutions	Insurers
Stockbrokers	X			
Investment banks	X	X		
Security dealers	X	X		
Private pension funds	X			X
Mutual funds	X			
Money-market mutual funds	X		X*	
Life insurance companies	X	X		X
Casualty insurance companies				X
Finance companies		X		
Commercial banks			X	
Savings and loans			X	
Mutual savings banks			X	
Credit unions			X	

*Money-market funds are not, strictly speaking, depository institutions, but function much like them.

Table 2.4   Assets of Selected Financial Institutions, 4th Quarter 1994

	Assets		
	Billions of $	Percent	Main Types of Assets
Depository Institutions			
Commercial banks	$4,161.7	76.2%	Mortgages, commercial loans, consumer loans, debt securities
Savings and loans and savings banks	1,013.1	18.5	Mortgages, U.S. gov. securities
Credit unions	294.4	5.4	Consumer loans, mortgage loans
Total	5,469.2	100.0	
Other Institutions			
Pension funds:			
Private	2,356.4	26.8	Stocks and bonds
State and local gov.	1,222.7	13.9	Stocks and bonds
Insurance companies:			
Life	1,887.9	21.5	Stocks and bonds, real estate
Other	669.5	7.6	Stocks and bonds, real estate
Mutual funds:			
Money market	605.3	6.9	Treasury bills, commercial paper
Other	857.7	9.8	Stocks and bonds
Finance companies	741.7	8.4	Consumer loans, business loans
Security brokers and dealers	443.4	5.0	Stocks and bonds
Total	8,784.6	100.0	

Source: Board of Governors, Federal Reserve System, *Flow of Funds Accounts, Flows and Stocks Outstanding,* Fourth Quarter 1994, pp. 86, 94, 96, 98, 100.

tion: (1) lower transactions costs, (2) the provision of long-term loans along with enhanced liquidity, and (3) reduced risk.

To see how financial intermediaries reduce information and transactions costs, consider the following example. Suppose a corporation wants to borrow $10 million. Since not many households are able to make a $10 million loan, the corporation would have to scurry around and borrow, say, an average of $10,000 from a thousand households. Since these households would not know that this corporation wants to borrow from them, the corporation would have to seek them out by extensive advertising. And then it would have to convince them that it is a sound borrower. A financial intermediary, say, a savings and loan, on the other hand, is set up to collect the funds of many small depositors.

It does not have to let households know that it wants their funds every time a borrower approaches it for a loan. The public already knows that the savings and loan would like its funds. Moreover, since the savings and loan's deposits are insured, depositors (except those with over $100,000 on deposit) do not have to investigate its credit standing. To be sure, the financial intermediary itself has to investigate the credit standing of the borrower, but a single investigation by an expert is much less costly than a thousand separate investigations by amateurs.

There is also a deeper sense in which financial intermediaries can be said to reduce transactions costs. It is difficult for lenders to judge the soundness of a potential borrower. The borrower has an incentive to go to considerable trouble to make his business look sound and creditworthy. He may, for example, adopt accounting procedures that make his business look more profitable than it actually is. How can the lender, who is after all an outsider to the business, judge? One possibility is for the lender to have an ongoing arrangement with the borrower whereby she makes frequent loans to this borrower. Over the years she then accumulates information about the borrower's soundness. Another way is to function as the borrower's depository institution and to use information about the borrower's deposit account to evaluate his soundness. For example, if a firm operates with such a low deposit level that it often has difficulty meeting its payroll, that suggests that this firm is not a good credit risk. Banks have available both their knowledge of the borrower's deposit behavior and what they have learned from previous dealings with him, and hence are in a good position to decide whether to make him a new loan.

Moreover, once a loan is made the lender should monitor the borrower's behavior to ensure that he does not take too many risks. The borrower may have an incentive to make risky investments because such investments promise a high yield. But the lender, who gets none of the gains if the risky investment turns out well and stands to lose if the borrower goes bankrupt, has an incentive to prevent such risk taking. Monitoring the borrower's behavior is often costly and time-consuming and hence not worthwhile for any small lender. But it is worthwhile for a financial intermediary that has made a large loan.

A second advantage of financial intermediaries is that they create liquidity by making it possible for lenders to lend short term and yet for borrowers to borrow long term. As we previously discussed, borrowers generally want to borrow longer term than lenders want to lend. Here is where the financial intermediary comes in. Despite the fact that it has used its depositors' funds to make long-term loans, a bank or a savings and loan association can promise its depositors that they can withdraw their deposits at any time. If it has many individually small depositors whose decisions whether to withdraw their deposits are independent of each other, then it can predict quite well the probability distribution of deposit withdrawals on any given day and hold small but sufficient reserves to meet such withdrawals.

However, this fortunate state of affairs does not *always* hold. Suppose, for example, that the public becomes afraid that a certain bank will fail. Large, and hence not fully insured, depositors will then try to withdraw their deposits on a massive scale. The financial intermediaries may not have sufficient liquid funds available to repay these deposits. Until 1934, when the federal government started to insure deposits, the United States suffered numerous financial panics in which many banks failed.

The third benefit of financial intermediation is that, by pooling a large number of loans, the intermediary reduces lenders' risk. Suppose that, in the absence of financial intermediaries, there are 100 lenders, each making one $1,000 loan. Suppose further that only 99 of these loans will be repaid. Every lender is then afraid that he or she will be the unlucky one. But if the lenders pool their funds, then each lender loses only 1 percent of his or her loan, and thus avoids the risk of a large loss in exchange for accepting a sure small loss. By depositing their funds into a financial intermediary, lenders, in effect, pool them; the depository institution pays them 1 percent less than the interest rate they would otherwise get and uses this 1 percent to offset the loss from the 1 percent of the loans that are not repaid.

Types of Financial Intermediaries

There are two types of financial intermediaries, depository and nondepository institutions. **Depository institutions** issue claims on themselves that are fixed in dollar terms. These are our familiar checking deposits and time deposits. The four depository institutions are commercial banks (usually just called "banks"), savings and loans, mutual savings banks, and credit unions. Since these institutions issue the major part of our money supply, they are extremely important. Hence, we will devote two whole chapters, Chapters 6 and 7, to them. The term **nondepository institutions** is used for a variety of institutions that have the common thread of providing financial services other than taking deposits. Any one firm may, of course, consist of more than a single type of institution. For example, some stockbrokers operate mutual stock funds and money-market mutual funds, and also act as security dealers.

Stockbrokers undertake purchases and sales of securities for their customers in exchange for a commission. In addition, most stockbrokers also provide their customers with investment advice. An individual investor cannot buy or sell securities directly on the stock exchanges, but must do so through a broker who is a member of the exchange.

Investment banks, also called "merchant banks," are not banks in the usual sense; they don't take deposits. Instead these archetypal Wall Street firms operate as advisers and agents for companies that want to issue more stock or other securities. The investment bank or often a group of investment banks called a **syndicate** may buy this stock from the company, expecting to sell it for a profit. This is called **underwriting.** Alternatively, the investment bank may just act as the company's agent and get a commission for selling the stock on behalf of the company. In addition, investment banks earn a substantial income by advising firms on, and arranging, mergers and acquisitions and by providing various other services.

Security dealers are to some extent similar to brokers. But they are not merely agents for buyers and sellers. They hold an inventory of securities, albeit one that is usually very small compared to the volume of their transactions. When approached by a buyer, they can sometimes sell the requested securities out of their inventory. Security dealers differ from investment bankers by dealing mainly in the secondary market, that is, in markets for "old" securities, while investment bankers operate in the primary market, that is, in markets for newly issued securities.

Private pension funds are administered by life insurance companies, banks, or specialized pension fund managers. Many corporations provide pensions for their employees. To do so, they have to set aside some funds. Although many put aside only relatively little and plan to pay the pensions largely out of future earnings, these pension funds have accumulated at a rapid rate. Pension funds hold primarily bonds and corporate stock.

Mutual funds are firms that invest the funds they receive from their customers in securities issued by a large number of companies. Most invest in stock, but there are also a number of mutual bond funds. Mutual funds provide a way for small investors to diversify their holdings over many corporations and yet avoid the high brokerage costs of buying small quantities of many stocks. In addition, they provide professional managers who buy or sell stock as they think appropriate. However, a theory that we will discuss in the next chapter (efficient-markets theory) tells us that, on the whole, professional managers will not consistently outperform the market as a whole, and the data show that they don't. Hence, a few mutual funds economize on costs by just buying and holding a portfolio that mirrors the market and then leaving it pretty much alone. Since mutual funds are legally owned by the people who invest in them, they pay out their earnings to their investors, except for their expenses, which include a fee that the mutual funds pay to the companies that administer them. So-called *load funds* also charge an often substantial fee to the buyer. *No-load funds* do not, but some funds that advertise themselves as "no-load" actually charge fees when the investor redeems (that is, sells) the stock.

Money-market mutual funds operate just like the mutual funds described above, except that they buy safe and highly liquid short-term securities, such as Treasury bills or bank CDs, instead of stocks or bonds. Since their assets are so safe and liquid, the interest received on the shares in a money-market fund is generally enough to absorb any losses of capital value. Hence someone who puts, say, $1,000 in a money-market fund can be almost certain that she has at least $1,000 in this account. Accordingly, money-market funds allow their customers to write checks against their accounts. Money-market funds are therefore very similar to depository institutions, and one could argue that even though they are not called "depository institutions," they qualify as such.

Life insurance companies provide several financial services. They sell term insurance, which is pure insurance, other insurance policies that have a savings feature, as well as annuities (guaranteed payments that begin at a specified age). They also administer pension funds. As providers of pure insurance and annuities, they make contingent payments. With regard to the savings feature of insurance policies, when they invest the temporarily excess premiums, they act as agents for the saver if they are mutual companies and as retailers of investments if they are stock companies (that is, companies owned by stockholders). Since their liabilities are long term, they invest primarily in illiquid assets, such as long-term corporate bonds, mortgages, and stock.

Casualty companies offer insurance against accidents, fire, theft, and other losses. Some of the events against which they insure, such as automobile accidents, generate liabilities that are steady and predictable, while others, such as insurance against hurricanes, result in erratic, more or less unpredictable losses. To be able to cover such losses, casualty companies hold large stocks of financial assets, assets that are more liquid than those of life insurance companies. Some are mutuals, that is, formally owned by their policyholders, and some are stock companies, meaning that, like most companies, they are owned by stockholders.

Finance companies are financial retailers. They obtain their funds on the wholesale market by selling both long-term and short-term securities and issuing stock, as well as by borrowing from banks. They then lend these funds to households that buy specific durables or want cash loans. They also make loans to firms, lease equipment to them, and provide them with cash backed by the firm's accounts receivable. Some, called *captive finance companies*, are owned by makers of durables, such as General Motors. Finance companies have grown rapidly. Currently, the total volume of their outstanding business loans equals about two-thirds of the business loans made by banks.

Government Credit Agencies

The federal government also has a number of credit agencies that provide a greater supply of credit or lower interest rates to particular sectors of the economy than the market provides. The sectors most favored in this way are housing and agriculture, though some other groups, such as college students and small businesses, also benefit.

Among the most important federal credit agencies dealing with the housing sector are the **Federal National Mortgage Association** (FNMA or "Fanny Mae"), the **Government National Mortgage Association** (GNMA or "Ginnie Mae"), and the **Federal Home Loan Mortgage Corporation** (FHLMC or "Freddie Mac"). These agencies sell securities and make the funds they thus obtain available to the mortgage market by buying up existing mortgages. Because it is widely believed that the federal government would not let them fail, they can sell securities at a low interest rate, and thus provide cheap funds to the mortgage market. The most important federal credit agencies for agriculture are three systems of twelve regional banks: the **Banks for Cooperatives,** the **Federal Intermediate Credit Banks,** and the **Federal Land Banks.**

The federal government also guarantees and insures loans. The most familiar examples of such loans are mortgage loans guaranteed or insured by the **Federal Housing Administration** (FHA) and the **Veterans Administration** (VA), as well as student loans. However, in the past the government has also guaranteed large loans to the Chrysler Corporation and to New York City to keep them out of bankruptcy.

Why does the government involve itself in supplying credit? One reason is a widespread (though perhaps questionable) belief that home owner-ship is beneficial not just to homeowners, but to the country as a whole. A second is the claim of farmers that private credit agencies do not meet their legitimate demand for funds. An alternative explanation, however, is the political strength of particular pressure groups, such as farmers, homeown-ers, and parents faced with college tuition bills, who want to obtain cheaper credit.

GOVERNMENT REGULATION OF FINANCIAL MARKETS

One reason for regulating the financial industry is to limit fraud and losses to creditors. Thus the federal government imposes strict regulations on the use of insider information in stock trading and on the claims that can be made in selling stocks and bonds, while the states try to ensure the soundness of insur-ance companies.

But it is the depository institutions, banks, savings and loans, mutual sav-ings banks, and credit unions that are most stringently regulated. We will now present the case for this regulation, a case that is widely accepted. Later in the book we will raise some questions about it.

There are several reasons for the extensive regulation of depository insti-tutions. One is **consumer ignorance.** For competition to work effectively the buyer must be able to evaluate the quality of the product with some degree of efficiency. Otherwise, various producers could succeed by offering a defective product at a low price. Consumers can evaluate most products in either, or both, of two ways. One is through experience. They buy, say, a quart of milk advertised by a new dairy. If they don't like it, not much is lost. The other way is by evaluating the product before purchase: for example, they may not buy a car that looks flimsy.

Unfortunately, neither method works well for deciding whether to buy the deposit services of a financial intermediary. The foremost characteristic most households look for in a financial intermediary is that it be safe and not fail. But experience provides little help here. Once a bank has failed, deposi-tors know that they should not have entrusted their funds to it, but by then it is too late.[2]

The other method of evaluating a product, inspecting to see whether it is flimsy, does not work for most depositors either. Extensive effort and technical knowledge are required to evaluate the soundness of a bank or other finan-cial intermediary. Just looking at the balance sheet won't do. Most depositors cannot tell whether the item listed as "loans" consists of loans to sound or to risky borrowers.

---

[2] Deposits are not the only example of large and infrequent expenditures on items whose technical soundness it is difficult to evaluate. This is so for houses, too. And here too we have government regulation (building codes) and inspection for safety and health defects that would not be obvious to the buyer. In the absence of such government regulations buyers would probably rely on pri-vate housing inspectors and on certificates by the builder. But the certificate of a failed bank would give a depositor little protection, and buildings are easier for a specialist to evaluate than banks are.

Unfortunately, the financial intermediary has an incentive to buy assets that are too risky from the point of view of the depositor and the economy as a whole. This is so, not because it wants to fail, but because if it makes a risky loan, all the additional interest the borrower pays because the loan is risky accrues to the intermediary. (The depositor, not knowing that the financial institution is taking these risks, does not ask for higher interest on the deposit.) But the institution does not bear all the corresponding potential loss, since large depositors and the deposit-insuring agency stand to lose too. Thus, for the depository institution itself, the cost of risk taking is less than it is for the economy as a whole. But in deciding how much risk to take, the depository institution sets the marginal revenue from taking risk equal to the marginal cost that the risk imposed on it alone and ignores the risk it imposes on the depositor and the insuring agency. Hence it takes more risk than is justified when one considers the cost of taking the risk to the economy as a whole.

Some mechanism is obviously needed to prevent financial intermediaries from taking too much risk. One possibility would be extensive consumer information. Thus, in principle, depositors could subscribe to reports, written by accountants and financial analysts, that evaluate banks and other financial intermediaries. However, such reports may not be reliable enough and may be expensive, both in terms of purchase price and in terms of the time it takes to read and evaluate their, perhaps conflicting, recommendations. But, even so, large firms that have deposits greatly exceeding the insurance limit do try to evaluate the soundness of their banks.

Another way to protect the depositor is to insure deposits. One possibility would be to have depository institutions insured by private insurance companies, but there would be the danger that if many large institutions fail, so would the insurance company. Bank failures cannot be predicted from actuarial tables the way deaths or car accidents can. However, the government is an institution that can always pay off its debts, and hence we have it insure deposits. But if the government insures deposits (up to $100,000), what protects the government against the danger of depository institutions taking excessive risks? The answer is that the government tries, not entirely successfully by any means, to limit the risk taking of depository institutions.

A second reason for government supervision of depository institutions is that they *create the major part of our money supply,* since, as we will explain in Chapter 13, they create deposits. Thus a wave of bank failures could wipe out a significant proportion of the money stock. Suppose that massive bank failures did reduce the supply of money. Since the money supply would then be smaller, it would no longer suffice to buy all the goods and services offered on the market. Production would be curtailed and unemployment would rise, perhaps substantially. During the Great Depression bank failures and the withdrawals of currency from banks reduced *M-1* by about one-quarter. This probably explains the extraordinary severity of this depression.

Firms make large payments to each other, while often holding only small deposits. They can do this because they can schedule their out-payments so that they are due only after the payments they are to receive from others have become due. If, because of a bank failure, a firm does not receive a payment due to it, it may have to default on a payment it is scheduled to make, and that, in turn, may well cause its creditor to miss a payment it has to make. The result of bank failures could therefore be a massive disruption of the financial system. The government has a responsibility to prevent this, similar to its responsibility to prevent disruptions in other essential services, like electricity or water.

A third reason for government supervision and insurance is that, without it, even sound, well-run banks might be in danger of failing when some other banks that took too much risk went under. The public cannot distinguish very well between sound and risky banks. The cost of being caught in a bank failure greatly exceeds the cost of withdrawing a deposit. Hence, in the absence of government supervision and insurance, when the public sees some banks fail it is likely to withdraw deposits from other banks too. Such runs on sound banks, due to contagion, may destroy well-run and safe banks. (Whether such contagion is likely to be a serious problem is far from certain.)

A fourth reason is that if a bank fails, firms, particularly small firms, that borrowed from it may now lose their access to credit. Hence, they may fail through no fault of their own. Their failures may worsen an ongoing recession.

These four reasons justify both deposit insurance and the accompanying regulations needed to ensure bank safety. Another set of regulations has been imposed for a variety of other reasons, such as constraining the growth of giant banks, protecting bank customers from discrimination, and lowering the cost of mortgages. To do the last of these, the government used to greatly limit the types of loans that savings and loans could make so that they would have little choice but to make mortgage loans.

Do these reasons provide a convincing case for government regulation of financial intermediaries? Or would we be better off with less regulation?

SUMMARY

1 The U.S. financial system, that is, the system for creating and trading in claims, is large and complex. A complex economy requires such a system to bring savers and investors together.

2 While bonds represent claims for fixed payments, equity represents an ownership claim. Bond prices vary inversely with the interest rate on newly issued bonds: the longer a bond's maturity, the greater the variation in its price as interest rates change.

3 Financial intermediaries serve to reduce transactions costs, to transform long-term loans into short-term liabilities and thus provide liquidity, and to pool risks.

4 Among the private institutions active in the financial market are stockbrokers, investment banks, security dealers, private pension funds, mutual funds, money-market mutual funds, life insurance companies, casualty companies, finance companies, commercial banks, savings and loans, mutual savings banks, and credit unions. Government agencies also make loans and guarantee or insure private loans.

5 Financial intermediaries are heavily regulated. Among the purposes of these regulations are to protect the money supply, to aid small depositors, and to favor the credit needs of certain sectors of the economy.

KEY TERMS

bonds	private pension funds
equity	mutual funds
coupon (coupon rate)	life insurance companies
money-market mutual funds	casualty insurance companies
financial intermediaries	commercial banks
stockbrokers	savings and loans
investment banks	mutual savings banks
security dealers	credit unions
transactions costs	duration

QUESTIONS AND EXERCISES

*1   In a number of countries the financial industry had been heavily taxed and its development held back. Write a memorandum to the minister of finance of such a country pointing out why this is a bad idea. (You didn't want the consulting contract in any case.)

2   Explain the distinction between stocks and bonds.

*3   Explain why bond prices vary inversely, but not strictly inversely, with interest rates.

4   Explain a firm's choice between issuing stock and selling bonds.

5   Describe the benefits of using financial intermediaries.

FURTHER READING

ALTMAN, EDWARD. *Handbook of Financial Markets and Institutions.* New York: Wiley, 1987.

STIGUM, MARCIA. *The Money Market.* Homewood, Ill.: Dow Jones–Irwin, 1990.

Financial Principles

After you have read this chapter, you will be able to:

- Discuss the nature and types of financial risk.
- Explain the basics of portfolio management and of various types of portfolio risk.
- Know what the Modigliani-Miller theorem says about the costs of financing by stocks and by bonds.
- Realize the implications of efficient-markets theory.
- Appreciate the completeness of markets.
- Understand the importance of moral hazard and asymmetric information.

Chapter 2 set forth the various types of assets, but it did not explain how savers can combine them into an efficient portfolio. In this chapter, which develops a basic theory of finance, we look at the portfolio and at the related question of the nature of risk. The other side of the market, and of the theory of finance, is the borrower's side. Corporate borrowers have to decide whether to issue stocks or bonds, and we look at that decision as well. With both sides of the market in place, we then ask some questions about how it operates. Are there opportunities for earning profits above the normal rate of return? Do all feasible types of markets and assets already exist? Do conflicts of interest between borrowers and lenders arise to create inefficiencies? We begin with the portfolio.

PORTFOLIOS

The term *portfolio,* originally a type of briefcase in which one could carry one's securities, also came to mean the assets in one's portfolio, the same way *wardrobe* came to mean the clothes kept in a wardrobe. It is the value and riskiness of the entire portfolio that matters to the investor, and not the value of any particular asset in it. If the value of half the assets in a portfolio declines by

10 percent and the value of the other half rises by 10 percent, the investor is no worse off than before.

The desirability of the entire portfolio depends on two factors, its yield and its riskiness. Calculating the yield of a portfolio is straightforward; the yield is the weighted average rate of return on the various assets that compose it. But calculating its risk is a more complex matter. The riskiness of a portfolio is generally *less* than the weighted average of the risks of the various assets in it. But before discussing why this is so, we will take up the notion of risk.

The Nature of Risk

The term *risk*, as used in economics, does not just mean the probability of a loss. Economists use this term to encompass both the probability of a gain and the probability of a loss—in other words, the deviation from certainty *in either direction*. For example, consider a bond that has the following characteristics: there is a zero probability of a loss, a 10 percent probability of a 3 percent yield, and a 90 percent probability of a 5 percent yield. This bond is considered riskier than another bond that has a 2 percent probability of a 2 percent loss and a 98 percent probability of a 2 percent yield.

Types of Risk

A supplier of funds takes three types of risk. First, there is **default risk.** A borrower may simply declare bankruptcy, perhaps due to unfavorable economic conditions, incompetence, or dishonesty, and not pay either the interest or the principal. Strictly speaking, a buyer of equity in a company does not face default risk, because the company is not legally obligated to make a payment. However, the risk that the company will earn a low, zero, or even negative rate of return can also be thought of as default risk.

The second type of risk is **purchasing-power risk.** For a loan it is the risk that the loan's *real* value, when it is repaid, as well as the *real* value of the interest payments received during its life are less than the lender expected, because the inflation rate was higher than he thought it would be. Someone who lends $1,000 at a 5 percent interest rate and expects the inflation rate to be 3 percent anticipates a 2 percent real rate of return. But if the inflation rate turns out to be 7 percent, then the real rate of return is −2 percent.

The third type of risk, **interest-rate risk** or **market risk,** is the risk that the price of a security may fall because interest rates have risen. At first glance one might object that this is not a genuine risk on par with the other types of risk, because if the lender does not sell the security, but waits until it matures, she does not lose anything. But this objection is not valid. First, many buyers of securities, particularly financial institutions, do not plan to hold them to maturity. Second, one advantage of holding a security is the feeling of safety it provides; even if one plans to hold it until maturity, the *possibility* of selling it if conditions change provides the owner with a margin of safety. Third, some people buy bonds in the expectation that bond prices will rise, so that they can sell the bonds at a capital gain. If bond prices do not rise and they hold the bonds to maturity, they earn less on them than they had anticipated and quite possibly less than they could have earned by buying another asset.

Portfolio Risk and Diversification

The riskiness of an entire portfolio is generally less than the average risk of the individual assets in it because the risks of various assets are not perfectly correlated; when the price of one asset goes down, the price of another asset may go up. The more diversified a portfolio is in this way, the lower its risk is. Note that to achieve diversification, you have to look at the risk characteristics of various assets, not at their other characteristics. In the 1980s some banks found this out the hard way. When oil prices were high, they had made many loans to oil drillers, as well as to owners of office buildings in Texas. Once oil prices fell and oil drillers went bankrupt and broke their leases, mortgage loans on buildings formerly occupied by oil drillers and mortgage loans on drilling rigs both went sour. The massive failure of savings and loans in the 1980s was due in good part to this lack of diversification. Most of their assets were long-term mortgages, whose values fell when interest rates rose.

In contrast, a proper diversification can greatly reduce risk. Suppose that your portfolio comprises two types of assets: stock in a machine-tool firm and stock in an economic consulting firm. Assume further that more people seek economic advice during bad times than during good times, while fewer people buy machine tools in bad times than in good times. So if times turn bad, the value of your machine-tool stock declines and the value of your consulting-firm stock rises, and if times turn good, the converse. Whichever happens, your portfolio shows some losses and some balancing gains. Hence the riskiness of your portfolio is less than the riskiness of either of the two stocks that compose it.

Indeed, if you hold just the right proportion of the two stocks, your portfolio will have the same value in good times as in bad times. As far as the alternation of good times and bad times is concerned, your portfolio is riskless, even though both the assets you are holding are risky.

Hedging. Surprising as it may seem, you can sometimes reduce the riskiness of your portfolio by adding to it an asset that is riskier than any of the assets it already contains. Suppose, for example, that the stock of the economic consulting firm is much riskier than the stock of the machine-tool firm. Even so, if you start out with just stock in the machine-tool firm, and you add a small amount of stock in the consulting firm, you reduce the riskiness of your portfolio because if times turn bad, the stock in the consulting company will rise by a much greater percentage than the stock in the machine-tool company will fall.

Reducing the riskiness of your portfolio by adding to it assets whose risk is negatively correlated with the riskiness of the assets you already hold is an example of **hedging.** The amount of each asset you should hold to hedge your portfolio with regard to an event, such as a rise in GDP (gross domestic product), depends on the susceptibility of each of the two assets with respect to this event. If a given rise in GDP causes the price of one asset to decline by 10 percent and raises the price of the other asset by 20 percent, then you can hedge fully with respect to a rise in GDP by holding twice as much of the first asset as of the second one.

Portfolio Management

An obvious implication of the difference in the riskiness of a portfolio and the riskiness of the individual assets that compose it is that with astute portfolio management one can hold a combination of risky assets, earn a high rate of return, and yet avoid excessive risk. This is how many financial managers earn high salaries.

Unfortunately, it is not always possible to hold some assets that benefit when Event A happens, and others that benefit by the appropriate amount when Event A does *not* happen. As a salient example, call Event A inflation. There are many assets, such as bonds, that lose real value when the inflation rate rises. But what asset benefits from inflation? At one time it was widely believed that stocks did, but the poor performance of the stock market in the 1970s put an end to that comforting belief. Real estate performed well during the inflation of the 1970s, but there is no assurance that it will do so again in the next inflation. Similarly, consider the concern about a global warming trend, or greenhouse effect. Someone who owns a farm in Kansas might consider it a good hedge to buy land in Canada. But we know little about how the greenhouse effect will affect wind patterns, and hence precipitation. If a serious greenhouse effect occurs, farmland in Canada might lose value even faster than farmland in Kansas. Hedging helps but cannot always eliminate all risk.

Holding a mixture of assets is not the only way to hedge a portfolio. One can also hedge by owing debts. Suppose, for example, that your salary does not rise during inflation. You can, at least partially, hedge against inflation by borrowing. Then, if inflation occurs, it lowers not only the real value of your salary, but also the real value of your debt and of your interest payments.

When using debts to hedge against the riskiness of one's assets, one should match the maturities of the assets and the debts. Consider a firm that builds a factory that it expects to be in operation for twenty years. Suppose it finances its construction by borrowing for one year only and plans to pay off the loan by borrowing again at the end of the year. This firm is assuming considerable interest-rate risk. At the end of the year when it has to borrow again, it may have to pay a much higher interest rate, a rate that may exceed what it earns from the factory. In contrast, had it borrowed at a fixed rate of interest by issuing a 20-year bond, the rise in the interest rate would not have affected it.

Reducing overall risk by hedging the risks of individual assets and liabilities is not the only consideration in managing one's portfolio. One must also determine how much risk to take, that is, at what point to balance off the conflicting objectives of maximizing returns and minimizing risks. One possibility is to hold assets with varying degrees of risk—to hold some extremely safe assets, and thus ensure at least a certain minimum income, and to take great risks with only a small proportion of one's assets. Doing so gives one both a feeling of security and the excitement of taking a gamble.

Contingent Claims

By selecting the right mixture of assets and liabilities, one can hedge against portfolio risk. But portfolio risk is only one of the many risks in life, and for most people by no means the biggest risk they face. Other risks include accidental damage to one's property, incapacitating illness, and death. Both households and firms therefore want to hold **contingent claims,** that is, rights to receive payments in case certain specified events occur. Familiar examples of contingent claims are life insurance and property insurance. Equity in a pension fund (that is, the accumulated present value of the pension payments due to a person) is also a contingent claim because the pension will be received only if the employee and other beneficiaries live long enough.

Optimal Portfolios and Security Prices

Suppliers of funds want to acquire assets that maximize yield and minimize the total risk of portfolios. Insofar as they can eliminate the risk of particular assets by diversification, that type of risk, called **diversifiable risk,** is harmless. Only **undiversifiable risk** imposes a burden. Suppose that the earnings of banks typically go up as interest rates rise, while the earnings of real-estate developers decline. Since you can hedge away the risk of changes in interest rates by holding a combination of stocks in both a bank and a real-estate development, you do not require an extra-high yield on the stock of real-estate developers to induce you to buy this stock, which is so sensitive to changes in interest rates. With others thinking the same way, competition for the available supply of this stock ensures that you will not get an extra premium on bank stock either.

In contrast, consider a risk that is not diversifiable, such as the risk that the stock market as a whole will decline. This is a risk you cannot avoid by diversifying and buying many different stocks. To induce you to take such *undiversifiable* risk, the average yield on stocks must exceed the yield on, say, savings deposits. And it does.

Apart from yield and undiversifiable risk there is a third characteristic of an asset that affects its value, and that is the asset's liquidity. As discussed in Chapter 1, liquidity has three dimensions: the speed with which you can sell the asset, the transactions cost of the sale, and the predictability of its price. The last of these can clearly be subsumed under risk. How quickly an asset can be sold is also a dimension of the risk of holding it because speed of sale only matters if there is a risk of incurring some loss by not selling the asset quickly. However, the transactions cost of buying or selling an asset is not part of its risk and thus contributes a distinct characteristic, along with yield and risk, that determines the desirability of the asset.

Transactions costs should be interpreted broadly enough to incude not only the actual dollars-and-cents cost of a purchase or sale but also the effort involved. This effort includes learning about the characteristics of the asset. Transactions costs can therefore be substantial, and indeed prohibitive for some buyers. Few urban households, for example, would buy farmland in a distant state, even if their best estimate is that for *carefully selected* farmland the yield is higher and the risk no greater than for corporate stock. Transactions costs, however, are usually not an important consideration for big financial institutions. They deal in such large dollar amounts that the cost of acquiring the needed expertise and the brokerage cost of buying the asset are only a trivial percentage of the value of their purchase.

The value of an asset to potential purchasers obviously serves to determine its price. Hence, the price of an asset depends positively on its yield, and negatively on its risk. The influence of transactions costs on price will depend on how great a factor households are in the market for the asset. This is equivalent to saying that the yield on an asset is a positive function of its risk, and in some cases of its transactions costs.[1]

But the price of an asset may vary substantially even if its yield, risk, and transactions costs are constant. One reason it may do so is that the yields, risks, and transactions costs of other assets may vary. If the yield on your asset is constant while the yield of other assets rises, the price of your asset will fall. Moreover, suppose the public becomes more risk averse. The price of your risky assets will fall even though their degree of risk has not changed. None of this should be surprising; the price of any good depends, in part, on the prices of competing goods and on tastes.

The dependence of the price of an asset on its expected yield and risk is formalized in the **capital assets pricing model** (**CAPM**). According to this model, the price of a stock is a function of its expected yield and its undiversifiable risk. This risk is measured by the *beta coefficient* (β), which shows how volatile the stock is relative to the average stock on the market. The stock of a highly cyclical company, such as a steel company, has a high beta, while the stock of a stable company, such as a food retailer, has a low beta. If one assumes that the stock's expected yield can be approximated by its actual yield, one can look at the data and see if stocks sell for what the CAPM says they should. The results are not very encouraging because the beta coefficient tells us little about a stock's price, and much work is being done to develop more sophisticated and, let us hope more successful, variants of the plain vanilla CAPM.

EQUITY VERSUS DEBT

So far we have looked at the financial market through the eyes of the supplier of funds who buys securities. On the demand side of the market are households, firms, and governments. As we mentioned earlier, households and governments can obtain funds only by borrowing, that is, by issuing promises to pay in the future; they do not have the choice of issuing equity. But corpora-

---

[1] To see why these two statements are equivalent, write the first one as $P = a + br - c$ Risk, where P is the price of the bond, r is the yield, and $a, b,$ and c are constants. For any given P, r and Risk must vary inversely.

tions do have that choice. How do they decide whether to borrow or issue equity?

Before taking up this question, we need to clarify the two ways that corporations can obtain equity capital. One, the obvious way, is to issue equity by selling additional stock on the market. Another is through **retained earnings,** that is, by not distributing all the earnings to the stockholders and ploughing some of them back into the business. In doing so corporations are, in effect, "selling" additional equity to their stockholders, since the shares each stockholder owns are now more valuable. Stockholders who do not wish to hold such additional equity can, of course, opt out by selling some of their stock. Suppose, for example, that a corporation earns a 10 percent rate of return, pays a 5 percent dividend, and retains the other 5 percent. Each of its shares is now worth 5 percent more. Stockholders can offset this automatic "purchase" of new equity by selling 5 percent of their stock, so that the total value of their stock is unchanged.

The Modigliani-Miller Theorem

In the previous chapter we described how a firm's risk grows as it borrows more and how that increases the interest rate it has to pay on other borrowing. This raises the possibility that borrowing by issuing bonds may ultimately be just as expensive for a firm as issuing more stock. This idea is developed in a basic theorem of finance, called the **Modigliani-Miller theorem** after its originators Franco Modigliani of MIT and Merton Miller of the University of Chicago. The theorem asserts that under certain conditions, which we will discuss shortly, it makes no difference to the firm's stockholders whether the firm finances itself by borrowing or by selling stock.

The intuitive idea behind the Modigliani-Miller theorem is that as a productive enterprise each firm has specific profit opportunities and risks and that these exist regardless of how the firm finances itself. For example, a shoe factory can sell shoes at a particular price and hire labor and buy materials at a certain cost. These factors determine its profits. It faces specific risks, such as a decline in the demand for shoes or a change in consumer tastes.

These irreducible risks must be shared somehow between stockholders and bondholders. Suppose the firm sells some additional stock and uses the funds it receives to buy up some bonds it had previously issued. The total risk of the firm has not changed. Some risk has merely been transferred from the remaining bondholders, who now feel safer because the firm has a bigger cushion of equity, to the new stockholders. Suppose further that everyone has the same aversion to assuming risk. If so, the firm has to pay the new stockholders exactly as much to induce them to assume an additional unit of risk as it gains from the bondholders' being willing to accept a lower interest rate because they now bear one less unit of risk.

The assumption that everyone has to be paid the same amount to assume a unit of risk may seem implausible. But remember in economics its what's true at the margin that counts. And the assumption that—at the margin—everyone has to be paid the same to induce them to assume a unit of risk is not unreasonable. Suppose Joe is a cautious person who does not like risk, while Jane is more venturesome. Despite this difference, at the margin, they will have the same aversion to risk, because Joe will own very few risky assets, while Jane will hold a large number of them. And the more risky assets relative to safe assets you hold, the greater the gamble you are taking, and hence the greater the amount you have to be paid to bear additional risk is. You might think of Jane and Joe exchanging assets until both have the same risk-return trade-off. (Until they do, they will not be in equilibrium.) Then, when our firm comes along and wants someone to bear the risk of holding its equity rather than its bonds, each requires the same compensation for bearing the additional risk. With the price of risk bearing therefore being the same regardless of whether the additional risk is borne by stockholders or by creditors, the firm's cost of obtaining funds is the same regardless of whether it sells stock or borrows. Hence, the firm should be indifferent between selling stock and selling bonds, and need not hire MBAs to tell it which it should do.

Nobody, including Modigliani and Miller themselves, believes that the Modigliani-Miller theorem is the complete story. Everyone recognizes that it leaves out three important elements, so that it *does* matter whether the firm sells stock or bonds. First, the U.S. tax laws are biased. They subsidize borrowing by allowing a firm to treat the interest that it pays as a deductible expense, but do not allow it to deduct its dividend payments on stock. They therefore subsidize borrowing, even though a high debt-equity ratio makes the financial system less secure.

Second, although markets move toward equilibrium over time, at any particular moment they are often significantly out of equilibrium, especially in situations in which there are sizable transactions costs. Thus, since Joe and Jane have not completed all their asset swaps, there are some people around who are willing to bear risk at a lower cost than others, and the firm can minimize its financing cost by selling them equity rather than bonds.

Third, firms have to worry about going bankrupt and having to sell their assets cheaply, rather than at prices that reflect their equilibrium values. This gives the firm and its stockholders an incentive to play it safe, which means to have more stocks and fewer bonds outstanding.

Does this mean that the Modigliani-Miller theorem is useless? No, it does not. Despite its qualifications it provides an insightful way of looking at financing costs. Prior to the Modigliani-Miller theorem, corporate treasurers would look at the yields on their stocks and their bonds. When the yield on their bonds was lower, the less-sophisticated treasurers would say: "Let's sell bonds; it's cheaper." The more-sophisticated ones would add a qualification: "But because it increases risk, selling bonds will drive up our future borrowing costs and depress the value of our stock." The Modigliani-Miller theorem gives financial managers an alternative window on the problem. Now the default setting, so to speak, is that these qualifications about future borrowing costs and stock prices make the costs of selling bonds and of selling equity equal, so that the three qualifications of the Modigliani-Miller theorem discussed above are qualifications to the conclusion that the costs are the same.

So much for the theory. Figure 3.1 shows how nonfinancial corporations have financed themselves over the last thirty years. They have generally obtained more funds by borrowing than by selling equity, and indeed, during most of the 1980s, their net receipts from selling stock were negative; that is, on the average they bought back more stock than they sold. But the other component of equity finance—retained earnings—has been significant. However, the data on retained earnings overstate their true amount. During inflation corporate earnings are overstated, and since retained earnings are defined as corporate earnings minus dividend payments, they are overstated too.

Why do corporations not issue more equity when equity is so much safer than debt? One reason is that retained earnings provide a tax-advantaged alternative to issuing new stock. Suppose a corporation pays you a dividend and you use your dividend to buy more stock. You have to pay income tax on this dividend. By contrast, if the corporation does not pay you a dividend and reinvests the funds in its business so that the price of its stock rises, then you pay no income tax on this. To be sure, when you sell the stock, you have to pay a capital-gains tax on its higher value, but it is better to pay taxes later than right now (and at death capital gains escape taxes). What is, therefore, puzzling is not that firms rely so much on retained earnings, but that they pay dividends at all.

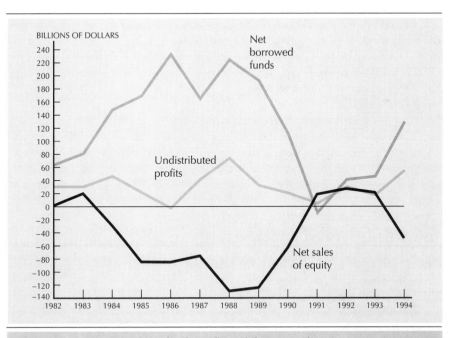

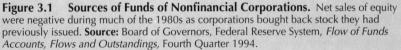

Figure 3.1   Sources of Funds of Nonfinancial Corporations. Net sales of equity were negative during much of the 1980s as corporations bought back stock they had previously issued. **Source:** Board of Governors, Federal Reserve System, *Flow of Funds Accounts, Flows and Outstandings,* Fourth Quarter 1994.

A second way in which the tax system discriminates against selling stock has already been mentioned: interest payments, unlike dividend payments, are deductible from the income on which the company pays corporate income tax. Moreover, capital gains are not taxed at such a high rate as ordinary income. Third, as will be explained below, if a company issues more equity, it is a sign of weakness.

Since the choice between issuing equity and borrowing is a hard one, it is not surprising that, as Figure 3.1 shows, the ratio of stock sales to borrowing varies a great deal. In the 1980s, as part of the takeover enthusiasm of the time, companies borrowed heavily to buy the stock of those companies they took over and as already mentioned, in some years net stock sales were negative. One can interpret such swings in financing in two ways. One is to say that conditions change. For example, as personal income-tax rates were cut in the 1980s, the tax bias in favor of borrowing became less important. The other way is to say that corporate managers, like other people, follow fads and fashions.

If a firm decides to sell equity, it still has to decide on some technical details, such as which investment banker to use and at which date to sell the stock. On the other hand if it decides to borrow, it still has to make one major decision, that is, whether to borrow short term, intermediate term, or long term. As we have already seen, the best way to minimize risk is to match the maturity of the debt to the useful life of the asset. However, since the short-term interest rate is usually below the long-term rate, firms are tempted to borrow short term. One compromise is a variable-rate loan. The interest rate on such a loan may be lower than on a fixed-rate loan, because the lender, say a bank, is itself borrowing largely short term and hence wants the interest rate that it receives to vary along with the rate it has to pay on its own borrowing. In that way it hedges.

But does not a variable-rate loan impose high risk on the borrowing firm because it may at some time have to pay a much higher rate than it anticipated? Not necessarily: as we will discuss in Chapter 16, one important reason why the interest rate may rise is that the inflation rate has risen. When inflation rises, the prices that firms receive rise along with their costs, such as the cost of borrowing.

HOW WELL DO FINANCIAL MARKETS FUNCTION?

Having looked at how suppliers of funds manage their portfolios and at how corporate demanders of funds decide what securities to issue, we can now look at the securities market as a whole. We first consider whether securities markets are efficient in the sense that they do not offer any easy opportunities for bargain hunters. We then ask whether financial markets are operating well in the sense of providing a reasonably comprehensive spectrum of assets and liabilities. Finally, we inquire whether a divergence of interests between borrowers and lenders creates impediments to the efficient flow of funds between potential borrowers and lenders.

Efficient-Markets Theory

The professionals who operate in financial markets are able and well trained, and most financial markets are highly competitive. Economic theory—specifically **efficient-markets theory**—therefore tells us that opportunities for excess profits, that is, profits in excess of the normal rate of return for the specific degree of risk, are quickly competed away. There are no five-dollar bills left lying on the pavement. This seems obvious and hardly worth bothering to point out, but it has far-reaching implications that are often ignored.

For example, the efficiency of markets means that the prices of financial assets already take account of all available information. This implies that it makes no sense to say "I will buy stock in Company X, because I know that X has a lot of monopoly power." This information is available to everyone in the market, and therefore is already embodied in the price of the stock. Similarly, since the market knows which companies are efficient, the stock of efficient companies is no better (or worse) a buy than the stock of inefficient companies!

Moreover, it suggests that projecting the price of a stock by looking at its past sales, profits, and so on, makes no sense. Since all the information that is available is already embodied in the current price of the stock, the only thing that *changes* its price is new, incoming information. Such information is distributed randomly, with positive and negative news being equally likely.[2] Hence, according to efficient-markets theory, asset prices move in a random walk. (In a situation described as a *random walk*, whether a price will rise or fall this period is unrelated to whether it rose or fell in the previous period.) Several implications follow.

First, one can use economic analysis much more readily to explain why asset prices are what they are than to predict how they will change. To predict the *change* in the price of an asset requires that one know what news about it will become available in the future. This applies not just to the prices of stocks, but to the prices of all assets, such as foreign currencies or wheat futures, that are traded in efficient markets.

Second, by speculating in asset markets, one should not expect to make a profit above the normal rate of return appropriate for the degree of risk, *unless* one has information that others don't have or one is able to interpret the existing information better, that is, unless one can predict what will happen better than others can. But these others may also employ economists. This answers for the economist the question "If you're so smart, why aren't you rich?" If economists know so much about the factors determining GDP and prices, why don't they clean up on the stock market? They don't because many people have the same information, so that the economists' knowledge is already embodied in stock prices.

A third implication is that in buying stocks someone without specialized knowledge can, on the average, generally earn as high a rate of return for a

---

[2] Strictly speaking this statement is correct only if all items of news are equally important, but it can readily be reformulated in terms of the number of items of news weighted by their importance.

given degree of risk as professional portfolio managers do, simply by picking a sample of stocks at random. This does not mean that portfolio managers are stupid. Just the opposite—the reason that choosing stocks at random is not such a silly idea is precisely because professional portfolio managers do a good job. They buy undervalued stocks and sell overvalued ones, so that stock prices are at a level that, given the available information, is the best estimate of their true value that can be formed. To be sure, because they spend much effort in selecting stocks, they tend to find undervalued stocks ahead of most other people and hence obtain a somewhat better yield, but they have to be paid for this effort, so that those who buy mutual fund shares earn no more on average than those who hold a randomly selected portfolio of equally risky stocks.

This does not necessarily mean that you should actually select stocks or other investments at random. It may be reasonable to develop a portfolio that suits your personal circumstances, such as the amount of risk you want to take. Or suppose that you derive your salary from selling oil-drilling equipment. You may then want to diversify by buying stocks in industries, such as airlines, that gain when oil prices decline.

Does efficient-markets theory imply that nobody can systematically make much money speculating in asset markets? Of course not. An obvious but sometimes overlooked point is that markets do not become efficient on their own. Someone has to buy or sell to bring prices into equilibrium, and the first ones to do so will earn a higher return, which may compensate them for their effort and ability. It, therefore, makes sense for financial institutions to employ securities analysts as stock pickers. But making more than the normal rate of return takes hard work or great ability—or luck.

Evaluating Efficient-Markets Theory

Efficient-markets theory appeals to economists because it is such an obvious and direct implication of the economist's basic tenet that people rationally maximize profits. But that does not necessarily mean that it is correct. We have to look at the empirical evidence. In deciding what this evidence shows, there is the problem of judging whether the glass is half full or half empty. On the whole, one might say that the theory works quite well. Easy ways of significantly beating asset markets do not abound—that much is clear. The more difficult question is whether there are a significant number of meaningful anomalies that contradict efficient-markets theory. The qualifications *significant* and *meaningful* are important. There are a large number of asset markets, and if, say, ten of them are not efficient, the efficient-markets theory is still valuable. We would also not reject the efficient-markets theory if we found that there were a way to earn 0.0001 percent more (after transactions costs) than the theory implies. For example, the average return from holding stocks is negative from the close of business on Friday until the close of business on Monday, so that it seems you could make money by systematically selling stocks on Fridays and buying them again on Tuesday mornings. But the fall between Friday and Monday is so small that nobody who has to pay brokerage costs can benefit from it. (See also the box on page 51.)

"Dart Board Beats Experts"

Each month the *Wall Street Journal* asks a group of stock market experts to select a portfolio consisting of their favorite stocks. It then "selects" a rival portfolio by throwing darts at a list of stocks and compares the performance of these two portfolios. Sometimes the experts win, sometimes the darts. This is consistent with what the efficient-markets theory tells us.

But suppose the data would show that, on the average over many months, the experts do much better. Suppose further that you are a firm believer in efficient-markets theory. How would you respond? Most likely, you would see whether there were any way you could protect your theory from the contrary data.

One thing you could do would be to challenge the experiment. Efficient-markets theory does not say that all stocks have similar rates of return. One gets paid for taking more risk; according to the theory only those stocks that are equally risky have the same expected rate of return. By taking more risk, one can, over the long run, beat the averages. Since the experts pick riskier stocks one would expect them to earn a higher return. Once one adjusts for differences in risk, the difference between the stocks selected by the experts and by the dartboard is very small and not statistically significant. And the small difference can easily be explained by buyers of stock bidding up the prices of those stocks that they read have been selected by the experts.

Another response would be to point out that efficient-markets theory does not deny that those who devote great ingenuity and much effort to the market do better than those who do not. If devotees did not do better, they would be foolish to spend their time trying to pick stocks. All that proponents of efficient-markets theory contend is that there are no abnormal returns to be earned, that the higher yields that the experts obtain are just sufficient to compensate them for their efforts.

There is considerable debate about whether efficient-markets theory is beset by anomalies (that is, contradictory evidence) that are significant. Much work is currently being done on this issue, and it has turned up a few anomalies. One is that the stocks that had a high growth rate of earnings or whose prices rose unusually fast in the past will subsequently have a lower yield than other comparable stocks. Another is that stock prices are affected by the weather in New York City—hardly an example of rational behavior! By making use of certain publicly available information, such as a stock's past dividend yield or its price-earnings ratio, one can earn a somewhat higher than normal rate of return. According to efficient-markets theory, there should be no seasonal variation in stock prices: if there were, someone could make money by buying stocks at the time at which they tend to be low and selling them at their seasonal highs. Yet there is some evidence for small seasonal variations for certain types of stocks.

Another objection that has been raised against efficient-markets theory is that the volatility of the stock market is much too great to be explained by any theory that assumes that investors behave rationally. Such extreme fluctuations can only be explained as the result of waves of optimism and pessimism sweeping the market. How else can one explain why on October 19, 1987 the stock market dropped by 22.6 percent on almost no news? But adherents of efficient-markets theory deny that the stock market is too volatile; they argue that reasonable changes in the discount rate of investors (to be explained in Chapter 5) can generate changes in the present value of future dividends that are large enough to explain the sharp fluctuations in stock values that we observe.

The Behavioral Theory of Finance

Suppose that because of the various anomalies just mentioned, we decide to reject efficient-markets theory. If so, we face a problem because efficient-markets theory follows naturally from the assumption that people rationally maximize their incomes. Hence, to reject efficient-markets theory, we must modify our usual assumption about rational income or utility maximization.

Some economists have developed such modifications. They have taken heed of the work of experimental psychologists that shows how people sometimes depart from rational behavior in certain persistent and systematic ways. For example, experiments have shown that most people read too much into small samples of data: they underestimate the probability that the behavior of the sample is just due to chance. Moreover, people are much more concerned about a loss they experience than about their failure to obtain an equivalent gain. In forecasting, they put too much emphasis on recent events relative to earlier events. And they attribute too large a proportion of their successes to ability rather than to good luck.

These insights, which fall under the general category of behavioral theory, have been used to explain the anomalies encountered by efficient-markets theory. Thus, to explain the high volatility of the stock market, one can modify the assumption of rational behavior to make allowance for our being excessively influenced by the opinions of others, in other words, by a herd instinct that makes us buy when others buy and sell when others sell. Similarly, if people underestimate the probability that something is merely due to chance, they are willing to pay too high a price for stocks that have shown high earnings growth, so that the yield on these stocks will then be less than the yield on other stocks. Furthermore, if people consistently underestimate the probability that they will borrow on their credit cards, they will be reluctant to

Play it Again, Sam

Doesn't it seem reasonable that a mutual fund that has had an unusually high yield in the past is likely to have an above average yield again? So why don't investors move massively into the best performing funds and abandon others? Doesn't their failure to do so show that efficient-markets theory is wrong?

Not quite. A study did find that mutual stock funds that performed unusually well last month are likely to continue their above average performances, but only for two months—which makes it hardly worth shifting one's funds.

shift from cards that charge a high interest rate to cards with a low interest rate. That could be the reason for the anomalous finding that despite much competition among credit card issuers, credit card rates stayed very high as interest rates fell in the 1990s.

Such reliance on irrational behavior is open to the response that while many people may act irrationally in psychological experiments, and perhaps as consumers, the sophisticated professionals who determine asset prices do not behave irrationally. If any did, they would lose money, or at least earn a lower rate of return than their competitors, and be put out of business. Behavioral finance theorists respond that if the naive amateurs in a market behave irrationally, then in many cases the sophisticated professionals have a rational incentive to do what the naive people do. Suppose I know that tomorrow an article in the *Wall Street Journal* will make many naive investors think GM's earnings will go up, and they will therefore buy GM stock. Even if I know that they are wrong, that GM's earnings will fall instead of rise, I will buy GM stock today because the naive investors will make GM stock rise tomorrow. The behavioral theory of finance is very much a minority approach in economics. But it *may* become more popular in the future.

Complete Financial Markets

Rational behavior implies that firms will continually seek new, profitable opportunities, so that all profitable niches are filled by a wide variety of different financial institutions and financial services.

What types of financial services should one therefore expect to find? Since financial markets are complicated, one would expect to see some institutions that advise borrowers and lenders and act as their agents. Then there should be institutions that operate as wholesalers and retailers and bring borrowers and lenders together. Financial intermediaries should interpose themselves between the ultimate borrowers and lenders.

As we saw in Chapter 2, these niches have generally been neatly filled. There is great variety among financial institutions, and the existence of every type of financial institution can be explained by the particular service that it offers. This does not mean that there are institutions that satisfy *all* the demands of borrowers and lenders. In particular, insurance markets are incomplete, mainly because of differences in the information possessed by insurance companies and those they insure.

But despite the inevitable absence of certain contingent markets, our financial system is remarkably elaborate and complete. This is a major source of strength of the U.S. economy. No other country has as complex a capital market. One might think that this is not important because finance is somehow not as "productive" an industry as, say, steel. But this is wrong. The capital market helps to determine where investment will take place and hence is a powerful determinant of the efficiency of a country's economy.

To illustrate the sophistication of U.S. capital markets, consider four relatively recent developments. One is the transformation of the mortgage market. Traditionally the mortgage market was highly specialized, both geographically and by the institutions that held mortgages. Real estate is not homogeneous, and mortgage lenders have to inspect the property, so mortgage credit was extended primarily by local lenders. As a result, in fast-growing areas mortgage rates would be high, while in slowly growing areas they would be low. Moreover, the volume of mortgage loans was to some extent inhibited by the limited funds available to the banks and savings and loan institutions in a particular area.

Fortunately, there was money to be made by eliminating these constraints, by unifying the mortgage market geographically, and by opening this market to lenders who are willing to *hold* mortgages but have no opportunity themselves to inspect the property and, hence, to *extend* mortgage credit. For example, suppose that the prevailing interest rate on mortgage loans charged by savings and loans is 10 percent, but that pension funds would be willing to grant mortgage loans at 8 percent if it were not for the difficulty they experience in initiating mortgage loans. Someone who could develop a way of shifting mortgages out of the portfolios of the savings and loans that originated them and into the portfolios of pension funds that will hold them could then make a lot of money. One possibility would be that she would buy a $100,000 mortgage from a savings and loan at, say, $105,000 and sell it to a pension fund at, say, $110,000. (The pension fund would be willing to pay that much for the mortgage because it is getting an asset with an interest rate of 10 percent.)

The procedure actually followed is somewhat different, but the principle remains the same. A financial institution, say a large brokerage firm, buys mortgages with similar risk characteristics from savings and loans and from other originators of mortgage loans, with an agreement that the originators will continue to service the loans; that is, they will do the necessary paperwork and will collect the interest and pass it on to the brokerage firm that bought the mortgages. This institution then issues its own bonds guaranteed by the bundle of mortgages it has bought and sells these bonds to pension funds, insurance companies, and other buyers. These buyers are willing to buy the bonds at a yield that is lower than that generally charged on mortgages because they are the liabilities of a respected brokerage firm and are secured by the mortgages. As a result, the brokerage firm is able to make a profit. Borrowers receive a substantial benefit too, because as brokers compete for bundles of mortgages, the prevailing interest rate on mortgages falls. This process of issuing securities backed by mortgages is called **securitization.**

Securitization was a substantial step forward, but it was not the last step. The next step was to extend the market for the mortgage bonds by letting small investors—not just insurance companies and pension funds—buy these bonds. This was done by selling some of the bonds in small denominations, as low as $1,000. Another, less obvious step was to reduce a problem that besets mortgage-backed bonds. When mortgage borrowers repay their loans ahead of time, their repayments are used to pay off some part of the outstanding bonds. Mortgage borrowers are likely to repay their mortgages as interest rates fall, and they can refinance their mortgages at a lower rate. Hence, the bondholders get some of their money back just at a time when interest rates on any new investments they make have declined, so that their interest income falls.

The ingenious response of brokers was to issue two distinct types of bonds against the pool of mortgages. As early repayments on mortgages are received, they are first used to retire one type of bond and not the other. Thus, those who want to protect themselves against early repayment can do so. In exchange they must, however, accept a lower yield on their bond.

Securitization has spread beyond the mortgage market. All sorts of loans, such as student loans, automobile loans, boat loans, and even certain business loans, are now being securitized, and that practice too is likely to grow. The only major limitation on the development of securitization is that the underlying loans must be fairly standardized so that purchasers of bonds backed by these loans can judge their safety.

The second example of market innovation is the **stripping** of bonds. Long-term government bonds have a potential for a big capital gain—or loss. This makes them attractive to some investors, but scares off others who want to tie down a fixed yield and avoid risk. Hence, brokers buy long-term government bonds and then sell off to one customer the right to any capital gain or loss on the bonds, while another customer buys the right to the bond's fixed interest payments.

A further example is the development of securities with contingent interest rates. Many of these are called **derivatives** because they are derived by splitting up an original security along the lines of the stripping of mortgage-backed bonds. Suppose that you have a portfolio that falls in value if interest rates rise, while my portfolio goes up when interest rates increase. We would both be better off if you would make a loan to me provided that this loan had an interest rate that rose should interest rates generally fall. In this way we would both hedge our portfolio risks. Many variants of such interest-rate hedges have now become available. Thus, one can buy securities whose interest rate goes up when a specified foreign currency rises against the dollar. One bank even sells a certificate of deposit (CD) that moves inversely to a stock market index, and thus allows the buyer to hedge against market declines.

The final instance of the market's sophistication is **interest-rate swaps.** If a company that borrowed at a variable interest rate would now prefer a fixed-rate loan instead, while another company is in the opposite situation, a bank can arrange for them to swap the interest payments they have to make. A similar swap can be arranged for firms that have to make interest payments in different currencies.

MARKET FAILURES: MORAL HAZARD, ASYMMETRIC INFORMATION, SIGNALING, AND PRINCIPAL-AGENT PROBLEMS

So far we have described a financial market that operates with remarkable efficiency. The profit motive drives market operators to set the prices of assets so that buyers can expect to earn a normal return for the level of risk that they are taking and no more. The profit motive also drives them to develop a wide variety of assets with different characteristics.

But financial markets also have their problems. Market operators behave in a way that maximizes their private benefits and not necessarily the benefits received by the whole economy. According to the invisible-hand theorem, under certain conditions the private welfare of market operators and the public's welfare coincide. One of these conditions is that everyone in the market possesses sufficient information. Obviously this condition does not fully hold in the financial market. Some investors are naive and uninformed: as the old proverb has it, "A fool and his money are soon parted." While the cheating of gullible people is a serious problem, it is more a problem of law enforcement and of writing effective laws than of economics, so we will pass it by. Instead, we will look at the problem created by **asymmetric information,** that is, by one party to a contract knowing something that the other party does not. But to explain the seriousness of the problem that asymmetric information creates, we must first explain **moral hazard.**

Moral Hazard

Once a loan is made or some other financial contract is signed, the interests of the two parties to the contract diverge. Suppose you have just taken out automobile insurance. You can now sleep easier, but that is not all; you can now also afford to be a little less careful about locking your car, about not parking it on dark streets, and so on. Obviously, you don't want your car to be stolen even though it is insured. But the cost to you of having your car stolen is now lower. Hence, it is rational for you to be less careful. But by being less careful, you impose a more onerous burden on the insurance company. This is an example of moral hazard. Other examples of moral hazard abound in financial markets. Suppose a bank makes a loan. It faces the moral hazard that the borrower, though capable of repaying, may decide instead to abscond with the funds. But even an honest borrower creates moral hazard: the riskier the investments that the borrower makes with a loan, the greater the chance that she will not be able to repay. But since risky investments, on the average, pay a higher rate of return, even allowing for the occasional failure, she has an incentive to use the loan to hold risky rather than safe assets. Consequently, the bank faces the problem of moral hazard even when the borrower is honest and fully intends to repay the loan.

Similarly, suppose a corporation sells bonds. If it has a history of being conservatively managed, it can borrow at a relatively low interest rate. But once it has sold the bonds, it then has an incentive to undertake riskier and, hence, more lucrative projects than before or to undertake additional borrowing, which makes the previously issued bonds riskier. Thus, in the corporate takeovers that were so prominent a feature of the financial landscape of the 1980s, many bondholders found that their previously safe bonds suddenly turned into risky bonds as the corporation that had issued these bonds sold additional bonds in the process of taking over another company.

Asymmetric Information

Moral hazard would not matter if the lender could anticipate correctly how much additional risk the borrower will assume. If she could, she would simply raise the interest rate enough to compensate for that risk. But generally the lender lacks sufficient information about the borrower's future behavior. The borrower may know what he intends to do, but he does not share all this information with the lender. This **asymmetric information** can affect prices substantially and greatly reduce the volume of transactions. Take, for example, the market for secondhand cars: someone buying a used car does not know whether the previous owner got rid of it because it ran badly or because he wanted to own a newer model. But what the buyer does know is that, since many cars are traded in because they do run badly, buying a used car involves substantial risk. This results in a low price for all used cars, even for those that run well. This low price then discourages owners from trading in cars that do run well, and this further lowers average quality and, hence, the price of used cars. Thus, asymmetric information results in what is called **adverse selection.**

Asymmetric information, and the related issues of moral hazard and adverse selection, are particularly troublesome in financial markets. What is traded is usually some form of IOU, in other words a promise, rather than an immediately available item, such as a car, that can be inspected or tried out. And the value of this promise depends, in part, on what the borrower will do in the future. As a result of this informational asymmetry, interest rates on what are actually safe loans are at least somewhat higher than they would be if the lender knew as much about the borrower's propensity to take risks as the borrower knows. Then, since interest rates are higher, fewer loans are taken out.

The Principal-Agent Problem

A special aspect of the asymmetric-information problem is the **principal-agent problem.** When one person (the principal) enlists another (the agent), conflicts of interest often arise. A good example of a principal-agent problem is how one should remunerate a law firm. The usual procedure is for the law firm (the agent) to bill its client (the principal) for each hour worked. But this gives the law firm an incentive to put in some unnecessary hours and to use high-priced lawyers to do what a paralegal could do just as well. On the other hand, if the client agrees to pay the law firm a fixed amount for handling a particular case, the firm has an incentive to do less work on this case than the client would like. Another possibility is for the client to agree to pay a bonus if the case is won. But how large should this bonus be? It depends on how difficult the case is. The client, not being an expert lawyer, does not know, and the law firm at least has an incentive not to tell him if it is an easy case. Similarly, the law firm cannot tell definitively how difficult the case is, in part because the client has an incentive to withhold information that would show it to be a very difficult case. Such ignorance makes it hard to agree on what the bonus should be.

A more obvious example of a principal-agent problem concerns executive perquisites, such as an executive who chooses to fly first class when a coach ticket would do just as well. Some executives of nonprofit institutions, who do not have stockholders breathing down their necks, may feel little pressure to do without ornate offices. A more serious problem is that corporate managers may maximize not stockholder profits but their own power and status by focusing on growth instead of on profits and by taking over other corporations even

How Not to Select the Best Portfolio Manager

A corporation that had to select a manager for its pension fund portfolio decided to rely on a contest. It gave a number of professional portfolio managers part of its portfolio to manage and told them that whoever earned the highest yield would get to manage the entire portfolio. Smart move? No, it was not. Can you figure out why?

Put yourself in the position of one of, say, a dozen competitors. Would you try to select a portfolio that achieves the appropriate balance between earnings and risk? Not if you were rational. In this contest you gain nothing unless you are number one; being number two or number twelve amounts to the same thing. So it would make sense to go for broke and load up on extremely risky stocks. As a result, the corporation is not likely to find out from this contest who the best portfolio manager is.

Moral of the story: Before you entrust your business to someone, ask yourself what he or she is maximizing.

though doing so may lower profits. Outright dishonesty, the proverbial "hand in the till," is also an instance of the principal-agent problem.

An example from financial markets is a stockbroker who induces a customer to do more trading than is wise. The customer will not gain from unnecessary trades (called "churning"), but the stockbroker will earn extra commissions. A more subtle example is a president of a bank who takes less risk than that which would maximize the income and welfare of the bank's stockholders. She stands to gain relatively little if a risky venture succeeds (she is "just doing her job"), but to lose her job if it does not. Similarly, a loan officer of a bank who has made a bad loan may well have an incentive to hide that fact from his manager, even if it means that the bank will lose more in the end, because he hopes to move on to another job before the loan goes into default.

Principal-agent problems may also lead to excessive risk taking. For example, mutual fund managers receive bonuses if their funds perform unusually well, but their salaries are not cut if they perform badly. This asymmetry gives them an incentive to take too much risk. As one money-market fund manager explained, when evaluating a risky new financial product, the fund's manager's "eyes go off to the side; they calculate in their heads what effect it has on their bonus."[3]

Not surprisingly many institutions and devices have been developed for mitigating the principal-agent problem. We will discuss only a few that have a bearing on financial markets. One possibility is continually to monitor the agent's behavior. But that can be expensive. A way to reduce the expense is to rely on others to do the monitoring. These others may be organizations that directly rate the quality of a firm's debt, such as Standard & Poor's, or organizations that do so indirectly, as when a bank makes a loan to a company and thus lets others know that it thinks that this company is creditworthy. An alter-

[3] Cited in Robert McGough, "Risk in Mutual Funds Is Rising as Managers Chase after Bonuses," *Wall Street Journal*, 81 (August 11, 1994), p. A5.

native method is to write detailed contracts that tie the agent's hands. For example, some bond issues contain covenants that constrain the amount of additional debt that the borrowing corporation can take on, and thus limit the risk it will fail or, if it does fail, the claims of other creditors to the borrower's assets. Similarly, the covenant of a bank loan may limit the amount of dividends paid out to stockholders, so that the firm's owners cannot drain it of most of its value and leave the bank to take possession of a firm that is virtually worthless. But constraining borrowers by detailed contracts has two problems. First, it limits the borrower's flexibility in meeting unforeseen events, and second, a clever borrower may find ways around the terms of the contract.

Yet another way of ameliorating the principal-agent problem is to tie the agent's rewards to the gains obtained by the principal. For example, some highly speculative mutual funds reward the manager only if the fund makes a certain minimum rate of return. Finally, government regulations, such as laws regarding fraud, may prohibit certain actions by agents.

Signaling

Given the problem of asymmetric information, borrowers have an incentive to persuade lenders that they are worthy customers. They do so by **signaling.** To see how signaling works, suppose that you are a manufacturer who has developed a new type of stereo. You have tested it, but you are not certain that it will perform well in actual use. Would you put your standard brand name on it or sell it under some other name? If you have serious doubts about how well it will function, you might decide to sell it under some other name to protect the good reputation of your brand. Brand names allow firms to signal the high quality of their brand-named products by putting their reputation on the line. An example of signaling outside economics comes from wars. Even with symmetric information a country may fight a war it knows it will probably lose rather than agree to surrender territory to an aggressor without a war. The reason? Because by not fighting, it signals other potential aggressors that they, too, could obtain territory from this country without the cost that a war imposes even on the victor.

Signaling in financial markets takes many guises. The owners of a small firm might invest a large proportion of their own wealth in it to indicate to lenders that they have a strong incentive not to take too much risk. A corporation might reinvest an unusually high proportion of its earnings to signal to prospective lenders that it expects its business to be unusually profitable. A firm that is about to issue bonds might take out a bank loan. The fact that the firm's bankers are willing to trust it signals the firm's soundness to prospective buyers of its bonds.

On the other hand, a firm can send a negative signal. If a firm sells stock when it can just as well finance itself by selling bonds, it signals that its own expectations of profitability are no higher than the market's expectations and may well be lower. If it thought that it would be more profitable, it would not be willing to cut new stockholders in on these higher earnings, but would reserve them for the existing stockholders by selling bonds instead of stock.

Another example of a negative signal is offering to pay a very high interest rate. After all, a corporation that would fail if it did not get a loan should be willing to pay any rate of interest it had to. Lenders know this and are therefore reluctant to make loans to borrowers who offer to pay extremely high interest rates. In the standard theory of markets, goods go to those willing to pay the highest price for them. This does not hold for the credit market. Credit is often rationed: at the going price (interest rate) demand exceeds supply, yet the price is not raised to equate supply and demand. A higher interest rate would discourage sound borrowers and attract too many unsound ones. As a result, those who want to finance high-risk, but worthwhile, ventures often find it hard to obtain loans.

To some extent government regulation may also be thought of as a signaling device. Thus, banks that are members of the Federal Reserve System, **member banks,** are regulated somewhat more strictly than other banks. A bank signals its greater safety by becoming a member bank.

Other Partial Solutions to the Asymmetric-Information Problem

Since signaling is so imperfect, other ways of ameliorating information asymmetries have been devised. An obvious one is to have someone specialize in ferreting out information and making it available to others. Thus, stockbrokers employ securities analysts, who research a stock by studying industry trends, interviewing the firm's managers, and so on, and then present their findings in newsletters sent to the broker's customers. There are also specialized firms, such as Standard & Poor's, that publish information about companies. But even such specialists usually cannot know as much about a firm as its managers do.

Another partial solution is something we have already discussed, the existence of financial intermediaries that pool the savings of many people, so that they have sufficient funds to make it worthwhile to undertake the expensive search for information. Few individuals can afford a staff of loan officers or securities analysts, but banks and mutual funds can.

Finally, the government forces large corporate borrowers to provide fairly detailed information. One reason why U.S. capital markets are more efficient than European ones is that, at least until recently, corporations selling stock in Europe did not have to provide much information. Hence, European investors had more reason to be concerned about asymmetric information and were therefore less willing to buy stock. While over 33 percent of U.S. households directly owns stocks, only about 6 percent of German households does.

SUMMARY

1 What matters to the owner of a portfolio is not the yield and risk on each asset taken separately, but the yield and risk on the entire portfolio. The types of risk are default risk, purchasing-power risk, and interest-rate risk.

2 The risk of a portfolio is not the same as the average of the risks of each of the assets in the portfolio. A portfolio composed of assets that are individually risky might,

under certain circumstances, be riskless. Portfolio risk can often, but not always, be hedged. Debts can be used to hedge assets. Contingent claims can be used to reduce risk.

3 The riskiness of a debt depends on how well its duration matches the duration of an asset that was bought with it. A variable-rate debt may well be less risky than a fixed-rate debt.

4 In deciding whether to borrow or to sell stock to obtain funds, a corporation should not just compare the interest rate with the yield on the stock, but should take into account the increased risk that results from borrowing, and, hence, the higher returns required by other lenders and by stockholders. These indirect effects are developed in the Modigliani-Miller theorem, which shows that under specified conditions the costs of bond finance and equity finance are the same.

5 Efficient-markets theory states that the price of assets already takes account of all *changes* in market price, that in speculating on the asset market, one should anticipate earning only a normal profit for a given degree of risk unless one has special information, and that selecting stocks at random is not necessarily foolish.

6 The behavioral theory of finance explains some seemingly anomalous findings by relaxing the rationality assumption.

7 The U.S. capital market is extensive and sophisticated. Subtle niches are exploited; examples include the securitization of mortgages and other loans, securities with contingent interest rates, and the stripping of bonds.

8 Moral hazard and asymmetric information create particularly severe problems in financial markets. To a limited extent, they can be ameliorated by signaling. Another source of inefficiencies is the principal-agent problem, which often arises when those who make the decisions and those who benefit or lose from them are not the same people.

KEY TERMS

portfolio	default risk
risk	purchasing-power risk
interest-rate risk (market risk)	efficient-markets theory
portfolio risk	behavioral theory of finance
hedging	securitization
portfolio management	moral hazard
contingent claims	asymmetric information
Modigliani-Miller theorem	signaling
capital assets pricing model	principal-agent problem
retained earnings	

QUESTIONS AND EXERCISES

1 Explain the various types of risk. Also, explain why a portfolio consisting of risky assets may be riskless.

*2 You cannot buy insurance against being fired. What are the reasons? (Note the plural.)

3 Why do so few people buy annuities that guarantee them a fixed income for as long as they live?

4 Explain the efficient-markets theory. How plausible is it?

*5 Give your own examples (not those from the chapter) of moral hazard, asymmetric information, and signaling.

FURTHER READING

FAMA, EUGENE. "Efficient Capital Markets II," *Journal of Finance,* 46 (December 1991), 1575–618. A detailed and useful survey.

The Journal of Economic Perspectives, 3 (Fall 1988), 99–158. The symposium offers an excellent, albeit advanced, discussion of the Modigliani-Miller theorem.

MALKIEL, BURTON. *A Random Walk Down Wall Street,* 5th ed. New York: Norton, 1990. A classic statement of efficient-markets theory.

THALER, RICHARD. *Advances in the Theory of Finance.* New York: Russell Sage Foundation, 1993. A stimulating collection of articles on the behavioral theory of finance.

Asset Markets

After you have read this chapter, you will be able to:

- **Understand the distinctions among the major types of financial securities.**
- **Discuss the differences between retail markets for securities and wholesale markets for securities.**
- **Compare and contrast over-the-counter markets and auction markets.**

The range of assets in the U.S. economy is large—from nonreproducible real assets like agricultural land and coal mines, to reproducible real assets like homes, office buildings, and business inventories, to many financial securities like demand and time deposits, Treasury bills, corporate and U.S. government bonds, and corporate shares. Each of these assets is traded—bought and sold—in a market, and each of these markets has its own unique characteristics. This chapter surveys the different assets, their characteristics, and the markets in which they are traded.

REAL AND FINANCIAL ASSETS

Assets are generally arranged into two main groups: **real assets,** which can be seen and touched, and **financial assets,** pieces of paper like currency, bank deposits, bonds, and shares that represent real assets. Among real assets are privately owned residential real estate, farms, office buildings, inventories in stores, and goods in process of production and publicly owned assets, including the interstate highway system, military bases, universities, national parks and forests, libraries, post offices, public schools, and fire stations. The list of publicly owned real assets is both much longer and more varied. All real assets have an owner; Americans "own shares" in the federal government and in thousands of state, city, and town governments, as well as in thousands of school districts and sewage districts, which in turn own these real assets.

The financial assets include various types of bonds (federal government, state and local governments, corporate), demand and savings deposits, deposits in nonbank financial intermediaries like the savings and loan associations, savings banks, credit unions, and the cash values of life insurance policies. Moreover, the financial assets include mortgages, shares in mutual funds, shares in pension funds, shares, both preferred and common, in both U.S. firms and foreign firms, and options on financial and real assets. Individuals own several hundred billions of dollars of currency, the note issues both of the U.S. Treasury and of the Federal Reserve Banks.

Most of these financial assets are indirect claims to the ownership of real assets. Thus the ownership of shares in tens of thousands of U.S. firms represents an indirect claim to the ownership of the factories and the warehouses that these firms own. And the bonds issued by these firms also represent an indirect claim to these same assets; frequently these assets have been pledged or mortgaged to the bondholder.

THE MAIN FEATURES OF ASSET MARKETS

The purchase and sale of assets occur in different markets and in different types of markets. Some markets are **wholesale,** and some are **retail.** This distinction is dependent on the attributes of the assets. If the attributes of the assets are homogenized, like pounds of copper or gallons of heating oil or 30-year U.S. government bonds, trading in these assets occurs in wholesale markets, because one unit of the asset is a perfect substitute for another unit. If instead, the attributes of the asset are variegated, so that the units traded are less than perfect substitutes for each other, the markets are retail and local. Real estate is a classic example of an asset traded in a retail market; each unit of real estate is location-specific. Even the various apartments in a large condominium building differ in terms of location and in most physical features, such as floor, view, and floor plan. Transactions in homes, apartments, factories, unimproved and improved land, and homes and office buildings occur primarily in retail markets. Similarly, the markets for racehorses, antique automobiles, art, and rare books are retail. The unique characteristics of each real asset mean that an extended period may pass between the time that the owner of the asset makes it known that the asset is for sale and the sale takes place, primarily because no buyer is willing to pay the seller's asking price.

In contrast, many financial securities are traded in wholesale markets. The two basic types are **over-the-counter,** or **telephone, markets** and **auction markets.** U.S. government bonds, foreign currencies, and the shares of 6,000 private firms are traded in over-the-counter markets. Corporate shares and futures contracts in commodities and in securities are traded in auction markets, typified by the New York Stock Exchange and the Chicago Board of Trade.

The dominant characteristic of auction markets is that the trading rules—covering the size of the trading unit (such as the number of shares, the number of ounces, or the number of gallons), the hours of trading, and the mechanisms for transferring money and securities between buyer and seller—are precisely specified. The number of "seats" in auction markets is also fixed. A second characteristic of auction markets is that the representatives of the buyers and the representatives of the sellers meet at a particular location, such as a trading desk or a trading pit, and loudly announce the price they are prepared to pay or the price at which they will sell, until they strike a deal; the descriptive term for this practice is **open-outcry.**

In contrast, the dominant characteristic of the over-the-counter market is that buyers and sellers communicate by phone or by computer, frequently with the assistance of brokers. The brokers that "make the market"—that hold in their own portfolios inventories of securities to be traded—are located in a number of different cities, including major financial centers like New York, Chicago, and Los Angeles, as well as more modest financial centers like Milwaukee, St. Louis, and Atlanta. The trading arrangements, in the sense of the duration of contracts, the size of the units traded, and the settlement mechanisms for exchanging money and securities, are less formal in the over-the-counter markets than in the auction markets, although certain conventions covering things such as the date of settlement and the mechanism of settlement have developed.

Historically the development of auction markets follows the development of over-the-counter markets. Once an over-the-counter market in an asset or a commodity has developed, a group of entrepreneurs organizes an auction market as a way to facilitate trading in this same asset or commodity—and to enhance their own income from providing trading facilities. The organizers usually believe that an auction market will encourage trading because of its greater liquidity—a given volume of purchases or sales will have a smaller impact on the price of the asset or commodity. The development of an auction market for trading in a security does not usually forestall trading the same security in the over-the-counter market. And investors may use the auction market rather than the over-the-counter market for one of several reasons—access to it may be easier or greater financing for their transactions may be more readily available.

The owners of the various commodity and financial-future exchanges compete vigorously to increase the volume of trading that occurs on their exchanges, because their incomes increase as the volume of trading commissions increases. Prices in auction markets for a security, such as a future contract to buy British pounds and the prices in the over-the-counter markets for *spot,* that is immediate, purchases of British pound forward-exchange contracts, are closely linked; if they got too far apart investors could profit by buying in one market and selling in the other. Because attributes of the securities traded in the auction and the over-the-counter markets may differ slightly, the actual price quotes may differ, but usually by no more than several one-hundredths of 1 percent. And the price changes in one market will be strongly correlated with price changes in the other market, except when the price changes are extremely small.

THE MARKET IN BANK DEPOSITS

Bank deposits are one of the largest classes of financial securities in the United States. They include both checkable and savings (or time) deposits sold by banks, savings and loan associations, mutual savings banks, and credit unions.

Bank deposits total $4,000 billion. The large number of advertisements in newspapers and on TV for bank deposits suggests the extensive size of the market—the advertisements stress the interest rates that each bank will pay on its deposits, the safety of each bank, and the flexibility in the terms of each deposit. The market in bank deposits is decentralized in that the deposit liabilities of each bank differ somewhat from those of other banks. Deposits are insured only up to $100,000; therefore, large deposits should not be considered perfect substitutes in terms of sensitivity to default risk.

The uniqueness of the market in bank deposits—and the reason the existence of the market is overlooked—is that these deposits almost always trade at face value; the buyer or owner of these deposits knows that he can sell the deposit back to the bank at its purchase price of $1.00—and receive 100 cents on the dollar, provided the deposit is held to its maturity.

The unique advantage of bank deposits as financial securities is their liquidity; the owner of these deposits has complete confidence in the value of the deposit (or much less uncertainty about the price at which the deposit can be exchanged for money). In some cases the owner of the deposit may request that the bank repay the deposit prior to maturity, although there may be a penalty for early withdrawal. Some certificates of deposit are negotiable; the owner of one of these might sell it prior to maturity to an investor willing to hold the security.

THE FOREIGN-EXCHANGE MARKET

The **foreign-exchange market** is the market for demand deposits denominated in the U.S. dollar, the Canadian dollar, the German mark, the Japanese yen, and most other currencies. It is the largest market in the world in terms of the volume of daily trading. This market is primarily an over-the-counter market, albeit an international one. Since the key participants are the large commercial banks, the market tends to be located in the major financial center in each country. But trading in foreign exchange occurs in some regional centers as well. Indeed, trading takes place wherever the brokers who are prepared to buy and sell foreign exchange are located. In the United States trading in foreign exchange occurs primarily in New York, although some trading is also undertaken in Boston, Philadelphia, Miami, Chicago, Detroit, Los Angeles, and San Francisco. The major international financial centers include London, Tokyo, Frankfurt, and Zurich. Participants communicate in this worldwide market by telex and telephone.

Banks specialize in trading their own currency, but each also has its own foreign-exchange trading department to buy and sell foreign exchange both for firms engaged in international trade and investment and for the bank's own account. Daily trading volume is at least twenty times larger than the volume of international trade and investment to be financed. This indicates that only a small percentage of transactions in the foreign-exchange market are made on behalf of customers needing foreign currency. Most of the transactions are made in anticipation of profits from changes in the exchange rate.

Some transactions in foreign exchange are **spot transactions,** with the exchange of deposits two business days after the parties agree to the transaction. Some transactions are **forward transactions,** with the exchange of deposits 30, 60, or 90 days after the parties agree to the transaction.

In the 1970s auction markets in foreign exchange were developed as a supplement to the over-the-counter market. They now account for 5 to 10 percent of the total volume of foreign-exchange trading. These markets—represented by the International Monetary Market (IMM) of the Chicago Mercantile Exchange, the New York Futures Exchange, the London International Financial Futures Exchange, and the Philadelphia Options Exchange—trade futures contracts in foreign exchange and options on futures contracts. A futures contract in foreign exchange is similar to a forward-exchange contract: the contract provides for an exchange of a specified amount of money at a particular date—the day the contract matures. At the Chicago IMM, futures contracts are available in six currencies—the British pound, the Japanese yen, the German mark, the Swiss franc, the Australian dollar, and the Canadian dollar. At any moment, there may be eight or ten different classes of futures contracts outstanding in each foreign currency. These futures contracts have standardized maturity dates; each contract is identified by the month in which it matures. They are also standardized in amount, typically about $50,000.

THE U.S. GOVERNMENT SECURITIES MARKET

The market in U.S. government bonds and bills is one of the largest in the world. The U.S. government's debt totaled $4,673 billion by June 1994, and the public held $3,310 billion of this debt. Together the Federal Reserve and the Social Security Trust Funds held nearly $700 billion of the debt. The publicly held federal debt includes many different maturities, from 90-day Treasury bills to 30-year bonds.

Trading in U.S. government securities occurs in an over-the-counter market. There are more than forty primary dealers, who have been approved by the Federal Reserve and can bid on *new* issues of U.S. government securities without having previously established deposits. In addition, four to five hundred dealers trade U.S. government securities to profit both from anticipating the changes in the prices of these securities and from handling the transactions with customers who wish to hold these securities in their portfolios.

The major buyers and holders of marketable U.S. government securities are the U.S. life insurance companies, U.S. commercial banks, and U.S. pension funds, as well as various foreign governments and central banks. The life insurance companies hold U.S. government securities because they have long-term liabilities to their policyholders; they seek to match the maturity of their securities with the maturity of their liabilities. Similarly, banks hold U.S. government securities because they wish to hold some low-risk assets. Both types of institutions are concerned with exposure to **market risk,** the likelihood of a change in interest rates on long-term securities relative to the interest rates on short-term securities. Life insurance companies have guaranteed payments to their policyholders; if interest rates on their securities should decline, their cash receipts would decline relative to their obligations. In the same way, if interest rates on bank deposits increased significantly relative to interest rates on the securities that the banks own, their cash payments would increase relative to their cash income.

Banks, life insurance companies, and other financial institutions trade securities extensively in an attempt to increase their total return; they "play the yield curve"—the relationship between interest rates on short-term securities relative to interest rates on long-term securities. Thus, if a life insurance company anticipates an increase in interest rates on long-term government securities, the firm will shorten the maturity of its portfolio; it will sell long-term securities and buy short-term securities in anticipation of being able to purchase long-term securities in the future when their prices are lower and their yields are higher. (If the firm continued to hold long-term securities while their prices declined, it would incur a loss.) In contrast, if the firm expects the prices of long-term securities to rise, it will buy more long-term securities in anticipation of realizing a capital gain as their prices increase.

STATE AND LOCAL GOVERNMENT BONDS

Outstanding state and local bonds in 1994 totaled over $1.2 trillion—about one-third the total value of federal government and government-guaranteed bonds. The key feature of state and local bonds is that the interest income on these bonds is not subject to federal income tax. Moreover, in some states the interest income is not subject to the state income tax. Residents who buy bonds issued by New York City pay neither city, state, nor federal income tax on the interest generated by those bonds. Hence, these bonds are likely to be acquired and held by individuals and firms that are obligated to pay federal income tax and especially those individuals who are subject to high income tax rates.

In contrast, institutions that are not subject to federal income tax because of their legal form of organization, such as college endowment funds or pension funds, are not likely to acquire nontaxable bonds; similarly foreign investors are not likely to acquire these bonds. Various mutual funds acquire these bonds and pass on the tax advantages to the investors in these funds, who are attracted by the additional advantages of diversification and professional risk appraisal. This tax-saving feature of state and local government securities can be considered a subsidy from the federal government to the state and local governments, since the interest rates that state and local governments offer on their bonds can be lower than they would otherwise have to be.

Some of the state and local government securities are **general obligation** bonds, or based on the full taxing power of the governments. Others are **revenue** bonds, and based only on the income of specified toll roads, airports, power-producing facilities, and other revenue-producing units of the government. And some of them are **industrial development** bonds, which are used to finance the development and construction of factory sites.

State and local government bonds are sold in an over-the-counter market. The market differs significantly from the market for federal government bonds because the individual bonds are so small that they are traded much less often. As a result, the market is much less liquid than the market for U.S. government securities.

THE CORPORATE BOND MARKET

Outstanding U.S. corporate bonds totaled $1,232 billion by June 1994. Public utility firms—railroads, electric power companies, telephone companies, and airlines—are major issuers of bonds; they sell these bonds to finance their expansion. Most of these bonds provide for a fixed interest payment.

The U.S. corporate bond market has two components. Some corporate bonds are traded on the auction market, along with preferred shares and common stock shares; the New York Stock Exchange is the principal auction market for trading in corporate securities. The remainder are traded in the over-the-counter market both in the United States and in the Euro-bond market—an offshore extension of the U.S. dollar bond market that is located in London, Zurich, and other European centers.[1] The Euro-bond market developed in response to the U.S. Interest Equalization Act of 1963 (which is no longer in effect); this act levied a tax of 1 to 2 percentage points on purchases of foreign securities by U.S. residents. The result was that foreign borrowers began to issue new U.S. dollar bonds in London or Luxembourg. The interest rates on these bonds were higher than they would have paid had the bonds been issued in the United States, but significantly below what they would have paid had they been denominated in the currency of one of the European countries. The buyers were foreigners—and those Americans who were evading payment of the tax. Euro-bonds have several advantages—tax on interest income is not withheld by the payer, and no record of bondholders' names is maintained; hence they are attractive to investors who wish anonymity.

U.S. corporate bonds are acquired by investors who want somewhat higher returns than those available on U.S. government bonds. And the buyers of these bonds can increase their interest return significantly by acquiring bonds that are considered less than "blue chip." Several rating agencies— Standard & Poor's, Moody's, Fitch—rank the bonds into one of eight categories on the basis of their risk. This is judged partly by the relation of the issuing firm's total income to its interest payments: the smaller the firm's income relative to its interest payments, the riskier the bonds, since the rating agencies are concerned that the borrower may not have sufficient cash receipts to pay interest. Many of the investors who own government bonds also hold large amounts of corporate bonds. However, the corporate bond market lacks the depth, breadth, and resiliency of the U.S. government securities market, and hence the liquidity of that market; modest changes in the amount of securities demanded or supplied can lead to a significant change in the price of these securities. Thus, corporate bonds are traded much less extensively than government bonds.

Apart from the debt instruments listed above, there is a type of bond that goes in and out of vogue in phase with the surges in corporate takeovers, about

[1] See Chapter 8 for a discussion and analysis of the offshore markets in U.S. dollar securities.

Suppose Your Uncle Gives You a Junk Bond: Should You Thank Him?

The term *junk bond* denotes any bond that is not classified as an investment-grade bond, and only unusually safe bonds are labeled investment grade. If a bond is classified investment grade, then a trustee can buy it for a trust fund and generally escape legal liability if the bond turns sour. Only about a thousand corporations in the United States can issue these investment-grade bonds; the bonds of all other corporations are junk bonds. They vary from bonds that are almost investment grade to bonds of bankrupt companies. Some junk bonds started out as investment-grade bonds, but were reclassified as the fortunes of the corporation that issued them deteriorated.

Are junk bonds a good investment? As usual you get nothing for nothing. The promised yield on junk bonds is higher than on investment-grade bonds, often much higher, but so is the risk. A study covering a long time span found that, on the average, junk bonds performed well. Someone who had bought a large sample of junk bonds would have incurred losses on some of them, but the higher rate of return on the others would have more than made up for that. That may, however, not be so for more recent issues of junk bonds. In the 1980s many junk bonds were issued and some of them were quite unsound.

Junk bonds have a bad reputation. Part of it is due to their unappetizing name. Who wants to own anything called "junk"? Another reason is that in the 1980s many people believed that numerous savings and loans that failed at a high cost to the taxpayer did so because of losses they sustained on their junk bonds. But as we will discuss in Chapter 9, they sustained large losses because they had an incentive to take excessive risks. If they had not taken these risks by buying junk bonds, they would have taken them some other way. A third reason is that in the 1980s illegalities sometimes occurred in connection with the sale of junk bonds. Michael Milken, who pioneered the great expansion of the junk-bond market and made an immense fortune on them, was sent to jail on various charges. But that should not hide the fact that the expansion of the junk-bond market allowed many corporations who previously could not issue bonds to do so now. This has enhanced the efficiency of the U.S. financial system.

So by all means thank your uncle.

every twenty years. Called a **junk bond,** it is the riskiest of all bonds, and therefore pays very high interest. Typically, these bonds are not rated by a rating agency. They are usually backed by a firm's investment bank. Throughout the late 1980s, more corporate junk bonds were issued than ever before. Most of these bonds were issued by Drexel, Burnham, Lambert, a large investment bank that has since ceased doing business. When Drexel closed, its junk-bond customers no longer had a venue in which to restructure their outstanding debt issues so that the bonds could remain solvent. As a result, many junk-bond holders defaulted in the early 1990s. Since then, these bonds have fallen out of fashion and are now viewed as too risky by many investors. But that does not necessarily mean that junk bonds are a bad investment; the higher yield of junk bonds *may* make them a better investment than a AAA bond for those who can stomach the risk.

THE MARKET IN CORPORATE SHARES

On a busy day, trading in corporate shares totals $5 billion and average daily volume hovers around 225 million shares, both in auction markets in the major U.S. cities and in the over-the-counter market. The New York Stock Exchange is the dominant market, and its auctions account for more than 90 percent of total trading. The American Stock Exchange, only a few blocks away in New York, specializes in trading shares of smaller firms, including many involved in energy production. Several of the regional stock exchanges—the Midwest Exchange in Chicago, the Pacific Exchange in Los Angeles and San Francisco—trade the shares of some of the firms listed in New York. And shares in a few small local firms are traded on the exchanges in Boston, Philadelphia, Baltimore, and Washington. The exchanges in Salt Lake City and Spokane specialize in trading shares in "penny stock," primarily of firms engaged in gold and silver mining.

Shares in more than four thousand firms are also traded in the over-the-counter market. Many of these shares are traded on a national basis, with buyers and sellers located in cities as far away as Miami and Seattle. But a large number of these firms are small, and their shares are likely to be traded primarily among local investors.

In recent years, a third, hybrid market in corporate shares has developed. This is an over-the-counter market that facilitates trading in the shares listed on the New York Stock Exchange in the hours after the exchange is closed.

Another recent extension is the development of financial futures contracts in corporate shares, using futures contracts in foreign exchange as a model. The buyer of the futures contract acquires the right to buy a package of corporate shares at a specified date—the maturity date of the contract. Investors who anticipate a significant increase in the general level of prices of corporate shares might find it more convenient and less costly to buy the index rather than the shares of individual firms. The sellers of stock price futures might be investors who anticipate a significant decline in the price of corporate shares and who hold a large and diversified set of shares.

DERIVATIVE AND SIMILAR MARKETS

Chapter 3 alluded to the creative ways in which financial markets meet a variety of needs. For example, some firms strip bonds so that one holder receives the interest on the bond, and the other the capital gains. The two new securities are called **derivatives** of the original bond. However, the term "derivatives" is often used loosely to include original securities with specialized features that make their value highly sensitive to changing conditions. These features may be tailored for a particular buyer of a security. In recent years the derivatives market has grown rapidly, and derivative securities now exist for a large variety of financial and real assets. For example, one type of derivative is a **floater.** This is a security whose interest payments change along with the interest rates on newly issued securities. Another is a **reverse floater,** whose interest payment goes *down* when market interest rates rise, and vice versa.

Orange County Goes Bankrupt

On December 6, 1994 Orange County, a wealthy county of over 2 million inhabitants near Los Angeles, filed for bankruptcy. How did this happen?

Robert Citron, the county's financial manager, had tried to keep taxes down and expenditures up by earning a high yield on the funds that the county was investing. The funds included not only the county's own funds but also those of various other government entities, such as local school districts. Even during the 1990–91 recession, Mr. Citron was earning an 8 to 9 percent return, much higher than the 5 to 6 percent that the state of California was earning at the time.

But there is no gain without pain. To earn such high yields, Mr. Citron took great risks. One way he did so was by holding derivatives, particularly negative floaters. Another way was through leverage and through trying to take advantage of the steepness of the yield curve. In effect, although the mechanics were different, the county purchased long-term securities, used them as collateral for short-term loans, and then used the loan receipts to purchase more long-term securities. As a result, the county had the equivalent of more than one-and-a-half dollars of debt outstanding for every dollar of equity.

As long as the interest rate on its long-term securities stayed much higher than the interest rate it was paying on its short-term borrowing, this was a highly successful strategy. But when interest rates rose in 1994, the values of its long-term securities fell. As a result, investment bankers wanted their money back, and so did the various government entities that were holding their funds with Orange County. Orange County had to declare bankruptcy. Nobody knows as yet how large the loss on its $20 billion portfolio will be, but some suspect that it will be about $2 billion. That is 10 percent of its portfolio, and more than one-quarter of its equity.

Derivatives can be used to hedge one's risks. For example, a firm that is borrowing short term, and hence loses when interest rates rise, can also issue reverse floater securities, so that some of its interest payments decline when its other interest payments go up. Derivatives can also be used to take on additional risk. For example, a firm that does not have short-term debt outstanding can buy reverse floater securities. In doing so, it takes on additional risk, since the value of these securities will decline sharply if interest rates rise.

Derivatives can have a large effect on a firm's riskiness, because in the process of splitting an original security into various parts, the major risk component can be isolated and sold separately. If a firm that is subject to one type of risk purchases a derivative with the opposite type of risk, it may substantially reduce that firm's riskiness. But if the firm buys a derivative with the same type of risk, it may substantially increase its own riskiness.

One important type of derivative is a **call option** on a stock. A so-called **European call option** gives you the right—but not the obligation—to purchase a specific amount of a stock at a fixed price, called the **strike price,** on a particular date, say, three months from today. Suppose the current price of common stock in the Acme Corporation is $9 and you buy a call option with a strike price of $10. If three months from today Acme stock trades for $12, you can buy a specific amount of this stock at $10 and make a tidy profit by reselling it at $12. You are therefore willing to pay a certain amount of money to someone who will sell you a "call." You may, of course, lose all you pay, because if three months from today the stock sells for $9, your right to buy it at $10 is worth nothing.

The opposite of a call is a **put option.** This gives you the right to sell a security at a fixed price on a particular date. Suppose you hold a stock currently selling for $20, but you are afraid that its price may fall sharply. You may not want to sell it because there is also a chance that its price will rise precipitously. By buying a put option that allows you to sell the stock, say, on October 1 at $17, you can hedge your risk since you can lose no more than $3 a share on the stock. You do, however, have to pay someone to enter into such a put contract, and if the price of the stock does not fall below $17 on the strike date, you will lose what you paid for the "put."

Derivatives are also important in other financial markets. Options exist not only for stocks, but for stock indexes, long-term bonds, commodity futures, and foreign currencies, to name but a few other possibilities. Suppose you think that the stock of Acme Corporation is undervalued relative to other stocks, but you are afraid to buy it because you think that the entire market is likely to decline. You can guard against that risk by selling a put on an index composed of the prices of most of the stocks in the market. Or an importer who has to make a payment next month in Japanese yen may want to avoid the risk that the price of yen in terms of dollars will rise. She can buy a currency call option that allows her to buy yen next month at a price fixed today.

Figure 4.1 provides an excerpt from the *New York Times* listing some options. Part A shows for both puts and calls the prices at which option contracts on the Standard & Poor's index were traded the previous day. It shows their dates horizontally, the strike prices vertically, and the price at which they traded in the body of the table. Some cells are empty because no contracts of that particular type were traded the day before. Part B shows option prices for a few particular stocks, while Part C shows the prices at which some currency futures traded.

GLOBAL TRENDS IN FINANCIAL MARKETS

The cliché that the world has become a smaller place is correct. Decreasing trade barriers have expanded the volume of international trade, while advances in telecommunications have made it easier and cheaper to obtain information on investment opportunities all over the world. Government restrictions on foreign investment have been reduced. At the same time, with income and wealth rising sharply in many countries, other financial markets, including those in Japan and Hong Kong, have grown rapidly to rival those in the United States and Europe.

As large and efficient stock markets develop in many countries, it becomes easier to invest in securities of firms around the world. For example, U.S. investors who are optimistic about the future of emerging markets in

A. Index Options

INDEX OPTIONS

S&P 100 (CBOE) Close: 429.17

Strike Price	Calls Jan	Feb	Mar	Puts Jan	Feb	Mar
380	r	r	r	$1/16$	$3/8$	$7/8$
385	r	r	r	$1/16$	$7/16$	r
390	r	r	r	$1/16$	$1/2$	$1\,1/4$
395	r	r	r	$1/8$	$11/16$	$1\,1/2$
400	r	r	r	$1/8$	$7/8$	2
405	r	r	r	$3/16$	$1\,1/16$	$2\,3/16$
410	$19\,7/8$	$22\,1/4$	r	$1/4$	$1\,3/8$	3
415	15	$17\,1/4$	r	$7/16$	$1\,15/16$	$3\,3/4$
420	$10\,1/2$	$12\,7/8$	r	$5/8$	$2\,3/4$	$4\,5/8$
425	6	9	12	$1\,3/16$	4	$5\,7/8$
430	$2\,5/8$	$5\,5/8$	$8\,1/2$	$2\,13/16$	$5\,1/2$	$7\,1/2$
435	$11/16$	$3\,1/8$	$5\,3/4$	$6\,1/8$	$8\,3/8$	$9\,3/4$
440	$3/16$	$1\,7/16$	$3\,1/2$	$10\,7/8$	$11\,3/4$	$12\,1/2$
445	$1/8$	$9/16$	$1\,7/8$	$15\,5/8$	$16\,1/2$	r
450	$1/16$	$1/4$	$15/16$	$20\,1/2$	r	$21\,1/8$
455	$1/16$	$1/8$	$7/16$	r	r	r
460	$1/16$	$1/8$	$5/16$	r	r	r
465	r	$1/16$	$1/4$	r	r	r
470	r	r	$1/4$	r	r	r

B. Stock Options

Stock Date	Exch Strike	Close Call	Put
Adapt	A	$24\,1/16$	
Jan. 95	$22\,1/2$	$1\,3/4$	r
Feb. 95	25	$1\,1/2$	$2\,3/16$
AdobeS	P	$31\,9/16$	
Jan. 95	35	$1/8$	$3\,5/8$
AdvMD	P	$31\,3/4$	
Jan. 95	25	$6\,7/8$	r
Jan. 95	30	$1\,7/8$	$5/16$
Jan. 95	35	$1/8$	$3\,1/4$
Feb. 95	25	$6\,3/4$	$1/8$
Feb. 95	30	$2\,3/4$	$3/4$
April 95	$22\,1/2$	$9\,5/8$	$3/16$
April 95	25	$7\,1/8$	$3/8$
April 95	30	$3\,7/8$	$1\,5/8$
April 95	30	$1\,5/8$	$4\,1/4$
July 95	30	$4\,5/8$	$2\,1/8$
July 95	35	$2\,1/2$	$5\,1/4$
Jan. 96	30	$6\,1/2$	$2\,3/4$
AetnLf	A	$49\,3/4$	

C. Foreign Currency Options

JAPANESE YEN (CME)
12.5 million yen; cents per 100 yen

Strike Price	Calls Feb	Mar	Apr	Puts Feb	Mar	Apr
1005	1.83	2.29	s	0.37	0.83	s
1010	1.48	1.98	s	0.51	1.02	s
1015	1.17	1.70	s	0.70	1.23	s
1020	0.90	1.44	s	0.93	1.47	s
1025	0.69	1.22	s	1.22	s	s

OPTIONS EXPLAINED

Options tables list consolidated prices for the most active stock options in U.S. trading. Long-term and short-term options are shown together. Volume criterion, for inclusion, is the total of "put" and "call" options for a given expiration date and exercise price.

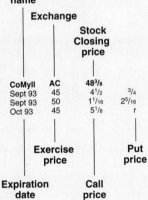

Exercise price: Amount for which shares can be bought or sold under the option.

Call price: Price of a "call" option, which is the right (but no obligation) to buy shares at the exercise price on or before the expiration date.

Put price: Price of a "put" option, which is the right (but no obligation) to sell shares at the exercise price on or before the expiration date.

r: Option that did not trade.

N.I.: New issue that began trading yesterday.

Percentage gainers list excludes options that closed under $1 the previous day or did not trade.

Percentage losers list excludes options that closed under $1 yesterday or did not trade.

Volume comparisons table includes trading in both long-term and short-term options.

Exchange: Where the company's options are traded. If the exchanges exceed three, the top three in volume are listed.
A American Stock Exchange
C Chicago Board Options Exchange
N New York Stock Exchange
P Pacific Stock Exchange
X Philadelphia Stock Exchange

Expiration date: Third Friday of the month shown.

Figure 4.1 Selected Option Prices, January 12, 1995. Source: *New York Times,* January 13, 1995, pp. C4, C13.

Southeast Asia and Russia can buy stock in companies in these countries at home or abroad, or they can invest in funds that gather together the stocks of companies located in, say, Singapore or Moscow. Similarly, it has become easier for foreigners to hold U.S. stocks and bonds. Thus foreigners and international agencies currently hold about 13 percent of federal debt, the same proportion they held twenty years ago, when the federal debt was about one-tenth of what it is now.

Nowadays, there is a major stock market open somewhere around the world at nearly any hour, and certain stocks can be traded for up to twenty hours a day. The major stock markets that compose this trading ring are the New York Stock Exchange, the London Stock Exchange, and the Tokyo Stock Exchange.

THE MARKETS IN MORTGAGES AND CONSUMER DEBT

People in the United States owe $4,280 billion of mortgage debt, both on residential real estate and on commercial buildings. The uniqueness of mortgage debt is that the borrower pledges real property if the terms of the loan are not fulfilled. Over the past 27 years, mortgages have been bought by government-sponsored agencies such as the Federal Home Loan Mortgage Corporation (FHLMC) and the Federal National Mortgage Association (FNMA). Consumer installment debt has some of the characteristics of mortgage debt, in that the borrower pledges the car or the diamond ring or the refrigerator to the lender if the terms of the loan are not fulfilled.

As we discussed in the previous chapter, both mortgage debt and consumer installment debt were highly illiquid until only recently; once the lender had acquired the loan, he was likely to hold the loan until maturity. But recently, thanks in part to the rapid declines in computer costs, this has changed. Through the process of securitization, mortgages, automobile loans, and student loans are now consolidated into packages against which securities are issued and traded. Like bonds, these securities are quoted daily in the newspapers, with information about their maturity dates and current yields. A package of securitized mortgages (or consumer loans) is analogous to a mutual fund; just as each owner of a mutual fund share holds a claim on the assets of the mutual fund, so the owner of a share in a securitized mortgage package holds a claim on all the mortgages in the package.

SUMMARY

1 If the attributes of assets are homogeneous, as with U.S. bonds of a specific maturity, they are traded in *wholesale* markets. If the attributes of assets are variegated, so that the units traded are less than perfect substitutes for each other, the markets are *retail*.
2 Financial asset markets include the market in bank deposits, the foreign-exchange market, the U.S. government securities market, the market for state and local government bonds, the corporate bond market, the stock market, derivative and similar markets, and markets in mortgage and consumer debt.

3   The dominant characteristic of *auction markets* is that the trading rules are precisely specified. A second characteristic is that the traders meet at a particular location. In contrast, the dominant characteristic of the *over-the-counter market* is that buyers and sellers communicate by phone or computer and negotiate the arrangements of the trade.

4   Spot foreign-exchange transactions trade one currency for another within two business days. Forward transactions set the exchange rate for a trade 30, 60, or 90 days hence. Options on foreign exchange give the holder of the option the right to trade one currency for another at a specified exchange rate, but not the obligation to do so.

5   Derivatives are special types of securities, often derived by splitting up other securities. Their value is highly sensitive to financial conditions. They can be used to hedge risk as well as to speculate.

6   International trade and investment have substantially expanded in recent decades as legal barriers have been removed and as the cost of communication has fallen.

KEY TERMS

real assets	call options
financial assets	derivatives
auction market	strike price
over-the-counter market	market risk
wholesale market	general obligation bonds
put options	junk bonds
Euro-bonds	

QUESTIONS AND EXERCISES

*1   What are the basic types of markets in which assets and liabilities are traded?

2   What is the key characteristic of the market for bank deposits?

*3   Discuss: "Derivatives are extremely risky," and "Derivatives are an efficient tool for reducing risk."

4   What is traded in the foreign-exchange market? How does a forward exchange contract differ from a spot exchange contract?

*5   What is the auction market in foreign exchange, and how does it differ from the over-the-counter market? What is the relationship between prices in these two markets?

6   List some of the basic characteristics of the market in U.S. government securities.

*7   What is a call option, what is a put option, and how do they differ?

FURTHER READING

CRABBE, LELAND, MARGARET PICKERING, and STEPHEN PROWSE. "Recent Developments in Corporate Finance," *Federal Reserve Bulletin*, 76 (August 1990), 593–603. A good survey of developments in the 1980s.

Federal Reserve Board publications provide comprehensive data on financial statistics. See the *Federal Reserve Bulletin*, which is published monthly.

FRIEDMAN, BENJAMIN M., ed. *Corporate Capital Structures in the United States*. Chicago: University of Chicago Press, 1985.

IBBOTSON, ROGER G., and GARY P. BRINSON. *Investment Markets*. New York: McGraw-Hill, 1987.

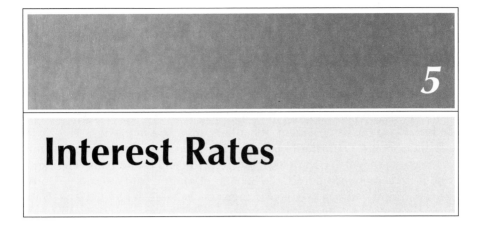

Interest Rates

After you have read this chapter, you will be able to:

- **Understand how interest rates and present value are calculated.**
- **Appreciate how differences in liquidity, tax treatment, default risk, political attributes, and currency attributes affect interest rates.**
- **Know what the yield curve is and gain an understanding of the factors that determine its slope.**

Virtually all loans involve not only the repayment of the principal amount loaned, but also the payment of interest. By not spending a dollar today and lending it out, you obtain more than a dollar to spend in the future. In other words, a dollar today exchanges for more than a dollar tomorrow. The interest rate measures this price of borrowing money, or looked at the other way around, the reward for lending money. As simple as the return on a savings account, the interest rate nonetheless plays a central role in the way the economy functions. In this chapter, we will investigate the way interest rates are calculated, look at the use of interest rates in figuring present values, and discuss the factors that cause interest rates to differ from each other. Later on, in Chapter 16, we will study the factors that determine the overall level of interest rates, and in Parts 3, 4, and 5, we will examine the ways in which changes in interest rates affect the economy.

COMPOUND INTEREST

Let's begin with a simple loan. Suppose you have $1,000 to lend and you find someone (a bank offering certificates of deposit, for instance) willing to pay you $1,100 a year from now for the use of your money. The **future value,** $1,100, includes the **present value,** or principal, $1,000, and the accrued interest for one year, $100.

The formula summarizing the simple, one-year loan is

$$\text{Present value} = \frac{\text{future value}}{1 + \text{interest rate}}.$$

In this case,

$$\$1,000 = \frac{\$1,100}{1+ \text{interest rate}}.$$

Solving for the interest rate i,

$$i = \frac{\$1,100 - 1,000}{\$1,000} = \frac{100}{1,000} = 10\%.$$

The simple loan gets its name mainly because it involves only one period, and hence one interest payment. What happens if you hold your CD for two years and continue to receive 10 percent interest on it? Assuming that the bank pays interest annually, you will have $1,210 at the end of two years. The extra $10 reflects **compound interest,** the benefits of interest paid over two periods. The 10 percent for the second year then produces $110, not $100, so your account is worth $1,210.

In mathematical terms, the compound interest formula is

$$\text{Present value} = \frac{\text{future value}}{(1 + \text{interest rate})^x},$$

where x is the number of periods. For the two-year loan,

$$\$1,000 = \frac{\text{future value}}{(1 + .10)^2},$$

so   Future value = $1,000 × 1.21 = $1,210.

With the more general formula, we can calculate loans of any length. In five years, the CD at 10 percent will be worth

$$\$1,000 = \frac{\text{future value}}{(1 + .10)^5},$$

so   Future value = $1,000(1.61) = $1,610.

Using the simple loan calculation for a single, five-year period would have produced only $1,500 [$1,000 × (1 + interest rate)]. Compound interest really does make a difference.

A common and vexing problem in business is how to compare investment alternatives that come to fruition at different points in time. Should an executive put $1 million into an asset that trustworthy experts tell her will be worth $1.5 million five years from now? After all, the half-million-dollar gain looks pretty good—or does it?

Our executive can measure the opportunity cost of her money by the interest rate. That is, she does not have to invest in the new asset; she could simply put the money into a bank account or some equally secure, interest-bearing investment. Suppose again that the interest rate is 10 percent. With interest compounded annually, her $1 million will produce

$$\$1,000,000 = \frac{\text{future value}}{(1+ .10)^5},$$

so   Future value = $1,610,000.

She is better off putting her firm's money in the bank.

Present Discounted Value

The interest rate, as we are beginning to see, forms the bridge between present and future values. For convenience, business analysts generally work all future values back to the present. Let's examine the case of a business executive with a $500,000 budget, one investment opportunity that will be worth $750,000 in five years, and another that will be worth $1,000,000 in seven. His first step will be to discount the two future values to their respective present values, using the present discounted value formula:

$$\text{Present discounted value} = \frac{\text{future value}}{(1 + \text{interest rate})^x},$$

where x is the number of periods. (It is no mistake that the present discounted value formula matches the one for interest rates.) Applying the formula and assuming an interest rate of 10 percent, $750,000 five years from now becomes

$$\text{Present value} = \frac{\text{future value}}{(1 + r)^5}$$

$$= \frac{750,000}{(1.10)^5}$$

$$= \$465,839.$$

The present discounted value, $465,839, is less than the present value of the cash, $500,000, so this investment is not worth undertaking.

The other opportunity will produce $1,000,000 in seven years. Its present discounted value is:

$$\text{Present value} = \frac{\text{future value}}{(1 + r)^7}$$

$$= \frac{\$1,000,000}{(1 + .10)^7}$$

$$= \$512,821.$$

Now the present value is greater than the cash, so the opportunity should be pursued. The rule is simple: if the present discounted value of the investment opportunity is greater than the cost of the investment, pursue it. If it is less, pass on it.

We can see how vital the prevailing rate of interest is. At 10 percent, the present discounted value of $1,000,000 seven years from now is $512,821. At 5 percent, the present value is:

$$\text{Present value} = \frac{\text{future value}}{(1 + r)^x}$$

$$= \frac{\$1,000,000}{(1.05)^7}$$

$$= \$709,220.$$

Example of Payments on an Amortized Loan

Suppose in December 2000 someone takes out a $100,000 amortized two-year loan at a 10 percent interest rate with monthly payments. Below are the payments she would make, broken down into interest payments and repayment of principal. Initially, most of the payments represent interest, and the outstanding principal shrinks slowly. But as time goes by, the principal shrinks more and more, so that a continually declining proportion of the monthly payments is needed to pay interest and therefore the outstanding principal shrinks at an accelerating rate.

Monthly Loan Payments—Interest versus Principal

Payment Number	Payment Date	Payment Amount			Balance Due
		Total	Interest	Principal	
1	Jan 2001	$4,614.49	$833.33	$3,781.16	$96,218.84
2	Feb 2001	4,614.49	801.82	3,812.67	92,406.17
3	Mar 2001	4,614.49	770.05	3,844.44	88,561.73
4	Apr 2001	4,614.49	738.01	3,876.48	84,685.25
5	May 2001	4,614.49	705.71	3,908.78	80,776.47
6	Jun 2001	4,614.49	673.14	3,941.35	76,835.12
7	Jul 2001	4,614.49	640.29	3,974.20	72,860.92
8	Aug 2001	4,614.49	607.17	4,007.32	68,853.60
9	Sep 2001	4,614.49	573.78	4,040.71	64,812.89
10	Oct 2001	4,614.49	540.11	4,074.38	60,738.51
11	Nov 2001	4,614.49	506.15	4,108.34	56,630.17
12	Dec 2001	4,614.49	471.92	4,142.57	52,487.60
13	Jan 2002	4,614.49	437.40	4,177.09	48,310.51
14	Feb 2002	4,614.49	402.59	4,211.90	44,098.61
15	Mar 2002	4,614.49	367.49	4,247.00	39,851.61
16	Apr 2002	4,614.49	332.10	4,282.39	35,569.22
17	May 2002	4,614.49	296.41	4,318.08	31,251.14
18	Jun 2002	4,614.49	260.43	4,354.06	26,897.08
19	Jul 2002	4,614.49	224.14	4,390.35	22,506.73
20	Aug 2002	4,614.49	187.56	4,426.93	18,079.80
21	Sep 2002	4,614.49	150.67	4,463.82	13,615.98
22	Oct 2002	4,614.49	113.47	4,501.02	9,114.96
23	Nov 2002	4,614.49	75.96	4,538.53	4,576.43
24	Dec 2002	4,614.49	38.14	4,576.35	0.00

Interest Rates and Discount Rates

Some loan contracts specify a discount rate rather than an interest rate. That means that the interest payment is made not, say, monthly or yearly or when the loan is repaid, but is made when the loan is received. For example, suppose you borrow $1,000 for a year and the discount rate is 8 percent. You sign a promisary note for $1,000, and the lender discounts it by giving you only $820 for this note. By paying interest in advance in this way, you are actually paying a 8.7 percent rate ($80/$920) rather than an 8 percent rate. Such discounting is not unusual for short term loans in large transactions. For example, Treasury bills are sold on a discount basis. Discounting reduces paperwork because no checks have to be written for interest payments. That facilitates trading in these securities.

Real and Nominal Rates

Suppose you cut your consumption by $100 and buy a CD that yields 4 percent. You might be in for a disappointment, because the $104 that you then have available next year might purchase no more than $100 does this year. In terms of purchasing power, that is in *real* terms, the interest rate you earned has been zero. In some years the real rate on Treasury bills has even been negative. It is therefore very important to distinguish between the **real interest rate,** which takes changes in purchasing power into account, and the **nominal interest rate,** which does not.

The real interest rate is equal to the nominal interest rate minus the percentage change in prices. For example, if the inflation rate is 3 percent, a nominal interest rate of 8 percent represents a real interest rate of 5 percent. Suppose you lend someone $1,000 and later get back $1,080 dollars. But what you could buy before for $1,000 now costs $1,030. Of the $80 nominal interest that you received, only $50 is genuine income; the other $30 merely compensates you for the decline in the purchasing power of the principal of the loan.

This is simple and straightforward. What is not so simple is to keep the distinction between the real rate and the nominal rate firmly in mind. For example, in 1980 when the interest rate on three-month Treasury bills was 11.5 percent, many people were complaining about high interest rates. But since the consumer price index was rising at a 12.5 percent rate that year, the real interest rate was minus 1 percent.

WHY INTEREST RATES DIFFER

The version of the interest rate that we have examined up to this point is sometimes referred to as the **pure rate of interest.** The pure rate of interest measures the cost of money tomorrow versus its cost today. Yet, on a typical day, the *Wall Street Journal* lists several hundred interest rates. There are interest rates on the forty-plus U.S. Treasury bills, thirty-plus note issues of the U.S. Treasury, and about forty bond issues of the U.S. Treasury. There are interest rates on the securities issued by various U.S. government agencies—the Federal Intermediate Credit Bank, the Federal Home Loan Bank, and so forth. There are the interest rates on fifty nontaxable revenue bonds sold by the agencies and governments of various states and localities, such as the New Jersey Turnpike, the Municipal Assistance Corporation (MAC) of New York, and the Washington Public Power Authority. There are the interest rates on three hundred corporate bonds traded on the New York Stock Exchange and forty corporate bonds traded on the American Stock Exchange.

Many interest rates are open-market rates and vary frequently, perhaps daily or even hourly, in response to changes in demand and supply. Several interest rates are managed, usually set by the banks or by a government agency; these posted interest rates might remain unchanged for an extended period. The **prime commercial loan rate,** which is the interest rate that banks charge on loans to their best commercial borrowers, is an example of a posted or managed rate. So is the Federal Reserve's discount rate. So are the interest rates on certificates of deposit and on the U.S. Treasury's savings bonds.

The key question is, why are there so many different interest rates at any one time? A related question is, why does the relationship among these interest rates change over time? The principal answer is that these securities differ in their attributes: some may promise to make repayment at a later date than others, some are riskier than others, and some carry tax advantages. Technically, the relevant attributes include liquidity, information cost, tax liability, default sensitivity, venue or political risk, currency, and maturity.

The Liquidity Attribute

Let's look first at how characteristics of markets influence interest rates. A main feature of markets is **liquidity.** As discussed in Chapter 1, liquidity involves the ease with which a security can be sold and the impact of a given volume of sales or purchases on the price of a security. The difference between the price paid when a security is purchased and the price received when the security is sold reflects the various charges or fees demanded by the brokers and the other intermediaries in the market; these charges and fees can be grouped as transactions costs. The size of these transactions costs measure the liquidity of the market.

The more liquid the market, the lower the transactions costs and the lower the interest rates attached to the securities traded in that market; the less liquid the market, the higher the interest rate the borrower must pay to sell securities to investors, for the investors want to be compensated for the costs they will incur when they sell the security.

Real estate is traded in retail markets, which are not liquid: a seller usually establishes a price and waits until a buyer makes an offer. (Occasionally there are real estate auctions, especially when the owners are in distress and need cash immediately.) The seller usually knows that it is unlikely that the property will be sold at the listed price, so the listed price is set to leave some room for negotiation; the seller cannot refer to a market price because there are no identical pieces of property available. The brokerage commissions on residential real estate generally range from 5 to 6 percent; the costs on a $100,000 transaction would amount to $5,000 or $6,000. And in addition buyers would incur the costs of identifying the property they wish to purchase and negotiating with the sellers. In contrast, markets in government bonds and foreign exchange are highly liquid, so that the costs associated with a $100,000 transaction would be $30 to $50—or 3/100ths to 5/100ths of 1 percent.

While the market in U.S. government securities is the most liquid, even within this market individual securities differ in terms of liquidity, depending on the amount of the security that remains outstanding and whether the security has been *seasoned,* or traded extensively. Securities issued by U.S. government agencies like the Federal Intermediate Credit Bank and the Federal Home Loan Bank generally pay a higher interest rate than those issued by the U.S. Treasury, since they are less liquid, primarily because the size or outstanding volume of the agency issues is smaller.

The Information Cost Attribute

No reasonable person will make a loan without having some information about whether the borrower is likely to repay. Such information may be costly to obtain. Risky borrowers have an incentive to masquerade as safe borrowers, so creditors may have to undertake an expensive effort to dig beneath the surface. These expenditures are known as **information costs,** and they increase the interest rate.

The concept of information costs leads to several further observations about why interest rates differ. First, since the cost of investigating a borrower's credit standing does not rise in proportion to the size of the loan, other things being equal, interest rates on large loans are lower than interest rates on small loans. Second, large, well-known firms can, again other things being equal, borrow at a lower rate than small, less well known firms. Third, the federal government, whose credit standing does not need to be investigated, can borrow at a rock-bottom rate. Fourth, since lenders usually have much less information about small firms than about large ones, small firms tend to borrow relatively less often on the large impersonal bond market and relatively more often from banks and other creditors who have a comparative advantage in obtaining information about them.

The Tax Liability Attribute

What matters to lenders is the **after-tax income.** Hence, another reason why interest rates on some securities are higher than on others is that the interest income on them may be subject to income tax, while the interest income on the others is not. A corporate bond with a 9 percent, taxable interest rate doesn't look as attractive to someone in the 39 percent marginal tax bracket as does a 7 percent, tax-free rate; for this investor, the after-tax return on the taxable security is 3.51 percent. Since each investor seeks to maximize the after-tax income or return, the investor is concerned with the effective tax rate on interest income, dividend income, and capital-gains income and compares various securities in terms of their tax liability. This determination is based on the **marginal tax rate,** not the average tax rate. The marginal tax rate is the tax rate on *changes* in one's income, not on the average dollar of income.

The interest income of the security issues of state governments and of the various subdivisions of state governments, such as cities, counties, and townships, are not subject to federal income taxes. (The reverse is not true; state governments tax the interest income of federal government securities.) As a result, some investors prefer nontaxable state and local government bonds

to the taxable bond issues of the U.S. government, of various foreign governments, and of various U.S. and foreign corporations, even though the interest
rates on the taxable bonds may be several percentage points higher than the
interest rates on the nontaxable state and local bonds.

Assume the interest rate on a taxable bond is 7.50 percent, while the
interest rate on a nontaxable bond is 6.20 percent. Whether the investor
should prefer the bond with the higher interest rate depends on the investor's
marginal tax rate. For each investor, the effective comparison is between the
after-tax return on the taxable security and the return on the tax-free security;
investors differ in their preferences or choices, because their marginal tax rates
differ. The higher the marginal tax rate of a given investor, the more likely,
given any particular set of interest rate differentials, that the investor will prefer the nontaxable security. Conversely, investors with low marginal tax rates
are unlikely to be attracted to tax-free securities; instead they will buy the taxable securities because the after-tax returns on the taxable securities are higher
for them than those on the tax-free securities.

At any one moment, the after-tax return on the taxable securities and
the return on the tax-free securities are similar or identical for one group of
investors; for these investors, the differences in before-tax interest rates more
or less compensate for the differences in tax rates. The preferences of these
investors may change if their marginal tax rate changes; as their marginal tax
rate increases, they will demand more nontaxable securities.

The difference between the interest rate on taxable securities and the
interest rate on tax-free securities varies as a result of changes in three factors—the level of the marginal tax rate, the level of interest rates, and the supply of tax-free securities relative to the supply of taxable securities. As marginal
tax rates increase, some investors in the highest marginal tax bracket will shift
from taxable securities toward tax-free securities because their return on these
securities will be higher. Thus, the borrowers that issue taxable bonds must
pay higher interest rates to compensate investors for the higher tax rates.
Increases in the supply of tax-free securities relative to the supply of taxable
securities lead to a decline in the difference between the interest rate on taxable and nontaxable securities. Finally, as the level of interest rates increases,
the interest rates on taxable securities must increase relative to the interest
rates on nontaxable securities in order to compensate investors for the larger
amount of tax they must pay on the higher interest income.

The Default-Sensitivity Attribute

A big risk in owning most securities is **credit risk;** in some cases the borrower
may not repay all the interest and principal. Because investors perceive that
individual securities differ in terms of their probability of default, the interest
rates on these securities differ. The least risky securities in terms of default are
those of the U.S. government, because the U.S. government can obtain the
funds to pay the interest on its outstanding securities from its power to tax and
from its control over the Federal Reserve System, our nation's central bank.
(The reliance on central-bank financing for the funds to pay the interest on

the U.S. Treasury's debt may be problematic because it may lead to an increase in the inflation rate, which we will study later in the book.)

Not surprisingly, rates on securities believed to be more sensitive to default are higher than those on securities judged less sensitive to this risk. And the greater the sensitivity of individual securities to default, the higher the interest rate attached to these securities. The key issue is whether the additional interest rate paid by borrowers in higher-risk categories more or less compensates the lenders for the higher risk. Some contend that differences in the interest rate, or differentials, are appropriately scaled to the probability of default and the losses that the borrowers are likely to incur, so that the holders of risky bonds are adequately compensated—but only adequately compensated—for the losses they will incur as a result of default by different borrowers. The implication is that the net income of those investors who choose the riskier bonds will not be significantly higher than the income of those investors who prefer the less risky securities. The competing view is that the interest-rate differentials are large relative to the losses on the riskier securities, because the **risk premium** embedded in the interest-rate differential represents additional compensation to investors for bearing the uncertainty associated with the probability of the loss, over and above the actuarial value of that probable loss.

In the previous chapter we discussed junk bonds. Yields on these bonds have been 3 to 4 percentage points higher than the interest rates on conventional bonds in order to induce investors to buy them. The rationale for such a large difference in interest rates was that these borrowers presented a significantly greater risk, and there was little experience to substantiate their ability to pay interest on a timely basis. The term *junk bonds* itself would seem detrimental to the interests of the borrowers, since investors would want a higher interest rate for buying a bond with "junk" in its name than they would for a bond with similar features and a less pejorative name.

When these junk bonds were first issued, the higher interest rates seemed more than adequate to compensate for the higher risk. But recent experience with junk bonds issued in the 1980s suggests that interest rates were too low to compensate investors for the losses that they have incurred: more than one-third of these bonds have gone into default.

The differential between interest rates on U.S. government bonds and those on corporate bonds—and between AAA corporate bonds and BBB corporate bonds—might change for several reasons, including changes in the relative supplies: the larger the volume of new corporate bond issues relative to the volume of new government bond issues, the larger the differential. Moreover, the differential increases during recessions or periods of slack business activity, for the likelihood of default decreases the more robust the level of business activity.

The Political Attribute

The volume of U.S. dollar–denominated bonds issued by U.S. and foreign firms in London, Zurich, and other offshore financial centers is about as large as the volume of U.S. dollar bonds issued in the United States.

Grading the Riskiness of Bonds

Suppose you are considering buying some bonds. Obviously you would like a way of telling with certainty just how risky these bonds are, but there is no way of doing that. For one thing, the general level of interest rates may rise while you hold the bond, and if they do, the value of your bond will decline. Here, all you can do is make a more or less informed guess.

When it comes to the credit risk of your bond, however, you will get more help. Moody's and Standard & Poor's publish credit-risk evaluations, which rate the likelihood that the issuing company or government will go bankrupt. Their evaluations are based on considerable research, but even so, they are sometimes incorrect. The companies use a grading system running from D (there is no F) to triple A. (Talk about grade inflation!) The table below describes the meaning of their grades.

Summary of Bond Ratings

Investment Grade	Moody's	S&P's
Highest quality	Aaa	AAA
High quality	Aa	AA
Upper medium	A	A
Medium	Baa	BBB
Lower quality:		
Moderately speculative	Ba	BB
Speculative	B	B
Highly speculative	Caa	CCC
Poor quality	Ca	CC
Lowest quality, no interest	C	C
In default, in arrears	—	D

Since interest rates on U.S. dollar bonds issued in London and Zurich are generally higher than those offered on comparable bonds issued in New York, the question that arises is why any investors hold New York dollar bonds—and forgo the higher income available on the offshore bonds. The answer is that investors—at least some of them—are concerned that a country's authorities might apply exchange controls, that is, controls over the repatriation of funds from the foreign financial center to the United States. The differential between the interest rate on Eurodollar bonds and the interest rate on comparable bonds issued in New York represents the payment demanded by the marginal investor for incurring the political risk associated with investing in offshore U.S. dollar bonds—the risk that some type of control might interfere with the use of funds received in payment of the interest. Variations in the differentials between interest rates on New York dollar bonds and comparable interest rates on dollar bonds available in a financial center in

Europe might reflect either changes in assessment of the political risk attached to offshore dollar bonds or, alternatively, changes in the supply of Eurodollar bonds relative to the supply of comparable bonds issued in the United States.

The Currency Attribute

Most of the securities noted in the *Wall Street Journal* and other U.S. newspapers are denominated in the U.S. dollar; interest is paid and principal repaid in U.S. dollar funds. But some of these securities provide for the payment of interest and principal in a foreign currency, such as the Swiss franc, the German mark, or the Japanese yen. The interest rates on these securities differ from those on comparable U.S. dollar securities for several reasons, including anticipated changes in the foreign-exchange value of the U.S. dollar in terms of the foreign currency. For example, if U.S. investors anticipate that the British pound will depreciate relative to the U.S. dollar, they will require a higher interest rate on British pound securities to compensate for the loss they might incur by holding them. (A similar statement can be made about British investors.) The implication is that the more rapid the anticipated rate of depreciation of the British pound is, the higher the interest rate on British pound securities relative to the interest rate on U.S. dollar securities will be.

Moreover, the interest-rate differential on comparable bonds denominated in different currencies may include a risk premium, similar in some ways to the risk premium that compensates investors in the bond market for the greater default sensitivity of somewhat riskier bonds. If investors conclude that securities denominated in a particular currency are riskier because that currency is more volatile in the foreign-exchange market, they may demand a premium to hold securities denominated in this currency as compensation for this greater risk: holdings of securities denominated in some currencies are riskier than holdings of comparable securities denominated in other currencies.

Changes in the differential between interest rates on U.S. dollar bonds and on comparable bonds denominated in other currencies primarily reflect anticipated changes in the foreign-exchange value of the U.S. dollar in terms of these currencies. As investors begin to anticipate that the U.S. inflation rate will increase relative to the inflation rates in Germany and Japan, interest rates on U.S. dollar securities will increase because investors will expect inflation to cause the U.S. dollar to depreciate in the foreign-exchange market, and these investors will require compensation for this change.

The Term Structure of Interest Rates

The phrase **term structure of interest rates** refers to the difference in interest rates for various maturities, for example, the differences among the interest rates of 90-day Treasury bills, 1-year Treasury notes, and 30-year Treasury bonds.

The term "structure" is important because the maturities of various securities vary widely. At one extreme there are loans, such as overnight federal funds and overnight repurchase agreements, that have a maturity of one day.

At the other extreme, there are some rare securities with a maturity of over ninety years. In between are 90-day Treasury bills, 9-month commercial paper, 30-year U.S. government bonds, and so on. A lender who wants to offer her funds for any specific length of time between one day and thirty years should be able to find some security that allows her to do just that.

What makes for such a wide spread of available maturities is not just that there are borrowers who issue securities with different maturities, but also that there is a large secondary market. Suppose you want to invest for exactly 9 years and 265 days. No borrower has issued a security with exactly that maturity. But, at various times borrowers have issued securities with maturities of 10 years. If you buy a 10-year security that was issued 100 days ago, then for your purposes, the maturity of this security is exactly equal to the 9 years and 265 days for which you want to invest.

The Yield Curve

Does the maturity of a security affect the interest rate you earn on it? The simplest and most naive answer one might give is that interest rates should be about the same for all maturities. If a firm pays you 7 percent, that is $70, for lending it $1,000 for one year, wouldn't the same firm pay you a total of $140 for lending the same amount for two years? No it will not, at least not most of the time. Interest rates vary depending on the maturity, or more precisely the duration, of the loan. This relation between the yield of securities and their maturity is depicted by a **yield curve.** Such a curve, shown in Figure 5.1, is published every weekday in the *Wall Street Journal.* As this figure shows, the yield curve is not fixed, but varies from time to time, occasionally even by enough to change the direction of the slope (see Figure 5.2). Although an upward-sloping yield curve is called a "normal yield curve," it is not unusual for the yield curve to be "inverted" shortly before the onset of a recession. Indeed a recent study found that whenever the federal-funds rate greatly exceeded the three-month Treasury bill rate, a recession soon followed.[1] What determines the slope of the yield curve? Many factors do, so many that just listing them would result in confusion. It is therefore better to simplify the story by looking at two extreme stories, neither of which is realistic, and then combine what we have learned from them into a more realistic theory.

Extreme Market Segmentation

The first extreme story treats long-term securities and short-term securities as though they were very different commodities, as different, say, as potato chips and motorbikes. Economic theory tells us that all markets are connected, that in principle, a rise in the price of potato chips affects the price of motorbikes. But we also know that as a practical matter, we can ignore such trivial effects. *If*

---

[1] A warning: While this relation has held in the past, it need not necessarily hold in the future. A plausible explanation of it is that spikes in the federal funds rate, and hence in the gap between the funds rate and the three-month Treasury bill rate, signify a shift to a highly restrictive monetary policy that will generate a recession.

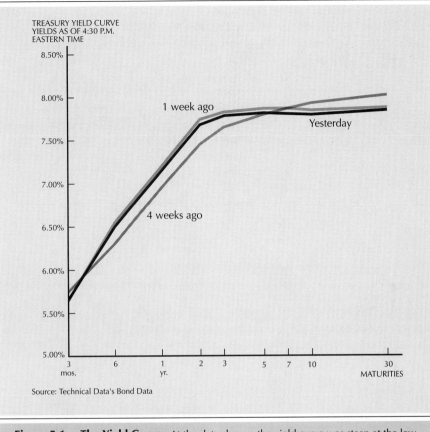

TREASURY YIELD CURVE
YIELDS AS OF 4:30 P.M.
EASTERN TIME

1 week ago

Yesterday

4 weeks ago

Source: Technical Data's Bond Data

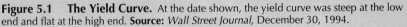

Figure 5.1   The Yield Curve. At the date shown, the yield curve was steep at the low end and flat at the high end. **Source:** *Wall Street Journal,* December 30, 1994.

long-term and short-term rates are thus determined essentially independently of each other, then the yield curve is not a meaningful concept. It is like looking at the ratio of the price of potato chips to the price of motorbikes. Yes, we can calculate this price ratio, but there is no reason to expect it to be stable or of any interest.

In this extreme story in which long- and short-term securities are treated as very different assets, there are some institutions, such as life insurance companies, that want to lend long term and some borrowers, such as households seeking fixed-rate mortgages, that want to borrow long term. Supply and demand in this long-term market determine the long-term rate. At the same time there are other lenders, such as households accumulating funds for near-term expenditures, that want to lend short term, and other borrowers, such as retailers needing to increase their inventories before Christmas, that want to borrow short term. Their supplies and demands determine the short-term rate. The two markets are entirely segregated, so that no borrower who prefers long-term financing will decide to borrow short term merely because the short-term

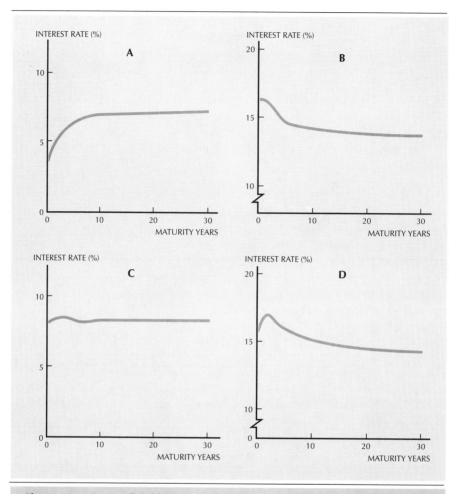

Figure 5.2   Types of Yield Curves. Panel A shows an upward-sloping yield curve, tracked in April 1994. Panel B shows a downward-sloping yield curve, tracked in May 1981. Panel C shows a flat yield curve, tracked in June 1989. Panel D shows a humped yield curve, tracked in August 1981.

rate is lower. Similarly, if the long-term rate is lower, no borrower will be enticed into borrowing long term, and no long-term lender will be tempted to switch to short-term lending. No matter how much the price of motorbikes falls, you will buy potato chips and not a motorbike. Long-term rates and short-term rates are unrelated.

Extreme Arbitrage Theory

The second extreme story treats long-term and short-term securities *not* as separate commodities, but as essentially the same commodity. So, we can apply the law of one price, which states that the same units of the same commodity in the same place at the same time must sell for the same price. If some units were to cost more than others, customers would buy the cheaper ones, or else traders, called arbitragers, would buy the cheaper units and thus raise their price, and then sell them in competition with the more expensive units and thereby bring down their price.

This *seems* to imply that the yield curve is flat, and since we know that it is usually not flat, the extreme arbitrage story seems useless. But that appearance is deceptive, because it fails to compare like with like. Consider, for example, one-year and two-year securities. The extreme arbitrage story says that the total yield on both securities must be equal. But how can we compare a 4 percent annual yield on a one-year security with a 5 percent annual yield on a two-year security? To decide whether one security is a better buy than the other, we have to compare the yields of the securities for the same time period. Suppose that the buyer of the one-year security could be certain that when her security is paid off at the end of the first year, she will reinvest for a second year, again at 4 percent. We could then say that the one-year security yields 4 percent, and thus 1 percent less per year than the two-year security. But with interest rates changing all the time, there is no reason to assume that next year's rate on one-year securities will again be 4 percent.

Suppose interest rates rise, so that in the second year a one-year security yields 8 percent. Then—ignoring compound interest—the average annual yield from investing in two successive one-year securities would be 6 percent, and thus higher than the 5 percent annual yield on the two-year security. Hence, even though we observe that the yields on one-year and two-year securities differ, it may still be true that investors expect to earn the same return by investing for one year at a time as they could earn by investing for two years. This principle can be generalized for longer maturities. Even if a 5-year bond pays a lower rate than a 30-year bond, investors might still expect to earn as much or more by buying the 5-year bond as by buying the 30-year bond because they expect interest rates to rise.

If the extreme arbitrage story were correct, borrowers and lenders would not care whether they borrowed (or lent) short term or long term. Rather, they would care only about the total yield they would earn. This means we can use the relation between the yields on short- and long-term securities that we observe in the market to tell us what the market expects short-term interest rates to be in the future. For example, again ignoring the compounding of interest, suppose that a two-year security pays 5 percent and a one-year security pays 3 percent. We can then say that the market expects the one-year interest rate to be 7 percent next year. If it expected the one-year rate a year from now to be less than that, then lenders would not be willing to buy a 3 percent one-year security this year, whereas if they expected it to be more than 7 percent, they would all want to buy a one-year security instead of a two-year security. (A similar argument applies to borrowers.) That would raise the one-year rate and lower the two-year rate. More generally, according to the extreme arbitrage story, the current long-term rate is an average of the expected future short-term rates over the life of the long-term security. *Thus, in the simple and extreme arbitrage story, if the yield curve slopes upward, the market must expect short-term rates to rise; if the yield curve slopes downward, it must expect short-term rates to fall; and if the yield curve is flat, then it must expect short-term rates to be stable.*

What Does Explain the Slope of the Yield Curve?

Both stories discussed so far were called "extreme," which suggests that they are wrong. But they have been useful in clarifying our thinking. We can now combine the valid components of each to come up with a much more defensible theory. This theory is called the **preferred habitat theory.** It recognizes that long- and short-term securities are not a single commodity, so that their prices—and hence long- and short-term rates—can differ. But it also recognizes that there is considerable connection between the two markets. The relevant comparison is not between motorbikes and potato chips, but between motorbikes and moderately priced cars. If the price of motorbikes rises, *some* of those who intended to buy motorbikes will now buy cars instead.

But we should try to go beyond the innocuous statement that both extreme views are partially valid. How close a substitute for long-term securities are short-term securities? The answer to this question will tell us how valid it is to read the market's prediction of future short-term rates into the slope of the yield curve. If long-term borrowers and lenders are reluctant to leave the long-term market, and short-term borrowers and lenders are reluctant to leave the short-term market, then the slope of the yield curve contains little information about expected future rates.

The extreme assumption that borrowers and lenders do not care whether they borrow or lend long term or short term is, of course, nonsense.

But a more moderate version of the arbitrage story does not require that *all* borrowers and lenders be willing to shift between markets at the slightest differential in interest rates. As so often in economics, what occurs depends on what happens at the margin. Suppose, for example, that the long-term rate is 7 percent and the short-term rate is 5 percent. Despite the higher cost of borrowing long term, the typical long-term borrower may be unwilling to borrow short term instead. But *some* long-term borrowers will decide to save themselves the extra 2 percent by shifting to the short-term market. In doing so, they will drive the long-term rate down and the short-term rate up, and *if* there are enough of them, the two rates will become practically equal.

Moreover, although the discussion has so far dealt only with two types of securities, long term and short term, there are also many securities with intermediate maturities. This continuum of maturities makes it much more likely that borrowers and lenders will switch between markets. Suppose, for example, that the interest rate on 30-year bonds rises by 2 percent. Those who normally buy 90-day Treasury bills are not likely to switch to 30-year bonds. But some of those who normally buy, say, 20-year bonds will be enticed by the higher interest rate into buying 30-year bonds instead. As they switch from 20-year bonds to 30-year bonds, the yield on 30-year bonds falls, and the yield on 20-year bonds rises. And with the yield on 20-year bonds rising, some of those who otherwise would have bought 15-year bonds now buy 20-year bonds, so that the yield on 15-year bonds also rises, and so on down the line. In this way, changes in long-term and short-term security markets are linked.

Liquidity Premium

The fact that markets are linked does not necessarily mean that the extreme arbitrage story is closer to the truth than the extreme segmentation story. One way in which the extreme arbitrage story fails is that the yield curve is usually upward sloping. It is hardly plausible that the market usually expects that short-term rates will rise since in actuality they sometimes rise and sometimes fall. A plausible explanation is that there is a **liquidity premium** in the market; on the margin, lenders prefer to lend short term, while borrowers prefer to borrow long term. Hence, to bring supply and demand in both markets into balance, the long-term rate usually exceeds the short-term rate. As a result, if the two-year rate is, say, a quarter of a percent higher than the one-year rate, that *may* be entirely consistent with the market expecting next year's one-year rate to be the same as, or even lower than, this year's.

Given the existence of a liquidity premium, that the yield curve becomes steeper does not necessarily mean that future short-term rates will rise. The increase in the short-term rates could instead be due to a rise in the liquidity premium. Changes in the liquidity premium can explain why it frequently happens that a steepening of the yield curve is *not* followed by a subsequent rise in the short-term rate, and a flattening of the yield curve is *not* followed by a fall in short-term rates.

The Liquidity Premium and the Flow of Funds

The liquidity premium is an important element in determining the slope of the yield curve. Hence, market analysts would like to be able to predict how it will behave.

The liquidity premium that is embodied in the long-term rate depends not only on the preferences with respect to liquidity of each of the individual lenders and borrowers, but also on the relative importance of each of them in the market. For example, the liquidity premium might rise, even though the individual lenders or borrowers have not changed their preferences for liquidity, if there is a shift in the distribution of loanable funds away from those lenders who have a low preference for liquidity toward those who have a high preference for liquidity.

There is no extensive set of data on the preferences for liquidity of individual borrowers and lenders. But there are detailed data on the distribution of liquid funds and of other financial assets, as well as liabilities, among various sectors of the economy, such as insurance companies, nonfinancial corporations, banks, state and local government retirement funds, and so on. The Board of Governors of the Federal Reserve System publishes these data as part of its *Flow of Funds* accounting system. For each of these sectors this data set lists the types of financial assets it holds, as well as the types of liabilities, and the quarterly changes in these assets and liabilities.

Financial analysts trying to predict the term structure of interest rates can use these data. Suppose, for example, that they see that the available funds of banks (institutions that like to lend relatively short term) are increasing more rapidly than they expected, while the available funds of state and local government retirement funds (which like to invest long term) are increasing at a slower rate. They may then revise their forecast of the term structure of interest rates.

SUMMARY

1   There are simple formulas for calculating the interest rate.
2   One can compare the yields of assets with different maturities by calculating their present values.
3   The real rate of interest is obtained by subtracting the inflation rate from the nominal interest rate.
4   The less liquid a security is, the greater the cost of investigating its safety is; and the higher its risk of default is, the higher the interest rate that has to be paid on it is. The political and currency attributes of securities also explain some of the differences in their yields, as do their tax attributes.
5   An important characteristic of securities is their maturity. The yield curve relates their maturity to their yield. Yield curves usually, but not always, slope upward.
6   The slope of the yield curve can be explained by the relative pressures of supply and demand for securities of various maturities, as well as by the market's expectations of future short-term rates.

KEY TERMS

compound interest   present discounted value
liquidity premium   market segmentation
risk premium   arbitrage
yield curve   preferred habitat theory
real interest rate   flow of funds
marginal tax rate   information costs

QUESTIONS AND EXERCISES

1   Explain *why* interest rates are affected by a security's liquidity, tax liability, political, and currency attributes.
*2   What factors determine the slope of the yield curve?
3   Why does the yield curve usually slope upward?
*4   What is wrong with the extreme market segmentation story?
5   What does the extreme arbitrage story contribute to our understanding of the yield curve?
*6   Suppose you observe that long-term interest rates rise much more than short-term rates. What, if anything, does this tell you about what will happen to short-term rates in the future?

FURTHER READING

HOMER, SYDNEY. *A History of Interest Rates*. New Brunswick, N.J.: Rutgers University Press, 1963.

HOMER, SYDNEY, and RICHARD I. JOHANNESEN. *The Price of Money 1946–69*. New Brunswick, N.J.: Rutgers University Press, 1969.

ROLL, RICHARD. *The Behavior of Interest Rates*. New York: Basic Books, 1970.

STIGUM, MARCIA. *The Money Markets*. New York: Dow Jones, Irwin, 1990.

The Depository Institutions Industry

After you have read this chapter, you will be able to:

- **Claim some familiarity with the history of banks and other depository institutions.**
- **Describe how governments charter, regulate, and insure depository institutions.**
- **Understand the significance of bank capital, check clearing, correspondent banking, and concentration in banking.**
- **List recent developments in the thrift industry.**

Depository institutions controlled four trillion dollars at the end of 1994, an amount equal to one-fifth the country's net wealth. In this chapter, we look at how the depository institutions industry as a whole is organized and regulated. This industry consists of four types of institutions: commercial banks, savings and loan associations, savings banks, and credit unions.[1] We divide the industry into two parts: **commercial banks** (usually just called banks) and **thrifts,** which include the other three types of institutions, but we will learn that the distinction has become blurry.

Banks are by far the most important depository institutions because of their size, the wide range of assets they hold, and their importance in financing small- and medium-size firms, as well as their role in both the payments mechanism and the creation of money. Hence, we discuss them in more detail than the thrifts. In the next chapter we will take a closer look at the operation of individual depository institutions, examining the types of assets that these firms hold and the types of liabilities that they issue.

---

[1] As discussed in Chapter 2, money-market mutual funds also function as depository institutions, but officially they are security firms, not depository institutions.

In recent years foreign banks have greatly expanded their role in the United States, and U.S. banks have become more active in foreign countries. In the appendix to this chapter we will discuss several alternative ways in which other countries have organized their banking systems in order to highlight the characteristics of the U.S. system. Chapter 8 deals with international banking.

BANKING HISTORY: A SKETCH

Historically, commercial banks differed sharply from thrifts. Their function was primarily to collect funds by providing checkable accounts and to make mostly business loans. The main function of thrifts, on the other hand, was to collect savings in the form of time deposits, that is, deposits against which one cannot write checks, and to make mortgage loans. Clearly, the distinction between banks and thrifts has eroded. Commercial banks have increased their lending to households, and now their checkable deposits account for only about one-quarter of their total deposits. Thrifts, on the other hand, have increased their lending to businesses and now provide checkable deposits. Indeed, some of them use the word *bank* in their title. But it is still true that banks make many more business loans, while thrifts focus on mortgage loans, and most checkable deposits are held in banks, not thrifts. Table 2.4 showed the relative importance of the various types of depository institutions.

We will get a better idea of where we stand now if we dig deeper into the history of banking. Banking is an old business. Banks existed that made loans and exchanged foreign currencies in ancient Babylon and in the classical civilizations, particularly Rome. But modern banking started in Renaissance Italy where bankers, apart from buying and selling foreign currencies, also took demand and time deposits. These deposits were usually transferred orally by the owner visiting the banker, who sat behind his bench or table, though checks were not unknown. (Our term *bankruptcy* comes from the Italian custom of breaking the bench of a banker who could not pay off his creditors.) The most famous of these Italian bankers were the Medici family, who for a time ruled Florence and made loans to princes and merchants both in Italy and in the rest of Europe.

In England banking grew out of the custom of goldsmiths, who took in their customers' gold and silver for safekeeping. They then discovered that they could lend such coins out, keeping just a certain proportion as a reserve, since not all customers would come in for repayment at the same time. Moreover, they gave their depositors receipts, which these depositors could pass on to other people, who were then entitled to collect the corresponding amount of gold or silver. Eventually, to make such transfers more convenient, they issued receipts in round-number sums. These receipts thus became private bank notes, that is, currency notes issued by and repayable on demand by the bankers.

In colonial America the first bank, in the modern sense of the term, was the Bank of North America, founded in 1782. Subsequently, banking spread rapidly as the states chartered more and more banks, some of them owned by the states themselves. Between 1781 and 1861 over twenty-five hundred banks were organized, but many of them were unsound; almost two-fifths of them had to close within ten years after they opened.[2]

In 1791, at the urging of Alexander Hamilton, Congress temporarily chartered a national bank, the First Bank of the United States, in part owned by the federal government. This bank, which was much larger than the state-chartered banks, held deposits of the federal government and transferred funds for it to various parts of the country. It also tried to discipline the state-chartered banks that had issued too many bank notes (that is, currency notes issued by banks), either by refusing to accept their notes in payment or by collecting a lot of them and presenting them all at once to the unfortunate bank for redemption in gold.

Not surprisingly, in 1811 when the charter of the First Bank of the United States came up in Congress for renewal, the state-chartered banks tried to kill it. Among the arguments against it were that it was, in part, owned by foreigners and that it had dabbled in politics. There was also some doubt as to whether the Constitution permitted Congress to charter a bank and a belief that the bank had too much monopoly power. These arguments were effective. Congress did not renew the First Bank's charter.

In 1816 the Second Bank of the United States was chartered with the federal government owning one-fifth of the stock and appointing one-fifth of the directors. Although it did a lot of good in curbing excessive expansion by state banks, its charter was allowed to expire in 1836. This occurred in good part because it was opposed by President Andrew Jackson, who was concerned about the concentration of economic power in the Northeast and was an opponent of the bank's president, Nicholas Biddle.

The 1830s also saw another important change in banking. Until then states could charter banks only by a special act of the legislature. This led to much corruption and favoritism. In 1837 Michigan led the way to a new system, called **free banking.** Under this system, anyone who met rather easy conditions could organize a bank and issue bank notes as well as take deposits; checks by this time had come into widespread usage. Although free banking avoided the scandals of the previous system, it developed its own problems. Many new banks were organized and issued their bank notes, and with so many different bank notes around, it was hard to differentiate between genuine and counterfeit notes, or even notes issued on nonexistent banks. Moreover, notes of certain banks, considered unsafe or located far away, circulated at less than full face value. Merchants had to look up in registers of bank notes the value of notes presented to them as payment. In addition, a few—though not very many—banks, the so-called wildcat banks, made it hard to present their bank notes to them for redemption in coin (that is, in legal tender) by locating in out-of-the-way places. As a result, some bank notes circulated well below their face value. Bank failures, too, were common. However, these losses from bank failures should not be exaggerated because most failed banks could pay off a substantial proportion of the face value of their notes. Moreover, these fail-

---

[2] Benjamin Klebaner, *Commercial Banking in the United States: A History* (Hansdale, Ill.: Dryden Press, 1974), p. 48.

ures were not primarily due to attempts to cheat the public or to banks' taking irresponsible risks. Instead, as Arthur Rolnick and Warren Weber of the Federal Reserve Bank of Minneapolis have pointed out, they resulted from the decline in prices of the state bonds that the banks were required by law to hold as collateral against their notes.

These problems, as well as the need to develop an additional market for government bonds to finance the Civil War, led Congress to establish the National Banking System, starting with the National Currency Act of 1863 (later amended and renamed the National Banking Act). The federal government now chartered **national banks,** which issued uniform bank notes. These notes were safe because each national bank had to deposit $10 of federal government bonds with the Comptroller of the Currency for each $9 of bank notes it issued. (Thus it would put up $1 of capital, borrow $9 from depositors, and hold $10 of interest-earning government bonds.) If a bank failed, the holders of its national bank notes were repaid by the Comptroller of the Currency out of the bonds the bank had deposited with him. State-chartered banks were effectively prevented from issuing bank notes by the imposition of an annual 10 percent tax on their notes. There was now a uniform and sound currency that, unlike the previous bank notes, was accepted at **par** (that is, at full value) throughout the country. Funds could be transferred all over the country at a cost that could not exceed the small cost of shipping bank notes and was frequently less. But state banks, though they could no longer issue bank notes, did not disappear, as had been thought they would, because, with the rapidly growing use of checks, they could still provide a medium of exchange—checking deposits.

Although the National Banking System solved the problem of there being too many types of bank notes and reduced the frequency of bank failures, it was far from perfect. For example, it did not provide an efficient system of check collection. Instead of sending a check that had been deposited with it directly to the bank on which the check had been drawn, the bank would send the check to another bank with which it had a "correspondence" relationship (which we will explain later in this chapter), and that bank would send it on the same way, so that a check would sometimes pass through many banks before reaching the bank on which it was drawn. Hence, it took much too long to discover whether a check had bounced.

Another problem was that the federal government required national banks to keep reserves against their deposits. Some of these reserves had to be kept as currency in the banks' vaults, but (except for banks in the three largest financial centers) banks could keep part of their reserves as deposits with banks in larger cities. A problem arose when these regional banks then withdrew these reserves: the banks in the financial centers would find themselves short of reserves and have to call in some of the short-term loans they had made to dealers in the money market and the stock market. As a result interest rates would rise sharply. Sometimes a financial panic—in which banks could not get at their reserves—would result.[3] Banks did, however, develop a device to ameliorate greatly the impact of financial panics. They would jointly stop

---

[3] Besides, some banks would close their doors and fail rather than touch their reserves, so these reserves did little good.

paying out currency to the public and would pay instead in **clearinghouse certificates,** which were notes that could be used to make deposits, and hence would be accepted as payments in many cases, albeit often at a discount. Moreover, payments could still be made by check. Had that system still been in effect in the 1930s, the Great Depression would have been much less severe.

Yet another problem was that there was no central bank to adjust the money supply to meet the need for money, so the money supply could not expand along with the demand for money. Hence, there were frequent complaints about a "shortage" of money in the fall when the harvesting season raised the demand for money, and interest rates would rise. A related complaint was that in a financial panic no additional currency was available to meet the increased demand that resulted as the public, afraid of bank failures, tried to shift out of deposits into currency. Bank failures were frequent, particularly among state banks, which, being less heavily regulated than national banks, had grown at a faster rate. (However, losses as a percent of total deposits were quite small.)

In 1907 a severe recession occurred, which, along with previous dissatisfaction with the banking system, resulted in the appointment of the National Monetary Commission. After exhaustive studies it recommended the establishment of a central banking system that was to become the Federal Reserve System. But there was a great deal of opposition to the creation of a central bank out of fear that it would be run by bankers and lead to a banking cartel. It was not until 1913 that this opposition was overcome and the Federal Reserve Act was signed by President Woodrow Wilson.

We will discuss the Federal Reserve System in considerable detail in Chapter 11, but we will note here the ways in which this new system was intended to solve the problems that beset the National Banking System. Checks could now be cleared through the Federal Reserve instead of being routed through a whole chain of banks. Required reserves had to be kept initially with the Federal Reserve rather than with other banks, and being centralized, the reserves could now be made more readily available to banks that needed them. (Subsequently banks were allowed also to keep them as currency in their vaults.) The money supply was made more responsive to the demand for money by enabling banks to borrow from the Federal Reserve. But the attempt to make banks safer failed miserably. There were many more bank failures in the period 1931 to 1933 than at any other time.

CHARTERING, EXAMINATION, AND FED MEMBERSHIP

Government control over banks comes in several layers. Initially, there is chartering. A prospective bank has to obtain a *charter, either from the federal government* (through the Comptroller of the Currency) as a **national bank,** *or from its state government* (through the state banking authority) as a **state bank.**

The second layer of government control is the Federal Reserve. Although its main function is the conduct of monetary policy, it also regulates banks. A national bank must, and a state bank may but need not, join the Federal Reserve System and become a **member bank**—this term *always refers to member-*

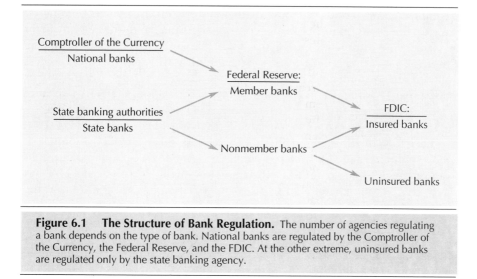

Figure 6.1   The Structure of Bank Regulation. The number of agencies regulating a bank depends on the type of bank. National banks are regulated by the Comptroller of the Currency, the Federal Reserve, and the FDIC. At the other extreme, uninsured banks are regulated only by the state banking agency.

ship in the Federal Reserve System. Third, there is the Federal Deposit Insurance Corporation (FDIC). All member banks *must* join the FDIC, and practically all other banks have joined too. The resultant structure of government contacts is shown in Figure 6.1.

Table 6.1 shows the distribution of banks by type. Nearly 40 percent of all banks are member banks, but they hold three-quarters of all assets. Almost one-third of all banks are national banks, and they hold close to 60 percent of all bank assets.

Once a national bank is in operation, it has many contacts with the government. One form of this contact is the **examination.** With a frequency depending on the perceived riskiness of the bank, employees of the Comptroller of the Currency, called **bank examiners,** make an unannounced visit to each national bank, and at other times a bank has to submit detailed information on its operations. Although preventing fraud is one of the purposes of bank examination, it is not the only one. Others are seeing whether the bank

Table 6.1   Distribution of Insured Commercial Banks by Type, December 1994

Type of Bank	Percentage of All Banks	Percentage of All Bank Assets
Member banks	38.7	77.3
National banks	29.4	56.2
State banks	9.3	21.1
Nonmember banks	61.2	22.7
Total	100.0	100.0

Source: FDIC, *Statistics on Banking,* 1994, p. B25.

is complying with various rules and regulations concerning its asset holdings, if it is carrying assets on its books at a conservative value, and whether any loans or security holdings involve excessive risks. If a security is deemed too speculative, the examiner can order the bank to sell it. If repayment of a loan is doubtful, the examiner can order the bank to classify it as "loss," "doubtful," or "substandard." Depending on the particular classification, the bank may have to stop treating the interest it receives on the loan as income, it may have to put aside, out of its profits, a special reserve against losses on the loan, or it may have to write off the loan altogether as a loss. Since a bank is required to keep a minimum ratio of capital to assets, the write-down of capital that results from writing off loan losses or from selling low-quality securities at a loss may force it to raise more capital or to curb the growth of its assets. Moreover, the fact that it has to write off loans can hurt a bank by reducing the price of its stock. Obviously, since the quality of loans and securities is a matter of opinion, disputes between banks and examiners do arise. However, in some cases bank officers welcome the advice of examiners who, as outsiders, can take a more objective view than do the bank's officers.[4]

The examiners classify banks into five categories depending on their *capital adequacy, management, earnings,* and *liquidity*. This rating, known by the acronym CAMEL, determines how often a bank is examined. If the news that it has been classified as a problem bank leaks out, as has happened occasionally, neither the bank's customers nor its stockholders are likely to react favorably.

Apart from the chartering authorities, the Federal Reserve has the right to examine member banks and the FDIC to examine insured banks. However, to avoid duplication or even triplication, the Fed usually leaves examination of national banks to the Comptroller of the Currency and examines only state member banks. Similarly, the FDIC usually examines only nonmember insured banks.

As Table 6.1 showed, more than one-third of all banks, but few state banks, are member banks. What kept many banks out of the Federal Reserve System in the past was that the Fed then imposed relatively high reserve requirements on member banks. By contrast, nonmember banks only had to meet the usually much less stringent reserve requirements set by their states. However, in 1980 the law was changed to impose the same reserve requirement on member banks and nonmember banks, so that the reserve requirement is no longer a deterrent to Fed membership. At the same time Fed membership lost one of its great attractions. Previously only member banks had normally been able to borrow from the Fed; now all banks can. However, member banks still have to meet some Fed regulations and restrictions on permitted activities that are stricter than the corresponding state regulations. The advantage of membership for larger banks is that it facilitates their acting as city correspondent banks, an activity we discuss later in this chapter. Moreover, Fed membership confers prestige and status on a bank.

---

[4] Since a bank examiner becomes familiar with operating methods and thus obtains a thorough knowledge of banking, some banks like to hire former bank examiners.

Why Does the United States Have So Many Banks?

The size of the U.S. economy alone cannot explain why the United States has so many more banks than other industrialized countries do. In Canada six banks with extensive branch systems account for much of the banking business, in Great Britain about six do so, and in Germany three banks do. One reason is that our federal system of government allows each state to charter banks. But there is more to it than that. After all, if it wanted to, the federal government could charter just a few national banks and allow them to do business in every state. It also has the constitutional power to eliminate state-chartered banks.

The central reason for the large number of banks in the United States probably has to do with the distrust of banks and of large aggregations of financial power that figures so prominently in our populist ideology. This distrust of banks was fed by the losses that depositors suffered from the frequent bank failures prior to 1934. Banks seemed not only coldhearted, but also dishonest, particularly those in distant, big cities. To curb the role of large banks and to keep banking as much as possible a local business, there were, until recently, severe constraints on the number of branches a bank could have; several states did not allow a bank to have any branches at all.

The irony is that a major reason for the frequency of bank failures was precisely that banks were kept small and not allowed to branch nationwide. Banks that must concentrate their loans in a small geographic area because they are not allowed to have branches elsewhere are more likely to fail than banks that can make loans over a diversified geographic area.

BANK CAPITAL

Capital requirements are such a crucial part of the U.S. system of bank regulation that we had better be clear what bank capital is and what it is not. Capital is *not* a specific asset that the bank owns. You cannot walk into a bank and see its capital the way you see its office equipment, the securities it owns, or its customers' loan documents. Capital is something very different. It is the claim that the owners of the bank, that is its stockholders, have on the bank. Suppose you and some rich friends start a bank. You put up, say, $10 million of capital, and once the bank is in operation, it gathers $90 million of deposits. It uses the whole $100 million to buy a building, make loans, buy securities, and so on. Ten percent of these assets belong to you and the other shareholders.

What happens if the bank makes a $1 million profit? The depositors' claims are unchanged at $90 million, and with the bank now being worth $101 million, the amount the shareholders own, that is their capital, has gone from $10 million to $11 million. (Conversely, had the bank made a $10 million loss, the shareholders' claims, that is, their capital would have been wiped out.)

Bank capital is divided into two classes: **core capital,** also called **primary capital** or **equity capital,** and **secondary capital.** Equity capital is, as the name implies, the equity that the stockholders have in the bank. Secondary capital includes, along with primary capital, certain long-term borrowing by the bank, such as its issuance of bonds with an average maturity of at least seven years, and its reserves against loan losses. It is mainly large banks that have such long-term bonds outstanding. Small banks are not well enough known to be able to issue such bonds.

The reason why the government imposes a capital requirement on banks is to provide a cushion of safety both for the FDIC and for uninsured depositors. A large capital stock helps to make a bank safe because capital represents those funds that the bank can lose without endangering its ability to repay its creditors. Suppose that a bank's capital is equal to 5 percent of its assets. Then, even if it loses 5 percent of its assets as a result of making unsound loans, its creditors are still covered because the value of the bank's remaining assets is sufficient to pay off its creditors. Only the stockholders lose. And protection of stockholders is not a legitimate reason for bank regulation; they are responsible for how they invest.

The Appropriate Capital Ratio

From the bank's point of view, a certain cushion of equity capital is clearly desirable. Not only does it help to protect the bank's stockholders against the danger of the bank failing by providing a buffer against some losses that would otherwise cause the bank to fail, it also lowers borrowing costs by reassuring the bank's creditors. In addition, it helps to draw customers because business borrowers, as well as large depositors, are reassured by a high capital ratio. Developing a borrowing relationship with a bank is time-consuming, and a firm prefers to borrow from a bank that is likely to be around next year. However, the marginal yield from adding capital declines after a certain point. Suppose, for example, that a bank already has a high stock of capital relative to its assets. The chance of its failing is already so low that adding even more capital does not influence its potential customers much.

At the same time, the more equity capital a bank has per dollar of assets, the greater the number of dollars of capital over which the bank's earnings have to be spread is. Assume, for example, that the bank earns a 1 percent profit on its total assets. If equity capital equals 10 percent of total assets, then this 1 percent yield on assets represents a 10 percent yield to the bank's stockholders; on the other hand, if the bank has the same earnings, but only half the ratio of equity capital to total assets (5 percent), then the stockholders earn not 10 percent but 20 percent on their capital. Thus when a high capital ratio imposes a cost on a bank and the benefit of additional capital declines the more capital a bank already has, each bank has an optimal ratio of capital to assets at which the marginal advantage of additional capital is just offset by its disadvantage.

But here is a problem, a problem that is basic to much of the difficulty in bank regulation: what constitutes an optimal capital stock, and hence the optimal amount of risk, from the bank's point of view is insufficient capital, and hence excessive risk, from the social standpoint. If a bank would be the only one to lose if it failed, the social and private costs of risk taking would be the same. But this is not so. If a bank fails, the FDIC has to step in and rescue the insured depositors and, in addition, depositors with accounts above the insurance ceiling may lose. Moreover, if a large bank fails or many smaller banks fail almost simultaneously, the public may lose confidence in other banks and try to withdraw its deposits, and thus cause them to fail.

When a bank decides how much risk it should accept, it does not take these *external* costs of its potential failure into account. It selects a level of risk at which the marginal loss from risk taking to it alone is just equal to the marginal yield from taking this risk. Hence, it takes more risk than is socially optimal. This is why the government is justified in stepping in and limiting the amount of risk a bank takes. It does this by limiting the riskiness of the bank's loans and securities and by requiring the bank to hold more capital than it would in the absence of regulations.

Since the function of capital is to protect the FDIC and large depositors, the amount of capital a bank needs depends on the riskiness of its assets. Accordingly, the capital-asset ratio that banks are required to meet depends in part on the assets they hold. Banks are required to hold a *risk-adjusted* capital-asset ratio of at least 8 percent. In calculating the denominator of this capital-asset ratio, riskless assets, such as holdings of currency and short-term U.S. government securities, have a weight of zero; that is, no capital at all is required against them. Somewhat riskier assets, for example, longer-term U.S. government securities, have a weight of 30 percent, so that 2.4 percent (30 percent × 8 percent) capital has to be held against them. Assets with greater risk have a weight of 60 percent, while assets with more risk still—for example, mortgage loans and business loans—have a weight of 100 percent. Of the 8 percent risk-adjusted capital required, 4 percent must be so-called Tier 1 capital, which is essentially equity capital, while the other 4 percent may (but does not have to) include long-term funds the bank has borrowed (see the box,

---

Will the Real Capital-Asset Ratio Please Stand Up

The main function of bank capital is to protect the FDIC and large depositors in case the bank fails. Taking this view, we should count as capital anything that offers such protection. Stockholders' equity should therefore be counted as capital. That much is clear. Beyond that it gets murky. In case the bank fails, bondholders get paid only after the claims of all depositors and the FDIC are satisfied. This suggests that the amount the bank has borrowed by issuing bonds be treated as capital, just like equity, since it too provides a cushion for losses and thus protects the FDIC and depositors. On the other hand, the bank is legally required to pay interest on the bonds, and if it fails to do so, it can be forced into bankruptcy. If that happens, the bank's assets may have to be sold at a price well below their prebankruptcy values, and that may result in losses to the FDIC and large depositors. This suggests that we should *not* treat the bank's bond issues as capital.

So what do the regulators do? They firmly straddle the issue by allowing the bank to count certain types of longer-term borrowing as part of its capital, but only up to a certain proportion of the required capital-asset ratio.

page 105)[5] An additional capital requirement is that the capital-asset ratio, unadjusted for risk, should be at least 3 percent for the soundest banks and may be set higher for others.

These are the minimum requirements, and the regulators can require banks with unusually risky assets to hold more capital. Moreover, banks that have capital well above the minimum requirement are allowed to do certain things, such as paying higher deposit rates, that others are not.

DEPOSIT INSURANCE

The Federal Deposit Insurance Corporation (FDIC) commenced operations in 1934 in response to massive bank failures that had occurred between 1930 and 1933. Almost all banks have joined the FDIC. This is not surprising since membership in the FDIC gives a bank a great advantage over an uninsured bank in competing for deposits. Since competitive pressures, as well as the unwillingness of states to charter uninsured banks, make FDIC membership necessary for practically every bank, the FDIC, in effect, has veto power over the formation of just about any new bank. In addition to insuring commercial banks, the FDIC also insures savings banks and operates the insurance funds for the savings and loans. It does so through two separate funds that it administers, the Bank Insurance Fund and the Savings Association Insurance Fund.

In return for an insurance premium paid by banks, the FDIC insures deposits up to $100,000. If a depositor has several accounts in his or her own name in one bank, the total that is insured is still $100,000. But if a person has several accounts under different names (for example, a personal account, a joint account with a business partner or a spouse) or if these accounts have different beneficiaries (as in the case of trust funds, for example), then each of these accounts is insured separately for $100,000. Similarly, if a person has accounts in several banks, all these accounts are insured. Although nearly all accounts are fully insured, the very few that are not include some very large accounts, so that only about two-thirds of the dollar value of deposits is insured. However, large depositors are frequently protected by the fact that if they have a loan from a failed bank, they can substract the amount of their deposits from what they owe to the bank.

The $100,000 ceiling does not mean that large depositors always suffer losses when their bank fails. In some cases they lose nothing because of the ways the FDIC handles bank failures. One way, called **deposit assumption,** is for the FDIC to merge the failing bank into a sound bank, which then takes over the liability for all deposits regardless of size. To induce a sound bank to undertake such a merger, the FDIC often provides a subsidy, such as taking over certain bad loans of the failing bank at 100 cents on the dollar. If so, large deposits are assessed a share of the FDIC's losses. But if the FDIC suffers no loss, they, too, lose nothing, though they may have to wait a long time before they are fully compensated.

---

[5] The denominator of the capital-asset ratio includes not just assets, but also certain "off-balance-sheet" items discussed in the next chapter.

A second way of handling bank failures is for the FDIC to let the bank fail and then pay off its depositors in full on the first $100,000 of their deposits. On any amount over $100,000, depositors share in what the FDIC gets when it sells the bank's assets. A third, much less frequently used method is for the FDIC to take over the bank and operate it temporarily before selling it.[6] The FDIC is generally required to use whichever method is the least costly.

Why is there a $100,000 ceiling? Why not insure all deposits fully? This would prevent all bank runs. The establishment of the FDIC eliminated runs by small depositors. But with a $100,000 ceiling, large depositors and other creditors of banks, such as those who sold it federal funds, will still run on a bank rumored to be failing.

The reason for not changing the law to insure all deposits fully is not the expense. It would cost the FDIC very little. Instead, the problem with covering all deposits is that this would remove an incentive that large depositors have to choose their banks carefully. As long as there is an insurance ceiling, large depositors, predominantly businesses, have an incentive to avoid banks that take too many risks. Hence, banks are under some pressure to follow safe policies. Depositor surveillance thus supplements the FDIC's surveillance. But it is far from obvious that depositor surveillance is effective.

CLEARING

An important task of the banking system is clearing checks and processing wire transfers. Since clearing runs smoothly, it is usually taken for granted, but were this process to break down or encounter substantial delays, we would have much to complain about.

Suppose that a check drawn on one bank is deposited in another one. How is this check cleared, that is, presented for payment? Since a vast number of checks have to be cleared, elaborate mechanisms for doing so have been developed. One such mechanism is a clearinghouse. This is usually an organization of local banks that meets every working day for a few hours. Each bank appears at the clearinghouse and presents the checks it has received that are drawn on the other banks belonging to the same clearinghouse. The banks then offset their claims and liabilities against each other, and any bank with a favorable net balance receives payment.

Many checks drawn on banks in other cities move through the Federal Reserve's clearing system. Suppose a check is deposited in a bank located in the same Federal Reserve District—there are 12—as the bank on which it is drawn. The Federal Reserve Bank then credits the account that this bank has with it and debits the account of the bank on which the check is drawn. If the check is drawn on a bank in another Federal Reserve District, the Federal Reserve Bank passes it on to the Federal Reserve Bank of that other district, and this Federal Reserve Bank then debits that bank's account. The depositing bank gets credit from the Fed after one or two days, depending on the dis-

[6] There are additional, though rarely used, ways in which the FDIC can treat a failing bank. For example, as will be discussed shortly, when Continental Illinois was failing, the FDIC provided it with funds in exchange for stock in the bank.

tance the check has been sent. The Fed also operates a system of automated clearinghouses for electronic transactions. Electronic clearing is spreading rapidly because clearing an electronic payment costs only about half as much as clearing a check.

The Fed has to compete for the clearing business with correspondent banks (which we will describe shortly) and with private check-clearing firms. The Fed handles about one-third of all checks and the majority of the nation's electronic transfers.

As already mentioned, large payments are made not by checks but by wire transfers. The volume of such wire transfers is immense, amounting on the average day to about four months' GDP. The Fed operates a wire system, called **Fedwire,** and the big banks run another system called **CHIPS** (Clearinghouse Interbank Payments System) used mainly for international transactions.

CORRESPONDENT BANKING

A private network called the **correspondent system** connects banks and eliminates many of the disadvantages that would otherwise follow from having so many small, isolated banks. Under this system, smaller banks, called country correspondent banks, keep deposits, primarily demand deposits, with large city correspondent banks, frequently with several of them.

The city banks pay for these deposits by providing their country correspondent banks with many services. One important service is clearing checks in a more convenient way than the Fed does. In addition, city banks provide direct loans to country banks and also participate with country banks in making loans that are too large for the country banks to make on their own. Or, conversely, country banks experiencing too little loan demand can participate in profitable loans made by their city correspondents. The numerous other services that city correspondent banks provide to country correspondent banks include the sale or purchase of securities, access to the market for federal funds, investment advice and general business advice, and buying or selling foreign exchange for its customers. Thus, city correspondent banks provide many of the services that the head office of a large branch bank provides for its branches.

CONCENTRATION IN BANKING

There are approximately eleven thousand commercial banks in the United States, ranging from very small banks to extremely large ones. The 45 largest banks in the United States (those holding assets of $10 billion or more in 1993) taken together hold only 44 percent of the total assets of insured commercial banks. Few other industries have that many firms and so little concentration, and one might think, therefore, that there is no monopoly problem in banking. Indeed, one might wonder whether the problem is rather that there are too many banks—too many, that is, to reap economies of scale and to be able to provide a sufficient range of services to bank customers. However, the empirical evidence suggests that once a bank gets above a fairly moderate size, economies of scale are at most modest, except for the small group of very large banks with between $5 billion and $25 billion in assets.

The fact that banking is an unconcentrated industry does not mean that the United States does not have a problem of insufficient banking competition. While large firms can borrow from banks anywhere in the country, small firms, being known only in their locality, can borrow only from a local bank. It is not worthwhile for banks elsewhere to acquire the information needed to lend to them. And within a firm's area there may be only one bank or a few banks. Hence, despite the large number of banks there is still a problem of market power on the lending side. On the deposit side, however, thrift institutions provide additional competition, and due to the prevalence of automatic teller machines, depositors can readily use banks outside their own locality if their local banks do not provide satisfactory service.

Branch Banking

One of the persistent controversial issues in banking in the United States has been branch banking. Should banks be allowed, like firms in other industries, to have as many branches as they wish and place them anywhere in the country? For a long time the answer was "no." Suspicions about the influence of "Wall Street" and distrust of large banks induced most states to limit branching. Some states, such as Illinois, did not allow banks to have any branches at all; many other states imposed severe limits on the location of branches, such as permitting a bank to have a branch only in the county in which it had its head offices and in adjacent counties. In 1927 the McFadden Act essentially prohibited national banks from opening branches in other states.

During the postwar period, restrictions on branch banking were whittled away, both by changes in banking laws and by the banks themselves, which made use of the legal loopholes they found. Finally, in 1994 Congress passed a law eliminating most restrictions on branching by national banks as of 1997. This law includes several stipulations: one gives states the right to prohibit out-of-state national banks from opening branches in their territory if they so chose (although it is unlikely that many states will take advantage of this option); another provides a barrier against excessive concentration in banking by disallowing any bank mergers that would give a bank control of 30 percent or more of deposits in a single state or 10 percent of deposits nationwide.

Does this mean that large banks will now open branches all over the country and put most small, local banks out of business? Probably not, because large banks do not benefit from great economies of scale. In California, the home of some giant branch-banking systems, small independent banks have been able to prosper alongside the giants. All the same, the number of banks in the United States is likely to decline, though to nowhere near the small number of banks in most industrialized countries.

SOCIAL REGULATION OF BANKING

Banks are subject to numerous regulations that focus on social objectives rather than on the soundness of banks. One type of regulation tries to protect bank customers from exploitation or discrimination. A good example is the federal **Truth in Lending Law,** which requires that borrowers be given sufficient information to compare readily the interest rates charged by different lenders. Prior to the passage of this law, such a comparison was often hard to make.

Discrimination in lending on the basis of race, sex, age, or creed is also prohibited by law. One of these laws specifically prohibits **redlining,** that is, refusing to make loans or being reluctant to make loans in certain areas, such as inner-city neighborhoods with large minority populations. The extent to which banks actually did and still do redline certain areas is a much-debated issue, but recent evidence suggests that redlining does occur.

Another type of regulation goes beyond prohibiting a bank from discriminating and requires banks to contribute to the improvement of social conditions. This regulation, the **Community Reinvestment Act,** states that banks and other insured lenders have an obligation to meet the reasonable credit needs of the low-income neighborhoods in which they are located or have a branch. When they apply for permission to open a new branch or to merge with another institution, the regulatory agencies are supposed to take into account how well they have served their low-income neighborhoods. Social activists have sometimes used threats to file complaints under the Community Reinvestment Act as a way to provide benefits to certain low-income people. Whether such a law is needed or the profit motive already gives banks enough of an incentive to meet the "reasonable credit needs" of low-income neighborhoods is under debate.

SAVINGS AND LOAN ASSOCIATIONS

The most important thrift institutions are savings and loans. The main way they differ from banks is that most of their loans are mortgage loans, and nearly all their deposits are time deposits. Legally, they differ from banks in having a different charter. Usually, but not always, they have the word *savings* somewhere in their title. But they can also call themselves *banks.* Thus, one large savings and loan is called First Nationwide Bank. This may sound confusing because it *is* confusing.

Chartering, Supervision, and Insurance

Savings and loans can be corporations owned by their stockholders or mutuals owned, at least nominally, by their depositors, although in reality, these depositors usually have no control over them. They can have either a federal or a state charter. Federally chartered savings and loans, and most state-chartered ones, are members of the Federal Home Loan Bank system. They are supervised and examined by one of the twelve Federal Home Loan Banks, from which they can borrow for fairly long periods, often at below-market rates. The Home Loan Banks themselves are supervised by the Office of Thrift Supervision. Deposits in savings and loans are insured in the same way as bank deposits, through the Savings Association Insurance Fund, which is part of the FDIC.

Banks and Social Objectives

Many people argue that banks should be required to contribute to the social goals of alleviating poverty and compensating for the effects of racism by making loans to the disadvantaged, even if such loans are less profitable than other loans. Others object to singling out banks to pay for society's problems. The debate has turned mainly on the issue of fairness. Those who favor imposing a social duty on banks argue that this is fair because banks receive many benefits from the government. Their opponents contend that the government does not provide many benefits to banks.

What are the benefits that banks are said to receive? Deposit insurance is often cited. There is no question that savings and loans and to a lesser extent savings banks have, at least until recently, received deposit insurance at a rate set way below the fair market rate. (As we will discuss in Chapter 9, their insurance system received a massive bailout from taxpayers.) In addition, savings and loans benefit indirectly from the government's homeownership subsidies because they can borrow cheaply from the Federal Home Loan Banks, and until the mid-1980s, they also benefited from a government-imposed ceiling on time deposit interest rates.

It is less clear, however, that banks have received special net benefits from the government. On the one hand, the banks' deposit insurance system (the FDIC) has not had to be bailed out. On the other hand, the Treasury has had to stand ready to make loans to the FDIC if the need ever arose. Without FDIC insurance, even if banks had been privately insured, there would probably have been runs on several large banks that had made unsound international loans in the 1980s, and these would have failed and possibly brought a substantial part of the banking system down with them. Moreover, if the banks had had to purchase deposit insurance from the private sector, their premiums would probably have been higher. Given these arguments, *perhaps* the government could be justified in charging banks more for deposit insurance than its cost—and one way to do that is to impose social duties on them.

Banks also benefit by being able to borrow cheaply from the Federal Reserve, and they probably gain something from the law that prohibits interest payments on demand deposits, although, as discussed in the next chapter, this regulation is not very effective. On the other hand, they are required to keep reserves on which they earn no interest, and thus, in effect, make an interest-free loan to the government. All in all, the fairness or unfairness of imposing on banks certain costs of alleviating bad social conditions is not as easy to determine as it might at first appear.

But fairness is not the only consideration. Efficiency also matters. Imposing a special tax on banks is inefficient, because it distorts resource allocation by raising the price of banking services above their marginal cost. For example, banks are then less able to compete with money-market funds and with finance companies. On the other hand, if bad social conditions are to be alleviated, the necessary funds have to be raised in some way, and that means distorting resource allocation somewhere. And there is always the possibility that if the burden is not imposed on banks, it will not be imposed to the same extent on anyone else either, and the bad conditions will fester unchecked.

A Sketch of Savings and Loan History

Savings and loans started out as associations of people with low and moderate incomes who pooled their funds to provide housing for themselves. Instead of all of them waiting until each had accumulated enough savings to buy a house, they would pool their savings and select, often through a lottery, one member who could borrow the pooled savings. The first U.S. savings and loan was the Oxford Building Society in Frankfort, Pennsylvania, in 1831.

The more recent history of savings and loans is closely tied to the government's policy on home ownership because that policy relied in large part on the thrifts to provide mortgage loans. The New Deal attempted to expand home ownership and succeeded: in 1930 about one-third of all households were homeowners; now about two-thirds are. To accomplish this goal, the prevailing type of mortgage was changed. Prior to the New Deal the typical mortgage was not the long-term amortized mortgage we know today, but a mortgage due in a lump sum, often after ten years. In practice, mortgages were frequently renewed, but, even so, this type of mortgage was better suited to the well-to-do than to the average person. To help more people buy houses, the federal government encouraged thrift institutions to make what is now known as the "traditional" type of mortgage, that is, a long-term, fixed-rate mortgage repayable in installments. The Federal Housing Administration (FHA) was set up to insure such mortgages. This policy was successful; families found long-term amortized mortgages manageable, and home ownership increased substantially after World War II. Savings and loans played a large role in this. The nominal dollar value of their residential mortgage holdings in 1965 was twenty times what it had been twenty years earlier, and they accounted for 41 percent of all outstanding residential mortgage debt (other than real-estate bonds). But, as we will show in Chapter 9, this seeming success turned out to be the sheep's clothing on a very dangerous wolf.

SAVINGS BANKS

Savings banks started as charitable institutions to provide low-income people with a secure place for their savings; hence some have names such as Dime Savings Bank or the Mechanics' Bank. Until the 1930s commercial banks did not want to bother with the small savings of low-income people, and since savings and loans were not available everywhere, many such people had no safe repositories for their savings. Hence some public-spirited people established savings banks. The early ones were organized as mutuals. They developed primarily in some eastern and midwestern states, and even now are highly concentrated in a few states. In other states savings and loans fill the niche that in their absence would be occupied by savings banks.

Savings banks now come with a variety of characteristics. They can be mutuals or stock companies, can hold federal or state charters, and are insured by one of the two FDIC funds, the Savings Association Insurance Fund or the Bank Insurance Fund. They can hold a more diversified menu of assets than can savings and loans, but not as diversified a one as commercial banks can. As a result, their assets are somewhat less concentrated in mortgages than are those of savings and loans, but mortgages are still by far their main asset. Their main liabilities are time deposits.

CREDIT UNIONS

Credit unions are the smallest of the three types of thrifts, but the fastest-growing ones. In 1994 their assets were almost four and a half times what they had been in 1980. At one time their customers, known as "members," had to have a common bond, such as working for the same firm or living in the same neighborhood, but this rule has been greatly relaxed in recent years. Many credit unions are sponsored by employers as an employee benefit and receive subsidies, such as free rent, from the employer. They also benefit by their earnings not being subject to federal income tax. Some of their (part-time) officers are endowed with missionary zeal and work without pay. All these factors reduce their operating costs, and so allow them to pay a relatively high rate to their depositors, while charging a relatively low rate to borrowers.

Credit unions can hold either a state or a federal charter. About two-thirds are federally chartered and are supervised by the National Credit Union Administration, which also insures the deposits of federally chartered credit unions (and many state-chartered ones) up to $100,000. Credit unions' main assets are consumer loans, and since these are short-term loans with little interest-rate risk, credit unions are not hurt by rising interest rates.

SUMMARY

1 Banking has a long history. In the United States there were two national banks chartered by the federal government, and their demise was followed by a period of free banking. This in turn was followed by the National Banking System that provided safer banks.
2 Banking is heavily regulated by federal or state chartering authorities, by the FDIC, and, for member banks, by the Federal Reserve.
3 Banks are required to maintain a capital-asset ratio to protect the FDIC and depositors. Since this ratio exceeds what banks would hold on their own, this is an area of continual conflict between banks and regulators. Nearly all deposits are now insured up to $100,000.
4 Checks are cleared by local clearinghouses, by the Federal Reserve, or by private firms. Wire transfers are undertaken through Fedwire or through CHIPS.
5 Banks have extensive correspondence relationships that provide small banks with services from large banks.
6 Although banking is an industry with many firms and with a low concentration ratio on the national level, there is still a problem of banks having excessive market power on a local level. Restrictions on branch banking have almost disappeared.
7 In recent years various types of discrimination in granting credit, such as redlining, have been outlawed. Lenders are also required to provide extensive information to borrowers.
8 Savings and loans are chartered by the federal and state governments. They played a large role in the federal government's attempt to foster home ownership.

9 Savings banks are chartered by the federal and state governments. They hold mainly mortgages.

10 Credit unions take deposits from and make consumer loans to people with a common bond. They are often subsidized by the depositors' employer and have grown rapidly.

11 Appendix: The British, Canadian, and German banking systems are highly concentrated. The German system is the primary example of universal banks that have wide powers and a close relation to industry. Many of the world's largest banks are Japanese.

KEY TERMS

Bank of United States	primary capital/equity capital
thrifts	secondary capital
free banking	appropriate capital ratio
bank chartering	deposit assumption
national banks	correspondent banks
state banks	Community Reinvestment Act
member banks	savings and loan associations
bank examination	Federal Home Loan Banks
FDIC	savings banks
CAMEL	credit unions
Truth in Lending Law	par value

QUESTIONS AND EXERCISES

1 Sketch the history of banking in the United States.

*2 Describe how banks are regulated.

3 Why do we regulate bank capital? What does capital consist of?

*4 Critically discuss:
  a. Banks should be allowed to decide on their own how much capital they want to keep; after all, they are the ones who lose if it turns out that they have insufficient capital.
  b. Capital requirements should be raised to 25 percent.

5 How does the FDIC handle bank failures?

6 What do you think is the most serious current problem in bank regulation? (Articles on current banking problems can be found in *Business Week, The American Banker,* and the *Wall Street Journal.*)

*7 Identify: (a) correspondent banks, (b) savings banks, and (c) credit unions.

FURTHER READING

FEDERAL RESERVE BANK OF CHICAGO. *Bank Structure and Competition.* Chicago, Ill.: Federal Reserve Bank of Chicago. This annually published volume contains interesting papers from annual conferences on banking.

KAUFMAN, GEORGE. *Banking Structures in Major Countries.* Boston: Kluwer Academic Publishers, 1992. A useful compilation of essays on various banking systems.

KLEBANER, BENJAMIN. *Commercial Banking in the United States.* Hinsdale, Ill.: Dryden Press, 1974. A compact and useful source.

NAKAMURA, LEONARD. "Small Borrowers and the Survival of the Small Bank: Is Mouse Bank Mighty or Mickey?" Federal Reserve Bank of Philadelphia, *Business Review,* December 1994, pp. 3–13. A good discussion of the future for small banks.

PIERCE, JAMES. *The Future of Banking.* New Haven: Yale University Press, 1991. An excellent discussion of banking and bank regulation.

ROBERDS, WILLIAM. "The Rise of Electronic Payments Networks and the Future Role of the Fed with Regard to Payment Finality," Federal Reserve Bank of Atlanta, *Economic Review,* 78 (March–April 1993), 13–22. A detailed discussion of the problems created by electronic transfers.

ROLNICK, ARTHUR, and WARREN WEBER. "Free Banking, Wildcat Banking and Shinplaster," Federal Reserve Bank of Minneapolis, *Quarterly Review,* Fall 1982, pp. 10–19. A stimulating discussion of free banking.

SHAFFER, SHERRILL. "Bank Competition in Concentrated Markets," Federal Reserve Bank of Philadelphia, *Business Review*, March–April 1994, pp. 3–16. An interesting discussion of whether banks have much market power.

APPENDIX: BANKING SYSTEMS IN SOME OTHER COUNTRIES

To understand the U.S. banking system it is useful to look at several foreign bank systems. By showing alternative ways in which banking can be organized, they illustrate the effects of the choices made by U.S. banking regulators.

Canada. The Canadian banking system differs sharply from that of the United States; it resembles the British system from which it was copied. A half-dozen federally chartered banks, which each have a large number of branches throughout the provinces, account for most of Canada's banking. Like the governments of other industrialized countries, the Canadian government provides deposit insurance and regulates its banks. The main regulator, the Superintendent of Financial Institutions, examines banks annually. Despite the differences in their banking structures, there is one important tie between banking in the United States and Canada. Under the U.S.-Canada free trade agreement, U.S. and Canadian banks have the same status and market access in each other's country.

Germany. The German banking system also differs sharply from that of the United States. Germany has what are called universal banks, that have a much greater scope of operation than U.S. banks. They can hold stock in nonfinancial corporations, and conversely, nonfinancial institutions can own banks. Moreover, most Germans who own stock keep their stock certificates with their bank for safekeeping and allow the bank to vote these shares in the election of directors. German banks, therefore, have about 40 percent of the votes in corporate elections, and one or more representatives of the bank sit on the boards of directors of about two-thirds of the hundred largest German corporations. In addition, there is a German tradition of a close relation between a firm and its bank. All in all, the large German banks have considerable influence on corporate decisions. German commercial banks can also carry out investment banking and are the dominant institutions in bringing new stock and bond issues to the market.

Such universal banks are not unique to Germany. They also exist in France, Holland, Italy, Spain, and Switzerland. British banks also have many of the powers of universal banks.

Another characteristic of the German commercial and savings bank system is that about a third of its assets are held by banks owned by the public sector, that is, by the states, cities, and districts. The German post office also takes savings deposits.

A third way that German and several other European banks differ from U.S. banks is in the way they transfer funds. Although checks are used in retail transactions in Europe, they play a much smaller role than in the United States. Under what is called a *Giro* system, instead of giving a check to the seller, who then deposits it in his bank for clearing, a German buyer orders her bank to make the payment, giving her bank the seller's Giro number.

Great Britain. London has a long tradition of being a world financial center, and despite the relative decline of the British economy in the postwar period, its efficiency and relative freedom from regulation has allowed London to remain much more of a hub of international finance than are Tokyo and Frankfurt (the financial center of Germany), despite their larger economies. The international role of the City (as London's financial district is called) is shown by the fact that in value terms, about half of all deposits in Britain are denominated in foreign currencies.

The British commercial-banking market is highly concentrated, with just six banks holding most of the deposits. However, as in the United States, banks face active competition from nonbanks such as the "building societies," which are similar to U.S. savings and loans. The British central bank, the Bank of England, is the main regulator, and it relies to a relatively large extent on informal pressures rather than on legal proceedings.

Japan. Japanese banks are the largest in the world. This is due not just to the size of the Japanese economy—which is after all much smaller than the U.S. economy—but also to the high Japanese savings ratio and to the fact that large Japanese banks have branches throughout the country. Japanese banks are very active internationally as well. They may hold a much greater selection of assets than U.S. banks and have large holdings of corporate stock and real estate. Over 40 percent of all the stock listed on Japanese stock exchanges is held by banks. As a result, banks were hurt very badly when the Japanese stock and real-estate markets fell sharply in the late 1980s. They were also hurt by the decline in the U.S. real-estate market. Large Japanese banks have a close relation with large firms because banks and some of the firms they lend to are members of the same groups (called *Keiretsu*); within each group, banks hold shares in the firms, and the firms hold shares in the banks.

The primary bank regulator in Japan is the Ministry of Finance, and the Japanese central bank, the Bank of Japan, plays a subsidiary role. These regulators have wide powers, not all of which are clearly specified, because under the Japanese system, informal nudges by government agencies, so-called "administrative guidance," play a large role. The government is a major competitor of banks for time deposits because it operates a large savings-bank system through the post office.

The European Community (EC). The development of a common market for banks in Europe is not an easy task because EC member countries regulate their banks in different ways. The three guiding principles that have been adopted are: (1) minimal harmonization of different national regulations, so that national autonomy is preserved to the maximum feasible extent; (2) mutual acceptance of other countries' rules and regulations; and (3) home country control. The first of these arises from the natural wish to allow each country to maintain the regulations it wants. Mutual acceptance of other countries' regulations is needed because otherwise a country could inhibit the activities of foreign banks within its territory, and thus violate the principle of having a common market. The third principle, home country control, means that one country has clear-cut responsibility for each bank. But it does require considerable harmonization of regulation (for example, similar capital requirements) both to provide a level playing field and to prevent "competition in laxity," that is, competition between the regulators for institutions by easing their application of the rules and regulations on them.

7

Inside the Depository Institution

After you have read this chapter, you will be able to:

- Explain the various items that appear on a depository institution's balance sheet.
- Show some basic knowledge of the characteristics of bank loans.
- Discuss some characteristics of the way banks make decisions.

The previous chapter discussed how the depository institution industry is organized. This chapter discusses what firms in this industry do to maximize their profits. Such a discussion has to be fairly general, because depository firms differ greatly in size and hence in the types of business they do. Even among commercial banks there is a wide range. Twenty percent of all commercial banks have less than $25 million of deposits, while 55 banks have deposits of over $10 billion.

There is, however, one characteristic that all depository institutions share: they are in the business of issuing their own debts in order to acquire the debts of others. What you and I think of as a deposit, the depository institution regards as a debt it has issued; it shows up as a *liability* on the depository institution's balance sheet. Conversely, what you and I think of as a loan by the depository institution, it regards as a debt it has purchased; the loan shows up as an *asset* on the depository institution's balance sheet. Since depository institutions are in the business of buying and selling debts, one can analyze the activities of depository institutions by looking at their balance sheets. This is what we will do, looking first at the balance sheets of banks, and then briefly at the balance sheets of the various kinds of thrifts.

THE BANK'S BALANCE SHEET

Table 7.1 shows the balance sheet of the banking industry as a whole. As any balance sheet, it lines up the assets on one side and the liabilities on the other and is arranged so that the two sides equal each other. The trick that makes them equal is the convention that the bank's capital is listed on the liabilities side, not the assets side of the balance sheet. To illustrate how this ensures that the two sides are equal, assume that the bank sells for $2,000 a bond that it bought and had carried on its books at $1,000. The bank's recorded assets now go up by $1,000. But so does its capital and hence the liabilities side of its balance sheet.

What is capital? Before looking at the individual items on the balance sheet, we must look at an important conceptual point. Calling capital, that is, the owners' equity, a liability may seem a bizarre use of the word *liability*. But

Table 7.1 Assets and Liabilities of Commercial Banks, February 1995

Assets	Percent	Liabilities and Capital	Percent
		Transactions deposits	20.3
Total cash assets (= cash in vault + reserves with Federal Reserve + deposits at U.S. depository institutions + cash items in the process of collection + other cash assets)		Time and savings deposits	44.1
		Borrowings[d]	22.6
		Other liabilities	4.8
		Capital	8.1
	5.5	Total	100.0
Securities:	23.7		
U.S. government	18.1		
Other securities	5.6		
Loans and leases	65.8		
Interbank[a]	4.5		
Commercial and industrial	17.0		
Real estate	25.8		
Consumer loans[b]	11.5		
Other	7.0		
Other assets	6.4		
Adjustments[c]	-1.4		
Total	100.0		

a: Includes federal funds sold to, reverse repurchase agreements with, and loans to commercial banks in the United States.
b: Includes loans for the purchase of securities.
c: Adjustments for unearned income, reserves for losses on loans and leases, and reserves for transfer risks.
d: Includes borrowings from related foreign offices of banks.
Source: Based on *Federal Reserve Bulletin,* May 1995, p. A18.

bizarre or not, that is the way the word is used. You might find it helpful to think of the balance sheet as listing what the bank owns (on the asset side) and listing the claims that various groups, such as its depositors and its owners, have on it (on the liabilities side). The bank's capital represents the claim that the stockholders have on the bank and is therefore a liability to the bank, though it is, of course, an asset to the stockholders. Another way of seeing why capital is on the liabilities side is to realize that the word "assets" can be replaced by the term "uses of funds" and the word "liabilities" by "sources of funds." It then becomes apparent why capital is listed as a liability, since it is a source of funds. Another way of seeing why capital is treated as a liability is to remember that the balance sheet shows the financial position of the bank itself, not the bank's owners. To the owners of the bank, the capital they have invested in it is an asset, but for the bank itself, it represents a claim someone has on it, and hence is a liability. A bank does not have a safety deposit box full of currency that is its capital. Instead, capital, originating in the funds that the owners provided, is invested in various assets, such as loans and the bank's building. Figure 7.1 illustrates this.

THE BANK'S LIABILITIES

Transactions Deposits

The first item on the liabilities side is **transactions deposits.** A transactions deposit is simply an account against which you can write a check. Such accounts are also called *checkable deposits,* and they come in several forms. First, there are *demand deposits* on which banks are not allowed to pay interest. However, as so often happens, the law is an imperfect barrier against economic pressures. Although banks cannot pay "explicit interest," that is, interest in money terms, they can pay "implicit interest" by providing free services. Many

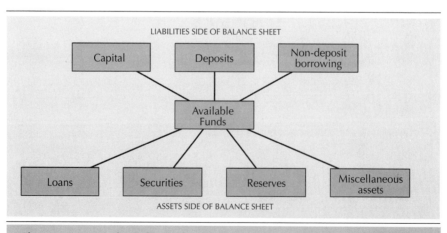

Figure 7.1   A Bank's Balance Sheet. Banks obtain funds from stockholders (capital), depositors, and other lenders and use them to make loans, hold securities and reserves, and acquire miscellaneous assets.

banks figure this quite precisely; they apply a certain interest rate to the deposits of their business customers and then provide them with free services, such as payroll preparation and purchases of foreign currencies, up to that amount. In addition, a bank often charges a lower rate of interest on loans to a firm that keeps a large demand deposit with it.

Another type of transactions deposit, called, not very imaginatively, *other checkable deposits,* consists of checkable deposits on which banks are allowed to pay interest. Only households and nonprofit organizations are allowed to hold such "other checkable deposits."

Savings and Other Time Deposits

One type of **savings deposit** is the passbook account, but savings accounts can also be set up by a written agreement between the depositor and the bank rather than by a passbook. Another type, the certificate of deposit, usually abbreviated as CD, is for a fixed sum. Although households can cash their CDs before the stated maturity date, there is usually an interest penalty for this. This penalty also exists for fixed-maturity passbook accounts but not for other passbook accounts.

Large depositors can purchase negotiable CDs, which are issued only by well-known banks. "Negotiable," a fancy term for saleable, means that the purchaser can reclaim the funds prior to the maturity date by selling the CD on the money market. Then, at maturity, the bank pays off the CD to whoever is holding it. Most negotiable CDs are purchased by businesses and governments, since the minimum denomination is $100,000 and the normal denomination is $1 million or more. They are highly liquid assets since there is an active market for them. The maturity of negotiable CDs is usually a year or less and is often set to suit the convenience of the particular purchaser.

Borrowings, Other Liabilities, and Capital

In addition to their deposits, banks have other liabilities. One of these is purchased **federal funds,** which, as explained in Chapter 4, are reserves at the Fed that can be transferred within one day.

The federal-funds market is a large one, and banks use it at times not just to obtain the funds to meet their reserve requirements, but also to obtain funds for additional lending. It is used particularly by the big banks, which often borrow more than their required reserves. Most loans are made on a one-day basis, and it is a way in which banks can quickly obtain more reserves or lend excess funds. Many small banks enter this market—typically as lenders—through their city correspondent banks. For them, it is a convenient way to earn interest on what would otherwise be excess reserves. The great majority of banks are active in this market. Although it is actually a market for loans, the language of the money market calls such transactions *sales* on one end and *purchases* on the other. The interest rate that the selling bank charges is called the **federal-funds rate.**

Another liability on the bank's balance sheet is securities sold under **repurchase agreements.** Repurchase agreements, also called *repos* or RPs, work as follows: Bank A sells a security to someone with an agreement to repurchase it at a certain date at an agreed-on price. In essence the repo is just a secured loan Bank A has received, since it has to repurchase the security. It is therefore a liability of the bank. Such repurchase agreements can be used to pay interest on what is actually a demand deposit in the following way. The bank makes an agreement with a customer corporation that toward the end of the day, when all incoming checks have already been cleared, it will "sell" the corporation a security for some of the funds in its demand deposit, with an agreement to repurchase the security the next morning. The corporation then has the funds available to meet incoming checks the next morning, when it needs them. The corporation also receives one day's interest on the overnight loan of its funds. Banks would prefer not to have to offer such overnight repos and, thus, not to have to pay interest. But competition among banks forces them to pay this interest.

Another liability item is outstanding acceptances. Acceptances arise in a rather complicated way. A firm selling to another firm on credit may not know enough about the buyer to feel safe in accepting a promise to pay. This is particularly likely with a foreign customer, in part because it is more difficult to sue in a foreign court than in a court in one's own country. But while the seller does not want to take the customer's IOU, he is willing to take the IOU of the customer's bank. Hence, a financial instrument, called a **banker's acceptance,** was developed. To explain it, let us back up and look first at a transaction *not* involving a bank. The seller draws up an order to the buyer to pay a sum of money by a certain date and releases ownership of the merchandise when the buyer accepts the order to pay by writing *accepted* across it. It is now a **trade acceptance** and is legally binding. Alternatively, the buyer can make an arrangement with her bank allowing the seller to draw the order to pay not on the buyer, but on the buyer's bank. When the bank writes *accepted* on this order to pay, it becomes a banker's acceptance. Since the bank is liable to make the payment on it, it is listed on the bank's balance sheet as a liability. However, the buyer is supposed to make payment to the bank by the date the bank has to make its payment on the acceptance. The bank lends its reputation, not its funds, to the buyer, who usually has to pay a small fee for this service. The seller receiving the banker's acceptance need not hold it to maturity but can sell it (at a discount from face value) in the money market.

The final item on the liabilities side is the **capital account.** It is calculated by summing assets and subtracting the liabilities owed to others from them.

THE BANK'S ASSETS

Primary Reserves

The first three assets listed on the left side of the balance sheet in Table 7.1 compose the bank's **primary reserves.** They are currency and coin held by the bank—called *vault cash*—reserves with the Fed, and demand deposits with other banks, that is, correspondent-bank balances. These three items form the first line of defense against a deposit or currency outflow.

Deposits with the Federal Reserve have two purposes. One is to satisfy the reserve requirement. Every depository institution that has checkable deposits of more than $4.2 million must keep a reserve against these deposits.[1] At present the required reserve ratio is 3 percent for the first $54 million and 10 percent above that. This reserve requirement can be met either with vault cash, and most of it is met that way, or through deposits at the Fed.[2]

The second purpose is to serve as a clearing balance, or cushion, for situations in which the bank is a net debtor in the clearing process. A bank wants such a cushion because the daily gross payments that it has to make are likely to be thousands of times larger than its reserve balance. Hence, small percentage differences in incoming and outgoing payments can have a great effect on its reserves. Fortunately, a bank does not have to meet its reserve requirements daily, but only as averages over a one- or two-week period, depending on its size. But it does have to pay a fee if its end-of-day balance is negative. While a bank does not earn anything on its required reserves, it does earn something on a part of its reserves in excess of its required reserves.[3] Sometimes the reserves that a bank wants to keep for clearing purposes exceed the reserves that it is legally required to keep, so that the legal reserve requirement is then not a restraining influence on the bank's portfolio decisions.

Obviously, vault cash, reserves with the Fed, and interbank deposits are all extremely liquid. Cash items in the process of collection are another highly liquid item on the balance sheet. These consist of checks and similar instruments which have just been deposited in the bank and which the bank has sent on for clearing.

Distinguishing Capital from Reserves

Although banks are required to keep both capital and reserves, they are quite different items. Capital represents the contribution of the owners of the bank. As already explained, it is an entry on the liabilities side of the balance sheet and cannot be identified with any particular item on the asset side of the balance sheet. A bank uses all its available funds, be they contributions of stockholders (capital) or of depositors, to buy various assets. It does not invest its capital in one asset and its deposits in another. By contrast, primary reserves are specific assets the bank holds: vault cash, deposits with the Fed, and checkable deposits with other banks.

Capital and reserves fulfill different functions. Capital acts as a cushion to absorb losses and, thus, to protect the FDIC and large depositors against the

---

[1] Money market funds are not required to keep reserves; but then they are not officially depository institutions. The cutoff point for reserve requirements is raised each year to take inflation into account. The figure in the text applies to 1995.

[2] Small institutions need not keep reserves with the Fed, but can keep them with another institution that then passes them on to the Fed.

[3] What they earn is credit toward purchases of Federal Reserve services, such as check clearing and currency shipment. For a description of the complex regulations see Edward Steven, "Required Clearing Balances," Federal Reserve Bank of Cleveland, *Economic Review*, Fourth Quarter 1993, pp. 2–14.

danger that the bank will become insolvent. Legally required reserves do not provide such a cushion. Suppose a bank loses 10 percent of its assets because it has made unsound loans. If its capital is only 8 percent, the bank's net worth is then −2 percent, regardless of the fact that it holds, say, 10 percent reserves. The only way the reserve requirement enhances the safety of a bank is by ensuring that some of the bank's assets are so safe that the bank cannot suffer a loss on them.[4] But since reserves are such a small percentage of total bank assets, this does not provide much reassurance. Chapter 23 will discuss the functions that the reserve requirement does serve.

Securities and Loans

Beyond its primary reserves a bank holds mainly loans and securities. These two items are known as **earning assets** because they bring the bank income. One part of these earning assets composes its **secondary reserves.** These are *assets that are not quite as liquid and safe as primary reserves, but still are very liquid.* They therefore provide the bank with a second line of defense if its primary reserves are insufficient. Unlike primary reserves, they earn a modest income, though their yield is usually lower than that on less liquid and less safe assets.

It is not possible to identify secondary reserves on a bank's balance sheet, since the items constituting the secondary reserves are classified as part of other items. One item included in secondary reserves is short-term government securities. Others are banker's acceptances, commercial paper, and call loans, which are loans mainly to brokers and security dealers on which the bank can demand repayment in a day.

Banks do not put all their available funds other than primary and secondary reserves into loans; they also hold fixed-income securities, such as bonds, mainly those issued by federal or state and local governments. Federal securities provide banks with assets that have no default risk and have a very wide market, so that they are more liquid than other securities with the same maturity. State and local government securities provide income that is exempt from federal taxes. State and local government securities, like federal securities, are, however, subject to interest-rate risk.

Loans involve personal relationships between the banker and the borrower. Hence, they differ sharply from security purchases. The bank usually buys securities from a dealer on the open market and does not know the borrower personally. Moreover, while a bank can sell a security again in the open market, there are fewer facilities for selling business and consumer loans, and the bank usually, though by no means always, holds them until maturity. There is, however, a growing tendency to securitize, and thus sell, consumer loans and business loans. Bank loans, other than interbank loans, fall under one of four broad categories: business loans, real-estate loans, consumer loans, or foreign loans.

Business Loans. **Banks** have a strong comparative advantage in making commercial and industrial loans. Many make most of their loans to fairly small, local borrowers. Such loan applications require evaluation by someone on the

[4] Vault cash is safe because banks are required to have insurance against theft.

spot, such as the local banker. This gives banks a powerful advantage over large, distant lenders, such as insurance companies. Compare, for example, the position of a bank and an insurance company in making a loan to a local grocery store and in buying a corporate bond. The bank knows much more about the local grocery store than the distant insurance company does and, hence, is in a much better position to decide whether to make it a loan. In contrast, the insurance company with its large staff of security analysts can reach a much more sophisticated decision about buying a corporate bond than can the typical bank.

An important characteristic of bank lending to business is **credit rationing.** A bank, unlike other firms, does not stand ready to provide as much of its product, loans, as the customer is willing to pay for. A fruit store will normally be happy to provide the buyer with, say, ten times as much as he normally buys, but a bank will usually not be ready to make a borrower ten times the normal loan. Similarly, a bank will not make loans to just anyone who applies for one, even if she is willing to pay an interest rate high enough to offset the fact that this loan is risky. Banks ration loans among applicants, both by turning away some loan customers and by limiting the size of loans to others. The basic reason that banks, unlike other sellers, limit the amount of the product (loans) they provide to each customer is that the bank takes a risk. It hands over its funds and cannot be certain that it will be repaid. As we discussed in Chapter 3, raising the interest rate to compensate for the higher risk is not a complete solution, because a high interest rate attracts those borrowers who know that their projects are extremely risky, while discouraging those whose projects are safer.

Credit rationing has both its defenders and its critics. The defenders point out that a banker's evaluation of loan requests acts as a check on the overoptimism of the firm's management. By scrutinizing loan requests, granting some and denying others, the banker provides potential borrowers with the services of a more or less objective outsider. The critics of credit rationing, on the other hand, point out that it allows banks to favor large depositors over other borrowers. Moreover, they argue, it gives bankers much arbitrary power, particularly in small towns, where there may be few or no competing banks, and it can be used as a weapon in forcing tie-in sales of bank services.

One factor that plays an important role in credit rationing is the existence of a customer relationship between the banker and the business borrower. Most of the business loans that banks make are to previous borrowers: banking is a repeat business. Firms establish a customer relationship with a particular bank (or in the case of a large firm, with several banks) and, as long as the arrangement is mutually satisfactory, continue both to borrow from this bank and to keep deposits with it. This customer relationship comprises more than just a borrower-lender relation. The firm also uses other services of the bank, such as the provision of foreign exchange, the preparation of payrolls, and so on. These services are often profitable and important for the bank. Large firms establish their customer relationships primarily with large and medium-size banks, not only because such banks can provide these ancillary services, but also because national banks (and in many states, state banks) are allowed (with some exceptions) to lend to any one borrower an amount equal to no more than 15 to 25 percent of the bank's capital, depending on the type of loan.

This customer relationship implies that the bank has an obligation, though not a legally binding one, to take care of the reasonable credit needs of its existing customers. A bank is therefore not a completely free agent in making loans. To accommodate its customers' reasonable demands, it might have to turn away new potential customers, even though these new customers would be willing to pay a higher interest rate than do existing customers. Similarly, it might have to ration loans among its existing customers rather than turn some of them down altogether. Or else it might have to sell some of its securities, or obtain the funds needed for extra loans by raising the interest rate it pays on large CDs. In the short run such actions may be costly for the bank, but are necessary to maximize long-run profits.

The existence of stable banking relations provides a major benefit: information. Over the years a bank learns much about its customers. If these customers were to change banks frequently, this information would become worthless to the firm's old bank, and its new bank would have to spend much effort to acquire this information.

The maturity of bank loans varies widely. Banks make many **term loans,** that is, loans *usually having a maturity of from one to five years.* Some are for even longer periods. A borrower can use these term loans to finance fixed investment. They are often **amortized**, that is, repaid in installments just like a consumer loan or a mortgage. On term loans the bank can protect itself by imposing certain restrictions on the borrower, such as limiting the amount of other debt that can be incurred. Another way banks sometimes take care of customers' needs for long-term capital is to purchase capital equipment and lease it to the customer. Thus banks own ships, airplanes, and even cows.

Instead of a term loan, a borrower may prefer to get frequent short-term loans. One way to do this is under a **line of credit.** This is an *arrangement whereby the bank agrees to make loans to a firm almost upon demand up to a certain amount.* Lines of credit are usually established for a year. Under a firm line of credit the bank is committed to make loans unless the firm's credit standing seriously deteriorates, and it frequently charges a fee on the amount of the line that is *not* used, in addition to the interest on the amount that *is* used. As an alternative, a firm may obtain a revolving credit arrangement whereby it can borrow up to a certain amount and then repay the loan at will without penalty. Later it can then borrow again up to the designated amount. A firm can also obtain a formal commitment from a bank to make it a loan in the future. For this it frequently has to pay a small fee. As Table 7.2 shows, in November 1994 about three-quarters of all business loans were made under some form of loan commitment such as a line of credit or revolving credit.

A bank frequently requires business borrowers who have a line of credit, and many who don't, to keep a **compensating** or **supporting balance** in the bank. This means that the firm has to keep as a demand deposit, say, 10 percent of its line of credit, or, under other arrangements, say, 15 percent of its outstanding loans. Compensating balances may be set as an *average* balance during the life of the line of credit or, more burdensomely, as a minimum balance. A compensating balance requirement is not legally binding, but if the borrower does not adhere to it, the bank may refuse further loans or may

Table 7.2   Commercial and Industrial Loans Made, November 7–11, 1994

Size of Loans (Thousands of Dollars)	Percentage of: Number of Loans Made	Value of Loans Made	Average Maturity*	Loan Rate (Weighted Average)	Percentage of Loans: Secured by Collateral	Made under Loan Commitment
Short-Term Loans						
All short term	81.8%	88.6%	56 days	6.37%	32.7%	67.7%
Made at Fixed Rates						
1–99	19.6	.7	151	7.8	89.1	43.4
100–499	1.5	.8	178	7.8	74.4	70.8
500–999	.5	.8	67	6.6	49.3	79.3
1,000–4,999	1.4	7.9	49	6.2	26.3	75.0
5,000–9,999	.5	9.3	32	5.7	13.1	69.0
10,000 and over	.6	62.6	20	5.4	7.2	63.1
Made at Floating Rates						
1–99	43.0	2.9	173	9.1	81.8	85.7
100–499	11.2	5.8	181	8.6	76.9	88.9
500–999	1.7	3.0	178	8.3	74.3	89.9
1,000–4,999	1.6	8.2	151	7.8	59.1	81.6
5,000–9,999	.2	3.9	139	6.9	55.6	75.7
10,000 and over	.2	12.7	75	6.0	43.6	44.3
Long-Term Loans						
All long term	18.0%	11.3%	43 months	7.5%	66.7%	79.5%
Made at Fixed Rates						
1–99	7.4	.3	52	9.4	93.2	26.7
100–499	.7	.3	61	8.7	89.3	38.7
500–999	.0	.1	47	7.0	45.2	93.1
1,000 and over	.2	1.8	40	6.7	43.3	70.4
Made at Floating Rates						
1–99	6.4	.4	43	9.2	84.6	60.3
100–499	2.1	1.2	40	8.4	80.5	84.3
500–999	0.5	.8	33	8.2	69.7	85.9
1,000 and over	0.7	6.4	44	7.3	66.9	86.2

*Average maturity weighted by loan size, excluding demand loans.
Source: Based on *Federal Reserve Bulletin,* February 1995, p. A68.

charge a higher interest rate on any subsequent loan. There is much variation in the compensating balance requirements of different banks. Some have rigid policies, while others merely consider the potential borrower's deposits as one factor in deciding on a loan request.

The compensating balance requirement raises the effective interest rate. Suppose a bank makes a $100,000 loan at an 8 percent interest rate with a 10 percent minimum compensating balance requirement. The borrower can then use only $90,000 of that, but still pays 8 percent on $100,000, or $8,000, which is equivalent to 8.9 percent on the $90,000 actually used. However, in many cases the borrower has a partially offsetting benefit: the compensating balance can be drawn on if things get really bad, and besides, as we mentioned above, banks provide free services to business depositors as implicit interest on their deposits.

Another requirement frequently imposed on a borrower is to provide the bank with collateral for the loan so that, in case it is not repaid, the bank can sell the collateral to pay it off. The collateral, which may consist of securities, inventory, and so on, often, though not always, exceeds the value of the loan. This protects the bank in case the collateral's market value declines.

The interest rate charged on bank loans varies of course, along with interest rates in general, though with a lag. Table 7.2 shows the interest rates charged on loans in November 1994. It shows that the larger the loan the lower the interest rate. This is not surprising since the interest rate paid has to compensate the bank for the cost of making the loan, and the cost of making a $10 million loan is not a thousand times the cost of making a $10,000 loan. This does not mean that a small borrower who obtains a small loan could lower the interest rate by taking out a large loan. Just the opposite—if the loan is made at all, the interest rate would be higher, because a large loan to a small firm is risky.

Many loans are made at the prime rate. This is a rate established by each bank for large loans to its better customers. The prime rates of various banks tend to move together. Typically, one large bank changes its prime rate and other banks follow. Loans to firms that do not receive the prime rate are often scaled up from the prime rate. For example, the loan agreement may state that the interest rate will be half a percent above the prime rate.

Since only the stronger firms can borrow at the prime rate, getting the prime rate is prized as an important symbol. However, particularly in periods when banks are scrambling for loan business, many top firms can borrow at (unannounced) rates below the prime rate. Some large firms are offered the alternative of borrowing at a small fixed margin over the **London Interbank Offered Rate** (LIBOR), that is, the rate at which large international banks lend to each other on the international market.

As Table 7.2 shows, the interest rate charged is frequently a variable rate, rather than a fixed rate; as the prime rate on newly contracted loans changes, the rate on many previously made business loans changes along with it. Sometimes, however, the loan agreement contains a "cap" on how high the interest rate can rise.

Real-Estate Loans. Traditionally mortgage loans were considered risky for banks because they involved considerable default and interest-rate risk, and were illiquid. Both the interest-rate risk and the illiquidity of real-estate loans is less of a problem now. Interest-rate risk has been reduced by the advent of variable-rate mortgages. However, because many variable-rate mortgages have caps that limit how high interest rates can rise, there is still some interest-rate risk. The illiquidity of mortgage loans, in particular of fixed-rate loans, has been reduced greatly by the development of the secondary market for mortgages through securitization. But default risk is still a serious problem. The real-estate market is volatile, with busts following booms. A bank that made what seemed like an eminently sound loan to a developer during a real-estate boom may find all of a sudden that the real-estate market has collapsed, that the developer cannot pay the interest on the loan, and that the collateral for the loan is worth much less than the loan itself. From 1990 to 1992 many banks suffered large losses on their real-estate loans, losses that some of them could not survive.

One type of real-estate loan is the **home-equity loan.** This is a loan secured by the borrower's home. It has the pleasant feature that, even though the funds can be used for any purpose, interest paid on it can, like most other mortgage interest, be treated as a deduction from income on the federal income tax. Nearly all home-equity loans have variable interest rates.

Consumer Loans. Another major outlet for bank funds is lending to consumers, which accounts for almost 20 percent of total bank loans. One substantial advantage of consumer loans for banks is that they are liquid because they are usually short term and amortized. Some are made at variable interest rates.

Many consumer loans are made for the purchase of durables, which then serve as collateral for the loan. Banks make consumer loans both directly to consumers and indirectly through durable-goods dealers (car dealers, for instance) by financing loans originated by the dealer. Banks also make general-purpose loans to consumers. Among these are credit-card loans on which the bank receives not only interest from the borrower, but also a commission from the vendor. Some banks have set up an arrangement by which credit-card holders can have their checking accounts credited and the card debited automatically if the balance in the checking account is insufficient to meet incoming checks. Other banks have set up similar arrangements for automatic loans to customers who do not have the bank's credit card. Another type of consumer loan is the federally subsidized student loan.

Banks also make loans for the purchase of securities. Such loans are made not only to households but also to security dealers and brokers who use them to finance their customers' purchases, as well as their own security holdings.

Foreign Loans. Many large banks, as well as some medium-size banks, have banded together into so-called syndicates to make large loans to foreign firms and foreign governments. Loans to foreign governments are safer than loans to foreign or domestic firms in one respect: a country—unlike a firm—is not likely to go out of business. However, they are riskier in another way since, if a foreign government refuses to repay, the bank cannot go to court, have the country declared bankrupt, and have all its assets distributed among its creditors. Instead, the sanctions against a country just walking away from its debts are twofold. First, its assets that are located elsewhere, for example, bank deposits in another country or ships in foreign ports, can be seized. This makes it hard for a country to carry on normal foreign trade. Second, a country that has defaulted on its debts will find it difficult to borrow abroad, even for the essential short-term financing of its imports. In Chapter 9 we will describe the great problem that foreign loans created for banks in the 1980s.

Other Assets

Apart from the major assets discussed so far, a bank's balance sheet contains a number of minor assets listed in Table 7.1 as "Other assets." Included in this category are items such as customers' liabilities on account of acceptances, which is the counterpart of the acceptances item listed as a liability. When a bank accepts a draft for a customer, the customer incurs a liability to the bank, and this is an asset for the bank. Additional examples of "Other assets" are federal funds sold and bank office buildings.

ASSET AND LIABILITY MANAGEMENT

Banks make a living borrowing at one price and lending at a higher price. They have to pay attention not only to how much they earn by lending, but also to how much they pay for the funds they borrow and hence from whom they borrow. Banks do not depend for their funds only on depositors who walk through their doors. They can buy funds in an open market. Even small banks can do so by buying federal funds from their city correspondent bank, by borrowing from the Fed, or by borrowing through a money broker. (Money brokerages split up large deposits into $100,000 units and deposit them into whichever banks pay the highest interest rate.) Medium-size and large banks can also buy funds in many other ways. One way is to issue what are called *large CDs*, that is, CDs for $100,000 or more. Such CDs have a national market, and, normally, if a bank offers a slightly higher rate in this market, it can readily obtain additional funds. In addition, banks can bid for funds on the national money market through repurchase agreements. Another way is for the bank's holding company to sell commercial paper (something the bank itself is not allowed to do) and to make the proceeds from this sale available to the bank. Still another way is to borrow so-called **Eurodollars,** that is, dollar-denominated deposits in European and Caribbean banks or in foreign branches of U.S. banks.

The business of a large bank therefore extends beyond the traditional making of loans. For example, the treasurer of a large bank that is $100 million short of funds will call another bank and inquire at what rate that bank is buying and selling funds. If the bank quotes rates that seem high, the treasurer, instead of buying, say, $50 million from it, may sell it $50 million, and hope to buy the now-required $150 million from other banks later on at a lower rate.

Reliance on purchased funds has both advantages and disadvantages for a bank. The advantage is that the bank can readily obtain funds that way. It does not, like the traditional bank, lend out its deposits. Instead, it will frequently make a loan and then raise its CD rate enough to get the deposits that make the loan possible. It can therefore make profitable loans it would otherwise have to turn down. On the other hand, living off purchased funds has its dangers. First, the interest rate that has to be paid to attract purchased funds may rise sharply. The suppliers of such funds provide them only because the bank pays a competitive interest rate, not because of loyalty to the bank or because it has a conveniently located branch! Hence, such purchased funds are at times much more expensive than are the so-called core deposits of households and firms that are the bank's regular customers. Second, suppose a rumor starts that the bank is unsound. Small depositors will stay with the bank, since their deposits are insured, but the providers of purchased funds will cut and run, and that may cause the bank to fail. In 1984 Continental Illinois, then the eighth-largest bank in the country, faced such a massive outflow of funds and was, in effect, taken over by the government for some time.

Matching the Maturities of Assets and Liabilities

A bank has to watch the relation between the maturities of its assets and of its liabilities. Several factors tempt it to hold assets that have much longer maturities than its liabilities. One is that its loan customers frequently want term loans at fixed interest rates, so that they can predict their future interest cost.

Financing a Loan

Suppose you are the CEO of a bank and a loan officer has just told you that she has finally succeeded in getting Solid Inc. to apply for a loan. But the data on your computer screen show that you do not have any excess funds. You don't want to turn the loan down if you can help it. So what should you do?

Could you borrow from the Fed? You are not supposed to borrow to make additional loans, and should borrow only to take care of unexpected drains of funds. But you think the Fed will not find out what you are doing. All the same, the Fed will lose patience if you borrow too frequently, and you don't want to use up your borrowing opportunities there. So, how about buying federal funds? That's a bit risky because the federal-funds rate may rise, and you might find that you are paying more for the funds than you get by lending them. Well, how about getting longer-term funds by raising the rate you pay on CDs? Usually that would be fine, but right now it is not, because an unusual number of CDs that you issued last year are coming due, and if you raise the CD rate, you will have to pay the higher rate on the renewal of all those old CDs.

So you decide to sell some of your Treasury bills. After all, you bought them not for their earnings, which are lower than on longer-term securities, but to maintain liquidity. And one of the reasons you wanted liquidity was precisely because a good loan opportunity might show up.

At the same time, its depositors and suppliers of purchased funds prefer short maturities for their claims on the bank. Moreover, since short-term interest rates are usually lower than long-term rates, a bank can often make a profit by lending long and borrowing short.

But such a maturity mismatch creates a serious risk. Suppose, for example, that a bank buys 5-year bonds paying 8 percent, and initially finances this purchase by issuing 90-day CDs at 7 percent. If interest rates then rise, so that the bank is now paying, say, 10 percent on the CDs it uses to finance its holdings of 8 percent bonds, it will not be a very happy bank. In the late 1970s First Pennsylvania, then the twentieth-largest bank, got into trouble that way and had to be rescued by the FDIC and a consortium of other banks. Hence, banks have been careful in recent years to limit the size of the maturity gap between their assets and liabilities. They have done so in large part by making loans at variable rather than at fixed rates.

RISKS IN BANKING

Banks have to face several types of risk. They obviously have to worry about default risk, whether their loans will be repaid on time. They also have to worry about the interest-rate risk that results from a maturity mismatch. A related risk is liquidity risk, that is, the risk that the bank will experience an unexpectedly large outflow of funds. Banks guard against that by holding liquid assets,

Banking in the Good Old Days

Nowadays, when banks pursue depositors with TV ads, it is hard to imagine that there was a time when banks sat back and expected depositors to come to them cap in hand. But there was. Here is a description of how to open a bank account, taken from a textbook published in 1916.*

There are so many ways in which a bank may be defrauded . . . that the officers must be very careful to whom they extend the privilege of opening an account. . . . One of the pleasantest ways to open an account with a bank is to be introduced by a depositor in good standing. . . . It is not always possible to arrange for a personal introduction. In such a case, a properly written letter addressed to an officer and signed by a depositor in good standing, or even by a mutual friend, will be of material assistance. . . . If it is impossible for a person to obtain either a personal or written introduction to the bank he had chosen, he may make application for the opening of an account without an introduction and have the assurance that such a procedure will not militate against him, if he presents his case properly. It is true that some banks will not, under any circumstances, open an account with a person unknown to them. In fact, it is good banking practice not to accept accounts from strangers. . . .

*Joseph F. Johnson, Howard M. Jefferson, and Franklin Escher, *Banking* (New York: Alexander Hamilton Institute, 1916), pp. 266–68.

as well as by having sources of borrowing available. The bigger banks that make international loans also have to worry about political, or country, risk, which is the risk that unfavorable developments in a country will prevent borrowers there from repaying their loans. A country may impose controls over foreign payments and make only limited amounts of dollars and other foreign exchange available to those who need to repay their bank loans. Another type is **payments** or **settlement risk.** This occurs if, perhaps due to some telecommunications breakdown or computer failure, a bank does not receive a large payment it had counted on.

OTHER ACTIVITIES OF BANKS

Banks have moved a substantial distance beyond their traditional business of merely borrowing funds and lending them out. They now provide numerous financial services for which they earn substantial fees. Some large banks now earn half or more of their income from fees. David Coultor, a BankAmerica vice chairman, explained that: "Once you get people hooked with credit, you have to sell them other services. . . . We have very few stand-alone credit customers. If we had them, we would have to have a conversation to get them to do more with us or we'd part ways."[5]

Among the services provided are buying and selling foreign exchange, preparing payrolls, acting as trustee of a company's pension fund and as registration agent for its stock, and providing companies with cash management plans and derivatives. Banks also sell households shares both in their own mutual funds and in other mutual funds that they sell on commission. They would also like to sell life insurance, and although they have not yet obtained the right to do so, they may receive it soon.

Off-Balance-Sheet Financing

Apart from lending funds, banks also lend their reputation in ways that leave no trace on their balance sheets. One example of off-balance-sheet financing is a **letter of credit,** whereby a bank guarantees that the recipient of the letter of credit will pay the bill for which it is issued. Another is a **standby letter of credit.** This is an arrangement whereby the bank guarantees (and hence assumes liability for) a customer's obligation, such as repaying a loan. In effect, the bank participates in the loan by assuming the risk of the loan, without actually having to provide any funds (as long as the debtor does not fail). Another example of off-balance-sheet financing is an **interest-rate swap.** Suppose one of the bank's customers has a variable-rate debt but would prefer to have a fixed-rate debt, while another customer is in the opposite position. The bank can arrange for them to swap their interest-rate liabilities. It can also arrange swaps for customers who have debts denominated in foreign currencies.

Although these activities do not show up on a bank's balance sheet, they

---

[5] Cited in Ralph King and Steven Lipin, "New Profit Center," *Wall Street Journal,* January 31, 1994, p. A6.

do create risks for the bank. If a customer defaults on a swap, the bank may be left holding the bag. These are not the only sources of risk that fail to show up on the bank's balance sheet. When a bank sells a loan it has made, it may seem that the bank has now got rid of the risk that this loan represented. But that is not so, because the loan contract usually obliges the bank to assume contingent liability in case the loan fails. To take account of such risks, the regulators include some off-balance-sheet items in the risk-adjusted assets against which a bank has to keep capital.

Other Risks

Banks also take risks by speculating in the foreign-exchange market and in the money market. For example, a bank that expects interest rates to rise may buy more federal funds than it needs early in the week in the hope of selling them at a profit later in the week. And it may also buy securities if it expects interest rates to fall.

As explained in the previous chapter, banks have an incentive to take more risk than the regulators consider appropriate, because the FDIC and large depositors bear some of the risk that banks take. When the regulators tell banks that they are not allowed to hold certain risky assets, the banks comply and sell these assets, but then take more risk on, say, interest-rate swaps to restore their risk position to its equilibrium value. When the regulators then crack down on those activities, the banks abandon them in favor of some other risky activities, until the regulators catch up with those, and so on.

Table 7.3 Balance Sheet of Thrift Institutions, Third Quarter 1994

Financial Assets	Percent	Liabilities	Percent
Reserves with the Federal Reserve	.2	Deposits	79.6
Currency, deposits, federal funds, and repurchase agreements	4.6	Credit market instruments	8.1
		Miscellaneous	12.3
U.S. government securities	19.2	Total	100.0
Corporate and foreign bonds	7.1		
Tax-exempt securities	.2		
Corporate securities	.8		
Mortgages	49.6		
Consumer credit	11.7		
Other Loans (to business)	.8		
Miscellaneous assets	5.8		
Total	100.0		

Source: Based on Board of Governors, Federal Reserve System, *Flow of Funds Accounts, Financial Assets and Liabilities*, Fourth Quarter 1994, p. 94.

Trust Departments

Large banks also earn fee income in a way that involves little risk by having a **trust department.** Trust departments administer funds for wealthy households, estates, pension funds, and other customers. For some trust funds the bank provides only investment advice, but more usually the bank has sole investment responsibility. Corporate trust departments administer corporate pension funds, send out interest and dividend payments, and register bond transfers. About one-quarter of all banks have trust departments, but these trust funds are highly concentrated in a relatively small number of large banks.

THE THRIFTS' BALANCE SHEET

The balance sheet of thrifts, shown in Table 7.3, is simpler than that of banks. The items on it either are self-explanatory or have been discussed already.

SUMMARY

1 Banks issue checkable deposits, and savings and time deposits. Other bank liabilities include federal funds bought, banker's acceptances, and capital.
2 All except the smallest depository institutions with transactions accounts must hold reserves set—within limits—by the Federal Reserve.
3 Bank loans are the biggest bank asset. Banks ration credit. Business firms have a customer relationship with banks and are able to get long-term as well as short-term loans. They often have a line of credit, but have to keep compensating balances and frequently have to offer collateral. The best customers can sometimes borrow below the prime rate. On term loans the interest rate is often variable.
4 Mortgage loans are an important part of a bank's assets, though they are relatively illiquid. In addition, banks make consumer loans and security loans.
5 Banks manage their liabilities by actively buying funds in the CD market and in the federal-funds market. Large banks rely heavily on such purchased funds.
6 Banks have to watch the maturity match between their assets and liabilities. They are tempted to hold assets that are much longer term than their liabilities, but this is risky.
7 Banks earn a significant proportion of their income from fees. They obtain fees from various types of off-balance-sheet financing, from trust departments, and from service charges on deposits.
8 Mortgage loans are the biggest assets of savings and loans and savings banks.
9 Banks can increase their earnings (and their risk) by off-balance-sheet financing.

KEY TERMS

demand deposits
certificates of deposit (CDs)
federal funds
repurchase agreements (RPs, repos)
banker's acceptances
primary reserves
secondary reserves

term loans
line of credit
compensating balance
prime rate
LIBOR
liability management
letter of credit

credit rationing

customer relationship

off-balance-sheet financing

interest-rate swaps

trust department

QUESTIONS AND EXERCISES

1 Describe the way banks manage their liabilities.

*2 Explain what both negotiable and nonnegotiable CDs are.

3 Describe:
   a. banker's acceptances
   b. repos
   c. federal funds
   d. primary reserves

*4 What is credit rationing. Why do banks do this?

5 Describe the following characteristics of business loans:
   a. lines of credit
   b. compensatory balances
   c. collateral
   d. the prime rate

6 Suppose a banker tells you that in his 25 years as a loan officer he has never made a loan that went into default. Should you congratulate him for sound business judgment?

*7 When banks sell loans, they retain liability if the loan turns sour. What is the reason for that arrangement?

8 Describe the functions of a bank's trust department.

*9 "Capital requirements on banks should be lowered. If they have a smaller proportion of their funds tied up in capital they can make more loans." Discuss.

10 Describe some methods of off-balance-sheet financing.

FURTHER READING

FEINMAN, JOSHUA. "Reserve Requirements: History, Current Practice, and Potential Reform," *Federal Reserve Bulletin,* 79 (June 1993), 569–89. A good discussion of reserve requirements.

JOHNSON, SYLVESTER, and AMELIA MURPHY. "Going Off the Balance Sheet," Federal Reserve Bank of Atlanta, *Economic Review,* 72 (September/October 1987), 23–35. A good survey and evaluation of various techniques.

MAYER, MARTIN. *The Money Bazaar,* Part 3. New York: Dutton, 1984. A fascinating description of how banks operate.

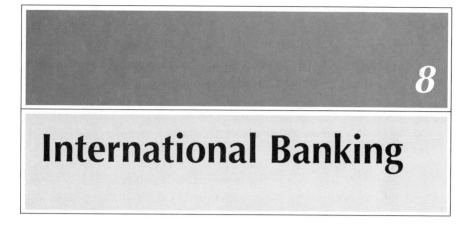

International Banking

8

After you have read this chapter, you will be able to:

- Understand what the offshore banking market is.
- Discuss what a Eurodollar is and how it differs from a domestic U.S. dollar.
- Have some understanding of why the growth of the market in Eurodollar deposits has been so important for the expansion of international banking.

The commercial banking systems of the major industrial countries have become internationalized in the last two decades, and banks headquartered in New York, Chicago, Los Angeles, Tokyo, Frankfurt, London, Zurich, and Toronto now compete aggressively in each other's domestic markets. U.S. banks now have nearly one thousand branches and subsidiaries in Western Europe, Asia, and Latin America. And banks headquartered in Western Europe and Japan have more than five hundred banking offices in New York, Chicago, San Francisco, and Los Angeles; these banks account for about a fifth of the value of bank loans in the United States.

One consequence of the internationalization of commercial banking is that there is now more extensive competition in the major national financial centers as foreign banks seek to increase their share of markets for domestic loans and domestic deposits. Banking in Great Britain may be dominated by a few banks, but many major non-British banks also compete for British pound deposits and the loans of major and modest customers alike. Similarly, the three big German banks (Deutsche, Dresdner, and Commerz) have encountered increased competition for loan and deposit business from fifty branches of foreign banks now open in Frankfurt, Dusseldorf, and Hamburg.

This chapter studies the growth and present structure of international banking. It goes on to analyze the relationship between interest rates on U.S. dollar deposits in New York and those on U.S. dollar deposits in London and other financial centers. The rapid increase in international banking poses special problems for policymakers, and these are also examined.

OFFSHORE BANKING AND THE INTERNATIONALIZATION OF COMMERCIAL BANKING

The surge in international banking competition has been facilitated by the growth of the external currency market called the **offshore banking market.** Offshore banks help bring lenders and borrowers together in basically the same way domestic banks do; the major difference is that they sell deposits and buy loans denominated in a currency other than that of the country in which they are located. The term *offshore* means that these banks are located beyond the legal jurisdiction of the country traditionally associated with deposits denominated in a particular currency. Thus, the London offices of U.S. and German banks sell deposits and buy loans denominated in U.S. dollars, German marks, and perhaps ten currencies other than the British pound. The terms *Eurodollar, Euromark,* and so on, are sometimes applied to these offshore deposits to distinguish deposits there from domestic bank deposits. Foreign banks with branches in New York and other U.S. cities get a substantial part of their funds for U.S. dollar loans by selling deposits denominated in the U.S. dollar in London and other offshore centers.

At the end of 1993, offshore deposits issued by banks in Western Europe totaled $7,000 billion. About 70 percent of these deposits were denominated in the U.S. dollar, 14 percent in the German mark, and 7 percent in the Swiss franc.

Offshore banking occurs in monetary havens, such as London, Luxembourg, Singapore, Panama, and the Cayman Islands. Firms and investors shift income to tax havens to take advantage of lower tax rates, just as firms in the shipping business, no matter where they are headquartered, register their vessels in Liberia or Panama to take advantage of less-restrictive regulations. Investors acquire offshore deposits primarily because interest rates on offshore deposits exceed those on domestic deposits by more than enough to compensate for the additional costs, inconveniences, and risks. The rapid growth of offshore deposits denominated in the U.S. dollar reflects the response of investors to the fact that interest rates on offshore deposits exceed the interest rates on comparable domestic deposits. The interest-rate differential exists because offshore banks incur lower costs than domestic banks. Competition for deposits among offshore banks means, too, that they pass on to investors or depositors most, if not all, of the savings associated with producing deposits in the offshore, rather than the domestic, market.

Offshore banks are virtually unregulated by the authorities of the countries in which they are located. The British authorities, for example, recognize that transactions denominated in the U.S. dollar, the German mark, the Swiss franc, and other foreign currencies in London have no more significance for the management of the British economy than if they had occurred in Luxembourg or New York. Great Britain benefits from these transactions because it exports more banking services. Indeed, to the extent that dollar banking services occur in London rather than New York, the British have "poached" banking activities that almost certainly would have occurred in New York or another U.S. city. As a result, employment in banking and related industries increases in London and drops in New York, Chicago, Los Angeles, and so on.

Fifty international banks—the major banks in each industrial country—are important competitors in London's offshore market in bank deposits, while another three hundred banks from various countries also participate. Competition among political jurisdictions such as Great Britain, Luxembourg, the Bahamas, and Singapore for offshore banking business means that each of these countries is reluctant to apply regulations on offshore transactions, because these banks might then move to even less regulated offshore centers.

THE STRUCTURE OF INTERNATIONAL BANKING

One of the striking differences between the domestic banking systems of the major countries is the number and size of banks. There are more banks in the United States than in all other industrialized countries combined. In most other countries, three, four, or five banks, each with hundreds of branches, account for 60 to 70 percent of bank deposits and loans. In the United States even the largest U.S. bank accounts for less than 10 percent of total U.S. deposits.

That U.S. banks are both large and yet much more numerous than in other countries reflects two factors. First, total bank deposits are much larger in the United States than elsewhere: the U.S. economy is at least twice the size of the Japanese economy, the next largest. Second, the United States has long been concerned with maintaining competition in banking. In the past this led to legislation greatly restricting branching by banks.

Paradoxically, in a few cases the large size of major U.S. banks encouraged the merging among and growth of foreign banks: foreign banks did not want to be at a size disadvantage in competing to meet the financial needs of large multinational firms. In Great Britain in the early 1970s, for example, the National Provincial Bank merged with Westminster Bank, while Lloyds merged with British and Overseas Bank. In the Netherlands, Amsterdam Bank and Rotterdam Bank merged.

Most of the foreign offices of U.S. banks are branches; they are not incorporated in the country in which they are located. These foreign branches have the same legal status as branches located in the United States; the only difference is where they are situated. In a few cases, however, the parent banks have set up subsidiaries that have a separate legal status abroad. Some countries, including Mexico and other developing countries, require that foreign-owned banks participate in a joint venture with a domestic bank, and then the subsidiary form is essential. For banks headquartered in the United States, the distinction between branch and subsidiary is important for determining U.S. corporate income-tax liability, for the income (or losses) of foreign branches is included in the bank's U.S. income in the year in which the income is earned, while the income of the foreign subsidiaries is subject to taxation in the United States only when subsidiaries pay dividends to their U.S. parent banks. Moreover, the distinction between branch and subsidiary is important to depositors who are concerned that the bank might incur losses: conceivably the subsidiary could close with a loss to its shareholders while the parent remained in business (although this seems unlikely); in contrast, a branch could not fail while the parent remained open for business.

The major expansion of U.S. banks abroad, which took place in the 1960s and 1970s (although several U.S. banks had established foreign branches in the latter part of the nineteenth century and a few more in the 1920s), occurred for several reasons. First, banks expanded to foreign shores to follow the foreign expansion of U.S. firms. Second, they did so to avoid domestic limits on growth; this was especially true for U.S. banks headquartered in New York City, where state and federal regulations at that time prohibited them from establishing branches in the United States outside New York City. Finally, a large number of U.S. banks went abroad to participate in the offshore money market; they especially wanted to avoid the loss of deposits to the branches of U.S. and foreign banks in London and other offshore centers that offered higher interest rates on U.S. dollar deposits than those U.S. banks could pay on domestic U.S. dollar deposits. In the late 1960s there was a ceiling on interest rates that American banks could pay on domestic deposits. This ceiling was eliminated for large deposits, and hence the deposits that compete with offshore deposits, in 1970. But even so, interest rates on domestic deposits were lower than on offshore deposits, because U.S. reserve requirements raised the cost of producing deposits in the United States. But the reserve requirements on time deposits has now been eliminated, and with it most of the cost advantage of offshore deposits. The distribution of foreign offices of U.S. banks matches the pattern of the foreign investment of U.S. firms with two exceptions: U.S. banks are underrepresented in those countries in which entry has been restricted, including Mexico and other developing countries, and overrepresented in London, Luxembourg, the Bahamas, and other monetary havens. Many U.S. and foreign banks established offices in these monetary havens to participate in the offshore market for deposits denominated in the U.S. dollar, the German mark, the Swiss franc, the Japanese yen, and a few other currencies. Setting up branches to participate in the offshore market was generally less costly or more profitable than setting up additional domestic offices to compete for deposits.

The major expansion of foreign banks in the United States, which took place in the 1970s, also occurred for several reasons. First, these banks were also trying to circumvent the domestic constraints on geographic expansion. Second, they wanted to participate directly in the dominant international center of finance. Third, they wanted to participate in the financing of international trade between their own countries and the United States: because much of the trade was denominated in the U.S. dollar, foreign banks were at a disadvantage in trade-financing, since they did not have direct access to U.S. dollar funds. Fourth, some wanted to serve particular ethnic markets in the United States, both the expatriate business community and immigrants. Moreover, firms headquartered in Western Europe, Japan, and Canada were increasing their investments in the United States, and the banks headquartered in these countries did not want to lose their customers to U.S. banks.

Foreign banks contemplating entering the United States faced a number of key decisions—one was whether to set up offices in New York or in a smaller U.S. financial center, a second was whether to enter the U.S. market by starting a new office or by purchasing a U.S. bank, and a third was whether to set up a branch or a subsidiary. Foreign banks initially had certain advantages in the United States. Although they were not allowed to branch across state lines, they might establish branches in one state and a subsidiary in another (or subsidiaries in several other states). Also, their U.S. branches were not required to join the Federal Reserve, nor were they required to hold reserves. Moreover, their required capital ratios were below those of U.S. banks; indeed the U.S. branches of foreign banks were not required to have any separate capital of their own.

INTERNATIONAL BANKING AND THE DOMESTIC BANKING SYSTEM

What controls should the United States place on the offshore branches of its banks? How should it treat branches of foreign banks in the United States? More broadly, what is the impact of the internationalization of commercial banking on U.S. monetary policy? These are some of the questions posed for domestic policymakers by international banking.

The rapid growth of foreign banks in the United States in the 1980s focused attention on whether foreign banks had regulatory advantages in the United States relative to U.S. banks. Moreover, their rapid growth led to the concern that the regulations applied by some foreign authorities to the activities of U.S. banks within their jurisdictions were more restrictive than the regulations applied to the activities of foreign banks within the United States and vice versa.

A key feature of banking regulation within the United States is the multiplicity of regulatory authorities. The regulatory dilemma the United States faced was that if U.S. regulation of foreign banks followed the principle of reciprocity, then the severity of regulations applied to U.S. offices of banks headquartered abroad might vary, depending on the country in which the foreign banks were headquartered. Thus, the United States was reluctant to adopt the principle of **reciprocity,** and instead applied the same regulations to all banks operating in the United States regardless of where those banks were headquartered and regardless of how U.S. banks were regulated in those foreign countries. This approach was formalized in the International Banking Act of 1978 (IBA), which reduced the competitive advantages previously available to foreign banks in the United States by treating them as if they were U.S. banks and established the principle of **national treatment.** All foreign banks operating in the United States now are treated as if they were U.S. banks, regardless of the treatment afforded U.S. banks in their host countries (the national-treatment principle has taken priority over the reciprocity principle). While foreign banks may not join the Federal Reserve, they are required to hold reserves there, comparable to those held there by U.S. banks, if their deposits exceed $1 billion. The U.S. branches of foreign banks are provided with the option of holding federal licenses; previously they were only allowed to hold state licenses. Those branches of foreign banks that are involved in selling deposits to U.S. residents are also required to participate in federal deposit insurance. And the U.S. branches of large foreign banks are now subject to the same supervisory and supervision requirements as comparable U.S. banks.

The IBA has slowed the expansion of foreign banks in the United States. Yet these banks are sufficiently numerous and large to increase competition in banking significantly, especially in loans to U.S. businesses and in the markets for deposits of and loans to individual households in New York and California. And because foreign-owned banks in the United States now must hold reserves at the Federal Reserve, the effectiveness of U.S. monetary control has been increased.

This brings us to the question of monetary policy and the internationalization of commercial banking. The growth of offshore deposits has decreased the significance of the barriers among currency areas. Both investors and banks are very conscious of the additional return they might earn by moving funds across borders between currency areas. And the resulting growth of offshore deposits has increased the willingness of firms to estimate the costs and risks associated with altering their currency exposures. Thus, with the decline in the segmentation of currency areas that the expansion of offshore banks

The Erosion of Banks and Bank Regulation

One day in the next year or two, one of the largest U.S. banks will decide to cease banking operations. This firm will have concluded that the benefits of being a bank—primarily government-supplied deposit insurance and access to the discount window of the Federal Reserve—are no longer worth the costs—including deposit-insurance premiums, reserve requirements, interest-rate ceilings, and asset-examination procedures. A small number of other U.S. banks will follow suit immediately.

Such a decision to cease banking operations follows the same logic as the rapid growth of offshore banking in the 1970s in response to the increased cost of bank regulation in a period of increasing inflation and higher interest rates: when the costs of avoiding regulation fall below the costs of regulation, more and more investors and financial institutions will opt to avoid the regulations. The deposits of the offshore branches of U.S. banks were not subject to interest-rate ceilings or reserve requirements, nor did these offshore offices have to pay deposit-insurance premiums. Because the offshore offices of these banks incurred lower costs than the domestic offices of these same banks, they could pay higher interest rates. This was good for business: large firms increasingly took advantage of the higher interest rates on offshore deposits; they shifted deposits from regulated banks in the United States to deposits in the offshore offices of these same banks.

Similarly, with the rapid growth of automatic teller machines (ATMs), more and more depositors are likely to take advantage of the higher interest rates offered by banks in distant locations. Proximity is far less important if cash can be obtained at an ATM. So more and more customers will find it worthwhile to undertake a larger share of their transactions with banks that pay higher interest rates, despite their locations. More and more customers will also be willing to undertake their transactions with unregulated financial institutions like the money-market accounts of various brokerage firms or of lenders like GE Capital or GMAC.

As the costs of avoiding regulation fall, more and more investors and financial institutions will choose to avoid the regulations. Then regulatory institutions will either have to reduce the costs of regulation or face a significant decline in the number of firms they regulate.

has brought, the scope for independent national monetary policies has also declined. The rapid growth of offshore deposits denominated in U.S. dollars in the 1970s generated controversy about the impact such offshore deposits would have on the stability of the international financial system and the effectiveness of national monetary control.

Since the major offshore banks are branches of the major international banks, the concern that their failure might trigger the collapse of the banking system is greatly exaggerated. Most offshore banks are unlikely to make riskier loans than their head offices; indeed the offshore branches of U.S. banks are examined by the same U.S. authorities that examine the domestic offices of these banks. Legally, holders of deposits in offshore offices are not likely to incur losses even if these offices make numerous loans that prove faulty: the solvency of these offshore offices is based on the solvency of their head offices. Finally, the central banks in the United States and other industrial countries have agreed that each central bank is responsible for the liquidity needs of the offshore offices of banks headquartered in its jurisdiction.

SUMMARY

1 In the last several decades, commercial banking has become much more international, as banks headquartered in the United States, Western Europe, and Japan have established systems of branches in other countries.
2 The growth in international banking has been facilitated by the expansion of offshore banking—banking offices operating in particular centers sell deposits denominated in a currency other than that of the country in which they are located. Thus, banks in London, including the London branches of U.S. banks, sell deposits denominated in the U.S. dollar or the German mark or the Swiss franc.
3 The growth in international banking has brought with it special regulatory and monetary policy questions, including whether regulations penalize domestic banks in their competition with foreign banks.

KEY TERMS

Eurodollar deposits
International Banking Act of 1978

principle of reciprocity
principle of national treatment
offshore deposits

QUESTIONS AND EXERCISES

*1 Discuss the conditions necessary for the growth of an external currency market. Why do interest rates on offshore deposits exceed those on comparable domestic deposits? What is the upper limit of this difference? If interest rates on external deposits are higher than those on domestic deposits denominated in the same currency, why does anyone continue to hold domestic deposits?
2 Is it likely that any financial collapse that might befall the offshore banking system would have little effect on the domestic banking system?
*3 Discuss the ways in which the growth of offshore dollar deposits has contributed to the growth of branches of foreign banks in the United States.

FURTHER READING

FIELEKE, NORMAN. *Key Issues in International Banking.* Boston: Federal Reserve Bank of Boston, 1977. A conference volume with good descriptive material.

LITTLE, JANE SNEDDON. *Eurodollars.* New York: Harper & Row, 1975. A descriptive survey of actors in the offshore money market.

U.S. CONGRESS, HOUSE COMMITTEE ON BANKING, CURRENCY, AND HOUSING. *International Banking.* Washington: Government Printing Office, 1976. A comprehensive survey of international banking and background materials for the International Banking Act of 1979.

The Failure of the Deposit-Insurance System

After you have read this chapter, you will be able to:

- Appreciate the magnitude of the greatest failure of the U.S. financial system since the Great Depression.
- Understand why such a breakdown was allowed to happen.
- Realize how the government tried to resolve the problem.

In the previous chapters the U.S. financial structure was described as an essentially well functioning system. Here, we'll see how, in a dramatic and extremely costly way, a major part of it broke down. The story is important not only in its own right, but also as a case study of how financial policies can fail. It is unlikely that we will experience the same type of breakdown again for a generation or for many generations. But other failures are likely to occur. And what we learn from this failure may prove useful for subsequent crises; past mistakes are good, though expensive, teachers. As you read this chapter you may feel that you are being asked to study a historical episode that is over and done with. But understanding how a disaster was allowed to happen may turn out to be practical, not useless, knowledge; things that happened a long time ago often provide more useful lessons than do recent events. The appendix discusses in some detail who should be blamed for the savings and loan debacle, and the discussion illustrates that it is not all that easy to assess blame.

From our 1990s perspective it may be hard to believe that the deposit-insurance system was ever highly praised. However, following its disastrous performance in the early part of the Great Depression, the depository system seemed to be on a sound footing. For forty years, from 1942 to 1981, only 255 bank failures occurred, and those involved primarily small institutions and hence were not costly to the insurance funds. But this happy situation did not last. In the 1980s not only did the failure rate of banks rise sharply, but some of the largest banks in the country were among the failures. By the early 1990s the FDIC's insurance fund was threatened with insolvency. The insurance premiums that banks paid had to be raised substantially. In 1991 Congress had to raise the FDIC's credit line at the Treasury from $5 billion to $30 billion. Investors showed their lack of confidence as prices of banks' shares dropped in the stock market.

For savings and loans the situation was even worse. There were widespread failures and the insurance agency, the **Federal Savings and Loan Insurance Corporation** (FSLIC), itself became insolvent and required a massive bailout by taxpayers.

To see why the deposit-insurance system collapsed, we have to look separately at banks and at savings and loans. But first we need to consider a problem that is endemic to the deposit-insurance system: as discussed in Chapter 3, insurance gives the insured institution an incentive to take too much risk.

DEPOSIT INSURANCE AND THE INCENTIVE TO TAKE TOO MUCH RISK

Those who in 1933 opposed the establishment of the FDIC, as many large banks did, had a good argument: deposit insurance encourages excessive risk taking. In the absence of deposit insurance, depositors have a strong incentive to choose their bank carefully and to avoid banks that take too much risk. Hence banks are under market pressure to play it safe. If they take a lot of risk, they will either lose depositors or else have to pay a higher interest rate to compensate depositors for the extra risk.

But doesn't a bank in any case have an incentive to avoid excessive risk taking because the bank's stockholders and managers lose if the bank fails? The answer to this question is both yes and no. It has an incentive to avoid risk, but that incentive is balanced by the fact that risky ventures, on the average, pay a higher rate of return. The bank chooses that level of risk at which the additional gain from holding riskier assets just balances the loss from doing so. If, due to deposit insurance, the depositors do not object to the bank's risk taking, the bank has no reason to take the potential losses to the FDIC into account in deciding how much risk to take. Consider the following analogy: a kind uncle lends you $10,000 to play the stock market and tells you that you get to keep all the gains if your stocks rise, but he will take the loss if the stocks fall. You then have a strong incentive to buy risky stocks, where the chances of large gains and losses are both high. In the game of heads I win, tails I don't lose, I might as well bet the family farm.

Suppose now that, instead of giving you the $10,000, your uncle gives it to your sister, but still lets you keep all the gains from the investment of this money without suffering any of the losses. You then have an incentive to make the following arrangement with your sister: "I will pay you something if you allow me to invest that money in extremely risky stocks." Since your sister does not stand to lose anything, she would agree to this. If your gamble turns out badly, neither you nor your sister, but only your uncle, is the loser. This is the trouble with deposit insurance; a bank has an incentive to make risky loans and the insured depositors have no reason to object. The deposit insurer sub-sidizes this risk taking.

Given this fundamental flaw, the interesting question is not why deposit insurance reached a crisis in the 1980s, but why it took so long for serious trouble to develop. The most obvious reason is that depository institutions are not entirely free to decide how much risk to take. Examiners have something to say about it too, but not all that much. First, a large bank is a complicated institution that is better understood by its president than by the examiners. Second, there is safety in numbers. An examiner can mount a strong argument when any one institution steps out of line and does what others do not do, but when most banks do the same thing, the examiner's complaint is not nearly so per-suasive. For example, in the 1970s, when the law did not set explicit minimum capital ratios but left them partly to the examiners' judgments despite com-plaints by the regulatory agencies, capital ratios generally fell. Third, as we dis-cussed in Chapter 6, if the examiners prevent a bank from taking on as much risk as it wants to in one way, such as buying risky securities, it will search for some other way of taking risks. Regulation curbs excessive risk taking to *some* extent, but to a considerable extent it merely changes the type rather than the amount of risk that banks take.

If regulatory pressure is much less potent than appears at first glance, what other factors curbed excessive risk taking and explain why the deposit-insurance system did not collapse much earlier? One factor is that, for a time, a bank or savings and loan had a strong incentive to play it safe because its charter was a valuable asset that it would have to relinquish if it failed. Charters were valuable because until the early 1960s the federal government severely restricted the number of bank charters it issued, in part to limit competition, so that banks often had considerable market power. But in the 1960s, the fed-eral government decided to make banking a more competitive industry and therefore issued more charters. Since charters then became less valuable, banks had less of an incentive to preserve their charters by not failing.

Another factor that may perhaps have inhibited risk taking in the past is the memory of the Great Depression. A banker who early in his career experi-enced the massive bank failures of the Great Depression may have been some-what leery about risk taking for the rest of his life. But eventually these bankers retired and were replaced by those who had encountered the Great Depres-sion only in history books and in stories.

But even those bank managers who do not personally remember the Great Depression may still be reluctant to take as much risk as is in the interest of the bank's stockholders, because their primary goal is to maximize their own welfare, not the stockholders'. Having somewhat lower earnings usually does not threaten a bank manager's job, but if a bank or thrift fails, its top man-agers are usually fired. Whether a wish to protect their jobs does make man-agers significantly more unwilling to take much risk is hard to say, but it might.

The three reasons just cited—the value of bank charters in previous years, memories of the Great Depression, and managers' wish for job security—may explain why the insurance system did not break down much earlier. But eventually it did break down. For the hows and whys we have to look separately at the recent histories of savings and loans and of banks. Moreover, we have to look a great deal deeper than at the antics of "a bunch of crooks." Crooks played their part, but the real roots of the disaster lie much deeper, in our housing policy.

A Sketch of Savings and Loan History

Starting in the 1930s, as part of its policy to encourage home ownership, the federal government encouraged thrift institutions to make what have become the standard: long-term, fixed-rate mortgages repayable in installments. The Federal Housing Administration (FHA) was set up to insure such mortgages and the Federal Savings and Loan Insurance Corporation (FSLIC) was created to insure savings and loan deposits.

But something was overlooked. The long-term, fixed-rate mortgage is feasible as long as interest rates are not rising fast and short-term rates are below long-term rates. The thrift institution borrows short and lends long, and with stable interest rates it has a predictable spread between what it receives on its loans and what it pays to its depositors.

Although interest rates did rise in the years between World War II and the Vietnam War, the rise was fairly modest. The rate on ten-year government bonds was 2.8 percent in 1953, and 4.0 percent in 1963, and short-term rates were below long-term rates in every year of this period. But after 1965 rates rose substantially; by 1982 the rate on ten-year government bonds was 13.9 percent, and the Treasury-bill rate was 14.0 percent. When interest rates rise this sharply, thrifts are in trouble. They have to pay the higher rate to their depositors, to avoid losing deposits, but earn only the old, lower rate on their outstanding mortgages. In 1981, savings and loans were, on the average, paying 10.92 percent for their funds but earning only 10.11 percent on their assets. Such a negative spread of .81 percent is hardly a good way to pay the rent!

What was to be done? Interest rates on outstanding mortgages obviously could not be raised. But interest rates paid on deposits could be kept from rising. The Banking Act of 1933 had ordered the Federal Reserve to set the maximum rates that banks could pay on time deposits. Until 1967 the Fed had enforced this rule, **Regulation Q,** with an easy hand, raising the ceiling whenever interest rates on securities rose high enough to make banks uncomfortable with them.[1] But in 1967 the thrifts were complaining bitterly that competition for deposits among themselves, as well as competition from banks, was forcing deposit rates to levels that would bankrupt many of them. That, in turn, would disrupt the flow of funds into mortgages, and hence reduce residential construction. So, instead of raising the Regulation Q ceiling, the Fed lowered it slightly to help the thrifts. Similar regulations were issued for non-member banks by the FDIC and for savings and loans by the FSLIC, which until 1989 insured savings and loan deposits.

---

[1] The *Q* in the term *Regulation Q* has no deep meaning. The Fed called its first regulation "Regulation A" and had reached the letter Q by the time it regulated deposit rates.

Rising interest rates were not the only problem that the industry faced. Technological changes in finance, such as the rise of money-market funds and the securitization of mortgages were eating away at the savings and loan industry's market. The industry would have had to shrink even if interest rates had not risen.

Problems with Regulation Q

Regulation Q took care of the immediate emergency in 1967, but as forward-looking policy it was defective. Yet it took 18 years of painful experience before Regulation Q was completely eliminated. In the meantime, Regulation Q did a great deal of damage. First, it was discriminatory. Wealthy households, for whom it is worthwhile to acquire financial sophistication, could earn a high rate of interest by buying securities, while the government held down the interest rate that the less financially sophisticated lower- and middle-income households received on savings deposits.

Second, when interest rates rose, the Regulation Q ceiling resulted in **disintermediation.** This ugly word describes the shift of funds out of financial intermediaries into direct investments. With rising interest rates on securities, it became worthwhile for depositors to withdraw their deposits and buy securities instead. Hence, whenever interest rates rose sufficiently, the net inflow of funds into thrift institutions fell drastically. As a result, these institutions had to cut back on their mortgage lending. This is hardly what Regulation Q was intended to do. It had been imposed not just out of concern for thrift institutions as such, but also so that they could continue to be a ready source of mortgage loans for the residential building industry. Instead, disintermediation occurred. This reflects a basic principle of economics: if you set the price, you lose control over the quantity, and vice versa.

Another basic principle of economics is that if you block one channel of competition, you stimulate others. When Regulation Q prohibited depository institutions from competing by price (i.e., by altering the interest rate on deposits), they competed by offering "free gifts" to depositors instead. In addition, they competed by opening many new branch offices. Beyond a certain point, such nonprice competition is wasteful.

Still another basic principle of economics is that if you impose controls on one type of institution, unregulated institutions offering similar products will flourish or new ones will appear. Thus Regulation Q caused money-market funds to grow from a trivial segment of the financial system to a substantial one. Money-market funds had the potential to drain deposits rapidly from both banks and thrift institutions.

More basically, Regulation Q did not address the issue that our whole system of thrift institutions was viable only under special conditions. As previously discussed, financing long-term, fixed-rate mortgages with short-term deposits works only if interest rates are not rising rapidly. But in the 1970s and early 1980s they *were* rising rapidly. As a result, in economic terms (though not in legal and accounting terms), most thrift institutions had a negative net worth. What saved them was that accountants valued the mortgages in their portfolios at acquisition prices, that is, at the amount for which the mortgages had originally been made, and not at the market prices, that is, at what the mortgages would fetch if sold. One study calculated that by 1981 insured savings and loans had had implicit losses (measured as the difference between the actual values and the book values of their portfolios) that were equivalent to what they would have lost had 35 percent of their mortgage loans been in default. For savings banks the equivalent figure was 39 percent.[2] What kept thrift institutions alive was an asset that never appears on their books: the value of the deposit-insurance guarantee. In the absence of insurance, sophisticated depositors would have started a run on the thrifts.

Phasing Out Regulation Q

Obviously, something had to be done, and many things were tried. One was price discrimination. Not all savers withdraw their deposits when market interest rates rise relative to the fixed Regulation Q rate. So, instead of raising all interest rates, which would have been expensive for thrifts, why not raise the Regulation Q ceiling rate only for those types of deposits that are sensitive to interest rates, that is, large deposits and long-term deposits. That was done. But when other depositors saw that rates on large deposits and long-term deposits were much higher than the rate they were getting, they too moved into long-term deposits and sometimes also into large deposits by combining several of their small deposits. Hence, paying higher rates on long-term deposits and large deposits became expensive for thrifts.

Another approach was to reduce the maturity gap between assets and liabilities by permitting thrift institutions to make consumer loans and even some types of business loans, which have much shorter maturities than mortgage loans, so that the interest rate they received on their assets would rise along with their deposit rates. But this did not help in the short run. Thrifts still had all those old mortgages on their books.

It became more and more obvious that Regulation Q, while a successful patch in the sense that it had prevented most thrifts from failing, was not a viable long-term solution. Hence, in 1980 a new law was passed requiring a phase-out of Regulation Q by March 1986. In return, thrift institutions were given the right to offer checkable deposits to households, just like banks, and also a wider choice of assets they could hold.

Problems with Maturity Mismatch

The phase-out of Regulation Q took care of disintermediation and the competition from money-market funds. But in the short run it did little to eliminate the maturity mismatch that still troubled thrift institutions. Most of them still had liabilities in excess of the true value of their assets. This problem was handled partly by merging weak institutions into stronger ones and partly by a policy of "say it ain't so." As long as a thrift's deposits are insured and it can

---

[2] See Edward Kane's *The Gathering Crisis in Deposit Insurance* (Cambridge, Mass.: MIT Press, 1985).

meet day-to-day cash outflows, it can stay afloat even with a negative net worth. Hence, the regulatory authorities allowed some institutions to remain open even if their net worth, as measured by standard accounting procedures, fell below the minimum set forth in the regulations. In addition, the FSLIC provided a few weak savings and loans with funds that they could apply toward their net worth requirements. They were obligated to pay interest on these funds only if they (ever) had income rather than losses. Another policy was to indulge in creative accounting, so that institutions that had a negative net worth could pretend to have a positive net worth. For example, by the miracle of creative accounting, two institutions with negative net worths would merge, and lo and behold, their joint net worth would become positive. Apparently the laws of arithmetic do not always hold. These ways of ignoring reality were only short-term palliatives. But they helped. As interest rates fell in 1982 and 1983 many institutions that had survived only due to the "let's pretend" policy became truly viable again. Honesty is not *always* the best policy.

But creative accounting did not save all thrift institutions. Some had a maturity mismatch that was too severe. Others suffered from a policy that was adopted to aid them: in 1980 and again in 1982 savings and loans were allowed a substantially wider choice of assets. But many lacked the expertise and, as we will explain later, even the incentive to distinguish between safe and risky assets. As a result many collapsed because of unsound loans rather than the initial maturity mismatch.

There was a sharp decline in the number of savings and loans. Some of this decline was the result of voluntary mergers, but much of it resulted from failures or from mergers forced by the threat of failure. Even if one looks just at formal failures and ignores those failures that are disguised as mergers, the failure rate rose drastically.

The Savings and Loan Crisis

As the 1980s came to a close, more and more savings and loans became insolvent. The appropriate response would have been for the FSLIC to close them all down before they piled up additional losses. But the FSLIC could not do this because its insurance fund was not large enough either to take over all insolvent institutions and pay off the depositors or to pay solvent institutions to merge with them. It did, however, take over many institutions. Thus between February and May 1989 it seized two hundred insolvent institutions (including the ninth-largest thrift institution) whose collective liabilities exceeded their assets by almost $30 billion.

Some savings and loans were insured by private, but state-sponsored, insurance funds instead of by the FSLIC. Some of these private insurance funds were sound, but others, such as those in Ohio and Maryland, were not, and they failed. Depositors, many of whom probably thought that their deposits were insured by a federal agency, now found their deposits temporarily frozen and unlikely to be fully repaid. (One outcome of the Ohio and Maryland experiences is that today all savings and loans are required to have federal insurance.)

The FSLIC itself was in trouble. It had neither the funds nor the personnel required to close down all the savings and loans that were insolvent. Many of these "zombies," as Edward Kane of Boston College has termed them, were allowed to stay open, with the losses that they were incurring adding to the total liabilities that the federal government would eventually have to pay off. In May 1989 there were almost six hundred insolvent savings and loans generating further losses, losses that by some estimates amounted to over three-quarters of a billion dollars a month. It was already clear by late 1988 that something drastic had to be done. Yet the upcoming election and the understandable congressional unwillingness to bite the bullet meant that reform was postponed until August 1989 when the **Financial Institutions Reform, Recovery and Enforcement Act** (FIRREA) was passed.

FIRREA

The new legislation had two purposes. The immediate one was to provide the funds needed to close down insolvent institutions that were continuing to incur large losses. The longer-run purpose was to prevent a recurrence of massive thrift failures. To do so, it established several new agencies. One was temporary: the **Resolution Trust Corporation** (RTC) was established to close down insolvent savings and loans. The FIRREA also established several permanent agencies. The **Office of Thrift Supervision** (OTS) was created to charter and supervise federal savings and loans and to supervise those savings and loans that have a state charter. Two other organizations that it created are the **Savings Association Insurance Fund** (SAIF) and the **Bank Insurance Fund** (BIF), both of which are administered by the FDIC.[3]

To avoid a repetition of the thrift crisis FIRREA instituted several reforms. The most important was to raise capital requirements. It set two capital requirements, both of which savings and loans must meet. The first is a risk-based capital requirement that is as stringent as that imposed on national banks. The second sets a 3 percent ratio of core capital to assets and a 1.5 percent ratio of tangible capital to assets. (Core capital consists primarily of equity and reserves against loan losses; tangible capital excludes loan loss reserves and good will.) An important aspect of the new capital requirement is that it eliminates the accounting gimmicks that thrifts had previously been permitted to use in calculating their capital ratios.

The FIRREA also tried to ensure the safety of thrifts in other ways. Thus it prohibited them from directly holding low-grade (junk) bonds. (Although junk bonds did not play a terribly large role in savings and loan failures, they have a bad reputation.) What is probably more important is that it imposed stricter limits on the proportion of their assets that thrifts can invest in various types of business and consumer loans. Moreover, if a savings and loan wants to make equity investments, it can no longer do so directly, but must do so

---

[3] It also instituted two supervisory agencies, the Resolution Trust Corporation Supervisory Board and the Federal Housing Finance Board. The former is to supervise the Resolution Trust Corporation, and the latter the Federal Home Loan Banks, thus taking over the functions of the discredited Federal Home Loan Bank Board, which, along with the FSLIC, was abolished.

through a separately capitalized subsidiary, so that any of its losses on such investments can no longer erode the capital that backs up its deposits. Other provisions of the law eliminate some of the investment powers that several states had bestowed upon the thrifts they had chartered and enhance the ability of the regulators to order savings and loans to cease unsafe operations.

Paying the Piper

The media first reported that resolving the savings and loan crisis would cost $500 billion. That was a gross overestimate, caused in good part by adding future and current dollars on a one-to-one basis instead of calculating the pre-

---

Here We Go Again?

"Lower Interest Rates Revive Fears for Banks and S. & L.s" ran a front page headline in the *New York Times* of January 13, 1992. At first glance that seems strange; what caused the savings and loan disaster in the 1960s and 1970s was rising not falling interest rates. But as the article explained, while in the short run banks and savings and loans are benefiting from a widening spread between the interest rates they receive on outstanding loans and the interest rates they pay on deposits, the long-run situation is dangerous. Many mortgage borrowers are taking out fixed-rate mortgages at these lower rates to pay off their initial higher-rate mortgages. Hence there is a danger that when interest rates rise again, depository institutions will again be squeezed between low earnings on their outstanding loans and the need to pay higher interest rates on their deposits.

But haven't they learned a lesson from their previous experience? The answer is yes and no. They are more cautious now and try to avoid maturity mismatch to a greater extent than before by balancing their long-term assets with long-term liabilities and with other hedges. Moreover, securitization has allowed them to sell many of their long-term mortgages. But even so, their unhedged holdings are increasing. This is not surprising since deposit insurance gives them an incentive to take excessive risk.

What then could be done to avoid a replay of the savings and loan debacle? One obvious possibility would be to limit the number of long-term fixed-rate mortgages that depository institutions are allowed to make, unless these mortgages are balanced by long-term liabilities. But it is most doubtful that the U.S. public would stand for a policy that would greatly limit the availability of fixed-rate, long-term mortgages. Another possibility would be to recognize that such mortgage loans are very risky and to impose special capital requirements on them. The regulators did propose the imposition of such capital requirements on savings and loans, but withdrew that proposal because of massive opposition by the industry.

Another possibility would be to require depository institutions to hedge by using appropriate derivatives or other contracts that pay them a certain sum if interest rates rise. Life insurance companies, which gain from rising interest rates, might be willing to enter such contracts at a price. But depository institutions would object to such a requirement.

sent value of a stream of future payments. It now looks as though the cost will be about $150 billion. But even that is hardly trivial. It amounts to about $570 per capita. Clearly, the savings and loan disaster was one of our greatest policy disasters of the postwar period.

Where Did All the Money Go?

The greater part of the losses from the savings and loan collapse came about when honest savings and loans got trapped between low-interest, fixed-rate mortgages and sharply rising interest rates. However, it is also interesting to examine the process by which dishonest savings and loan managers (and a few honest ones) added to these losses.

Most of the losses that the crooks imposed on the savings and loans came about through indirect theft. For example, a savings and loan manager would make a loan to a less-than-honest developer at a very high interest rate. Both borrower and lender knew that the loan was unlikely to be repaid, because the project was very risky and would probably fail. The savings and loan would, however, book the initial interest that was due plus various other charges as current income and thus show a spurious profit. The manager could use that profit to pay himself a higher salary and to pay big dividends on the stock in the savings and loan of which he owned shares, as well as to finance personal expenses disguised as business expenses. Moreover, he might sell some real estate that he owned to the developer at an exorbitant price. The developer would also benefit by draining off part of the loan in the form of a higher salary and higher dividends. But these ill-gotten gains of the savings and loan manager and the developer represented only a part, and probably a small part, of the total loss that resulted from the deal. Most of the loss showed up as a bad investment, such as an office building that stayed largely empty or an incomplete housing tract.

Losses piled up, not only because it might have taken, say, a $10 loss to the savings and loan to put $1 into the manager's pocket, but also because the market system was not operating the way it normally does. Ordinarily when a business does badly, the manager has no incentive to expand since that would just lead to bigger losses. To be sure, she might want to expand if she were operating primarily with borrowed funds and if the lenders were naive enough to lend her more at the previous interest rate despite her losses. But such obliging lenders are hard to find—except when the government steps in and guarantees their funds, as the FSLIC did.

If, like the savings and loans, you can borrow more at the prevailing interest rate despite your losses, then the profit-maximizing response to losses that reduce your net worth is to borrow more, and use the borrowed funds to undertake very risky investments. If the gamble turns out badly, as is likely, and you lose the additional money, all that means is when you eventually go bankrupt, it will be a bigger bankruptcy. Why not go out with a bang instead of a whimper? But if the gamble turns out well, you can offset the losses you previously incurred, and thus avoid bankruptcy. This strategy is known as "gambling for resurrection." Even honest savings and loan managers might do this in the hope of salvaging their institutions, and thus preserving not only their own jobs, but also the jobs of their employees and the availability of mortgage funds in their community. Crooks, of course, had another incentive: to keep their savings and loans alive as long as possible so that they had more time in which to loot them.

The result was that the number of failing savings and loans, instead of contracting, grew at startling rates, sometimes increasing 100 percent or more per year. And since most of the risky gambles did not pay off, the losses just became larger and larger.

The bizarre effect of the government guarantee of deposits combined with extraordinarily lax supervision and regulation was that the savings and loan industry grew rapidly at a time when it should have been contracting because of the competitive pressures from money-market funds on the deposit side and mortgage companies on the lending side. If an industry expands rapidly when the fundamentals argue for contraction, eventually someone will be presented with a large bill.

COMMERCIAL BANKS

Figure 9.1 shows that the FDIC's experience with commercial banks has been broadly similar to the FSLIC's experience with savings and loans—few and relatively small failures in the 1942 to 1981 period followed by a massive rise in both the number of failures and their liabilities in the late 1980s. But the magnitude of the problem differed. The banking industry was hurt but not devastated. Moreover, the stories behind the failures differ. Banks did not fail because they held long-term, fixed-rate mortgages at a time when interest rates rose. Because they were able to hold a wide variety of assets, banks had matched the maturities of their assets and liabilities much better than savings and loans had done. While for small banks dishonest dealings continued to play an important role in failures, as it had done all along, most of the bigger banks that failed in the 1970s, 1980s, and early 1990s did so because they had made risky loans.

Continental Illinois

The most dramatic case among the big banks that failed in this period was Continental Illinois, then the country's eighth-largest bank, with over $40 billion of deposits. What set off its failure in 1984 was the failure of a medium-size Oklahoma bank, Penn Square. At least in part because that bank's books were unclear at best, the FDIC could not merge Penn Square into another bank. Instead, the FDIC chose to pay off Penn Square's deposits up to $100,000 and let the large depositors take their losses. This scared some large depositors who had assumed that, to avoid the danger of a panic, the FDIC would protect all deposits in a bank that large. Penn Square had made many more loans than it had the funds for and had done so by selling off many of its loans to other

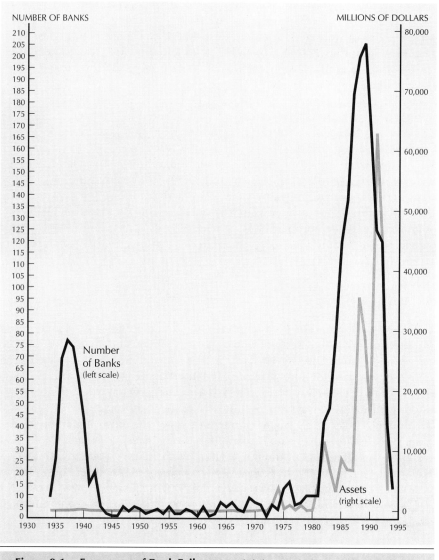

NUMBER OF BANKS

MILLIONS OF DOLLARS

Number
of Banks
(left scale)

Assets
(right scale)

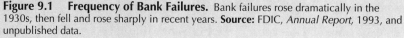

Figure 9.1   Frequency of Bank Failures. Bank failures rose dramatically in the 1930s, then fell and rose sharply in recent years. **Source:** FDIC, *Annual Report,* 1993, and unpublished data.

banks. Depositors in the banks that had bought these loans now became concerned that their bank might have bought many unsound loans and hence might no longer be solvent.

One bank that had bought many loans from Penn Square was Continental Illinois. This bank was vulnerable in any case because it had made many unsound loans on its own, and also because it had obtained an unusually large proportion of its funds from large depositors and from loans by other banks.

Large creditors, not being insured, will withdraw their funds as soon as they hear that a bank *might* be in trouble. (As someone remarked at the time, money managers are people specially trained to panic at the slightest opportunity.)

Hence, in May 1984, Continental Illinois faced a massive outflow of funds. To meet this outflow, it borrowed an extraordinary amount from the Fed—$4 billion. In addition, a consortium of large banks granted it a line of credit up to $5.3 billion. Moreover, the regulatory agencies and some large banks provided a capital infusion of $2 billion. But even these measures did not stop the run. So the FDIC took the unprecedented step of guaranteeing all deposits and other debts of the bank, no matter how large. Still the run continued. Presumably creditors were afraid that in case of failure the FDIC might keep them waiting for their funds.

Something had to be done. Continental Illinois was a big bite to swallow, and no bank was willing to risk merging with it on terms acceptable to the FDIC. Hence, in July 1984 the FDIC took the drastic step of restructuring the bank. It provided $1 billion of additional capital and bought from the bank $4.5 billion of shaky loans at full face value. In return the FDIC got 80 percent ownership of the bank. The FDIC also fired the top management. (Subsequently it sold all its stock in the bank at a loss.)

The Continental Illinois episode raised some big, as yet unanswered, questions regarding the FDIC's handling of bank failures. Did the FDIC do the right thing in effectively nationalizing this bank? Should it have protected the large depositors of this bank when it sometimes lets the large depositors of smaller banks suffer losses? Or should it have let Continental Illinois fail and take the risk that this might start runs on other large banks?

LDC Loans Turn Sour

The collapse of Continental Illinois was only one of the disasters that struck U.S. banking in the 1980s. We touched on a much more expensive disaster briefly in Chapter 7. That mess occurred when many less-developed countries (LDCs), in effect, defaulted on their loans from U.S. banks.

In 1973–74 oil prices quadrupled. For some LDCs, like Mexico, this was a bonanza, but for oil importers, like Brazil, it was a disaster. To pay their higher oil bills, they had to either cut their living standards or borrow massively abroad. Not surprisingly, they were tempted to do the latter. This temptation was hard to resist because at the time the *real* interest rate, that is, the interest rate adjusted for inflation, was negative, so that borrowing seemed a great bargain.

At the same time the banks were eager to lend to the LDCs. Oil exporters were depositing vast sums in U.S. banks, so that banks were awash with funds they wanted to lend. In addition, those oil-producing LDCs, such as Mexico, that were currently selling only fairly moderate amounts of oil, but had large oil reserves in the ground, suddenly seemed like good credit risks.

One might think that the bank regulators would have had enough foresight to see that the LDC loans involved much risk and so put reasonable limits on them. But they did not. Why not is unclear. One factor was that the Federal Reserve saw the bright side of these loans. By taking the deposits of oil exporters and lending them to oil importers, the banks were recycling the funds in a way that ameliorated the oil importers' current problem. Had they not done so, the oil-importing countries would have faced a severe crisis.

Moreover, with oil exporters demanding dollars to buy the CDs of U.S. banks, the dollar tended to rise on the foreign-exchange market. Such a rise in the dollar makes U.S. exports less competitive and also generates a flood of imports. However, when U.S. banks make loans to foreigners, these borrowers sell the dollars on the foreign-exchange market, which forces the dollar down. Hence, the LDC loans prevented an undesirable rise in the dollar on the foreign-exchange market. And, it must be admitted, loans to some large LDC debtors, such as Korea, did not become a problem subsequently.

The usual story, though not necessarily the correct story (see the box below), is that the borrowers, the banks, and the regulators all made what by hindsight can be called bizarre mistakes. Many borrowers probably underestimated greatly the risk that real interest rates would rise again and make the

Should One Pity the Banks?

The usual story of the debt crisis pictures the banks as bunglers who made loans without carefully considering the risks. There are stories of young, inexperienced loan officers being rewarded with rapid promotions for making massive loans, even though these loans soon thereafter went into de facto default.

Dennis Logue of Dartmouth College and Pietra Rivoli of the Board of Governors have challenged this story.* They argue that, although the LDC loans were not a good investment for banks, banks behaved rationally and, though "slightly wounded," were not "substantially damaged" by the loans. Their argument is that banks were aware that these loans were risky; therefore, over the period in which they made the largest proportion of their loans, they charged a sufficiently high risk premium (1 to 2 percent above LIBOR) to cover their risk.

To be sure, the loans made after 1982 were generally not profitable. However, the larger portion of these later loans was not new money, but was deferred interest due on prior loans. Overall, despite the concessions that they later made to the debtors, the banks earned about as much on the initial loans as they would have on U.S. government securities. (Of course, these loans were much riskier than government securities, and therefore should have paid a higher rate.) Therefore, it is not so surprising that, despite the massive de facto defaults on LDC loans, in general bank stocks rose almost as much as stock prices between 1975 and 1988. However, the stock of banks with heavy LDC involvement rose less than the stock of relatively smaller banks that had lower LDC exposure. So banks with massive LDC loans were not happy banks, but neither were they the incompetent fools they are often made out to be.

*Dennis Logue and Pietra Rivoli, "Some Consequences of Banks' LDC Loans: A Note," *Journal of Financial Services Research,* 6 (May 1992), 37–47.

debts they were incurring an unmanageable burden.[4] Banks did not investigate the loans sufficiently, often greatly underestimating the amount that the countries were borrowing from other banks and thus their total indebtedness. And at least one leading bank, Citibank, believed that loans to governments were always safe. Finally, the regulators did not look far enough beyond the current situation to see what would happen if real interest rates rose sharply or if a recession lowered the prices of LDC exports.

In the early 1980s the banks received a rude shock. Argentina and Brazil, both massive borrowers, threatened to default on their loans. Other countries, such Mexico and Peru, followed their example. At least in hindsight this was not surprising. The recessions of the early 1980s had sharply reduced both the prices and the volume of the raw materials these countries were exporting. Moreover, their debts had been contracted at variable interest rates. Hence when in the early 1980s the inflation rate was falling much faster than the nominal interest rate, these countries were paying a much higher real interest rate than they had anticipated. Furthermore, they stood to lose relatively little by defaulting. A foreign government, unlike a private domestic borrower, cannot be forced into bankruptcy. The main sanctions against defaulting are that the creditors may seize its assets in foreign countries (such as ships in foreign ports) and that a country that is in default usually finds international capital markets closed to it. But if it has a large debt outstanding, the inability to borrow more may be a lesser burden than servicing the existing debt.

All the same, most debtor countries did not go into legal default. Instead, they announced that they could not service their loans, that is, make the required interest payments and the repayments of the principal that were due. Hence they wanted to renegotiate the terms of the loans.

The banks had two choices. One was to accede to the borrowing countries' demands to stretch out the maturity of the debts and make them further loans, which these countries could then use to "pay" the interest on the debts. (In effect, the banks would themselves be paying the interest they received.) The other choice was to declare the borrowing countries in default. The banks decided that the lesser evil was to stretch out the debts and to make additional loans.[5] Though the lesser evil, it was still extremely painful for the banks. Not only were they extending the life of loans whose repayment had become highly doubtful, they were making additional loans to these borrowers and making

---

[4] In addition, borrowers probably underestimated the probability that the prices of their raw-material exports would fall as much as they did. Misappropriation of funds and other forms of corruption also played an unknown, but probably not trivial, role in inducing LDCs to borrow excessively.

[5] The government encouraged them to do so under the Baker plan (named after the then secretary of the treasury, James Baker). In exchange for the additional loans the debtor countries were to undertake reforms that would increase their productivity, so that they would eventually be able to manage their debt. But reforms, such as privatizing inefficient state-owned industries, proved much more difficult to enact than to talk about, living standards fell, and the size of the outstanding debt rose. Subsequently, the Brady plan (named after Baker's successor as secretary of the treasury) proposed that the banks write down the principal of the debt or lower the interest rates, in return for a pledge by the debtor countries actually to make the lower payments called for by agreements. Such arrangements were made in some cases, and they did reduce the burden on some countries.

Charting the End of a Bank

In 1991 the Bank of New England, then the third-largest bank in that region, failed. New England had been hit hard by the 1990–91 recession and the price of New England's real estate fell sharply. The Bank of New England, which had a large portfolio of real-estate loans, now found that many of its borrowers could not service their debts. Since it did not have enough capital to cover these losses, it failed. Below is the *New York Times'* analysis of that failure.

A Year in the Life of a Troubled Bank*

Dec. 15, 1989: Bank of New England announced that its bad loans would rise to $1.6 billion for 1989, that it might rescind a 34-cents-a-share dividend, and that it was considering a merger and sale of assets.

Dec. 22: Bank of New England canceled the dividend.

Dec. 26: Walter J. Connolly, Jr., said he would relinquish his position as chief executive "when the board has selected a candidate" to replace him.

Jan. 17, 1990: Shares fell on fears that federal regulators would delay or stop the rumored sale of the bank's subsidiary operations to the Fleet/Norstar Financial Group.

Jan. 19: Bank put its 1989 loss at $1.05 billion and its fourth-quarter loss at about $1.2 billion. Nonperforming loans were estimated at $2.25 billion. A plan to sell $6 billion in assets was unveiled.

Jan. 26: Bank announced that it had begun to borrow from the Federal Reserve Bank of Boston. The board requested the resignation of Mr. Connolly. H. Ridgely Bullock was named as interim chairman.

Jan. 29: Citicorp bought the bank's consumer credit-card business for $828 million.

Jan. 31: Bank completed sale of the United States portion of McCullagh Leasing to GE Capital for $350 million.

Feb. 8: The bank revised its agreement to sell its Banc New England Leasing unit and $500 million of the lease portfolio to Bank of Tokyo for $92.5 million.

Feb. 15: Canadian Imperial Bank of Commerce bought about $1 billion of the portfolio of the bank's communications lending group.

Feb. 22: Bank reported $1.11 billion loss for 1989.

March 1: In an agreement with federal regulators, the bank agreed to increase its capital and reduce its assets so that capital equals 3 percent of assets by the end of May and 5 percent by year-end.

March 9: Lawrence K. Fish named chairman and chief executive.

April 4: Bank said it would cut 5,600 jobs by the end of the year.

April 27: Bank reported a first-quarter loss of $46.6 million.

*From the *New York Times,* January 8, 1991.

June 15: At the annual meeting, Mr. Fish told shareholders that deposits had stabilized.

July 23: Saying it was unable to reach an agreement on an acceptable price, the bank took Maine National Bank off the block.

Aug. 3: Bank reported a second-quarter loss of $33.3 million. Nonperforming assets rose to $2.78 billion, from $2.67 billion.

Aug. 20: Share prices hit a low after Ted DiMauro, a Massachusetts congressional candidate, announced erroneously that the bank would be seized by federal regulators.

Sept. 4: Citizens Financial Group of Providence, Rhode Island, agreed to buy most of the bank's Rhode Island operation for $75 million.

Oct. 19: Bank reported a third-quarter loss of $123.2 million. Bad loans rose $65 million to $2.84 billion in the quarter.

Dec. 20: Bondholders proposed a debt-for-equity swap that would give bondholders 92 percent of the company's common stock in exchange for $705 million in debentures.

Jan. 4, 1991: The bank estimated its fourth-quarter loss at $450 million and said nonperforming assets would rise $500 million to $3.3 billion. The news led depositors to withdraw about $1 billion.

Jan. 6: Bank of New England's three major units were declared insolvent and taken over by federal regulators, who injected $750 million into two of the units.

Jan. 7: The bank holding company filed for bankruptcy. Bank's subsidiaries were reopened under FDIC control.

---

them at interest rates that did not come anywhere near reflecting the additional risk that such LDC loans were now seen to have.

But the alternative of declaring the borrowers in default would have been even worse, because the banks would then have had to acknowledge on their balance sheets losses that in many cases would have been large enough to destroy the banks. (It has been said that if you owe a small amount to a bank, you have to be polite to the banker, but if you owe a large amount, then the banker has to be polite to you.) The outstanding debts of 15 heavily indebted countries to the 9 largest banks equaled 143 percent of the equity capital plus loan loss reserves of those banks. Writing down these debts to a realistic value would therefore have forced many, perhaps all, of these banks into insolvency. Hence they stretched out maturities, made additional loans, and pretended everything was fine. That gave them a breathing spell in which they could accumulate additional equity, both by plowing back earnings and by selling new stock, which they used to build up their loss reserves against these loans.

As the economies of some large debtor countries improved, they were in a better position to shoulder at least part of the debt. Hence they made arrangements with the banks for repaying part of their debt, in which the banks forgave the rest or exchanged the loans for longer-term bonds. By spring 1992 the LDC debt problem was no longer a significant threat to the U.S. banking system.

Previously in this chapter we discussed how this very same policy of not acknowledging losses was a disaster when it was followed by the savings and loans. In that case it added substantially to the losses that the deposit insurer ultimately had to cover. In the case of the banks it worked. Had the banks been forced to recognize the losses at the time they incurred them (that is, when the LDC borrowers announced that they could not service their debt), a substantial part of our banking system would probably have failed, with losses greater than the assets in the FDIC's insurance fund.

It is interesting to speculate what would have happened in the absence of deposit insurance. Here is one scenario: as soon as it appeared that the LDC borrowers could not or would not service their debts, there would have been a massive run on banks, both by depositors and by other suppliers of funds. Perhaps even those banks without any exposure to LDC debtors would have been run, on the grounds that they might experience large losses on their interbank deposits if their correspondent banks were to fail. Hence, one can make a case that deposit insurance averted a disaster.

But this scenario is not all that plausible. In the absence of deposit insurance, banks might well have decided not to make all these loans to LDC countries, because they would have known that they faced the danger of a run. Moreover, even if the banks themselves had ignored the riskiness of their LDC loans at the time they were made, these loans would still have worried their depositors. Hence, to hold on to their depositors, banks would have been forced to limit their LDC loans. If this is the case, then deposit insurance was a major cause of the unwise lending to LDCs.

Oil Troubles and Real-Estate Losses

The next major blow or series of blows started in the Southwest, especially in Texas. Oil prices fell in the second half of the 1980s. As a result, many firms in oil-related industries that had borrowed in the expectation that oil prices would continue to stay high could no longer service their bank loans. It was not just companies directly engaged in the oil industry that were unable to meet their obligations. As companies producing drilling equipment went out of business, developers from whom they had leased office space suffered losses and had to renege on *their* loans. As this first group of developers cut rents in an effort to fill their buildings, other developers, who also had to cut rents to remain competitive, took losses. As a result, many large Texas banks and bank holding companies failed, among them First City Bankcorporation, with assets of $12.2 billion, and MCorp, a bank holding company with assets of $15.4 billion. Nine of the ten largest Texas bank holding companies ran into trouble and had to obtain assistance from either the FDIC or other outsiders to meet their obligations.

Falling energy prices were by no means the cause of all of the problem loans at the time. Extensive overbuilding caused a severe slump in commercial real estate that was not just confined to the Southwest, but struck virtually the whole country. Before 1986 the tax laws had favored real-estate investment. The 1986 tax-reform law withdrew many of the implicit subsidies and also, by lowering tax rates, made the favorable tax treatment of real-estate investment less valuable. As a result, real-estate prices fell, with losses not just to developers and holders of real estate but also to those who had lent to them.

The losses that banks suffered on their energy loans and real-estate loans may well have been smaller than the losses they had previously taken on their LDC loans. Yet they pulled down many more banks. The reason is that when a domestic commercial loan turns sour, it is a *relatively* straightforward situation, and clear-cut precedents exist that tell the bank's auditors and examiners that the loan's value must be written down on the bank's books; that is, the bank's capital is reduced. The inability of the LDC debtors to repay presented a more complex and unfamiliar case, and that allowed the regulators and the banks to pretend that nothing had happened.

CONGRESS STEPS IN: THE FDIC IMPROVEMENT ACT OF 1991

As a result of the massive bank failures of the eighties and early nineties, the FDIC's bank-insurance fund proved insufficient. In December 1991 Congress increased the FDIC's credit limit at the Treasury to $30 billion. Not surprisingly, in return Congress insisted on tightening regulations.

One way regulations were tightened was by a system of trip wires. Previously, the regulators were not legally required to impose serious sanctions on banks that were incurring losses and thereby reducing their capital below the required level. The new law requires them to impose specific sanctions when a bank's capital ratio is too low or when its losses indicate that it is likely to fail. Such sanctions can take several forms. The FDIC can require a change in the bank's management. It can also require the bank to increase its capital by selling additional stock, to limit its rate of growth, or to cut or even eliminate its dividend. Moreover, regulators are now required to close a bank when its capital-asset ratio falls below 2 percent. This is an important provision because previously, at least in part for legal reasons, regulators would normally not close an institution until its book value was zero, and (as will be discussed in Chapter 10) by that time its economic value was usually negative.

In the discussion of the savings and loan debacle, we pointed out that the regulators had not been tough enough, that they had exercised excessive forbearance in the hope that the sick savings and loans would recover. By prohibiting such forbearance, Congress tried to avoid letting the banks' losses reach the same dimensions as the savings and loans' losses.

Congress also tried to correct the basic flaw of the deposit-insurance system: its encouragement of excessive risk taking. For example, members of Congress reasoned that if large depositors were likely to suffer from their banks' imprudent practices, they would keep a close eye on their banks and withdraw their money should those banks take on too much risk. Thus, Congress decided to change the policy that tended to protect both large and small depositors when the FDIC merged a failing bank with a sound one. Now large depositors have to bear a proportionate share of the FDIC's costs in such mergers.

"Congress' R$_x$ a Fatal Dose?"

So ran the headline of an article in the *American Banker*, the trade paper of the banking industry.* The article expressed concern about the insurance premium that the FDIC charged banks. This premium, which was 8.3¢ per $100 of deposits in 1989, had risen to 23¢ per $100 by the end of 1991, and the author, Robert Dugger, was afraid that the FDIC would raise it to 30¢. Some bankers suggested that such a rise would be counterproductive; by reducing bank profits, it would cause some banks to fail and hence might cost the FDIC more than it brought in.

At first glance such a concern seems ludicrous—30¢ per $100 (0.3 of 1 percent) of deposits is surely a trivial amount. Raising the premium 0.07 of 1 percent would surely not cause many banks to fail.

But first glances can be deceiving, so let us take a second glance. When expressed as a percent of deposits, 30¢ per $100 is a trivial amount, but is it right to express the insurance premium as a percent of deposits? Perhaps it should instead be expressed as a percent of bank profits. Banks' profits represent about 1 percent of deposits for a reasonably profitable bank. An insurance premium of 0.3 of 1 percent of deposits therefore represents about one-third of banks' profits— a far from trivial proportion.

But even a second glance may not tell the *whole* story. Initially banks may have to pay the higher premium out of their profits. In response to this lower profitability the banking industry will shrink, and as that happens, decreased competition for deposits and for loan customers will allow banks to pass the premium increase on to their customers. Suppose that they pass it all on to their depositors. A reduction of 0.3 of 1 percent in the interest rate depositors receive is not likely to drive many depositors away from banks. Hence, the banking industry may shrink by only a modest amount. Until they can pass on the higher premium, however, bank profits will fall significantly.

*December 20, 1991.

Moreover, Congress severely limited the FDIC's "too-big-to-fail" policy, a policy that the FDIC had adopted at the time of the Continental Illinois debacle. This policy had promised that large as well as small depositors and other creditors of a dozen or so of the country's largest banks would be fully protected in case of failure. The rationale was that a failure of such a large bank could cause large depositors to run other banks, and thus set off a financial crisis. Now the FDIC can offer such protection to large depositors in the largest banks only under very special conditions.[6] Finally, the FDIC now charges riskier banks a somewhat higher insurance premium than safe ones (currently 31¢ per $100 of deposits versus 23¢), and has raised the insurance premiums for all banks.

[6] One is that the Secretary of the Treasury, on recommendation of the Board of Governors and of the FDIC directors (each recommendation being based on a two-thirds vote), decides that it would be too risky to let the bank fail. The other is that the Secretary of the Treasury, in consultation with the President, decides that the failure would have serious enough adverse consequences to warrant deviation from policy.

Despite these reforms, by 1990 a number of observers expected a surge in bank failures. But this surge never came. As short-term interest rates fell in the early 1990s and the yield curve steepened, the spread between what banks earned on their assets and what they paid on their deposits widened. As banking thus became more profitable, bank failures declined, and the FDIC did not have to use its right to borrow from the Treasury. From a negative balance of $7 billion at the end of 1991, the FDIC went to a positive balance of $13 billion by the end of 1993. For the time being at least, there is no sign of an impending banking crisis.

SUMMARY

1 Deposit insurance induces banks to take too much risk. Bank examination is not a sufficient safeguard against excessive risk taking, though it was supplemented for a time by the banks' reluctance to risk losing their charters and perhaps by memories of the Great Depression.

2 When interest rates rose sharply in the 1970s, many savings and loans became, in effect, insolvent. The imposition of ceilings on deposit rates (Regulation Q) was not a long-run solution since it led to disintermediation, alternative forms of competition, and discrimination against poor households. For a time the insolvencies of thrifts were covered up by creative accounting, but that merely raised the cost of the payment that ultimately had to be made. In the end, the FSLIC itself became insolvent.

3 FIRREA replaced the FSLIC with a new insurance system, provided Treasury funds for this agency, and established new agencies to dispose of the assets of closed institutions. It imposed stricter capital requirements and regulations on savings and loans.

4 The massive taxpayer funding of FIRREA that was required by the savings and loan crisis caused much indignation. But blaming crooked managers and bought politicians is simplistic. The whole system of fixed-rate mortgages financed by short-term deposits is a more fundamental cause.

5 The failure of the nation's eighth-largest bank, Continental Illinois, in 1984 was followed by the failure of other large banks. Prior to that, the inability of LDCs to service their debts had endangered many big banks, but that problem had been covered up by extending the maturity of the debts and by making additional loans to the LDCs. When energy prices fell in the 1980s and when in the late 1980s and early 1990s overbuilding caused domestic borrowers to default on their bank loans, the problem could no longer be papered over, and many banks, both large and small, failed.

6 In 1991 Congress had to provide additional borrowing authority for the FDIC, and in doing so, it imposed stricter regulations. A system of trip wires now requires specific regulatory action before a bank's capital is exhausted, large deposits are no longer fully protected, the too-big-to-fail doctrine is severely curbed, and the insurance premium that banks pay depends on their riskiness. Falling interest rates in the early 1990s rescued banks that would otherwise have failed.

KEY TERMS

Regulation Q
FIRREA
Resolution Trust Corporation

Bank Insurance Fund
Savings Association Insurance Fund
Office of Thrift Supervision

QUESTIONS AND EXERCISES

*1 Discuss: "Deposit insurance does not induce banks to take excessive risks. The wish to avoid failure provides banks with a sufficient motive to avoid excessive risk taking."

2 Discuss: "The savings and loan industry was bound to collapse when interest rates rose sharply."

*3 Explain whether you think deregulation, that is, the removal of deposit ceilings and the extended investment powers of savings and loans, was a mistake.

4 Describe the problems that beset banks in the 1970s and 1980s.

FURTHER READING

BRUMBAUGH, R. DAVID. *Thrifts under Siege.* Cambridge, Mass.: Ballinger Publishing Co., 1988. Chapters 2 and 3 provide an excellent discussion of the thrift institutions' crisis.

KANE, EDWARD. *The Gathering Crisis in Deposit Insurance.* Cambridge, Mass.: MIT Press, 1985. A good discussion of current problems with deposit insurance, in a spirited style.

LINDERT, PETER, and PETER MORTON. "How Sovereign Debt Has Worked," in *Developing Country Debt and Economic Performance,* Jeffry Sachs, ed. Chicago: Chicago University Press, 1989, pp. 39–106. A fascinating discussion of previous experience with debt default.

NATIONAL COMMISSION ON FINANCIAL INSTITUTION REFORM, RECOVERY, AND ENFORCEMENT. *Origins and Causes of the S & L Debacle: A Blueprint for Reform.* Washington, DC: Government Printing Office, 1993. A fine analysis of the savings and loan disaster.

WHITE, LAWRENCE. *The S & L Debacle.* New York: Oxford University Press, 1991. A worthwhile treatment by an economist who served as a director of the Federal Home Loan Bank Board.

APPENDIX: WHO IS TO BLAME?

When taxpayers are suddenly confronted with a large bill, there is a natural tendency to get angry and to look for someone to blame. It is tempting to look for a single villain rather than to allocate the blame more generally. But, as this appendix demonstrates, this temptation should be resisted, at least with respect to the savings and loan debacle.

Blaming the Crooks and Politicians

The media blamed the savings and loan disaster on crooked managers who robbed the savings and loans they worked for and on politicians who allowed these managers to do so in exchange for "campaign contributions" (read *bribes*). Much attention has been given to the case of Charles Keating who is accused of mismanaging Lincoln Savings and Loan, and five senators, the "Keating Five," who intervened with bank regulators on his behalf. One certainly cannot deny that crooked managers did steal a lot of money from the savings and loans. But one should be at least somewhat suspicious of attempts to blame crooks for all or most of the savings and loan debacle, because such an explanation accords so well with the self-interest of the parties who advocate it.

The media have an incentive to blame crooks. Fraud and other forms of dishonesty are much easier to explain—and much more exciting to read about—than are things like the specific changes in arcane accounting rules that played a large role in bringing about the debacle. Who wants to read about the difference between GAAP (generally accepted accounting principles) and RAP (regulatory accounting principles) instead of about extravagant mansions and wild parties?

Moreover, the public has an entirely natural urge to seek an outlet for its indignation about this costly debacle, and hence it *wants* to read stories that blame the problem on crooks rather than on hard-to-evaluate decisions that the regulators had made over many years. Like politicians, journalists prefer to tell the public what it wants to hear. And the regulators, who prepare hand-outs for the media, have no incentive to direct the public's attention to the bad decisions that their agencies have made.

How much of the problem is due to crooked managers? Bert Ely, a leading expert on the savings and loan industry, estimates losses due *directly* to fraud as $5 billion, that is, about 3 percent of total losses.[7] But that figure does not include the total costs of fraud. Fraudulent bank managers and bank owners, seeking to drain additional deposits out of their failing savings and loans, paid higher interest rates to depositors. To counter this competition for deposits, some other savings and loans that were run honestly also offered to pay higher rates to their depositors. Hence, the crooks are responsible, directly or indirectly, for some, but not all, of the losses that savings and loans suffered because of the excessive interest rates they were paying to depositors. Ely estimates the total losses that are due to excessive interest rates as $14 billion. He also estimates that savings and loans experienced losses of some $14 billion due to excessive operating costs. A substantial part, but not all, of these costs results from excess capacity in the savings and loan industry due to the existence of so many insolvent, but still operating, savings and loans. Some of it is due to expensive managerial perquisites and to incompetence. Hence, the $5 billion in losses that Ely estimates as the *direct* cost of fraud is probably a substantial underestimate of the total losses due to fraud and self-dealing.

If one goes to the other extreme and makes the unwarranted assumption that the crooked managers were responsible for all the excess interest and operating costs, one gets a total of $33 billion, which amounts to 22 percent of Ely's estimate of the total loss. Such a wide range, between 3 percent and 22 percent, is broadly in line with the estimate of another leading authority on the savings and loan debacle, Edward Kane. He attributes no more than 10 or 20 percent of the FSLIC's losses to "violations of law or stockholder rights."[8] A commission set up by Congress, the National Commission on Financial Institution Reform, Recovery, and Enforcement, puts the figure at 10 to 15 percent.[9] Such figures are much lower than those suggested by news reports. What

[7] Bert Ely, "Where Did All the Money Go?" unpublished.

[8] Edward Kane, "The Unending Deposit-Insurance Mess," *Science,* 246 (October 27, 1989), 452.

[9] National Commission on Financial Institution Reform, Recovery, and Enforcement, *Origin and Causes of the S & L Debacle: A Blueprint for Reform* (Washington, DC.: Government Printing Office, 1993), p. 8.

makes the lower figures plausible is that by 1980, when deregulation started to make massive fraud possible, there was not all that much money left in the till. Savings and loans that accounted for a substantial proportion of the industry's total assets already were insolvent in economic terms: these "zombies" were kept alive only by the fact that they could carry their assets on their books at more than their true market value.

All the same, a vast amount was stolen. What accounted for it? One might claim, as some have done, that the 1980s was the decade of rampant greed. But we know of no evidence whatsoever that people were any less greedy in prior decades or are any less greedy now. A much more plausible explanation is that in the 1970s and 1980s it was easy to steal from the savings and loans. Given the extremely low capital-asset ratios that the regulators had set, with a small investment in the stock of an S & L fast-buck artists could control a vast volume of assets. Hence, instead of plying their trade elsewhere, they concentrated on savings and loans. The crooks were not the lions who killed the savings and loans, but were the jackals who feasted off them after the lions of rising interest rates and bad investments had left them either dead or dying.

That fraud was not the main cause of the debacle does not, of course, excuse it. Still, there were deeper reasons for the failure.

Blaming Congress

The public blames the savings and loan debacle not just on thieving managers but also on politicians. The trade associations of the savings and loan industry, as well as individual savings and loan officers, made large campaign contributions. Some senators and representatives, such as the famous "Keating Five" and Representative Jim Wright, who lost the speakership of the House as a result of the savings and loan scandal, put pressure on the regulators to take it easy on particular savings and loans, and not to close them down. This may *seem* like a simple and straightforward case of bribe taking, but again it is more complex. First, regardless of what one thinks about political contributions by political action committees (PACs), and large contributions in general, it is not only a legal way but also a standard way of financing political campaigns. Second, for better or worse, in our system it is the duty of senators and representatives to take up the case of a constituent who has been treated unfairly by a regulatory agency. Some of the politicians who pressured the FSLIC on behalf of savings and loans may have done so in good faith, uninfluenced by the campaign contributions that they received. Others may well have acted from baser motives.

Congress also contributed to some extent to the thrift debacle by raising the insurance ceiling from $40,000 to $100,000 in 1980. With a higher ceiling, fewer depositors had an incentive to confine their deposits to those thrifts that followed safe policies. Many congresspeople who voted for this change did so to enhance the availability of mortgage funds, and others did so to protect depositors.

Another way in which Congress contributed to the problem was by opposing for too long suggestions that savings and loans be allowed to offer variable-rate mortgages. Such mortgages would have reduced the losses of savings and loans as interest rates rose. In trying to preserve the long-term fixed-rate mortgage, Congress was probably reflecting the will of the people. But even so, that may not be an adequate excuse.

Finally, and perhaps most importantly, Congress failed in its responsibility to take timely action. While losses to the FSLIC were piling up as more and more savings and loans became insolvent, Congress did not act to stop these losses. To be sure, the administration did not provide all the leadership it should have. But not only did Congress fail to act on its own, it also blocked some badly needed proposals that the administration did make. In particular, it was very slow to give the FSLIC the funds that it needed to close failing institutions, whose operations were adding every day to the losses that would ultimately have to be paid off. It gave in to the political power of an industry that not only provided campaign funds, but was also highly regarded by the public.

Blaming the Regulators

The regulators, specifically the late FSLIC, deserve much blame—for their actions, as well as their inactions, prior to 1985, when several corrective moves were finally made. As we discussed in Chapter 6, what protects the deposit-insurance funds is the depository institution's capital cushion. As savings and loans incurred large losses due at first to rising interest rates and later to low-quality investments, the capital requirements should have been raised. Instead they were eased, both by lowering the required capital ratio from 5 to 3 percent and by expanding the items that could be counted as capital. Creative accounting was the rule of the day.

The regulators should also be faulted for not closing down much earlier many of the insolvent thrifts that were piling up further losses. They allowed them to stay open in the hope that many of them would recover. The FSLIC procrastinated until the losses became so large that it lacked the funds needed to close down most of the insolvent savings and loans. Furthermore, it hid the deteriorating position of the insurance fund from Congress and the public.

Why did the regulators adopt such an attitude of "What, me worry?" One reason is that the managers of a regulatory agency do not want to admit that they did something wrong, that their agency made any mistakes. It is better to procrastinate and hope that even if things do not get better on their own, cosmetic solutions will suffice for the time being. Heads of regulatory agencies do not serve forever. If they can paper over a problem for a few years, it will become someone else's problem. Such an attitude of "not on my watch" is only natural and surely not unique to regulatory agencies.

Moreover, who knows, with a great deal of luck, the problem *might* have solved itself. Thus, in 1980 it was not unreasonable to expect that interest rates would soon decline greatly. Had they done so, a large proportion of the sick savings and loans would have recovered. And when interest rates declined in the mid-1980s, many savings and loans did recover only to be sunk by the unwise or dishonest investments they had made. Sometimes procrastination works. Consider the situation of banks in 1983. Had the FDIC forced banks to write down their loans to less-developed countries to a realistic figure, some of the country's largest banks might have failed. Instead, the FDIC played a "let's pretend" game, and did so successfully.

A second reason for the inadequate response of the FSLIC was that its parent agency, the Federal Home Loan Bank Board (FHLBB), like many other regulatory agencies, was excessively influenced by the industry it was supposed to regulate. It is unlikely that anyone would have been appointed to the Home Loan Bank Board to whom the industry objected. The savings and loan industry, along with its ally, the residential construction industry, possessed great political power. One source of this power was that in the 1970s, even more than now, the public was strongly imbued with the belief that home ownership should be a basic national goal. Hence, unlike now, it looked with favor on the savings and loan industry that provided a ready supply of mortgage funds. Even if he had wanted to, it would have been most difficult in the 1970s for a FHLBB chairman to take on the savings and loan industry in a fundamental way. The industry could probably have hounded him out of office. Perhaps some regulators also treated the industry too gently because they hoped to get jobs there after they left government service.

A third reason for inadequate regulation—an insufficient number of examiners—was less the fault of the regulators than of the Office of Management and Budget (a White House agency) and of Congress, which did not permit the FSLIC to hire enough examiners and to pay salaries sufficient to attract the required staff.

Federal regulators were not the only regulators at fault. Some state regulators, such as those in California and Texas, eagerly granted wide-ranging power to state-chartered thrifts. After all, if some of these thrifts failed, it would not be the state but the FSLIC, and ultimately taxpayers nationwide, who would pay the cost. In the meantime lax regulations would generate additional capital for the local housing industry. They would also generate more requests for state charters and thus enhance the state regulator's domain. The federal regulators were hardly pleased to see their domain shrink as savings and loans switched from federal to state charters, so they, too, eased their regulations to induce savings and loans to stay in the federal system. The role of the state regulators should not be underestimated. Over 40 percent of all taxpayer losses were generated by savings and loans in Texas.

The role that the regulators played can also be seen by comparing what happened to the savings banks with what happened to the savings and loans. Savings banks were not quite as vulnerable as savings and loans because they were not as heavily concentrated in mortgages. But that difference is not large enough to explain why their losses were so much smaller. The main explanation is that they were regulated not by the FSLIC but by the FDIC. The FDIC did not allow savings banks to use all the accounting gimmicks that the savings and loans were allowed to use or to expand as much as savings and loans, and thus to take on so much additional risk.

Another reason why the FSLIC regulators failed is that many examiners were ill trained for the job they were supposed to do. In the good old days when savings and loans made only low-risk home mortgages, the safety of their assets did not present a serious problem as long as the S & Ls obeyed regulations. Moreover, examiners were trained to check for that, and not for complex issues about asset safety that arose once S & Ls made the more complicated and risky types of loans that the new legislation allowed them to make.

Blaming the Administrations

Various administrations, from Roosevelt to Reagan, also deserve much blame. As already mentioned, the foundation of the problem was laid by the Roosevelt administration when it fostered long-term, fixed-rate mortgages and insured the deposits of savings and loans without charging the riskier ones a higher insurance premium. Then, in 1966, when interest rates rose sharply, the latent problem created by the savings and loans' long-term mortgages and short-term deposits became an actual one as many thrift institutions were threatened with failure. In hindsight we would have been better off had the Johnson administration let them fail, because the clean-up cost then would have been much less. But neither the White House nor the public supported such a policy, and the savings and loans were propped up by ceilings on deposit rates under Regulation Q.

One might have defended the imposition of Regulation Q ceilings in 1966 had this been treated as a temporary measure to gain time until a permanent solution could be put in place. Since a genuine solution would inevitably have imposed large losses on someone, it would have met with much opposition, opposition that only the White House might have had a chance to overcome. But various administrations did nothing to foster such a solution.

Finally, when it became clear that Regulation Q was breaking down, the Reagan administration rightly supported deregulation, but failed to support it with adequate funds for enhanced supervision. It might seem obvious at first glance that with less regulation fewer regulators would be needed, but this is wrong. Easier regulation will sometimes require more regulators. Suppose, for example, that bank regulations were eased by allowing banks to hold any assets that were safe. Such a relaxation of regulations would require a substantial increase in the number of bank examiners because it would take examiners a great deal of time to determine whether certain assets that banks would then hold were safe. By contrast, suppose that regulations were tightened substantially by permitting banks to hold only three types of assets: cash, reserves with the Federal Reserve, and Treasury bills. Most bank examiners could then be dismissed because it would be very easy to determine whether banks were meeting these requirements. Unfortunately, this relationship between the severity of regulation and the number of examiners needed was not understood or at least taken seriously enough by the administration. On the other hand, Ely has argued that the FSLIC and the Federal Home Loan Bank Board did not use the resources they had efficiently, that supervisors in many cases failed to act on the examiners' recommendations that certain savings and loans be closed down.[10]

[10] Bert Ely, "Fifteen Sets of Public Policy Failures that Have Largely Caused the FSLIC Crisis," unpublished.

Blaming Economists

Academic economists, too, deserve some blame. In general, they seemed to support deregulation, at least in part because most believe in market solutions. Not being lawyers or accountants, they did not realize the great potential for fraud that would result from the deregulation of thrifts that were failing and hence did not press for enhanced supervision and control over risk taking. Moreover, they advocated the elimination of Regulation Q without initially taking into account that in the absence of Regulation Q, high-risk institutions would be able to bid funds away from more conservative ones, so that the average degree of risk taking in the industry would rise. In addition, they were slow to warn the public about the potential trouble that the holding of fixed-rate mortgages would create for thrifts if interest rates were to rise sharply. (On this issue one of us who coauthored a study of savings and loans at that time must plead mea culpa.)

Blaming the Public

Americans have a strong tradition of thinking of the public as an innocent victim of the evil deeds of others. Liberals tend to blame greedy corporations for what goes wrong, while conservatives tend to blame politicians and bureaucrats. The present account has been broadminded and blamed the dishonest managers as well as the politicians and bureaucrats. But the public too deserves some blame. It wanted to subsidize homeownership—after all, most people are at some time in their lives homeowners—and besides, homeownership is a widely proclaimed part of the American Dream. But while the public was willing to give some subsidy to homeownership through the tax system, it wanted to provide a bigger subsidy than it was willing to pay for in that way. So it tried to provide the subsidy on the cheap by requiring savings and loans to devote nearly all their funds to making long-term fixed-rate mortgage loans. That seemed like a costless way of providing a subsidy, but as so often happens, what seems free in the short run turns out to be costly in the long run. But perhaps blaming the public is unfair because neither the news media nor professional economists issued sufficient warning. As the National Commission on Financial Institution Reform, Recovery, and Enforcement put it: "Unlike bankers, who were seen as driven by profits and self-interest, S & Ls were viewed as partners in pursuing the American Dream. The S & L industry . . . did a masterful job of wrapping itself in the mantle of housing. . . . What was good for S & Ls was good for housing."[11] That made it hard for the administration, Congress, and the regulators to crack down on the S & Ls as they should have.

---

[11] National Commission on Financial Institution Reform, Recovery, and Enforcement, *Origin and Causes of the S & L Debacle*, p. 20.

Financial Policy: Some Remaining Issues

After you have read this chapter, you will be able to:

- Evaluate the pros and cons of various proposals for reforming the deposit-insurance system.
- Appreciate the problems of an overlapping regulatory structure.
- Understand the debate about whether the role of banks is declining.
- Discern the issues raised by allowing banks to undertake new financial activities and by relaxing the barriers separating banks from other commercial activities.

The U.S. financial system is not static. Problems arise and are eventually resolved, but the solutions then create new problems. For example, in the 1930s setting up the FDIC was an effective response to the problem of massive bank failures, but it led to excessive risk taking by banks in the 1970s and 1980s.

By no means are all the problems that arise the result of previous fixes. Some are due to economic or technological change. For example, in the 1970s sharply rising interest rates provided an incentive to get around Regulation Q, which capped the interest rate on deposits. Anyone who could offer what are, in effect (though not under law), deposits could garner much business. Thus a potential niche developed for money-market funds, and the falling costs of electronic bookkeeping turned the potential niche into a profitable area. As money-market funds grew, Regulation Q, which in 1967 had saved the thrifts, was no longer viable.

One must therefore take an evolutionary view of the financial structure. We do not solve problems once and for all, and then live happily ever after. Today's solutions generate tomorrow's problems. Or, even if harmless in themselves, today's solutions may be outdated by tomorrow. Mathematical problems have lasting solutions; problems of economic policy often do not. In particular, the inability to fix the problems of depository institutions is hardly surprising because policymakers aim at having institutions that fulfill two conflicting goals: taking some risk on the asset side of their balance sheets and yet, with little government intervention, providing totally safe deposits.

The last chapter examined the inherent flaw in our deposit-insurance system, how it caused large losses, and how policymakers therefore undertook some reforms. These reforms were hardly fundamental, and may not suffice. Accordingly, in this chapter we will discuss several proposals for a more basic reform of the deposit-insurance system.

The defects of the deposit-insurance system are not the only problem besetting our financial structure. Another problem is the confused nature of our regulatory system. Still another, more fundamental problem is the declining role of banking in our financial structure. This raises the question of whether banks should be allowed to expand their reach beyond their traditional bailiwick.

FIXING THE DEPOSIT-INSURANCE SYSTEM

We will now review several proposals that have been made for improving the deposit insurance system. They range from moderate to radical.

Improved Administration

What might seem the obvious solution to excessive risk taking by depository institutions is to have more and better-trained examiners. But increasing the frequency of examination is costly. Apart from the direct cost of paying the examiners, examinations disrupt the day-to-day activities of the institution being examined.

Moreover, even strenuous examination may fail to prevent serious problems. New financial instruments are being developed all the time, and it is often hard to tell how risky they will turn out to be. Even though examiners knew in, say, 1962 that savings and loans had a severe maturity mismatch, it wasn't until we actually experienced the great inflation of the 1960s and 1970s and learned the gravity of the problem this posed for the savings and loans that examiners realized how much of a danger such mismatch created. Who knows which practices that the examiners—and the rest of us—now consider safe will turn out to have been highly risky?

Furthermore, a large bank is a complex institution, and it is hard for examiners to acquire enough knowledge about its operations to successfully dispute with its executives and lawyers. And even in those cases in which examiners do catch excessive risk taking, they have not necessarily won the battle. Banks, like everyone else, have a constitutional right to be protected from arbitrary and capricious actions by the government. Hence, if they want to fight to the finish, they can file suit alleging that the examiner's decision is arbitrary and hence legally void. Moreover, banks can develop practices and acquire assets that look safer to the examiners than they actually are. But if the examiners respond to this challenge by preventing banks from developing new types of financial services, then they will frequently stifle what would have been useful financial innovation.

Risk-Related Insurance Premiums

A number of economists have urged the FDIC to require banks that take more risk to pay a higher insurance premium. In principle this scheme looks fine. Banks that want to take more risk can pay for the right to do so. Private insurance companies do not charge all drivers the same premium. If bad drivers have to pay more for car insurance, why shouldn't banks that take a good deal of risk pay higher insurance premiums too? In December 1991 Congress legislated such a system. However, the risk differential that the FDIC has imposed is fairly small.

This sounds like a good idea, but there are problems; it is by no means obvious that the risk-adjusted system of premiums will work well. First, it is difficult—though not necessarily impossible—to determine the risk that a bank imposes on the FDIC. It is not just the difficulty of estimating the riskiness of a bank's individual assets; it is also the fact that the riskiness of these individual assets is often a poor guide to the riskiness of the bank's balance sheet. The latter, as discussed in Chapter 3, depends also on the correlation between the risks of various assets, that is, how well the bank has hedged its investments. The liabilities side of the balance sheet is also relevant. For a bank with many long-term, fixed-rate deposits, long-term, fixed-rate assets are less risky than they are for a bank with few such liabilities. Furthermore, the risk that matters in assessing a bank's premium is not the risk of the institution failing, but the risk that the FDIC has to pay out a large sum of money. This depends on how quickly the regulators find out that the institution is unsafe and close it down. Suppose a bank uses 90 percent of its assets to play roulette in Las Vegas. If the FDIC closes it before its capital is all gone, there are no losses to the FDIC. But measuring the potential loss to the FDIC is even harder than measuring the riskiness of an institution's balance sheet. Moreover, the premium would have to be adjusted quickly as an institution takes more risk—by the time the examiners come around it may be too late.

An additional difficulty is that since premiums depend on the outcome of the examination process, it may be necessary to develop fairly mechanistic rules for grading banks, so that a bank could not argue that it is being placed into a higher risk class arbitrarily. Yet reducing the role of the examiner's personal judgment may significantly weaken the whole examination process. Furthermore, imposing a higher insurance premium on a bank that is already in difficulty may cause it to fail.

These objections to a risk-related insurance premium do not necessarily mean that such a system is unworkable. The risk-related insurance premium may improve our deposit-insurance system, but it is not the answer to our prayers.

Higher Capital-Asset Ratios and Marking to Market

A seemingly obvious solution is to raise the required capital-asset ratio, and this was indeed the approach followed by the 1989 legislation. With more of their own capital at stake, insured institutions have less of an incentive to take risk. In the extreme case in which a bank has no capital of its own and relies entirely on the funds of insured depositors, a bank has an incentive to hold the riskiest assets available. In the opposite extreme case a lender who relies entirely on his own capital has no incentive to take excessive risk.

Second, the higher its capital-asset ratio, the greater the probability that the institution will be able to ride out temporary adversities and not fail. As we discussed in Chapter 6, the main function of capital is to absorb losses and thus to allow the institution to continue to operate for some time despite losses.

Third, higher capital requirements reduce the losses suffered by the insuring agency if the institution does fail. Assume, for example, that the required capital-asset ratio is, say, 2 percent. Suppose further that in the time between examinations a bank could lose as much as 3 percent of its assets. Then, by the time the examiners notice that a bank is failing and have it closed down, the FDIC could already have incurred losses equal to 1 percent of the bank's assets. But suppose that the required capital-asset ratio had been 6 percent. Then, when the bank is closed (or, more likely, merged with another bank because it lacks sufficient capital), the FDIC suffers no losses.

But relying on a high capital-asset ratio to protect the FDIC has some problems. One is that a bank's capital is measured by subtracting the value of its liabilities from the value of its assets. But the data used for assessing its liabilities and assets are book values, not actual market values. A bank that bought a 7 percent bond five years ago for $1,000 and watched its value fall to, say, $800 because interest rates rose to 9 percent, would still value it at $1,000. But if the bank fails, all the FDIC gets for the bond is $800. Book-value accounting may substantially overstate or understate a bank's true capital.

There are two possible solutions to this problem. One is to require depository institutions to maintain a sufficiently high book-value capital-asset ratio. Then, even if their capital-asset ratios are overstated because some of their assets are worth less in the market than their book value, their capital would still be sufficient to cover their losses. Suppose, for example, that the required capital-asset ratio is 20 percent and that banks are closed down if their capital-asset ratio falls below that level. Suppose further that, due to the infrequency of examinations, by the time the FDIC notices that a bank is not meeting its capital requirement, the book value of its capital has shrunk to 10 percent. Then even if the market value of the bank's capital is only half its book value, the bank's capital is still positive (5 percent), so the FDIC does not suffer any losses.

However, there is a drawback in raising the capital-asset ratio so high that, despite the potential overstatement inherent in book-value accounting, the true value of capital is nearly always positive. Since equity capital costs banks more than deposits do, requiring a higher capital-asset ratio, and thus forcing banks to finance themselves more with equity and less with deposits, would raise the banks' costs.[1] As a result, banks would charge borrowers a higher interest rate, as well as paying a lower interest rate on deposits. The banking industry would then shrink as it loses both deposit and loan customers. Put another way, the higher the ratio of banks' capital to their assets, and hence to their liabilities, the less intermediation services banks are providing. And, as we saw in Chapter 2, financial intermediation is a valuable service.

All the same, many experts consider a higher capital-asset ratio the best way to protect the FDIC. They point out that prior to the 1930s capital-asset ratios were much higher than they are now. And, as we saw, one of the major reforms of FIRREA was that it raised the capital-asset ratio of savings and loans. But there is much opposition from depository institutions to raising the capital-asset ratios beyond the levels set by FIRREA. It might take another crisis to overcome this opposition.

Given these serious obstacles to raising the *quantity* of capital across the board, perhaps the way to proceed is to raise the *quality* of bank capital. Suppose that three conditions are met: (1) the FDIC is given immediate on-line information on a bank's capital, (2) this capital is measured at its true market value rather than at its book value—this is called **marking to market**—and (3) once the FDIC takes over a bank, the market value of that bank's assets do not deteriorate any further. In that case, if a bank is in danger of failing, the FDIC could give the bank the maximum opportunity to recover by delaying a takeover until the moment its capital reaches zero. And the FDIC could do so without any risk to its own funds.

In actuality these three conditions are not met. The bank's capital is measured at book not market value, the FDIC does not have on-line information on a bank's capital, and the market value of a bank's assets can deteriorate significantly between the time the FDIC takes over a bank and the time it sells its assets. Nothing can be done about the last two conditions. But something can perhaps be done about the first condition: the measurement of capital at market rather than at book value.

If the capital requirement that banks have to meet were measured by its true market value, then the FDIC's losses in bank failures would be substantially reduced, even if the capital-asset ratio were lower than it is now. On this there is little disagreement.

But there is much disagreement about the feasibility of measuring, at a reasonable cost, the true market value of a bank's assets. Marking to market is easy for those assets for which there exists a ready market, such as government bonds. But it is much more difficult for those assets that are heterogeneous or traded only infrequently, such as business loans. Techniques for valuing such assets exist, but the resulting values may not be sufficiently accurate. (One

---

[1] The Modigliani-Miller theorem's conclusion that equity financing and debt financing are equally costly is not relevant because, due to deposit insurance, depository institutions can borrow cheaply from depositors. Besides, as discussed in the text, factors like taxes, bankruptcy costs, and imperfect capital markets mean that the Modigliani-Miller theorem does not hold completely even without deposit insurance.

might reply, however, that they are likely to be more accurate reflections of true market value than are book values.)[2]

Those who oppose market-value accounting, and that seems to include most banks, argue that it is subjective and inaccurate, as well as very costly. They also argue that it makes little sense to close an institution merely because the market value of its assets is *temporarily* less than its liabilities. As long as a bank does not intend to sell its assets right now, when their prices are low, these temporarily low prices are irrelevant. What underlies this argument is the assumption that the price of the assets is low only temporarily and soon will rise again. But that assumption reflects a belief that markets are not entirely rational and efficient, because if the available information indicates that the price of an asset will be substantially higher next year, speculators will buy it this year and thus raise its current price. If one believes that prices efficiently embody the information available, then the current price of an asset should be a good indication of its worth in the future, and marking to market makes sense. In contrast, if market prices are much affected by waves of optimism and pessimism, then marking to market is inappropriate.[3]

Secondary Capital

Another proposal would require depository institutions to have outstanding secondary capital, such as long-term bonds, that in case of bankruptcy, would be paid off only after the claims of the depositors and the FDIC are met. These subordinate bonds (or other borrowed capital) would protect the FDIC the same way primary capital does. They would also make it more costly for depository institutions to assume too much risk, because the bondholders who provide the secondary capital would then require a higher interest rate on their bonds to compensate them for the greater risk. Presumably these bondholders would look beyond the book value of a bank's assets, and if they thought that the true value of a bank's capital was zero, they would not buy its bonds. In addition, if the bonds that a bank has issued suddenly drop in value, this might provide a useful signal to the FDIC that this bank bears close watching.

But here, too, there are problems. First and foremost, there is a good chance that there would be no market for the bonds issued by small, local banks because the small size of the bond issues would not make it worthwhile for investors to take the trouble of evaluating the banks. Second, past experience with the secondary debt of banks suggests that the bonds would be held in large part by insiders, such as the bank's own holding company or the bank's stockholders. Such insiders have little incentive to discipline the bank if it takes excessive risk. And even if an "outsider" market could be developed, it

---

[2] Marking to market would not only help regulators but would also help private investors who want to evaluate the profitability and soundness of a bank. Moreover, it would end the practice of artificially raising book capital by selling assets whose price has risen, while holding on to those whose price has fallen.

[3] To be consistent, the liabilities side of the balance sheet should also be marked to market. The bank's core deposits (that is, the deposits of interest-insensitive holders) become more valuable to it when interest rates rise. A bank with a large volume of such deposits is then a more valuable merger partner, and this should be recognized when measuring that bank's capital.

is by no means clear that the bondholders would possess enough information to exercise much control over the bank's risk taking. They would, however, provide an extra cushion of capital that would protect the FDIC in case the bank became insolvent.

Lowering the Insurance Ceiling

The main problem created by deposit insurance is that it greatly reduces the incentive depositors have to monitor their banks and thrifts and to withdraw their deposits from those that take too much risk. Hence, to restore such depositor supervision some economists have advocated lowering the insurance ceiling to perhaps $50,000 or even less. As we discussed in the last chapter, Congress went part of the way in 1991 by making the $100,000 limit more binding.

Even with a $50,000 ceiling, however, the great majority of depositors would be fully covered and hence have no incentive to monitor their bank. But that does not matter much because it is primarily the large depositors and not the small ones who are likely to possess the necessary knowledge to monitor their banks. Moreover, one purpose of deposit insurance is to protect small, financially unsophisticated depositors and not those who can, or should be able to, protect themselves.

Like the other proposed reforms, lowering the deposit ceiling has disadvantages as well as advantages. First, it is by no means obvious that even large depositors can evaluate the riskiness of their banks. A number of empirical studies have investigated whether the prices of a bank's outstanding stocks and bonds fall ahead of the announcement that the bank is in trouble. If they do not, then even the holders of the bank's securities are apparently unable to determine the soundness of a bank. The empirical evidence, while mixed, suggests that this is so. However, one might object with some justice that it is not ability but motivation that is lacking: if the FDIC lowered its deposit coverage, more depositors would lose; these losses would greatly increase the incentive for large depositors and security holders to watch the bank more carefully. As a result, better information would become available.

Another serious problem with lowering the deposit-insurance ceiling is that it might take us back to the days when depositors would run banks: deposit insurance was introduced to prevent runs, as well as to protect small depositors. It may well be that lowering the ceiling to, say, $50,000 would not result in any runs, but it would be a risky experiment.

The Narrow Bank

A more fundamental reform than lowering the insurance ceiling would be to limit deposit insurance to only a special, new category of bank. A so-called **narrow bank** would issue checkable deposits and hold extremely safe assets, such as Treasury bills or highly rated commercial paper.[4] Since all the assets of such a bank are extremely safe, the FDIC's commitment to insure deposits would be

[4] Alternatively, narrow banks could be allowed to hold riskier assets, such as corporate bonds with a broad market, if they marked them to market daily.

almost costless. Only in the case of criminal activities, such as absconding with the bank's funds, could such a bank sustain significant losses. Other banks, let us call them **business banks,** could hold riskier assets and offer uninsured time deposits. This proposal has the advantage of maintaining the two major benefits of deposit insurance—a run-proof system of transactions deposits and a safe depository for the funds of small savers—while avoiding the potential for large losses to the FDIC.

Like other reform proposals, however, the narrow-bank idea has disadvantages. First, there would be a strong incentive to develop financial instruments that, while not legally classified as checkable deposits, would function much as they do. Business banks would then market these instruments by paying a higher rate of interest than could narrow banks with their extremely safe assets. Second, splitting the banking system would be costly, particularly because people would have to spend a good deal of time learning about the new types of banks.

Privatizing Deposit Insurance

Until the crises that beset first the FSLIC and later the FDIC, federal deposit insurance was generally considered an outstanding example of a successful government program. While probably most economists and surely most of the

Isn't a Bank a Strange Creature?

The proposal for a narrow bank raises a basic question. Why aren't banks already narrow banks? Certainly they obtain most of their funds by taking deposits and offering the public a very safe and highly liquid asset. Wouldn't one expect them to hold a portfolio of safe and liquid assets rather than of loans that involve significant risk and are not very liquid? How, then, can one explain that banks often make fairly risky and not very liquid loans?

Two explanations focus on the special information possessed by banks. First, as the holder of a firm's deposits, a bank can learn much about the firm: it can notice whether the firm can afford to keep adequate balances or sometimes comes close to missing a payroll and whether its deposits (which measure its receipts from sales) are rising or falling. Hence, the bank is in a good position to decide whether the firm is creditworthy and is therefore the natural institution to make business loans. How valid this explanation is depends on an empirical question: just how much does a bank learn about a firm from being the keeper of its deposits?

Second, making business loans is inherently risky and can best be done by a financial intermediary that has expert knowledge rather than by individual savers. But how can the savers be assured that this intermediary will not take undue risks? One possibility is that the savers have the right to withdraw their deposits on demand. If they find out that the institution is taking excessive risk, they can protect themselves by withdrawing their funds. And the intermediary, knowing that they will do so, is forced to avoid excessive risk. Hence it makes sense for checkable deposits and risky business loans to be combined in one institution, a bank.

public still consider federal deposit insurance useful, a number of proposals for fully or partially privatizing deposit insurance have emerged.

Some argue, for example, that a private insurance company would be able to operate more flexibly than a governmental one. It could, for example, cancel the insurance of a bank without the bank being able to challenge this action in court as an exercise of arbitrary governmental power. Prior to federal deposit insurance some states had insurance systems in which the banks mutually guaranteed each other's deposits. This system seemed to be effective. Bankers often knew which banks were taking excessive risks and could threaten to exclude them from the guarantee system.

But a private insurance system also has its problems. Unlike the federal government, private insurance companies can go bankrupt. Who would insure the insurers? Would depositors feel safe with private insurance, or would they run their bank as soon as they heard rumors of its possible failure, out of fear that the insurance company would also fail? One possible solution would be to have the insurance company itself insured by the government. Granted, that would not get rid of government insurance entirely, but it would impose some private capital and hence private supervision, between the bank's capital cushion and the ultimate obligation of the federal government to make good on deposits. Another possibility is to require banks to insure a certain amount, say $3,000, per deposit with a private insurance company and the rest with the FDIC. Such a limitation on the liabilities of private insurance companies should calm fears that they would not be able to meet their obligations. Moreover, the FDIC could then more easily use risk-related premiums, because it could use the insurance premiums that private insurers charge as an indicator of the premiums that it should charge.[5]

An Assessment

Partisans of one or the other of the proposals reviewed above would argue that it offers *the* solution. Skeptics may conclude that *none* of them would be an improvement over the present system. Still other observers may decide that, while none of the proposals offers a complete solution, one or a combination of several proposals would be helpful. However, if the current system continues to work, it is unlikely that any of them will be adopted in the foreseeable future. But if the deposit-insurance system faces another crisis, then we may have the opportunity to see how one or the other actually works.

SIMPLIFYING THE REGULATORY SYSTEM

Depository institutions are regulated in a complex and cumbersome way. Some banks are chartered by state authorities, and others by the federal government. Some state banks are regulated by the Federal Reserve and some are not. And

---

[5] A less radical variant of private insurance is the previously discussed proposal for requiring banks to use secondary capital as subordinate debt. In both cases private capital—and hence private-sector supervision—is used to protect the FDIC from losses up to a certain amount. The subordinate-debt proposal has the advantage that since the funds are there the moment the subordinate debt is bought, there is no question about the private-sector entity not being able to meet its commitment in a crisis.

the FDIC adds another layer of supervision. Similarly, some savings and loans are chartered by their state authorities and some by the Office of Thrift Supervision, which also supervises the state-chartered thrifts.

Such a system is not only complex, but it also allows depository institutions to select, within limits, who their regulators will be. Since the regulators want to have as many institutions as possible under their sway, they are tempted to compete by relaxing their rules. We already encountered an example of such "competition in laxity" in Chapter 6 when we discussed how state regulators, particularly those in Texas and California, expanded the portfolio choices of their savings and loans in a dangerous way. Another example comes from New York. When the state banking commissioner did not allow a large bank, Marine Midland, to merge with a foreign bank, the Hong Kong and Shanghai Banking Corporation, Marine Midland simply handed in its state charter and took out a national bank charter instead.

By no means do all economists agree that such alleged competition in laxity is bad. Many argue that it provides a useful counterweight to the inherent tendency of bank regulators to impose excessive regulation, and to discourage risk taking too much. Bank regulators have an incentive to be too severe because they get blamed if they allow banks to do something that results in some bank failures. But they do *not* get blamed by the public if they prohibit something, say, a new type of loan, that would actually have been quite safe. If they prohibit it, nobody ever finds out about its safety. Insofar as this bias in the regulators' own reward and punishment system outweighs the bias that results from the pressures brought to bear by the banking industry and from the regulators' tendency to be "nice" to their industry, regulations tend to be too severe, and some competition among regulating agencies is desirable. For example, interest payments on checkable deposits developed when some savings banks in New Hampshire and Massachusetts that were insured by a state agency instead of the FDIC were able to ignore the FDIC's edict and pay such interest.

Competition in laxity is not the only problem that the overlapping system of regulation creates. It also introduces complexity, despite the efforts of the various regulators to coordinate their examinations and regulations.

It is therefore not surprising that from time to time, attempts are made to simplify the regulatory system. Thus in 1993 President Clinton proposed setting up a Federal Banking Commission that would combine the regulatory functions of the Comptroller of the Currency, the Office of Thrift Supervision, the FDIC, and the Federal Reserve. This proposal was criticized by small banks fearful of losing their present influence on the regulators. Much more damaging was the opposition of the Federal Reserve, which (rightly or wrongly) argued vehemently that to respond effectively to potential financial crises, it needs the hands-on knowledge and insight it obtains from its supervision of banks.

THE DECLINING ROLE OF BANKS

The share of banks in the U.S. financial system has shrunk sharply over the long run. Thirty years ago they accounted for three-quarters of all short- and medium-term business credit; now they account for only a bit more than half.

Currently the volume of outstanding commercial paper is roughly equal to the outstanding commercial and industrial loans of banks; thirty years ago it was only one-tenth. As Table 10.1 (page 184) shows, in 1900 banks accounted for 55 percent of all the assets of financial intermediaries; by 1990 their share had fallen to about half that, 27 percent. Their loss of market share was particularly sharp in the 1980s, when it fell from 37 to 27 percent. This long-run loss in market share cannot be attributed to the rise of thrift institutions, because thrifts also lost market share between 1900 and 1949 and, after a surge between 1949 and 1980, lost it again in the 1980s, so they ended up with the same market share in 1990 as they had had in 1900. Over the whole period it was the nondepository institutions—insurance companies, pensions and trusts, investment companies, and finance companies—that gained market share.

These data are, however, subject to a serious qualification. They overstate the losses of banks, because they do not take account of their off-balance-sheet activities. A company that in 1950 might have borrowed from its bank now sells commercial paper instead. But to do so, it takes out a loan commitment from its bank in case it cannot roll over its commercial paper at maturity. This loan commitment generates a fee for the bank, something that Table 10.1 does not take into account.

All the same, there is little doubt that the market share of banks has declined, not only in the United States, but also in many other countries. And the troubles of banks may grow. Brokerage firms, whose money-market funds already compete with banks for deposits, have also started to compete with banks in offering business and mortgage loans. Moreover, as memories of what happened in the 1970s and 1980s fade, the junk-bond market is likely to revive and become a strong competitor of banks for business loans.

One can explain the decline in the role of banks in two, not mutually exclusive, ways. The first way ascribes it to market forces. Over the long run, as households have acquired both more wealth and greater financial sophistication, they have shifted away from banks, which offer ease of investment but a somewhat lower yield, toward more specialized financial institutions, which offer a higher yield. Moreover, the rise of pension funds and the rise of life insurance companies, both connected with the rises in income and wealth, mean that a larger share of financial assets is administered by professional portfolio managers, who are less likely than households to hold bank CDs. In addition, falling costs of data processing and other innovations fuel the rapid growth of money-market and other mutual funds that compete directly with bank deposits. Meanwhile, on the other side of the balance sheet, as lower costs of communications and data processing enable investors to evaluate and buy the securities issued by the ultimate borrowers, so that these ultimate borrowers can finance themselves at a lower cost that way than by borrowing from banks.

The second way the role of banks has declined is that banks are treated unfairly. They are subject to reserve requirements, minimum capital requirements, FDIC insurance premiums, and various regulatory burdens, such as those imposed by the Community Reinvestment Act. Their competitors, for example, money-market funds and finance companies, are not subject to these

Table 10.1 Relative Shares of Total Financial Intermediary Assets, 1900–1990 (percent)

	1900	1912	1922	1929	1939	1949	1960	1970	1980	1990
Commercial banks	55.2%	55.3%	54.9%	45.9%	40.0%	42.3%	38.6%	38.5%	37.2%	26.8%
Thrifts:	16.0	12.7	10.9	12.0	10.6	9.9	20.1	20.8	23.3	16.0
Savings & loans	2.8	2.5	3.2	5.1	3.3	3.9	12.1	13.4	16.9	11.1
Mutual savings banks	13.3	10.2	7.6	6.9	7.2	5.8	6.9	6.0	4.6	2.7
Credit unions	0.0	0.0	0.0	0.0	0.1	0.2	1.1	1.4	1.9	2.2
Insurance companies:	12.2	14.2	12.9	16.0	21.2	19.7	24.0	19.1	17.4	19.1
Life insurance	9.4	11.2	10.1	12.1	17.6	16.0	19.6	15.3	12.6	13.8
Other insurance	2.8	3.0	2.9	3.8	3.6	3.8	4.4	3.8	4.8	5.2
Pensions and trusts:	16.6	17.8	21.2	22.2	25.5	25.5	9.8	13.0	13.0	19.3
Personal	16.6	17.8	20.8	20.8	21.1	13.4	0.0	0.0	0.0	0.0
Private	0.0	0.0	0.0	0.3	0.6	1.6	6.4	8.4	7.7	11.8
Public	0.0	0.0	0.3	1.0	3.7	10.5	3.3	4.6	5.3	7.5
Investment companies:	0.0	0.0	0.1	2.1	1.0	0.9	2.9	3.7	3.7	10.9
Mutual fund	NA	NA	NA	NA	NA	NA	2.9	3.6	1.7	5.9
Money market	NA	NA	NA	NA	NA	NA	0.0	0.2	2.0	5.1
Finance companies	0.0	0.0	0.0	1.8	1.8	1.7	4.7	4.9	5.3	7.9

Note: Money Market data starts in 1974.

Source: Franklin Edwards, "Financial Markets in Transition—Or the Decline of Commercial Banking," in *Changing Capital Markets: Implications for Monetary Policy,* Federal Reserve Bank of Kansas City, p. 9.

burdens and can therefore out-compete them. The question here is whether the special burdens that are imposed on banks are greater than the special benefits that banks receive and their competitors do not: FDIC insurance and the ability to borrow from the Fed. This is a question we have encountered before and for which there is no definite answer (see the box on page 111).

Does the declining share of banks create a problem that needs to be addressed, or should it be treated like the decline of any other industry and left to the market? At first glance it may seem that this depends on which of the above ways of explaining the decline is correct: if the decline of the banks' share is due to market forces, there is no reason to counteract it. But for several reasons that is a facile answer. First, regardless of what is causing the relative decline of the banks' market share, if their profitability declines at the same time, they will be tempted to take on more risk, and that might eventually lead to a taxpayer bailout, as well as to economic instability.

Second, as banks lose out to unregulated competitors whose liabilities are riskier than those of the banks, the danger of a financial crisis that might set off a recession increases. Compare insured bank deposits with money-market shares. The former are perfectly safe, while it is possible that holders of money-market shares may suffer a loss. So far that has not happened, but only because in the few cases where a money-market fund had capital losses that exceeded its interest earnings, the companies that managed these funds swallowed the losses instead of passing them on to the shareholders. They may not always be willing to do that. If not, how will the shareholders react to losses? Will they run money-market funds?

Third, some of the burdens imposed on banks provide special benefits to others, and a decline in these benefits as the banking industry shrinks has a social cost, regardless of why the industry is shrinking. For example, the Community Reinvestment Act subsidizes loans to minorities, and (as we will explain in Chapter 23) the reserve requirement provides funds for the federal government. If these interventions have positive externalities, the market solution is not the optimal one. In addition, there is some concern that the declining market share of banks may make monetary policy less effective, though that is still a highly controversial claim.

Opening New Markets for Banks: The Demise of Glass-Steagall Restrictions

Banks have responded to the challenge of the relative decline for their core services by increasing their efforts to provide other financial services, some of which, such as trust departments, we have already described. But in doing so banks faced a legal barrier. In the 1920s banks were allowed to have affiliates that dealt in securities. But in the 1930s many people claimed that fraudulent dealings by banks and their security affiliates were responsible for the Great Depression. As a result, in 1933 Congress passed the Glass-Steagall Act separating commercial banking from investment banking, so that banks had to get out of the securities business. We have known for a long time that this explanation of the Great Depression is wrong, but that did not suffice to get rid of the constraints the Glass-Steagall Act imposed on banks. The investment banks that profited from keeping commercial banks off their turf had a strong incentive to persuade Congress to maintain the act. Similarly, insurance agents urged Congress to maintain the prohibition against banks' selling insurance.

Arguments Pro and Con. There has been much debate about the wisdom of restricting commercial banks within the narrow confines that the Glass-Steagall Act set for them. Several reasons can be given for letting commercial banks deal in securities the same way investment banks do. One is that, in general, competition is good, and the more competition there is in investment banking, the better. Moreover, if commercial banks can make a good profit in the securities business, that would help to reduce bank failures. Third, there may be significant synergy between commercial and investment banking; for example, some of the information that banks have about their customers may help them in investment banking activities, so that combining commercial and investment banking would lower the cost of security underwriting. In addition, if banks can switch some of their activities into investment banking, then the resources devoted to commercial banking can shrink without individual banks having to shrink. That way the commercial banking industry can contract in a relatively painless way.

But there are also some arguments on the other side. The most obvious one is that if banks deal in securities, they take on additional risk, and hence more banks will fail. Is that correct? As the discussion of portfolio risk in Chapter 3 shows, this depends on the relative riskiness of commercial and investment banking and on the correlation of these risks. While far from conclusive, the evidence suggests that a commercial bank's risk is not increased if it enters the securities business.

A stronger argument against allowing commercial banks to do investment banking is that it is not fair to ask investment banks to compete with institutions that have cheap access to funds because their deposits are insured. This problem can be avoided at least to *some* extent by requiring a commercial bank to carry out its investment banking in a separately capitalized subsidiary of its holding company. Since that subsidiary cannot issue insured deposits, it has to borrow at an interest rate that reflects the market's evaluation of its riskiness and so it does not have any special advantage over a competing investment bank.

However, there is a danger that those who lend to a subsidiary of a bank holding company do so in the belief that the bank will not allow the subsidiary to fail, that it will provide the subsidiary with whatever funds it needs to stay afloat. If so, deposit insurance indirectly subsidizes the investment-banking subsidiary, since it would be called on should the subsidiary's losses drag down the bank. Banks reply that the law authorizing their investment banking activities can contain certain provisions, called **firewalls,** to prevent the channeling of bank funds into an ailing subsidiary. The question is whether the law is written tightly enough to make these firewalls fully effective.

Another argument against allowing commercial banks to undertake investment banking is that the commercial bank can threaten to cut off loans to firms that do not use its investment-banking subsidiary and thus provide unfair competition to investment banks. Applying such pressure is illegal, but laws against such activity are hard to enforce. A more plausible response is that banks are unlikely to have the required market power. A sound borrower who is refused a loan by one bank can go to another bank.

Commercial banks have also tried to obtain permission to sell a broad range of insurance products and to undertake real-estate brokerage. Many of the previous arguments for and against allowing commercial banks to exercise investment-banking powers apply here, too. On the one hand, bank profits may increase, and thus reduce the probability of bank failures, and banks could reduce excess capacity in banking by directing some of their assets toward insurance and real-estate brokerage. In addition, banks and firms that sell insurance or broker real estate probably replicate many of the same tasks, so combining all these activities in one organization cuts costs by reducing duplication of effort. Besides, it is convenient for households to buy their insurance where they do their banking. Finally, there is no reason to think that selling insurance and acting as real-estate brokers would increase the riskiness of banks. On the other hand, those who object to banks selling insurance and real estate argue that banks can pressure consumers who apply for loans to switch their insurance and real-estate business to the bank, and thus create unfair competition for other insurance salespeople and real estate brokers.

The Separation of Banking and Commerce

A related issue is whether firms in other industries, say the steel industry, should be allowed to own banks. An argument for this is that some firms would buy banks and thus bring new capital into banking, capital that could absorb losses that otherwise the FDIC would have to absorb. Moreover, since we generally allow firms to enter various industries, why make an exception to exclude them from banking?

Opponents respond that banking is different because banks benefit from a federal safety net: they can borrow from the Fed and their deposits are insured. There is general agreement that this federal safety net should not be extended to firms that own banks. So the debate concerns whether it is possible to write laws and regulations that provide effective firewalls between a bank and the commercial firm that owns it (or that is owned by the same holding company). Can a bank find ways of channeling funds to its commercial parent company, for example, by making loans on favorable terms to customers of that firm? If so, the bank might weaken itself so much by bailing out the commercial firm that the FDIC would have to bail the *bank* out, and thus, in effect, extend the safety net to the commercial firm. Or is it possible to build firewalls that prevent any such dissipation of bank assets, without these firewalls' separating the bank's business from the commercial firm's business so much that most of the efficiencies of combining the bank and the commercial firm are lost? In addition to these fears, opponents of such combinations also worry that allowing commercial firms to enter banking could lead to a dangerous concentration of economic power and give an unfair competitive advantage to commercial firms that own banks. Moreover, they argue that such combinations cannot result in much inflow of capital into banking, unless banking is

Universal Banking

Should the United States allow universal banking as, for example, Germany and Switzerland do (see page 115)? The close connections that universal banks have with many of the firms that borrow from them avoid some of the asymmetric-information problems discussed in Chapter 3, since a universal bank knows the borrower's business from the inside and has a long-term stake in the company. For example, a universal bank is more likely than the average stockholder to know when a firm tries to make itself look creditworthy by undertaking activities that raise its short-run profitability at the expense of its long-run profitability. Moreover, a universal bank that holds a significant part of a company's outstanding stock is in a better position to monitor the behavior of its executives, and to fire them if that is needed.

However, if representatives of a bank sit on the boards of several firms in the same industry, they might work to reduce competition. Moreover, allowing banks to hold stock in commercial firms would increase the riskiness of their portfolios. In addition, banks might favor the loan applications of firms whose stock they hold, and thus reduce the availability of loans to other firms. For these reasons, as well as because of the widespread distrust of large and powerful banks, it is unlikely that universal banks will be permitted in the United States, although some economists have advocated such a change in regulations.

profitable. And if that is the case, capital flows into banking in any case. So why take the risks entailed in what would be the hard-to-reverse step of allowing the combination of commercial firms and banks?

Legislative Changes. Some of these arguments, on both sides of the issue of eliminating the Glass-Steagall prohibitions deserve to be taken seriously. But such issues are decided in good part by the relative political power of banks and their opponents. In the 1980s and 1990s the regulators and the courts chipped away at the scope of the Glass-Steagall Act and interpreted it narrowly, so that the banks received considerable investment-banking power.

SUMMARY

1 The most obvious answer to the deposit-insurance problem is to say that the regulators should do a better job. But there are severe limits to what better regulators could accomplish; problems are hard to anticipate, the soundness of banks is not easily determined, and banks can dispute the regulators' orders.

2 Another answer to the deposit-insurance problem would be to impose higher insurance premiums on risky institutions. But the risk banks present to the FDIC is hard to measure; it is not just the average risk on assets.

3 Higher capital-asset ratios are another possible solution. The higher a depository institution's capital-asset ratio, the less incentive it has to take excessive risk. More capital also makes failure less likely and protects the FDIC in case of failure. But requiring higher capital-asset ratios would be costly to depositors and borrowers and would reduce the size of the banking system. Marking to market would improve the quality of the capital shown on an institution's books, but it would be hard to

accomplish. Also, it is useful only if market values are the best available estimates of true values.

4 A proposal related to that made above is to require depository institutions to have subordinated secondary capital outstanding. But it is far from obvious that small institutions could sell such securities.

5 To induce people to pay more attention to the soundness of their depository institutions, the insurance ceiling could be lowered. But it is not obvious that depositors could discriminate between sound and unsound institutions, and, also, lowering the ceiling might result in runs.

6 A more radical idea is to insure only *narrow* banks, banks that hold very safe assets, and not to allow other banks to issue checkable deposits. But it would be costly to split our banking system in that way, and there would be a strong incentive to develop hybrid types of deposits.

7 Another radical proposal is to substitute private insurance for government insurance of deposits. But the private insurer might then have to be reinsured by the government.

8 President Clinton proposed a reorganization of the bank regulatory system. However, the Fed objected to losing regulatory power.

9 The market share of banks has shrunk substantially. The extent to which this is due to regulatory burdens is debatable.

10 There has been much discussion about the appropriate frontier between banks and other types of business. Should commercial banks be allowed to undertake investment banking, to sell insurance, and to act as real-estate brokers? Should firms primarily engage in commerce be allowed to own banks? These issues are still under debate.

KEY TERMS

risk-adjusted insurance premiums	insurance ceiling
marking to market	narrow banks
secondary subordinated capital	competition in laxity
firewalls	universal banks

QUESTIONS AND EXERCISES

1 Argue for one of the proposals to improve the deposit-insurance system.

2 Criticize one of the proposals for improving the deposit-insurance system.

*3 Discuss: "Life and casualty insurance companies prevent policyholders from taking excessive risk by charging a risk-adjusted insurance premium. What works for them would also work for the FDIC."

*4 Many economists favor raising the capital requirements of banks. Why?

5 Do you favor allowing banks to enter any industry they wish and allowing firms in any other industries to own banks? Why or why not?

FURTHER READING

CORRIGAN, E. GERALD. "Balancing Progressive Change and Caution in Reforming the Financial System," Federal Reserve Bank of New York, *Quarterly Review,* 16 (Summer 1991), 1–13. A strong argument against allowing commercial firms to own banks.

EDWARDS, FRANKLIN. "Financial Markets in Transition—Or the Decline of Commercial

Banking," in *Changing Capital Markets,* Federal Reserve Bank of Kansas City, 1993, pp. 5–62. A very good survey of the relative decline of banks.

FEDERAL RESERVE BANK OF ATLANTA. *Economic Review,* March 1984. This issue has several good articles on deposit insurance.

GREENSPAN, ALAN. "Testimony," *Federal Reserve Bulletin,* 77 (June 1991), 430–43. This testimony presents the Fed chairman's evaluation of various proposals for reforming deposit insurance and the banking system.

Journal of Banking and Finance, 15, no. 2 (1991). This issue has several excellent articles on deposit insurance.

LITTAN, ROBERT. *What Should Banks Do?* Washington, D.C.: Brookings Institution, 1987. An excellent discussion of the appropriate domain for banks.

PIERCE, JAMES. *The Future of Banking.* New Haven: Yale University Press, 1991. Chapters 4 and 5 present a strong case for limiting deposit insurance to transaction accounts.

U.S. TREASURY DEPARTMENT. *Modernizing the Financial System: Recommendations for Safer, More Competitive Banking.* Washington, D.C.: U.S. Treasury Department, 1991. The Treasury Department's recommendations for financial reform, accompanied by a set of comprehensive study papers that provide valuable surveys of proposed deposit-insurance reforms.

WHEELOCK, DAVID. "Is the Banking Industry in Decline? Recent Trends and Future Prospects From a Historical Perspective," Federal Reserve Bank of St. Louis, *Review,* 75 (September–October 1993), 3–22. An informative historical account.

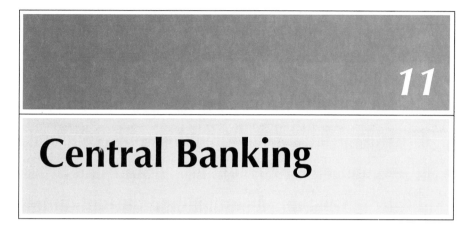

Central Banking

11

After you have read this chapter, you will be able to:

- Explain what a central bank is and what it does.
- Describe both the formal and informal aspects of the Federal Reserve's structure, and the extent of its independence.
- Assess the case for and against central-bank independence.

With money, capital markets, interest rates, depository institutions, and international banking introduced in earlier chapters, the cast of characters in the financial system is almost complete. One player is missing, however: the central bank. In this chapter we will discuss our own central bank, the Federal Reserve System, in some detail. Before doing so, however, we have to look more generally at what central banks in developed countries do.

THE CENTRAL BANK: A PROFILE

Despite their name, central banks are not banks in the sense that commercial banks are. They are governmental institutions that are not concerned with maximizing their profits, but with achieving certain goals for the entire economy, such as preventing massive commercial bank failures, high unemployment, and so on. Central banks, even if in a formal sense owned by private stockholders, carry out governmental functions and are therefore part of the government. When a bank acts as a central bank, that is, determines its actions on the basis of the public interest rather than its stockholders' interest, it operates as a public institution.

Origin of Central Banks

Central banks have developed in two ways. One is a slow evolutionary process; the prime example is the Bank of England, which started out as a commercial bank, but over the years acquired the added powers and responsibilities of a central bank. In this process of evolution it is hard to say when the Bank of

England ceased to be a commercial bank and became a central bank. In contrast many central banks, like the Fed, were central banks right from the start. Such a central bank is actually owned by the government, although it may, like the Fed, have private stockholders.

Purposes and Functions of a Central Bank

The two most important functions of central banks are to control the quantity of money and interest rates and to prevent massive bank failures. But they also have certain "chore" functions. Central banks also act as advisers to their governments, particularly in the area of international finance. To do so, many central banks have large research staffs.

Controlling the Money Supply. It is widely, though not universally (see pages 511–12), believed that as the nineteenth-century British economist and financial journalist Walter Bagehot wrote, "Money will not manage itself." Each commercial bank, as it obtains reserves, expands its deposits and—in the absence of some mechanism for controlling the volume of reserves, deposits, and hence the money stock—could grow at an inappropriate rate. One way of controlling the growth rate of deposits is to require banks to stand ready to redeem their deposits in some valuable commodity, such as gold. Another is to institute a central bank charged with keeping reserves, and hence deposits and the money supply, growing at an appropriate rate. This does not mean that central banks always succeed in keeping the growth rate of money on the right track. The history of the Federal Reserve's policies (discussed in Chapter 27) leaves open to dispute whether, on the whole, the Fed has done more good than harm. Since credit, like money, can be used to buy goods and services, central banks are also concerned with the supply of credit.

Preventing Bank Failures. One aspect of controlling the money supply is the need to guard against bank failures. This is not to say that central banks have always prevented widespread bank failures; the Fed certainly did not do so in the 1930s. But a central bank *should* act as a **lender of last resort,** that is, as an institution able and willing to make loans to banks in a crisis, when other banks cannot or will not do so, or to provide liquidity to the banking system through open-market operations when this is needed. (Being a lender of last resort is one reason why a central bank cannot be a profit-maximizing institution. Such an institution would lend at all times, not just in crises.) The reason the central bank is able to make loans at such a time is that (as we will see in Chapter 14) it has the power to create reserves. In the United States, one defense against bank failures is, of course, the FDIC, but the Fed stands ready to support the FDIC by acting as a lender of last resort. If a sound bank is short of liquidity, the Fed can make a loan to keep it alive until either it can obtain liquid funds or the FDIC can deal with it.

Being ready to act as a lender of last resort is an extremely important function of a central bank. It is easy to forget this because the threat of financial panic arises only rarely. Hence, when one looks at the day-to-day activities of a central bank, its function as a lender of last resort seems irrelevant and unimportant. But one can say the same thing about a fire extinguisher! Don't forget, therefore, that, although a central bank does not *normally* act as a lender of last resort to the banking system, it must always stand ready to do so, even if doing so means that it must temporarily abandon other goals such as fighting inflation.

Setting and Maintaining Exchange Rates. Most central banks, along with other governmental agencies such as treasury departments, are concerned with the appropriate exchange rate for their currencies. (In this context the term *currency* is used in a broad sense to denote a country's money, not just paper money and coin.) In many cases, though by no means in all, a central bank maintains this exchange rate by intervening on the foreign-exchange market. If the value of the country's currency in terms of foreign currencies falls below the target range, the central bank buys its own currency, and thus raises the price. Since in buying its own currency, the central bank must pay out foreign currencies, it must maintain a stock of foreign currencies or be able to borrow such currencies, often from foreign central banks. Conversely, if the country's currency rises too high, a central bank will sell it and thus push the price down. Foreign central banks pay much more attention to the exchange rate than does the Federal Reserve here in the United States. This is because foreign trade accounts for a much larger proportion of GDP in those countries than it does for the United States and because many other countries peg the value of their currency to the currency of another country. The Federal Reserve will often pay little, if any attention to the exchange rate of the dollar.

Chore Functions. One of a central bank's chore functions consists of maintaining the payments mechanism. Thus the Federal Reserve issues **Federal Reserve notes**—our paper currency—and withdraws worn notes from circulation in exchange for new ones. When a bank needs additional currency, the Federal Reserve ships it currency and debits the bank's account. As we explained in Chapter 6, the Fed also clears checks and performs wire transfers among banks. Not all central banks do all these things.

Another set of chore functions consists of services the central bank provides for commercial banks. Thus it acts as a banker's bank, holding most of the reserves of commercial banks. As we will explain later, these reserves have no physical existence; they are just entries on the liabilities side of a central bank's balance sheet.

In addition to its services for commercial banks, a central bank provides many services to the government. Thus it acts as the government's bank. The government keeps an account at the central bank, writes its checks on this account, and, in some countries, sells its securities through the central bank.

Another group of services it provides to the government arises directly out of the central bank's close relation with commercial banks. Thus the central bank typically administers certain controls over commercial banks. For example, the Fed controls bank mergers and examines member banks.

In some countries, in particular the less-developed countries, the central bank also makes loans to the Treasury. In fact, a number of central banks—the Bank of England again is the prime example—started as commercial banks that made loans to the government and got certain privileges in exchange. But having the central bank make loans to the Treasury can be highly inflationary since it does so by creating new money, and such an increase in the money supply often results in inflation. The central bank often would prefer not to make such inflationary loans, but in some countries it lacks the power to resist the Treasury. To prevent this, in the United States the Treasury cannot just ask the Fed for a loan. However, what cannot be done openly can be, and is, done indirectly by using the public as an intermediary; the Treasury sells securities to the public, while the Fed buys the same amount of government securities from the public.

Other Aspects of Central Banking

Before leaving the topic of central banks in general, there are two more items to be discussed: the relation of central banks to the rest of the government and their ability to create reserves.

Relations between the central bank and the government are complex. Although central banks are part of the government, they maintain a certain detachment from the rest of it. They usually have much more independence than do such government agencies as the Treasury Department.

Central banks have the power to create reserves. Unless there is a law stating that the central bank must keep, say, twenty cents in gold for each dollar of its outstanding currency notes or deposits, it can create as many reserves for the commercial banks as it wants to. After all, these reserves consist, apart from currency, merely of entries on the central bank's books. Hence, if a central bank wants banks to have more reserves, all it has to do is to buy securities from them and pay for the securities by writing up their reserves on its books.

THE FORMAL STRUCTURE OF THE FEDERAL RESERVE SYSTEM

Although other developed countries generally had central banks much earlier, it was not until 1913 that the United States established the Federal Reserve System. Until then, the Treasury carried out some quasi-central-banking functions, but it did so only in a rudimentary way. One reason the United States had not established a central bank was the traditional U.S. fear of concentrated financial power. Populists were worried that a central bank would be dominated by the big banks, which would employ it as an instrument of monopolistic control, or more generally that Wall Street would use it to dominate Main Street. Conservatives, on the other hand, were worried that a central bank would be dominated by politicians beholden to debtor interests, who would use it to pursue inflationary policies.

Those who urged the establishment of a central bank pointed to the waves of bank failures and the resulting financial crises that from time to time plagued the U.S. economy. Other countries, they said, avoided these problems because they had central banks. In addition, without a central bank, check clearing was cumbersome and slow. In 1907 an unusually severe financial crisis provided the final push needed to establish a central bank. Even then, six years went by before President Wilson signed the Federal Reserve Act in December 1913. The Federal Reserve Act was a carefully crafted compromise that tried to allay the fears of both populists and conservatives by an elaborate system of checks and balances.

Figure 11.1 summarizes the structure of the Federal Reserve System. Instead of a monolithic central bank, the act resulted in the establishment of

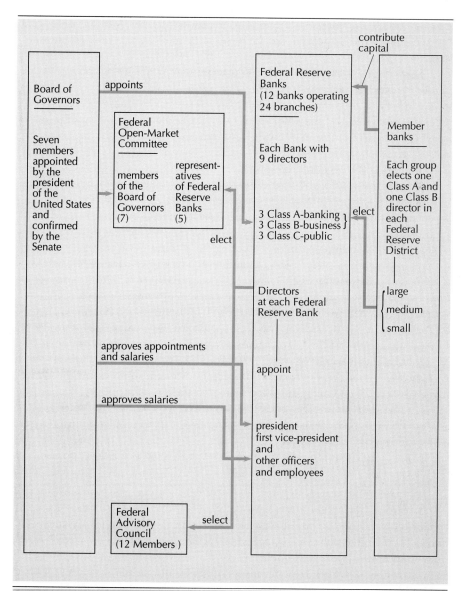

Figure 11.1   The Structure of the Federal Reserve System. A system of checks and balances disperses power in the Federal Reserve System. **Source:** Board of Governors, Federal Reserve System, *The Federal Reserve System, Purposes and Functions* (Washington, D.C.: 1974), p. 18.

12 Federal Reserve Banks located in various parts of the country, with a **Federal Reserve Board** in Washington, D.C., to coordinate them and to provide some supervision. Thus power was decentralized geographically and was shared between the Federal Reserve Banks, which were close to the bankers in their districts, and the presidentially appointed Federal Reserve Board. It was not clear at first whether it was more accurate to describe this system as a single central bank with 12 branches, or as 12 coordinated central banks. It was also not clear for some years which was more powerful—the New York Federal Reserve Bank (the largest of the 12 Reserve Banks) or the Federal Reserve Board.

The Federal Reserve System was established primarily as a way of pooling the reserves of member banks. It was supposed to make loans out of these pooled reserves to banks that were short of reserves. By being pooled in the Federal Reserve Banks, the reserves of member banks could be mobilized for use where they were most needed. Solvent banks would no longer be destroyed by bank runs when there were other banks that had large reserves that they did not need and thus could be lent.

The high hopes of the founders of the Federal Reserve System were not met. In the 1930s the Federal Reserve did much too little to meet the demand for reserves, and the United States experienced the worst financial crisis and the most severe series of bank failures in its history. Largely as a result of this experience, the Federal Reserve System we have today is quite different from the one instituted in 1913. It has been changed both by important legislation in 1935 and 1980 and by that slow evolution in modes of functioning that is a matter of internal organization and practices rather than of statutory change. Thus the 1935 Banking Act centralized power in the Fed's **Board of Governors** (the successor to the Federal Reserve Board) by reducing the power of the Federal Reserve Banks. It also made the Fed more independent of the President by eliminating the appointment of the Secretary of the Treasury and the Comptroller of the Currency (both presidential appointees) to the Board of Governors. The 1980 legislation eliminated the most important distinction between member banks and other banks, since it required all banks (as well as thrifts with checkable deposits) to meet the same reserve requirements, regardless of membership in the Fed.

We will now examine the Federal Reserve System as it exists at present.

The Federal Reserve Banks

The locations of the 12 Federal Reserve Banks and their branches are shown in Figure 11.2. The assets of various Federal Reserve Banks are far from equal. More than half the assets are held by just three: New York, Chicago, and San Francisco. The New York bank alone accounts for about 30 percent of all Federal Reserve assets. Apart from its size, the New York bank is the "first among equals" because its location gives it direct contact with the country's main money market. Hence, this bank carries out all the purchases and sales of securities on behalf of the whole Federal Reserve System. In addition, it is the Fed-

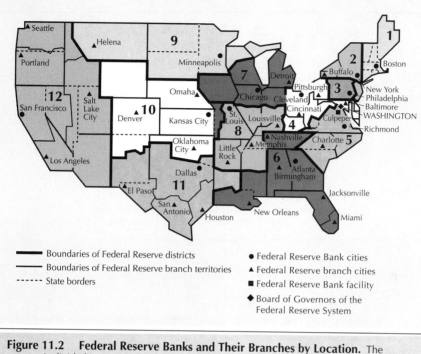

Figure 11.2   Federal Reserve Banks and Their Branches by Location. The country is divided into 12 Federal Reserve Districts: Alaska and Hawaii are in the twelfth district.

eral Reserve System's contact point in many, though not all, of the Fed's dealings with foreign central banks and international institutions.

Each of these Federal Reserve Banks is controlled by a board of nine part-time directors. Three of these directors, called Class A directors, are elected by the member banks and are bankers themselves. Member banks also elect three Class B directors. These directors may not be officers or employees of banks, but are people active in business or agriculture; they thus bring to the Fed the viewpoint of business borrowers. To prevent domination by any group of particular-size banks, member banks are divided into large, medium, and small banks, and each of these groups votes for one Class A and one Class B director. But actually, neither Class A nor Class B directors are "elected" in the proper sense of the term, since there is usually only a single candidate for each "election." Frequently the single candidate for election as a Class B director, and often also the single candidate for the Class A directorship, is someone suggested to the banks by the president of the Federal Reserve Bank.

Finally, there are three Class C directors. These are not elected by the member banks. They are appointed by the Board of Governors to embody the broader public interest beyond that of banks and their borrowers. One of these Class C directors becomes the chairman of the board and another the vice-chairman.

It is sometimes said that the member banks elect the majority of the Federal Reserve Banks' directors, but this is misleading. When one takes account of the fact that, in addition to the appointed Class C directors, the president of the bank often in fact nominates the Class B directors and apparently in many cases even the Class A directors, it is more accurate to say that in actuality the Federal Reserve System selects the majority of the directors.

In describing the various classes of directors, we avoid saying that any of the three classes "represents" a particular group, because all directors are supposed to represent the public interest rather than the narrow interests of bankers or borrowers. The public interest, however, is like the proverbial elephant described by the blind men. One's associations and experiences affect one's perception of the public interest.

The chief executive officer of each Federal Reserve Bank is its president, chosen by the directors with the approval of the Board of Governors. In recent years the president has frequently been someone initially suggested to the directors by the Board of Governors.

The Federal Reserve Banks examine member banks, approve or disapprove some bank-merger applications, clear checks, withdraw worn currency from circulation, and issue new currency. In addition to these chore functions, the Federal Reserve Banks have some policy functions too. Each sets a **discount rate,** that is, *the rate the Fed charges on its loans to banks and other depository institutions in its district.* This rate has to be approved by the Board of Governors, which, by its power to approve or disapprove the existing discount rate, can force a Federal Reserve Bank to change its current rate. Hence, the only real power the Federal Reserve Banks have over the discount rate is the power to advise and to delay a change in the discount rate for as long as two weeks. However, each Federal Reserve Bank decides which banks are allowed to borrow; that is, under general rules applicable to all Federal Reserve Banks, each makes the particular decision when a bank or other depository institution in its district applies for a loan. A more important policy role of the Federal Reserve Banks is, as will be described later, to participate in the Federal Open-Market Committee (FOMC).

Still another function of the Federal Reserve Banks is to provide the Federal Reserve System with local contacts. Most statistical data become available only with a delay. However, by talking to local business managers, the directors and the presidents of the Reserve Banks hear of economic developments before they are reflected in the statistics. For example, the head of a major corporation may tell them that it plans to cut back on production and employment. The Federal Reserve Banks make such information available to all the Federal Reserve's policymakers. A related function of the Federal Reserve Banks is to carry out research on problems of banking and monetary policy. The Federal Reserve Banks have capable staffs of economists who work on these problems. (The Federal Reserve Banks publish some of this research in their *Reviews,* which are available to the public at no cost. At the end of this chapter, you will find the addresses to write to for a free subscription to these *Reviews.*)

Another important function of the Federal Reserve Banks is to explain *and justify* Fed actions to the local business community, and thus generate political support for the Fed. The Fed needs such support to fight pressures brought to bear on it by some members of Congress and sometimes by the White House. Like any other policy-making agency, the Fed has to act as a political animal.

The Board of Governors

At the apex of the Federal Reserve System is the Board of Governors (sometimes still called the Federal Reserve Board), located in Washington, D.C. The seven governors are appointed by the President of the United States with the advice and consent of the Senate. They can be removed only for cause, something that, so far, has never happened. In recent years, the majority of the governors have been professional economists. A full term of office is 14 years, and governors cannot be reappointed after serving a full term. This is supposed to remove them from needing to seek the president's favor or to fear the president's displeasure. In the ideal case all governors would serve out their full 14-year terms, which are staggered. If so, there would be only two vacancies on the Board every four years, so that within a single term a president could not dominate the Board. But the chairman's term—as chairman, not as Board member—is only four years so that each president can appoint a chairman. These provisions are examples of the checks and balances built into the Federal Reserve System.

However, not all of them have worked well. Board members usually retire before their full 14-year terms are up, sometimes because of age and sometimes for financial reasons. In the period 1970 to 1994, of the 26 governors who left the Board only 10 had served for as long as seven years. Hence, usually more than two vacancies occur on the Board during any one presidential term. For example, there were four vacancies on the Board during President Carter's first three years in office. Moreover, when a governor resigns, the president usually appoints someone to the remaining years of the former governor's term, rather than to a new and complete 14-year term. This not only means that most governors have less than a 14-year term, but also that they are then eligible for reappointment to a full term of their own and might therefore be tempted to favor the president's view. The provision that gives the chairman a term as long as the president's has also not worked out as intended. For example, if a chairman resigns in the third year of a president's second term, the new chairman can serve for three years of the next president's term.

The governors make monetary policy; they control the discount rate and, within limits, can change reserve requirements. Together with other members of the Federal Open-Market Committee they control the most important tool of monetary policy, open-market operations. In addition, the chairman is one of the main economic advisers to the president, as well as to Congress. And governors sometimes also act as U.S. representatives in negotiations with foreign central banks and governments. Beyond this, chairmen frequently press their views on fiscal policy and other economic issues in statements to Congress and to the general public. The news media pay much attention to the chairman's statements. The Board has a large and competent staff of economists to aid it in this work.

Despite the fact that determining monetary policy is by far the Board's most important task, much of its time is spent on bank regulatory problems. For example, it passes judgment on many bank-merger applications and decides the permissible lines of nonbank activity for bank holding companies. It also administers the laws that prohibit discrimination and untruthful statements in lending. In these activities the Board of Governors' control extends beyond banking to credit in general. Since the Federal Reserve has a reputation as an efficient agency, it tends to have many peripheral tasks thrust upon it. Closer to home, it exercises some supervision over the Federal Reserve Banks, which have to submit their budgets for Board approval.

The Federal Open-Market Committee

The focal point for policy making within the Federal Reserve System is the FOMC, the **Federal Open-Market Committee.** This committee consists of the seven members of the Board of Governors, whose chairman is also chairman of the FOMC, and five of the presidents of the Federal Reserve Banks.[1] The Federal Reserve Banks rotate in these five slots on the FOMC except for the New York Bank, which has a permanent slot. However, even those Federal Reserve Bank presidents who are not currently members of the FOMC are usually present at its meetings and participate in its discussions, though, of course, they do not vote. But since the FOMC tries to reach a consensus rather than just rely on a majority, their presence, even in a nonvoting capacity, gives all Federal Reserve Bank presidents some influence over FOMC decisions. The FOMC currently meets about eight times a year, that is, roughly every six weeks, and sometimes holds telephone conferences between meetings.

The FOMC's function is to decide on **open-market operations,** that is, on *Federal Reserve purchases and sales of securities.* The FOMC does not carry out security purchases or sales itself. Instead, it issues a "directive" telling the New York Federal Reserve Bank the open-market policy it should follow for the accounts of all the Federal Reserve Banks.

There are some other Federal Reserve components, but they are *much* less important than the FOMC. One is the Federal Advisory Council, which consists of one commercial banker (usually a president of a large commercial bank) from each district. As the name implies, this committee advises the Board of Governors, but that is all.

THE INFORMAL STRUCTURE OF THE FEDERAL RESERVE SYSTEM

Merely to know the formal, legal aspects of an organization is rarely sufficient. The Fed, as any other organization, has developed certain traditions and other attributes that strongly affect its operations. These informal aspects are nei-

---

[1] Although the law permits the first vice-president of a Federal Reserve Bank to serve on the FOMC in place of its president, this is normally not done, except when a president is unable to attend a meeting.

ther definite nor clear-cut. One of these is the distribution of power within the Federal Reserve System.

Distribution of Power within the Federal Reserve

Although the distribution of power over monetary policy within the Federal Reserve System and among "outsiders" is a matter of judgment, former Fed governor Sherman Maisel has given an estimate of the distribution of power, shown in Table 11.1. However, there are two qualifications to Table 11.1. First, the distribution of power cannot be quantified precisely; as Maisel states, "Other knowledgeable persons would certainly draw charts with different weights."[2] For example, one former senior Fed official believes that the chairman has more power than Table 11.1 suggests. Second, the distribution of power depends, in part, on the personalities involved. For example, a president who takes great interest in monetary policy exercises more influence than one whose main concern is foreign policy. Similarly, the influence of the chairman became less pronounced in 1987, when Alan Greenspan, who believes in consensual management, took over from Paul Volcker, who was more attuned to strong leadership. Most chairmen have been strong leaders. The distribution of power also depends on the particular issue. The FDIC, for example, has influence on matters like banks' capital-asset ratios, but not on monetary policy.

The chairman's power is based on five sources. First, as the head of the Board, his or her opinions and statements carry great weight with the public. Second, a number of decisions do not even come before the Board, but are made by the chairman solely as the Board's representative, and it is the chairman, not the whole Board, who meets with the president. Third, the chairman arranges the agenda and exercises the leadership role at the Board's meetings. Fourth, the chairman maintains supervisory powers over the Board's staff members, who therefore have a greater incentive to please the chairman than

Table 11.1   An Estimate of the Distribution of Power over Federal Reserve Policy

Insiders	Percent	Outsiders	Percent
Chairman	45%	Administration	35%
Staff of the Board and FOMC	25	Congress	25
Other governors	20	Public directly*	20
Federal Reserve Banks	10	Financial interests	10
		Foreign interests	5
		Other regulatory agencies	5
Total	100		100

*Includes the press, economists, lobbyists, and general public.
Source: Sherman Maisel, *Managing the Dollar* (New York: Norton, 1973), p. 110.

---

[2] Sherman Maisel, *Managing the Dollar* (New York: Norton, 1973), pp. 109–11.

other Board members. Essentially, the staff works for the chairman, not the Board. So in trying to debate with the chairman, the other governors are severely limited by a lack of staff support. Finally, the foregoing powers of the chairman give him or her an aura of authority, which tends to induce other Board members to vote the way the chairman does. But the chairman does not always get his or her way. For example, in 1986 Chairman Volcker was out-voted at a Board meeting, and even though a compromise was worked out a few days later, this was widely considered a blow to Chairman Volcker's stature.

The Federal Reserve's Constituency

To refer to the Fed's *constituency* is to use the term in a broader sense than one would when applying it to the geographic constituency of a member of Congress. When applying it to a governmental agency, one generally means that this agency views itself as speaking for a particular group and tries to represent this group's interests within the government. In return, the agency receives political support from its constituency. As former Secretary of the Treasury George Shultz put it: "Advocacy government is part of our unwritten constitution."[3] The Department of Agriculture, for example, acts as a voice for farmers and receives support from congressional representatives from rural districts. The Department of Labor has a similar relation to labor unions. This does not mean that these agencies necessarily disregard the public interest; rather, the public interest is supposed to emerge as a consensus of the views of various groups as expressed by "their" government agencies. Admittedly, the view of the public interest that does emerge can too often be summarized as "more for me," and the power of various groups is not always appropriate.

It seems plausible that the Fed views itself as having two major, and perhaps two minor, partly overlapping constituencies. One major constituency is obvious: it consists of banks and the financial community. The other major constituency is less obvious: it is composed of the fixed-income groups who stand to lose by inflation. Several government agencies (such as the Departments of Agriculture and Labor) represent producer groups, who want higher prices. So someone is needed to represent those who lose when producers raise their prices or the government adopts excessively expansionary policies. The Fed has assumed some of this task, at least in the sense of worrying more about inflation than most other government agencies do. Whether it has worried sufficiently about inflation or has sometimes become an engine for inflation is another issue.

Two other, though minor, constituencies that the Fed *may* have are the financial press and academic economists. Since the Fed is in the public eye so much, it obviously wants to get a favorable reception by the press and also by academic economists, who, at times, have been sharply critical of it, both in their writings and in their testimony before Congress. But it is hard to say to what extent, if any, the Fed's policy has been influenced by its concern about the opinions of these two groups.

---

[3] "Reflections on Political Economy," *Journal of Finance,* 29 (May 1974), 325.

FINANCES OF THE FEDERAL RESERVE SYSTEM

The outstanding stock of the Federal Reserve Banks is owned by its member banks, who receive a fixed 6 percent dividend on this stock. The fact that the member banks own all the stock of the Federal Reserve Banks is sometimes taken to mean that they own these Federal Reserve Banks. This is wrong. Ownership means two things: the right to appropriate all the net earnings and the right to control the property. Member banks have no claim on the residual earnings of the Federal Reserve Banks. They get their 6 percent dividend, regardless of the Fed's earnings. Similarly, they have *very* little control over the Federal Reserve Banks and none over the Board of Governors. Hence, they do *not* control the Fed.

The net earnings of the Federal Reserve Banks come from the securities they hold and, to a much smaller extent, from interest on the loans they make. They also charge financial institutions for the services they perform for them, such as clearing checks. But where do the funds that the Fed invests in securities come from? The main source is the issuance of Federal Reserve notes, that is, the currency notes that we carry in our wallets. Suppose the Fed prints $1 million of Federal Reserve notes and ships them to a bank whose customers ask for them. It then debits the bank's reserve account. If it wants to keep total bank reserves constant, it then offsets this decline in bank reserves by buying $1 million of securities in the open market. Hence, on its books its liabilities for outstanding Federal Reserve notes are up by $1 million, but so are its government security holdings. Apart from this, the Fed can buy securities in a way akin to deposit creation by banks. It simply pays for the securities by giving banks credit on their reserve accounts. Similarly, when the Fed makes loans to member banks, it just writes up their reserve account.[4]

Out of the earnings on this capital the Fed pays its dividends on member bank stock (which amount to about 1 percent or so of the Fed's income). After taking care of this item, it places a relatively small amount into its surplus account and turns the great bulk of net earnings over to the U.S. Treasury. There is no law requiring the Fed to do this, though, if it did not, there would soon be one.

FEDERAL RESERVE INDEPENDENCE

The Fed has a great deal of independence, much more than other government agencies. While the president, with the advice and consent of the Senate, appoints new governors as vacancies occur and chooses a chairman, once these selections are made, *officially* the president does not have any more power over them. Once appointed, they can ignore the president's wishes. This may well happen because new governors tend to become co-opted by the Fed, that is, to

---

[4] It may seem that when a member bank deposits reserves with the Fed, the Fed obtains funds, which it can invest and hence earn interest on. But the total amount of currency and reserves is fixed. Assuming that there is no change in the amount of currency held by the public, then the only way one bank can obtain more reserves is for another bank's reserves to decline. Hence, there is no change in the total reserves, and therefore in the earning assets, held by the Federal Reserve.

accept the prevailing Fed view. Governors rarely dissent from the Fed's line, at least in public. When Governor Nancy Teeters was being considered for appointment to the Board, she told the Board's chairman, Arthur Burns: "Arthur, you don't want someone on the Board with my liberal background." Burns replied: "Don't worry, Nancy, within six months, you will think just like a central banker."[5]

In a formal sense, Congress can control the Fed. The Fed has been set up to be a "creature of Congress," as Congress likes to remind it. But Congress is not organized to exercise day-to-day control over it, nor, under present legislation, does it have the right to do so. Thus, while the Fed reports its targets for the growth rate of the money stock to Congress, *in principle* it could ignore any congressional reactions to these targets.

Actual Independence

But, as usual, the formal situation as set forth in legislation is only part of the story. Actually, the president and Congress have considerable influence over the Fed. One source of the president's influence is moral suasion; the governors are reluctant to oppose the views of the one person elected by the whole nation; they go along if they feel they can do so without dereliction of duty. Second, the Fed is continually active in Congress, trying to obtain certain legislation that would help it in regulating banks or trying to block other legislation. It wants the support of the president in these legislative struggles and hence has an incentive to keep on good terms with him or her. Third, the chairman wants the president's goodwill, so that when the president appoints a new governor, it will be someone to the chairman's liking. As John Woolley, a leading authority on the politics of the Fed, has put it: "Rather than conclude that the presidents generally get the monetary policy they want, it would be more accurate to say that only infrequently are presidents extremely unhappy with the monetary policy they get."[6]

In general, the Fed cannot take the continuation of its independence for granted. It is to some extent a prisoner of its independence. It may have to give in on some issues to prevent Congress from taking away some of its independence. But the influence of the president and Congress should not be overestimated; on some issues the Fed can mobilize an extraordinarily powerful lobby of bankers in each congressional district to pressure Congress into preserving its independence. Congress, by and large, doubts its ability to challenge the Federal Reserve, in part because the Fed claims to possess esoteric knowledge about monetary policy and in part because the Fed claims that it is our protector from explosive inflation. Moreover, members of Congress would reap little political benefit from becoming informed enough about monetary policy to challenge the Fed in a sophisticated way. Demagogic attacks on the Fed may win plaudits from some people back home, but the Fed can usually show that these attacks are naive. However, at times when sharply rising interest rates upset many voters, the Fed is vulnerable to congressional pressures.

[5] Cited in William Greider, *Secrets of the Temple* (New York: Simon & Schuster, 1987), pp. 73–74.

[6] John Woolley, *Monetary Politics* (New York: Cambridge University Press, 1984), p. 111.

Delineating the Fed's Autonomy

Just how much independence the Fed has is hard to pin down because its independence is, in part, a matter of tradition and accepted practice and not something one can look up in the statutes. One way of judging its independence is to look at what happened in those cases in which the White House and the Fed were in conflict. Who won? The trouble is that many cases of conflict are hashed out in private meetings over breakfast or lunch, and such meetings do not leave a trace unless someone knocks over a coffee cup. There are only a few examples of major conflicts that are public knowledge, so we have to go back quite a ways in history to get a sample.

One such example comes from the early 1950s. During World War II and for a few years thereafter the Fed had agreed to maintain the prices of government securities at par; this meant that it could not allow interest rates to rise. The Fed became more and more dissatisfied with this arrangement, which was feeding inflation, so in April 1951 it revolted, and despite strong opposition from President Truman and the Treasury, it raised interest rates and let government securities fall below par. President Truman was furious. There was a big uproar. But the Fed had the support of Congress, the financial community, economists, and informed opinion in general. President Truman did not get his way. The Fed and the Treasury settled on an agreement (called the "Accord") that allowed the Fed significantly more leeway to set interest rates than it had had before.

Another example comes from the mid-sixties. In 1965 President Johnson urged the Fed not to raise the discount rate. The Fed went ahead and did so anyway. President Johnson was furious. He called Fed chairman William McChesney Martin down to his Texas ranch for a tongue-lashing. But the Fed did not reverse itself, and the higher discount rate stuck. Perhaps the tongue-lashing prevented the Fed from raising the discount rate subsequently; that we cannot know.

In 1967 when Chairman Martin's term as chairman came up for renewal, President Johnson wanted the Fed to adopt a more expansionary policy. Because he was afraid that he might not be reappointed, Chairman Martin went along.

In October 1979, the Fed considered adopting a new operating procedure that would allow interest rates to fluctuate much more. The White House staff was adamantly opposed, although President Carter himself did not get involved in the dispute. The Fed then adopted the new procedure. Had the president been strongly opposed to the procedure, it is not at all clear what the Fed would have done because the FOMC itself was split on the issue.

More recently, in March 1994, when President Clinton invited Fed chairman Greenspan to a White House meeting, this was interpreted as White House pressure on the Fed to keep interest rates low, and hence as a threat to Fed independence. Bond prices fell. At least some observers believed that the meeting made it more likely that the Fed would raise interest rates to show that it was not under the president's thumb.

Thus Federal Reserve independence is a subtle thing. To say that the Fed is independent is wrong. And so is to say that it has no independence.

Fortunately for the Fed, such periods of rapidly rising interest rates usually pass before its opponents can mobilize public opinion.

The Fed fosters its independence from Congress and from political pressures in general by providing little information. Compared to foreign central banks, the Fed is much more open, but that is not saying much. One of the necessary skills of a Fed chairman is the ability to evade giving clear answers. Chairman Greenspan once remarked: "Since I have become a central banker I've learned to mumble with great incoherence. If I seem unduly clear to you, you must have misunderstood what I have said."[7] At a congressional hearing former Senator William Proxmire once told former Chairman William McChesney Martin:

> I have the greatest respect for your ability, and I think that you are an outstanding and competent person, and everybody agrees with that, but the fact is, that when you try to come down and discuss this in meaningful specific terms, it is like nailing a custard pie to the wall. . . . And frankly, Mr. Martin, without specific goals, criteria, guidelines, it is impossible to exercise any Congressional oversight over you, and I think you know it.[8]

All in all, as Sherman Maisel has written:

> . . . independence is both ill-defined and circumscribed. . . . Although no legal method exists for the President to issue a directive to the System, its independence in fact is not so great that it can use monetary policy as a club or threat to veto Administration action. The System's latitude for action is rather circumscribed. . . . In any showdown, no nonrepresentative group such as the Fed can or should be allowed to pursue its own goals in opposition to those of the elected officials.[9]

The Subtlety of the Fed's Independence

Here is an illustration of how ill-defined the Fed's independence is. Officially, the extent to which the Fed is independent is set by law. Since Congress changes the relevant laws infrequently, one might expect that the extent of the Fed's independence is constant. But the laws only set the framework. As we mentioned above, both tradition and unfolding events play an important role in determining the actual degree of the Fed's independence.

In 1987 the Fed for a short time lost much of its control over monetary policy. This came about not because the law was changed. Instead, the United States made an informal agreement with other industrialized nations to keep the value of the dollar on the foreign-exchange market stable. As will be explained later, a stable exchange rate of the dollar requires the Fed to keep interest rates and the growth rate of money at certain levels. It is the Treasury Department, not the Federal Reserve, that determines what the particular exchange rate of the dollar should be. Hence, by agreeing with other coun-

---

[7] *Wall Street Journal,* September 22, 1987, p. 31.

[8] Cited in John Culbertson, *Full Employment or Stagnation?* (New York: McGraw-Hill, 1964), pp. 154–55.

[9] Sherman Maisel, *Managing the Dollar,* pp. 24, 136.

tries to keep the exchange rate of the dollar within a certain range, the Treasury, in effect, took over much of the control over monetary policy. But since situations in which monetary policy focuses on keeping the exchange rate fixed are rare, the Treasury dominates monetary policy only rarely.

INDEPENDENCE: PROS AND CONS

Does the Fed have too much or too little independence? From time to time this question becomes a political issue, and it *may* sooner or later become a major issue in a presidential election. Political debates about the Fed's independence do not result so much from fundamental disagreements about the proper role of the Fed in the government (an issue that evokes little public excitement) as from strong disagreement about whatever policy the Fed is following. One way to change the Fed's direction is to bring it under control of those in Congress or the administration who oppose its policy. Another way is to frighten the Fed enough so that it will change its policy. Thus, in 1982, when interest rates were extraordinarily high, several bills to reduce the Fed's independence gained much support in Congress. Shortly thereafter the Fed changed its policy, perhaps in part because of these threats.

We discuss the pros and cons of monetary policies in Part Four. Here we will discuss more general arguments about the Fed's independence. Although these arguments sound abstract, they are relevant to what may sooner or later become a major political issue.

The Case for Independence

There are several arguments on both sides of the independence issue. Supporters of independence argue that monetary policy, and hence the value of the dollar, is too important and too complex an issue to be left to the play of political forces. As former Chairman of the Board Martin put it:

> An independent Federal Reserve System is the primary bulwark of the free-enterprise system and when it succumbs to the pressures of political expediency or the dictates of private interest, the groundwork of sound money is undermined.[10]

In this view the political process is myopic: being overly concerned with the next election, it overplays the importance of short-term benefits and hence is unwilling to make those hard and unpopular decisions—such as tolerating more unemployment in the short run—that are needed to obtain the long-run benefits of a stable price level. Moreover, politicians, if they can, are likely to use the central bank to finance increased government expenditures without raising taxes.[11] In addition, pressure groups impart an inflationary bias to

---

[10] Quoted in A. Jerome Clifford, *The Independence of the Federal Reserve System* (Philadelphia: University of Pennsylvania Press, 1965), p. 18.

[11] The way this works is as follows. Inflation raises the demand for (nominal) currency, since the public needs more currency to pay the higher prices. As the Fed issues more currency, its earnings rise and it turns them over to the Treasury. In addition, real interest payments on the federal debt decline, so that the government has more money available for other expenditures.

government policy. Hence an independent central bank largely removed from political pressures is needed to ensure justice to those who lose from inflation.

In addition, even if the politicians' desire for a certain monetary policy accurately reflects the public's wishes, it is not obvious that the Fed should necessarily go along. One might argue that the public has better things to do with its time than study economics (bizarre as that seems to us). It therefore delegates certain decisions to the Fed. Specifically, the public suffers from what William Poole of Brown University has referred to as the "number one problem syndrome"—during a recession all that seems to matter is to lower the unemployment rate, while during an inflationary expansion, reducing the inflation rate is all that matters. But an overly expansionary policy to fight unemployment ultimately results in too much inflation, and a restrictive policy that lowers the inflation rate also raises unemployment temporarily. Hence, the public may well prefer to have the Fed pay less attention to its temporary policy preferences.

Furthermore, for a reason discussed in Chapter 26, central banks are tempted to aim at a level of unemployment that is too low to be feasible in the long run. The unfortunate result is a higher inflation rate with no matching decline in unemployment. In addition, as discussed in the appendix to this chapter, there is the danger that a politically influenced central bank will try to overstimulate the economy before elections. It is widely believed that an independent central bank is less subject to these temptations.

It is therefore not all that surprising that the statistical evidence for developed countries shows that those countries with relatively independent central banks have a lower inflation rate (see Figure 11.3A). That does not necessarily imply a cause-and-effect relationship. It *might* be the case that countries that are inflation averse not only have lower inflation rates, but have also decided to give their central banks much independence. Even so, the negative correlation between inflation and central-bank independence is, at the least, consistent with the theoretical arguments that central-bank independence leads to a lower inflation rate. And as Figure 11.3B shows, this lower inflation rate does *not* come at the cost of a lower growth rate of output.

The Case against Independence

Critics of central-bank independence reject these arguments. They believe that it is fundamentally undemocratic to say that elected officials should not be trusted to judge monetary policy. To be sure, monetary policy involves difficult decisions that need a long-run point of view, but the same thing is true of foreign policy or defense policy. Moreover, for better or worse, the public holds the president responsible for the economic conditions that result from *all* the policies followed during his or her administration. Hence, the president should have control over monetary policy, one of the most important of these policies.

In addition, some economists maintain that the Fed has not used its independence well and therefore should be deprived of it. At times it has tolerated inflation, as in the late 1960s and 1970s, and in other years, the 1930s for

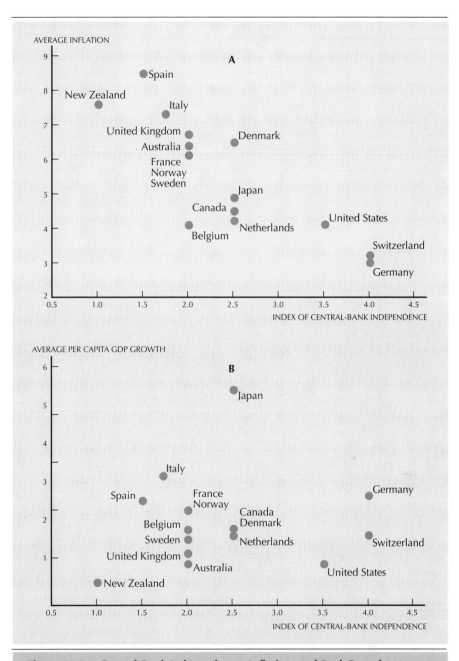

Figure 11.3   Central-Bank Independence, Inflation, and Real Growth. There
was a strong, negative correlation between central-bank independence and the average
inflation rate from 1955 to 1988. But central-bank independence is essentially
uncorrelated with the growth rate of real GDP. **Source:** Alberto Alesina and Lawrence
Summers, "Central Bank Independence and Macroeconomic Performance," *Journal of
Money, Credit and Banking,* 25 (May 1993), 155–56.

example, it has had a deflationary bias and allowed too much unemployment to develop. In addition, its independence has not really removed it from politics. Instead, to defend both its actions and its independence, it has had to become a political animal. Moreover, its independence allows the Fed too much leeway to indulge in that characteristic weakness of a bureaucracy, continuous overemphasis on narrow, parochial interests.

Finally, monetary and fiscal policies should be integrated, and adequate integration cannot be achieved, the opponents of Fed independence claim, merely by a process of informal consultation. Rather, it requires that the Fed be part of the administration. Giving the president control over the Fed need not necessarily weaken its influence and might even strengthen it. If it were part of the administration, the Fed's counsel would then be better heeded by the administration.

Possible Compromises

These arguments for and against the Fed's independence may give the misleading impression that the choice is between two irreconcilable extremes. But this is not so. Even if the Fed were to lose its formal independence and become part of the administration, there would still be at least an attempt to keep it out of partisan politics. Moreover, as just pointed out, the independence that the Fed currently has is far from complete.

On a more practical level, the debate is not between those who want the Fed to be totally independent and those who want it to have no independence at all. Instead, it focuses on proposals for relatively minor reductions in the Fed's independence. For example, one proposal would make the chairman's term of office coincide better with the president's so that each president could appoint his or her own chairman a year after taking office. Other proposals would shorten the term of the governors or eliminate the FOMC and shift its work to the Board of Governors. A more radical proposal would put the Secretary of the Treasury on the FOMC, and an even more radical one would make the Fed turn all its gross earnings over to the Treasury and finance its activities through congressional appropriations. This would give Congress much more control over the Fed.

OTHER CENTRAL BANKS

As we mentioned previously nearly all countries have central banks; the prime exception is Hong Kong, where a commercial bank undertakes some central-banking functions. The three most important central banks, apart from the Federal Reserve, are the Bank of Japan, the German Bundesbank, and the Bank of England. The Bank of Japan and the Bundesbank are important, not just because of the size of their countries' economies, but also because the successful anti-inflationary policies that they have followed have made them models for many other central banks. The Bank of England is important because London is a leading center of international finance.

The degree of independence held by any given central bank varies widely. Among the major central banks, the most independent are the Bundesbank, the Federal Reserve, and *perhaps* the Bank of Japan. The Bundesbank has a legal mandate to prevent inflation. In contrast, the Bank of England is under the control of the British cabinet; the Chancellor of the Exchequer (whose office more or less resembles that of the U.S. Secretary of the Treasury) can give it binding orders. Among the smaller central banks the Swiss National Bank and the Austrian National Bank have great independence.

The countries of the European Community plan to establish a European central bank by January 1, 1998, a target date they may or may not achieve. According to the plan, this bank will carry out a single monetary policy for all the EC countries. Such a joint monetary policy is needed, because the EC countries want to maintain fixed exchange rates among their currencies as a way of facilitating trade and investment. As will become apparent later in this book, this requires that they all have essentially the same inflation rate, and that, in turn, requires similar or at least coordinated monetary policies. The best way to ensure that different countries do not follow divergent monetary policies is to vest monetary policy in a single, supranational central bank.

If all works well, the EC countries may eventually go beyond having a single monetary policy and use a common currency. Whether this will happen is hard to tell. It is also possible that some countries will consider the European central bank's policy to be inappropriate and will therefore decide to go their own way, even though this means both abrogating a treaty and sacrificing the fixed value of their currency in terms of other European currencies. Indeed, in 1992 the move to a common central bank had a severe setback, when European monetary policies diverged sharply and some countries devalued.

The European central bank will presumably look much like the Federal Reserve in one respect: it will have a fairly decentralized structure. Indeed, the proposed central bank is sometimes referred to informally as the "Euro-Fed." However, it will differ from the Fed in one important way. It will have something the Fed does not have: the single primary goal of price stability. The Euro-Fed will also be much influenced by the model of the Bundesbank, because of the Bundesbank's reputation as an anti-inflationary central bank.

In general, countries that in recent years have set up new central banks or have modified existing central banks have tended to give them considerable independence. This is due, at least in part, to a growing belief that the primary goal of a central bank should be price stability and that independent central banks are better able to achieve this goal.

SUMMARY

1 Central banks are not banks in the conventional sense; they are institutions concerned with managing the money stock, preventing financial panics by acting as lenders of last resort, and performing other governmental tasks.

2 Central banks perform services, such as holding reserves and clearing checks for banks, and also act as the government's bank, doing such chores as issuing currency. Central banks can create reserves for the banking system.

3 The Federal Reserve System has become more centralized since its establishment in 1913. Its current organization is shown in Figure 11.2.

4 Each Federal Reserve Bank has nine directors chosen in a way that provides checks and balances. While formally the Federal Reserve Banks are "owned" by member banks, this does not give member banks ownership in any meaningful sense.

5 The Board of Governors consists of seven members appointed by the president. Together with five Reserve Bank presidents, they make up the Federal Open-Market Committee (FOMC). This committee controls the Fed's most important tool, open-market operations.

6 Within the Federal Reserve, the chairman has a great deal of power; among outsiders, the administration and Congress have the most power over the Fed. The major constituencies of the Fed are the financial community and fixed-income groups.

7 The Fed's independence is circumscribed. It prefers to go along with the president's overall views on monetary policy. The president's power arises in large part from moral suasion. There are numerous arguments for and against Fed independence.

8 The most important foreign central banks are the German Bundesbank, the Bank of Japan, and the Bank of England. The European Community countries are currently in the process of setting up a common central bank. Most foreign central banks have less independence than the Fed, but there is a trend toward more central-bank independence and toward giving central banks a price-stabilization goal.

KEY TERMS

central bank	Federal Reserve Banks
lender of last resort	Board of Governors
chore functions	FOMC

QUESTIONS AND EXERCISES

*1 Discuss the extent to which this statement is true for the Federal Reserve System: The term *central bank* is a misnomer; it is nothing like a bank.

2 Why do countries have central banks?

*3 What does the phrase *lender of last resort* mean?

4 Discuss the chore functions of the Federal Reserve.

*5 What monetary policy functions are carried out by:
   a. the Federal Reserve Banks
   b. the Board of Governors
   c. the FOMC

6 Discuss critically: "The Federal Reserve Banks have nothing at all to do with monetary policy; they only undertake the chore functions of the Federal Reserve System."

*7 The Federal Reserve System is an example of a system of checks and balances. Describe these checks and balances.

8 What does it mean to say that the Federal Reserve has constituencies? What are they?

9 Write an essay either defending or criticizing central-bank independence.

FURTHER READING

CUKIERMAN, ALEX. *Central Bank Strategy, Credibility, and Independence.* Cambridge, Mass.: MIT Press, 1992. A comprehensive, advanced treatise.

GALBRAITH, JOHN A. *The Economics of Banking Operations.* Montreal: McGill University Press, 1963. Chapter 7 gives a useful and compact discussion of central banking.

HAVRILESKY, THOMAS. *The Pressures on American Monetary Policy.* Boston: Kluwer Academic Publishers, 1992. A detailed discussion of political pressures on the Federal Reserve.

KANE, EDWARD. "External Pressures and the Operations of the Fed," in *The Political Economy of Domestic and International Monetary Relations,* eds. Raymond Lombra and Willard Witte. Iowa City: University of Iowa Press, 1982. A superb discussion of the Fed as a political animal.

KAUFMAN, GEORGE. "Lender of Last Resort: A Contemporary Perspective," *Journal of Financial Services Research,* 5 (October 1991), 95–110. An evaluation of the appropriate way to conduct a basic central-bank function.

MAISEL, SHERMAN. *Managing the Dollar.* New York: Norton, 1973. Provides important insights into Fed behavior by a former member of the Board of Governors.

MAYER, THOMAS, ed. *The Political Economy of American Monetary Policy.* New York: Cambridge University Press, 1990. Many of the essays in this book discuss the Fed's independence.

SYLLA, RICHARD. "The Autonomy of Monetary Authorities: The Case of the U.S. Federal Reserve System," in *The Central Bank's Independence in Historical Perspective,* ed. Gianni Toniolo. New York: Walter de Gruyter, 1988, pp. 17–38. A good discussion of the evolution of Fed independence.

WOOLLEY, JOHN. "The Politics of Monetary Policy: A Critical Review," *Journal of Public Policy,* 14 (January–March 1994), 57–85. An excellent survey.

Also note: The Federal Reserve Banks publish reviews of their research findings and these are available free of charge. Requests for *Reviews* should be addressed as follows:

Bank and Public Information Center
Federal Reserve Bank of Boston
600 Atlantic Avenue
Boston, Massachusetts 02106

Bank and Public Relations Department
Federal Reserve Bank of Richmond
P.O. Box 27622
Richmond, Virginia 23261

Public Information Department
Federal Reserve Bank of New York
33 Liberty Street
New York, New York 10045

Information Center
Federal Reserve Bank of Atlanta
104 Marietta Street, N.W.
Atlanta, Georgia 30303

Public Information Center
Federal Reserve Bank of Chicago
P.O. Box 834
Chicago, Illinois 60690

Office of Public Information
Federal Reserve Bank of Minneapolis
250 Marquette Avenue
Minneapolis, Minnesota 55480

Public Information Department
Federal Reserve Bank of St. Louis
P.O. Box 442
St. Louis, Missouri 63166

Public Information
Federal Reserve Bank of Kansas City
925 Grand Avenue
Kansas City, Missouri 64198

Public Services Department
Federal Reserve Bank of Philadelphia
P.O. Box 66
Philadelphia, Pennsylvania 19105

Public Affairs Department
Federal Reserve Bank of Dallas
Station K
Dallas, Texas 75222

Publications Section
Research Department
Federal Reserve Bank of Cleveland
P.O. Box 6387
Cleveland, Ohio 44101

Public Information Section
Federal Reserve Bank of San Francisco
P.O. Box 7702
San Francisco, California 94120

APPENDIX: EXPLAINING CENTRAL-BANK BEHAVIOR

What matters much more than the way central banks are organized is how they behave. But a central bank's behavior, unlike its organization, cannot be understood just by reading the applicable laws. It has to be surmised by looking at what the central bank has done in the past and by applying the theories that explain behavior to central banks. But there is a problem in applying these theories. When dealing with firms, one can, at least as a first approximation, assume that they try to maximize profit and build an explanation of their behavior on that basis. Similarly, one can explain much of the behavior of households by assuming that they try to maximize utility, which is a positive function of their income and leisure. But what does a government agency such as a central bank maximize? This is by no means an easy question to answer, and the answer may well differ in different countries and at different times. We will therefore take up five explanations of central-bank behavior, two of which consider the central bank as essentially independent and autonomous and three of which treat it as carrying out the orders of its political masters.

The Public-Interest Explanation

In this view the central bank acts as a skilled technician who tries to maximize the public's welfare. It accepts as its goals the value judgments and preferences of the public (judiciously blending majority and minority views) and tries its best to achieve these goals. The flavor of this theory is expressed well by a phrase used by one of the founders of the Federal Reserve System, Senator Carter Glass, when he referred to the Fed as a "Supreme Court of finance."

One can defend this theory by pointing out that the president has a strong incentive to appoint governors who are dedicated to the public interest. After all, the President gets blamed if a recession occurs or if inflation accelerates. Once they are appointed, the governors have an incentive to follow the right policies, both because, like most people, they want the public to be better off and because they are concerned with their own reputations. Moreover, there is little reason for them to do anything except serve the public interest; their nominal salaries are fixed and do not go up if they adopt bad policies. To be sure, sometimes what is good for the Fed is bad for the country, but why should the governors prefer the Fed's welfare to the country's?

The Public-Choice Explanation

Another theory of how government agencies behave, somewhat misleadingly called "public-choice theory," sees government officials as driven by self-interest and as trying to maximize not the public's welfare, but their personal welfare and the welfare of their own agencies. To be sure, they do not ignore the public's welfare entirely, but in many cases of conflict, they give preference to their agencies' welfare. This does not require that government officials consciously put the interests of their agencies above the public's interests. All that is needed is that they make the common mistake of overestimating the importance of their agencies and the good they can do. As a result, they ambitiously promote their agencies and try to enhance their agencies' powers. And the actions of the officials of a government agency, taken collectively, are the actions of that agency. This theory was developed, in large part, to explain why governmental agencies usually try to increase their budgets. But since the Fed sets its own budget, this theory's direct applicability to the Fed is more controversial. However, it can be reformulated in terms of the Fed's trying to increase its power, autonomy, and prestige.

Assuming that the Fed has such bureaucratic motives, how would one expect it to behave? First, it would, whenever possible, avoid conflicts with powerful people who could harm it. In practical terms this means that it would, for example, be tempted to follow expansionary policies that in the short run would meet Congress' and the administration's wish to keep interest rates down. Second, one would expect it to try to maintain its power and autonomy: to be unwilling, for example, to give up any of its policy tools, even those tools that are not useful. Third, it would be unlikely to admit that it had made mistakes in the past and, in general, would limit the information it provides the public.

A fourth way for an organization to protect itself from criticism is to act myopically, that is, to pay a great deal of attention to the direct and immediate impact of its policies and to pay too little attention to the longer-run or less direct damage these policies may do. This is so because the organization is more likely to be blamed for those bad effects of its policies that are immediately visible and clearly its fault than for those bad effects that could be the result of many other causes.

Finally, the Fed would have an incentive to announce vague targets, so that if it missed its target this would not be obvious. In any case, many central bankers tend to think of their task as an art that is inherently vague and is practiced better by relying on the intuition of knowledgeable people than on rigorous analysis. For example, the preeminent central banker of the pre-World War II period, Sir Montague Norman, was once asked the reason for a decision he had made. He replied: "Reasons, Mr. Chairman? I don't have reasons. I have instincts."[12]

One can readily find instances in which the Fed behaves in the ways predicted by public-choice theory. For example, to avoid public scrutiny, the Fed is reluctant to reveal some information that would draw media attention. But these are often essentially minor matters. The more serious and much more controversial question is whether the major decisions that the Fed makes about monetary policy are significantly influenced by its self-interest as contrasted with the public's interest, and if so, whether it matters. After all, if the Fed makes the right decisions because it realizes that a well-functioning economy is in its own self-interest because it raises its power and prestige, then it does not matter whether it is motivated by its self-interest or by the public's interest.

---

[12] Quoted in Andrew Boyle, *Montague Norman* (London: Cassel, 1967), p. 327.

The Political-Business-Cycle Explanation

The two explanations we have considered so far treat the central bank as though it had complete autonomy. The three alternative explanations deny that the central bank has much independence, and see it as carrying out the wishes of elected officials.

One possibility here is the occurrence of a **political business cycle.** This is a situation in which the president induces the Fed to adopt an overly expansionary policy before an election, so that interest rates and unemployment are low as election day approaches. After the election the Fed has to become restrictive, and interest rates and unemployment rise. But voters forget this before the next election comes around.

Fortunately, such political business cycles are not as likely to occur as might seem at first glance. They require several conditions. First, voters must be influenced by recent economic conditions, rather than by conditions shortly after the previous election. This seems plausible. Second, a political business cycle benefits a President only if the voters are unaware of it. Many economists object, rightly or wrongly, that this is inconsistent with rational behavior, and therefore implausible.

Third, the Fed must be willing to do the president's bidding. But will it? Much of the president's influence over the Fed is moral suasion. But it is hard to argue on the basis of moral suasion when asking the Fed to trick the public into voting for you. Furthermore, the Fed's own interests tell it not to generate political business cycles. Its prestige and hence some of its influence derive largely from its reputation as an objective, technical agency, removed from the political process. Why should it risk this reputation? Moreover, if it generates a political business cycle and the incumbent president loses all the same, the new president will hardly be well disposed toward it. It could also lose support in Congress. So, unless the Fed perceives the opposition candidate to be a threat to it, it has an incentive to do as little as possible before an election, to lie low, and to try to keep out of the news.

Fourth, for a political business cycle to work, the Fed would have to be able to time the impact of its policies well. Otherwise such policies would backfire. Assume, for example, that the Fed becomes expansionary too early. The expansionary policy might then create inflation and rising interest rates before election day and therefore hurt the president. Conversely, if it waits too long, the decline in unemployment might appear only after the election, and thus be too late. Since the lag in the effect of monetary policy is hard to estimate, it may simply not be possible for the Fed to play the political-business-cycle game effectively. Bad intentions are not enough.

Whether political business cycles occur is an empirical issue, so it might seem that close analysis of the data could provide the answer. But empirical testing of the hypothesis that political business cycles exist is difficult. It is not clear precisely what hypothesis is to be tested. Is it that there have been political business cycles before every presidential election, before some elections, or before at least one presidential election? The "every election" hypothesis is clearly wrong. The "at least one" hypothesis does not lend itself readily to econometric testing because it refers to a single case. The "some" hypothesis is hard to test because there have been only ten presidential elections since 1953, hardly a large sample.[13]

On the whole, the empirical evidence does seem to suggest that political business cycles do occur. But it is important to note that the tests that have been undertaken have achieved mixed results: some have found evidence of political business cycles; others have found no evidence. One version of the political-business-cycle hypothesis that does seem to perform relatively well is a complex version that introduces fiscal policy. It states that prior to elections fiscal policy becomes more expansionary and the deficit increases. In response to a large deficit the Fed then increases its open-market purchases, and the money supply expands.

This discussion of political business cycles has dealt only with the United States. For some other countries the evidence for political business cycles may be stronger. For example, the 1994 Mexican peso crisis was due, at least in part, to the (officially independent) Mexican central bank adopting a much too expansionary policy before the election, and also postponing a necessary devaluation until after the election.

A Rational-Expectations Version of Political Business Cycles. There is a version of the political business cycle that is consistent with rational behavior by voters. In this theory, elections trigger fluctuations in employment, but not because anyone tries to hoodwink voters.

Suppose that there are two parties. One, called D, prefers a more expansionary monetary policy than its rival, called R. In unionized industries some long-run wage contracts have to be made before the election. Unions and management finally agree on a real wage, but do not know the appropriate money wage. If the Ds win, the inflation rate will be higher than if the Rs win, and so will the money wage that corresponds to the agreed-on real wage. But unions and management do not know who will win. Given risk aversion, the rational response to this problem is to use an estimate of the inflation rate that corresponds neither to the best guess of what the inflation rate will be if the Ds win nor to what it will be if the Rs win, but to something in between. Hence, they settle on a money wage that is between the one that is appropriate if the Ds win and the one that is appropriate if the Rs win.

Suppose now that the Ds win. The inflation rate is higher and real wages are lower than was anticipated when the contract was signed. With real wages now being lower, employment expands. Alternatively, assume that the Rs win. Real wages are now higher and hence employment falls.

This theory is ingenious. However, it may not be able to explain much of the observed changes in employment because only a relatively small proportion of U.S. workers are covered by long-run union contracts.

---

[13] The year 1953 is a good starting date because, as will be explained later, that is when the Fed became free to pursue a flexible policy.

Curbing Political Business Cycles

Political business cycles, if they do exist, are obviously undesirable. How can we minimize the probability that one will occur? There may seem to be an obvious answer: inform the public. Once voters know that the administration is trying to fool them by hyping the economy before an election, they will not be swayed by good conditions during an election year.

A nice idea, but it probably wouldn't work. Suppose voters have read about political business cycles and expect economic conditions to be unusually good in an election year. If so, they will tend to vote against the president if economic conditions are just average. Hence, the president has a strong incentive to hype the economy. And with the public thinking that the Fed is playing partisan politics, the Fed has no reputation to lose if it does so. So it is likely to go along with the President.

Only if the public could distinguish between those cases in which prosperity is due to a political business cycle and those in which it is due to other factors would increased public awareness of political business cycles help to prevent them. And that distinction is hard to make. There is usually much uncertainty about what the appropriate monetary policy is. If policy becomes more expansionary during an election year, some more or less plausible justification can usually be given. Voters would have to be able to evaluate economic forecasts and also be experts on monetary policy to know whether this justification is genuine or whether it is just a cover for a political business cycle. Unless the public can draw such a distinction, widespread knowledge that political business cycles may exist will make it more likely, not less likely, that they occur. "A little knowledge is a dang'rous thing."

Inflation as a Hidden Tax

Governments can enhance their popularity by raising expenditures or by cutting taxes. But being seen to raise taxes or the deficit reduces popularity. Hence governments have an incentive to garner additional revenue in ways that are hidden. Inflation provides such a way.

Inflation increases governmental revenue by increasing the demand for currency as prices and nominal income rise. As will be discussed in Chapter 13, the government gains revenue from the resulting **seigniorage.** A second reason the government gains from inflation is that part of the tax system is set in nominal terms, so that it is nominal capital gains and not just real capital gains that are taxed. Thus someone who buys stock for $1,000 when the price index is 100 and sells it for $2,000 when the price index stands at 200 is taxed on $1,000 of spurious capital gains. Similarly, lenders are taxed on spurious interest income as inflation raises the nominal, but not the real, interest rate.[14] The third reason inflation benefits the government is that the government is the biggest debtor in the economy, and as inflation rises, it lowers the real value of the government's outstanding debt.

[14] This is partially offset by the fact that many borrowers are able to treat interest payments as deductions from gross income. But the private sector is a net earner of interest due to its holdings of government securities and hence a net loser from the higher tax on real interest income.

These potential gains from inflation give the government an incentive to press the central bank into adopting inflationary policies. On the other hand, inflation or at least a rise in the inflation rate is widely unpopular. One might argue that a government therefore has more to lose than to gain from inflation. That would be an effective answer if the choice were a clear-cut one between, say, 3 percent and 5 percent inflation, all other things being equal. But that is not always the case. There is often much uncertainty about the direction the economy is going and therefore whether a more expansionary or a less expansionary policy is the appropriate stabilization policy. Since the government obtains revenue from inflation, one would expect it to pressure the Fed to be more expansionary than it would be if it were only concerned with stabilization. This may explain why our macropolicies have generally leaned more toward accepting the dangers of inflation than is consistent with the public's preferences.

The Partisan Monetary Policy Explanation

The final theory of central-bank behavior that we consider starts from the proposition that political parties differ in their relative concern about inflation and unemployment. In the United States, by and large, Republicans show relatively more concern about inflation, and Democrats about unemployment. In Europe, too, left-wing parties tend to focus on the evils of unemployment, while right-wing parties focus on the evils of inflation, though neither in the United States nor in Europe is this an ironclad rule.

This difference between right- and left-wing parties has been attributed to differences in the classes whose interests they represent. The well-to-do, who tend to support right-wing parties, have much to lose from inflation because they hold financial assets whose real value is reduced by inflation. They have

---

Explaining U.S. Macropolicies

Douglas Hibbs of Harvard University has provided empirical evidence for the partisan theory.* He shows that when Democratic administrations succeed Republican administrations, macropolicy tends to become more expansionary and output tends to rise. But, after some time, inflation also rises, and that causes a shift to more restrictive policies, which lower output later in the Democratic president's term. When a Republican administration takes over, the slowdown in aggregate demand is intensified and output contracts. The inflation rate then falls, so that in the second part of its term a Republican administration can shift to expansionary policies, which increase output.

Hibbs concludes that the Democrats are more likely to get into trouble with the voters because their overly ambitious attempt to lower unemployment creates inflation, while the Republicans are more likely to get into trouble because their preference for restrictive policies increases unemployment.

*Douglas Hibbs, "The Partisan Model of Macroeconomic Cycles: More Theory and Evidence for the United States," *Economics and Politics,* 6 (March 1994), 1–21.

less to lose from unemployment because highly skilled employees are less likely to lose their jobs than low-skilled ones. In contrast, lower-paid individuals who tend to support left-wing parties have more reason to fear unemployment, and, since they hold fewer financial assets, have less to fear from inflation. This class-interest view is probably more applicable to Europe than to the United States, since in Europe political parties are usually much more closely aligned with different economic classes than in the United States. And even for Europe one has to treat the class interpretation with some caution because, as we will show later, in the long run a rise in the inflation rate does not reduce unemployment, so that it helps low-income groups only temporarily (except insofar as higher government revenues lead to an expansion of certain welfare-state programs). Moreover, recessions and higher unemployment reduce profits, and thereby hurt the well-to-do, even if they do not lose their jobs. All the same, it is possible that low-income groups and their political parties perceive inflation to be in their interest, while the well-to-do and their political parties do not.[15]

Suppose the central bank gives in to such partisan pressures, and becomes more expansionary when the Democrats win the White House and Congress. Is this appropriate, or should the Fed be criticized for yielding to partisan influence? That is hard to say. Those who think that the Fed should be independent and act as a "Supreme Court of finance" might condemn it, while those who think that the Fed should not be so independent would commend it.

---

[15] One might also explain the greater emphasis of left-wing parties on unemployment and the greater emphasis of right-wing parties on inflation in another way. Left-wing parties believe that the government can improve the functioning of the economy; hence they support policies that lower unemployment. Right-wing parties doubt the efficacy of government policies.

TWO

THE
SUPPLY
OF
MONEY

The Measurement of Money

After you have read this chapter, you will be able to:

- Understand the distinction between the a priori and empirical definitions of money.
- Know the compositions of *M-1*, *M-2*, and *M-3*.
- Show some familiarity with alternative ways of measuring money.

In Chapter 1 we talked about money in general terms. Now, in preparation for discussing how money affects interest rates, employment, and prices, we have to be much more specific. So in this chapter we take up how money is measured. Chapter 13 explains how money is created, that is, how depository institutions can create several dollars of money for each additional dollar of reserves they receive. Chapter 14, the last chapter in Part Two, then explains where the reserves come from.

This chapter starts by discussing a dispute that is based on different views about what a definition of money should accomplish. We then discuss the specific items that should be included in money and conclude with a look at the accuracy of the data on money.

THE A PRIORI AND EMPIRICAL APPROACHES

There are two major approaches to defining money. The first, called the **a priori approach,** is rather philosophical and *focuses on the nature of money.* Those who use an a priori approach search for the particular characteristic that distinguishes money from other things and then define money in terms of this characteristic. This is the way we usually define something.

To the question "What is *the* distinguishing characteristic of money?" there is a simple answer: its medium-of-exchange function. This function is unique to money; nothing else is a general medium of exchange. By contrast, the store-of-wealth function is not unique to money; money shares this function with many other things, such as stocks, bonds, and diamonds. Hence, those who use the a priori approach define money as anything that is a generally accepted medium of exchange.[1]

The a priori definition of money has the advantage of providing, at least on an abstract level, a fairly clear-cut differentiation between those items that are money and those that are not. Items that can normally be used to make payments, such as checking deposits and traveler's checks, are money, while time deposits are not. Hence, this approach defines money as *M-1*.

While the a priori approach to defining money focuses on what is distinctive about it, that is, on the essence of money, the rival **empirical approach** *focuses on those attributes of money that make the money supply important for macroeconomic policy.* These are, first, that changes in the money supply have a major, and many economists would say dominating, impact on nominal income and, second, that the Fed can control the supply of money. The empirical definition of money therefore defines money not by any inherent characteristics, but as that liquid asset or collection of liquid assets that (1) has the most predictable influence on nominal income and (2) can be controlled by the Fed. If these two criteria are met best by two different measures of money, rather than by a single one, then a painful trade-off is required.

At one time it seemed that *M-1*, that is, currency and checkable deposits, had a closer relation to GDP than the broader measures of money that include time deposits *(M-2* and *M-3)* had. But in 1981–82 the old stable relationship between *M-1* and GDP disappeared, so that now the broader measures have a closer relationship to GDP than *M-1* does. Unfortunately, they are harder for the Fed to control than *M-1* is, so that we face a painful trade-off in trying to control GDP by changing the quantity of money. At present, the Federal Reserve uses the broader measures, and not *M-1*, to formulate policy. It is possible that in the future the relation between the broader measures of money and GDP will become less stable, or *M-1* or some other measure of money will again have a stable relation to GDP.

Which is better, the empirical or the a priori definition? Those who adhere to the a priori definition argue that the empirical definition is inadequate because it misses the essence of money and hence is subject to erratic shifts. Thus, it may define money as *M-1* at one time and as *M-2* at another time, depending on which of these shows a closer correlation with income. This seems arbitrary to supporters of the a priori definition. Supporters of the empirical definition, on the other hand, see nothing wrong with the definition of money changing from time to time.

Fortunately, this disagreement is unimportant. It is essentially a dispute about how to use the word *money* and is not a disagreement about how the economy operates. Thus, one could accept the a priori definition of money as *M-1*, and yet, since *M-2* has the more predictable effect on income, think and

---

[1] The standard-of-value function is also unique to money. But one cannot use it to measure money since it is an abstraction rather than a concrete unit. Thus, it is meaningless to ask, for example, whether the standard of value increased at a 5 percent rate last year.

Table 12.1   Measures of Money, January 1995

	Billions of Dollars (not seasonally adjusted)	Percent
M-1:		
Currency	$355.9	30.7%
Traveler's checks	8.1	.7
Demand deposits	388.8	33.6
Other checkable deposits	405.7	35.0
Total	$1,158.5	100.0
M-2:		
M-1	$1,158.5	31.9%
Small time deposits	832.7	22.9
Savings deposits and money-market deposit accounts	1,122.4	30.9
Money-market mutual funds*	393.3	10.8
Overnight repurchase agreements and overnight Eurodollars†	125.5	3.5
Total	$3,632.3	100.0
M-3:		
M-2	$3,632.3	83.8%
Large time deposits	359.9	8.3
Money-market mutual funds (institutions only)	192.4	4.4
Term repurchase agreements and term Eurodollars†	288.2	6.6
Technical adjustment‡	−138.1	−3.2
Total	$4,334.7	100.0

*General purpose and broker-dealer only.
†Eurodollars of U.S. residents only.
‡Includes adjustments for double counting.
Source: *Federal Reserve Bulletin,* April 1995, p. A14.

talk mainly about *M-2,* using some word other than *money*—say, *bread*—if one wants to talk about the essential characteristics of the medium of exchange.

M-1, sometimes called *narrow money,* was already defined in Chapter 1 in general terms. More specifically it consists of items that can be spent immediately, that is, currency, traveler's checks, and those deposits in commercial banks, mutual savings banks, and savings and loan associations against which unlimited checks can be written, as well as share drafts in credit unions.

As Table 12.1 shows, *M-2,* also called *broad money,* adds to *M-1* various items that are almost as liquid as checkable deposits. These are small time deposits, that is, time deposits of less than $100,000, which, at a small penalty, can usually be redeemed on demand, and money-market deposit accounts, which are time deposits against which a limited number of checks can be written. It also includes savings deposits, which can be cashed by presenting the passbook at the bank, and shares in money-market mutual funds (which often have a minimum value on checks that can be written on them), as well as overnight repurchase agreements and Eurodollar deposits, redeemable overnight.

Large time deposits cannot be redeemed, though they are often negotiable, which means that they can be sold in the secondary market and hence are similar to securities. Therefore they are included in *M-3*, but not in *M-2*. *M-3* also includes Eurodollars, repurchase agreements for longer than overnight, and shares in those money-market funds that deal with institutions but not with the general public.

Figure 12.1 shows the behavior of *M-1*, *M-2*, and *M-3* in recent years and illustrates the considerable divergence in their growth rates: it *does* make a difference how money is defined. For example, in 1993 *M-1* grew rapidly, but *M-2* grew slowly. Was monetary policy easy or tight?

AN ALTERNATIVE DEFINITION

The definitions currently used by the Fed are not etched in stone. Over time the financial system changes, new financial instruments are developed, and economists learn more about the relation between various measures of money

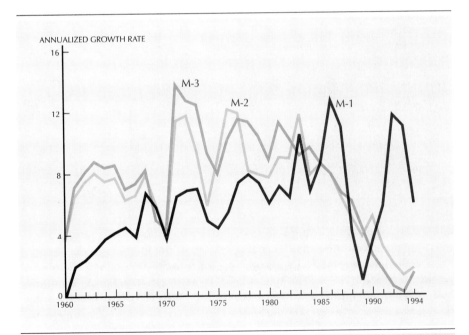

Figure 12.1   Growth Rates of *M-1*, *M-2*, and *M-3*. The growth rates of these measures of money have diverged substantially in recent years. **Source:** Federal Reserve Bank of St. Louis.

and income. All these may call for new measures of money. And from time to time, new measures of money are proposed, such as currency plus those deposits that do not pay interest, or *M-2* plus mutual funds that hold bonds. If such a measure continues to show a close correlation with GDP, it will gain support.

TWO SIMPLE BUT INAPPROPRIATE DEFINITIONS

Why not simply define money as currency? Such a definition would be simple and obvious, and what is more important, currency has a close relation to GDP. But there are some problems. First, economic theory tells us that when people find that they have more money, they will exchange some of this money for other things; that is, they will spend more. But why should you increase your expenditures on goods and services and on securities merely because you hold more currency, without your money holdings having changed? Wouldn't you just deposit the excess currency?

Why, then, do the data show such a close relation between currency holdings and GDP? The likely answer is that it is not the holding of currency that stimulates expenditures, but the other way around; when you plan to spend, you draw more currency out of the bank. The second problem with defining money as currency is that the Fed has no direct way of controlling currency holdings. Any depositor can go into a bank and withdraw or deposit currency regardless of the Fed's wishes.

Well, then, how about defining money as that total that the Fed can control most accurately—reserves of banks and other depository institutions? Here the problem is that reserves are less closely related to expenditures, and hence GDP, than *M-1* is. Changes in reserves affect aggregate demand indirectly by changing the money supply and hence are likely to be less closely related to aggregate demand than the money supply itself is. Another measure, the monetary base (sometimes denoted by M_0), which consists of reserves plus currency, does have a close statistical relationship to GDP. But since it consists mainly of currency it is open to the same objection as currency. All the same, some economists consider the base the most useful measure.

MONEY SUBSTITUTES

Whichever way one defines money, there will be some near-monies that are similar to it and that make its measurement rather arbitrary. The most obvious example is credit cards. One can think of a credit-card line of credit as a substitute for holding money—or else as money itself. Lines of credit, such as those provided by credit cards, are like money in the sense of providing a widely, though not quite generally, accepted medium of exchange. However, they differ from money in one important way: money is part of a person's wealth, but a line of credit is not; for example, wouldn't it be better to receive a $1,000 check as a gift than have the ceiling on a credit card raised by $1,000?

Another money substitute that does represent wealth is a short-term government security. There is a saying on Wall Street that one can sell a Treasury bill even on a Sunday. For large holders the cost of selling Treasury bills is low, and the prices of Treasury bills are very stable. So, for many holders a Treasury bill is so highly liquid that it does not differ much from deposits. Similarly, large time deposits, which are excluded from *M-2*, are often highly liquid. There is an active market for them, and for those with a short maturity the price is quite stable. Moreover, as some economists point out, large firms can hold foreign currencies to meet their needs for transactions balances by selling them on the foreign-exchange market just before they make payments in dollars. Such assets illustrate that, as discussed in Chapter 1, one cannot draw a sharp line of distinction between the items that should be included in money and those that should not.

MEASURING MONEY AS A WEIGHTED AGGREGATE

Perhaps the solution is to measure money in a more sophisticated way. So far the discussion has been in terms of a simple dichotomy: an item either is—or is not—money, with nothing in between. But this is a crude procedure. Why not allow for the obvious fact that for the empirical definition of money the difference between those items included in money and other highly liquid assets is a matter of degree rather than of kind? This suggests that one should measure money as a *weighted average* of various components rather than as their simple sum. For example, currency might be given a weight of 1, and savings deposits a weight of, say, 0.3. The problem is then to find some way of assigning appropriate weights to various monetary components. One way is by constructing an index that uses the interest rate paid by a monetary asset as an (inverse) measure of its *moneyness,* or "liquidity." Financial assets provide liquidity (which is what we mean by moneyness) and interest. In equilibrium the total of these two yields must be equal for each asset; otherwise, people would switch out of the lower-yielding asset into the higher-yielding one. Thus, the lower the interest rate an asset pays, the greater must be its perceived liquidity. Hence, by using the interest rates paid on an asset as an (inverse) weight of its moneyness, one can combine various assets into a monetary total.

REFINING THE MONEY MEASUREMENTS

So far we have discussed some broad issues in defining and measuring money. Now we get more specific. It is easy to say that checkable deposits should be counted as part of the money stock, but do we really want to include all types of checkable deposits? No, we do not. We are interested in the size of the money supply, because changes in the money supply bring about changes in expenditures and hence in nominal income. This suggests that we should include only those deposits that affect expenditures.

It follows that the deposits of the federal government should not be counted. Federal government expenditures are totally unaffected by the Treasury's money holdings. They are set by congressional authorization and, in some cases, by the behavior of the economy. The U.S. Treasury is never constrained in its expenditures by having insufficient money; it can always borrow. For this reason U.S. government deposits—but not state and local government deposits—are excluded from the money supply.

So Who Has the Cash?

The Treasury Department and the Fed keep close tabs on the amount of currency that the Treasury has produced. (If they did not, an employee might be tempted to walk off with some of it.) So we know precisely how much currency has been issued. In January 1995, it corresponded to about $1,365 per capita, that is, to about $5,460 for a family of four. That sounds bizarre. Surely few people hold that much currency, if only because they are afraid of theft. In fact, according to a household survey, the amount of currency that people hold is not much more than 10 percent of the currency that is supposed to be in circulation.

So what accounts for the difference? Some currency is held by the *underground economy*, that is, by those who are engaged in illegal activities, such as drug dealing, tax evasion, prostitution, or handling stolen property. One sometimes hears about drug dealers caught with immense amounts of currency. But it is unlikely that these activities account for more than a small percentage of the missing currency. Business holdings of currency probably account for another 3 percent. Some currency has been lost or destroyed, but, on the other hand, counterfeiting has added to the currency in circulation.

So where is the rest? We don't know. One hypothesis is that it is held by people who are evading taxes and who therefore prefer currency, which cannot be traced, to bank deposits, which can be. Another hypothesis is that much, if not most, of it is held in foreign countries. In countries where the inflation rate is very high or property rights are insecure, people have a strong incentive to hold foreign currency as a store of wealth, rather than to hold their own currency. If that is a major part of the explanation, one would expect the problem of missing currency to show up not only in the United States, but also in other countries that have a relatively stable, well-regarded currency, such as Germany. And it does.

Another item that is excluded is currency held by banks in their vaults. We exclude this because it too does not affect anyone's expenditures. And for the same reason, interbank deposits are also excluded. In addition, we exclude cash items in the process of collection, that is, checks, etc., currently in the process of clearing. This is done on the (perhaps somewhat doubtful) assumption that those who wrote the checks have already deducted them from their outstanding balances. And what affects expenditures are the deposits that people *think* they have.

HOW RELIABLE ARE THE DATA?

If economists want to use changes in the growth rate of the money supply to predict GDP, they must know what the growth rate of the money supply is. Similarly if, as we will discuss in Chapter 24, the Fed wants to set a certain target for the growth rate of the money supply, it must know how fast the money supply is growing. Can one measure the growth rate of the money supply accurately enough?

There are several practical problems in measuring the money supply. One relates to the data on currency; see the box above. Another problem is created by the seasonal adjustment of money data. These data, like most economic time series, are adjusted for seasonal variations. For example, the demand for money increases before Christmas, and to prevent a sharp rise in the interest rate at that time, the Fed increases the money supply in December. Then, when the Fed publishes the data on the money supply, it provides seasonally adjusted data, as well as seasonally unadjusted data. The former are adjusted to eliminate, as best as one can, the effect of such normal seasonal fluctuations in the money supply. But such adjustments are subject to large errors, particularly for *M-1*. Errors in the seasonal adjustment are much more serious the shorter the period over which the growth rate of money is measured, since over the whole year positive and negative errors in the seasonal adjustment cancel each other out. Even for quarterly data there is considerable cancellation of errors. But monthly data are subject to serious errors in the seasonal adjustment, and the preliminary estimates of the seasonally adjusted weekly growth rates of money are very poor indeed. In addition, the early estimates of the monetary growth rate have to be revised as the Fed gets reports from banks on their actual deposit levels; for the smaller banks the Fed has had to estimate these in calculating the preliminary estimates.

All this suggests that one should not get exercised about preliminary estimates of weekly or monthly growth rates of the money supply. What may seem like wholly inappropriate changes in the money supply may turn out, after the data are revised, to have been quite appropriate changes.

SUMMARY

1   There are two general approaches to defining money. The a priori approach focuses on the essence of money. This leads to the *M-1* definition. The empirical approach focuses on that collection of monetary assets that has the closest correlation with nominal income and is readily controlled by the Fed.
2   *M-1* is defined as currency, checkable deposits, and traveler's checks. *M-2* adds to *M-1* savings deposits, small time deposits, money-market fund shares, overnight repurchase agreements, and overnight Eurodollar deposits. *M-3* adds to this large time deposits and term repurchase agreements and some other items.
3   The most common measure of money is *M-2*, but it is not clear which is the best measure. The existence of near-monies complicates the measurement of money. One approach to measuring money tries to resolve the problem by assigning the various components different weights and then combining them.
4   Federal government deposits, vault cash, interbank deposits, and cash items in the process of collection are excluded from all definitions of money.
5   The short-run growth rates of seasonally adjusted money are not measured accurately.

KEY TERMS

a priori definition of money
empirical definition of money
M-1
M-2

M-3
narrow money
broad money
seasonal adjustment errors

QUESTIONS AND EXERCISES

1 Write an essay defending:
   a. the a priori approach to the definition of money
   b. the empirical approach to the definition of money
*2 Describe a change in Federal Reserve or FDIC regulations that would induce you to make a change in the definition of money.
3 Explain why federal government deposits, vault cash, interbank deposits, and cash items in the process of collection are excluded from the money supply.
*4 Should food stamps be included in *M-1* or *M-2?*

FURTHER READING

ADVISORY COMMITTEE ON MONETARY STATISTICS. *Improving the Monetary Aggregates.* Washington, D.C.: Board of Governors, Federal Reserve System, 1976. A storehouse of technical details on how the money data are constructed and on how they could be improved.

BARNETT, WILLIAM, EDWARD OFFENBACHER, and PAUL SPINDT. "New Concepts of Aggregate Money," *Journal of Finance,* 36 (May 1981), 497–505. A good discussion of measuring money as a weighted aggregate.

BRYANT, WILLIAM. *Money and Monetary Policy in Interdependent Nations.* Washington, D.C.: Brookings Institution, 1980. An argument that one needs to look beyond a country's borders in defining money.

FRIEDMAN, MILTON, and ANNA SCHWARTZ. *Monetary Statistics of the United States.* New York: Columbia University Press, 1970. Chapter 3 gives a cogent and powerful defense of the empirical approach to the definition of money.

HART, ALBERT. "Regaining Control over an Open-Ended Money Supply," in U.S. Congress Joint Economic Committee, *Special Study on Economic Change,* Vol. 4. Washington, D.C.: 1980, pp. 85–143. An important discussion on the erosion of the concept of money.

SIMPSON, THOMAS. "The Redefinition of Monetary Aggregates," *Federal Reserve Bulletin,* 66 (February 1980), 97–114. This is the Fed's statement of how it defines money, and its reasons for adopting its definitions.

U.S. CONGRESS, HOUSE, SUBCOMMITTEE ON DOMESTIC MONETARY POLICY, COMMITTEE ON BANKING, FINANCE, AND URBAN AFFAIRS. *Measuring the Monetary Aggregates,* 96th Congress, 2nd session, February 1980. A useful compendium of economists' views.

YEAGER, LELAND B. "The Medium of Exchange," in *Monetary Theory,* ed. Robert Clower. Baltimore: Penguin Books, 1969, pp. 37–60. A rousing and subtle defense of the a priori approach to defining money.

The Creation of Money

After you have read this chapter, you will be able to:

- Realize that there is nothing mysterious about multiple deposit creation.
- Understand how and why multiple deposit creation is possible.
- Explain the various leakages to the deposit creation process and how they limit the deposit multiplier.
- Derive the money multiplier from the deposit multiplier.
- Spell out money supply theory and the endogenous view of money.

Having looked at the definition of money, we will now see how it is created. A basic point is that by far the biggest component of our money supply—deposits—is created by depository institutions. These institutions do not just increase deposits and the money supply by a dollar when their reserves go up by a dollar. Instead, as they act to maximize their profits, they collectively raise deposits and the money supply by more than one dollar. But first let us look at the creation of the other component of money—currency.

CURRENCY CREATION

The first step in the creation of currency notes (dollar bills, etc.) is that the Bureau of Printing and Engraving, an agency of the U.S. Treasury Department, produces currency notes. It then sells them to the Federal Reserve, which pays for them by crediting them to the Treasury's account. Then when a bank needs currency, it calls the Fed. The Fed ships it currency and debits its reserve account. The bank then puts this currency into circulation by paying it out to customers. At that point, when the currency gets into the hands of the nonbank public, it becomes part of the money supply. Coins, too, become money in this way.

The amount of currency in circulation therefore depends on how much currency the public wants to hold. People can always turn any checkable deposits they own into currency. Monetary policy does not operate by controlling the quantity of currency directly; instead, it controls the supply of deposits by controlling the reserves of banks.[1]

The creation of currency is a very profitable activity for the government. It can produce a dollar bill for a few cents, and then get a dollar's worth of goods and services for the bill. The way this works is that when the public wants more currency and withdraws it from the banks, the banks buy currency from the Federal Reserve, which debits their reserve accounts for it. The Fed then restores bank reserves by buying an equivalent amount of securities from the banks or the public. As a result, some of the interest that the Treasury previously paid to banks or the public it now pays to the Fed. And it gets back what it pays to the Fed when the Fed turns over its earnings to the Treasury. The gain the government obtains from creating currency is called **seigniorage**, a term that hearkens back to the Middle Ages when the right to coin precious metals belonged to each feudal lord, called *seigniore* in French.

The creation of deposits by banks is also profitable for the government because it increases the banks' demand for reserves, and, as just described, when the Fed provides banks with additional reserves, the Treasury benefits.

MULTIPLE DEPOSIT CREATION

By **multiple deposit creation** we mean that, if banks obtain an additional dollar of reserves, for example, by someone depositing a dollar of currency, total deposits eventually go up by more than one dollar. To understand how this occurs, three things must be kept in mind. One is the nature of deposits. Unless you understand just what a deposit is—and that is not obvious—you will never understand multiple deposit creation. The second relates to two cases in which multiple deposit creation does *not* occur. These cases may provide an intuitive understanding of why deposit creation occurs in other situations. The third is the equilibrium level of deposits when the deposit creation process is finished.

The Nature of Deposits

What actually is a **deposit?** It is not a physical object like currency, but merely *a property right evidenced by an entry in the bank's books.* You cannot see a deposit, or hold it in your hand, any more than you can hold in your hand the right to a jury trial or someone's promise. This is confusing because when we speak of someone drawing a deposit out and receiving currency in exchange for the deposit, there certainly is a tangible item, currency, being withdrawn. But when you "draw out your deposit" what you are actually doing is *exchanging* your right to receive payment from the bank in the future for currency right now. When banks create deposits, they no more create something out of nothing than the Supreme Court does when it creates a new legal right. In neither

---

[1] There are good reasons for this. Suppose that, to limit the money supply, the Fed provided no additional currency to banks. Banks would then not be able to meet their legal obligation to pay out demand deposits on demand and would be closed. Conversely, if the Fed tried to raise the money supply by increasing outstanding currency, it would have no way of getting this currency to the public, and, even if it did, the public could get rid of the currency by depositing it.

case does what is created have any physical existence. It is important to keep this in mind; otherwise, the subsequent discussion of deposit creation becomes incomprehensible.

Two Special Cases: 100 Percent Reserves and 100 Percent Currency Drain

As another preliminary to multiple deposit creation, consider two special cases in which multiple deposits are *not* created. These cases provide a clue why multiple deposit creation occurs in more realistic situations.

100 Percent Reserves. The first special case is one in which the law in its awful majesty requires that the bank keep 100 percent reserves against its deposits. Consider what happens when someone deposits $10,000 of currency. We can see this best by looking at a **T account,** *a condensed version of the bank's balance sheet,* which leaves out all previous entries and shows just the ones we are currently considering. Such a T account now shows:

(1)

Assets		Liabilities	
currency	$10,000	deposits	$10,000

This bank is in equilibrium; it has exactly the reserves that the law says it must hold against its deposit. Has there been multiple deposit creation? Certainly not. A $10,000 deposit has been created against $10,000 of currency, which functions as reserves. This is a one-to-one ratio; there is nothing multiple about it.

Loans as Currency Only. Consider another unrealistic case in which the required reserve ratio is only, say, 20 percent, but in which a borrower, when granted a loan, takes the proceeds entirely in the form of currency and continues to hold this currency. In this case, since the required reserve ratio is less than 100 percent, the above T account does not represent an equilibrium for the bank. It can increase its profits by lending out $8,000 of the initial $10,000 deposit, keeping the other $2,000 as a reserve against its deposits. Its T account now, after it has made a loan, looks as follows:

(2)

Assets		Liabilities	
currency	$2,000	deposits	$10,000
loan outstanding	$8,000		

This bank is now in equilibrium; it holds just the reserves (currency) it must hold against its deposit. But again, there has been no multiple deposit creation: the bank initially received $10,000 of currency, that is, reserves, and has $10,000 of deposits outstanding, so that deposits have increased in a one-to-one ratio to reserves.

The Equilibrium Level of Deposits

Now drop the unrealistic assumptions that banks have to keep 100 percent reserves and that borrowers take out their loans entirely as currency.

Assume instead that—in equilibrium—banks keep as reserves only, say, 10 percent of their deposits, and also assume that as deposits increase, people do not decide to hold more currency.

Suppose now that someone deposits in a bank or other depository institution a $1,000 check obtained by selling a Treasury bill to the Federal Reserve. When the bank sends the check to the Federal Reserve for clearing, the Fed credits the bank's account for it, so that its reserves with the Fed go up by $1,000. Since, by assumption, reserves are 10 percent of deposits, deposits must eventually go up by ten times that amount, or $10,000. How does this happen?

It cannot happen by the bank itself lending out $10,000. If it were to lend out $10,000, then as the borrowers write checks and the recipients of these checks deposit them in other banks, the bank would face a demand from these other banks for $10,000. But it has only the original $1,000 available to meet these claims. So this does not work.

What does explain multiple deposit creation is the following principle. *When a bank makes a loan or buys a security, it loses an equivalent amount of reserves. However, it loses these reserves not into thin air, but to another depository institution, which now makes a loan. This loan ends up in another institution, and so on. The reserves stay within the depository system and generate additional deposits until finally deposits are equal to ten times reserves.* (Had we used a reserve ratio of, say, 20 percent in this example, the process would end when deposits are equal to five times reserves.)

Now let us follow the process through step by step. In doing so, we will assume that, as a bank makes loans or purchases securities, all the money that is received from the bank is redeposited in a checkable deposit, either by the original recipient or by someone from whom the original recipient buys something. This assumption is not quite correct and we will modify it later. However, it is a reasonable first approximation, because few people are willing to borrow and pay interest merely to hold currency. We will also assume quite arbitrarily that there is a 10 percent reserve requirement. Finally, we will assume that depository institutions use all their available reserves to make loans or to buy securities instead of holding some idle reserves.

Assume now that someone deposits a $10,000 check obtained from selling a security to the Fed into Bank A. When the check has cleared, this bank's T account looks as follows:

Bank A

(3)	Assets		Liabilities	
	reserves with Federal Reserve	$10,000	deposits	$10,000

As before, since the bank has $9,000 more than the required 10 percent reserves, it increases its loans and writes up the borrower's deposit account by the amount of the loan. Its T account is:

Bank A

(4)

Assets		Liabilities	
reserves with			
Federal Reserve	$10,000	deposits	$19,000
loans outstanding	$9,000		

The borrower does not keep the loan idle, but uses it to make a purchase. And the seller now deposits the $9,000 check received into, say, Savings and Loan B, which sends it to the Fed for clearing. After it clears, Bank A's T account is:

Bank A

(5)

Assets		Liabilities	
loans outstanding	$9,000	deposits	$10,000
reserves with			
Federal Reserve	$1,000		

Its reserves, $1,000, are now just sufficient to cover the $10,000 deposit it has outstanding, so it is in equilibrium. However, Savings and Loan B has now received $9,000 of deposits and reserves, which gives it the following T account:

Savings and Loan B

(6)

Assets		Liabilities	
reserves with			
Federal Reserve	$9,000	deposits	$9,000

But there is no reason why B should want to keep 100 percent reserves against the deposit. It needs to keep only $900 ($9,000 times 10 percent) as reserves and can use the remainder, $8,100, to make a loan or buy a security. When the borrower, or the seller of the security, spends the $8,100, the recipient deposits the check into Bank C, which sends it to the Federal Reserve for clearing. As a result, B's T account becomes:

Savings and Loan B

(7)

Assets		Liabilities	
reserves with			
Federal Reserve	$900	deposits	$9,000
loans outstanding	$8,100		

B is now in equilibrium, having just the $900 reserves it needs and no more. But the story continues with C, which has received $8,100 of deposits and reserves. It, too, will keep only 10 percent, that is, $810, as a reserve against the $8,100 deposit and use $7,290 to buy a security or make a loan, which, by the now familiar process, will become a deposit in D, so that D can now lend out 90 percent of it, $6,561, which, in turn, will become a deposit in E, and that depository institution will again lend out, or buy a security with, 90 percent of this, and so on.[2]

In this process, deposits are being created by every depository institution in the chain; there are deposits of $10,000 in A, $9,000 in B, $8,100 in C, $7,290 in D, $6,561 in E, and so on. In other words, there is **multiple deposit creation:** *the initial increase in reserves has called forth a series of subsequent deposits.* The two essential reasons this occurs are that, first, no institution keeps a 100 percent reserve against its deposit and, second, while each one loses an equivalent amount of reserves when it makes a loan or buys a security, these reserves are received by another institution.

The story told so far may seem clearly unrealistic in one way. Bank B received $9,000 of reserves and deposits and then lent out exactly $8,100. Obviously, it is not likely to make a loan of just that amount. In actuality, banks do not look at particular receipts of reserves and deposits, and then try to lend out 90 percent of these particular receipts. Instead, banks have a continual inflow and outflow from a large number of transactions. There is no reason to tie particular loans closely to particular reserve receipts.

The Deposit Multiplier

How much does the multiple deposit creation amount to? We have a series here that goes as follows: $10,000, $9,000, $8,100, $7,290, $6,561, and so on, each figure being 90 percent of the preceding one. (There is, of course, nothing special about the 10 percent reserve ratio. It is just a number picked arbitrarily. Had a 50 percent reserve ratio been used, the sequence of deposits would have been $10,000, $5,000, $2,500, $1,250, ...) Such a sequence forms the geometric progression

$$R\,[1 + (1 - rr) + (1 - rr)^2 + (1 - rr)^3 + \cdots],$$

and its sum is

$$D = \frac{1}{rr}\,R,$$

where D stands for the dollar volume of deposits, rr is the reserve ratio, and R is the initial increase in reserves that occurred when Bank A obtained a $10,000 deposit. With a 10 percent reserve ratio, deposit creation amounts to $(1/0.1) \times \$10,000$, that is, $100,000. Hence, we have here a **deposit multiplier** $(1/rr)$ of 10. The deposit multiplier is the *change in deposits per dollar change in reserves.* (Unlike the Keynesian multiplier that relates some autonomous expen-

---

[2] As an exercise, write out the T accounts for C, D, and E.

diture item, such as investment, to income, this multiplier relates reserves to deposits.)

MULTIPLE DEPOSIT CONTRACTION

Now take the opposite case where reserves decrease. To get some variation into the figures, assume that the reserve ratio is 25 percent. Assume again that no excess reserves are held. When a customer of Mutual Savings Bank A buys a $10,000 security from the Fed, the Fed debits A's reserve account as the customer's check is cleared. Its T account now looks as follows:

Mutual Savings Bank A

(8)

Assets		Liabilities	
reserves with Federal Reserve	−$10,000	deposits	−$10,000

Since A kept only $2,500 of reserves against the $10,000 deposit, it is short $7,500 of reserves and has to replenish them by selling a security or calling in a loan for $7,500. When it does so and the check it receives is credited to its account, its T account—considering both the initial and the new transaction—becomes:

Mutual Savings Bank A

(9)

Assets		Liabilities	
reserves with Federal Reserve	−$10,000 +$ 7,500	deposits	−$10,000
loans and securities	−$ 7,500		

The first entry on the asset side shows the initial loss of reserves as the customer's check cleared, and the next two entries show the effect of the bank's sale of a security or calling in a loan. Mutual Savings Bank A is now in equilibrium. It has lost $10,000 of reserves and made this up both by reducing its required reserves and by obtaining new reserves. But in doing so it has shifted part of its reserve shortage to another depository institution since by selling a security, or calling a loan, it received a check drawn on Bank B.

As this check clears, Bank B's T account becomes:

Bank B

(10)

Assets		Liabilities	
reserves with Federal Reserve	−$7,500	deposits	−$7,500

Bank B kept $1,875 (= $7,500 × .25) against the $7,500 deposit, and it is now short $5,625 (= $7,500 − $1,875) of reserves. Hence, it too sells a security or calls in a loan for $5,625. Its T account becomes:

Bank B

(11)	Assets		Liabilities	
reserves with			deposits	−$7,500
Federal Reserve	−$1,875			
	(= −$7,500 + $5,625)			
loans and securities	−$5,625			

Bank B has therefore lost reserves equal to exactly 25 percent of the decline in its deposits and hence is not short of reserves anymore. But when it obtained $5,625 by selling a security, it received a check drawn on a deposit in Bank C. As this check is cleared, Bank C is short of reserves, its T account looking like this:

Bank C

(12)	Assets		Liabilities	
reserves with			deposits	−$5,625
Federal Reserve	−$5,625			

Bank C does not have to worry about $1,406 (= $5,625 × .25) of this loss in its reserves because its deposits have fallen too. But it is still short $4,219 of reserves. So, suppose that it sells a security for $4,219 to a customer of Savings and Loan D. It now has sufficient reserves again, but D is short $3,164 ($4,219 × .75) of reserves. So *it* sells a security, and thus passes the problem on to Bank E, and so on.

In this process, deposits are decreasing in a geometrically declining sequence. They fell by $10,000 in A, by $7,500 in B, by $5,625 in C, and so on. Applying the equation for the sum of a declining geometric series, we can see that checkable deposits must fall by $40,000, or

$$\frac{1}{rr} R = \frac{1}{.25} \$10{,}000.$$

Thus, multiple deposit contraction is just as possible as multiple deposit creation, and not surprisingly, the two are symmetrical, though the numbers differ here because we used different reserve ratios.

LEAKAGES FROM THE DEPOSIT CREATION PROCESS

The story told so far is that of a multiplier process in which required reserves are the only leakage that absorbs the reserves with which the story started out. But there are also two other leakages, which we now take up: excess reserves and currency holdings by the public.

Excess Reserves

A bank or other depository institution will frequently hold excess reserves to avoid having to borrow from the Fed, to buy deposits in the CD market, or to sell short-term securities. After all, although depository institutions are not legally required to keep reserves against time deposits, they want to keep *some* reserves against these deposits, too. However, excess reserves are typically small. From 1985 to 1994 they averaged 2.5 percent of total reserves.

How can we introduce excess reserves into the story of how deposits are created? The simplest way is to think of them as functioning just as required reserves. Suppose a bank gets a $10,000 deposit and lends out only, say, 85 percent of it, holding 15 percent as reserves against this deposit. It does not matter in the least for the deposit creation process whether all the 15 percent is required reserves or whether, say, 14 percent is legally required and 1 percent is excess reserves. In either case, as the bank lends out $8,500, the next bank receives an $8,500 deposit. Hence, now that banks hold some excess reserves, the deposit multiplier is not $d = 1/rr$, but

$$d = \frac{1}{rr + e},$$

where e is the *percent of a dollar of deposit that banks hold voluntarily* as **excess reserves.** If the required reserve ratio is 14 percent and banks hold 1 percent excess reserves, the deposit multiplier is $1/.14 + .01$, or 6.67.

Deposits into Currency

As the volume of deposits expands and income rises along with it, people exchange some of their additional deposits for currency. Suppose that for each dollar of deposits, the public wants to hold, say, 30 cents more currency. The 30 cents of currency that depository institutions have to pay out to the public for every dollar of new deposits are lost to the deposit creation process just as much as are the 14 cents that, in this example, they have to keep as required reserves. A bank receiving a $10,000 deposit keeps $1,400 as a legal reserve, $100 as an excess reserve, and pays out to the public $3,000 as currency. Hence it can lend only $5,500, which then becomes a deposit in the next bank. So the deposit multiplier now becomes

$$d = \frac{1}{rr + e + k},$$

where k is the proportion of each dollar of deposits, d, that the public withdraws as currency. In this example, we have

$$d = \frac{1}{.14 + .01 + .30} = 2.22.$$

FROM THE MULTIPLIER TO THE STOCK OF DEPOSITS: THE MULTIPLICAND

Just what is it that we multiply by the deposit multiplier to get the total stock of deposits (both time and checkable deposits)? Consider first a simplified world in which there are checkable and time deposits but no currency. Then the multiplicand is the total volume of reserves, so that total deposits are equal to

$$D = \frac{1}{rr + e} R,$$

where D is total deposits and R is the total volume of reserves. When reserves increase, the deposit creation process continues until all the new reserves have been absorbed in additional holdings either of required reserves or of excess reserves.

If we now introduce currency, there are two effects. First, there is an additional leakage, the leakage into currency, and second, the stock of currency can now be used, along with reserves, to meet one of the leakages, the public's demand for currency. Hence, the multiplicand becomes not just reserves, but reserves plus the currency held by the public, a sum we will call the **base** in the next chapter.[3] Deposits are now equal to

$$D = \frac{1}{rr + e + \ell} (R + C).$$

FROM THE DEPOSIT SUPPLY TO THE MONEY SUPPLY

The main reason for discussing the deposit multiplier is that it permits one to calculate the money multiplier. That is not a simple step because we have three measures of money, *M-1*, *M-2*, and *M-3*. We therefore work out the analysis initially for a simple monetary system in which there is only a single type of deposit, and "money" is defined as such deposits plus currency.

So we have to add currency to the deposits whose creation we previously discussed.[4] Since the public is holding a proportion ℓ of its checkable deposits as currency, each dollar of checkable deposits results in ℓ dollars of currency being held. Total currency holdings are

$$\ell D = \ell \frac{1}{rr + e + \ell} (R + C) = \frac{\ell}{rr + e + \ell} (R + C).$$

Adding this to deposits, which are

$$D = \frac{1}{rr + e + \ell} (R + C),$$

one gets

$$M = \frac{1 + \ell}{rr + e + \ell} (R + C).$$

The Multipliers for *M-1*, *M-2*, and *M-3*

The money multiplier we have derived so far does not correspond exactly to the money multiplier we need for any of the standard definitions of money. It is closest to the multiplier applicable to *M-3*, but differs slightly from it because

---

[3] We describe here what is called the *base multiplier*. There is also a *reserves multiplier*, which omits the currency ratio and is therefore equal to total deposits divided by reserves.

[4] We ignore the complication that the money stock includes traveler's checks, but excludes interbank and federal government deposits.

M-3 includes repurchase agreements, which need not all be with depository institutions. But if we ignore this detail and if we define *depository institutions* broadly enough to include money-market mutual funds, then the multiplier we have derived so far corresponds to the money multiplier applicable to *M-3*.

Fortunately, it is not difficult to modify our *M-3* multiplier to obtain the multipliers we need for *M-1* and *M-2*. To obtain the *M-1* multiplier two additional steps are needed. One is to redefine the currency ratio as the ratio of currency to checkable deposits, rather than to all deposits, as well as to redefine the excess reserve ratio as the ratio of excess reserves to checkable deposits.

Second, since certain deposits, such as time deposits and deposits in money-market funds, are excluded from *M-1*, we must take account of the fact that during the deposit creation process some funds will leak into these deposits. But the effect this has on the deposit creation process is more complex than the leakage into reserves or currency. When banks hold a dollar more of reserves or when the public decides to hold an additional dollar of currency, a whole dollar is lost to the deposit creation process. But when the public decides to hold an additional dollar of time deposits, the banking system does not lose a whole dollar, because it can lend out almost all the funds that it received as time deposits. It is only the *reserves* (all of which are excess reserves, since depository institutions are not required to hold reserves against time deposits) that banks decide to hold against these deposits that are lost to the deposit creation process. Hence, let us do two things. First, let us redefine *e*, the excess reserve ratio, as the excess reserves ratio for checkable deposits and define e_t as the excess reserves ratio held against time deposits. Second, to obtain the *M-1* multiplier, let us add to the previously discussed leakages an additional term, te_t. Here *t* measures the leakage into time deposits (and all other items that are included in *M-3*, but not in *M-1*). The *M-1* money supply is therefore

$$M\text{-}1 = \frac{1 + \ell}{rr + e + \ell + te_t}\,(R + C).$$

Since *M-2* includes certain types of time deposits, such as small time deposits and money-market deposit accounts, the deposit multiplier for *M-2* has to take into account only the leakage into other types of deposits, mainly large time deposits. Hence, for the *M-2* multiplier we have to define *t* as the leakage into these other deposits and *e* as the reserve ratio held against these deposits. We also have again to redefine the required reserve ratio, the excess reserve ratio, and the currency ratio as ratios in which the denominator consists of the deposits included in *M-2*.

MONEY SUPPLY THEORY

We could end the story at this point and say that there is a fixed money multiplier determined by *rr*, *e*, *ℓ*, *t*, and te_t. One could take the average values of these coefficients and easily calculate the money multiplier. But why assume that the values of these leakage coefficients are fixed? While the reserve requirement is set by the Fed, the other coefficients depend on how the public and the banks want to hold their assets. Since the public's decisions are open to economic analysis, we need not take these leakage coefficients as given, but can see how they change with economic conditions.

The excess reserve ratio e that banks want to hold depends, on the one hand, on the interest rate that banks could earn by investing these excess reserves and, on the other hand, on the benefits that banks expect to obtain from holding them. A profit-maximizing bank keeps excess reserves up to a point at which the cost of idle reserves (the yield obtained from investing them minus the cost of investing) is equal to the benefit to the bank (avoidance of the cost of obtaining additional reserves if the bank runs short of reserves, multiplied by the probability that the bank will run short).

The public's desired currency ratio ℓ depends on the cost of holding currency, that is, on the interest rate paid on deposits. It does so in two ways. First, the higher the interest rate paid on deposits, the greater the incentive to hold deposits rather than currency, to go to the bank several times a month, rather than to draw out at the beginning of the month all the currency one will need for the whole month. The second way is more subtle. The higher the interest rate on securities relative to the interest rate paid on deposits, the greater is the incentive to switch out of money into securities. But when people decide to hold more securities and less money, they are much more likely to reduce their deposits than their currency holdings. Hence, as rising interest rates induce people to switch into securities, deposits fall more than currency, so that the currency ratio rises. The currency ratio also depends on income or wealth, because these variables measure the extent to which people can afford to forgo earning interest on deposits or securities to obtain the convenience of holding currency, and on retail sales, the variable that measures the work to be done by currency. Some economists believe that the currency ratio also varies with tax rates because in transactions where taxes are evaded, it is safer to use currency than checks, which leave records. Another factor influencing the currency ratio is the size of the drug trade and other illegal transactions in which payment is made by currency and not by check.

The time deposit ratio t depends on the interest rate on time deposits compared to the yields on checkable deposits and on securities. Obviously, if banks raise the interest rate they pay on time deposits, and neither the yields on checkable deposits nor the yields on securities rise, the public will want to hold more time deposits. The time deposit ratio also depends on total wealth, since time deposits are one way of holding wealth.

Thus, income, wealth, and interest rates are factors determining e, ℓ, and t, and hence the money multiplier. As income rises and interest rates increase, one would expect e to decline somewhat. But since it is already small to start with, this does not make much difference. At the same time, with income and retail sales as well as interest rates on securities all rising, ℓ rises too.

Hence, the deposit multiplier is **endogenous,** that is, affected by income, so that, even if the Fed keeps bank reserves constant, the stock of money tends to rise as income increases and fall as income falls—in other words, to behave **procyclically.**

This analysis of money creation, which makes the *money multiplier endogenous by allowing* e, ℓ, *and* t *to vary,* is called **money supply theory** to distinguish

Monetary Policy, Bank Reserves, and Deposit Creation

In the 1990–91 recession many people argued that the Fed's attempt to stimulate the economy by lowering interest rates and increasing bank reserves would fail because banks were reluctant to lend. Many banks were in a precarious financial position because of unsound loans they had made in the 1980s, and, it was said, bank examiners had raised their standards and hence were unduly critical of loans the banks were currently making. Moreover, some banks had to scramble to meet the higher capital requirements that had recently been imposed. Under such conditions would multiple deposit creation work the usual way, or would the money supply fail to respond to the infusion of additional reserves?

A straightforward answer is that the money multiplier would be more or less unaffected. If banks decide not to make loans, they still have to do *something* with their excess reserves, and they may buy securities instead. When a bank buys a $10,000 security from someone, it gives that person a check for (or wire-transfers) $10,000, which then become deposits in another bank, just as if the bank had made a $10,000 loan.

The money multiplier cannot decline unless the leakages increase. It is possible that, given the above scenario, some banks would keep slightly more excess reserves, out of fear that their precarious position might not allow them to borrow in the federal funds market, if they should run short of reserves. Moreover, if banks make fewer loans, and instead buy more securities, the interest rate on securities falls. With the cost of holding excess reserves dropping, banks would have an incentive to hold more excess reserves. But since the excess reserve ratio is very low, it seems most unlikely that the money multiplier would be much affected. Nor should the currency ratio or the time deposit ratio change significantly. Hence, one would expect the money multiplier to remain more or less unchanged, so that the Fed could, as before, raise the money supply by pumping more reserves into the banking system.

However, that does not mean that the Fed's ability to stimulate the economy was unaffected by the troubles of the banking industry. Bank loans have some special features. Many small firms that borrow from banks cannot readily raise funds in the bond market or the stock market. Hence if banks cut back on their loans and buy securities, some firms that previously borrowed from banks are not able to obtain funds, and hence have to scale back.

The question is therefore not whether the Fed can induce an increase in the money supply—it can. Nor is it whether expanding the money supply in 1990–91 was as stimulating as it usually is—it was not. The real question is whether the difference was large enough to matter. That is a harder question to answer.

it from a mechanistic approach that takes the money multiplier to be a constant.

WHAT DOMINATES, SUPPLY OR DEMAND?

So far we have told a story in which depository institutions receive some reserves and then create deposits. Such a supply-based story is not just a useful way to learn about the relation between reserves and deposits. It also describes a situation that occurs at least some of the time. But at other times the sequence is different. Suppose that the Fed wants the money supply to grow at a certain rate. It will then provide all the reserves that depository institutions need to create that supply of money. In this case it is the money supply the Fed wants that determines the volume of reserves, not the volume of reserves that determines the money supply. Suppose, for example, that in such a situation the money multiplier falls, say, because the currency ratio rises. The result will be not a lower money supply, but a higher volume of reserves, since the Fed will supply more reserves to compensate for the decline in the money multiplier. The same is true if the Fed decides to aim not at a particular supply of money, but at a particular interest rate. As we will discuss later, there is a demand curve for money that determines the demand for money at each interest rate. To keep the interest rate at a particular level, the supply of money must be equal to the amount demanded at that interest rate. Hence, if the Fed wants a particular interest rate, it must set the money supply at the appropriate level by providing the right amount of reserves. Here, too, if the money multiplier declines, the result is not a decline in the money supply, but a rise in the amount of reserves.

Can the money supply change even if the Fed does nothing, just because the public wants to hold more (or less) money? Yes, to some extent it can. Suppose that incomes rise and, as a result, people want to hold more money to finance an increase in their purchases. To obtain additional money, they will try to sell securities. As they sell securities, the price of securities will fall and interest rates will rise. As described in the previous section, a rise in the interest rate will then give banks an incentive to lower their excess reserves. Hence, the money supply will expand.

There is no disagreement in principle about this process: the money supply will change in accordance with the public's demand for money, even if the Fed does not change reserves. But there is disagreement about the *extent* to which the money supply adjusts to the public's demand for money if the Fed does not change reserves. Many economists think that it adjusts only slightly. But some hold a different view.

IS MONEY ENDOGENOUS OR EXOGENOUS?

Some of the time the money supply is endogenous with respect to income and the interest rate. A change in either of these variables generates a change in the money multiplier. Moreover, since the Fed is likely to respond to an increase in the interest rate by raising reserves and thus the money stock, we may add an equation for Federal Reserve behavior to our model, so that the money supply becomes endogenous also through the actions of the Fed.

But at other times the money stock is exogenous. The Fed may change its policy and reduce the growth of reserves, even though the interest rate is rising, because it has become afraid of excessive inflation. Or the currency ratio may fall because news reports about dramatic thefts have made people afraid to keep much currency at home.

Moreover, even though the money supply is usually endogenous, one can still hold the Fed responsible for an inappropriate growth rate of the money stock, because the Fed has the power to offset endogenous changes in the money multiplier by changing reserves. We do not absolve a fire department from blame if it lets a building burn down, even though the fire department did not set the blaze.

SUMMARY

1   Currency notes are created by the Bureau of Printing and Engraving. Banks buy them from the Fed and put them into circulation.
2   Multiple deposit creation is best understood by focusing on a set of rules that explains under what conditions banks can make certain book entries. What makes multiple deposit creation possible is that the funds one depository institution loses when it makes a loan or buys a security are received by another one.
3   Simple examples of multiple deposit creation show a chain of decreasing deposits created by various depository institutions. Multiple deposit contraction operates by the same mechanism as deposit expansion.
4   There are various leakages in the deposit creation process: required reserves, excess reserves, and the flows into currency.
5   For the *M-1* multiplier one must also include a leakage into time deposits, and for the *M-2* multiplier, a leakage into large time deposits.
6   Money supply theory explains why all the leakages other than required reserves are functions of income and the interest rate.
7   The money multiplier tells us how much reserves have to increase to generate a specific increase in the money supply. But more commonly, the causation runs the other way; a desired change in the money supply determines the reserves the Fed has to supply.

KEY TERMS

deposit multiplier   money supply theory
money multiplier   endogenous-money view
leakages

QUESTIONS AND EXERCISES

*1   Carry out the example set out on pages 235 to 236 through to Bank G. Assume that G just holds the reserves it receives and does not make additional loans. On this assumption, what is the deposit multiplier?
 2   What happens in the example of deposit creation on page 236 if the proceeds of the loan made by B are redeposited in B?
*3   Set up an example of the deposit creation process using a 50 percent reserve ratio. Work it through for four banks.
*4   Work out an example of deposit *contraction* using a 15 percent reserve ratio. Follow it through for six banks.
 5   How would you answer a banker who claims that banks cannot create deposits, that they can lend out only the money deposited with them?
*6   Carry the example of deposit contraction on pages 238 to 239 forward and assume that F has excess reserves and hence does not have to call a loan. What is the deposit multiplier now?

7 Suppose that we have an economy in which there is only a single bank, which has a reserve ratio of 20 percent. If someone deposits $1,000 of currency in this bank, how much can this bank lend out?

8 Why do changes in income and wealth affect e, ℓ, and t?

FURTHER READING

BURGER, ALBERT E. *Money Supply Process.* Belmont, Calif.: Wadsworth Publishing Co., 1971. Chapters 1 to 4 give an extremely thorough and detailed discussion of the deposit and money multipliers.

FEDERAL RESERVE BANK OF CHICAGO. *Modern Money Mechanism: Workbook.* Chicago: Federal Reserve Bank of Chicago, 1961, pp. 1–14. A very clear and lucid discussion of deposit creation.

PESEK, BORIS. "Monetary Theory in the Post-Robertsonian 'Alice in Wonderland' Era," *Journal of Economic Literature,* 14 (September 1976), 867 ff. The latter part of this article is a forceful and stimulating criticism of the traditional view of deposit creation. For the traditionalist's response, see the debate in the *Journal of Economic Literature,* 15 (September 1977), 909–27.

TOBIN, JAMES. "Commercial Banks as Creators of 'Money,'" in *Banking and Monetary Studies,* ed. Deane Carson. Homewood, Ill.: Irwin, 1963, pp. 408–19. A sharp critique of the traditional explanation of deposit creation.

Bank Reserves and Related Measures

After you have read this chapter, you will be able to:

- Understand where reserves come from.
- Explain how the Fed creates and extinguishes reserves.
- Distinguish between various measures of reserves.

If you read the appendix, you will be able to:

- Illustrate how each of the market factors affects bank reserves.

In the previous chapter we discussed how depository institutions use their reserves to create deposits. In this chapter we see where these reserves come from. Any individual depository institution can obtain reserves by competing them away from another institution, perhaps by selling CDs to its customers. But obviously, all depository institutions taken together cannot obtain reserves this way. They can gain reserves only from some outside entity, that is, from either (1) the Fed, (2) the Treasury, (3) the domestic public, or (4) foreigners.

The way in which reserves change is set out in a standardized accounting framework, published each Friday in the *Wall Street Journal*. Table 14.1 shows a condensed example. The first two items in this table are the changes in reserves brought about by the Fed. The other items, called *market factors*, are outside the Fed's control. We will discuss the first two items in the body of the chapter and the market factors in the appendix to this chapter.

FEDERAL RESERVE ACTIONS AND RESERVES

The main way the Fed changes reserves to undertake monetary policy is through open-market operations in which the Fed buys securities from, or sells securities to, banks or to the public. Suppose that the Fed buys securities

Table 14.1 Factors Changing Reserves, Week ending April 27, 1995 (millions of dollars)

Purchases of U.S. government securities, securities of U.S. government agencies, and acceptances*	$31,342
Borrowings from the Federal Reserve	72
Float	61
Other Federal Reserve assets	1,510
Gold stock	3
Special Drawing Right (SDR) certificates	0
Treasury currency outstanding	882
Currency in circulation	35,203
Treasury cash holdings	22
Treasury, foreign, and other deposits with the Federal Reserve	1,578
Other Federal Reserve liabilities and capital	2,707
Service-related balance adjustments	−2,788

*Includes securities bought under repurchase agreements.
Source: *Wall Street Journal*, April 28, 1995, p. C15.

directly from a bank. It pays for the securities it buys by crediting that bank's reserve account, so that the bank's reserves go up automatically. The T accounts of the bank and the Fed look as follows:

Bank

(1)

Assets		Liabilities
reserves with Federal Reserve	+	(unchanged)
securities held	−	

Federal Reserve

Assets		Liabilities	
securities held	+	deposits of banks (= reserves)	+

Suppose now that the Fed had bought these securities not from a bank, but from General Motors. General Motors gets a check, which it deposits in its bank, and the bank clears the check by sending it to the Fed for credit. The bank's T account becomes:

Bank

(2)

Assets		Liabilities	
reserves with Federal Reserve	+	deposits	+

The Fed's T account becomes:

Federal Reserve

Assets		Liabilities	
securities held	+	deposits of banks (= reserves)	+

In both of these cases the bank's reserve account goes up. The only difference is that in the second case deposits go up automatically, whereas in the first case where the Fed bought the securities from a bank, deposits go up only when the bank uses the reserves to make a loan or to buy another security. (The Fed's balance sheet is the same in both cases.) Conversely, when the Fed sells a security to a nonbank, bank reserves fall, and the T account of the buyer's bank shows:

Bank

(3)

Assets		Liabilities	
reserves with Federal Reserve	−	deposits	−

The next item, borrowings, refers to the loans that depository institutions can obtain from their Federal Reserve Banks. The Fed makes these loans by crediting the borrowing institution's reserve account, so that we have the following T account entries:

Bank

(4)

Assets		Liabilities	
reserves with Federal Reserve	+	borrowings from Federal Reserve	+

Federal Reserve Bank

Assets		Liabilities	
loans to banks	+	deposits	+

When the bank repays the loan, the Fed will take the amount of the loan out of the bank's reserve account, so that the T account will show negative entries for this item: the reserves will therefore disappear.

THE FED'S CONTROL OVER RESERVES

The Fed obviously controls its own open-market operations. It can also influence borrowing at the discount window by changing the discount rate and by bringing pressure to bear on banks that borrow too much. This might give the impression that the Fed has no problem in controlling reserves.

Such an impression would be misleading. The Fed is not the only one whose actions change bank reserves. As will be explained in the appendix, market factors, such as the public depositing or withdrawing currency, change reserves independently of the Fed's actions. Hence, if the Fed wants to control the amount of reserves, it has to forecast the effects of these market factors on reserves and then, if necessary, offset them by open-market operations.

If the Fed could predict the impact of the market factors precisely, they would create no problem. But market factors are hard to predict. Hence, over the short run, such as a week, the Fed's control over reserves is far from perfect. However, over a longer period, say, a calendar quarter, the Fed can control the growth rate of reserves well because it then has enough time to make up for errors in its predictions.

MEASURES OF RESERVES AND THE BASE

There are several important concepts related to reserves that are used in discussing monetary policy. They are the **base** (sometimes also called the *monetary base* or *high-powered money*), **total reserves, unborrowed reserves, excess reserves,** and **free reserves.**

Base. This widely used measure of the stance of Fed policy consists of the reserves of depository institutions plus the currency held by the public. About 85 percent of it consists of outstanding currency. But if one makes a rough allowance for currency held abroad, the proportion of the base that consists of *domestically* held currency is less, perhaps very substantially less.[1]

Total Reserves. These are the sum of required and excess reserves. They consist of reserves with the Federal Reserve and vault cash.

Unborrowed Reserves. Depository institutions are, at least to some extent, reluctant to be in debt to the Fed. To the extent that this is so, when they obtain additional reserves, the first thing they do is repay these loans rather than use these reserves to make loans or buy securities. If this view is correct—and this is disputed—then deposit creation depends less on total reserves than on *unborrowed reserves,* sometimes called *owned reserves.* To obtain owned reserves, all one has to do is to subtract from total reserves the amount that depository institutions have borrowed from the Fed.[2]

Excess Reserves. These are total reserves minus the reserves depository institutions are required to keep against their deposits.

Free Reserves. This measure subtracts from unborrowed reserves the reserves that have to be kept against existing deposits in an attempt to measure the reserves that are available to expand deposits.

Table 14.2 gives the various reserve and base measures. Which of these is best for predicting how the money stock will change? This is an unsettled issue. The base has an advantage over bank reserves because it takes account of cur-

---

[1] A related concept is the *adjusted base,* which takes account of changes in reserve requirements. Thus, if the Fed lowers the required reserve ratio, an amount equal to the reduction in the dollar volume of required reserves is added to the base.

[2] *Seasonal borrowings* as well as *extended borrowings* (both of which will be discussed in Chapter 23) are not subtracted since they do not generate such strong pressure to repay.

Table 14.2 Reserve Concepts	
Measure	Definition
Base or monetary base or high-powered money	Reserves of depository institutions plus currency held by the public
Reserves	Reserves of depository institutions
Unborrowed reserves	Reserves minus borrowings from the Fed*
Excess reserves	Total reserves minus required reserves
Free reserves	Excess reserves minus borrowings from the Fed*

*The borrowings that are subtracted do not include seasonal and extended borrowings.

rency holdings of the public, which are ignored by reserves. But, on the other hand, it gives currency holdings too much importance by counting a dollar of currency held by the public as equal to a dollar of reserves held by banks, despite the fact that a dollar of bank reserves, unlike a dollar of currency, results in several dollars of money.

Unborrowed reserves and the unborrowed base are better measures than total reserves or the total base if—*but only if*—depository institutions are reluctant to expand deposits on the basis of the reserves they have borrowed from the Fed.

Excess reserves and free reserves are measures with a potential problem. Suppose the data show that excess reserves have increased. This need not be a signal that deposits will increase; excess reserves may have increased just because the federal-funds rate has fallen, while the discount rate has not, so that banks find it worthwhile to hold more excess reserves.

THE IMPORTANCE OF DISTINGUISHING BETWEEN VARIOUS RESERVE MEASURES

Why bother to learn all these different reserve measures? Does it really matter which one we use? Yes, it does. Suppose that the Fed uses free reserves as its measure and undertakes open-market purchases to make free reserves rise by, say, $100 million. However, at the prevailing federal-funds rate and discount rate, banks do not want to hold any additional free reserves. Hence when they obtain the additional reserves, they go ahead and make additional loans. Free reserves are back at their previous level, so the Fed tries to raise them again. And again, banks use the additional reserves to create more deposits, so that free reserves do not rise. The Fed now pumps in even more reserves. This could go on for a long time, and while it does, the money supply rises at an excessive rate. This actually happened in the 1960s.

Or suppose that the Fed sets a target for the base at the same time that the currency ratio shifts substantially. Since the Fed is targeting the base, it does not offset these changes in the currency ratio and hence the money supply fluctuates more than if the Fed had targeted total reserves.

THE RESERVE BASE, THE MONEY MULTIPLIER, AND THE MONEY STOCK

Over a reasonable period, the Fed can exercise good control over the monetary base or reserves through its open-market operations by offsetting changes in reserves induced by market factors. Does this mean that it also has good control over the supply of money? This depends on its ability to predict changes in the money multiplier. If the money multiplier is stable or otherwise highly predictable, the Fed could attain its target for the money supply very easily. If it wants the money supply to increase by, say, $10 billion and it knows that the money multiplier applicable to the base is 2.5, it would simply raise the base by $4 billion. But is the money multiplier so highly predictable? As Figure 14.1 shows, it is not very stable. Indeed, changes in the money multiplier account for a larger proportion of the year-to-year changes in *M-2* than do changes in the base. So if the Fed wants to control money by controlling the base, it needs an equation to predict variations in the money multiplier. The question becomes, how well can the Fed predict the change in the money multiplier?

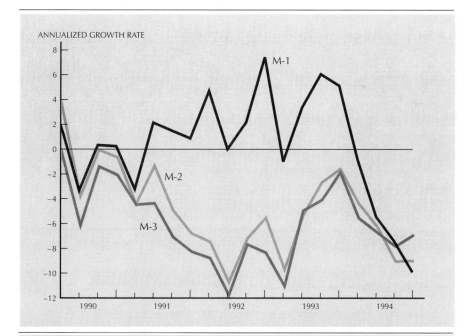

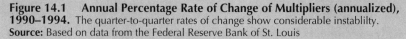

Figure 14.1   Annual Percentage Rate of Change of Multipliers (annualized), 1990–1994. The quarter-to-quarter rates of change show considerable instablilty.
Source: Based on data from the Federal Reserve Bank of St. Louis

SUMMARY

1   Reserves are created or destroyed by Fed security purchases and loans.
2   Important measures of reserves are the base, total reserves, unborrowed reserves, excess reserves, and free reserves.
3   The growth rates of the money multipliers are quite variable.

KEY TERMS

base	unborrowed reserves
reserves	excess reserves
total reserves	free reserves
money multiplier	

QUESTIONS AND EXERCISES

*1   Describe how open-market sales affect bank reserves. Use T accounts. Does it matter whether the Fed sells securities to banks or to the public?
 2   Describe how bank borrowing from the Fed affects reserves.
*3   How do the following differ from each other: total reserves and base; total reserves and free reserves?
*4   Look at the data in the *Federal Reserve Bulletin* to calculate the money multiplier for the last few years. Can you guess, by looking at each of the leakages, why it has changed the way it has?

FURTHER READING

BERGER, ALBERT. *The Money Supply Process.* Belmont, Calif.: Wadsworth, 1971. A very thorough and comprehensive survey of the factors that determine the money stock.
MELTON, WILLIAM. *Inside the Fed.* Homewood, Ill.: Dow Jones-Irwin, 1985. Chapters 7 and 8 offer an excellent discussion of how the Fed operates in the money market.
NICHOLS, DOROTHY (Federal Reserve Bank of Chicago). *Modern Money Mechanism.* Chicago: Federal Reserve Bank of Chicago, 1971. A simple and clear discussion of deposit creation and of the factors changing bank reserves.

APPENDIX: MARKET FACTORS THAT CHANGE RESERVES

In the chapter we took up two factors that generate changes in reserves, open-market operations, and discounting. We now look at the other factors listed in Table 14.1. This table starts with the factors that, if positive, raise reserves.

Factors that Increase Reserves

One of these is **float.** This item works as a loan from the Fed. If the Fed were to give credit for a check it has been sent for clearing at exactly the same time that it debits the account of the institution on which the check is drawn, then there would be no float. But the Fed credits the account of the depositing institution after one or two days, despite the fact that, due to transportation delays and so on, it sometimes takes longer for the check to be debited against the account of the institution on which it is drawn. As a result of one reserve account's having been credited for the check, while the other has not yet been debited, total reserves increase for a time. Thus the T account of the institution that received the check and that of the one on which the check was drawn look as follows:

Receiving Bank

(1)

Assets	Liabilities
reserves with Federal Reserve +	deposits +

Drawer Bank

Assets	Liabilities
reserves with Federal Reserve unchanged	deposits unchanged

For both banks together, reserves have temporarily increased. When the check finally is debited to the bank on which it is drawn, the bank's reserve account is debited and the increased reserves and deposits generated by float disappear.

Another factor raising bank reserves is an increase in "other Federal Reserve assets." Whether the Fed buys paper clips from a local store or foreign currency from another central bank, it does so by drawing a check on itself. When the check is deposited and cleared, the Fed credits the reserve account of the institution that received it. Here are the relevant T accounts when the seller has deposited the Federal Reserve check and it has cleared:

Savings and Loan

(2)

Assets	Liabilities
reserves with Federal Reserve +	deposits +

Federal Reserve Bank

Assets	Liabilities
paper clips +	deposits +

Then there are various U.S. Treasury operations that change bank reserves. The first of these results from changes in the U.S. gold stock. If the Treasury sells gold, the check it receives in payment is debited against the reserve account of the institution on which it is drawn.

The next item, Special Drawing Right (SDR) certificates, we will defer until later (see Footnote 4) and turn now to Treasury currency in circulation. Since currency held by depository institutions is part of reserves, an increase in outstanding Treasury currency that ends up in depository institutions obviously increases their reserves. But how about Treasury currency that is held by the general public? We will make allowance for that part of Treasury currency by subsequently subtracting currency held by the public.[3]

Factors that Decrease Reserves

Bank reserves *decrease* if certain items increase. One of these is currency in circulation, that is, currency held by the public. Clearly, if someone withdraws $1,000 from a bank, then vault cash and as a result reserves decrease by $1,000. A similar story applies to the next item—Treasury cash holdings. If the Treasury's currency holdings increase and the public's currency holdings are constant, then the depository institutions must be holding less currency and hence fewer reserves. (If the increase in the Treasury's currency holdings comes from a reduction in the public's currency holdings, then a rise in one factor that decreases reserves—Treasury cash holdings—is offset by a fall in another factor that decreases reserves—currency held by the public.)

The Treasury deposits tax payments and receipts from sales of its securities initially into depository institutions. But since it writes its checks on its account with the Fed, from time to time it has to transfer funds from its accounts with depository institutions to its account with the Fed. When this happens, the Fed credits the Treasury's account and debits the accounts of the depository institutions.[4]

The T accounts are:

Depository Institutions

(3)	Assets		Liabilities	
	reserves with Federal Reserve	−	deposits of U.S. Treasury	−

Federal Reserve Bank

	Assets	Liabilities	
	(unchanged)	member bank deposits	−
		U.S. Treasury deposits	+

---

[3] What about Federal Reserve currency in circulation? This is already taken care of indirectly by taking account of the factors that change the Fed's balance sheet, such as loans. The proceeds of these loans can be taken either as a credit to the bank's reserve account with the Fed or, if the bank wants to, by having the Fed ship Federal Reserve currency to it.

[4] Now consider SDR certificates. These are Special Drawing Rights, a form of international reserves created by the International Monetary Fund (IMF). When the IMF distributes additional SDRs, as it does from time to time, the Treasury as a matter of government bookkeeping adds their dollar equivalent to its account at the Fed. Hence, occasionally there is an increase in Treasury deposits with the Fed that does not result in a decrease in bank reserves. To make up for the fact that we are treating *all* increases in the Treasury deposits at the Fed as though they were decreases in bank reserves, we have to add increases in SDRs back in by treating them as a factor that increases bank reserves.

Some foreign governments also keep accounts with the Fed. When they transfer funds from their deposits with banks to the Fed, then bank reserves fall the same way as they do when the U.S. Treasury transfers deposits to the Fed. And the same is true when certain other institutions that hold deposits with the Fed, such as the United Nations or the FDIC, increase their deposits with the Fed.

The next item is "other Federal Reserve liabilities and capital." Suppose that a new member bank buys stock in the Fed, and thus raises Fed capital. It pays for this stock by having the Fed debit its reserve account, so that total bank reserves fall. "Other Federal Reserve liabilities" are brought in to keep the books straight. Previously we treated all the increase in other Fed assets as though it meant an increase in bank reserves because the Fed pays for these assets. But insofar as these assets have not yet been paid for—so that Federal Reserve liabilities increase—bank reserves have actually not yet increased. Hence, we now compensate for this by subtracting the increase in Fed liabilities.

Finally, depository institutions that clear through the Fed have to keep sufficient balances to meet their clearing obligations. When these balances (service-related balances and adjustments) increase, bank reserves fall.

Questions and Exercises for Appendix

*1 Given the following data, calculate the change in bank reserves:

	Change
1. Fed security purchases (including repurchase agreements)	10
2. Gold stock	−10
3. Currency in circulation	15
4. Acceptances bought by the Federal Reserve	−3
5. Treasury currency	10
6. Float	−3
7. Other Federal Reserve liabilities and capital	1
8. Other deposits with the Federal Reserve	−1
9. Other Federal Reserve assets	5
10. Foreign deposits with the Federal Reserve	5
11. Federal Reserve loans	20
12. Treasury deposits with the Federal Reserve	−5
13. Treasury cash holdings	−5

2 Take the data given in the previous example and: (a) eliminate the figure shown for Fed security purchases and (b) add the following:

14. Member bank deposits at the Fed	−3
15. Currency held by banks	−2
16. Currency held by the nonbank public	5

Now calculate Fed purchases of securities.

3 Take each of the items in Question 1 and explain in your own words the effects of this item on bank reserves. Do not merely state whether it raises or lowers reserves, but explain why.

*4 Evaluate the following statements:
   a. When the Treasury buys gold, the money stock increases because the country now has more gold.

b. An increase in float increases the money stock because it means that there are more checks in transit. This in turn means that people are receiving more money, and this increases the money stock.

c. An increase in currency in circulation raises bank reserves because some of this currency will be deposited in banks.

d. When Federal Reserve loans increase, bank reserves decline because, by increasing the liabilities of banks to the Fed, a rise in Federal Reserve loans reduces the net assets that banks have with the Fed.

THREE

MONEY, NATIONAL INCOME, AND THE PRICE LEVEL

The Determinants of Aggregate Expenditures

After you have read this chapter, you will be able to:

- **Explain the quantity theory equations and the quantity theory itself.**
- **Discuss the income-expenditure approach.**
- **List the determinants of consumption and investment.**

We are now in a position to discuss a set of problems that are basic to our well-being. One is what determines the inflation rate and the price level over the long run. The other is what determines shorter-run fluctuations in the inflation rate, which, in turn, is connected to fluctuations in output and employment. Together, these successive expansions and contractions are called **business cycles** or, more accurately, **business fluctuations.** Since 1854 we have experienced at least 31 successive waves of expansion and recession. These fluctuations generate much personal hardship. In one such cycle, during 1932 and 1933, almost one-quarter of the nonfarm labor force was unemployed. More recently, in 1982, one out of ten members of the labor force could not find a job. To take a different example, consider the fact that in 1994, the consumer price index was about six times what it had been in 1950. Within a nine year period, from 1972 to 1981, the price index had more than doubled. This means that someone who retired on a pension fixed in dollar terms in 1972 could buy nine years later, in 1981, less than half of what he could buy with his pension when he retired.

Before seeing in Part Four how monetary policy can be used to ameliorate such problems, we have to ask what causes them. Are they primarily due to bad monetary or fiscal policies? Are they due to fluctuations in aggregate demand that arise spontaneously in a market economy? Or are they due to fluctuations in the growth rate of productivity?

Several theories have been put forward to explain business fluctuations. One is the **Keynesian,** or **income-expenditure,** theory, developed by the great English economist John Maynard Keynes and his followers. It explains aggregate demand by focusing on the incentives to consume and invest. Another is the **monetarist** theory, identified with the work of Nobel laureate Milton Friedman, currently at Stanford University's Hoover Institution, and the late Karl Brunner, and Allan Meltzer, of Carnegie-Mellon University. Monetarists, or **quantity theorists,** relate changes in aggregate demand primarily to changes in the supply of money. A third theory, **the credit view,** of which Ben Bernanke of Princeton University is the leading exponent, focuses on the availability of credit to explain aggregate demand. A fourth theory, **new classical** theory, developed mainly by Robert Lucas of the University of Chicago, Thomas Sargent of the Hoover Institution, Neil Wallace and Edward Prescott, both of the University of Minnesota, and Robert King of the University of Rochester, explains fluctuations in output primarily by supply-side factors.

A LOOK AHEAD AT PART THREE

Although there is much dispute about how our financial system should be managed, many facts about the financial system can be readily observed, so that there is little disagreement about them. Hence, the previous chapters have been mainly descriptive. When one says that banks offer checkable deposits, nobody will disagree. But about macroeconomic theory there is disagreement. In this part we will set out the broad areas of agreement, while explaining how and why economists differ on other issues.

In explaining the behavior of real income and prices, we are explaining the behavior of nominal income, because total output (which is the same as real income) times prices is equal to nominal income. Nominal income is usually measured by nominal gross domestic product (GDP), which is the dollar value of all final output before subtracting depreciation. As Figure 15.1 shows, both nominal GDP and real GDP have fluctuated substantially. Although these fluctuations are sometimes called "business cycles," the term "cycle" conveys an unwarranted impression of regularity. The majority of economists attribute these fluctuations not to variations in the capacity to produce, but primarily to variations in the demand for goods and services, that is, variations in aggregate demand.

What accounts for these changes in aggregate demand? To answer this question we will cover essentially the same ground as macroeconomics courses, but we will focus on the role of money in determining aggregate demand. We start in this chapter by dealing with both the quantity theory of money and the variables stressed by the Keynesian, income-expenditure theory. We then delve more deeply into the income-expenditure theory, with successive chapters on how it explains the interest rate, the role it attributes to changes in the demand for money, and its policy implications. Chapter 19 follows, with a closer look at the critical policy issues of unemployment and inflation. The following chapter then deals with monetarism and the credit view. The final chapter of this part discusses new classical theory, and a variant of the income-expenditure theory, called **post-Keynesian** theory.

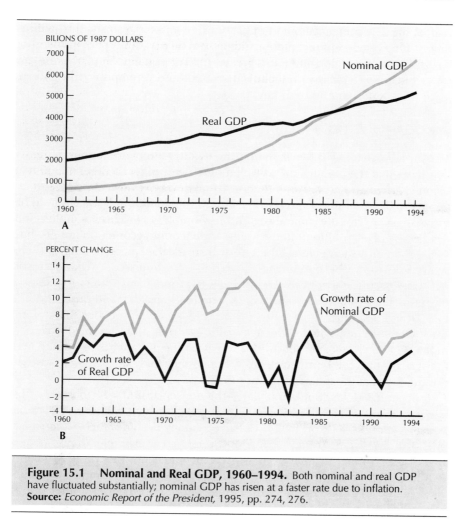

BILIONS OF 1987 DOLLARS

A

PERCENT CHANGE

B

Figure 15.1   Nominal and Real GDP, 1960–1994. Both nominal and real GDP have fluctuated substantially; nominal GDP has risen at a faster rate due to inflation. **Source:** *Economic Report of the President,* 1995, pp. 274, 276.

Before taking up any of these theories, a warning is in order: do not read politics into economic analysis. Some conservatives' teeth are set on edge as soon as one mentions Keynes. Doesn't acceptance of Keynesian theory require one to accept a large role for the government in managing the economy? No, it does not. The essence of Keynesian *theory* is the analysis of aggregate demand by looking at its components—linking consumption with income and investment with consumer demand and interest rates. Many Keynesians conclude from such an analysis that the economy is unstable. But one can accept the Keynesian method of analysis without necessarily concluding that the economy is unstable. Moreover, even if one concludes that the economy is unstable, that by itself does not make the case for stabilization policy. The economy may be inherently unstable, but, as we will explain in Chapter 26, government intervention *may* exacerbate rather than moderate such instability.

Similarly, the fact that the quantity theory is associated with Milton Friedman, who is widely known for his advocacy of free markets and for his criticism of big government, should not bias anyone for—or against—the quantity theory. One can accept the quantity theory and be a socialist, perhaps because one dislikes competition and wants greater income equality. Similarly, one can reject the quantity theory on technical grounds and yet oppose most government intervention in the economy.

THE QUANTITY THEORY EQUATIONS

The monetarist approach is based on the quantity theory of money, a theory that states that the nominal quantity of money determines the level of nominal income. Suppose you want to relate nominal income (YP, real income times prices) to the quantity of money (M). The simplest and crudest way would be to say that they are the same thing and to write $M = YP$. This is simple—and dead wrong. Dollar bills, or deposits in a transactions account, do not just buy some good and then give up the ghost. Instead, the recipient spends them again, so that they become income a second time, and so on. What occurs is illustrated by the story of two moonshiners (Jim and Tom) who were going to town to sell a $10 bottle of moonshine. The road was long and dusty and Jim told Tom: "I am thirsty and want a drink; here is a dollar for your share of it." After a few minutes, Tom felt thirsty too, took a drink, and gave the dollar back to Jim. Jim then took another drink and passed the dollar back to Tom. When they got to town the bottle was empty, but all they had between them was $1, not the $10 that the moonshine was worth.

What has to be done is to change the nonsensical $M = YP$ to $MV = YP$ by adding a term, V, for **velocity** (sometimes called **income velocity**). This term measures the number of times a dollar of money becomes income to someone during a given period, say, a year.[1] Suppose, for example, that someone spends $100 to buy a camera. The store's income is not the whole $100, but only its markup on the camera, say, $30. (The other $70 of receipts represents an exchange of assets, a camera for money.) Sooner or later two other things happen. One is that the owner of the store spends some of the $30 of income she received, so that someone else's income goes up by his markup. Second, the store orders a new camera from the manufacturer, whose income rises by her markup and who then buys materials and hires workers to produce another camera. As a result, income rises again. Currently, a dollar of money (M-2) becomes income (GDP) about two times a year.

The Cambridge Equation

An alternative formulation of this equation is called the "Cambridge equation," after Cambridge University where it was developed by Alfred Marshall and A. C. Pigou. It is written as $M = kYP$ where k is the proportion of a year's (or other period's) nominal income that people keep as money. For example, if people hold, on the average, an amount of money equal to six months' income, then $k = \frac{1}{2}$.

---

[1] Velocity, having the dimension of number of times per year, is a flow variable that allows one to relate a stock variable, money, to a flow variable, income.

Since $MV = YP$, and $M = kYP$, k must equal $1/V$. To illustrate, if people hold six months' income as money, so that $k = \frac{1}{2}$, then, on the average, a dollar of money enters someone's income twice a year.

Although the two equations formally say the same thing, the Cambridge equation is more insightful. When one talks about velocity, it is easy to think of velocity as a more or less mechanical thing; velocity just happens to be, say, 2, and that is all there is to it. In contrast, when talking about k, the proportion of their incomes that people want to hold as money, it is natural to think about this in terms of human choice. Hence, we treat it as governed by the same factors that govern our holdings of any other durable good, that is, as determined by income and by cost. However, discussions of monetary theory use both the velocity and the Cambridge k formulations, often interchangeably, so you must know both.

The Transactions Version

An earlier version of the quantity theory equations is called the **Fisher equation,** after Irving Fisher (1867–1947), its leading proponent. It is $MV' = PT$, where M is again money, T all the transactions undertaken with money, and P the average price of all items included in T. The V' of this equation is called **transactions velocity** and represents the number of times a dollar of money becomes *receipts* to someone even if it does not become income. Thus in our previous example of someone's buying a camera, the whole price of the camera—$100—is counted as soon as the camera is bought. So T encompasses not only the items included in GDP, but also intermediate products, purchases of secondhand goods (such as previously existing stocks and bonds), and factor services (such as wages, etc.). It even includes financial transactions, for example, transfers of funds from a checking account to a money-market fund. Transactions velocity is much greater than income velocity.

Transactions velocity V' is used much less frequently than income velocity V for two reasons. First, we are much more interested in predicting nominal GDP than we are in predicting total transactions. For example, we would hardly say that economic growth is satisfactory if output fell by 10 percent, while stock market sales rose by a more than offsetting 2 percent.

Second, there is a statistical problem. We can measure income velocity by writing $V = YP/M$, and then using readily available data on nominal GDP for YP and on M-2 for M. To use the transactions equation is much messier. We do not have good data on total transactions. And while we do have good data on the turnover of deposits, we can only guess at the turnover of the other component of money, currency. Hence, from now on, when we say "velocity," we will always mean income velocity.

All these equations are really *identities,* or tautologies, that is, statements that are true by definition. Like other identities they cannot *by themselves* tell us anything about the real world. To obtain empirical statements (that is, statements about the real world), one has to add some assumptions to them. Thus, the income-velocity equation is extremely *useful* if income velocity is stable or otherwise predictable. The equation is still true but *not useful* if velocity behaves unpredictably. The quantity theory of money asserts that velocity is predictable, so that if one knows the nominal supply of money, one can predict nominal income.

THE QUANTITY THEORY: AN OVERVIEW

Households and firms have an idea about the optimal value of their monetary holdings as a percentage of their income, or, in economic terminology, their Cambridge *k*. They continually adjust their actual balances to attain this optimal balance. They do so by reducing their net expenditures when they want to build up their monetary balances and by increasing their expenditures on goods, services, and securities when their monetary balances are too high. Hence aggregate demand, and thus income, depend on the interplay of the supply of and demand for money. In describing how this process operates we will first assume that the demand for money does not depend on the interest rate; we will remove this assumption later.

Suppose now that the Federal Reserve provides banks with more reserves and they make additional loans or buy securities so that deposits increase. As these deposits are spent by those who sold the securities or received the loans, some firms and households now find that they hold more money than they want to. Accordingly, these firms and households increase their own expenditures on goods and services or on securities. Thus they reduce their own monetary balances back to the optimum level, but in doing so they also raise the monetary balances of those from whom they have bought. These recipients now hold more money than they consider appropriate and hence increase *their* expenditures. The excess money is like the proverbial hot potato.

As the additional money is spent, income rises. The part that is spent on goods and services raises income directly, while expenditures on securities raise income indirectly by lowering interest rates, and thus induce households and firms to spend more.

How far will income rise? Consider three alternative situations. In the first there is full employment. The extra spending thus cannot help expand output, so real income is constant and the increased expenditures raise only prices. The rise in prices works to reduce the value of monetary holdings in real terms. This process of rising prices and falling real monetary balances will continue until real balances are back at their previous level because the nominal money supply and prices have risen proportionately. Only then will people hold no more real money than they wanted to hold and hence be back in equilibrium.

So in this case when all the adjustment is in prices, it is the public that determines the *real* money supply, even though it is the Federal Reserve that determines the *nominal* money supply. The price level changes to make the nominal supply of money as determined by the Fed equal to the real supply of money as determined by the public. *Hence, one can explain changes in the price level as resulting from changes in the nominal amount of money supplied by the Federal Reserve and the banks and from changes in the real quantity of money demanded by the public.*

For the second case consider the opposite extreme; there is a substantial excess supply of labor and productive facilities, and increased expenditures result, not in higher prices, but in higher output. As output and real income rise, the demand for money rises too, so that once real income has increased by enough to induce the public to want to hold additional money, the economy is back in equilibrium. How much real income has to rise to restore equilibrium depends on two factors: the increase in the money supply and the percentage change in the quantity of money demanded per 1 percent change in the real income, or *the real income elasticity of demand for money*. Suppose that the money supply has risen by, say, 10 percent and that the real income elasticity of demand for money is 0.9. Real income will then have to rise by 11 percent (10/9) to make the public willing to hold all the additional money.

The third case, the more relevant one for the *short run*, is an intermediate one. As expenditures increase, both prices and output rise. In this case, both the demand for real money balances increases as real income rises and the supply of real money declines as prices rise. So both terminate the rise in nominal income.

So far we have assumed that the public wants to hold the same amount of money regardless of the interest rate it could earn by holding securities instead. Obviously, this is not the case. If interest rates on securities rise relative to the interest rates earned on money, people will want to exchange some of their money holdings for securities, so that they can earn the higher interest rate. In terms of the Cambridge equation, k will fall so that for any given M, YP will be greater. Suppose, for example, that initially M was 100 and k ⅕, so that YP was 500. If the interest rate rises, k might fall to, say, ⅙, so that YP will be 600.

Now, as we will show in the next chapter, the *initial* effect of an increase in the money supply is to lower the interest rate. Hence, as the money supply increases, the *initial* rise in prices and real income will be less than what we stated for each of the three cases just discussed. Thus the quantity theory will not provide an accurate prediction. However, as we will also show in the next chapter, although the nominal interest rate falls at first when the money supply increases, it then rises again toward its previous level and may surpass it. Hence, quantity theorists argue, after a short transition period the traditional quantity theory result still holds. Quantity theorists say that if prices are flexible, as in the first case, then, at least as a first approximation, after some time prices will have risen proportionately to the increase in the quantity of money. Keynesian critics of the quantity theory do not deny that this will happen— eventually. But they argue that it will take a long time and that we are primarily interested in what happens over the next few years. Some of the debate between Keynesians and quantity theorists is therefore a dispute about how long it takes to reach the result the quantity theory predicts. It is a disagreement over how long the "short" run is.

So far we have discussed only one type of change in the market for money, an increase in the *supply* of money. If instead the *demand* for real money increases, then prices or real income (or a combination of the two) will have to fall to restore equilibrium.

If the supply of money changes only infrequently and by small amounts, while the demand for money changes frequently and substantially (due, for example, to financial innovations), then the quantity theory would not be useful. It would not explain most of the observed changes in real income and in prices. But quantity theorists believe that the demand function for money is stable and predictable and that it is changes in the supply of nominal money that primarily explain changes in income.

An Example of the Quantity Theory in Action: $P*$

Economists at the Fed recently developed an interesting longer-run version of the quantity theory, usually referred to as $P*$, the symbol they use for the long-run equilibrium price level.[2] In the first instance they try to explain the price *level* rather than the inflation rate. Since for many years the velocity of *M-2* has had an essentially flat trend, they take it as a constant. They also take the growth rate of real income to be equal to the growth rate of potential real GNP during the sample period. With Y and V thus fixed, $P*$ is determined by *M-2*. Taking the growth rate of real income as equal to the growth of potential output means that business cycles are ignored. But this is acceptable because this model tries primarily to explain the behavior of the price level only over a long enough period for cyclical changes to wash out. The authors then supplement this long-run theory with a theory of short-run dynamics that shows by how much prices adjust from their current level toward the level indicated by $P*$.

THE INCOME-EXPENDITURE APPROACH: BASIC IDEAS

The income-expenditure theory received its greatest impetus from Keynes's *The General Theory of Employment, Interest and Money* (published in 1936), but many other economists, some of them sharp critics of Keynes, have also left their mark. Its basic equation is

$$Y = C + I + G + X,$$

where Y is nominal income, C is consumption, I is investment, G is government expenditures, and X is net exports. This too is an identity. It is true by definition because we define C, I, G, and X so that together they encompass all expenditures. And since aggregate income is equal to total receipts from sales (that is, to aggregate expenditures), Y must equal $C + I + G + X$.

Another way of understanding this identity is to look at it from the side of output. All output must go to someone. One part, C, goes to consumers; another part, G, is used by the government. Some output, X, represents net exports and goes to foreigners. Business holds on to another part, I, for investment. This part has a special characteristic. The other sectors of the economy—consumers, government, and foreigners—decide how much they want to buy and go ahead and buy it. Business is in a different position because it is

[2] See Jeffrey Hallman, Richard Porter, and David Small, *M2 per Unit of Potential GNP as an Anchor for the Price Level* (Board of Governors, Federal Reserve System, Staff Economic Study, 1989), p. 157.

the seller of output. And sometimes it cannot sell all it thought it would. It then ends up with unsold output in its inventories. Such unintended increases in inventories, just like intended increases in inventories, count as investment. Thus, a retailer who expected to sell 100 dresses but sold only 50 is an (unhappy) investor in 50 dresses.

If firms find that their inventories have risen because they cannot sell as much as they thought they would, they respond by cutting back on production. Income now falls. Conversely, suppose that sales increase unexpectedly. When firms realize that they have sold more of their inventories than they expected, they restore their depleted inventories by raising production. Income now rises.

This critical role of inventories is shown in Figure 15.2, called the *45-degree diagram* or the *Keynesian cross*. Income Y, that is, $C + I + G + X$, is measured along the horizontal axis. The vertical axis measures $C + I' + G + X$, where I' is not actual investment, but the amount that business wants to invest. It therefore excludes the unintended changes in inventories described previously. A 45-degree line allows one to "translate" from one axis to the other,

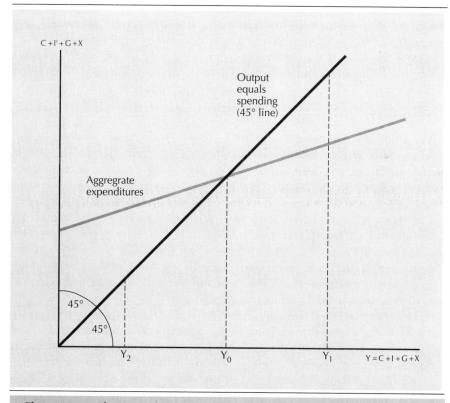

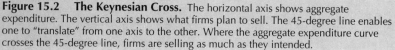

Figure 15.2   The Keynesian Cross. The horizontal axis shows aggregate expenditure. The vertical axis shows what firms plan to sell. The 45-degree line enables one to "translate" from one axis to the other. Where the aggregate expenditure curve crosses the 45-degree line, firms are selling as much as they intended.

because vertical and horizontal lines drawn from the 45-degree line to the axes mark off equal distances. At any point above this 45-degree line $C + I + G + X$ is less than $C + I' + G + X$. Hence I', the amount that firms want to invest, is greater than I, the amount they actually do invest. They therefore increase output to restore their depleted inventories. Similarly, at any point below this 45-degree line actual investment exceeds intended investment. Firms then try to reduce their inventories by cutting back production. Only at points along the 45-degree line are firms in equilibrium, meaning that they are adding to inventories exactly as much as they want to and no more.

Now introduce aggregate expenditure into this diagram. It is shown by the $C + I + G + X$ line. This line slopes upward because if income is higher, households consume more and firms invest more. At the point where this aggregate expenditure line crosses the 45-degree line, aggregate expenditure is just high enough for business to sell all it wants to. As a whole, it neither accumulates unwanted inventories nor runs down its intended inventories. At Y_0 the economy is therefore in macroeconomic equilibrium. If business were to produce more, so that income would be, say, Y_1, total demand would not be sufficient. Firms would accumulate excess inventories, and hence cut production. Similarly, at Y_2 sales would exceed what firms expected, and they would run down their inventories faster than intended. Hence they would raise production. Only at Y_0 are production and demand in equilibrium.

We now look at the determinants of the aggregate expenditure curve, starting with consumption.

Consumption

Households allocate their disposable income (income after personal taxes) either to current consumption or, through the act of saving, to future consumption. Thus, consumption depends (1) on the amount of disposable income and (2) on the proportion of disposable income withheld from current consumption, that is, saved. What is not saved is consumed; hence, one can explain the proportion of income consumed by looking at the factors that determine the savings ratio. What are they?

In part they are broadly sociological and historical. In some countries the urge for instant gratification is treated with tolerance, while in other countries (or in other historical periods) thrift and foresight are regarded as important virtues. Such sociological factors change only slowly, so that, for most purposes, economists can disregard them.

Another factor is the age composition of the population. For most households income rises into middle age and then drops sharply at retirement. At the same time, a household's needs are high in its early years when it equips itself with durables and bears some of the costs of raising children. Hence, both young households and old households tend to save little, while middle-aged households save much. Since the age composition of the population is not constant—think of the baby boom—the savings ratio and thus the propensity to consume are significantly affected by the age composition of the population.

The stock of wealth, or total assets, is another important determinant of the savings ratio. Consider a household that does not intend to leave any bequests but saves only to finance its consumption during retirement. The more wealth it already possesses the less it has to save to assure itself of a given standard of living in retirement. Similarly, someone who saves to leave a particular bequest obviously needs to save less if her wealth is already high. The same is true for someone who saves for unexpected emergencies. Since the only purpose of saving is to build up wealth, one would therefore expect changes in wealth, due, for example, to a rise in stock prices, to have an effect on saving.

In its effect on consumption and saving not all wealth is alike. Liquid wealth, such as holdings of deposits and short-term securities, has a greater effect on consumption than do holdings of illiquid wealth, such as a house or equity in a pension plan. This comes about because when we say "savings" we mean net savings, that is, the positive savings of some households minus the negative savings, or dissavings, of other households. Anything that makes it easier for some households to dissave (consume in excess of income) will reduce the overall savings ratio. And the possession of liquid wealth does make it easier to dissave. Someone without liquid wealth may not be able to obtain enough credit to dissave as much as she wants to, or may be discouraged from dissaving by the high cost of credit. By contrast, the possessor of liquid wealth can readily sell it and dissave.

The proportion of income saved is also affected by the reward for saving, the after-tax real rate of interest. The relation between saving and the interest rate is complex. But since money has much of its impact on consumption by changing interest rates, this relation cannot be passed over lightly.

Consumption and the Rate of Interest

Real interest rates affect consumption in several ways. One effect operates by increasing the reward for saving. It may seem surprising at first glance, but the direction of this effect is hard to determine. A fall in the interest rate lowers the reward for saving, which, taken by itself, should cause people to lower their savings ratio. At the same time, if interest rates fall, interest recipients are poorer and, hence, to restore some of their income losses, they try to increase their incomes again. One way to increase one's income is to save more. To take an extreme example, suppose someone insists on accumulating an estate of, say, $1 million in twenty years. Such a person must save substantially more if the interest rate falls from 10 percent to 5 percent.[3]

A second way in which a change in interest rates affects consumption has to do with the way in which households want to hold their wealth. They divide their wealth so that, at the margin, the imputed yield they obtain from consumer durables is just equal to the yield they obtain by holding financial assets, such as securities or bank deposits. When the interest rate on securities and bank deposits falls, households have an incentive to hold fewer of these assets and to buy more consumer durables. Hence consumer expenditures increase.

[3] Put in terms of microeconomic theory, the income effect here outweighs the substitution effect.

Third, with interest rates falling, the value of securities rises, so that households feel richer. And the higher their perceived wealth, the greater is their consumption. This may be a very strong effect. Fourth, a rise in the value of any of its assets raises a household's liquidity in the sense of raising its ratio of net worth to liabilities. And if households become more liquid, they are more ready to trade some of their liquid assets for such illiquid assets as consumer durables. A fifth way operates through a change in income. Since households are net creditors, a rise in the interest rate raises their incomes and hence both their consumption and their saving.

The Consumption Function

In summary then, one can write the consumption function as

$$C = a + c(Y' - T) + bW + dL + er_r + fA,$$

where C is aggregate consumption, Y' is personal income, T is personal taxes (so that $Y' - T$ equals disposable personal income), W is wealth, L is a measure of the liquidity of wealth, r_r is the real interest rate, A is a measure of the age of the population, and a, b, c, d, e, and f are constants.[4] Or one can use a simpler, but less precise version that treats all the independent variables, other than income, as though they were constant. If so, the consumption function becomes just $C = a + cY'$. Parameter a is called **autonomous consumption** because it is independent of income, while c is called the **marginal propensity to consume** since it measures the dollar change in consumption per dollar change in income.[5] The **average propensity to consume** is just C/Y'.

Permanent Income, the Life Cycle, and Wealth

So far when discussing the relation between income and consumption, we have not said whether consumption depends on income of the same period or on income over a longer period. At first economists took the seemingly obvious route of relating consumption and saving in one year to the income of that particular year. But this was then challenged by the **permanent-income theory** developed by Milton Friedman and the **life-cycle hypothesis** developed by Nobel laureate Franco Modigliani. Both theories point out that we save to accumulate wealth, so that we can consume in the future. An important motive, probably the most important motive, for saving is to even out consumption over time. This suggests that the relevant income is not the income of the current year, but income over the whole lifetime of the household. An alternative way of making this point is to say that consumption depends not on current income, but on the household's total wealth including its human wealth. (Human wealth is the present value of future earnings.)

But treating consumption as depending not at all on current income per se, but only on discounted lifetime income or total wealth may be going too

---

[4] If the equation is written in natural logs, then c becomes the income elasticity of consumption.

[5] The factors discussed so far are not the only ones that can affect consumption. Other variables that many empirical studies have found to be important include the rate of income growth and the relative levels of income.

Consumer Sentiment and the 1990–91 Recession

During the 1990–91 recession the newspapers carried many stories about the pessimism of consumers. This is not surprising. From August 1990 (two months into the recession) to October 1990 consumer sentiment, as measured by a survey undertaken by the University of Michigan for the past 44 years, had its biggest drop ever. No wonder the news media and some economists considered consumer pessimism to be a major factor in the recession.

A household's optimism or pessimism about its future income, and about the economic situation in general, can have a major influence on its spending. In deciding what it can afford, a household looks not just at its past and current income, but also at its probable future income. Someone who expects to lose his job in a few months is not likely to buy a new car or a new boat, and so commit himself to making a stream of payments. Moreover, most expenditures on durables are postponable. One can often make do with the old car for another year. So one would expect that if people become pessimistic, expenditures on durables will fall. And this is what the data show. But not all the money that would have been spent on durables is saved. Some of it is spent for nondurables because they do not involve a commitment as the purchase of a durable does. Suppose you decide not to buy a stereo and instead plan to go to a fancy restaurant each of the next twenty Sundays. Then, if you lose your job next week, you can cancel your plans to eat out. But had you bought the stereo, you would be stuck. Hence, when people become more pessimistic, total consumption does not fall as much as the consumption of durables does.

But since households do not spend on nondurables everything they save by postponing the purchase of durables, total consumption does fall when pessimism increases. Hence, an index of consumer sentiment does help to predict aggregate expenditure.

far. Some people, most students for example, are capital rationed. Their lifetime income is high enough that they could afford to consume more now than they actually do. But they cannot increase their current consumption because they cannot borrow enough against their future income. Besides, future income is uncertain and some people may use their current income as a rough guide to how much they can afford to consume. Hence, it seems plausible that current and permanent income both belong in the consumption function.

INVESTMENT

In this discussion we will make much use of the term **investment.** With that we do not mean just any employment of a person's savings, but something very specific—*additions to the capital stock.* Hence, we do not include in *investment* the purchase of CDs, bonds, or even stock. Only when a firm uses the funds it got from selling stock or bonds to build up its capital stock—by purchasing, say, machinery or inventory—or to undertake research on new products, do we count it as investment. This has an important implication: the reward that a firm receives when it invests is called *profit* (or *capital gain*) not *interest*. Interest is what the firm pays out to obtain the funds that it invests. Hence, when the interest rate falls, firms invest more. If one thinks of investment as the purchase of, say, a bond, that statement makes no sense. One reason why it is important to keep the definition of investment in mind is that we will later show how an increase in interest rates lowers investment. This does not contradict the obvious point that people buy more bonds when the interest rate on bonds rises: bonds are not counted as investment. To reiterate, an investor, in the sense we are using the term here, does not get *interest* on her investment, she gets *profits* (dividends and capital gains). Interest is what she *pays* to obtain the funds she invests in physical assets, either directly or through stock.

Figure 15.3 shows the fluctuations of various types of investment. They are large, particularly the fluctuations of inventory investment and net foreign investment.

Firms add to capital, that is, they invest, up to the point at which the expected yield on investment is just equal to the **user cost** of the additional capital (that is, the cost of investment). User cost has three components. One, **depreciation,** consists of obsolescence as well as wear and tear. The second is the **interest rate** that the firm must pay to borrow the funds that it invests or the imputed interest rate it charges itself when it invests some of its undistributed profits. The third is a **risk premium** that compensates the firm for venturing its funds. We will discuss these costs in more detail shortly.

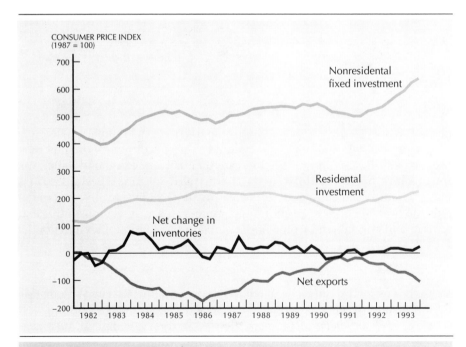

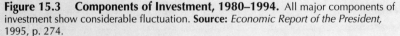

Figure 15.3   Components of Investment, 1980–1994. All major components of investment show considerable fluctuation. **Source:** *Economic Report of the President,* 1995, p. 274.

The Marginal Productivity of Capital and the Pace of Investment

Figure 15.4 shows the yield on capital as a function of the existing stock of capital. As additional capital is added, its yield, the marginal productivity of capital, declines. Given the declining marginal productivity of capital shown in the figure, one might expect that, over time, as the capital stock rises, the marginal productivity of capital continually falls. But Figure 15.4 shows the marginal productivity of capital only on the unrealistic assumptions that the size of the labor force is constant and that technology is unchanged. A growing labor force raises the demand for capital, and new technology often does so too, and thus shifts the marginal productivity of capital curve outward.[6] As a result, despite the growing stock of capital, there is no reason to assume that the marginal productivity of capital falls over time.

If some factor, such as new technology, raises the marginal productivity of capital, or if the user cost of capital falls, firms undertake new investment until the marginal yield on capital once again equals the marginal user cost of capital. But here we run into a complication. A firm's capital is a stock—say, $10 million—while investment is a flow, and thus has a time dimension—say,

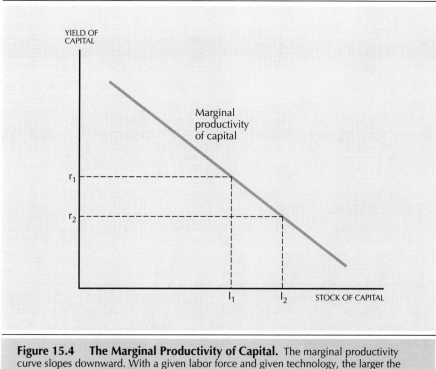

Figure 15.4   The Marginal Productivity of Capital. The marginal productivity curve slopes downward. With a given labor force and given technology, the larger the stock of capital, the lower is the yield per dollar of capital.

[6] By no means do all innovations raise the demand for capital; some save capital in the sense of requiring less capital per dollar of output. The computing power that required the purchase of a mainframe some years ago can now be obtained for a much smaller capital outlay from a PC.

$2 million per year. Hence, even if one knows how much additional capital a firm wants, one does not know its rate of investment. A firm that increases its capital stock from, say, $20 million to $30 million can invest for one month at the rate of $10 million per month or for five years at the rate of $2 million per year. How fast a firm attains its optimal stock of capital depends on the relative costs of operating for some time with insufficient capital versus the costs that result from speeding up the pace of investment. One can draw a curve relating the yield from investment not to the capital stock, but to the amount that is invested each year. This curve, shown in Figure 15.5, measures the marginal efficiency of investment. It is this curve, and not the marginal productivity of capital curve, that directly determines investment. It shows that as the interest rate falls, investment increases. As long as investment takes place, the capital stock rises, and as the capital stock rises, the marginal productivity of capital falls. The curve of the marginal efficiency of investment therefore shifts inward. Eventually, in equilibrium, net investment no longer takes place, because the capital stock has reached its new equilibrium, though gross investment is higher because the increase in the stock of capital means that replacement demand is greater.

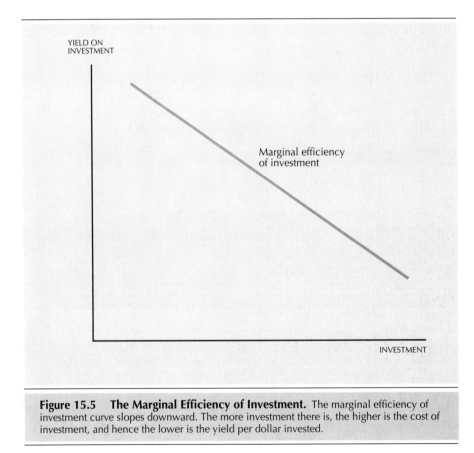

Figure 15.5   The Marginal Efficiency of Investment. The marginal efficiency of investment curve slopes downward. The more investment there is, the higher is the cost of investment, and hence the lower is the yield per dollar invested.

The User Cost of Capital

One of the components of the user cost of capital, the depreciation rate, depends on technology, a topic economists tend to ignore, feeling that it is more the province of engineers. Another component is the real rate of interest: here economists are on surer ground. The higher the interest rate, the lower the *present* value of the stream of income that capital will yield in the future. As previously discussed, the present value of a future payments stream of $\$Y$ per year is $PV = Y/(1 + r) + Y/(1 + r)^2 + Y/(1 + r)^3 + \cdots + Y/(1 + r)^n$. Obviously, the higher r is, the lower the present value of such a sum is. In particular, as Table 15.1 shows, the more distant payments lose value quite rapidly as the interest rate rises. Thus, at an interest rate of 5 percent, $\$100$ ten years from now has a present value of $\$61$; at a 10 percent interest rate, its present value is only $\$39$, and at a 20 percent rate it falls to $\$16$. Hence, for some types of investments that will begin to generate returns only, say, five years from now and then do so for twenty years, the rate of interest is of overwhelming importance.

The interest rate that should be used to discount future receipts is often a complex mixture of various yields. One component is the imputed interest rate on the undistributed profits that a firm invests rather than paying them out to its stockholders. Since its stockholders prefer receiving a dollar of dividends today rather than next year, the firm should charge itself an imputed interest rate on its own funds. Otherwise it would invest too much and pay too little in dividends.

Another component of the cost of capital is the cost of borrowed funds. This is more than just the interest rate. Suppose a firm borrows $\$5$ million at 10 percent. The true cost of this loan is greater than 10 percent, perhaps substantially greater. As discussed in Chapter 2, the more a firm borrows, the greater the risk its stockholders, as well as its creditors, take. That increased risk depresses the price of its stock and also raises the rate of interest it has to pay on further borrowing. So, instead of borrowing, the firm may decide to

Table 15.1   Present Value of $1 Received at Various Dates

Number of Years from Now	Discounted at Interest Rate of:		
	20%	10%	5%
1	$0.83	$0.91	$0.95
2	.69	.83	.91
3	.58	.75	.86
4	.48	.68	.82
5	.40	.62	.78
6	.33	.56	.75
7	.28	.52	.71
8	.23	.46	.68
9	.19	.42	.65
10	.16	.39	.61

issue more stock, even though its current stockholders then have to share the firm's earnings with the new stockholders. The burden of the increased risk if the firm borrows and the burden of diluting the current stockholders' equity if it sells stock are both part of the cost of capital.

Output and Investment

Since the only reason for using capital is to produce output, the marginal productivity of capital, and hence the rate of investment, depend on the volume of output as well as on the user cost of capital. Assume that real wages, the user cost of capital, and technology are all constant. Consider net investment (that is, investment beyond what is needed to take care of depreciation): how much will a firm invest? If its output is constant, its net investment will not be just constant; it will be zero. With constant output the firm's desired capital stock remains constant too, so that it does not have to add capital by investing. If output falls, then the firm has more capital than it wants and will disinvest by not replacing depreciating capital. Such disinvestment is a slow process.

Only if output increases will the firm undertake net investment. How much it then invests depends, in part, on its optimal capital coefficient, that is, its optimal amount of capital per dollar of output. If output accelerates, then the rise in investment can be dramatic. Table 15.2 gives an example. As long as output is constant at $100, the only investment that occurs is $50 of replacement investment. But when output rises from $100 to $120, the firm adds $100 of new capital. As a result, gross investment (new investment plus replacement investment) rises to $150. Thus a 20 percent increase in output has not raised investment just by 20 percent, but has tripled it.

The Stability of Investment

Since, from time to time, output does rise at an accelerating rate, the so-called **accelerator,** or **acceleration principle,** seems to imply that investment is highly erratic. This suggests that, in the absence of government stabilization policy, the economy would be unstable. But there is an ameliorating factor. Firms are

---

Table 15.2 Output and Investment

Value of Output	Value of Machines Needed*	Replacement Investment†	New Investment	Gross Investment‡
$100	$500	$50	$0	$+50
100	500	50	0	+50
120	600	50	100	+150

*$5 of machines are required to produce $1 of output.
†Depreciation is equal to 10 percent of the last period's machines.
‡Replacement investment plus new investment.

likely to move slowly toward their optimal capital stock, so that investment *per year* is not all that variable. There are several reasons for this.

First, a firm does not react mindlessly, as a badly programmed computer, to a suboptimal capital stock. Instead, it operates with the old capital stock if it expects the higher demand to be only temporary: toy makers do not raise their investment massively in December when demand rises. Second, a high rate of investment disrupts the firm's other activities, so that firms try to spread out investment over time. Third, the cost of obtaining funds may rise sharply as the firm invests more. It can finance a limited amount of investment from its retained earnings. To invest more than that, it may have to rely on bank loans. But capital rationing by its banks may limit the funds it can obtain that way. Other sources of funds, such as issuing bonds, may be more expensive. Hence, a firm's investment may be constrained by a rising cost of funds.

Fourth, when many firms try to invest at the same time, the cost of capital goods may rise substantially and induce some firms to postpone investment. Moreover, if many firms try to borrow more, the interest rate rises, and this discourages firms from investing. If the supply of funds available for investment is unresponsive to the demand for borrowing, then investment is not likely to increase much.[7]

But investment may also be unstable for reasons other than the acceleration principle. Some economists believe that the marginal productivity of capital curve, as it is perceived by firms, is highly unstable. Thus Keynes wrote:

> Our knowledge of the factors that will govern the yield of an investment some years hence is usually very slight and often negligible. . . . We have to admit that our basis of knowledge for estimating the yield ten years hence of a railway, a copper mine, a textile factory . . . amounts to little and sometimes nothing.[8]

If we lack reliable knowledge, then our opinions are not firmly anchored and thus are subject to radical revisions. Hence, some economists have argued that irrational waves of optimism and pessimism cause violent swings in investment that destabilize the economy. Other economists doubt that firms behave so irrationally and emotionally in their investment decisions.

Another Way of Looking at Investment: The *q* Theory

One theory of investment, called the q *theory*, was developed by Nobel laureate James Tobin of Yale University. It focuses on the stock market. This market sets a certain value on the outstanding stock of a firm. Suppose that this value is greater than what it costs to develop a similar firm, that is, to put up the buildings, buy the machinery, and hire the staff. If so, entrepreneurs can make a profit by undertaking the required investment, and they will do so. In con-

---

[7] Although the competition for capital goods and for financing suggests that investment for all firms jointly is more stable than for each firm individually, there is also a way in which the interaction of firms makes investment more unstable. When one firm purchases capital goods to undertake investment, it generates demand, and hence an incentive to invest, for the firms producing the capital goods.

[8] John Maynard Keynes, *The General Theory of Employment, Interest and Money* (New York: Harcourt, Brace, 1936), pp. 149–50.

trast, if it costs less to buy the stock of an existing firm than to start a similar firm, then those who want to hold claims to physical capital will buy stock in existing firms rather than initiating investment in new firms.

Hence, Tobin tries to explain the level of investment by a ratio q, which is the market value of firms divided by the costs of reproducing such firms. This q theory does not ignore any of the previously discussed factors and hence is consistent with our preceding discussion of what drives investment. These factors enter q by affecting the market value of firms. Tobin's theory is appealing because it is hard to see how it could *not* be right. However, the trick in constructing a theory is to use variables that can be measured with sufficient accuracy, and the reproduction costs of firms are hard to measure.

THE INTERACTION OF INVESTMENT AND CONSUMPTION: THE INVESTMENT MULTIPLIER

From the acceleration principle we know that changes in expenditures, and hence in output, bring about changes in investment. And the investment multiplier, which we now take up, shows how changes in investment generate changes in consumption. (Caution: do not confuse the investment multiplier with the money multiplier of Chapter 13. The former shows the relation between investment and income, and the latter the relation between reserves, or the base, and the money supply. They are similar only in that both show a geometric sequence.)

The basic idea of the investment multiplier is simple and obvious. When a firm undertakes investment, its spending generates income. When it puts up a building, it employs labor, and so do the suppliers of building material. When it buys machinery, the incomes of those who produce the machines go up. As these people spend their increased incomes, those who produce the goods they buy then experience an increase in *their* incomes and so on.

At first glance it might seem that $1 of investment spending would generate a continuous $1 flow of income as it is spent by a chain of recipients. Not so. The recipients of the additional income, all along the chain, do not typically consume 100 percent of their increased income. They save some of it. Moreover, not all the increased income represents disposable income. Some goes to pay personal taxes. Hence, at each link in the chain only one part of the increased receipts is consumed, so that the sequence of expenditures is decreasing. The chain of expenditures is

$$\$1c + \$1c^2 + \$1c^3 + \cdots + \$1c^n,$$

where c is the marginal propensity to consume.[9] Such a series approaches a sum of $1/(1-c)$.

Such a multiplier is applicable not just to investment, but to any change in exogenous expenditures, that is to any change in expenditures other than the consumption induced by a change in income. It therefore applies to a

---

[9] To take account of the fact that expenditures on imports do not directly become income to residents in the United States, c can be defined as the marginal propensity to consume domestically produced goods and services.

change in government expenditures or net exports, as well as to a change in consumption induced by some factor other than a change in income, for example to a rise in consumption due to a fall in the interest rate.

GOVERNMENT EXPENDITURES, TAXES, AND EXPORTS

Suppose the government buys more goods and services. Like the investment expenditures of firms, such expenditures become income to someone. These recipients consume it in the same way they consume income that results from private investment. Hence, the investment multiplier applies to government expenditures for goods and services just as much as it applies to private investment.[10] On the other hand, a rise in income taxes lowers aggregate expenditures by reducing the value of the multiplier. At each step in the chain the leakage into taxes is now greater, so that the percentage of total income that is consumed at each step is less. This decreases the multiplier and lowers income.

Thus, both higher government expenditures and lower tax rates increase nominal income. Since the excess of government expenditures over government receipts is the **deficit,** this implies that a rise in the deficit raises nominal income. But, as we will see in the next chapter, a higher deficit also raises interest rates. The effect of higher interest rates then offsets part of the expansionary effect of the deficit, perhaps a large part of it.

Although the view that deficits raise nominal income is widely accepted by economists, not all economists accept it. It has been challenged by Robert Barro of Harvard University. His argument, called the **Ricardian equivalence theorem,** is that people look far ahead into the future. When the government runs a deficit, they realize that either they or their descendants will have to pay off this debt or else pay interest on it continually. Since they do not want to impose such a burden on their heirs, they raise their savings by an amount sufficient to leave their heirs as well off as before. To do this, they cut their own consumption by an amount equal to the government's deficit. As a result, a deficit does not raise income. This argument is hotly disputed by many economists who doubt that people are that farsighted and well informed about the deficit and that concerned about their heirs.

The final component of aggregate expenditures is net exports, or exports minus imports. Suppose U.S. exports increase. Those who produced these exports now have a higher income and consume some of it, so that there is again a multiplier sequence. The other—negative—component of net exports is imports. One can think of the payments made to foreigners as a subtraction from income payments made in the United States and hence subtract imports from aggregate expenditures and nominal income in the United States. (This does not necessarily mean that higher imports reduce *real* income.)

---

[10] It is different for transfer payments. Suppose the government expenditures consist of transfer payments. These are not considered part of GDP. Hence GDP rises only when the recipients spend them. With the first term in the above sequence missing, the multiplier for government transfer payments is lower than it is for government purchases of newly produced goods and services.

The Stock Market and the Economy

A sharp drop in stock prices has several effects on the economy. First, the fall in wealth reduces consumption. Second, the cost of financing rises as firms have to give new stockholders a larger slice of the pie than before to obtain a given amount of equity capital. As a result, investment falls. Third, uncertainty increases and pessimism spreads; this reduces both consumption and investment. All this is pretty obvious. What is not obvious is how large these effects are.

Arguably the most dramatic event during the Great Depression was the stock market crash of 1929. Some people have therefore attributed much of the length and severity of this depression to it, and, more generally, have concluded that the stock market has a substantial effect on the economy.

But there is a problem with this argument. In 1966 the stock market fell more than 20 percent, and in 1987 it had its greatest one-day decline ever. So what happened at those times? Nothing, or at least not much that we can detect. To be sure, it is highly likely that in both cases income was subsequently at least a bit lower than it would otherwise have been, but in neither case did a recession follow.

Does that mean that the 1929 crash, too, had only a small effect on the economy? Not necessarily. Conditions were different then. A much larger proportion of stock purchases had been financed by borrowing, so that as stock prices fell, many more people not only lost some of their wealth, but were driven into bankruptcy. It is one thing to maintain your consumption as your wealth falls, and quite another to maintain it when you become bankrupt. And in 1929 the forced sales of the houses and other assets of insolvent borrowers *may* have had serious effects on asset markets. So, the importance of the 1929 crash is still open to debate. But regardless of what happened then, nowadays, while a stock market crash depresses income at least to *some* extent, it is far from being a reliable harbinger of an impending recession.

THE STABILITY OF INCOME

The multiplier tells us that a dollar of investment raises nominal income by more than a dollar. The accelerator tells us that increased consumption raises investment. This could lead to an explosive situation. Suppose that investment increases by $1 billion. With a multiplier of 2, this raises aggregate expenditure by $2 billion. The resulting demand for capital to produce this increased output could then raise investment by, say, $3 billion, which then raises income and consumption again. With high enough values for the marginal propensity to consume and the capital coefficient, the interaction of the multiplier and the accelerator could cause income to shoot up or down dramatically.

This could happen, but it need not. If people looked only at their current incomes in deciding how much to consume, then the marginal propensity to consume would be high. But suppose consumption depends on income over the long run or on wealth, as the permanent-income and life-cycle theories suggest. If so, consumption will not rise by much when income increases temporarily. As a result, the short-run marginal propensity to consume is low, so that the multiplier is less. Similarly, suppose that instead of responding immediately to a rise in demand, firms adjust their capital stock only slowly for the reasons discussed previously, so that the short-run accelerator effect is small. This too reduces the probability of violent fluctuations. Moreover, as we will discuss in Chapter 18, when either consumption or investment rises, interest rates rise, and this then dampens the rise in income.

THE QUANTITY THEORY AND THE INCOME-EXPENDITURE THEORY

In this chapter we have presented two theories, the quantity theory and the income-expenditure theory. The obvious question now seems to be which one is correct? But it is not necessarily the case that one of these theories is right and the other wrong. They might both be useful, and usefulness rather than rightness is a reasonable criterion for choosing a theory.

Neither theory is so narrow or specific that it merely says "If x occurs, y will happen." Rather, both are research strategies that tell us what variables are important in explaining or predicting changes in income. The quantity theory tells us to look at prior changes in the quantity of money, while the income-expenditure theory directs our attention toward the incentives that determine consumption and investment, that is, to the marginal propensity to consume, the marginal efficiency of investment, the interest rate, etc. But as we will explain in the next chapter, the interest rate depends, in part, on the real quantity of money. Hence, in the income-expenditure theory, the real quantity of money is one of several variables that explain income. Most economists who adhere to the income-expenditure theory believe that changes in the quantity of money are a major factor, but usually not the dominating factor, in explaining changes in income.

On the other side of the debate, quantity theorists focus on the supply of and demand for money. They do not deny that variables such as the marginal propensity to consume and the marginal efficiency of investment can, in principle, account for some of the variation in income. These variables operate by changing interest rates. Suppose that government expenditures increase. As the government sells bonds to finance the increased expenditures, the interest rate rises. This causes a fall in the Cambridge k, so that income increases. Similarly, a rise in the incentives to invest or to consume raises income according to the quantity theory, as well as according to the Keynesian theory. But quantity theorists believe that the effects on income of changes in the interest rate are relatively minor, either because velocity responds little to changes in the interest rate or because the relevant interest rate, the expected real rate of interest, itself changes little. At the same time, relatively large changes in the quantity of money occur and have substantial effects on nominal income. Hence, quantity theorists believe that changes in the quantity of money are the dominant, though not the sole, factor that changes nominal income.

A related facet of the dispute is the reliability with which certain variables can be predicted. Macroeconomic theory derives its justification not from being an elegant theory that is beautiful to behold, like some mathematical theorem, but from being useful for practical purposes, that is, for predicting changes in nominal income and thus for guiding policy. Quantity theorists believe that one can predict better how nominal income will change by estimating changes in the quantity of money and in velocity. Income-expenditure theorists, on the other hand, believe that to estimate variables like the marginal propensity to consume is the better strategy. Remember, too, that theories are tools and that it is often useful to have more than one tool in one's toolbox. Someone may therefore use the quantity theory when explaining the behavior of GDP in one period or in one country and the income-expenditure approach when dealing with a different period or a different country.

The dispute between income-expenditure theorists and quantity theorists is not a debate about whether a certain chain of logic is valid. If it were, it would have been settled long ago since all economists accept the same rules of logic. Instead, it is, in large part, a debate about empirical issues. Such issues are more difficult to settle. We will discuss them again in Chapter 20.

SUMMARY

1 Aggregate expenditure is identical with nominal income.
2 Aggregate expenditure can be analyzed from the money side using the quantity theory equations, $MV = YP$ or $M = kYP$.
3 The quantity theory explains changes in nominal income by changes in the supply of money. In it, changes in "Keynesian variables," such as government expenditures and the marginal propensity to consume, have an effect on income that works through the interest rate. But quantity theorists believe that these effects are much less important than the effects of changes in the supply of money.
4 Consumption depends on disposable income, wealth, liquidity, interest rates, and the age of the population. The permanent-income theory asserts that the relevant income measure is long-term income, and the life-cycle hypothesis uses the household's total, lifetime wealth instead of its current income to determine consumption.
5 Investment is the process of increasing the capital stock. It depends on the marginal efficiency of investment and the user cost of capital. The accelerator principle relates the desired capital stock to output. Despite this, investment need not be highly volatile.
6 The q theory provides a way of formulating the theory of investment in terms of stock market values. Investment takes place when the cost of creating a new firm is less than the price for which the stock representing the new firm can be sold.
7 The investment multiplier relates consumption to investment, government expenditures, and net exports. The interaction of the multiplier and the accelerator could, in principle, cause dramatic movements in income. But this is less likely if there are lags in investment and if consumption depends on long-run income or on wealth rather than on current income.

KEY TERMS

Cambridge equation
Cambridge k
income velocity
transactions velocity

income-expenditure theory
quantity theory
consumption function
permanent-income theory

life-cycle hypothesis
marginal productivity of capital
marginal efficiency of investment
user cost of capital

Tobin's q theory
accelerator
multiplier

QUESTIONS AND EXERCISES

*1 Explain the relation between aggregate expenditure and nominal income.
 2 Explain the meaning of "income velocity." Suppose you want to set up an equation relating money to the output and prices of consumer goods. How would you do it?
 3 Explain—in your own words—the basic idea of the quantity theory.
*4 What does the quantity theory predict will happen to income if the marginal efficiency of investment increases? Why?
*5 Suppose that the real income elasticity of the demand for money is 2 and that half the change in nominal GDP is due to real income and half is due to a change in prices. Suppose that the money supply rises by 10 percent. By how much will nominal GDP rise?
 6 What are the main differences between the quantity theory and the income-expenditure theory?
 7 What is the user cost of capital?
 8 Discuss the relation between output and investment.
*9 What factors tend to stabilize income despite the operation of the multiplier and the accelerator?

FURTHER READING

Several excellent macroeconomics textbooks discuss in detail the material taken up in this chapter. Among them are recent editions of:

DORNBUSCH, RUDIGER, and STANLEY FISCHER. *Macroeconomics*. New York: McGraw-Hill.
HALL, ROBERT, and JOHN TAYLOR. *Macroeconomics*. New York: Norton.
GORDON, ROBERT. *Macroeconomics*. Boston: Little, Brown.
MANKIW, GREGORY. *Macroeconomics*. New York: Worth Publishers.

For the classic discussion of the quantity theory, see IRVING FISHER, *The Purchasing Power of Money*, New York: Macmillan Co., 1991. For other references to the quantity theory see "Further Reading" in Chapter 20.

Aggregate Expenditures and the Interest Rate

After you have read this chapter, you will be able to:

- List the factors that determine interest rates.
- Realize why an increase in the money supply lowers the real interest rate only temporarily.
- Understand why an increase in the growth rate of money raises the nominal interest rate.
- Discuss the Fisher effect.
- Explain what difference it makes to interest rates if expectations are rational rather than adaptive.

If you read the appendix, you will be able to:

- Explain the relation between loanable-funds theory and liquidity-preference theory of interest-rate determination.

As explained in the previous chapter, one of the variables determining aggregate expenditure is the interest rate, a variable that deserves special attention in a book dealing with money and banking. We first examined interest rates in Chapter 5, where we looked at relative interest rates on various types of securities. Now we look at the determinants of the "pure" rate of interest, which is the hypothetical interest rate on riskless assets without transactions costs.

The determination of the interest rate is a difficult topic. To look at all the relevant factors at the same time would make for some very hard reading. So, to simplify, we will consider five different cases. We start with a simple, quite unrealistic case and then remove various simplifying assumptions as we go from one case to the next. In Case I, we assume that both the supply of and demand for money are constant. We also assume that interest income is not taxed and that changes in the inflation rate do not affect the propensity to consume or the marginal efficiency of investment. Case II drops the assumption that the supply of and demand for money are constant, but assumes instead that prices are fixed. This assumption is then dropped in Case III, which assumes instead that prices are completely free to respond to market forces. Neither fixed prices nor completely flexible prices are realistic assumptions. Hence, Case IV assumes that prices are "sticky," that is, that they adjust slowly. Finally, in Case V, we introduce income taxes and the effects of expected inflation on consumption and investment. In all these cases we will use as our example an increase in the supply of money. However, the same analysis can readily be applied to a change in the demand for money. But before considering these five cases, let us see why the interest rate is so important.

THE IMPORTANCE OF THE INTEREST RATE

Changes in the interest rate have an important effect on the economy. For example, thrift institutions were devastated when interest rates rose unexpectedly in the 1970s and early 1980s. Had they realized how variable interest rates could become, they would not have taken on so much interest-rate risk. Similarly, in the 1970s the debts of the less-developed countries would not have grown the way they did had either the borrowers or the lenders known how high the real interest rate would be in the early 1980s.

More generally, the interest rate is important for two reasons. First, *the interest rate is the price of obtaining goods, or resources, now instead of in the future.* In other words, the interest rate measures the price of future goods and resources in terms of current ones. Even if there is no inflation, a dollar next year is worth less to you now than a dollar this year. Exchanges of future goods against current goods pervade our economy. Households have to decide whether to consume more now or to save and consume more in the future, whether to work more this year or more next year. Firms have to make payments now to produce goods that will be finished in the future. Hence, the interest rate is one price that, usually implicitly, enters just about every nook and cranny of the economy.

Second, the more variable a price is, the more impact it has on the economy. And, as shown on the endpaper (located inside the back cover of this book), interest rates are highly variable. Our language hides the magnitude of changes in interest rates. Suppose that the price of butter rises from $1 to $2. We call this a 100 percent rise. But when the interest rate increases from, say, 6 percent to 12 percent, we usually call this a 6 percentage point rise and overlook that it is a 100 percent rise in the interest rate.

THE INTEREST RATE AS A PRICE

The interest rate is a price like any other. Hence, it is determined by supply and demand. Figure 16.1 shows the supply and demand for loanable funds. At r_1 the supply of loanable funds exceeds the demand for them, so the interest rate falls as suppliers offer successively lower prices (interest rates). At r_2

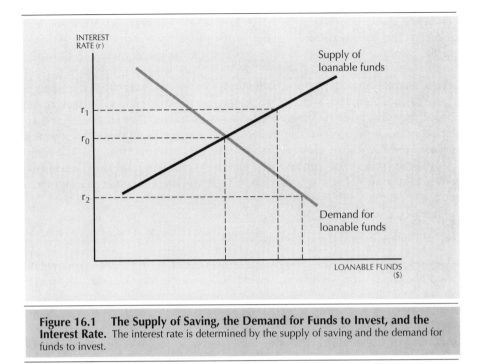

Figure 16.1   The Supply of Saving, the Demand for Funds to Invest, and the Interest Rate. The interest rate is determined by the supply of saving and the demand for funds to invest.

the demand for funds exceeds the supply, so the interest rate is driven up. Only at r_0, where supply and demand are equal, is the interest rate in equilibrium.

Alternatively, one can treat interest rates as determined by the supply of and demand for money. There is a certain quantity of money in existence, and there is a demand to hold money that depends on the interest rate. The interest rate, like any other price, then reaches equilibrium at the point where demand equals supply. (In the appendix to this chapter we discuss this theory of interest-rate determination and show that it yields the same results as the theory we take up now.)

CASE I: A SIMPLE ECONOMY

In this case we start with a simple economy in which the supply of and demand for money are constant and look at a situation in which there are no international capital flows (that is, no foreign investment). In such an economy there are several sources of loanable funds: many households save some of their incomes; so do businesses and even some governments. They offer these savings on the market for loanable funds. At the same time other households seek funds so that they can spend in excess of their incomes, and businesses borrow to invest in everything from nuclear power plants to a florist's inventory of roses, while many governments borrow to cover their deficits. The interest rate settles at the point at which the sum of these supplies equals the sum of these demands.

Now let us take account of the fact that our economy does not exist in isolation, that international capital flows do occur. Foreigners want to invest a certain proportion of their wealth in U.S. securities. This proportion depends in part on the interest rate paid on U.S. securities relative to the interest rate on foreign securities, as well as on expected changes in the exchange rate. Suppose, for example, that the interest rate on U.S. bonds is 8 percent and on British bonds is 6 percent. If the dollar appreciates or depreciates by less than 2 percent, one can earn a higher return by holding a U.S. bond than a British bond.

There is, however, some risk in holding one's assets in a bond denominated in a foreign currency. This is because the value of the foreign currency relative to one's own currency may decline. This exchange-rate risk makes it possible for the expected yield on U.S. securities to differ from that on foreign securities *somewhat* without setting off large continual capital flows. But large differences in yield can generate substantial capital flows (that is, U.S. purchases of foreign assets or foreign purchases of U.S. assets) for quite some time. Table 16.1 shows that from 1986 to 1989, capital inflows into the United States were almost equal to personal savings and after 1989 they declined sharply. In contrast from World War I to 1977 capital inflows were usually negative; that is, Americans invested more in foreign countries than foreigners invested in the United States.

Given the existence of such international capital flows, the interest rate now settles at the point at which both the domestic and the foreign demand for funds equal the domestic and the foreign supply of funds.

CASE II: THE FIXED-PRICE ECONOMY WITH CHANGES IN THE SUPPLY OF AND DEMAND FOR MONEY

It is, of course, unrealistic to expect any actual economy to have a constant supply of or demand for money, as was assumed in Case I. We now take the next step and in this case allow the supply of money and the demand for money to change. Suppose that the Federal Reserve increases bank reserves, with the result that banks increase the money supply by making loans or buying securities. In either case the supply of loanable funds increases and, as shown in Figure 16.2, the interest rate has to fall to bring the supply of and the demand for loanable funds back into equilibrium.

Similarly, suppose that the public wants to hold more money. To do this, people either refrain from lending money or they borrow money. In either case, the amount that people want to borrow rises relative to what they want to lend, so the interest rate rises.

As usual we can put supply and demand together in a diagram, such as Figure 16.3 in which we take income, wealth, and other prices as constant. Why do the curves in this figure slope the way they do? Let's look at the supply curve first. As discussed in the previous chapter, it is not necessarily the case that people save a larger proportion of their incomes as the interest rate rises, but we will make the assumption that they do. As already discussed, given a rise in the interest rate, capital inflows increase. The supply of money also rises

Table 16.1   Composition of Gross Savings and Capital Inflow, 1980–94

	Personal Savings	Gross Business Savings*	Federal Government Savings	State and Local Government Savings	Capital Inflows†	Total
			Billions of Dollars			
1980	$153.8	$345.7	$–60.1	$24.8	$–11.5	$452.7
1981	191.8	394.1	–58.8	28.5	–9.5	546.1
1982	199.5	417.5	–135.5	26.9	2.5	510.9
1983	168.7	472.7	–180.1	40.3	35.0	536.6
1984	222.0	520.7	–166.9	58.1	94.0	727.9
1985	189.3	546.4	–181.4	56.1	118.1	728.5
1986	187.5	533.9	–201.0	54.3	141.7	716.4
1987	142.0	588.7	–151.8	40.1	155.1	774.1
1988	155.7	646.6	–136.6	38.4	118.0	822.1
1989	152.1	667.3	–122.3	44.8	89.3	831.2
1990	170.0	691.2	–163.5	25.1	78.5	801.3
1991	211.6	725.7	–202.9	17.0	–8.1	743.3
1992	247.9	732.8	–282.7	24.8	56.6	779.4
1993	192.6	809.9	–241.4	26.3	92.3	879.7
1994‡	193.3	850.5	–158.4	25.3	135.0	1045.7
			Percent			
1980	34.0%	76.4%	–13.3%	5.5%	–2.5%	100.0%
1981	35.1	72.2	–10.8	5.2	–1.7	100.0
1982	39.0	81.7	–26.5	5.3	.5	100.0
1983	31.4	88.1	–33.6	7.5	6.5	100.0
1984	30.5	71.5	–22.9	8.0	12.9	100.0
1985	26.0	75.0	–24.9	7.7	16.2	100.0
1986	26.2	74.5	–28.1	7.6	19.8	100.0
1987	18.3	76.0	–19.6	5.2	20.0	100.0
1988	18.9	78.7	–16.6	4.7	14.4	100.0
1989	18.3	80.3	–14.7	5.4	10.7	100.0
1990	21.2	86.3	–20.4	3.1	9.8	100.0
1991	28.5	97.6	–27.3	2.3	–1.1	100.0
1992	31.8	94.0	–36.3	3.2	7.3	100.0
1993	21.9	92.1	–27.4	3.0	10.5	100.0
1994‡	18.5	81.3	–15.1	2.4	12.9	100.0

*Gross business savings including depreciation allowances.
†Equals net foreign investment.
‡First three-quarters of 1994 at annualized rates.
Source: *Economic Report of the President*, 1995.

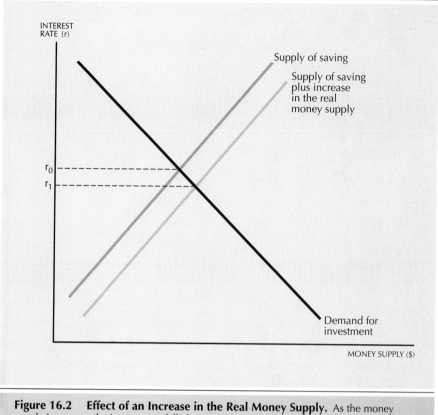

Figure 16.2   Effect of an Increase in the Real Money Supply. As the money supply increases, the interest rate falls from r_0 to r_1.

as interest rates go up (given a constant monetary base) because, as was explained in Chapter 13, the money multiplier increases as the interest rate rises. For all these reasons, the supply of loanable funds goes up as interest rates rise.[1]

On the demand side, investment declines as the interest rate rises. Similarly, the higher the interest rate, the less real money people want to hold because it now costs more in forgone interest to hold money.[2] The federal government's deficit is insensitive, or more likely, sensitive in a perverse way, to interest rates. It does not borrow less because interest rates have risen (though some state and local governments may). On the contrary, it may borrow more to meet the higher interest costs of its debt, while more or less maintaining

[1] Instead of assuming that the interest elasticity of saving is positive, we could assume that the effect of the capital inflow and the rise in the money supply more than offset the effect of a negative interest elasticity of saving.

[2] But don't some types of money pay interest too, so that a rise in the interest rate provides little incentive to switch from money to bonds? Not quite. The rate of interest on money lags behind the interest rate paid on securities. Hence, when bond rates rise, it is profitable to switch out of money into bonds.

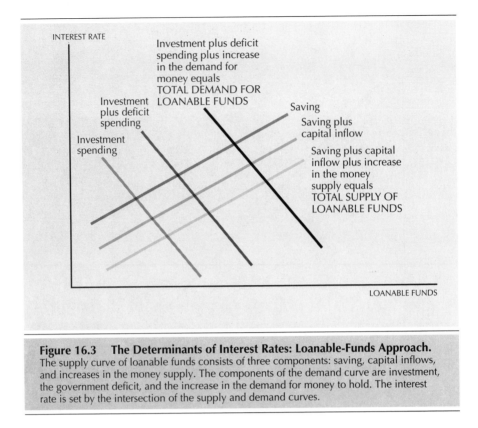

Figure 16.3   The Determinants of Interest Rates: Loanable-Funds Approach.
The supply curve of loanable funds consists of three components: saving, capital inflows, and increases in the money supply. The components of the demand curve are investment, the government deficit, and the increase in the demand for money to hold. The interest rate is set by the intersection of the supply and demand curves.

other expenditures. Despite this, the sum total of these effects probably is that the demand for money declines as interest rates rise.

Where does the Fed fit into this? News reports often say that the Fed has raised or lowered interest rates. It does so by changing the money supply in one of three ways. The most important way is for it to enter the market as a buyer or seller of securities and thereby change bank reserves. As it buys securities, it raises security prices directly (lowering interest rates), and as banks use their additional reserves to buy securities or make loans, interest rates fall further. Another way, which we will discuss in Chapter 23, is for the Fed to change the discount rate. Finally, it can change the public's expectations of future interest rates. Insofar as the expectations theory of the term structure is correct, the current long-term rate depends mainly on what interest rates are expected to be in the future. The Fed can influence these expectations through its ability to manipulate the money supply.

In this third case, where prices are taken as fixed, the interest rate must fall as the Fed generates a rise in the money supply. Only if the interest rate is lower will the public demand all the additional money that has been created. This decline in the interest rate is called the **liquidity effect.** In response to this decline in the interest rate, both consumption and investment rise, so that income increases. This increase in income, in turn, increases the demand for money, and hence the interest rate bounces back *part* of the way.[3]

CASE III: THE FLEXIBLE-PRICE ECONOMY

We start the discussion of this case with the assumption that people anticipate the inflation rate correctly, an assumption we then remove. But throughout this section we assume that prices are completely flexible, meaning that they move freely to their new equilibrium level and do so right away. With completely flexible prices, equilibrium can exist only if there is no idle capacity or involuntary unemployment. If there were any idle capacity, its owners would cut prices to get resources working again and unemployed workers would take jobs at lower wages.

Suppose that the nominal money stock rises in such a flexible-price economy. As before, at first the interest rate falls and aggregate expenditures increase. But since output is already at the full-employment level, it cannot expand to meet the increased expenditures, so that it is prices, and only prices, that rise.

They continue to rise as long as aggregate expenditures are above their previous levels. And as long as the interest rate is below its previous level, aggregate expenditures will be above their previous levels.

But as prices continue to rise, the *real* money stock falls. Eventually it returns to its initial level. At that point the interest rate, too, is what it was before the increase in the nominal money supply. This must be so because the only factor that caused the interest rate to fall was the greater real money supply, and now that supply has shrunk back to its previous level.

Figure 16.4 shows what occurs. Initially, the money supply increases from M_0/P_0 to M_1/P_0. (Right after the money supply has increased, the price level is still P_0 because prices have not yet had time to adjust.) With the real money supply rising to M_1/P_0, the interest rate falls from r_0 to r_1. As a result, aggregate expenditures increase. Firms, faced with an increase in demand and a fixed supply, raise prices to P_1, so that the real money stock falls to M_1/P_1 and the interest rate rises to r_2. But since it is still below r_0, prices continue to rise and the real money stock continues to fall. The same is true at r_3. This process ends only when the interest rate is back at r_0 and the real money supply has returned to M_0. The increase in nominal money has raised prices proportionately and left the real interest rate unchanged.

With changes in the supply of and demand for money having no effect on the interest rate, Case III yields the same result as Case I: the equilibrium

---

[3] To see why it cannot bounce all the way back, imagine that it were to do so. With the interest rate then being back at its previous level, consumption and investment, and thus income, would be back at their previous levels too. After all, the only reason they had risen is that the interest rate had fallen. But with income and the interest rate now having returned to their previous levels, who would want to hold the increased supply of money? Previously, people wanted to hold more money because income was higher and the interest rate was lower. But in the hypothetical situation in which the interest rate goes all the way back to its previous level, these incentives to hold more money no longer exist. Hence, the supply of money would exceed the demand for it and the interest rate would fall again.

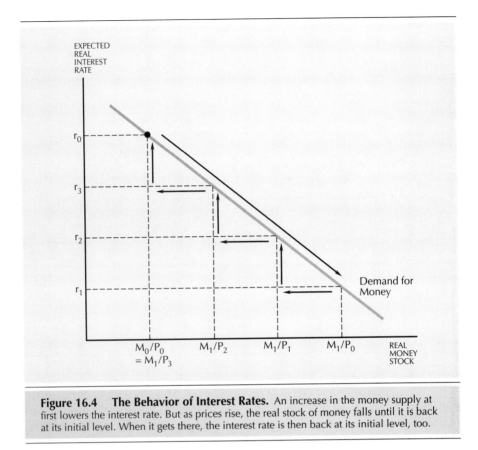

Figure 16.4   The Behavior of Interest Rates. An increase in the money supply at first lowers the interest rate. But as prices rise, the real stock of money falls until it is back at its initial level. When it gets there, the interest rate is then back at its initial level, too.

interest rate is determined only by saving and investment. This similarity of Cases I and III should not be surprising because in Case III, as in Case I, the *real* money supply and the *real* demand for money are ultimately unchanged. The only major difference between the two cases is that while in Case I the *nominal* money supply is constant, in Case III the nominal money supply increases. But since what determines the interest rate is the *real* money supply, the equilibrium positions of the interest rate are the same in both cases.[4]

Nominal and Real Interest Rates

In Case II, where prices were fixed, we did not have to distinguish between the real and the nominal interest rate, but now we have to. The real interest rate is the nominal interest rate adjusted to remove the effects of inflation; that is,

Real interest rate = nominal interest rate − inflation rate,

[4] To see why it is the *real* money supply and not the *nominal* money supply that matters, ask yourself the following question: suppose that the nominal money supply, all prices, all incomes, and all wealth were to double. Why should this change saving, investment, or the demand for money in real terms?

or in symbols,

$$r_r = r - p,$$

where r_r is the real interest rate, r the nominal rate, and p the inflation rate.[5] Why one has to subtract the inflation rate from the nominal interest rate to get the real rate is best explained by an example. Suppose that you lend someone $100 at an 8 percent interest rate when the inflation rate is 5 percent. At the end of the year you get back $108, but not all the extra $8 is genuine income to you. The $100 of returned capital will purchase only as much as $95 did at the beginning of the year, so that you should treat $5 of your nominal interest payment as part of the return of your capital, and only $3 as genuine interest income.

The distinction between the real rate and the nominal rate is important. As Figure 16.5 shows, these two rates often diverge. Thus, in the early 1930s during the Great Depression, the real rate of interest was very high, despite

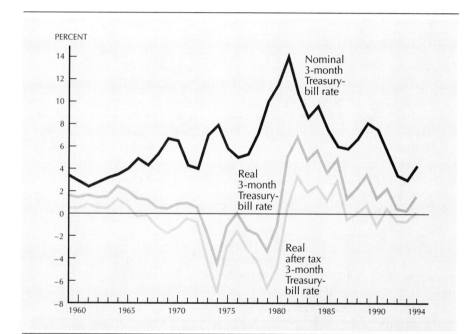

PERCENT

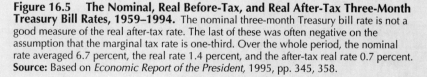

Figure 16.5   The Nominal, Real Before-Tax, and Real After-Tax Three-Month Treasury Bill Rates, 1959–1994. The nominal three-month Treasury bill rate is not a good measure of the real after-tax rate. The last of these was often negative on the assumption that the marginal tax rate is one-third. Over the whole period, the nominal rate averaged 6.7 percent, the real rate 1.4 percent, and the after-tax real rate 0.7 percent. **Source:** Based on *Economic Report of the President,* 1995, pp. 345, 358.

[5] Strictly speaking, this is only an approximation because it ignores the effect of inflation on the interest payment itself. But for the type of inflation we are familiar with in the United States, it is a close enough approximation.

the fact that the nominal rate was low. In the 1970s, when those who looked at the nominal rate were bitterly complaining about high interest rates, the real rate was extraordinarily low, and in fact, as Figure 16.5 shows, was negative in some years. (Figure 16.5 also shows the after-tax real rate, which we will discuss later.)

Which is more important, the nominal or the real interest rate? For most purposes the real rate is. Certainly, when considering whether a particular interest rate is fair, it is the real rate that counts. Even a 50 percent interest rate represents only a moderate real income to the lender when the inflation rate is 48 percent, while a 2 percent nominal rate provides the lender with a high real rate of return if prices are falling at a 10 percent rate. For determining aggregate expenditure, too, it is the real rate, or more precisely the expected real rate, that matters. A firm that expects the inflation rate to be 10 percent will not be deterred from investing by a 12 percent interest rate, while a firm that expects only a 2 percent inflation rate will be deterred. Similarly, a household may be willing to pay 15 percent to purchase a car if it expects that this car will cost 12 percent more next year.

THE FISHER EFFECT

Suppose the inflation rate, which had previously been zero, rises to 3 percent and everyone is aware of this. Lenders will now want a 3 percent higher nominal interest rate to compensate them for the 3 percent annual loss in the real value of their principal. Will they be able to get it? That depends on whether the factors that determine the equilibrium *real* rate of interest (the propensity to consume, the marginal efficiency of investment, capital inflows, the government deficit, and the supply of and demand for real money) are constant. If they are, and we will assume that they are throughout Case III, then the real rate will be constant, and hence the nominal rate will rise by 3 percent. More generally, we have

$$r = r_r + p^e,$$

where p^e indicates the expected inflation rate. Such an add-on to the real rate to take account of inflation is called the **inflation premium.** If (1) the expected inflation rate p^e is equal to the actual inflation rate and (2) the real rate is constant as the inflation rate changes, then the nominal rate changes point for point with the inflation rate. This is known as the **Fisher effect,** after Irving Fisher, who taught at Yale University in the first part of this century.

Note an important qualification to the Fisher effect: For it to be fully effective requires that the determinants of the real interest rate are unaffected by the inflation rate. For example, if the 3 percent rise in the inflation rate discourages investment, the real rate will fall, and hence the nominal rate will rise by less than 3 percent. Similarly, if nobody expects the 3 percent rise in inflation, the nominal rate will not change. What is therefore of great importance in determining the nominal interest rate is the way in which people form their expectations of inflation. So we have to digress and see how people form their expectations.

Adaptive Expectations

It is very difficult to determine how people form their expectations. Asking them runs into the problem that expectations are formed in large part in an unconscious way that people often cannot verbalize. At one time most economists used a simple model of expectations formation called the *error-learning model* or **adaptive expectations.** According to this model, people initially assume that the future will be like the past: if the inflation rate has been 5 percent in the past, it will be 5 percent next year. Suppose that this turns out to be wrong, that next year's inflation rate is actually 7 percent. People then adjust their expectations of the following year's inflation upward to reflect the error they have made. Thus they may expect the inflation rate now to be, say, 6 percent instead of 5 percent.[6] Hence when the inflation rate is changing, the inflation premium lags behind the actual inflation rate. As a result the nominal rate does not adjust quickly enough: the real rate of interest falls when the inflation rate is rising and rises when the inflation rate is falling.

This adaptive-expectations model is simple and may well be adequate for some purposes, but it has two serious faults. It assumes that people form their expectations only by looking at what has happened in the past, so that their expectations always lag behind actual events. This need not be. Suppose that a new administration pledged to a higher rate of economic expansion takes office. People should now expect the inflation rate to increase. More generally, the inflation rate of previous years is only one part of all the information that is available to estimate next year's inflation. If, as we generally assume in economics, people behave rationally, then they do not ignore all the other information. And if they do take account of all the information about future inflation that is readily available, then they are no more likely to underestimate the inflation rate than to overestimate it.

Rational Expectations

Recognizing these faults, today economists stress the theory of **rational expectations.** According to rational-expectations theory, people forecast in an efficient way, using all the information available to them. To do so, they must use some model of the economy that allows them to interpret incoming information. For example, using what they have learned from their economics courses, if they observe that the monetary growth rate is increasing and interest rates are falling, they predict that inflation will accelerate. But how about those who have never taken an economics course or who took one, but have forgotten everything from it? They, too, will have some (perhaps only implicit) theoretical framework that they will use to interpret incoming information.

Economics would be much further advanced if we knew these (largely inchoate) theories that people use. But we do not, so we have to make some assumptions. One possible assumption is that people's theories correspond

---

[6] Why don't people adjust their expectations all the way to 7 percent? The reason is that they used quite a lot of information in deciding that prices will increase at a 5 percent rate. They don't discard all this information merely because they were wrong in one year.

Forecasting Interest Rates

Suppose you hear from a secret but trustworthy source that the Fed will undertake large-scale open-market purchases tomorrow. Right after that your boss asks you what will happen tomorrow to Treasury bills and long-term bonds. Assuming that you remember what you have learned so far (economists assume all sorts of things), you will probably tell her that Treasury bill prices will rise substantially and long-term security prices will rise, but by much less. Usually you will be right. But not always.

Suppose that this time you are wrong: Treasury bills rise very little, and as a result, your company loses a lot of money. What will you tell your boss? The most likely explanation you could give is that the market expected the Fed action, and had already raised Treasury bill prices in anticipation.

Or suppose that you are right about Treasury bills, but wrong about bonds: Long-term bonds rise substantially. How would you explain that? One possible explanation is that the market interpreted the open-market operations as the beginning of an extensive and long-lasting expansionary policy, in other words as a harbinger of further cuts in short rates, which according to the expectations theory of the term structure, raises the prices of long-term bonds. Another possibility is that the Fed action was not the only factor affecting the prices of long-term bonds, that much of the rise in long-term bond prices was due to some other shock, such as news about increased demand for capital by firms.

Finally suppose you are wrong in a more serious way: bond prices fall instead of rising as the Fed undertakes its open-market purchases. You could explain by again saying that something else overrode the effect of the Fed's expansionary policy, but if bond prices fell just at the time that the Fed undertook its expansionary policy, that explanation would sound hollow. A more plausible explanation is that the market interpreted the Fed's action as the beginning of a more expansionary, and hence more inflationary, policy. The Fisher effect then worked to raise the nominal interest rate.

Usually none of these happens. Usually you are right in expecting bill prices to rise significantly and bond prices to rise to a very small extent. But "usually" is not "always." Forecasting is a risky business.

fairly well to economists' theories. This does not mean that everyone reasons the way economists do, but merely that their conclusions *average out* to what is shown by economists' models. This is not as unrealistic as it sounds at first, because the most important decisions are made by experienced managers who have reached their positions because they usually predict correctly. These managers can reach the same conclusions as economists without having the economists' theories in their toolboxes. For example, someone may not know the theories that explain the term structure of interest rates, but may simply observe that long-term interest rates behave in a certain way when short-term rates change; birds can fly without having studied aerodynamics.

Moreover, assuming that expectations are rational is not the same thing as assuming that people have perfect foresight; economic models certainly do not endow economists with such a useful quality. What it does mean is that, as opposed to the error-learning model, people will not make *systematic* errors for any length of time. They will still make errors, but these errors will be random, and, at least over the longer run, will balance one another out. People do not continually underestimate (or overestimate). To illustrate, here is an example from everyday life. Suppose that without it being announced, trains are now running more slowly so that the average trip takes half an hour longer. On the first day almost everyone will arrive at work late. Someone using an error-learning model will leave the next day, say, 10 minutes earlier and be 20 minutes late. But someone operating according to rational expectations may remember that in previous years when the weather was like this, trains were usually half an hour late, or else may call the railroad for information. Such a person will not always be exactly on time; some days the train will be slower, some days faster. But he or she will be late no more frequently than before.

How plausible is the rational-expectations approach? This is a hotly debated issue. Economists like the idea that people behave rationally. Indeed, this assumption forms the basis of economics. More specifically, it seems implausible that people forecast the inflation rate merely by looking at past rates.

The critics of the rational-expectations approach do not deny that people behave more or less rationally, but emphasize the "more or less." Since it is costly to obtain and process information, it may be *rational* to operate by a rule of thumb, such as projecting the past rate of inflation, perhaps with some adjustment for previous forecasting errors. The loss that results from such a rule of thumb may be so small that it is entirely rational to use such a crude rule. Why indulge in what J. M. Clark called the "irrational passion for dispassionate rationality"? It is therefore not so surprising that the empirical evidence does not provide strong support for the rationality of expectations.

Rational Expectations and the Inflation Premium

How can we apply the idea of rational expectations to the inflation premium? Since people's information is incomplete and their models imperfect, they will not estimate the future inflation rate with great accuracy. Sometimes they will make large errors. But since these errors tend to cancel out over the longer run, *on the average* their expectations will be correct. Hence, the inflation premium embodied in the nominal interest rate will—on the average—be correct, and—again, on the average—the real interest rate will be independent of the growth rate of the money supply or of changes in the demand for money.

Summary of Case III

With completely flexible prices—and a correctly anticipated inflation rate—the real rate of interest is unaffected by changes in the supply of nominal money because prices adjust to keep the real quantity of money constant. But in any particular case the public may well overestimate or underestimate the inflation rate and therefore add the wrong inflation premium in calculating the appropriate nominal rate. Hence, in individual cases the real rate of interest will change when the growth rate of money changes. But if expectations are rational, then—on the average—the inflation premium will be correct and the real interest rate will be unaffected by changes in the supply of money.

CASE IV: THE STICKY-PRICES ECONOMY

In Case II prices are fixed, and in Case III they are completely flexible, responding immediately to changes in the money supply. Neither of these cases is plausible. A more realistic case is one in which prices adjust fully, but only after some lag. Since ultimately they adjust fully, the final equilibrium in this more realistic case is the same as in Case III, and Figure 16.4 applies. But until we reach final equilibrium, we have a mixture of Cases II and III. So let us look at the sequence of changes in the interest rate when the money supply increases. We deal first with the case in which the inflation rate is anticipated correctly.

As in Case II the initial effect of an increase in the money supply is the liquidity effect, a drop in the real interest rate. Then, as real income and prices rise, the real interest rate rebounds. This is called the **income and price effect.** Since prices as well as real income rise, there is nothing to constrain the real interest rate from reaching its previous level; in fact, to reestablish equilibrium, it will ultimately have to return to its prior level. As long as the real rate is below that level, aggregate expenditures will be greater than before, and the greater aggregate expenditures are, the higher the inflation rate will be. Hence, prices, the demand for money, and thus the interest rate will continue to rise until the real interest rate is back at its previous level.

The nominal interest rate will be above the real rate by the amount of the inflation premium. This **expectations effect** could dominate the liquidity effect, so that in some cases a rise in the monetary growth rate *might* be accompanied by a rise rather than a fall in the nominal interest rate.

CASE V: AN ECONOMY WITH INCOME TAXES AND INFLATION EFFECTS

In the four previous cases we ignored the troublesome "detail" that our tax system does not respond correctly to inflation. Suppose that the real rate of interest is 3 percent and the inflation rate is 6 percent, so that the nominal interest rate is 9 percent. Although the true earnings of the lender are only 3 cents for every dollar lent, the tax system ignores this fact. It taxes a lender not only on the 3 cents of genuine income, but on the whole 9 cents she received. At the same time it allows a borrower to deduct from his taxable income not only the 3 cents of genuine interest, but the whole 9 cents.[7] Hence the income tax, in effect, imposes a special tax on lenders while subsidizing borrowers.

To see what this does to the interest rate, imagine an analogous situation: suppose that every time a book is sold the government taxes the buyer $1 and gives this dollar to the seller. Since there is no reason for the equilib-

---

[7] Throughout this discussion we will assume that lenders and borrowers are in the same tax bracket and will ignore the complication created by some types of income not being taxed.

rium price of a book to change, the market would negate the government's action. The price of a book would simply decline by $1, so that the after-tax cost to the buyer and the after-subsidy receipts of the seller would be the same as before. Hence, the inflation premium that is added to the real interest rate should exceed the inflation rate by enough to compensate the lender for the higher tax burden. Instead of being $r_r + p$, the nominal rate should be

$$r = r_r + p/(1 - T),$$

where T is the marginal tax rate. Suppose, for example, that the marginal tax rate is ⅓. Then if the inflation rate rises by 2 percent, the nominal interest rate should rise not by 2 percent, but by 3 percent, so that the *after-tax* inflation premium will be equal to the inflation rate. Whether during periods of inflation the nominal rate has actually risen enough to keep the real after-tax rate constant is another question. The empirical evidence that it does is plausible but not compelling.

Doesn't our theory say that it should rise enough to maintain the after-tax rate? The answer is that so far we have assumed that inflation does not affect the incentives to save and invest. Suppose inflation stimulates saving or discourages investment. If so, inflation would lower the equilibrium real interest rate. It is by no means obvious that inflation substantially affects either saving or investment in that way, but it might.

In the first place, when prices rise the real value of a person's stock of currency and government bonds falls. In response, households are likely to save more. In the second place, higher inflation creates greater uncertainty, and thus provides a good reason for saving more, just in case things go wrong. On the other hand, inflation *may* reduce the real return from saving, and that could affect the percent of income saved. It is far from clear what the net effect of all these factors is, but there is no reason to assume that a rise in the inflation rate leaves the savings rate unchanged.

Inflation also affects investment in several ways. A rise in the inflation rate generates uncertainty for firms. Will costs rise faster than prices? Will the Fed react by adopting a strongly restrictive policy to bring the inflation rate down again, and in the process cause a recession? Such uncertainties may well reduce investment. Moreover, as we will explain in Chapter 22, inflation raises the tax burden on some corporations. This, too, may lower investment.

In addition, a rise in the inflation rate affects two other determinants of the supply of and demand for loanable funds. Since, as we will explain in Chapter 26, a rise in the inflation rate reduces the federal deficit, rising inflation reduces the demand for funds, and hence lowers the equilibrium real interest rate. On the other hand, a rise in the inflation rate may (though it need not) scare off foreign investors, as well as induce Americans to place more of their funds abroad, and thus reduce the supply of loanable funds.

The upshot of all this is that once one allows for the effects of inflation on the incentives to save and invest, on the deficit, and on foreign investment, a rise in the inflation rate may either raise or lower the real interest rate, so that there is no presumption that the nominal after-tax rate will rise by exactly as much as the inflation rate.

That interest-rate theory leaves us with such a vague conclusion should not be surprising because the effects of inflation are likely to vary from case to case. For example, they are likely to be different in a country in which the government usually responds to a rise in inflation with a vigorous policy to lower it, than in a country in which a rise in the inflation rate usually signals that the inflation rate will rise even more in the future.

What interest-rate theory *can* tell us is about the very long run. After people have become accustomed to a higher inflation rate and have restored their stock of wealth to its previous level, after the uncertainty that concerns both domestic and foreign investors has disappeared, after tax laws have been adjusted to the higher inflation rate so that only real income and capital gains are taxed, and after the government's gains from inflation have been eliminated, then the Fisher effect will be in full operation, and inflation will only affect the nominal rate of interest, and not the real rate.

Where Are Interest Rates Going?

Real interest rates in 1994 were relatively low. Where will they be five or ten years from now? Though this question cannot be answered with precision, the work we have done so far suggests several trends to track.

One popular theory is that interest rates will rise because there will be a worldwide shortage of capital. As China, the countries of the former Soviet Union, and the other formerly Communist countries liberalize their economies, the marginal productivity of capital in these countries will rise sharply. Developing countries will also increase their demands for capital as memories of the debt crisis of the 1980s fade. Once upon a time such developments would have raised interest rates only in these countries, but now the world is one gigantic capital market, so if entrepreneurs in Moscow or Shanghai want to build steel plants, John and Mary Jones in Iowa City have to pay a higher interest rate on their mortgage.

Maybe interest rates will therefore rise. But maybe not. To be sure, world capital markets are much more integrated now than they were in 1950, though not as integrated as they were in the late nineteenth century. Significant barriers to international capital flows still exist. Investors may well be reluctant to invest in the formerly Communist countries because they fear a political upheaval could bring to power a regime that would prohibit them from sending their profits back home, and might even seize their property. That does not seem likely, but experienced investors know that politics is full of surprises.

Moreover, interest rates depend not only on the demand for capital, but also on the supply. Who knows, the U.S. savings ratio, which is unusually low now, may start to rise sharply, and as incomes rise in China, so will the supply of Chinese savings.

So while we are not in a position to make a forecast of real interest rates, a good first step is to identify the market and the demand and supply factors within it. Experts would want to track these factors in making their estimates.

A POLICY IMPLICATION: THE FED AND HIGH INTEREST RATES

When nominal interest rates are high the Fed gets blamed. Does that make sense? Perhaps, but not in the way most of the Fed's critics think. They argue that the Fed should increase the money supply to lower interest rates. In doing so, they make two mistakes. First and foremost, they focus on the nominal interest rate instead of on the much more relevant after-tax real rate, which is what borrowers consider in deciding how much to borrow. As Figure 16.5 (page 295) shows, the after-tax real rate was low during much of the 1970s, a time when there were vehement complaints about how high interest rates were. Second, they assume that the Fed could lower nominal interest rates by raising the growth rate of money. Any liquidity effect, however, is only temporary. In addition, the higher the monetary growth rate, and hence the greater the inflation rate, the higher the inflation premium. Therefore, at least after some time, a rise in the growth rate of money raises rather than lowers the nominal interest rate. Someone who wants to blame the Fed for high nominal interest rates should complain not that the Fed has kept the growth rate of money too low, but that it has previously kept it too high, so that now the nominal interest rate contains a large inflation premium. It is a high, not a low, growth rate of money that raises the nominal interest rate. The story is different for the real rate for which the empirical evidence is less clear.

SUMMARY

1 The interest rate is an important variable because, usually implicitly, it enters most transactions and also because interest rates are highly volatile.
2 A major issue in explaining interest rates are the conditions under which changes in the supply of or demand for money affect interest rates. If prices are fixed, then such changes affect interest rates permanently. If prices are completely flexible, they have no effect on interest rates. If prices are sticky, then they affect interest rates temporarily.
3 It is important to distinguish between nominal and real interest rates. The real rate is equal to the nominal rate minus the inflation rate. If people estimate the inflation rate incorrectly, they will add the wrong inflation premium to the real rate.
4 The error-learning model of expectations assumes that the public estimates inflation by looking only at previous inflation rates. But according to the rational-expectations theory, people look at a much wider variety of information in forming their expectations. Moreover, their errors show no systematic bias.
5 What affects decisions to save and invest is the after-tax real rate of interest. The way in which our tax system treats interest income means that when the inflation rate rises, the before-tax nominal interest rate should rise by more than the increase in the inflation rate.
6 If the marginal propensity to consume and the marginal efficiency of investment depend on the inflation rate, then changes in the growth rate of money will affect the real interest rate.

KEY TERMS

liquidity effect
real interest rate
Fisher effect
error-learning model
adaptive expectations

rational expectations
expectations effect
after-tax real interest rate
inflation premium

QUESTIONS AND EXERCISES

*1   The payment of net interest accounts for a smaller proportion of GDP than does payment for food. Why then do newspapers pay so much more attention to interest rates than to the price of food?

2   Explain how the following affect the rate of interest:
a. a tax on purchases of corporate stock
b. a reduction in government expenditures with no change in tax rates

*3   Discuss: "In an economy with flexible prices an increase in the growth rate of nominal money will raise nominal interest rates."

4   Discuss: "Our tax system ensures that the interest rate does not rise exactly in proportion to an increase in the inflation rate, but rises more than that."

*5   What difference does it make for the behavior of interest rates whether expectations are rational or not?

6   Offer some arguments that might suggest that expectations are not rational. How convincing are these arguments?

FURTHER READING

CONARD, JOSEPH. *An Introduction to the Theory of Interest.* Berkeley: University of California Press, 1959. A classic treatise on interest rates.

FRIEDMAN, MILTON. "Factors Affecting the Level of Interest Rates," in *Proceedings of a Conference on Savings and Residential Financing,* United States Savings and Loan League. Chicago: United States Savings and Loan League, 1969, pp. 11–27. An important analysis of how interest rates respond to changes in money growth.

MEHRA, YASH. "Inflationary Expectations, Money Growth and the Vanishing Liquidity Effect of Money on Interest: A Further Investigation," Federal Reserve Bank of Richmond, *Economic Review,* 71, no. 2 (March–April 1985), 23–35. A useful exposition, but it requires material which will be taken up only in Chapter 18.

THORNTON, DANIEL. "The Effect of Monetary Policy on Short-Term Interest Rates," Federal Reserve Bank of St. Louis, *Review,* 70 (May–June 1988), 53–72. A thorough analysis, but parts of it will not be comprehensible to someone who has not read the material in Chapter 18.

APPENDIX: THE LIQUIDITY-PREFERENCE APPROACH TO INTEREST RATES

In this chapter we have looked at interest rates as determined by the supply of and demand for loanable funds. Another way of looking at interest-rate determination is the liquidity-preference approach. This theory yields the same answers as the loanable-funds theory does, but describes the process in different terms. For some purposes this approach may be more convenient.

Unlike the loanable-funds theory, which is formulated in terms of *flows* (such as the flows of saving and investment), the liquidity-preference theory runs in terms of stocks. A supply of money, stated as a stock, confronts a demand for money, also stated as a stock. This difference between the two theories is just a matter of exposition. Since a flow represents a change in stocks, one can always reformulate a flow theory in terms of stocks and vice versa.

The reason the liquidity-preference theory is consistent with the loanable-funds theory is that the factors that determine the interest rate according to one theory also determine it according to the other. To illustrate this, suppose that real saving increases. As people cut their consumption, they also reduce the amount of money they hold to undertake consumption; their demand for money falls. Hence, according to the liquidity-preference theory (as well as the loanable-funds theory), as the liquidity-preference curve shifts down, the interest rate falls. Second, suppose that foreign capital flows into the United States. As will be explained in Chapter 29, U.S. exports then fall and imports rise; hence, U.S. income falls. When income falls, so does the demand for real money. The liquidity-preference curve again shifts down and the interest rate falls. Third, assume that the real money supply increases. Again, the interest rate falls.

Fourth, suppose that investment increases. To invest, firms temporarily need to hold more real money. This shifts the liquidity-preference curve upward, so that the interest rate rises. Fifth, if the government runs a deficit by buying more goods and services, the sellers of these goods and services now have higher incomes and hence a greater demand for real money. Again, the liquidity-preference curve shifts upward and the interest rate rises.[8] Finally, assume that people want to hold more real money. This is simply another way of saying that the liquidity-preference curve has shifted upward.

Hence, all the variables that according to the loanable-funds theory change interest rates also do so according to the liquidity-preference theory. Conversely, the two variables of the liquidity-preference theory, the supply of money and the demand for money, are part of the loanable-funds theory.

---

[8] In principle, a rise in government expenditures also has a direct effect on interest rates, since to spend more, the government must hold more money. But the amount of money the federal government holds per dollar of expenditure is trivial, and besides, the standard definition of money excludes balances held by the government.

Aggregate Expenditures and the Demand for Money

After you have read this chapter, you will be able to:

- **Understand the transactions, precautionary, and savings demands for money.**
- **Discuss what a money demand function is.**
- **Explain what happened to the stability of the demand function for money and to the stability of velocity.**

If you read the appendixes, you will be able to:

- **Describe the Baumol model of transactions demand, the speculative demand for money, and the liquidity trap.**

Two of the factors that determine interest rates—the supply of money and the demand for money—deserve particular attention. We discussed the supply of money in Chapters 13 and 14, and will discuss it again in Part Four. This chapter deals with the demand for money. The demand for money may seem a silly topic. Don't most people want as much money as they can get? Maybe so, but not in the way we are using the term *demand for money*. As usual in economics the term *demand* here does not mean demand in the sense of how much one would like of a good if it were free, but demand for a good relative to the other goods one wants. We ask, "How much money do you wish to hold, given that the more money you hold the less you can hold of other assets?"

The demand for money is related to the velocity of money and to the amount of money demanded per dollar of income (the Cambridge k). This chapter therefore discusses velocity, along with the demand for money. It starts with the demand for money in general, and then looks at money demand functions and velocity.

A SIMPLEMINDED STORY

Consider a person who holds money only for anticipated transactions in a purely mechanical way. He receives an income of, say, $3,000 each month and spends it at an even rate during the month. Until the last day of the month, he holds some money to cover expenditures. His money holdings are illustrated in Figure 17.1. On the first day he holds $3,000, and at the end of the last day $0. Since he spends his $3,000 at an even rate, his average money holdings are equal to ($3,000 + $0)/2, that is, $1,500.

    Someone who conducts his business in this way can hardly be said to have a demand for money that is worth discussing. The amount of money he holds is determined purely mechanically by his income and by the number of days remaining in the month. His mechanical behavior is inconsistent in two ways with maximizing utility. First, he pays no attention to the benefits and costs he might obtain from investing some of his income for part of the month.

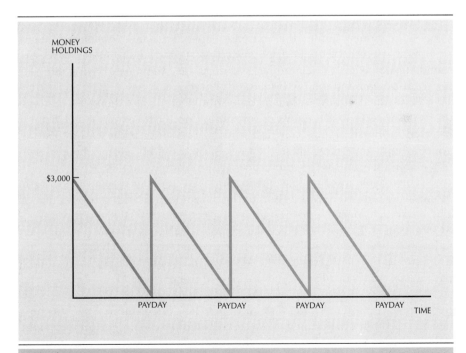

Figure 17.1   Time Pattern of Money Holdings: Simple Mechanistic Model.
Households receive a sum of money on payday and, in this example, run it down at a smooth rate over the pay period, so they hold zero money at the end of the period.

Second, he has only a **transactions demand** for money; that is, he holds money only for those transactions he anticipates, and ignores the fact that he may have an unexpected need for money.

Undoubtedly many people decide on their money holdings in this crude mechanistic way because it is not worth the cost and trouble to handle their cash balances in any other way. But a substantial part of the money supply is held in accounts large enough to make it worthwhile to manage them in a more sophisticated way.

Moreover, households keep much more money than can be explained by the need to hold some money until the next payday. Their money holdings, even if measured just by *M-1* and not *M-2,* amount to about one and three-quarters times monthly income, more than three times as much as one would expect from Figure 17.1. Obviously, the need to hold money until the next payday does not explain money holdings adequately. So let's see how those people who plan their money holdings carefully decide on them.

TRANSACTIONS DEMAND

There are many ways someone can take care of her transactions needs. At one extreme she can, as already discussed, keep all her receipts as money and then spend this money in the period between receipts. This avoids the trouble and cost of investing in securities or in near-monies, such as Treasury bills. But it has a disadvantage—forgoing the higher interest she could earn by investing some of the money. At the other extreme someone could invest all her income as soon as she receives it and sell a security whenever she needs money to spend. This maximizes her interest earnings, but frequently buying and selling securities generates large brokerage charges.

How much, if any, of her income should she invest therefore depends on two factors. One is the cost of investing, that is, the expense and trouble involved in investing and later disinvesting. The other is the *net* interest forgone by holding money, that is, the interest that could be earned on a security or a near-money minus the interest earned by holding money.

The trouble involved in acquiring and later liquidating securities or near-money does not rise in proportion to the amount involved, nor does the cost. The brokerage charge is not 100 times as great for a $100,000 security as for a $1,000 security. Hence, holders of large money balances are much more likely to invest their transactions balances than are holders of small balances. At current interest rates it does not make sense for most people to put some of their pay into securities or near-monies for part of the pay period.

But this does not mean that the transactions demand for money is independent of the interest rate. First, for large holders of money, such as businesses, it is often worthwhile to invest excess money even if just for overnight. And they are more likely to do so the higher the net interest rate. Second, households maintain transactions balances for occasional large purchases they plan to make some time in the future. The higher the net interest rate, the less likely they are to hold these funds in the form of money. Third, they also accumulate funds in their transactions accounts until it is worthwhile for them to buy securities. The higher the net interest rate, the smaller the amount of money required to make such a shift worth undertaking despite the cost and trouble involved in buying securities.

Fourth, the size of compensatory balances that firms hold also depends on the interest rate. The higher the interest rate, the greater the "free" services that banks provide per dollar of compensatory balance and, hence, the smaller are the compensatory balances that firms need to hold. Therefore, the transactions demand for money depends on the interest rate, even if nobody ever acquires securities on payday with the intention of turning them back into money before the next payday.

Apart from the net interest rate, the transactions demand for money also depends on the volume of intended transactions and hence on income. Obviously, the more money you plan to spend, the larger your transactions demand for money. The transactions demand for money is also a function of the cost and trouble of investing funds. This will vary with the value that people attach to their time, with the brokerage cost of buying and then selling securities, and with the available alternatives to holding money. Appendix A describes a model for determining the optimal level of transactions balances.

PRECAUTIONARY DEMAND

It usually makes sense to hold more money than you anticipate spending. As all of us have found out, frequently one spends more than one expects. Anything from car trouble to an unexpectedly high price for a purchase can force one to spend more than intended. Or a pleasant surprise may occur: an unexpected chance to snap up a bargain. Firms and some households also need to hold money because of the danger that they will not receive anticipated payments on time.

There are five ways to take care of such contingencies. One is to hold more money than one expects to spend, that is, to hold a **precautionary balance.** The second is to cut planned expenditures to make room for the unexpected ones as they arise. The third is to sell some asset, such as a bond or even physical capital, and the fourth is to borrow. A final possibility is to refrain from making a payment, a possibility that ranges all the way from just passing up a bargain to declaring bankruptcy.

All these responses have their costs. Holding a precautionary balance means forgoing some net interest. Cutting planned expenditures is usually painful and sometimes may not suffice to meet the unexpected need. For some assets, selling them quickly means selling them for substantially less than they would fetch in a more leisurely sale. Borrowing may be expensive. Passing up a bargain has an obvious cost. Reneging on a payment can involve embarrassment and a loss of reputation, as well as legal penalties.

It will usually pay to hold a precautionary balance, but how large should it be? The benefit from holding such a balance is that this avoids the costs of the other four alternatives just discussed, while the cost is the forgone net interest, say, 3 percent. As usual in economics the answer to the question "How big should it be?" is to set marginal cost equal to marginal revenue. Consider one of these costs, the cost of borrowing, say, at an 18 percent interest rate. The revenue you receive from holding a precautionary balance is then equal to the probability that you will actually use the precautionary balance times the 18 percent interest you avoid having to pay in this contingency. Since it is the essence of a precautionary balance that you hold it to guard against uncertain events, there will be times when you will not draw on it, and hence receive no benefit from it, while at other times it will save you a lot, 18 percent in this example.

Many unexpected events happen, but the probability that a household will have such bad luck that it has to make a large number of unexpected payments is much less than the probability that it will have to make just a few such payments. Similarly, a firm whose receipts from sales and whose required payments to other firms are not fully predictable will occasionally have the unpleasant experience that very few of its expected receipts are coming in, while very many of its bills are. But there is only a small chance that nearly all the bills it has to pay will arrive before any of its receipts do. Thus, both for firms and for households, the larger your precautionary balance is, the smaller the probability that you will actually use the last dollar in it. As a result, the marginal productivity of a dollar in a precautionary balance is less the greater the precautionary balance.

The marginal cost of holding a dollar in precautionary balances is constant, 3 percent forgone interest in this example. Hence, as you increase your precautionary balance, there comes a point at which the marginal productivity of a dollar in your precautionary balance is no greater than its 3 percent marginal cost. At this point your precautionary balance is just the right size. In our example, the marginal revenue of a dollar of precautionary balances is 18 percent times the probability of having to use that dollar. The marginal cost is 3 percent. To find the optimal balance, set marginal cost equal to marginal revenue. This means that 3 percent equals 18 percent times the probability of using the dollar. Solving for the probability, we find that the precautionary balance in this example should be large enough so that the probability of using its last dollar is $\frac{1}{6}$.

The same principle applies to the other costs of running out of money. Suppose, for example, that you can sell an asset right away for almost the same amount as you would get if you took your time selling it. In this case your response to running out of money would be to sell that asset rather than to borrow. The relevant marginal cost of having an insufficient precautionary balance is then the small amount you would lose by selling the asset quickly. Obviously, when faced with a shortage of money, you should choose the cheapest solution, whether it is borrowing, selling an asset, cutting expenditures, or delaying payment, and it is the cost of this cheapest solution that, along with the probability of using the last dollar and the net interest rate, determines the optimal size of precautionary balances.

So far we have looked at precautionary balances only as a device for meeting unexpected needs to make payments or delays in getting paid. But there is an additional way in which the need to take precautions makes people hold money rather than bonds. Holding bonds involves the risk that interest rates may rise and the price of your bond may fall. Hence, you balance off the risk of holding bonds against the higher return you obtain from bonds. As a result you may want to hold some money (or near-money) rather than bonds.[1] The lower the interest rate on bonds, the fewer bonds and the more money you will want to hold.

Thus, the size of precautionary balances depends on numerous factors. Some of them—the probability of having to make unexpected payments or the costs of cutting back on expenditures or of delaying payments—are usually constant. Hence we can assume that normally precautionary balances are not affected by variations in these factors.

However, the cost of selling assets does vary from time to time, depending on the public's security holdings. When households and firms are holding a large volume of liquid assets, such as Treasury bills, they have less need for precautionary balances, since these assets can be turned into cash at little cost. Similarly, the demand for precautionary balances falls when the net interest rate rises or when the rate at which firms and households can borrow decreases.

On the other hand, the demand for precautionary balances will increase if interest rates start to fluctuate more, so that the market values of securities, particularly long-term securities, become less stable. Moreover, in a sharp recession, the precautionary demand for money may increase. With unemployment widespread, households may decide to save more. Since for many wage earners it may not be worthwhile to hold near-monies, they may hold these savings as money instead. Businesses, too, may hold more precautionary balances because they are afraid that their customers may not be able to pay on time.

THE SAVINGS DEMAND FOR MONEY

Many people accumulate savings in their checkable deposits as their monthly expenditures fall short of their receipts. It is often reasonable for them to keep these balances where they are for some time, accumulate more funds, and then move them to a more permanent repository. One should therefore add a **savings demand** to the traditional transactions and precautionary demands for money. This demand for money depends on the gap between the interest rate paid on deposits and the rates on alternative stores of savings, such as securities. Since rates paid on many types of deposits are inflexible, it is the changes in the rates paid on time deposits and on securities that dominate this gap.

THE MONEY DEMAND FUNCTION

A more formal way of looking at the demand for money is to use the standard demand function of microeconomic theory. A rational household or firm will decide on its money holdings in the same way that it decides on its holdings of all other goods. Hence, the same factors that explain the demand for harpsichords and bubble gum also explain the demand for money. These factors can be set out in a generalized demand function:

$$D_A = f(P_A, P_S, P_C, YP, Z),$$

---

[1] It might seem that if people decide it is too risky to hold bonds, they will hold near-monies, say, Treasury bills, rather than money, so that the demand for money is unaffected. But this is wrong. If people switch out of bonds into Treasury bills the price of Treasury bills rises and their yield falls. As a result, some other people decide to hold money rather than Treasury bills.

where D_A is the demand for item A, P_A is its price, P_S represents the price of a substitute commodity, P_C represents the price of a complement (e.g., butter in a demand function for bread), YP is nominal income, and Z is a catchall variable called "tastes." Z includes not just what we normally think of as "tastes," but also technological factors. For example, if the demand for gasoline falls because cars become more fuel efficient, this is called a change in tastes. Anything that affects demand and is not part of the other variables in the demand function is dumped into the garbage-can variable, "tastes."

Applying this demand function to money, the price of holding money is the yield on the assets that you would otherwise hold minus the yield on money. For example, if the alternative asset is a bond, the expected cost of holding money is the net interest rate on bonds plus the expected capital gain (or loss) on these bonds minus the interest rate on money. For some people, however, the alternative asset is not bonds, but common stock or physical capital. Then the net yields on these assets are the relevant costs of holding money.

The cost of money substitutes is more complex. One money substitute for firms is maintaining a line of credit with an unused balance. The cost of this is the bank's charge for the unused part of the credit line. For households a credit card is a money substitute, and its cost is the annual fee plus the potential cost if the card is used. Another money substitute is holding a liquid asset instead of a higher-yielding, less-liquid asset. The cost of this money substitute is the difference in the interest rates on the liquid and the less-liquid asset. A clear-cut example of a money complement is hard to find, and hence money complements are usually ignored.

Income and wealth affect the demand for money in two ways. One is through the work that money has to do. Obviously, the larger your expenditures, the larger are the transactions balances and the precautionary balances you want. Second, the higher your income and wealth, the more you can afford of the good things of life, and one of these good things is not having to chase after every little bit of interest income. A poor person may balance his checkbook every day and frequently transfer funds between a transactions account and a savings account to earn as much interest as possible. By contrast, a wealthy person can treat her time as more valuable and forgo some interest income to avoid the bother of continually adjusting her money holdings.

The final variable, tastes, includes a whole set of factors, such as the payments technology that determines how fast payment can be made, payments habits that determine whether people are paid monthly or weekly, the availability of credit and money substitutes, attitudes toward delaying payments, etc.

Changes in tastes *might* cause sharp swings in the amount of money demanded. If this were the case, the money demand function would not be so useful because we cannot predict, or even measure, many of the factors included in the tastes variable. One could still say that if the net interest rate falls or if income rises, then, *other things being equal,* the demand for money will increase. This is far from useless, but it would not allow the Fed to predict what the demand for money will be, because it could not predict how the demand for money will vary due to changes in tastes. The quantity theory of money would then be of little use. With the demand for money, and hence velocity, fluctuating a great deal, knowing the supply of money would not allow one to predict income.

In contrast, if the demand for money is stable and predictable, then the quantity theory can be used to forecast nominal income. Using a simplified money demand function

$$M = a + bYP + cr,$$

suppose that the coefficients a, b, and c are stable. Then, if one knows what M and r will be, one can calculate YP. It is this ability to predict nominal income from a knowledge of the money supply that makes money demand functions so important. If the Fed can predict the demand for money accurately, it can then change the supply of money by the amount needed to generate the level of money income it desires.

STATISTICAL MONEY DEMAND FUNCTIONS

To see whether the demand for money is predictable, the generalized money demand function must be simplified. First, the empty box of money complements can be dropped. Most economists have also dropped the money substitutes variable. In principle, money substitutes belong in the money demand function, but if the demand for money is highly unresponsive to the price of money substitutes or if the price of money substitutes shows little variation, then one can dispense with this variable. Moreover, the tastes variable is usually omitted because it is too difficult to measure and changes in tastes are captured in the error term.

This leaves the interest rate and income or wealth. Most statistical money demand functions, though not all, measure the interest rate by short-term rates, such as the Treasury bill rate. This is far from ideal. In principle the demand for money depends on many interest rates, as well as on the yields of other assets, such as common stock. But most economists believe that these other rates are correlated closely enough with the Treasury bill rate so that this rate can serve as a reasonable proxy for interest rates in general. Income is often measured by current GDP. This is more or less correct if the reason for including income in the money demand function is that one needs money to undertake transactions. But if income is included because the higher one's income, the better one can afford the luxury of holding money rather than higher-yielding near-monies, then one should not use current GDP. Either permanent income or wealth is then a better measure. While some money demand functions use current GDP, others use permanent income.

The goodness of the fit of such money demand functions for M-1, which was the main measure until the mid-1980s, varies from time to time. It is not good from 1915 until the early 1950s, but then is excellent until the early 1970s. After that it degenerates. Starting around 1973 the amount of money demanded fell greatly below what most money demand functions were predicting. The "case of the missing money" became a standard puzzle in economics. Then, in the early 1980s, the demand for money grew more rapidly than predicted and became more unstable.

What caused these large errors? It is by no means certain, but it seems that the main explanations for the overestimation of money demand in the 1970s were financial innovations and high interest rates. Improvements in computer technology and falling costs of telecommunications provided the means for economizing on money holdings, and very high nominal interest rates provided the incentive to search out and use such innovations. Hence less money was demanded than the money demand functions predicted.

Then in the 1980s, there were two important legal innovations. First, banks were allowed to pay explicit interest on the checkable deposits of households. As a result, households began to hold more of their savings in checkable deposits and the demand for *M-1* grew. Second, interest rates paid on time deposits were deregulated and could therefore rise relative to other interest rates, so that the demand for time deposits, and hence for *M-2*, also grew. Moreover, the payment of interest on checkable deposits blurred the distinction between *M-1* and *M-2*. When *M-1* consisted primarily of funds held for transactions and precautionary reasons, it was much more distinct from other financial assets than it is currently. Now shifts in the demand for other financial assets affect the demand for *M-1* more than they used to do, and this makes the demand for *M-1* less stable.

The demand for *M-1* has also become more interest elastic because the demand for savings is more interest elastic than is the demand for funds that are held for transactions and precautionary purposes. At first glance it might seem that a greater responsiveness to interest rates simply changes the coefficient of the interest-rate term in the money demand function, without necessarily making the function fit any worse than before. But this is not so. Since, as a repository of savings, money competes with many assets, the demand for money depends on numerous interest rates. They cannot all be included in a money demand function, and that makes this function predict less effectively than it did when money was used less as a store of savings.

One possible solution is to define money as *M-2* rather than as *M-1*. Then it does not matter if people shift funds between checkable deposits and, say, savings accounts, because *M-2* internalizes such shifts; that is, while these shifts affect the composition of *M-2*, they do not affect the totals. Hence, it is not surprising that demand functions for *M-2* have been stabler than those for *M-1*. And that is the reason why many economists now measure money by *M-2* and why we do so in this book.

However, this solution also has its problems. An *M-2* demand function has to include the interest rate paid on *M-2*. This means that someone who wants to use such a demand function has to predict this interest rate so that she can plug it into the equation for *M-2*, and that is not easy. Moreover, an important purpose of a money demand function is to help the Fed make monetary policy, to let it know by how much it should change the money supply to generate the change in GDP that it wants to bring about. Hence, a money demand function should, if possible, use a measure of money that the Fed can control well. And the Fed can probably not control *M-2* as well as *M-1*. Last, but not least, although the demand function for *M-2* is stabler than the demand function for *M-1* it, too, has become much less stable than it used to be.

Economists are expending considerable effort trying to find a money demand function that is stable, and sometimes they do find functions that predict previous money holdings well. But as data for additional years become available, these functions usually cease to give a good fit.[2] All the same, it is quite possible that eventually we will find a stable demand function.

THE BEHAVIOR OF VELOCITY

In the 1970s, when *M-1* money demand functions were found to predict badly, some economists responded by saying that it does not matter much. *M-1* velocity was growing at a stable rate of about 3.2 percent per year. Hence, they said, you do not need a money demand function to predict GDP. All you have to do is to assume that velocity will be 3.2 percent higher next year than it is this year. If you know the change in the supply of money, you can predict income without having to use a money demand function. This approach looked promising in the 1960s and 1970s when *M-1* velocity was growing at a remarkably stable rate. But what worked so well in the 1970s has not worked since the early 1980s when *M-1* velocity fell and became erratic (see Figure 17.2).

The cessation of *M-1* velocity growth was unfortunate, not only for economists who had not predicted it, but also for many people who lost their jobs

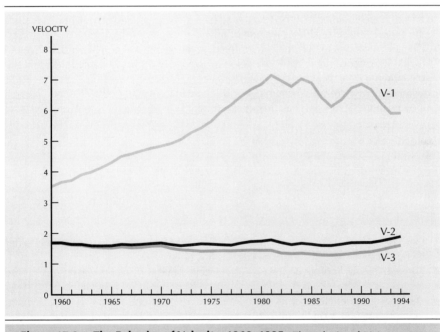

Figure 17.2   The Behavior of Velocity, 1960–1995. The velocity of *M-1* grew at a remarkably stable rate until the 1980s, while the velocity of *M-2* was stable until the early 1990s. The trend of *M-3* velocity changed in the mid-1980s. **Sources:** Based on the Federal Reserve Bank of St. Louis and *Economic Report of the President,* 1995, pp. 274, 353.

---

[2] This is a common problem in economics. It is easier to "predict" the past than the future. When dealing with past data, we can adjust our equation by adding additional variables, etc., until it gives a good fit to the data that we have. But we cannot make such adjustments for future errors.

because the Fed had set monetary policy on the assumption that velocity would continue growing. What might appear to be economic abstractions can have some powerful real-world effects.

SUMMARY

1 Transactions balances are held to avoid the cost and trouble of frequently acquiring and then liquidating a near-money or a security. The volume of transactions balances depends on the cost and trouble of investing and disinvesting, on the net interest rate of money, and on the planned volume of transactions.

2 People hold precautionary balances to meet unexpected needs. These balances provide an alternative to cutting planned expenditures, selling assets, borrowing, or not making payments. The amount held depends on a comparison of the lowest of these costs with the net interest rate and on the probability of having to make unexpected payments. Precautionary balances, too, are therefore a function of the net interest rate.

3 Money is also held as a repository for savings. This demand, too, depends on the interest rate.

4 The demand for money can also be explained by use of a money demand function that includes the cost of holding money, the price of money substitutes, income or wealth, and tastes. Statistical money demand functions usually include the interest rate and income.

5 Functions for M-1 demand gave a good fit for the 1950s and 1960s, but overpredicted money holdings for the 1970s, and have underpredicted money holdings since the early 1980s, probably as a result of financial innovations.

6 Demand functions for M-2 have performed better than those for M-1, and M-2 velocity has been more stable than M-1 velocity. Even so, M-2 has become much less stable than it used to be.

7 Velocity of M-1 grew at a remarkably stable rate in the 1960s and 1970s, but then fell sharply in the 1980s and became more erratic.

KEY TERMS

transactions demand	money demand function
precautionary demand	money substitutes

QUESTIONS AND EXERCISES

*1 Describe how you decide how much money to hold. How would your answer differ if your income were five times as large as it is now?

2 The demand for money depends on the interest rate for several reasons. What are they?

*3 Discuss: "This chapter spends much unnecessary effort on showing that the demand for money depends on the interest rate. This elaborate discussion is not needed; elementary microeconomics makes it obvious that the demand for money depends on the interest rate."

4 How will you decide the size of your precautionary balance once you graduate and earn a high income?

*5 Statistical money demand functions generally use either current GDP or a permanent-income measure of GDP. Is GDP necessarily the correct variable to measure income? What are other plausible alternatives?

6 Explain the problem of the "missing money" of the 1970s.

FURTHER READING

Journal of Policy Modeling (Summer 1990). This issue is devoted to modeling the behavior of velocity and, for those who have some training in econometrics, provides a useful survey of current research on velocity.

JUDD, JOHN, and JOHN SCADDING. "The Search for a Stable Money Demand Function," *Journal of Economic Literature*, 20 (September 1982), 993–1023. An authoritative survey of the "missing money" problem.

LAIDLER, DAVID. *The Demand for Money*, 4th ed. New York: Harper & Row, 1993. An excellent survey of the theoretical and econometric literature on money demand.

APPENDIX A:
A MODEL OF TRANSACTIONS DEMAND

Many sophisticated models have been constructed telling firms how much money to hold for the transactions motive. We illustrate the principle involved by looking at a simple version devised by William Baumol, then of Princeton University.

Assume that you finance a continuous flow of expenditures by selling securities or near-monies that you own. Assume also that the brokerage cost and other costs of selling securities are a fixed amount per sale, independent of the number of securities you sell.

How frequently should you sell securities or near-monies? On the one hand, if you sell all your securities the very first time you need money, you will have to pay the brokerage charge only once. But obtaining all the money you need right away has a high cost in another way: you forgo some interest income you could earn by holding on to most of your securities for a longer time. To minimize the opportunity cost of losing interest, you would want to sell them one at a time.

The best policy is to minimize the sum of both your costs, the brokerage cost and the opportunity cost of forgone interest. This total cost can be written as

$$Q = bT/C + rC/2,$$

where Q is the total cost, b the brokerage charge, T the amount of securities you will sell over the whole year, and C the amount of securities you sell at each sale, so that T/C represents the number of times per year that you will sell securities and pay a brokerage charge. The interest rate is r. The first term, bT/C, measures your brokerage cost. The second term, $rC/2$, measures the forgone interest. If you sell C dollars of securities at each sale and spend these proceeds at an even rate, you hold, on the average day, $C/2$ dollars. Hence your forgone interest is $rC/2$.

There is a mathematical technique (setting the first derivative at zero) that allows you to find the minimum value for Q. This minimum is reached at

$$C = \sqrt{2bT/r}.$$

Thus, the number of securities you should sell each time you sell is greater the higher the fixed brokerage cost and the lower the interest rate. Correspondingly, you should sell securities less frequently and in larger lots when you do sell, the higher the fixed brokerage cost and the lower the interest rate.

More specifically, the second equation tells you the interest elasticity of your cash holdings. Since C is a function of the square root of r, the interest elasticity is $-\frac{1}{2}$. Similarly, if one identifies the number of securities you will sell with your income, your income elasticity of demand for money is $\frac{1}{2}$.

These results should be interpreted with caution for two reasons. First, they apply only to the transactions demand for money. Firms hold much more money than that, in part because they are required to hold compensating balances. Second, we started out the story with you holding securities and selling them during the year to meet expenses. But most of us meet expenses not by selling a portfolio of securities, but out of income that is paid in cash. Interest rates would have to be extraordinarily high to make it worthwhile for the average person to buy securities on payday, and then sell them during the pay period. However, for those corporations or wealthy persons who receive their incomes in lumpy form, it might be worth doing so. For example, for a manufacturer of Christmas tree ornaments who receives most of his income in November and December, it may be worthwhile to buy securities at that time, and then sell them off during the year in accordance with the second equation.

APPENDIX B:
THE SPECULATIVE DEMAND FOR MONEY AND THE LIQUIDITY TRAP

In his book *The General Theory of Employment, Interest and Money,* Keynes introduced another demand for money, the **speculative demand.** He argued that an additional reason some people hold money rather than securities is because they expect security prices to fall. Suppose that the interest rate on a bond is 6 percent and you expect the price of such a bond to fall by 8 percent over the next year. You would be better off forgoing the 6 percent interest and holding a deposit than buying the bond and incurring an 8 percent capital loss. Keynes believed that people have an idea of what the *normal* rate of interest is. Hence, at times when the interest rate is below this level, relatively few people will want to hold bonds. What will they do with their assets instead? Keynes argued that instead of bonds they will hold "money." Money is in quotation marks here because Keynes defined money much more broadly than we do now. He included not only items in *M-3,* but even short-term securities, such as Treasury bills.

Most economists no longer ascribe much of a role to this speculative demand for "money," in large part because we now define money much more narrowly.[3] Someone who expects bond prices to fall is more likely to hold short-term securities than *M-2.* Moreover, in laying the foundation for the income-expenditure theory, Keynes had to work with a relatively simple portfolio model in which people must hold either bonds or "money." He did not consider the possibility that instead of holding either bonds or money, they might hold physical assets or claims to physical assets, such as stocks.

Keynes used the speculative demand for money to suggest that at certain

[3] However, the term *speculative demand for money* is often used to designate something we have included in the precautionary demand, holding money to avoid the risk of holding bonds, even when bond prices are just as likely to rise as to fall.

times the demand for money *might* become perfectly elastic, a condition known as **absolute liquidity preference** or as the **liquidity trap.** If everyone expects bond prices to fall at a rate that exceeds the additional interest that can be earned by holding bonds, nobody will want to hold bonds, and everybody will hold money instead. Keynes stated that he did not know of any instance when this had actually happened, but some economists have argued that it did happen for a few years during the Great Depression. Many others dispute this.

In any case, the idea of absolute liquidity preference got much attention as an interesting theoretical exercise. It was used to illustrate a hypothetical case in which changes in the supply of money have no effect on the interest rate. If the money supply is increased, the public simply holds the additional money and does not use it to buy either securities or goods, so that income does not respond to the increased money supply. (It is an extreme anti-quantity-theory case.) Similarly, if the government sells bonds to finance additional expenditures, this bond sale does not drive up the interest rate significantly, since people are willing to move out of money into bonds at an interest rate that is only trivially above the prevailing level.

Aggregate Expenditures: The Complete Model

After you have read this chapter, you will be able to:

- Explain how the IS and LM curves are derived and how their interaction determines the equilibrium level of income.
- Understand what determines the slopes and positions of the IS and LM curves.
- Use the IS and LM curves to determine the effects of monetary and fiscal policies on income.
- Explain the limitations of the IS-LM analysis.

Having dealt with each of the components of the income-expenditure model, we can now look at the complete model on the assumption that the inflation rate is fixed. (Given this assumption, one can say that an increase in the money supply reduces the interest rate permanently since it does not affect the inflation rate.) We then use this model to consider how monetary and fiscal policies change aggregate expenditures.

COMBINING THE ELEMENTS

Suppose the marginal efficiency of investment increases. Investment rises by, say, $10 billion per year. If the multiplier is 2, shouldn't income rise by $20 billion annually? No, it shouldn't, because the simple multiplier story leaves something out. This is the response of the interest rate to the increase in investment and income, and the feedback effect on income of this change in the interest rate. With investment and income rising, the demand for money increases, and hence the interest rate rises. This then reduces income again. So with income first rising and then falling, how can one be sure that a rise in investment really increases income?

More generally, we seem to be caught in a circularity. To know what income is, one has to know what the interest rate is. But the interest rate depends, in part, on what income is. Fortunately, one can solve for income and the interest rate simultaneously by looking, *at the same time*, at both the market for goods and services and at the market for money. This ensures that the interest rate that we are assuming in the process of determining income is the same interest rate that we get when we let income, along with other variables, determine the interest rate. This way of looking jointly at the determinants of income and the interest rate is illustrated by the **IS-LM diagram,** which shows equilibrium in both the market for goods and services and in the market for money at the same time.

In this discussion the term *interest rate* should be interpreted not just as the Treasury bill rate or the prime rate, but more broadly as a measure of the total cost and difficulty of borrowing. If a firm can no longer borrow because money has become tight, we call this a rise in the interest rate.

The Goods and Services Market

We now relate changes in the interest rate to changes in investment. Part A of Figure 18.1 shows the relation between the interest rate and investment. As the interest rate falls from r_0 to r_1 investment rises from I_0 to I_1. Part B transfers I_0 and I_1 from the horizontal axis to the vertical axis by means of a 45-degree line.[1] Part C then uses the Keynesian cross diagram of Chapter 15 to show how income responds to the change in investment. Thus, every interest rate implies a particular income. Figure 18.2 shows a curve, called the **IS curve,** that relates each interest rate to its corresponding level of income.[2] Put another way, the interest rate determines investment, and then investment, in combination with the multiplier, determines income.

So far we have assumed, quite incorrectly, that changes in the interest rate affect only investment and no other expenditures. But, as previously discussed, the interest rate affects consumption too. It also has an effect on imports and exports. If interest rates rise in the United States, foreigners want to buy more U.S. securities and need dollars to do so. At the same time, Americans want to buy fewer foreign securities, so they demand less foreign currency. With the demand for dollars increasing and the demand for foreign currencies decreasing, the dollar rises on the foreign-exchange market. Now U.S. goods become more expensive to foreigners and foreign goods become cheaper in the United States. Exports fall and imports rise. The demand for U.S. output, and hence U.S. GDP, falls.

Even government expenditures on goods and services (the only government expenditures that are counted as part of GDP) *could* be influenced by

---

[1] It is a geometric property of a 45-degree line diagram that straight lines drawn from the 45-degree line to the two axes mark off equal distances on both axes.

[2] The name IS comes from the fact that when the market for goods and services is in equilibrium planned *investment* equals planned *saving*. At one time macroeconomics was formulated in a way that focused on this equality, hence an I(nvestment)-S(aving) curve. The term LM, to which we will come soon, is derived from "*money* and *liquidity* preference."

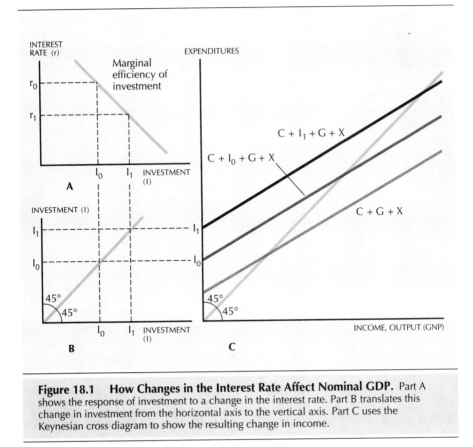

Figure 18.1   How Changes in the Interest Rate Affect Nominal GDP. Part A shows the response of investment to a change in the interest rate. Part B translates this change in investment from the horizontal axis to the vertical axis. Part C uses the Keynesian cross diagram to show the resulting change in income.

the interest rate. The higher the interest rate, the more it costs the government to service the national debt. *If* there is some political or legal constraint on the size of the deficit, the more interest the government pays, the smaller its expenditures on goods and services are.[3]

Hence, it is not just the interest elasticity of investment, but also the interest elasticities of consumption and government expenditures that make the IS curve slope downward and relate a lower interest rate to a higher income.

The Money Market

In a textbook or in class, one can say: "Pick any interest rate and . . . ." But in the real world the interest rate is not arbitrary. It is determined by the variables discussed in Chapter 16. By holding all but one of them constant, one can see how changes in this particular variable affect the interest rate. The variable we select is income.

---

[3] At the same time, however, the increased payments raise the deficit, and this raises income, and hence consumption.

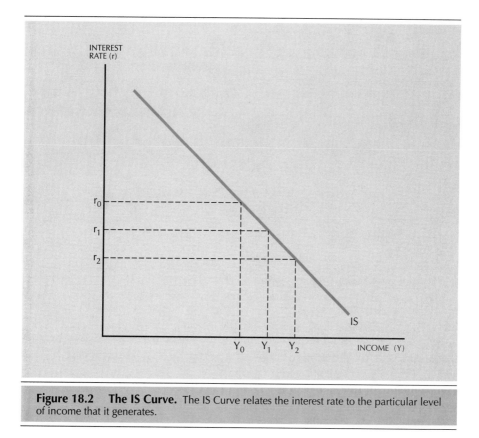

Figure 18.2   The IS Curve. The IS Curve relates the interest rate to the particular level of income that it generates.

Income and the interest rate are related by the **LM curve.** It is important to realize that, unlike most curves encountered in economics textbooks, it is neither a supply curve nor a demand curve. Instead, it is a **market equilibrium curve,** *that is, a curve showing all those particular combinations of interest rates and incomes at which the supply of and demand for money are equal.* It slopes upward because the higher income is, the greater the demand for money is. Hence, at a higher income level it takes a higher interest rate to make the public demand no more than the existing supply of money. In other words, *the demand for money depends positively on income and negatively on the interest rate; hence there exists some combination of income and interest rate that makes the demand for money just equal to any given supply of money.* Figure 18.3 shows the derivation of the LM curve. Part A shows how, for a given supply of money, the interest rate depends on the level of income. With income at $100 billion, the demand for money is equal to the fixed supply of money when the interest rate is 5 percent. But when income rises to $200 billion, the demand for money exceeds the supply. The interest rate has to rise to 8 percent to make the demand for money equal the fixed supply of money.

In Part B, which, unlike Part A, has income on the x axis, we chart all the points of intersection derived in Part A.

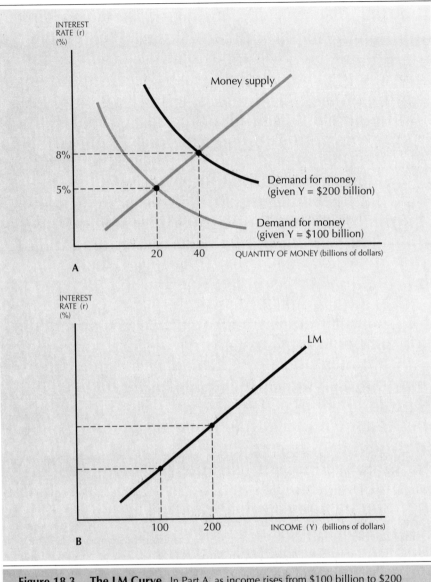

Figure 18.3   The LM Curve. In Part A, as income rises from $100 billion to $200 billion, the demand for money rises from $20 billion to $40 billion. As a result, the interest rate rises from 5 percent to 8 percent. Part B shows this relation between income and the interest rate. As income rises, the interest rate rises too.

So far, we have assumed that the supply of money is fixed. In principle, an increase in the interest rate results in an increase in the money supply. As we saw in Chapter 13, the money multiplier is a function of the interest rate, and in Part Four we will learn why the Fed is likely to raise reserves, and hence the money supply, when interest rates rise. But for the time being, we can ignore this complication since it does not change anything of substance as far as the present discussion is concerned. We will, however, have to introduce it later in this chapter.

Combining the IS and LM Curves

Since Figures 18.2 and 18.3 have the same variables on their axes, they can be combined into a single diagram, Figure 18.4. The market for goods and services is in equilibrium anywhere along the IS curve. Similarly, at any point on the LM curve the money market is in equilibrium. Hence, only at the point at which the two curves intersect is there equilibrium in both the commodity market and the money market—and thus in the whole economy. *In other words, only at the point of intersection does the interest rate that was arbitrarily assumed in drawing the IS curve correspond to the interest rate actually set in the money market.* Put another way, there are two unknowns, income and the interest rate, and two equations, the IS equation ($Y = a + br$) and the LM equation ($Y = c + dr$).

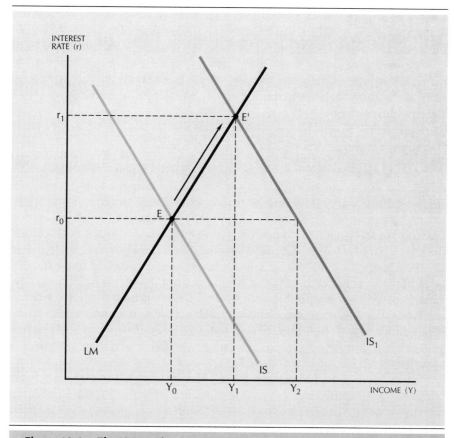

Figure 18.4   The IS-LM Diagram. When the IS and LM curves are combined, their point of intersection determines the interest rate and income. If the IS curve shifts upward, both income and the interest rate rise.

Taking the coefficients a, b, c, and d as known, these two equations can be solved simultaneously for both income and the interest rate.

The problem raised at the start of this chapter is now solved. Suppose the marginal efficiency of investment rises. At each interest rate firms now invest more, so that the income that corresponds to each interest rate rises. With the IS curve in Figure 18.4 shifting from IS to IS_1, income rises from Y_0 to Y_1. This raises the interest rate from r_0 to r_1. But this cannot reduce income back to its previous level, though it does reduce it some. If the increase in income had not raised the interest rate, perhaps because the Fed increased the supply of money enough to keep the interest rate at r_0, then income would have risen to Y_2 instead of just to Y_1.

To see why only the point of intersection of IS and LM is an equilibrium, consider what happens at other points. In Part A of Figure 18.5, at point A the interest rate r_1 is so high that it would require an income of Y_1 to make people willing to hold all the existing supply of money. But the IS curve tells us that with an interest rate of r_1 income would be only Y_2. Hence, if the interest rate were somehow to be at r_1, income would not stay at Y_1, but would fall. With income declining, the interest rate would also fall. Thus, both income and the interest rate would move toward their equilibrium values of Y_0 and r_0. Now consider point B in Part B of Figure 18.5. If the interest rate would somehow be at r_1, this would generate an income of Y_1 according to the IS curve. But the LM curve tells us that with an interest rate of r_1, it would take an income of Y_2 to make the supply of and demand for money equal. Hence, point B cannot be the equilibrium point.

Determinants of the Slopes of the IS and LM Curves

The IS curve is constructed by taking the increase in expenditures that results from a fall in the interest rate and applying the multiplier to it. Hence, the slope of the IS curve depends on the responsiveness of expenditures to a change in the interest rate, which we will call the **expenditures slope,** and on the value of the multiplier. The greater the expenditures slope or the larger the multiplier, the bigger the rise in income that occurs when the interest rate falls by a given amount and hence the flatter the IS curve. At one extreme, expenditures do not respond at all to changes in the interest rate, so that the expenditures slope is zero. In this case the IS curve is a vertical line. A fall in the interest rate leaves income entirely unchanged. At the other extreme, the expenditures slope is infinite. If so, an infinitely small drop in the interest rate generates an infinitely great rise in income. The IS curve is then a horizontal line.

The slope of the LM curve is more complex. The LM curve shows those combinations of interest rates and income levels that induce the public to demand just the existing supply of money. Suppose that people increase their demand for money very much when income rises by a dollar. The interest rate then has to rise a lot to prevent the demand for money from exceeding the supply as income rises. With even a small movement along the x (income) axis thus being associated with a large movement along the y (interest-rate) axis, the LM curve is steep.

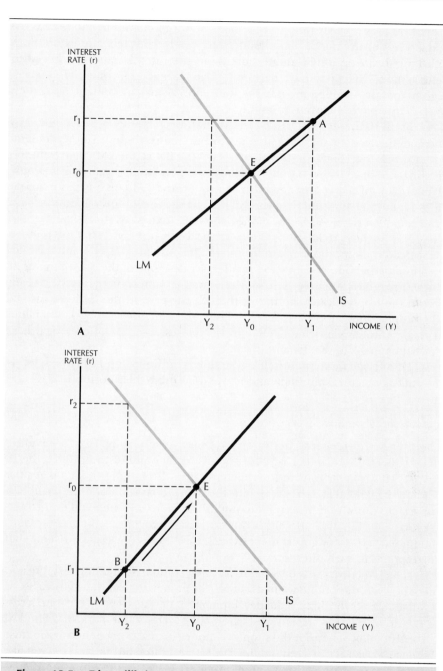

Figure 18.5   Disequilibrium Points in the IS-LM Diagram. Point *A* is a
disequilibrium point. If the interest rate is r_1, then as the LM curve tells us, income has to
be Y_1. Given the high interest rate r_1, that high a level of income is required to make the
public willing to hold all the supply of money. But such a high interest rate discourages
expenditures. The IS curve tells us that at a rate of r_1 income is only Y_2. In Part B at point
B, at an interest rate of r_1, income is Y_2. But if income is Y_2, it takes an interest rate of r_2 to
equate the supply of and demand for money. Since the interest rate cannot be both r_1 and
r_2 at the same time, the economy cannot be in equilibrium at point *B*. Only at r_0 are both
the commodity market and the money market in equilibrium.

Now look at the response of the demand for money to the interest rate. If a small rise in the interest rate induces people to cut their money holdings substantially, then only a small increase in the interest rate is required to release the additional money that people want to hold as income rises. Hence, a given movement along the x axis requires only a small movement along the y axis, so that the LM curve is relatively flat.

Thus, the more responsive the demand for money is to a change in income, the steeper the LM curve is. And the more responsive the demand for money is to a change in the interest rate, the flatter the LM curve is. In the limiting case in which an infinitely small drop in the interest rate makes people demand an infinitely great amount of money, the LM curve is a horizontal line. In another limiting case in which a change in the interest rate has no effect at all on the demand for money, the LM curve is a vertical line.

Now we have to allow for the fact, previously put aside, that the interest rate affects not only the demand for money, but also the supply of money. The response of the money supply to the interest rate is one of the determinants of the slope of the LM curve. The more the money supply increases for a given rise in the interest rate, the flatter the LM curve is. In the limiting case in which the money supply is infinitely elastic, the LM curve is a horizontal line. With an infinitely elastic money supply the interest rate cannot rise, regardless of what happens to the demand for money.

Having seen what determines the slopes of the IS and LM curves, let us look at what factors shift them and hence determine their positions.

Shifts of the IS and LM Curves

The IS curve relates each interest rate to a particular income. Hence, anything that changes the income that corresponds to each interest rate shifts the IS curve. (This is analogous to the demand curve. Everything that changes the amount demanded at each price shifts the demand curve.) For example, the IS curve shifts outward if firms want to undertake more investment at every interest rate. The IS curve also shifts outward if an exogenous increase in consumption, exports, or government expenditures raises the level of income that corresponds to each interest rate.

The LM curve shifts outward if, for each combination of interest rate and income level, the public wants to hold less money than it did before. Some possible reasons for this are the development of new near-monies, easier access to credit, or a fall in the interest rate paid on checkable deposits. The LM curve also shifts outward if the supply of money increases exogenously, because this curve shows all the combinations of interest rates and incomes that make the demand for money equal to the supply. The greater the supply of money, the lower must be the interest rate or else the higher must be income to make the demand for money equal to the supply.

As an exercise let's use the IS-LM diagram to describe what happens if there are large-scale bank failures. (Before reading on, try to work it out on your own.) If the FDIC pays off only insured depositors (so that large depositors lose), wealth is reduced and the IS curve shifts inward. Unless other banks receive enough reserves to allow them to expand their deposits by an amount equal to the loss of deposits in the failed banks, the money supply falls and the LM curve also shifts inward. (See if you can think of any other effects.)

FISCAL AND MONETARY POLICIES IN THE IS-LM FRAMEWORK

The IS-LM framework can be used to sketch how fiscal and monetary policies affect GDP.

Fiscal Policy

Since government expenditures are part of aggregate demand, the obvious effect of increased government expenditures is to shift the IS curve outward. (We will deal with the less obvious effects later.) In Figure 18.6A, as government expenditures shift the IS curve to IS_1, income rises from Y_0 to Y_1. It does *not* rise to Y_2 as it would according to the simpleminded multiplier formula, $Y = G/(1 - c)$, where G is government expenditures and c the marginal propensity to consume out of GDP. The reason is that, as income rises, so does the interest rate. Only if the LM curve were horizontal, like LM_1, would income rise as much as the simple multiplier formula predicts. Given that the LM curve is not horizontal, the rise in the interest rate *crowds out* $Y_2 - Y_1$ of income. The steeper the LM curve, the greater is this **crowding out.** In the limiting case of a totally interest-inelastic LM curve, shown in Figure 18.6B as LM_2, higher government expenditures have no effect on income; they just raise the interest rate from r_0 to r_2.

Tax cuts also shift the IS curve. If personal income taxes are cut, disposable personal income rises. Households respond by raising consumption. In Figure 18.7A, tax cuts raise income and the interest rate by shifting the IS curve to IS_1. Again, if the LM curve were completely vertical, income would not change. But the LM curve is not completely vertical since the demand for money is not completely interest inelastic.

Hence, someone who wants to argue that fiscal policy has no effect on nominal income has to do so on other grounds. One possibility is the Ricardian equivalence proposition discussed in Chapter 15. Another possibility is **portfolio crowding out:** as the government spends more, it must finance this increased expenditure either by selling securities or by creating new money to pay for it. Suppose it sells more securities. What does this do to the LM curve? One possibility is that as people hold more securities, they also want to hold more money, either because they are wealthier or because money and securities are complements. If so, government expenditures, and the associated issues of government securities, do not just shift the IS curve to the right, they also shift the LM curve to the left. If the LM curve shifts far enough to the left, say to LM_1 in Figure 18.7A, income falls to Y_2, less than it was before government expenditures rose. This is crowding out with a vengeance.

But the opposite possibility exists too. Suppose that people treat government securities (which could be highly liquid Treasury bills) as a good substitute for money. Hence, when they hold more government securities, their

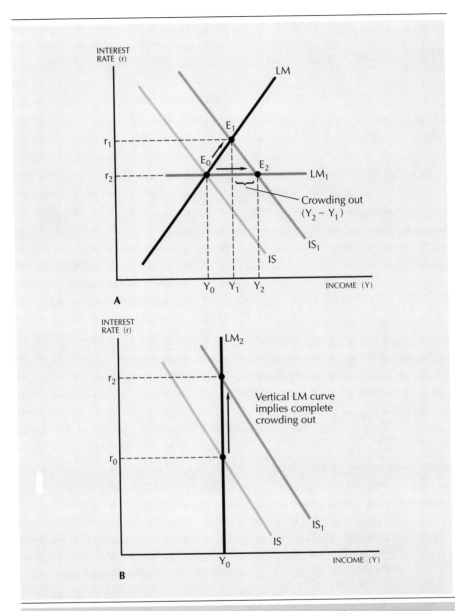

Figure 18.6   Crowding Out. We start with LM and IS (Part A). The government now raises expenditures or lowers taxes; this shifts the IS curve to IS_1. Income rises from Y_0 to Y_1. In a simplified multiplier analysis in which the interest rate is taken as fixed, the LM curve would have been horizontal (LM_1) and the change in government expenditures would be fully translated into a change in income. Income would have risen to Y_2. The difference between Y_2 and Y_1 is the "crowding out" of private investment that occurs as government finances its spending. Part B illustrates the extreme case of complete crowding out because the demand for money is completely unresponsive to the interest rate. Fiscal policy cannot increase income.

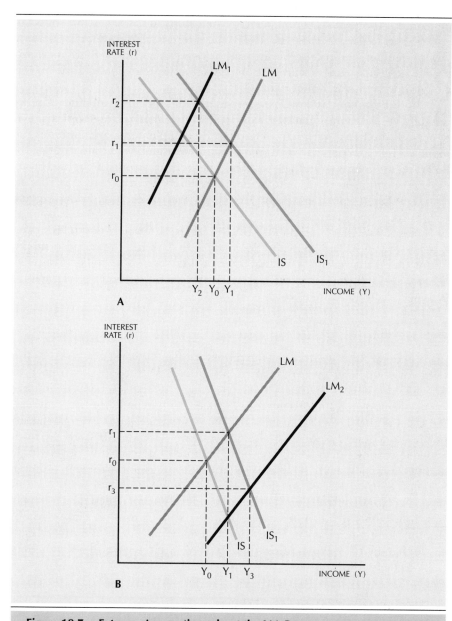

Figure 18.7   Extreme Assumptions about the LM Curve. The greater deficit that results from higher government expenditures or lower taxes could either raise or lower the demand for money. It is conceivable that an increase in government expenditures would shift the LM curve to LM_1, as in Part A; this would imply a fall in income. Alternatively, the LM curve could shift to LM_2, as in Part B, so that income would increase because of a shift in both the IS and LM curves.

demand for money falls. The LM curve then shifts to the right. If it shifts far enough, say to LM_2 as in Figure 18.7B, the interest rate falls to r_3. Instead of government expenditures crowding out private expenditures, there is **crowding in;** aggregate expenditure rises by an amount greater than government expenditures times the multiplier.

Both crowding out and crowding in are theoretical possibilities. Unfortunately, it has proven extremely difficult to find convincing empirical evidence on whether government securities are complements or substitutes for money.[4] Hence, economists disagree about the existence of significant portfolio crowding in and (if it does exist) on whether it is strong enough to offset the movement *along* the LM curve that raises interest rates.

But there is much less dispute about a way in which *partial* crowding out occurs. As the government spends more and income rises, interest rates rise. This causes foreigners to buy more U.S. securities, and Americans to buy fewer foreign securities. The increased demand for dollars and the reduced supply of dollars on the foreign-exchange market then cause the dollar to rise. So U.S. exports fall while imports rise. With exports falling and imports rising, income falls in the United States.

Monetary Policy

If the Federal Reserve increases the money supply, the LM curve shifts to the right, for example, from LM to LM_1 as in Figure 18.8A. Income rises from Y_0 to Y_1, while the interest rate falls from r_0 to r_1. Figure 18.8B shows the limiting case of a completely interest-inelastic IS curve. With expenditures not increasing at all as the interest rate falls, the increase in the money supply has no effect on income. The other limiting case shown in Figure 18.8B is the horizontal IS curve. With expenditures being infinitely interest elastic, it takes only an infinitesimally small decline in the interest rate to increase expenditures enough for the increase in the demand for money induced by the rise in income to absorb all the increased money supply. The increased money supply now translates fully into increased income, from Y_0 to Y_1 in Figure 18.8B. Another limiting case is one in which the demand for money is infinitely elastic, so that the LM curve is horizontal.[5] We saw this in Figure 18.6A: monetary policy is then powerless.

CRITICISMS OF THE IS-LM ANALYSIS

Although the IS-LM mechanism is widely used, it has some serious limitations. One is that the IS-LM diagram is valid only if the inflation rate is given exogenously. This is so because the *y* axis of the IS-LM diagram has to show both the

---

[4] It seems plausible that Treasury bills are a money substitute since they are so liquid, while a 30-year bond is more likely to be a money complement. However, the econometric evidence for this is far from compelling.

[5] In principle this special case would arise only under the very special condition that people have become convinced that the interest rate has hit bottom. If so, they would not want to buy bonds at a lower interest rate because they would be convinced that the market value of bonds will fall as interest rates rise again.

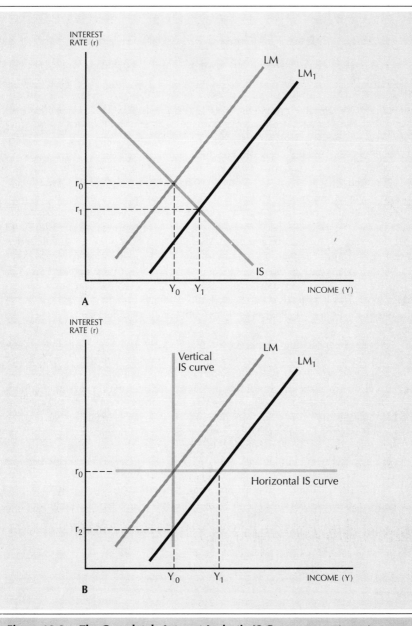

Figure 18.8   The Completely Interest-Inelastic IS Curve. Part A shows the normal case of an increase in the money supply: LM shifts to LM_1, and income increases. If expenditures are completely unresponsive to the interest rate, as in Part B, then shifts in the supply of money, and hence in the LM curve, have no effect on income.

Let's Go Back to Clay Tablets

Suppose people decide to buy fewer cars and to buy an equivalent amount of furniture instead. Aggregate expenditure is unchanged. Unemployment increases in Detroit, but falls in Tennessee where the additional furniture is produced. If there are enough unemployed workers in Tennessee to allow the furniture companies to hire as many workers as they need, then to a first approximation, unemployment does not rise. In other words, with aggregate expenditure constant, employment should change little.

What, then, is it about aggregate expenditure that makes it so important for explaining unemployment? Why does it matter whether the people who decide not to buy cars buy furniture or decide to save? As people save, two things happen: demand for consumer goods falls and demand for securities increases as the savers buy more stocks and bonds. Given the greater demand for stocks and bonds, prices of stocks and bonds rise. With the cost of capital now being lower, and the discount rate that firms use to evaluate future yields being lower too, firms have an incentive to invest more. (At the same time, with the demand for consumer goods falling, they may want to invest less because their factories are less busy, but let us assume that things work out well and that the favorable effect of falling interest rates outweighs the unfavorable effect of falling sales of consumer goods.)

So far so good. But there is something else that also happens. With the interest rate on securities, and thus the opportunity cost of holding money, being lower, people now have an incentive to hold more money. And when expenditures shift away from, say, automobiles toward holding money, something happens that does not happen when expenditures shift from, say, buying automobiles to buying furniture. A piece of furniture, like an automobile, is a produced good: labor is employed in making it. But that is not so for money. The creation of, say, $10,000 of currency or bank deposits requires practically no labor. Hence, the decline of employment in Detroit, as people buy fewer cars, is not offset by rising employment elsewhere.

Suppose that instead of currency and deposits with practically zero production costs, the economy used as money clay tablets with a cost of production equal to their monetary value. Clay is found just about everywhere in the United States. Hence, if we were on such a clay standard, those who lost their jobs could go out, dig up clay, and take it to the Treasury to be coined as money. Thus, if people decided to buy fewer goods and hold more money instead, it would be like a shift of expenditure from automobiles to furniture: unemployment would not rise.

real interest rate and the nominal interest rate. The real interest rate, or more precisely the expected real interest rate, is the appropriate rate to use when drawing the IS curve because investment depends on the expected real interest rate. But the demand for money, and hence the LM curve, depend mainly on the nominal interest rate.[6] If the inflation rate is constant, then one can accom-

---

[6] If the utility of the last dollar in your cash balance is 5 percent, and the nominal interest rate on a security is 6 percent, then (assuming no transactions costs) you should buy the security regardless of the inflation rate. Inflation will hurt you just as much if you hold money as if you hold a security.

modate both the nominal and the real interest rates on the same axis. Suppose, for example, that the inflation rate is 5 percent. Then the point on the y axis that is marked as an 8 percent nominal rate also serves as a 3 percent real rate. But this does not work if the inflation rate is not constant, so that the two scales do not have a unique relationship. If, as is actually the case, the inflation rate is greater when income is higher, then the relation between the two interest-rate scales on the y axis depends on where you are on the y axis. This means that you cannot draw the IS and LM curves without already knowing what income is. This problem could be handled, however, by adding a third dimension that has the inflation rate on the z axis.

The second problem is that physical capital has not been fitted into the story. One need not choose just between holding money and buying an interest-yielding asset as the LM curve has it. Instead, one can buy physical capital, such as some common stock or a house. This would not matter if the return on physical capital always moves in step with the return on interest-yielding assets. The interest rate on these assets could then serve, in part, as a proxy for the yield on capital. But the two yields might diverge.

Another problem with the IS-LM mechanism is that it pays no attention to expectations. Suppose that the money supply suddenly increases. The public may see this as a harbinger of future inflation, so that the IS curve and not just the LM curve will shift. Moreover, the IS-LM mechanism is not applicable to the long run because of its assumption that an increase in the money supply lowers the interest rate.

SUMMARY

1   Given the interaction between interest rates and income, we have to look at both of them at the same time to determine either one. This can be done in a diagram that has the interest rate on the y axis and income on the x axis.

2   The IS curve relates all consistent levels of interest rates and incomes, and thus connects all equilibrium points in the market for goods and services. A lower interest rate stimulates expenditures, and this, together with its multiplier effect, raises income. Hence, the IS curve slopes downward. Its slope depends on the response of expenditures to the interest rate and on the multiplier.

3   The LM curve relates all interest rates and income levels at which the supply of and demand for money are equal. Its slope depends on the responsiveness of monetary demand to changes in interest rates and in income, and on the response of the money supply to changes in interest rates.

4   The IS and LM curves show that, except in limiting cases, both monetary and fiscal policies change income. Fiscal policy may crowd out, or crowd in, private expenditures, depending on whether money and government securities are substitutes or complements. The effect of fiscal policy also depends on whether people cut their consumption as the national debt rises, as well as on the slopes of the IS and LM curves.

KEY TERMS

IS curve   crowding out
LM curve   crowding in

QUESTIONS AND EXERCISES

1　Explain in your own words why the IS curve slopes downward and the LM curve slopes upward.

*2　Explain why the IS curve and the LM curve can intersect at only one point.

3　What factors shift the IS and LM curves?

*4　Apart from an infinitely interest-elastic demand for money, what other assumption would give you the limiting case of a horizontal LM curve?

5　Add a point E somewhere to Figure 18.4 and show why it is not at equilibrium. (If you pick a point that is off both the IS and LM curves, you have to make some assumption about the relative speed at which the money market and the commodity market equilibrate.)

*6　Explain why government expenditures can crowd out, or crowd in, private expenditures.

FURTHER READING

FRIEDMAN, BENJAMIN. "Crowding Out or Crowding In? The Economic Consequences of Financing Government Debt," *Brookings Papers on Economic Activity*, 1978, pp. 593–664. A classic discussion of crowding out.

KING, ROBERT. "Will the New Keynesian Macroeconomics Resurrect the IS-LM Model?" *Journal of Economic Perspectives*, 7 (Winter 1993), 67–82. A criticism of the IS-LM model for its treatment of expectations.

Most intermediate macroeconomics texts have a chapter on the IS-LM model. See, for example, the texts cited under "Further Reading" in Chapter 15.

Inflation and Unemployment

After you have read this chapter, you will be able to:

- **Describe various types of inflation.**
- **Appreciate the workings of the Phillips curve and the NAIRU.**
- **Explain the aggregate supply curve, the effect of supply shocks, and incomes policies.**

Having looked at what determines aggregate expenditure and hence nominal income, we now ask how changes in nominal income are divided between prices and output. This matters: a 5 percent increase in nominal income is good if it is all a rise in real income, but not if it is simply a rise in prices. The extent to which an increase in aggregate expenditure results in rising output rather than in rising prices depends on the aggregate supply curve. Before we look at this curve, though, a description of inflation and unemployment is in order.

INFLATION: DEFINITION AND TYPES

Inflation is a significant and persistent increase in the price level. Unless prices are rising at a significant rate, say, more than 1 percent per year, it makes no more sense to talk about inflation than it does to call someone overweight because he exceeds the appropriate weight by 3 ounces. Besides, our price indexes are not all that accurate (see the box on page 338). They make insufficient allowance for quality improvements and for the benefits obtained from new goods. Hence the consumer price index (CPI) might show a small rise (perhaps as high as 1 or 1.5 percent, or possibly even more) at a time when consumer prices are actually stable.

Moreover, although most people call any significant increase in prices "inflation," in economics that word is used only for *persistent* increases in the price level. How long prices have to rise before one can speak of inflation is somewhat arbitrary; some economists would say at least three years, while others would draw the line at perhaps one year. The reason for drawing this distinction between sustained and episodic increases in prices is that the theories required to explain them differ. Many factors that can produce episodic price increases cannot account for sustained increases.

A sustained inflation, even at a moderate rate, can have a strong effect in the long run. At a 3 percent inflation rate a dollar has lost half its value after 24 years. (There is a simple way of approximating how long it will take a growing series to double: divide 72 by the growth rate. Since a doubling of the price level means a halving of the value of money, this rule of 72 can be used to calculate when money loses half its value.) Even after only three years of 4 percent inflation, the purchasing power of a dollar has fallen to 85 cents.

There is a special name for an extremely severe inflation: **hyperinflation.** There is no hard and fast line of demarcation, but one common criterion is price increases of more than 50 percent per month. It is hard to visualize the severity of some hyperinflations. For example, the German wholesale price index, which had been 70 in June 1922, was 1.3 trillion in December 1923. In such a situation someone going shopping has to carry his money in a suitcase. At the height of the German hyperinflation workers were paid twice a day because by the end of the working day their morning's earnings would have lost too much value. There is a story about someone who went shopping with a suitcase full of money and put the suitcase down to watch an accident in the road. When he looked again, he found the money dumped out in the street and the suitcase gone. During the hyperinflation in Yugoslavia, the government in Belgrade issued in the last week of December 1993 a 500 billion dinar

Measuring Inflation

How reliable are the price indexes, such as the CPI, that we use to measure inflation? Unfortunately, not very reliable. One major problem is the treatment of new products. They are added to the CPI only when they have been on the market long enough to have come into ordinary use. Hence the CPI does not catch the sharp decline in a product's price that usually happens early in its life cycle.

The second problem is that the CPI cannot make adequate allowance for quality improvements. This is a particularly serious problem for the prices of services, such as medical care. Suppose the cost of an office visit doubles, but the physician can now cure a disease after one visit instead of after four visits as before. The price index records a 100 percent increase in medical care costs, instead of a 50 percent drop. A third problem is that the price index does not make allowance for the public's shift to lower-priced stores, such as Wal-Mart or Price Club. The CPI is constructed in a way that does not take the lower prices charged by such outlets fully into account.

Table 19.1 Inflation Rates in Selected Countries*

Period	Britain	Canada	France	Germany	Italy	Japan	United States
1970–74	9.2%	5.7%	7.2%	5.5%	7.9%	10.0%	4.8%
1975–79	14.5	8.5	9.6	4.1	15.0	7.2	7.7
1980–84	9.1	8.3	10.6	4.4	15.2	3.8	7.2
1985–89	5.1	4.2	3.5	1.2	6.0	1.1	3.5
1990–94	4.5	2.7	2.5	3.4	5.0	2.0	3.6
1994 price index as % of 1960 index	777	422	508	245	1152	310	382

*Except for the last row, data are average annual percent changes in the consumer price index, with the percent change in the first year of the periods being the percent change from the last year of the prior five-year period.
Source: *Economic Report of the President,* 1995.

note, then worth about $5. About four weeks later, it was worth one one-thousandth of a cent!

Although during hyperinflations money is still used as a medium of exchange, it is no longer a standard of value. Instead, people figure in terms of a stable foreign currency, which becomes worth more of the inflated domestic currency every day.

Turning from the drama of hyperinflation to the more mundane events of recent years, Table 19.1 shows the recent inflation rates in the United States and some other major industrialized countries. It demonstrates that inflation is a common disease.

The history of inflation in the United States shows two major breaks. One came after World War II. Until then, as Figure 19.1 shows, prices rose as a concomitant of major wars, but then fell again afterward. As a result, consumer prices in 1929 were approximately what they had been 129 years earlier! As Table 19.2 shows, in terms of year-to-year changes prices in the 1870s were about as variable as in recent years, so that there was some uncertainty about the near-term inflation rate. But someone who contemplated buying a $1,000 thirty-year bond in 1870 might reasonably have figured that when the bond matured in 1900, her $1,000 would buy as much as it did in 1870. But after World War II prices did not decline to offset the war-induced inflation.

Until about 1965 it was reasonable to say that the United States was immune to peacetime inflation. Significant inflations occurred only during or right after major wars. The second major break occurred in the mid-1960s. The Vietnam War was not a major war as far as the U.S. economy was concerned: defense expenditures in 1967 were the same percentage of GDP in 1967 as in the early 1960s. Yet prices rose significantly and without letup. Indeed, until the 1980s, not only was the inflation rate high, it was accelerating. This pattern was broken only in the early 1980s when the inflation rate

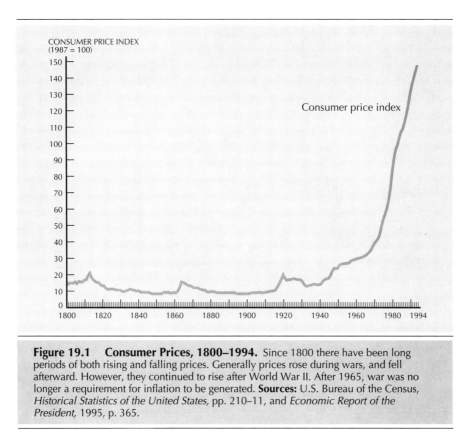

Figure 19.1   Consumer Prices, 1800–1994. Since 1800 there have been long periods of both rising and falling prices. Generally prices rose during wars, and fell afterward. However, they continued to rise after World War II. After 1965, war was no longer a requirement for inflation to be generated. **Sources:** U.S. Bureau of the Census, *Historical Statistics of the United States,* pp. 210–11, and *Economic Report of the President,* 1995, p. 365.

fell substantially. Since then inflation has been moderate, at least by the standards of the late 1960s and 1970s.

Will inflation continue to be moderate? One can tell two stories here. One is that the Great Inflation of the late 1960s and 1970s taught us a lesson that we will not soon forget. The Federal Reserve now seems committed to holding the inflation rate low, and even to reducing it to an average annual rate of perhaps 2 to 4 percent. The other story is that the lesson of the Great Inflation will wear off over time, so that monetary policy will once again take an excessive inflation risk in the hope of reducing unemployment. Which of these stories is more likely is hard to say. It depends on political attitudes more than on strictly economic factors.

UNEMPLOYMENT

At first glance it might seem that unemployment is an obvious condition that is easy to define, but as so often happens, what is obvious at first glance ceases to be obvious once one looks at it carefully. For example, should workers who are laid off, but will be recalled to their jobs within a month, be counted as unemployed? How about someone who has turned down a job because it offers a wage much below her previous wage? Is an engineer who refuses to take a job pumping gas at the minimum wage suffering involuntary or volun-

Table 19.2   Annual Inflation Rates, 1870–1994

	Mean	Maximum	Minimum	Standard Deviation*
1870–74	−3.3	.0	−5.7	2.9
1875–79	−3.9	.0	−9.8	3.6
1880–84	−.7	3.5	−3.6	3.0
1885–89	.0	.0	.0	.0
1890–94	−.8	.0	−3.8	1.7
1895–99	−.8	.0	−3.9	1.8
1900–04	1.5	3.9	.0	2.1
1905–09	.0	3.6	−3.6	2.6
1910–14	2.2	3.6	.0	1.5
1915–19	10.9	16.1	1.0	6.6
1920–24	−.2	14.7	−11.3	9.9
1925–29	.0	2.5	−1.9	1.8
1930–34	4.9	3.3	−10.9	5.6
1935–39	.7	3.6	−1.9	2.4
1940–44	4.7	10.1	1.0	3.7
1945–49	6.1	13.4	−1.0	5.6
1950–54	2.4	7.6	.7	2.9
1955–59	1.6	3.3	−.4	1.5
1960–64	1.3	1.7	1.0	.3
1965–69	3.4	5.3	1.6	1.4
1970–74	5.9	10.5	3.2	2.8
1975–79	7.7	10.8	5.6	2.1
1980–84	7.2	12.7	3.2	4.0
1985–89	3.5	4.7	1.8	1.1
1990–94	3.5	6.1	2.7	1.5

*The standard deviation is the square root of the sum of the squared deviation of each of the five yearly inflation rates from their mean, divided by five.
Note: Inflation is measured by the CPI.
Sources: Based on U. S. Bureau of the Census, *Historical Statistics of the United States,* pp. 210–11, and *Economic Report of the President,* 1995, p. 345.

tary unemployment? How about workers who are employed part-time but would prefer full-time jobs, or those no longer looking for work because they do not think they can find it? Our data, which are obtained from household surveys, count among the unemployed anyone who is on temporary layoff or who has turned down or quit a job and is looking for another one. But they exclude anyone who has given up and is no longer looking for a job. Are they measuring the right thing?

Since unemployment causes human suffering, one might say the less, the better. But zero unemployment is not a meaningful target. There is some unemployment, called **frictional unemployment,** even when the demand for labor greatly exceeds the supply. Some workers may have quit their jobs to look for new ones, while others have just entered the labor force but not yet found jobs. (In 1944, at the height of World War II when there was a great labor shortage, the officially measured unemployment rate was still 1.9 percent.)

Some unemployment is needed for an efficient economy. By analogy, consider the rental market. If the vacancy rate for apartments were zero, then newcomers and those who want to move to another apartment would be in trouble. The *apparent* waste of having some apartments stand idle is not really a waste. Similarly, firms keep inventories of finished goods to meet their customers' needs. Such "idle" inventories may seem a waste, but without them an economy could not function efficiently. Microeconomic efficiency requires some unemployment to provide flexibility as well as labor discipline. But this does not mean that unemployment is not a serious problem. First, unemployment is probably much higher than is required for efficiency. Second, the fact that some unemployment increases the economy's productivity does not reduce the suffering of those who are unemployed. Why should they have to bear the cost?

Still, microeconomic efficiency clearly requires some unemployment. But microeconomic efficiency is not the only criterion for the appropriate rate of unemployment. Another criterion is the prevention of accelerating inflation. This is related to the Phillips curve to which we now turn, starting with a situation in which prices are expected to be constant.

THE PHILLIPS CURVE WITH EXPECTATIONS OF CONSTANT PRICES

How fast wages rise depends on the unemployment rate. Expanding firms can either spend time and effort to search for additional employees at the prevailing wage or get more applicants, as well as reduce quits of already employed workers, by offering a higher wage. When unemployment is high, a little recruiting effort suffices to obtain additional employees, but when the pool of unemployed workers is low, then it is more efficient for firms to offer a higher wage. Hence, if unemployment falls low enough, employers raise wages faster than productivity is growing.

Moreover, in unionized industries, as unemployment falls, wages rise because the bargaining power of unions increases. With fewer unemployed workers around, unions are less afraid that an excessive wage increase will cost them jobs by creating opportunities for nonunionized firms to expand. Moreover, with many available jobs, unemployment is not so terrible a threat. In addition, employers are more reluctant to endure strikes at a time of high employment when demand for their output is high, so they are more willing to settle on the union's terms.

As a result one can find a relation, shown in Figure 19.2, called a **short-run Phillips curve**, after the late Professor A. W. Phillips. It shows that the lower the unemployment rate, the faster wages increase. Such Phillips curves, though not necessarily stable ones, have been found for several countries. The equation for this Phillips curve, in which prices are expected to be constant, is

(1) $w = a - bu + cq,$

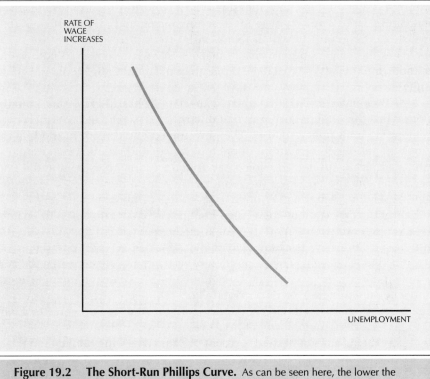

RATE OF
WAGE
INCREASES

UNEMPLOYMENT

Figure 19.2   The Short-Run Phillips Curve. As can be seen here, the lower the
unemployment rate, the faster wages rise.

where w is the rate of wage increases, u the unemployment rate, q the rate of
productivity increase, a a constant, b the coefficient relating wage increases to
the unemployment rate, and c a parameter that measures the extent to which
increases in labor productivity are passed on as higher wages. If firms set their
prices primarily as a markup on their longer-run labor costs, there is also a
simple Phillips equation for prices:

(2) $p = g - bu - hq$,

where p measures the inflation rate, g is a constant, and h is the proportion of
the increase in productivity that is passed on through lower prices.

The Expectations-Augmented Phillips Curve

In the much more realistic case in which prices are expected to change, the
Phillips curve needs an additional term. Surely wages rise faster if prices are
expected to rise at a 20 percent rate than if they are expected to rise at a 2 percent rate. Hence we now write the Phillips curve for wages as

(3) $w = a - bu + cq + dp^e$

and the Phillips curve for prices as

(4) $p = g - bu - hq + fp^e$,

where *d* is a coefficient that measures the extent to which expected price increases *p^e* are taken into account in setting wages, and *f* is a coefficient that measures the extent to which firms raise prices in response to the price increases they expect other firms to make. Since what matters to both workers and employers is the real wage rather than the money wage, *d* should equal unity.

This adjustment for inflationary expectations has an important implication. When the Phillips curve was first discovered, it seemed to provide a convenient menu of policy choices. The government could read off the Phillips curve the various combinations of unemployment and inflation that were feasible and pick its preferred choice, say, 5 percent unemployment and 4 percent inflation. It could then use monetary and fiscal policies to keep aggregate expenditures just high enough to reach this combination.

But the **expectations-augmented Phillips curve** does not allow this game. One can tell two stories about this inflation-augmented Phillips curve. In the first, expectations are backward looking and formed according to the error-learning model. Starting from a position of zero inflation, assume that the government raises aggregate expenditure enough to get 5 percent unemployment and 4 percent inflation. As prices rise by 4 percent people expect prices to rise again next year, say, by 2 percent. Hence, with the *p^e* term now equal to 2 percent, at 5 percent unemployment prices rise not by the planned 4 percent but by 6 percent. As a result of this 6 percent price increase, the public then raises its estimate of next year's inflation rate to, say, 4 percent. That year prices rise by 8 percent, and people once again raise their expectations of inflation. The closer expectations get to reality, the higher the inflation rate needed to maintain a 5 percent unemployment rate. There is an ever-accelerating inflation until the government finally gives up its goal of a 5 percent unemployment rate. This problem would not have arisen had the government chosen an unemployment target equal to, or greater than, that required to keep inflation from accelerating.

But this story in which expectations continually lag behind reality is not plausible. Rational people would realize that the inflation rate is accelerating and hence raise their estimates of next year's inflation rate enough so that, *on the average,* they would estimate it correctly. To be sure, some would still underestimate it, but others would overestimate it. Some years most would underestimate it; in other years most would overestimate it. But there would be no consistent error. In this second story, where expectations are rational, the Phillips curve is a vertical line; on the average, the unemployment rate is the same regardless of the inflation rate.

A situation in which expectations of inflation are formed rationally does not allow one to trade off inflation against unemployment. But the rationality of expectations also has a favorable side. If the government could convince the public that it would persevere with an anti-inflationary policy, it could bring the inflation rate down with less unemployment than would be required if people did not change their expectations. But usually the government cannot make its policy credible. Throughout the inflation it has promised to do something about the problem, so how can it now convince anyone that this time it really means it?

The classic example of terminating an inflation through a credible policy was the end of the German hyperinflation in 1924. When the German government, which previously had not claimed to be fighting inflation, adopted a credible anti-inflation policy, the public believed it and the hyperinflation ended quickly. What helped was that the inflation had become so extraordinarily severe and was causing so much damage that the government's announcement became a plausible response. Moreover, during a hyperinflation, contracts and wage arrangements are, in effect, indexed. There were no three-year labor agreements setting a certain increase in the money wage each January. In an economy suffering from a lesser inflation, such contracts can delay the adjustment to a lower inflation rate. Unless they are renegotiated, the scheduled rise in money wages results in real wages rising faster than planned and hence in unemployment. Pneumonia can be cured, but a cold cannot!

Figure 19.3 demonstrates a simple Phillips curve without an adjustment for price expectations. In Part A, which covers the years 1948 to 1965 when inflation and hence expected inflation were fairly low, this Phillips curve gives

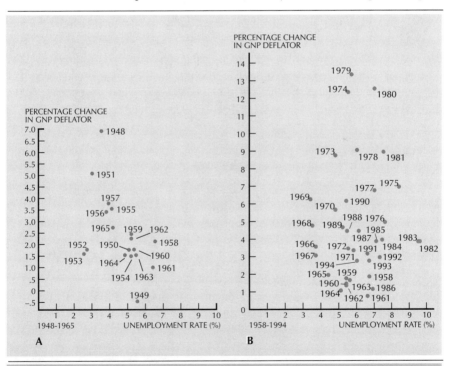

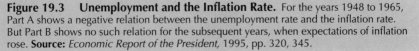

Figure 19.3   Unemployment and the Inflation Rate. For the years 1948 to 1965, Part A shows a negative relation between the unemployment rate and the inflation rate. But Part B shows no such relation for the subsequent years, when expectations of inflation rose. **Source:** *Economic Report of the President,* 1995, pp. 320, 345.

a fairly good fit. But when, as in Part B, the observations for 1966 to 1994 are added, this simple Phillips curve falls apart. Not all its collapse should be attributed to its failure to allow for expectations of inflation. Some of it, though only a minor part, is due to the rising *natural rate of unemployment,* to which we now turn.

THE NONACCELERATING INFLATION RATE OF UNEMPLOYMENT

If unemployment falls below a certain rate, there is ever-accelerating inflation. The unemployment rate that is just high enough to avoid this is called the **NAIRU** (for **nonaccelerating inflation rate of unemployment**) or the natural unemployment rate. This NAIRU need not be the unemployment rate consistent with zero inflation. It is just the rate at which unemployment is neither so

---

Is High Unemployment a Characteristic of Recessions?

After the recovery from the 1990–91 recession was well under way, many people still believed that the economy was in a recession. As evidence they pointed to the high unemployment rate. Were they right? No, they were not, for two reasons. One is that turning points in the unemployment rate typically lag behind the cyclical turning points in the other economic indicators, such as retail sales and personal income, that we use to delineate business fluctuations. When demand falls, firms typically cut back on overtime before they fire workers, and when demand increases, they initially meet this demand by increasing the number of hours worked. Only when they see that demand continues to stay high, do they usually hire more workers.

The other reason is more fundamental. It relates to the distinction between levels and rates of change. We generally look at unemployment as a level, not a rate of change: when many people are unemployed we (rightly) worry about unemployment being high, even though it may be falling. In contrast, recessions are defined primarily, not by the *level* of income or output, but as periods when output is *falling,* while expansions are essentially defined as periods when output is *rising* toward its potential. With expansions and recessions thus being defined by the direction of change, and not the level, of income, it follows that the level of income is high, not low, during the first part of the recession, when it has not yet had time to fall very far. Similarly, the level of income is low in the first part of an expansion, when it has not yet risen much.

During the last nine recessions the unemployment rate averaged 5.5 percent in the first six months of each recession, but 7.3 percent in the first six months of each subsequent expansion. Since the cyclical peak in 1948, the unemployment rate has been lower every time in the first six months of the recession than it was in the six months following the start of the recovery. (If one starts counting with the 1949 expansion instead of the 1948 recession, then there is one exception.) Even nine months after the start of the expansions, the average unemployment rate was still higher than it was nine months after the start of the recessions: 7.1 percent versus 5.9 percent. This shows the importance of distinguishing "high" from "rising" and "low" from "falling."

low that inflation accelerates, nor so high that the pressure of unemployed workers lowers the inflation rate. If an economy that is at the NAIRU has an ongoing 5 percent inflation rate, inflation will continue at this 5 percent rate. Only if its inflation rate is zero to start with will there be neither inflation nor deflation at the NAIRU.

The term *natural rate* does not mean that this particular unemployment rate is ordained by nature. Various policies such as the elimination of minimum-wage laws, more stringent job-search requirements for those receiving unemployment compensation, a decline in racial discrimination, and programs to retrain the unemployed might all lower the NAIRU.

Estimates of the natural rate now usually range between 5½ and 6½ percent. This is a disturbingly wide range. Should the Fed aim at a GDP level corresponding to 5½ or 6½ percent unemployment? Moreover, there is no reason to assume that the NAIRU is stable. That we lack reliable and precise knowledge of the NAIRU has an important implication for policy. If we set macro policy to aim at full employment, defined as the NAIRU, we may well end up either tolerating too much unemployment or setting off an accelerating inflation. It seems likely that in the 1970s a reason for high inflation was that the government had underestimated the NAIRU.

In the long run the actual rate of unemployment gravitates toward the NAIRU. It cannot stay any lower because that would set off an ever-accelerating inflation. This would eventually result in a restrictive monetary policy that would raise unemployment again. Conversely, when the unemployment rate is above the NAIRU, the search for jobs by unemployed workers puts downward pressure on wages and prices, and, as will be explained shortly, lower wages and prices lead to lower unemployment.

High unemployment—unemployment obviously in excess of the NAIRU—is not a new phenomenon. Prior to the Great Depression unemployment rose sharply during severe recessions. Economic historians disagree about whether, on the average, the unemployment rate was all that much higher before 1929 than it was after World War II. Clearly, the Great Depression was an extreme, quite atypical case. We will consider the causes of massive unemployment later; now we will consider the causes of inflation.

BEYOND THE SIMPLE, EXPECTATIONS-AUGMENTED PHILLIPS CURVE

There are two straightforward ways in which the Phillips curve that we have discussed so far can be improved. One is to make allowance for supply shocks. The other is to remove the assumption that prices are set by adding a constant markup to wages.

Supply Shocks

Between 1973 and 1975 the unemployment rate rose from 4.9 to 8.5 percent. Our Phillips curve suggests that the inflation rate should have fallen. But instead it rose substantially. The inflation rate (as measured by the consumer price index), which had been 3.4 percent in 1972, was much higher in the fol-

Unemployment Hysteresis

In the 1960s unemployment rates in the leading European countries were much lower than in the United States. Then, following the 1973–74 oil shock, European unemployment rose sharply. That is not surprising. What is surprising is that unemployment stayed high and did not decline as it did in the United States following the 1975–76 recession.

One of several explanations that has been given is *hysteresis*. This is a situation in which the previous value of a variable has a significant effect on its current value.

By and large, economic theory depicts a timeless state. Thus, the slope of the demand curve is taken as independent of past prices. It shows how much is bought at each price without taking into account what the price was previously. If a hundred units are bought at a price of $5, this is so regardless of whether the price in the previous period was $2 or $10. For many purposes this is a useful simplification, but in some cases it is not. Suppose that during a drought people are asked to conserve water. Demand for water falls. The next year, when rainfall is normal, the demand for water will not fully return to its previous level. Those who have installed water-saving devices will not rip them out.

Unemployment *may* be affected by hysteresis, so that the NAIRU is higher if the actual unemployment rate was higher recently. There are several possible reasons for this. One is that prolonged unemployment makes some workers unemployable; during long periods of unemployment their skills or their work ethic may deteriorate. Another possibility, more applicable to highly unionized European countries than to the United States, is that unions care primarily about their employed members and not about those who lost their jobs and hence may no longer be dues-paying members. If demand increases, they respond by demanding higher wages for their employed members and not by letting the increase in demand raise employment. Whether these or other factors actually result in significant unemployment hysteresis is as yet an unanswered question.

---

lowing three years of high unemployment, 8.7 percent in 1973, 12.3 percent in 1974, and 6.9 percent in 1975. How could that happen? It happened as a result of a series of severe supply shocks, in particular a quadrupling of oil prices by OPEC (Organization of Petroleum Exporting Countries) and widespread bad harvests. With the price of oil and food rising sharply, money wages and the inflation rate also rose substantially, despite the downward pressure on wages and prices exerted by higher unemployment and greater excess capacity.

Fortunately, such dramatic supply shocks as those we experienced in 1973–74 are rare, but smaller supply shocks occur with some frequency. Sometimes they raise the inflation rate, and sometimes, as when oil prices are falling, they lower it. Hence, it is useful to add another term to the price equation that takes account of supply shocks. Such a term might be a weighted average of the price of oil and food, two items particularly subject to supply shocks, or it might be a more comprehensive term that also includes the change in the foreign-exchange rate, since the exchange rate affects import prices and can be quite volatile. Between 1980 and 1985 the dollar rose by 64 percent relative to the currencies of our major trading partners, and then between 1985 and 1990 it fell by 38 percent.

Flexible Markups

A recession affects not just wages; it also affects the profit margin that firms earn. Excess capacity forces firms to cut their markups. Hence, the assumption made so far, that markups are constant, is, at best, just a first approximation. Fortunately, there is a simple way to take variable markups into account. Since we are trying to explain the inflation rate and not the wage rate, we can drop the wage version of the Phillips curve and go directly to the price version given on page 343. In this equation, (4) $p = g - bu - hq + dp^f$, we can now interpret the coefficient b as the effect that unemployment and excess capacity have on prices, without bothering with whether this effect comes from changes in wage costs or from changes in markups.

THE CAUSES OF INFLATION

A useful way to explain inflation is to look at an **aggregate supply curve**. This is a curve, such as S in Figure 19.4, that relates the price level to output. In discussing the Phillips curve, we explained why wages increase faster when unem-

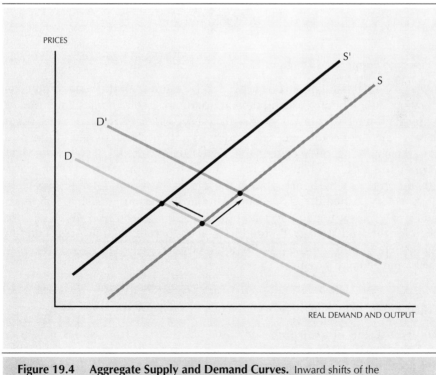

Figure 19.4   Aggregate Supply and Demand Curves. Inward shifts of the aggregate supply curve raise prices and lower real income. Upward shifts of the aggregate demand curve raise both prices and output.

ployment is low. An analogous relation holds for the level of wages. When unemployment is low and has been low for some time, wages will have risen more than they otherwise would have. Hence, wages and prices will be higher when unemployment is low and output is high. So the aggregate supply curve slopes upward. In the long run the aggregate supply curve is vertical. How long it takes for the short-run supply curve to evolve into the vertical long-run supply curve depends, in large part, on how fast expectations adjust to changes in the inflation rate and on how fast prices and wages adjust to these changed expectations.

For a given stock of nominal money, the real stock of money varies inversely with the price level. As explained in Chapter 15, aggregate demand (that is, aggregate expenditure) is a positive function of the real stock of money and therefore a negative function of the price level.[1] Hence, the aggregate demand curve shown in Figure 19.4 slopes downward; the higher the price level, the lower the real demand and, hence, output.

Several factors can shift the aggregate demand curve. One is a change in the money supply. If the money supply increases, the aggregate demand curve shifts outward, from D to D' in Figure 19.4, for example. With a given money supply anything that changes velocity, such as a change in the interest rate, will also shift the aggregate demand curve. Suppose, for example, that the marginal efficiency of investment increases. Interest rates would rise as firms borrow more to undertake investment, and hence velocity would increase. The aggregate demand curve would then shift outward.

Aggregate Supply and Demand Curves: An Application

In August 1990 Saddam Hussein invaded Kuwait. Given the volatile political situation in the Middle East and the importance of its oil supplies, this invasion generated much anxiety among both households and firms in the United States. Consumer confidence fell sharply, as did purchases of new houses and cars. Such a reduction in aggregate demand is illustrated by a shift from D' to D in Figure 19.4. By creating fears of reduced oil supplies, the invasion also raised oil prices and, hence, shifted the aggregate supply curve from S to S'. Both factors pushed the U.S. economy toward lower output. The 1990 recession is dated as starting in July, a month earlier, but it is possible that had it not been for the Gulf War, GDP would have been high enough in August and in subsequent months for the July dip not to be counted as a recession. Whether this would actually have been the case is hard to say.

PRICE INCREASES AND INFLATION: SUPPLY-SIDE SHOCKS

An upward shift of the supply curve, such as the shift from S to S' in Figure 19.4, raises prices. Many factors can generate such a shift. As we mentioned in our discussion of the Phillips curve, supply shocks like the one occasioned by OPEC in its stronger days can have such an effect; so can a fall of the dollar on

---

[1] It is also a positive function of the stock of wealth, and the higher the price level, the lower the real value of the wealth represented by the stocks of money and government bonds.

the foreign-exchange market. Other examples of possible supply shocks are rising labor costs due to increased union power, increased markups of prices resulting from a decline in competition, and pervasive crop failures.

Nobody denies that such supply shocks can temporarily raise the price level. Can they also cause inflation, that is, a *continual* increase in the price level? Such inflations, sometimes called *cost-push* inflations, can occur in principle, but for two reasons they are not likely. First, supply shocks are often events that occur quickly and are not repeated in the following year. Prices rise and can stay at the higher level for a long time, but they do not continue to rise. Second, as the aggregate demand curve tells us, when the price level rises real income falls. The resulting unemployment then creates downward pressure on wages and prices.

If one wants to blame supply shocks for inflation, one has to take an indirect approach. One way is to say that the rise in unemployment that often accompanies a supply shock will induce the Fed to adopt a more expansionary policy. The resulting increase in the monetary growth rate may raise the inflation rate for several years. But one might then want to attribute the inflation to the Fed's policy rather than to the supply shock.

Another way is to point out that often employees strongly resist any reduction in real wages. Hence if, say, oil prices rise, they demand wage increases to offset the higher prices. Firms then pass these higher labor costs on by raising prices, and this generates further wage demands. Such a *price-wage-price* spiral cannot be ruled out entirely. Had OPEC not raised oil prices in 1973–74 and 1979–80, money wages would have risen less than they did in subsequent years. All the same, as a general description of inflation, the price-wage-price spiral explanation of inflation is not entirely persuasive. Unions account for less than a quarter of the labor force. Moreover, the higher unemployment that results from rising wages and prices curbs wage increases. Hence, without denying that a supply shock can, in principle, cause some inflation, one might doubt that supply shocks, unless accommodated by expansionary monetary policy, can be an important cause of inflation in the United States. In Europe, where unions are more powerful and resistance to real wage cuts seems stronger, supply shocks may play more of a role.

Relative Prices and the Price Level

Suppose that OPEC doubles oil prices. Obviously, the *relative* price of oil has now risen, but how about the price level? Assume that the Fed does not increase the money supply to accommodate this supply shock. The price level starts to rise as the prices of oil and oil-related products go up. The real money supply falls, and this lowers aggregate expenditure. Initially, most of this reduction in aggregate expenditure results in falling output and employment. But, eventually, this rise in unemployment reduces the growth rate of money wages enough so that the price level is no higher than it would have been had oil prices not risen. This scenario is highly improbable because the Fed is likely to respond to a rise in unemployment by increasing the growth rate of money at least to some extent. But it does demonstrate the distinction between a rise in a relative price and a rise in the price *level*.

PRICE INCREASES AND INFLATION: THE EXPENDITURES SIDE

If the aggregate demand curve in Figure 19.4 shifts upward, say, from D to D', prices rise. Inflations due to upward shifts of the aggregate demand curve are sometimes referred to as **demand-pull** inflations. Such a shift could be due to increases in any of the following: the propensity to consume, the marginal efficiency of investment, government expenditures, exports, and the money supply. The aggregate demand curve also shifts upward if taxes, imports, or the demand for money decrease.

To account for inflation rather than just for a one-time increase in the price level, these factors would have to continue to change for some time. For example, suppose government expenditures increase and stay at their higher level. Aggregate expenditure rises, and so do prices, but once having risen, prices do not rise any further. Expressed in quantity theory terms, as government expenditures increase, the interest rate rises, which in turn raises velocity. Aggregate expenditures and prices go up as MV rises. But since there is only a one-time rise in the interest rate, prices increase only once and not continuously. Of course, this rise in prices would be spread out over time. Even so, a prolonged, demand-pull inflation would occur only if government expenditures rise for a long time and at a high rate. This is possible, but not very likely. It is also possible, but again not very likely, that increases in government expenditures would set off a longer-lasting price-wage-price spiral.

Similarly, a substantial inflation is not likely to result from changes in the propensity to consume or in the demand for money or in exports and imports. Changes in the marginal efficiency of investment are a more controversial issue. Many Keynesians believe that the marginal efficiency of investment is highly unstable, that occasionally there occur prolonged and substantial investment booms that are inflationary. But, all in all, by far the most likely suspect in inflation is the supply of money. First, increases in the money supply have a powerful effect on income; in the long run a 10 percent rise in the money supply leads to a 10 percent higher price level. Second, the monetary growth rate does vary substantially, with the variations sometimes persisting for fairly long periods. Third, by and large, the empirical evidence demonstrates a close correlation between movements in money and in prices. It is therefore not surprising that Milton Friedman has said that "inflation is always and everywhere a monetary phenomenon." By no means are all economists willing to go that far, but just about all would agree that a *major* inflation requires an increase in the money supply.

Is Money *the* Cause?

Although agreeing that major inflations cannot occur without an increase in the money supply, some economists are reluctant to say that money is *the* cause of inflation. They argue that attributing inflation to a rise in the money supply is superficial. Suppose, for example, that oil prices double and that the Fed increases the money supply to avoid the unemployment that would otherwise occur. Shouldn't one blame the resulting inflation on OPEC rather than on the faster growth of the money supply? Similarly, suppose that those who are relatively more concerned about unemployment than about inflation obtain greater political power. The Fed then becomes more expansionary and inflation results. It is hard to imagine that the Great Inflation of the late 1960s and 1970s could have been nearly as severe had the public, and hence the politicians, been much more strongly opposed to inflation. Isn't it therefore superficial to say that the inflation is "caused" by a rise in the monetary growth rate?

Not really: causes have other causes that underlie them. When someone explains why he got wet, he says that it is raining, not that there is a high-pressure area to the south or that gravitational forces cause clouds to shed moisture. *If* inflation occurs whenever the growth rate of money is high, why not say that high monetary growth is the cause? Pointing toward monetary growth has the advantage of explaining all, or most, inflations by a single cause. And a theory that points to the same cause in a wide variety of cases is (if correct) usually preferable to one that explains each case differently. Moreover, the monetary growth rate is a useful variable to focus on because the Fed can control it. This is not to deny that we should also ask what caused the money supply to increase.

POLICIES TO FIGHT INFLATION

If inflation has taken hold, two types of policies can be used to try to bring the inflation rate down. One is an indirect policy of lowering aggregate expenditures; the other is a policy of exercising direct control or suasion over wages and prices.

Reducing Aggregate Expenditures

If it is the excessive rise in aggregate expenditures that generates inflation, an obvious policy is to reduce aggregate expenditures. But such a policy is costly. The initial effect of a reduction in expenditures is a decrease in output and employment more than in prices, unless this anti-inflationary policy is highly credible or wages are flexible. In October 1979 the Fed changed to a more restrictive policy that, together with the cessation of unfavorable supply shocks, brought the inflation rate (as measured by the GDP deflator) down from 9.7 percent in 1981 to 3.8 percent by 1983. But the unemployment rate rose from 5.8 percent in 1979 to 9.5 percent in 1982 and 1983, a terrible cost in lost output and human misery.

The cost in terms of forgone output of reducing the inflation rate by 1 percentage point is known as the **sacrifice ratio**. This ratio is disconcertingly high. For example, one estimate puts it at 2.4.[2] Thus, to reduce the inflation rate, say from 4 to 2 percent, would mean losing the equivalent of 4.8 percent of one year's output, though this cost can be spread over several years. Indeed, one of the issues in macroeconomic policy making is whether it is better to

---

[2] Laurence Ball, "How Costly Is Disinflation? The Historical Evidence," Federal Reserve Bank of Philadelphia, *Business Review*, November–December 1993, pp. 17–28.

bring down a high inflation rate cold turkey or to do so more gradually. Proponents of gradual adjustment argue that this is less costly because it provides the time that is needed for sticky wages and prices to adjust. Proponents of the cold-turkey treatment, on the other hand, argue that an abrupt turn in policy is needed to change people's expectations, that people will not believe that the government will adhere to a gradual policy long enough to lower inflation to its target rate.

Incomes Policy

An alternative type of policy, **incomes policy**, tries to reduce the cost of bringing down the inflation rate. Recall the Phillips curve equation: $w = a - bu + cq + dp^e$. Instead of operating on the unemployment term, incomes policy focuses on the price-expectations term. Much of inflation is defensive because those involved—employees raising their wage demands and firms raising their prices—expect others to do so and don't want to be left behind. It is like everyone at a parade standing up to see better. It seems obvious that a prohibition of excessive wage and price increases could stop inflation at relatively little cost.

One form of incomes policy is therefore outright wage and price controls. This was last tried by President Richard Nixon in 1971 and had previously been used during the Korean War and both world wars. Wage and price controls are the most rigid form of incomes policy. At the other extreme is *jawboning*, that is, the president urging wage and price setters to behave responsibly and to keep the public interest in mind. In between are such policies as taking government contracts away from firms that raise prices excessively or offering tax cuts to firms that stay within certain wage and price guidelines. Incomes policy is sometimes formulated as a social contract whereby unions agree to settle for lower wage increases in exchange for price restraints by firms or for a full-employment policy, etc. Such social contracts are more applicable in many European countries that have a higher degree of unionization and highly centralized union decision making than in the United States.

Incomes policies suffer from three major defects. First, a mild incomes policy, such as jawboning, may have little impact. There is much dispute about whether it made much difference when Presidents John F. Kennedy and Lyndon B. Johnson tried it. Second, a much stronger policy, such as wage and price controls, interferes with resource allocation. We rely on relative prices to guide production. Resources flow to where they are needed mainly because prices rise in those sectors. By prohibiting price increases, price controls eliminate this incentive to shift resources.

Third, suppose that the inflation results from money growing too rapidly. Since people do not want to hold all this extra money, they spend some, and thus drive up prices in those sectors in which prices are not controlled. There will also be some evasion of controls. One way price controls can be evaded is to reduce the quality of the product while keeping the price fixed. Worse than that, eventually, when the controls are taken off, these large money balances cause a price explosion. The obvious answer is that controls should be accompanied by a monetary policy that is restrictive enough to eliminate the inflationary fuel. But this probably won't happen, for reasons explained in the box below.

INDEXING: GOOD OR BAD?

Many union contracts contain a so-called COLA (cost-of-living adjustment) clause that automatically adjusts wages, at least part of the way, for changes in the cost of living. Some economists have advocated indexing all wages. This would have two major advantages. First, it would make it much easier to curb inflation. Long-term labor contracts without COLAs contain an implicit allowance for rising prices. If the government then adopts an unanticipated policy to curb inflation, wages under these contracts still rise. As a result, real wages are then too high and unemployment develops. But with contracts containing COLAs nominal wages rise less if prices rise less. Second, COLAs avoid unwarranted gains or losses to some parties when the actual inflation rate differs from the one that was assumed in making indexed long-term contracts.

Price Controls and Inflation

Suppose as the inflation rate rises to, say, 8 percent, the government imposes wage and price controls that permit prices to rise only by 4 percent per year. Would this raise or lower your expectation of inflation over the next five years? It should obviously lower your price expectation for the immediate future, but you could reasonably argue that it will lead to higher, not lower, prices five years from now.

The argument is as follows: Since price controls create shortages and other serious distortions in resource allocation, they will probably be removed in a few years. When that happens, prices will rise in proportion to the increase that has occurred in the money supply. Hence, if the imposition of price controls induces a faster rise in the money supply than would otherwise have occurred, the price level five years from now will be higher than it would have been had price controls not been imposed.

And for two reasons price controls are likely to lead to a higher growth rate of money. First, the existence of price controls and the immediate decline in the inflation rate will make the public less willing to put up with a restrictive monetary policy. The Fed may then feel encouraged to lower interest rates. Second, if wage and price controls or some other type of strong incomes policy holds down wages, it is only fair that interest rates should be held down too. But how can this be done? One possibility is to limit the demand for loanable funds by a system of credit allocation, such as limiting the amount that banks can lend to certain types of borrowers. But credit allocation is cumbersome and has many disadvantages. A tempting alternative is to depress interest rates temporarily by increasing the monetary growth rate. In this way incomes policy ultimately increased the inflation rate during the 1970s.

But indexing also has its problems. Suppose that an unexpected decline in productivity growth or some other supply shock reduces output. This requires someone to sacrifice some real income. But with indexing protecting the real wages of most employees, those whose incomes are not indexed have to bear all the loss. To carry this point to its extreme, suppose that *all* incomes are indexed. Then, even a small supply shock would send the economy off into hyperinflation if the central bank accommodates the resulting increase in the demand for money as indexing raises incomes. Moreover, when an inflation gets started, indexing makes it worse, because it makes wages respond much more readily to the inflation.

THE CAUSES OF UNEMPLOYMENT

The obvious explanation of a rise in unemployment is that aggregate expenditure has fallen. Any of the variables that determines aggregate expenditure, such as the marginal efficiency of investment or the propensity to consume, may be responsible. Unemployment, unlike inflation, does not require a continuous change in these variables. For example, if government expenditures fall and stay at the lower level, unemployment rises and remains high for some time.[3]

Supply shocks can also result in unemployment. If productivity falls, firms demand less labor at the old real wage. Prolonged absolute declines in productivity are rare. But if productivity rises at a slower rate than was assumed when wage contracts were signed, then real wages will rise too fast, and unemployment will increase. A rise in import prices can have a similar effect. To protect their real wages as import prices rise, workers demand a higher money wage. But since there has been no offsetting increase in their productivity, employers hire fewer workers at that wage. In the United States these supply-side factors probably do not result in much unemployment, in part because unions are weak and in part because unions tend to focus on money wages rather than on real wages. But in Europe workers stress real wages more and unions are stronger. There, excessive real wage demands are a more plausible, though still a disputed, cause of substantial unemployment.

In one sense nearly all unemployment can be blamed on excessive *money* wage demands. Imagine that money wages are completely flexible, as unemployed workers are willing to work for whatever wage they can get. Suppose that in such an economy the money stock drops by 10 percent. As aggregate expenditures fall, unemployment develops, but after wages and prices have fallen by 10 percent, this unemployment disappears. Similarly, if the marginal efficiency of investment falls, there is *some* reduction in wages and prices that raises the money supply enough, and lowers interest rates enough, to restore full employment. In one sense it can be said that were it not for minimum-wage laws, nearly all unemployment would be voluntary since most of the unemployed could get jobs at *some* wage. This does not mean that those who say that they are unemployed are lying; it is just that they are leaving out part of

---

[3] Unemployment and inflation differ in this respect because unemployment refers to the level of a variable, whereas inflation refers to the change in a variable, the price level.

the story. They should not say that they cannot find work, but that they cannot find work at a wage they consider to be reasonable.

Most economists, and probably most other people, treat this as a semantic quibble. They talk of unemployment when someone cannot find work at a wage reasonably related to her previous wage, her experience, and her training. Moreover, they point out, minimum-wage legislation limits the ability of workers to accept lower wages.

SUMMARY

1   Inflation is a persistent and significant rise in the price level. Inflations range from moderate inflations to hyperinflations. Until the 1960s it seemed that the U.S. economy was immune from peacetime inflations. This is no longer so.
2   Some unemployment is needed for efficiency, and if unemployment falls below the NAIRU, accelerating inflation results. Eventually the Phillips curve becomes vertical and does not provide a menu of trade-offs.
3   The aggregate demand curve, drawn in the price–real output plane, is downward sloping. The aggregate supply curve slopes upward.
4   Prices rise if either the aggregate demand curve or the aggregate supply curve shifts upward. But unless these shifts persist, they only cause a blip in the price level, not inflation. The most likely culprit in inflation is the money supply. Supply shocks are more likely to account for high prices than for inflation.
5   Inflation can be fought either by reducing aggregate expenditure or by incomes policy. Reducing aggregate expenditure causes unemployment. There are reasons to question whether incomes policies would work.
6   Declines in aggregate expenditure create unemployment, but would not do so if wages were downwardly flexible. Supply shocks too can create unemployment.

KEY TERMS

inflation	natural rate of unemployment
sacrifice ratio	aggregate supply curve
hyperinflation	aggregate demand curve
Phillips curve	incomes policy
expectations-augmented Phillips curve	indexing
NAIRU	COLA

QUESTIONS AND EXERCISES

1   Look at data on the unemployment rate and on inflation (shown in the *Economic Report of the President*) for the last ten years. Do they describe a stable Phillips curve?
*2   Discuss: "The Phillips curve allows the government to select its preferred menu of inflation and unemployment."
3   The United States used to be immune to peacetime inflation. This is no longer true. Why do you think this is?
*4   Explain why the aggregate demand curve drawn in the price–real income plane slopes downward while the aggregate supply curve slopes upward.
*5   Discuss whether supply shocks can cause inflation. Are they likely to?
6   Suppose an unemployed person can only get a job by taking a 20 percent wage cut and refuses to do so. Would you classify him as involuntarily unemployed? How *do* you define involuntary unemployment?

FURTHER READING

BALL, LAURENCE. "How Costly Is Disinflation? The Historical Evidence," Federal Reserve Bank of Philadelphia, *Business Review*, November–December 1993, pp. 17–28. Provides a stimulating discussion of the sacrifice ratio.

EBERTS, RANDALL, and ERICA GROSHEN. "The Causes and Consequences of Structural Changes in U.S. Labor Markets: A Review," Federal Reserve Bank of Cleveland, *Economic Review* 26, (First Quarter 1992), 18–25. An informative discussion of factors changing the Phillips curve.

MCCULLOCH, HUGH. *Money and Inflation.* New York: Academic Press, 1975. A well-written and simple account.

TALLMAN, ELLIS. "Inflation: How Long Has This Been Going On?" Federal Reserve Bank of Atlanta, *Economic Review*, 78 (November–December 1993), 1–12. An informative survey of past inflations.

WEINER, STUART. "New Estimates of the Natural Rate of Unemployment," Federal Reserve Bank of Kansas City, *Economic Review*, 78 (Fourth Quarter 1993), 53–69. An interesting estimate of the Phillips curve.

The Quantity Theory, Monetarism, and the Credit View

After you have read this chapter, you will be able to:

- Explain the Chicago version of the quantity theory, its transmission process, and the evidence advanced for it.
- Distinguish between monetarist theory and Keynesian theory.
- Discern why it is so hard to determine whether the private sector is inherently stable.
- Appreciate the credit view.

If you read the appendixes, you will be able to:

- Present the Brunner-Meltzer model, as well as the Patinkin version of the quantity theory.

In this chapter, we return to the quantity theory, which we first encountered in Chapter 15. Milton Friedman, while at the University of Chicago, breathed new life into the quantity theory by finding in it a useful explanation of changes in GDP. We look at Friedman's "Chicago" version of this theory first. Then we turn to the empirical evidence that quantity theorists have provided. After that we look at a broader set of propositions that define the monetarist position and compare the monetarist and Keynesian views. We conclude with a consideration of an alternative approach that looks at credit rather than money. The appendixes discuss Don Patinkin's exposition of the quantity theory and the theory of two leading monetarists, Karl Brunner and Allan Meltzer.

DEVELOPMENT OF THE QUANTITY THEORY

The quantity theory has a long history. The great Scottish philosopher David Hume, a friend of Adam Smith, published a quite sophisticated version of this theory in the 1750s. It received masterly restatements by A. C. Pigou in Cambridge, England, in 1917, and by the great American economist Irving Fisher in 1911.

The quantity theory fell into disrepute during the Great Depression. It did not seem able to explain what was occurring because it depended on constant velocity, and velocity was falling rapidly. As we will discuss in Chapter 27, there is now much evidence that the quantity theory has much to contribute to understanding the Great Depression, but that was not appreciated at the time. Perhaps even more important was the publication in 1936 of Keynes's *General Theory of Employment, Interest and Money,* which provided an exciting alternative to the quantity theory. Most young economists became Keynesians. At only a few universities, notably the University of Chicago, was the quantity theory taught as a reputable theory rather than treated as an old, exploded fallacy.

The Chicago Approach

The quantity theory was revived in the 1950s by Milton Friedman and his students at the University of Chicago. They abandoned the older mechanistic approach that had assumed that velocity was constant. Instead, influenced by Keynesian theory, they treated the demand for money like the demand for any other capital good. (Money is a capital good because we do not consume it directly, but rather consume the service, liquidity, that it yields.) Hence, instead of assuming, as previous quantity theorists had done, that the Cambridge k was some fixed number, they assumed that it depended on income or wealth and on the cost of holding money, that is, on the yield you would forgo if you held money rather than some other asset. This is, after all, the way we treat the demand for other capital goods; we do not assume that the demand for houses is some fixed number, but assume instead that it depends on the price of houses and income or wealth.

If the demand for money is, in fact, a stable function of a few predictable variables, then, if one knows the values of these variables, one can predict how much money will be demanded. Suppose, as we did in drawing the LM curve, that the demand for nominal money is a function of nominal income (YP) and the nominal interest rate (r); that is,

(1) $M_D = f(YP, r)$.

If we assume that the supply of and demand for money are equilibrated by the money market, we can write

(2) $M_S = M_D = f(YP, r)$,

or, more specifically,

(3) $M_S = M_D = a + bYP + cr$,

where *a*, *b*, and *c* are coefficients that can be estimated statistically. Now suppose that we also know *r*. In this case, *once we are told what will happen to the nominal money stock* M_S, *we know how nominal income must change to make Equation (3) hold.*

This is the approach of Friedman's refurbished quantity theory. How does it relate to Keynesian theory? Keynesian theory tells us that income depends not only on the supply of and demand for money (the LM curve), but also on IS-curve variables such as the propensity to consume and the marginal efficiency of investment. What happens to these variables in the quantity theory? They enter indirectly. Suppose that the marginal propensity to consume or the marginal efficiency of investment increases. Nominal income rises. But Equation (3) tells us that if income rises while the money supply is constant, then the interest rate must rise too. This, in turn, reduces the Cambridge *k;* that is, it raises velocity. Thus, since changes in the propensity to consume and in the marginal efficiency of investment enter Friedman's analysis indirectly, there is no substantive difference between the two theories on this formal, abstract level.

The real disagreement relates to two empirical issues. First, quantity theorists believe that the demand function for money is stable, while Keynesians think it varies. In terms of Equation (3), Keynesians argue that the coefficients *a*, *b*, and *c* are less predictable than monetarists claim.

Second, as already discussed in Chapter 15, Keynesians point out that an increase in the quantity of money, because it lowers the interest rate, lowers velocity so that *MV*, and thus income, rise less than proportionately to the increase in the money supply. Quantity theorists reply that the interest rate declines only temporarily. The crucial issue here is how long it takes for the

---

Explaining Hyperinflations

After World War I a number of the defeated countries, such as Germany, Russia, and Austria, experienced hyperinflation. One peculiarity of such hyperinflation is that prices rise at a faster rate than the quantity of money does. On the surface that seems to invalidate the quantity theory of money. But actually it does not: the *modern* quantity theory can explain why prices rose much faster than the quantity of money. As Phillip Cagan of Columbia University has pointed out, the modern quantity theory does not assume that the velocity of money is constant. Instead, it makes velocity a function of the cost of holding money. This cost is usually measured by the interest rate and is relatively low and stable, so that velocity is fairly stable too. But during hyperinflations a much greater cost of holding money is its loss of purchasing power because interest rates lag way behind the inflation rate. Hence, Cagan ignored the interest rate and made the demand for money, and hence the velocity of money, functions of the expected inflation rate, which he estimated using an adaptive-expectations model.

By showing that the quantity theory is flexible enough to explain even situations where the velocity of money is highly variable, Cagan substantially increased the credibility of the modern quantity theory.

interest rate to return to its previous level. This issue is hard to resolve. To be sure, we can observe the nominal interest rate. But what affects expenditures is the expected after-tax real interest rate.

The Transmission Process

The income-expenditure theory describes a complex **transmission process**, set out in the preceding chapters, by which changes in the money supply affect income. Milton Friedman's discussion of the transmission process is different.

The main difference is that Friedman believes that changes in the money stock affect expenditures in so many and such complicated ways that it is useless to try to discover them all. Any attempt to do so would surely fail to find some of them and would therefore underestimate the total effect that money has on nominal income. Hence, instead of setting up an ambitious econometric model, Friedman (who, in any case, has little faith in large econometric models) prefers a different approach. This is to compare changes in the money supply and in nominal income over time without trying to trace through the particular channels by which money affects income.

This has caused many economists to criticize him for relying on a sort of "black box," where changes in the money stock are seen going in at one end and changes in nominal income are seen emerging at the other end without anyone knowing how the process works. This point is often put by saying that Friedman is relying on a mere correlation of changes in money and in income and that there are numerous examples in economics of correlations that do not prove that one variable is causing the other. For example, there is a correlation between the number of schoolteachers in a city and per capita alcohol consumption, but few would suggest that schoolteachers cause the drinking.

Quantity theorists reply that Friedman is not relying on some unexplained correlation between money and income. Economic theory tells us that if the supply of a good increases, its price falls. This can be applied directly to explain why the purchasing power of money falls, that is, prices rise, when the supply of money increases. Do we really need much more than that?

Fiscal Policy

Chapter 18 described how fiscal policy affects GDP according to the income-expenditure theory. Milton Friedman, on the other hand, believes that while fiscal policy can have some effect on GDP, this effect is quite small. One reason is that when the government runs a deficit, people decide to save more and therefore cut their expenditures. This is the Ricardian equivalence theorem discussed in Chapter 15. Second, insofar as private savings do not increase enough to balance fully the direct effect of a government deficit, so that the IS curve does shift outward, interest rates rise and expenditures fall. Friedman thinks that the LM curve is fairly steep and the IS curve fairly flat. Hence, as discussed in Chapter 18, much, though not all, of the expansionary effect of the outward shift of the IS curve is offset by a contradictory movement along the LM curve.

Some Empirical Evidence on the Importance of Money

Figure 20.1 shows the close relation between movements in money and nominal income in the United States. Such a relationship exists also for other countries, for example, Japan, and Friedman and Anna Schwartz (of the National Bureau of Economic Research) have found a very high correlation between money and nominal income in Britain. Similarly, as Figure 20.2 shows, differences in the growth rate of money in a sample of countries account for most of the difference in the growth rates of their nominal incomes.

Does this high correlation between money and nominal income mean that changes in the growth rate of money cause changes in nominal income, or should the correlation be interpreted the other way around, as changes in income causing changes in the monetary growth rate? In the latter case the correlation would certainly not be evidence supporting the quantity theory. Friedman and Schwartz support the hypothesis that causation runs from money to income in several ways. One is that they, as well as Phillip Cagan of Columbia University, have undertaken extensive historical studies of what factors have caused the U.S. money stock to change. They conclude that in severe recessions like those that occurred in 1920 to 1921 or 1929 to 1933 the money stock fell for some specific reason other than a fall in income, such as widespread bank failures or a restrictive Fed policy. Hence, they argue, in these

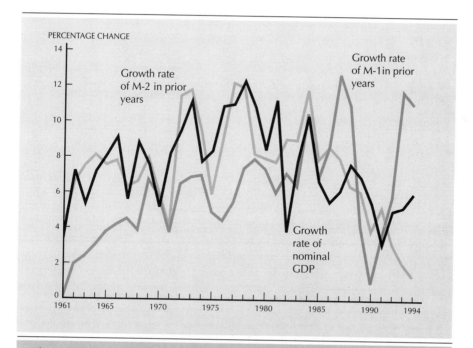

Figure 20.1   Growth Rates of Nominal GDP and *M-1* and *M-2*, 1961–1994.
Until the early 1980s, there was a close correlation between the growth of money and GDP growth the following year. This changed in the early 1980s. **Source:** *Economic Report of the President,* 1995, pp. 274, 353.

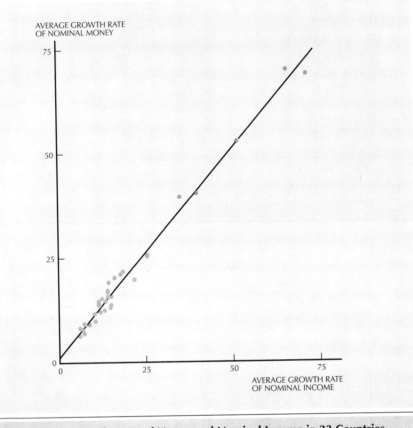

Figure 20.2   Growth Rates of Money and Nominal Income in 33 Countries.
There is a high correlation between the average growth rates of nominal income and of
money during the period covered, roughly 1962 to 1988. **Source:** Based on Nigel Duck,
"Some International Evidence on the Quantity Theory of Money," *Journal of Money,
Credit and Banking,* 25 (February 1993), 15.

cases causation could only have run from money to income, since we know
that what caused the decline in the money stock was something other than the
drop in income. Similarly, large increases in the money stock can be explained
by factors other than a change in income, such as the development of new
techniques for refining gold. For minor business recessions—by far the more
common ones—Friedman and Schwartz concede that the historical evidence is
not nearly so clear-cut.[1] This allows one to develop a compromise between the

---

[1] Friedman and Schwartz have also pointed to the fact that the peak in the growth rate of the
money stock usually occurs prior to the peak in business cycles, but they consider this to be
much less important evidence for their hypothesis that causation runs from money to income
than the just-discussed historical evidence. In any case, as James Tobin ("Money and Income:
Post Hoc, Ergo Propter Hoc," *Quarterly Journal of Economics,* 84 [May 1970], 301–17) has
shown, this evidence is of doubtful value because one can develop a model in which income
change is the cause and the change in the monetary growth rate the effect, and yet the monetary
growth rate shows an earlier peak than does income.

Keynesian and Friedmanian theories by saying that Keynesian theory can explain the usual minor recessions, but that major recessions are due to a decline in the monetary growth rate.

Critics of the quantity theory, on the other hand, have argued that a rise in income can bring about a rise in the money stock. The money multiplier increases to some extent when interest rates and income do. Moreover, the Fed has tended to increase the growth rate of the base when the growth rate of income increases. However, as already discussed, Friedman and Schwartz can point to specific instances when the growth rate of money changed for other reasons. Thus, Milton Friedman points to many different observations that support the quantity theory.[2] One is that the quantity theory seems to predict prices not only in a modern economy, but also in previous times when money consisted of, or was backed by, gold or silver. Rightly or wrongly, one might argue that at present the central bank increases reserves, and thus the money supply, when income is rising, so that causation runs from income to money rather than from money to income. But it is hard to see how, for the world as a whole, such reverse causation could have occurred under a gold or silver standard, since an increase in income could not have increased the production or importation of gold and silver.

In addition, Friedman cites the experience during hyperinflations when prices rose at such high rates that money lost virtually all its value. The quantity theory explains the behavior of prices in such situations with remarkable accuracy. He also points to cross-country comparisons of inflation rates and to the historical pattern of the behavior of money and GDP, such as are shown in Figure 20.1. He further states that the historical record shows that substantial declines in the quantity of money are both a necessary and a sufficient condition for severe depressions.

All in all, quantity theorists rely on the accumulated weight of many different pieces of evidence, any single one of which, by itself, would probably not convince many people. In economics, as in the physical sciences, theories usually do not stand or fall on the basis of a single crucial "experiment." However, some pieces of evidence are more notable and influential than others. Until the 1980s the stability of velocity in the United States provided a persuasive argument for monetarism. Not surprisingly, since then the instability of velocity and the poor fit of money demand functions (see Chapter 17) have substantially weakened the attraction of monetarism.

It is useful to distinguish three monetarist hypotheses. One is that changes in nominal income can be predicted accurately from a knowledge of how the money supply will change. This hypothesis held in the past and *perhaps* will hold again in the future, but it does not hold now. It is true that even now we can make very loose predictions along these lines, such as, if the money supply grows by 3 percent, it is extremely unlikely that nominal income will grow by more than 10 percent. But such predictions are too loose to be of much use.

---

[2] Friedman, "The Quantity Theory of Money," in *The New Palgrave: Money,* eds. John Eatwell, Murray Milgate, and Peter Newman (New York: Norton, 1989), pp. 28–32.

Fortunately, monetarism does more than just predict nominal income. Another monetarist hypothesis looks at the effect of a given change in the money supply on nominal income. For example, if the growth rate of money increases from 2 to 5 percent, nominal income will grow at an approximately 3 percent higher rate than it otherwise would have. This prediction differs sharply from the first hypothesis that one can predict changes in income by knowing the change in the money supply. Suppose that some factor, say, a financial innovation, greatly reduces the demand for money. Then, even if the change in the money supply is known, the change in income cannot be predicted accurately. But it can still be said that nominal income will be higher if the money supply increases sharply than if it does not, because the effects of the increase in the money supply will be added to the effect of the financial innovation. Hence the prediction that an increase in the money supply tends to raise nominal income more or less proportionately has not been seriously impaired by the recent instability in the demand for money.

The third monetarist hypothesis concerns economic history. It says that, at least in the United States, until recently most of the substantial changes in nominal income that occurred were due to, or made possible by, corresponding changes in the money supply.

KEYNESIAN VERSUS MONETARIST VIEWS

There is more to monetarism than just the quantity theory. We can isolate six major theoretical issues in the Keynesian-monetarist dispute.[3] Underlying the debate on these issues is a basic difference relating to the length of the horizon of one's analysis and the speed with which the economy adapts. Keynesians accept many monetarist views as correct in the long run, but not in the shorter run that is relevant for economic policy.

The first and most basic difference is the monetarist's belief in the quantity theory. The second is a hypothesis about the way in which changes in the money stock affect income, that is, the transmission process. We have already discussed Friedman's version of the transmission process, and in Appendix B at the end of this chapter we will look at the transmission process as proposed by two other prominent monetarists, Karl Brunner and Allan Meltzer.

Third, monetarists believe that the private sector of the economy is inherently stable. If the government would not destabilize the economy by ill-considered monetary policies, there would still be *some* fluctuations in income but we would have tolerable levels of unemployment and little inflation. Keynesians, on the other hand, by and large, believe that the private economy is inherently unstable and that fiscal and monetary policies are therefore needed to stabilize it.

Fourth, as already discussed, there is the monetarist research strategy of focusing on the supply of and demand for money. As a result, there is a fifth difference: while Keynesians generally use large-scale econometric models that

---

[3] For a further discussion of these issues, see Thomas Mayer, et al., *The Structure of Monetarism* (New York: Norton, 1978).

describe various sectors of the economy in detail, monetarists prefer to use smaller, highly aggregated models that relate the money supply directly to GDP.

Finally, monetarists and Keynesians view the price level in different ways; monetarists believe that prices are more flexible—downwardly as well as upwardly—than Keynesians do. For example, suppose that the price of oil rises by, say, 20 percent. Keynesians tend to say that if oil accounts directly, and indirectly as a raw material, for, say, 10 percent of GDP, then this 20 percent rise in oil prices will raise the overall price level by 2 percent. Monetarists, on the other hand, say that, with the nominal money stock held constant, much of the rise in the price of oil and oil products will be offset by declines in other prices from what they would otherwise be. This is so because if, as oil prices rise, the price level were to rise by 2 percent, then the demand for nominal money would exceed the supply, with the result that aggregate expenditure would fall and prices would decline again.

THE STABILITY ISSUE

We now look further at one issue that divides monetarists and Keynesians: the stability of a private enterprise economy, that is, its ability to avoid—without the help of governmental stabilization policies—substantial periods of extensive unemployment and severe inflations.[4] The Keynesian approach developed as a response to the unstable behavior of the economy. For nearly two hundred years before World War II, the progress of capitalist countries was periodically interrupted by panics, recessions, and depressions. The Great Depression of the 1930s was the last straw. Although monetarists attribute this and other severe depressions to sharp declines in the growth rate of the money stock, the Great Depression was widely interpreted as a result not of poor monetary arrangements, but of an inherent fault in the capitalist system. Governments in developed market economies became committed to interventionist policies aimed at preventing or limiting the erratic movements of production and employment that had caused so much waste and suffering in the past. Keynesian income-expenditure analysis provided a rationale for interventionist stabilization policy and a paradigm for the analysis of alternative stabilization policies.

Keynes's theory emphasizes the instability of private investment and at the same time deprecates the notion that the private economy contains sufficiently strong adjustment mechanisms to keep fluctuations in output and employment within tolerable limits. Keynesians attribute the instability of investment to variations in the investment opportunities generated by new techniques and new products. They also suppose that those variations in investment are accentuated by speculation in security markets. Moreover, Keynes and his followers emphasize the tendency for swings in investment to feed on themselves. Increasing investment would increase consumption spending through the multiplier, and the resulting improvement in capacity utilization

---

[4] For an example of the Keynesian view, see Hyman Minsky, *John Maynard Keynes* (New York: Columbia University Press, 1975).

would cause further increases in investment in sectors not originally involved in the investment boom. When the original impetus weakens, the whole process goes into reverse.

In analyzing the sources of instability in an economic system, we have to make a distinction between primary causes of instability and the secondary responses of the system to those primary impulses. The oil shock of 1973–74 stands as a classic example of a primary shock, or cause of instability. Multiplier response to a change in investment is a simple example of a secondary response.

Inventory cycles provide a more complex case of primary and secondary causes of instability. A rise in the rate of growth of income will tend to increase the rate of inventory investment, and that, in turn, will contribute to a further increase in the rate of growth of income. Exhaustion of the original impulse that set off the boom not only slows down the rate of growth of income directly, but will also cause inventory investment to decline and might even cause an absolute drop in output. In that case, producers will have excessive inventories and will for a time attempt to reduce them so that inventory investment becomes negative. That, of course, will make the situation even worse, causing a further decline in income and accentuating inventory problems. Because inventory investment is only a small part of total GDP, it will usually be possible to work off excess inventories. Nonetheless, the inventory mechanism can cause a fluctuation in output out of proportion to the original impulse that changed investment and the rate of growth of output.

Monetarists agree with Keynesians that all these factors can, *in principle,* create economic fluctuations. However, they argue that *as an empirical proposition* most of the income fluctuations we have experienced have been due to variations in the growth rate of the money supply and hence are the fault of the central bank. Second, monetarists put less emphasis than do Keynesians on the *macroeconomic* effects of a given exogenous shock because they focus on the supply of and demand for money, which work as automatic stabilizers. Suppose, for example, that an innovation greatly raises investment in the airline industry. This tends to raise nominal income. But, since $M = kYP$, with the money stock constant and nominal income rising, k must be falling. Ignoring changing interest rates for the moment, why should the public be willing to reduce its k? Since people are initially holding their desired ratio of money to nominal income, as nominal income rises they will try to increase their money holdings. And they do this by cutting expenditures (or selling assets), so that the increases in output and prices in the industries producing the new capital goods for the airlines are offset by falling output or prices in other industries.

To be sure, the assumption that the public wants its k to remain constant, despite the rise in the interest rate, is unwarranted. But monetarists believe that the interest elasticity of the demand for money is not very great, so that an investment boom and its resulting rise in interest rates lowers k only moderately. With the money stock constant and k falling only moderately, income rises only moderately. In monetarist analyses shocks, such as innovations, have much more effect on *relative* outputs and *relative* prices than they do on total output and the overall price level.

The question of whether a capitalist economy is stable or needs governmental intervention to avoid an unacceptable level of unemployment or inflation is obviously an extremely important one. Unfortunately, it is a question easier to pose than to answer. There is no convincing empirical evidence that would allow one to decide who is right. The following illustrate some of the problems encountered in trying to answer this question. One possible approach is to take an econometric model and put into it a stable monetary and fiscal policy in place of the policy actually followed, to see if the model then shows less fluctuation in income than was actually experienced. But the answer depends on the model used and the specifics of the simulation. Moreover, monetarists doubt that these models are reliable enough to evaluate the effects of various policies. Another possible approach is to ask whether the economy has been more stable in the postwar years, in which stabilization policy was used, than before 1929, when it was not used. The answer is yes, but monetarists can reply that the greater instability in the pre-1929 period was due to the fact that the growth rate of the money supply was more erratic then than it is now. A third approach is to ask whether, in those countries in which the government does relatively little to stabilize income, income is more stable than it is in those countries that follow stronger stabilization policies. But the problem here is to determine the direction of causation. Certain countries may follow stronger stabilization policies precisely because they experience more income fluctuations. For the question of whether a capitalist economy is inherently stable, every solution has its problems.

RECONCILING MONETARIST AND KEYNESIAN THEORIES

It is sometimes difficult to get a clear view of the differences between monetarists and those who use the income-expenditure approach, because they appear to be using different languages to express their views. To compare their views, it is necessary to translate from one language to another, and there is always the danger that something will be lost in the translation.

In the income-expenditure approach, each component of the expenditure side of the national income accounts is "explained" in terms of other variables. Thus, consumer expenditures are explained in terms of disposable income, wealth, and perhaps some other factors. Investment is supposed to vary with capacity utilization and interest rates. Price changes reflect changes in wages and in capacity utilization, but are also influenced by "exogenous" changes in food prices, taxes, and other factors. All these linkages interact with one another in the complex system sketched out in Chapters 15 through 18. In that kind of system, prices, output, and unemployment are strongly influenced by both monetary and fiscal policies, but they can be influenced by many other variables as well. Moreover, the structure of the system itself is subject to change without notice. The relations between unemployment and wage increases can be influenced by changes in the strength of trade unions, by import competition, and by changes in regulation as well as by expectations of future governmental policy. Investment expenditures can be influenced by speculation about the rapid growth of new industries, by threats of war, and by confidence or lack of confidence in governmental policy.

The income-expenditure approach is built up from a great many pieces. Economists who use this approach have disagreements about the relative importance of the many variables entering the system. For example, some think that changes in wealth have a powerful influence on consumer expenditures. Others are skeptical about the effect of wealth. Statistical studies do not yield sufficiently precise results to resolve the controversy. The result is that there can be considerable differences in judgments about the effects of any proposed policy. What links Keynesians is not their conclusions but their basic way of approaching the analysis of the economy.

Much the same thing can be said of monetarists. They too have their differences, but they share a belief in the critical importance of variations in the rate of monetary growth in the explanation of changes in prices and output. They tend to emphasize the existence of direct links between money on the one hand and expenditures, prices, and output on the other, and thus bypass the complex causal chains appearing in Keynesian models. Some of the direct linkages relate prices and outputs to actual and expected changes in asset markets, particularly money markets. They give great weight to the role of stocks of assets in determining flows of expenditures so that, for example, they emphasize the link between stocks of wealth and flows of consumer expenditures. In addition, they consider that prices and wages are relatively flexible, that is, more flexible than Keynesians usually assume. And they also think of the private economy as relatively stable. Finally, monetarists tend to have a longer time horizon than Keynesians. Some misunderstandings arise from these differing views of time, because the short-run effect of a policy change may be quite different from its long-run effect.

For practical purposes, it is necessary to simplify things to some extent. Interactions considered to have minor effects must be neglected. The result is that Keynesians often neglect matters that monetarists consider important and vice versa. In using different simplifications, they often appear to be talking different languages. But the difference between moderate Keynesians and moderate monetarists is not all that great—it is not always possible to tell which moderate is a Keynesian and which is a monetarist. Still, between more extreme Keynesians and more extreme monetarists the differences are substantial.

THE CREDIT VIEW

In our discussions of the income-expenditure theory and the monetarist theory we talked about the money supply as a determinant of expenditures. But, as we all know, one can buy without handing over money. One can use credit. The **credit view** tries to correct for the omission of credit and stresses the role of lending in the determination of nominal income.[5]

Proponents of the credit view point out an important way in which

---

[5] Among the leading contemporary credit theorists are Alan Blinder and Ben Bernanke, both of Princeton University, Benjamin Friedman of Harvard University, and James Tobin of Yale University.

money and credit differ. Money is homogeneous: one person's supply of money or demand for money has essentially the same effect on GDP as another person's. Credit is different: the credit market is segmented. It does matter—and according to an important version of the credit view, very much—who the suppliers and demanders of credit are because the markets for credit are different for each. Sharecroppers do not borrow by issuing commercial paper, and investment bankers do not obtain their funds from pawnshops. A major reason why credit markets are segmented is riskiness and consequently the precautions that lenders must take. When someone offers the asked-for amount of money in exchange for a commodity, his offer will be accepted, but not necessarily when he offers to pay at some future date, that is, asks for credit. Dollar bills offered by Bill Gates of Microsoft and by a homeless person have the same value, but their promises to pay do not.

Not only do promises to pay by borrowers differ, but so do offers of credit by various lenders. Many lenders specialize with respect to the riskiness of the loans they make. Some make relatively risky loans because they have little risk aversion; for example, venture capital firms finance start-up companies. Others, such as commercial banks, make loans to relatively risky borrowers, not because they have little risk aversion, but because they are able to screen and monitor borrowers effectively. As a result, if banks are short of funds, those borrowers whose credit ratings do not permit them to sell commercial paper or other securities may not be able to obtain financing and have to reduce planned expenditures, even though at the same time an excess of funds may be driving down interest rates in security markets.

Hence, say adherents of the credit view, financial pressures cannot be gauged correctly simply by looking at the supply of and demand for money or at interest rates on Treasury bills. One must also see how well the distribution of loanable funds among creditors matches the demand for loanable funds among borrowers.

Like the quantity theory and income-expenditure theory, the credit theory therefore pays much attention to banks. But it does so for different reasons. The quantity theory and the income-expenditure theory pay attention to banks because banks and other depository institutions create the dominant part of our money supply. In contrast, credit theorists look not at the liability side of the bank's balance sheet but at the asset side. They consider banks so important because banks provide funds not only to large firms with high credit ratings, but also to those that cannot tap the securities market. Small firms have no easy substitute for bank credit because banks, unlike other lenders, have intimate knowledge of firms, knowledge derived from long-standing credit relationships, as well as from information garnered as the keeper of the firms' deposits and from contacts with the local business community.

Hence, shocks to the banking industry, such as disintermediation, may lower GDP even if interest rates are constant. Or if banks, perhaps prodded by their regulators, become more cautious and switch from loans to government securities, the money supply is unchanged and interest rates on securities fall. Yet, say credit theorists, there is now a financial stringency that may result in a recession.

The Credit Crumble

During the 1990–91 recession, despite an expansionary monetary policy, the growth rate of credit declined sharply. Some decline is normal in recessions because the demand for credit goes down. But this time the decline was unusually severe. A greater than normal decline was to be expected because prior to the recession, credit had been growing at an unsustainable rate. But the decline was greater than can be explained that way. This "credit crumble," as it was sometimes called, evoked much concern because it was seen as exacerbating the recession and slowing the recovery.

What caused it? One factor was the collapse of the savings and loan industry discussed in Chapter 9. Between 1989 and 1992, savings and loan credit dropped by 45 percent. Another reason was that banks rationed credit more severely than usual because they were concerned about the bad loans already on their books. Moreover, their regulators, influenced by what had happened to the savings and loans, became tougher. In addition, banks had to raise their capital-asset ratios to meet the new capital standards, and one way to do that was to slow the growth of their assets. Banks therefore not only tightened their credit standards, but also charged an interest rate on their loans that was unusually high relative to their own cost of funds.

At the same time some other lenders were also under pressure to limit their lending. The rating agencies lowered the credit ratings of many finance companies because they had large losses and weak balance sheets. This raised the costs of their funds and made them cautious about additional lending. Life insurance companies, too, had serious losses, some even failed, and their regulators became stricter—all of which discouraged the growth of their lending. Even the commercial paper market became a weaker source of credit as the rating agencies downgraded the ratings of numerous issues and as some issuers of commercial papers actually failed, so that potential investors in commercial paper lost confidence and reduced their purchases.

It is not possible to determine just how much these credit problems contributed to the 1990–91 recession and to the unusually slow pace of the subsequent recovery. But a study by the New York Federal Reserve Bank suggests that "credit constraints are likely to have made at least some contribution to the economic slowdown."*

*M. A. Akhtar, "Causes and Consequences of the 1989–92 Credit Slowdown," in *Studies on Causes and Consequences of the 1989–92 Credit Slowdown,* Federal Reserve Bank of New York, (New York: 1994), p. 26.

Here is an illustration. During the second part of the Great Depression, starting in 1934, both nominal and real short-term interest rates were usually very low, and the real money supply was growing. Does this necessarily mean that monetary policy was easy, that funds were readily and cheaply available to any reasonably sound firm that wanted to borrow? No, it does not. To be sure, the government could borrow cheaply. But many banks had failed, and thus broken the customer relationship between firms and their banks. Moreover, the surviving banks, like other lenders, became very cautious. A more recent example is the credit crunch of the early 1990s discussed in the box on page 372.

Although many advocates of the credit view focus on bank credit, others do not. Thus Benjamin Friedman of Harvard University focuses on total non-financial debt, that is, on the credit extended to everyone in the economy except to financial institutions.[6] He found that for the 1960s and 1970s this measure predicted nominal GDP as well or better than money did. Unfortunately, in the 1980s, when money ceased to predict income, the predictions obtained from total nonfinancial debt also deteriorated.

SUMMARY

1 The quantity theory went into a decline in the 1930s, but was revived in the postwar period largely by Milton Friedman and his students. Their version of the quantity theory made the demand for money a function of other variables—primarily permanent income and interest rates—rather than treating it as a constant.

2 Dependence of the demand for money on the interest rate is consistent with the quantity theory if a change in the quantity of money changes the interest rate for only a short time. By the time the expected real interest rate has returned to its previous level, nominal income and money have changed proportionately.

3 The transmission mechanism of the Chicago approach is formulated in terms of changes in the quantity of money rather than in terms of interest rates, and it does not try to analyze the particular channels by which money affects income in detail, in part because there are too many of them.

4 There is much empirical evidence showing a close correlation between nominal money and nominal income or prices. A debated issue is the direction of causation.

5 Monetarism can be described as a conjunction of several related propositions. Leaving aside the ones relating to policy, they are the validity of the quantity theory, a particular transmission process, the stability of the private sector, a focus on aggregate expenditure as a whole rather than on demand in particular sectors, a focus on the price level as a unit, and a skeptical attitude toward large econometric models.

6 In the Keynesian view the economy is unstable, due both to external shocks and to internal factors, such as inventory cycles. Monetarists question the empirical significance of such destabilizing factors.

7 The credit view focuses on credit as a determinant of aggregate demand and stresses segmentation in the credit market. Banks are important because of the type of credit they provide.

KEY TERMS

Keynesians
monetarists
quantity theory of money
Chicago school

transmission process
monetarist hypotheses
credit view

---

[6] Suppose you deposit $10,000 in a bank which then lends $8,000, buys a $1,000 security, and holds $1,000 as a reserve. Total credit has expanded by $19,000 dollars: your $10,000 "loan" to the bank plus the bank's $8,000 loan and $1,000 security purchase. But since this involves counting the deposit as credit both when it is made and when it is lent by the bank, Friedman's measure excludes it. He counts only the $9,000 credit—loan plus security purchase—extended by the bank.

QUESTIONS AND EXERCISES

*1 How does Friedman's analysis of the transmission process differ from the Keynesian version?

*2 Imagine that you were asked to undertake an empirical test of the quantity theory. How would you go about it?

*3 Discuss: "In both the quantity theory and the Keynesian theory an increase in the quantity of money generates an increase in nominal income. Hence these theories are basically the same."

4 Describe three monetarist hypotheses.

5 Discuss: "There is no way we can determine with any degree of certitude whether the private sector is inherently stable."

6 State the credit view in your own words. What type of evidence would make a convincing case for it?

FURTHER READING

BERNANKE, BEN, and ALAN BLINDER. "Credit, Money and Aggregate Demand," *American Economic Review,* 78 (May 1988), 435–39. An important statement of the credit view.

BRUNNER, KARL, and ALLAN MELTZER. *Monetary Economics.* Oxford: Blackwell, 1989. A collection of important articles by two leading monetarists.

FRIEDMAN, MILTON. "The Quantity Theory of Money," in *The New Palgrave: Money,* eds. John Eatwell, Murray Milgate, and Peter Newman. New York: Norton, 1989, pp. 1–40. A masterly discussion by the world's leading quantity theorist.

———. *Studies in the Quantity Theory of Money.* Chicago: University of Chicago Press, 1956. A classic statement of Friedman's view together with essays by his students providing empirical evidence. Chapter 1 is particularly useful.

FRIEDMAN, MILTON, and ANNA SCHWARTZ. *Monetary Trends in the United States and the United Kingdom.* Chicago: University of Chicago Press, 1982. An outstanding piece of scholarship. (For review articles that survey its highlights see the December 1982 issue of the *Journal of Economic Literature.*)

———. "Money and Business Cycles," *Review of Economics and Statistics,* 45 (February 1963), supplement, 32–64. An important survey of the empirical evidence for the quantity theory.

LAIDLER, DAVID. "Money and Money Income: An Essay on the Transmission Mechanism," *Journal of Monetary Economics,* 4 (April 1978), 151–92. An excellent survey of one of the major disputes about the quantity theory.

MAYER, THOMAS. "Monetarism and its Rhetoric," in *The Role of Economic Theory,* ed. Phillip Klein. Boston: Kluwer, 1994. A look at some broader aspects of monetarism.

———, et al. *The Structure of Monetarism.* New York: Norton, 1978. A survey of the broader aspects of monetarism including debate on the topic by both monetarist and nonmonetarist economists.

MOORE, BASIL. "Monetary Trends in the United States and United Kingdom," *Financial Review,* 18 (September 1983), 146–66. This is a good critical review.

PATINKIN, DON. *Money, Interest and Prices.* New York: Harper & Row, 1965. A brilliant treatise.

ROMER, CHRISTINA, and DAVID ROMER. "Does Monetary Policy Matter?" in *Macroeconomic Annual,* eds. O. Blanchard and S. Fischer. Cambridge, Mass.: MIT Press, 1989, pp. 121–69. An impressive analysis of postwar cycles in income and money.

APPENDIX A:
THE REAL BALANCE EFFECT

A rigorous approach to the quantity theory, called the "real balance approach," has been developed by Don Patinkin of Hebrew University. This is concerned primarily with establishing two propositions. The first is that under certain specified conditions a change in the stock of money brings about a strictly proportional change in the price level, and the second is that Keynes was wrong when he claimed that there could be an equilibrium at less than full employment in an economy in which wages and prices are *completely* flexible. Patinkin does not deny that reestablishing full employment when, say, the marginal efficiency of investment falls may *perhaps* mean a much greater drop in wages than would be feasible; he is just concerned with showing that, in principle, falling wages and prices would bring about full employment.

Patinkin organized his analysis around the real balance effect. As a convenient, though hardly realistic, expository device, suppose that a helicopter flies over a country and drops currency. The lucky inhabitants now find that they hold more money than they desire to hold, given their incomes, their wealth, and the interest rate. Hence, they use this excess money to buy securities and physical assets. This basic idea of the real balance effect is obvious, and we have already discussed it at various points. But to understand it fully, one must put it into a model that starts out with certain quite specific assumptions.

The Assumptions

The most dramatic assumption is that wages and prices are completely flexible so that, as long as the supply of labor exceeds the demand for labor, wages continue to fall. Patinkin is not saying that this is the way wages actually behave; he is merely trying to show what would happen if this assumption were to hold.

The second assumption is that people do not suffer from a *money illusion*. This needs explaining. Suppose that prices double but that your income and wealth double also, so that you are as well-off as before. Will you also double the *nominal* value of your expenditures, and thus keep your real expenditures constant? If you are fully aware of what has happened and behave rationally, you will do so. Your propensity to consume depends on your real income, your real wealth, and the real interest rate, and these variables are all unchanged. But it is certainly possible that you may not be fully aware that your real income and wealth are unchanged; for example, you may underestimate the rise in prices, and hence believe that your real income and wealth have risen. If so, you are said to suffer from a money illusion.

As prices rise or fall some redistribution of income takes place, and if gainers and losers have different marginal propensities to consume or to invest, aggregate expenditure is affected. But to simplify the analysis, Patinkin assumes such redistribution effects do not occur. In addition, he assumes that as prices change, people do not hold back or accelerate purchases in the expectation of further price changes. For expository convenience, he also assumes that the government's budget is balanced. In addition to these assumptions, we will assume *temporarily* that there are no government bonds outstanding and that all the money in existence is outside money, specifically, for example, currency. Later, when introducing government bonds, we will also assume that taxpayers are indifferent to the real value of the government's debt and do not feel poorer (and hence cut their consumption) when the real value of the government's debt rises.

The Model

Divide all the numerous markets in the economy into three. One is the commodity market in which a person's real expenditures on consumer goods and a firm's expenditures on capital goods are functions of real income, real wealth, and the interest rate.

The second market is the labor market in which both the supply of and demand for labor depend on the real wage; the higher the real wage, the greater the supply of labor willing to work, but the smaller the demand for labor.

Third is the money market in which the real interest rate depends on nominal income and the nominal money stock. The higher nominal income, the greater the demand for money and, hence, the higher the interest rate. And the greater the supply of money, the lower the interest rate.

Another aspect of the model is that real expenditures (that is, consumption plus investment) are functions of real income and real wealth. This is not so much an assumption as something that follows directly from microeconomic theory. Real wealth consists of three types of assets: physical capital or claims thereon (e.g., stock), claims that the public has on the government (currency, government securities, and reserves that depository institutions hold with the Fed), and claims that one member of the public has on another (e.g., corporate bonds or mortgages). For the public as a whole, these latter claims wash out, since each person's claim is balanced by some other person's debt. We first consider a model in which there are no government bonds and no reserves with the Fed, so that net wealth for the public as a whole consists only of capital and currency, and money is the same as currency.

Workings of the Model

We now put this model through its paces by considering five cases: an expansion of the labor force, a rise in the nominal money stock, an increase in the demand for money, a rise in the average propensity to consume, and an exogenous rise in prices. To simplify, we describe some processes that actually operate simultaneously as though they operate sequentially.

An Expanded Labor Force. As more people seek work, wages fall. And given our assumption of complete wage and price flexibility, wages must fall until all those who want jobs have them. But with wages and, hence, aggregate expenditure falling, won't prices fall too, so that real wages are constant and firms have no incentive to employ the additional workers? To see why this will *not* happen, assume at first that it *does* happen and then see why this situation cannot be an equilibrium. Suppose that both wages and prices fall equally by, say, 10 percent. Real income is then constant. But real wealth has increased. With the money stock being constant in nominal terms, the real money stock has risen 10 percent, so that both the economy's wealth and liquidity have risen. This increased liquidity lowers the interest rate, and this induces a rise in expenditures. The increase in wealth also raises consumption expenditures. These increases in expenditures in turn raise prices. Hence, in equilibrium, prices fall less than wages. The resulting decline in real wages permits the additional workers to find jobs.

A Rise in the Nominal Money Stock. Suppose that, due to a benevolent helicopter, the money stock increases 10 percent. People now try to get rid of their excess money holdings by raising expenditures. As long as their real money balances are higher than before, their expenditures will also be greater than before. Only after prices have risen by 10 percent, too, will real money balances be back in equilibrium.

What happens to the real rate of interest? The factors that determine it are saving, the yield on capital (and hence the demand for capital), and any gap that exists between the real quantity of money demanded and supplied. In the Patinkin model a rise in the supply of money does not change the flow of savings or the yield on capital. And, as just discussed, the price level adjusts to eliminate the gap between the real quantities of money demanded and supplied. Hence, with none of the determinants of the interest rate being different, the real rate of interest must be the same as it was before the money stock increased.

An Increased Demand for Money. Suppose people want to hold 10 percent more real money. To do so, they must reduce their demand for something else since their total assets are fixed. We assume that they reduce their demand for commodities and bonds proportionately. As they reduce their expenditures on commodities, unemployment develops so that wages and prices fall. Once prices have fallen by 10 percent, the real quantity of money available has risen by 10 percent; this matches the 10 percent increase in the demand for real money. The economy is back in full-employment equilibrium and wages and prices no longer fall. In addition, as in the previous case of an increase in the supply of money, the interest rate must be back at its previous level too.

An Increase in the Average Propensity to Consume. Initially the rise in consumption raises prices. However, this reduces the real money stock, and with falling wealth and rising interest rates, there is downward pressure on prices. But prices do not fall all the way back to their initial level. With the propensity to consume being higher, there is, of course, less saving. Hence, the interest rate rises, and at the higher interest rate the public wants to hold less real money. But the nominal stock of money is unchanged, and to make this unchanged nominal stock of money correspond to the desired smaller stock of real money, prices have to rise. So an increase in the propensity to consume raises prices.

An Exogenous Increase in Prices. Suppose that for some reason producers mistakenly believe that the equilibrium price level has risen and accordingly raise prices. This reduces real wealth and also the real money stock, so that the interest rate rises. Both the rise in the interest rate and the decline in wealth reduce expenditures. As expenditures fall, prices are forced down again. Equilibrium is restored only at the previous price level and interest rate.

Concluding Note. In two of these five cases, an increase in the money stock and an increase in the demand for money, there were no effects on the real economy. In this model purely monetary changes such as these have no *real* effects; money is just a veil. But in two other cases, an increase in the labor force and a rise in the propensity to consume, the interest rate changed too. These were cases of changes in the real factors (the supply of labor and the supply of saving) so that one would expect a change in the relative price of labor and capital, and not just in the price level. In the final case, an autonomous price increase, neither the interest rate nor the equilibrium price level changed because all that had happened was that prices had been raised by mistake.

Inside Money, Outside Money, and Government Bonds

The time has come to remove two assumptions—that there are no government bonds outstanding and that currency is the only type of money. (Currency is *outside money* because it is not the debt of anyone in the private economy. In contrast, deposits, being debts of banks, are *inside money*.) If there are government bonds denominated, as they usually are, in nominal terms, then a 10 percent increase in the money stock must raise prices by *less* than 10 percent. Suppose prices rise by 10 percent. The real value of government bonds would then fall by 10 percent, so that the public would be poorer. It would therefore cut consumption. This, in turn, would force down prices. Hence, a new equilibrium can be reached only when prices have risen less than proportionately to the rise in the money stock.

Now assume that inside money exists, that is, money that is a claim on someone within the private sector, such as deposits, which are claims on banks. Assume that such inside money increases by 10 percent while currency and government bonds are constant. If prices were to rise by 10 percent too, then people would be poorer, because the real value of their currency plus government bonds would then have fallen by 10 percent, and they would cut their consumption. Hence, when inside money increases by 10 percent, prices must rise by less than 10 percent. (Prices will rise to some extent because, since the money stock has increased, the interest rate will fall so that expenditures will rise.)

The upshot of all this is that, if there are government bonds or inside money, money and prices will generally not change proportionately as they do in the Chicago version of the quantity theory. But we must qualify this last statement by saying that some economists believe that inside money is also net wealth, and others believe that taxpayers do treat an increase in the real value of the government debt as a corresponding reduction in their wealth. If they are right, the above discussion has to be modified.

APPENDIX B:
THE BRUNNER-MELTZER MODEL

When we discussed Friedman's monetary theory, we mentioned that (rightly or wrongly) he is often criticized for not sufficiently explaining *how* money affects income and for relying on "mere correlations." But this criticism is certainly not applicable to the work of two other leading monetarists, Karl Brunner and Allan Meltzer. They have developed an extensive and very complex analysis of the transmission process.

Brunner and Meltzer reject the standard Keynesian IS-LM transmission mechanism as oversimplified. So they developed a different transmission mechanism, one that stresses changes in the stock of assets and in the relative prices of assets. In their model (built on some earlier work of Carl Christ of Johns Hopkins University), suppose that government expenditures increase. There is, as in the standard Keynesian model, a direct expansionary effect and also a multiplier effect. But in addition, Brunner and Meltzer point out, there is a stock effect. The government has to finance the deficit; it must pay for the increased expenditures by issuing either bonds or money.[7]

Consider first the case in which it issues money. Microeconomics tells us that if the supply of any one item increases, its *relative* price must fall to clear the market. But an increase in the supply of money cannot lower the price of money in dollar terms; a dollar always sells for a dollar. However, it can lower the *relative* price of money by raising the prices of all other items, that is, of consumer goods, capital goods, and bonds. As the prices of both consumer goods and capital goods rise, it becomes profitable to produce more of them, so that output now increases. And, similarly, the rise in bond prices makes it profitable for firms to issue more bonds and to buy capital goods with the proceeds of these bond sales. (Or, to express this in Keynesian terminology, the fall in the interest rate stimulates spending.) At first, all this results in both output and prices rising. But output rises only as long as it is profitable to produce more because the price of output is high relative to the price of labor and other inputs needed to produce it. Once wages and other costs rise in proportion to the increase in output prices, the additional production is no longer profitable, so that output now falls back to its previous equilibrium level. Thus, an increase in the money stock raises real income only temporarily, but prices, and hence nominal income, rise permanently.

Consider now the opposite case in which the government finances its rising expenditures by selling bonds to the public, instead of increasing the money stock. The increased supply of bonds lowers bond prices relative to the prices of other assets. The critical question is now what this fall in bond prices does to the demand for capital and hence to investment. If one assumes, as the IS-LM model does, that bonds and capital are similar and therefore good substitutes for each other, then as the public holds more bonds, its demand for capital is reduced. Hence, stock prices and prices of capital goods such as

---

[7] Actually the Treasury does not, except to a trivial extent, pay for its expenditures by issuing money. What happens is that the Treasury issues bonds, and, at the same time, to keep the interest rate stable, the Fed buys government securities in the open market. But as a result of the Fed's security purchases, bank reserves, and hence the money stock, increase.

houses fall, and firms cut their investment. But Brunner and Meltzer (as well as some Keynesians, such as James Tobin of Yale University) make the opposite assumption. In their view government bonds and capital are complements rather than substitutes. Hence, an increase in the supply of government bonds *raises* the demand for capital as the public tries to sell its excess government bonds to buy corporate stock and physical capital instead. As a result, stock prices rise, so that corporations now have an incentive to issue more stock and build more plants and equipment. Investment and income therefore increase. Thus, in the Brunner-Meltzer model, not only monetary policy, but also the size of the government deficit—fiscal policy—and the way it is financed can, at least in principle, have a powerful effect via an increased stock of government bonds.

Another important role that fiscal policy plays in the Brunner-Meltzer model arises from the fact that this model takes account of disequilibrium in the government sector. Most macroeconomic models look at the commodity and labor markets, and at money or bond markets, and say that the economy is in equilibrium if all these markets are. But suppose the government is running a deficit. Can one still say that the economy is in equilibrium? Brunner and Meltzer say no because the government has to finance the deficit by issuing bonds or money, and hence—as long as there is a deficit—the public's stock of bonds or money must be growing. And since its wealth is growing this way, the public's expenditures will be growing too. As long as the government runs a deficit, the IS and LM curves are continually shifting upward so that the economy is not in equilibrium. And the same is true (though now with wealth and expenditures falling) if there is a surplus. Equilibrium requires a balanced budget.

How is it then that so many other economic models ignore the need for a balanced budget in equilibrium?[8] The answer is that they define equilibrium less comprehensively. They treat the rise in the public's stock of bonds and money due to the deficit in one period as an exogenous factor that disrupts equilibrium in the next period, and therefore they analyze the effects of the increase in these stocks separately. In contrast, Brunner and Meltzer look at the whole process as a single unit.

What makes equilibrium analysis so attractive to economists is that there usually exist forces that move the economy toward equilibrium. In the absence of new shocks, one can predict where the economy will end up. Does this work for the Brunner-Meltzer model? What mechanisms, if any, bring the economy to such a broader equilibrium in which the government's budget is just balanced?

Assume the government raises its expenditures, and thus runs a deficit. This has several effects. It increases aggregate expenditure both directly and also through multiplier effects as consumption increases. Since income is rising, tax receipts rise too. But they do not rise by enough to balance the budget. There are, however, additional effects. One is that the deficit, by raising the public's holdings of bonds and money and hence its wealth, raises the pro-

[8] Not all other models ignore the effects of the deficit. Some Keynesian economists have built models incorporating these effects much along the lines of Brunner and Meltzer.

portion of income consumed. Second, investment also increases as the rise in the stocks of money lowers interest rates. Both the rise in consumption and the rise in investment raise nominal income and, hence, tax receipts. Moreover, rising prices lower the real value of the interest payments the government makes on its debts. For all these reasons the increase in aggregate expenditure reduces the deficit. And since aggregate expenditure continues to increase as long as there is a deficit, eventually the deficit is eliminated entirely. At this point the economy is in equilibrium. A similar analysis applies if the government cuts its expenditures or raises taxes so that it runs a surplus; this too will be eliminated.

In this model where equilibrium requires that the government's budget be balanced, fiscal factors, such as the progressivity of the tax system, play an important role. The more progressive the tax system, the smaller the rise in income required to generate the revenue needed to eliminate a given deficit. Such a large role for fiscal policy has caused some economists to question whether the Brunner-Meltzer model is really monetarist and not Keynesian. *In principle,* their model could even produce the old-fashioned and rigid Keynesian conclusion that fiscal policy has a powerful effect on income, while monetary policy is almost powerless. But Brunner and Meltzer believe that this is as it should be: a theory sets out various possibilities, and empirical tests then determine which of these possibilities correspond to the real world. Brunner and Meltzer have undertaken extensive empirical tests from which they conclude that the dominant impulse that drives nominal income is not fiscal policy, but changes in the nominal money stock. Since they have also shown that the Fed, if it wants to, can control the nominal money stock, they hold the Fed largely responsible for inflation and for fluctuations in real income.

Other Perspectives: New Classical, Real Business Cycle, New Keynesian, and Post-Keynesian

After you have read this chapter, you will be able to:

- Appreciate the role of rapid market clearing in new classical theory and the debate about the rapidity of market clearing.
- Explain real business cycle theory.
- Understand the new Keynesian response.
- Discuss post-Keynesian theory and how it differs from traditional income-expenditure theory.

Monetarists are by no means the only critics of the standard income-expenditure theory. We cannot take up all the criticisms, but two have emerged that deserve our attention. They are the so-called new classical theory, including a variant known as real business cycle theory and the post-Keynesian theory. In response to new classical theory, a number of income-expenditure theorists developed a new variant of the income-expenditure theory known as "new Keynesian theory." This chapter deals with all three of these developments.

NEW CLASSICAL THEORY

A number of economists, led by Robert Barro (Harvard University), Robert Lucas (University of Chicago), Thomas Sargent (Hoover Institution and Stanford University), and Neil Wallace (University of Minnesota), have sharply challenged what used to be the prevailing macroeconomic theory. Their objection to the then-prevailing versions of the income-expenditure theory and monetarist theory was in part methodological. The proponents of these theories were primarily concerned with predicting and explaining changes in aggregate income, unemployment, and inflation. Although they used economic theory to do so, they were not all that concerned with rigorously deducing every macroeconomic proposition from microeconomic principles. The new classical economists, on the other hand, insisted that macroeconomics start with the axiom of rational utility maximization and deduce economic theory from it, that is, that macroeconomics be built on sound microeconomic foundations. Since, in their view, income-expenditure theorists had not provided such foundations, they accused them of sloppy theorizing. They focused their criticism on two points, the treatment of expectations and the Keynesian and monetarist assumption that wages and prices are sticky.

The way people form their expectations is an important but exceedingly difficult topic. It is important because households and firms obviously make their decisions not on the basis of what actually *will* happen, but on the basis of what they *expect* to happen. Whether a firm invests depends not on whether this investment *will* actually be profitable, but on whether the firm *thinks* that it will be profitable. Hence, to predict how much investment will take place, one should know how firms form their expectations. But we have no way of finding this out precisely, so we have to use some more or less arbitrary rule of thumb.[1] For many years the rule of thumb that both Keynesians and monetarists used has been to assume that people form their expectations by extrapolating from the past, perhaps by using the error-learning model described in Chapter 16. But this implies that people behave irrationally, that, as discussed in Chapter 16, they ignore much available information. All the same, both Keynesians and monetarists were willing to use the simple, easy-to-handle, error-learning model, in part because they thought that it would provide sufficiently accurate answers.

The new classical economists reject this approach. They point out that the assumption that people form their expectations simply by extrapolating from the past implies that they are not maximizing their utility or profits. And utility or profit maximization forms the core of economic theory! They have, therefore, replaced the error-learning model with the rational-expectations model that we also first encountered in Chapter 16. By now this reasoning has proved persuasive to many economists, be they Keynesians or monetarists. Despite the great difficulty of building economic models that embody rational expectations, this is now the preferred procedure in economics.[2]

The second focus of new classical theory, the insistence that wages and prices are flexible, is more problematic. To be sure, price flexibility does not mean that prices change all the time; they change only if supply or demand

[1] Why not ask firms and households about how they form their expectations? It is very difficult, if not impossible, to formulate questions in a way that provides meaningful information about why people think the way they do.

[2] Rational-expectations models are extremely difficult to construct because they include a recursive process. Being rational, the public, on the average, predicts correctly what will happen; that is, what the model shows will happen. But what the model shows as happening depends on what the public predicts will happen. Sometimes one cannot rule out multiple solutions to such models.

changes. But it does mean that prices adjust quickly to changes in supply and demand, so that buyers can buy as much as they want and sellers can sell as much as they want. Simple economic theory suggests that markets should clear in this way, since it is in the self-interest of buyers and sellers to adjust prices until supply equals demand. But if markets do clear rapidly, one cannot explain unemployment and business fluctuations by a lack of demand as income-expenditure theorists try to do. New classical economists therefore challenged the income-expenditure and monetarist explanations of economic fluctuations by saying that they are based on the entirely arbitrary assumption that wages and prices are sticky. And arbitrary assumptions (usually called "ad hoc assumptions") do not make for good theory.

Later in this chapter we will discuss how income-expenditure theorists responded to this challenge, but first we will discuss how new classical theory tries to explain changes in income and employment.

The New Classical Theory in Action

To understand the new classical view, let us now make the new classical assumption that money wages *are* flexible, both upwardly and downwardly. If so, those changes in aggregate expenditures that people can observe should not generate any unemployment. Suppose, for example, that the marginal efficiency of investment declines. Firms therefore invest less, and the demand for labor falls. Employers threaten to fire workers unless they take a cut in their nominal wages. Workers generally respond by taking a wage cut, and thus preserve their jobs. They do so for two reasons. First, a wage cut usually results in a much smaller drop in nominal income than does unemployment. Second, workers know that the decline in investment, and hence in aggregate nominal expenditures, will result in a fall in prices. Since workers behave rationally and are therefore concerned with real wages instead of their money wages, they do not object to a cut in nominal wages.

If the decline in investment lowers productivity, and therefore does mean a cut in real wages, then some workers will decide to quit. But they are not *involuntarily* unemployed. They are not working because, in their view, the marginal utility of leisure exceeds the marginal utility of the wage that they are offered. They may prefer to take leisure rather than the lower wage because they can use their leisure time to look for better-paying jobs.[3]

Similarly, suppose that the money supply expands and that the public is aware of this. Realizing that prices will rise, workers now demand higher money wages, and employers, knowing that they can sell their output at higher prices, agree to pay these higher money wages. Employment does not expand because people, being aware that the higher money wage corresponds to an unchanged real wage, have no incentive to work more.

If so, then what causes the fluctuations in unemployment that we do observe? Robert Lucas has offered an explanation, known as the **Lucas supply function.** He points out that many changes in aggregate expenditures are not

---

[3] But the idea that people quit their jobs to look for better ones should not be overemphasized; many people look for other jobs while still employed.

correctly interpreted by the public. Firms observe the price of the products they make, but they do not observe the *general* price level as quickly and as accurately. Hence, when aggregate expenditures fall, each individual firm knows only that the price of its own product is falling. Such a fall could be due either to a shift in the demand for the individual firm's product or to an overall drop in aggregate expenditures. The firm does not know for sure which it is. If it is aggregate expenditures that have fallen, then the firm should cut its price and maintain its output. By doing so each firm keeps its price constant relative to the prices of all other goods. This is the correct response because the relative demand for the firm's product is unchanged. But if the drop in the price of the firm's output is due to a decline in the demand for its product, perhaps because consumer tastes have changed, then the firm should cut its output.

Not knowing whether it is aggregate expenditures or the demand for its individual products that has changed, the firm straddles and does a bit of what is appropriate if aggregate expenditures have fallen and a bit of what is appropriate if the relative demand for its product has declined. Hence, when aggregate expenditures fall, the firm reduces its output as well as its prices.

Workers are in a similar position; when their employer demands a nominal wage cut, they do not know whether this is an economywide phenomenon that will result in a fall in prices and an unchanged real wage or just an employer-specific phenomenon that would mean a cut in real wages. Hence, some refuse to take such a cut in their nominal wages and decide to look for jobs elsewhere, so that unemployment increases.

Many economists have criticized this theory. One objection is that much information on economywide movements in aggregate expenditures is readily available. Firms can subscribe to forecasting services or at least read the summary of forecasts in the *Wall Street Journal*. A related criticism is that errors in differentiating between economywide changes in prices and changes in relative prices could not persist for long enough to explain recessions. The new classical economists reply that after output and employment are cut, it may take some time to restore them to their previous levels. Thus, before raising employment, firms may need to work off inventories that have piled up in the period between the decline in demand and the time at which the firm cut its production. But can such adjustment lags explain why, during the Great Depression, unemployment exceeded 20 percent for some years? Even the much lower unemployment rates of the early 1980s—9.7 percent in 1982, 9.6 percent in 1983, and 7.5 percent in 1984—seem hard to explain just by adjustment lags.

One way of distinguishing between the Keynesian, monetarist, and new classical economics is in terms of the lags in the adjustment of wages and other prices. Keynesians believe that wages and prices are so slow to adjust to a fall in aggregate expenditures that if left to itself, our economy would, from time to time, experience massive unemployment lasting for many years. Eventually wages and prices would fall by enough to raise the real money stock sufficiently to restore high employment, but this process could take many years. As Keynes once wrote about the quantity theory's adjustment process, "In the long run we are all dead."[4] Monetarists believe that the lag in wage and price adjustments exists, but that this lag is much shorter than Keynesians think, while the new classicals set the adjustment lag at close to zero.

REAL BUSINESS CYCLES

As the various criticisms of the Lucas supply function were raised, many new classical economists developed another explanation of economic fluctuations and unemployment known as **real business-cycle theory.**

It is *not* true that good scientific procedure tells you *always* to discard your theory when the "facts," that is, empirical observations, contradict it. Perhaps these observations are wrong; perhaps they are being misinterpreted. So let us see if we can maintain our theory of rational utility-maximizing agents (that is, households and firms) by showing that the seemingly plain "fact" that from time to time there is much more unemployment than just frictional unemployment is actually not a fact at all. This has been the response of many new classical economists.

The Behavior of Real GDP

Let us make a detour and look at a highly stylized picture of business cycles. Part A of Figure 21.1 shows such business cycles as they have been traditionally conceived. Here GDP oscillates smoothly around its trend. Monetarists explain these oscillations in large part by changes in the growth rate of money. Some Keynesians, on the other hand, might say that during booms, eventually the marginal efficiency of investment falls temporarily as the capital stock, particularly the stock of inventories, rises; the result is a recession. In either case, sooner or later, the recession comes to an end, perhaps because the monetary growth rate has stopped falling or perhaps because the marginal efficiency of investment is rising again. An expansion then occurs, and the economy moves back to full employment and high utilization of capacity. The fall in aggregate expenditures has reduced output only temporarily. Since during this process *potential* output has continued to grow at its normal rate, the new peak lies on the same trend line as the previous peaks. In such an economy in which changes in GDP are due to changes in aggregate expenditures, a rise in GDP above its trend during the expansion will be followed by a decline during the recession.

Now imagine a very different situation. Suppose that there are shocks to the economy's productive capacity. For example, in 1973–74 OPEC raised oil prices sharply, and as a result some capital equipment that used a lot of petroleum products could no longer be employed profitably. Until oil prices fell again, it was as though this capital had been destroyed by an earthquake. Such shocks might be permanent or at least long lasting. Hence, after a negative productivity shock has reduced output, there is no reason to expect that output will return to the trend line of previous peaks. Similarly, if a positive productivity shock occurs, output will stay above its previous peak at least until a

---

[4] John M. Keynes, *A Tract on Monetary Reform* (London: Macmillan & Co., 1924), p. 80.

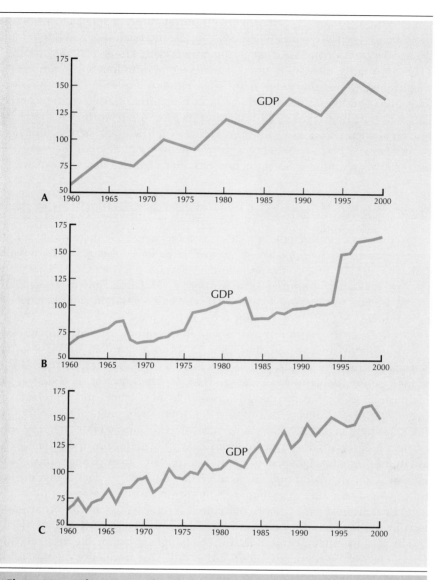

Figure 21.1   Three Types of Cycles in GDP. Part A shows cycles that oscillate smoothly around a trend. Part B shows a GDP series that is subject to productivity shocks. Part C illustrates a case where GDP has a trend and is subject to purely random shocks.

negative productivity shock happens to come along. GDP will then behave as pictured in Part B of Figure 21.1. Fluctuations in output are therefore explained by successive positive and negative shocks to productivity, and not by changes in aggregate expenditures.

Which of these two pictures represents our economy better? Surprisingly, this is hard to say. To see why, look at Part C of Figure 20.1. It *seems* to show fairly regular cycles in GDP which, like the cycles of Part A, could readily be attributed to cycles in aggregate expenditures. But what it *actually* shows is the same trend as in Part B, combined with purely random shocks.[5] No cyclical movements, such as one might expect from the interaction of a multiplier and the accelerator or from a change in the growth rate of money, underlie Part C. (The appearance of cycles in series that are actually random is a common optical illusion and one that keeps many stock market "experts" in business.)

Much highly sophisticated work has been done to determine whether Part A or Part B of Figure 21.1 is a better picture of our world. This work has not yet yielded a conclusive answer. Hence, the fluctuations of GDP in our economy *could* be due to changes in productivity rather than to changes in aggregate expenditures. Such fluctuations are called **real business cycles.**

The Real Business Cycle Theory

Let us therefore look at a theory, called **real business cycle theory,** that tries to make sense of fluctuations like those in Part B. These fluctuations consist of shifts in real GDP that do not show any self-reversing tendencies. If GDP rises, it is just as likely to continue to rise further as it is to fall. Hence, ignoring the trend, the best forecast one can make on the basis of the previous behavior of GDP is to say that GDP will remain at its current level.

Consider an economy with no unemployment other than frictional unemployment, and assume that some shock to technology occurs—say, an innovation that raises the productivity of labor. Real wages rise and that induces more people to enter the labor force. Employment then stays at this higher level as long as the marginal productivity of labor, and therefore real wages, stay high. Conversely, suppose that some technological shock reduces the marginal productivity of labor. Wages decline, and so does employment. Someone observing these fluctuations in employment may quite mistakenly attribute them to changes in aggregate expenditures, whereas in reality employment fluctuated only because people decided to work more at those times when real wages were higher. Nobody was involuntarily unemployed.

Real business cycle theory therefore presents a radically different way of looking at the economy. Both Keynesians and monetarists see fluctuations in output and in unemployment as due to changes in aggregate expenditures. Output falls when aggregate expenditures fall. The productive capacity of the economy is unchanged; just less of it is being used when aggregate expenditures fall. In contrast, real business cycle theorists believe that aggregate expenditures are always sufficient to purchase the total of goods and services that people want to produce. (If they were not, wages and prices would fall, and the resulting rise in the real money supply would raise aggregate expenditures to make them sufficient.) Recessions are simply periods in which the productivity of the economy has declined. Since productivity, and hence real wages,

---

[5] The following procedure was used to construct the curve in Part C. The cycles shown in Part A were generated by multiplying the trend value of GDP in each of eight successive periods by 1.00, 1.05, 1.10, 1.15, 1.20, 1.15, 1.10, and 1.05. To construct the GDP curve for Part C, the trend value of GDP in each period was multiplied by any one of these eight values chosen at random. The occurrence of seeming cycles is not the result of repeated efforts to get a curve that looks cyclical. Part C shows the only "run" that was tried.

are lower, fewer people want to work. It makes sense for people to work less at times when their real wages are lower and to work more at times when their real wages are higher.[6]

But how about the Great Depression? In 1932 and 1933 unemployment exceeded 20 percent of the civilian labor force. Had all these people decided to enjoy leisure in those years? Of course not. Thus Edward Prescott of the University of Minnesota, an originator of real business cycle theory, does not deny that there was genuine involuntary unemployment during the Great Depression. He does not claim that real business cycle theory explains all the fluctuations in the U.S. economy, but he believes that it explains about half the fluctuations in the prewar period and about three-quarters in the postwar period.

Critics of real business cycle theory raise a number of issues. One is to question the assumption that there exist technological shocks powerful enough to trigger cycles as large as the ones actually observed. Real business cycle theorists have not provided convincing evidence that such large technological shocks occur. In particular, it is hard to imagine that there are many technological shocks that *reduce* productivity, and thus generate a recession. A second problem relates to the new classical claim that the drop in employment during recessions is the result of workers' quitting their jobs because they prefer to work less now and work more in the future when they expect their wages to be higher. This assumes a great readiness to shift their time between working and taking leisure, something that is hard to reconcile with the data, particularly say the critics, since there is no evidence that real wages are much lower in recessions than in expansions.

Moreover, the critics say real business cycle theory implies that people want to work fewer hours during recessions, but recessions are characterized less by a drop in the average number of hours that employees work than by a rise in the number of people who are unemployed. Real business cycle theorists respond that due to commuting costs and other fixed costs of employment, it makes sense either to work full time or not to work at all. Hence, instead of most people cutting back somewhat on the number of hours they work, those who previously were only marginally better-off by working full time than by not working at all now decide to drop out of the labor force entirely, while others continue to work full time.

A different type of real business cycle theory focuses on frictional unemployment. Most economists assume that frictional unemployment is fairly constant. But this need not be the case. There may be times when consumer demand, technology, or changes in foreign trade bring about rapid declines in some industries and rapid increases in others. It takes time for workers to shift to new jobs, and in the meantime unemployment rises.

---

[6] To talk of the unemployed taking leisure time seems to fly in the face of how the unemployed themselves experience their situation. But, at least to some extent, it is possible to reconcile what the unemployed believe about their situation with real business cycle theory. Suppose that a technological change greatly reduces a worker's equilibrium wage. Rather than take a wage cut, she quits her job, since, not knowing about the technological change, she expects to find another job at her previous wage. But her equilibrium wage has fallen so she cannot find that other job, and hence considers herself unemployed.

The debate about real business cycles is still going strong, and it is too early to know where it will end. But even if the real business cycle theorists lose the debate, their work may still be useful in explaining certain fluctuations that have occurred. It is highly probable that we experience both types of fluctuations—traditional expenditure-driven business cycles and shifts in productivity. The critical question is their relative importance.

NEW KEYNESIAN THEORY

Apart from criticizing new classical theory in the ways just described, Keynesians responded by providing their own microeconomic underpinnings. In what has come to be known as **new Keynesian theory,** they justified the assumption of wage and price stickiness, which forms an important part of both Keynesian and monetarist theory. To do this, they had to show that wage and price inflexibility was consistent with the basic assumption of economics, rational utility maximization.

One obvious reason why some wages do not fall during recessions is that they are set by contracts lasting several years. One might, of course, ask why employers and employees do not renegotiate these contracts as demand falls during recessions. One answer is that contract negotiations are time-consuming and hence costly. An additional reason may be that unions may be concerned primarily with the interests of their members, who are employed, and not with the interests of those who are unemployed and no longer paying union dues.

Another explanation, which Keynes himself had advanced, is that workers are concerned not just with the absolute levels of their real wages, but also with their real wages relative to those of other workers. This would not prevent wage cuts if all wages could be cut at the same time. But in the U.S. economy wages are negotiated at different times, so that wage contracts overlap. Workers who are considering whether to accept a wage cut do not know whether other workers will accept a wage cut too, so that they can take a wage cut without lowering their relative wages.

Moreover, even if it is only absolute real wages and not relative wages that matter to workers, overlapping contracts still create a serious obstacle to wage cutting in a recession. If contracts in other industries still have, say, a year to run, those whose contracts expire now and are asked to take a nominal wage cut know that, at least for a year, their real wages will fall along with their nominal wages. And in a year the recession may be over, so that there will be no wage and price cuts in other industries. In that case, anyone who accepts a lower wage contract during the recession will be taking a cut in real wages for the entire length of the contract. The source of the problem is the absence of a coordinating mechanism for wages across industries.

Formal wage contracts are only a small part of the story, since less than one-quarter of the U.S. labor force is unionized. So how else can one explain wage stickiness? One likely possibility is the existence of informal **implicit contracts.** Those who are not covered by an explicit and formal contract still have an expectation that their employer will treat them in a certain way. In exchange for what they consider fair treatment they put in a fair day's work. The relationship established is valuable to both employer and employee, and it keeps the employer from replacing his workers every time a lower-priced applicant becomes available. Moreover, if the employer were to fire some workers and replace them with others willing to work for a lower wage, the remaining employees might be unwilling to provide the new ones with the training and information they need to work effectively. The existence of explicit and implicit contracts does not mean that nominal wages are totally rigid. For example, in the 1980s, money wages were cut in a number of industries, such as airlines and trucking, that were being deregulated. It was clear to both employers and employees that deregulation, by eliminating cartel-like price setting, had lowered the wage rates that the industry could pay. But under other conditions, getting money wages to fall can be a slow process.

The strategy of cutting prices during a recession runs into some of the same obstacles that wage cutting does. Just as coordination problems may thwart wage cuts, they may also thwart price cuts. Suppose that steel companies cut prices as demand for steel falls. Would that result in an increased demand for steel since the prices of goods made from steel would then fall? Not necessarily. The producers of automobiles, washing machines, and so on, might gratefully pocket the savings from the cheaper steel instead of passing them on to their consumers. Similarly, price setters, when considering whether to lower their prices, face a problem analogous to the implicit contract problem that wage negotiators face. In some industries firms have tacit understandings about not trying to undercut each other's prices, and any firm that does cut its price might set off a price war.

Moreover, the benefits that firms could obtain from cutting prices may be quite small. Suppose that as demand falls, a firm realizes that its prices are now above the point where marginal revenue exceeds marginal cost, so that it could raise its profits by cutting its prices. This potential rise in its profits may be too small to induce the firm to cut its prices. A price cut affects profits in two ways: the firm gains because it sells more units, and the firm loses because it gets less for each unit it sells. Its net gain from cutting its prices may therefore be small. To be sure, even a small gain is better than nothing, but the firm has to consider two additional factors. One is the costs of changing prices, such as informing buyers, though that cost is probably fairly small. However, it is possible buyers will resent continual price changes, since they make it harder to decide what to buy.

A probably more serious problem is that cutting prices is risky for the firm. Just how large is its elasticity of demand? Will its rivals respond by cutting their prices? Will its creditors take a price cut to be a sign of desperation, and hence be unwilling to renew loans? Will customers consider the lower prices to be a sign of lower quality? The safe thing may be to keep prices fixed and to cut output and employment instead.

Thus one can give many reasons why it is possible that wages and prices do not fall enough in recessions for markets to clear. And these reasons are consistent with rational utility maximization. This does not mean, however, that new Keynesian economists have been entirely successful in explaining wage and price stickiness. They have offered many divergent explanations instead of a more intellectually satisfying unified theory. Also, they have not provided much empirical evidence about which, if any, of their proffered explanations explain wage and price stickiness in the real world and which are just theoretical possibilities. Much work remains to be done.

Although the debate between new classical economists and their critics is therefore still unsettled, it has already increased our understanding of how the economy functions. The introduction of rational expectations is an important innovation, and while it may well turn out that new classical economists have greatly exaggerated the importance of shocks to productivity, they may well have corrected a previous underemphasis on such shocks. Moreover, they have forced their opponents to place their macroeconomics on much better micro-foundations.

POST-KEYNESIAN THEORY

New classical theory takes the assumption of rational behavior most seriously and argues that the instability of aggregate expenditures is not as serious a problem as both Keynesians and monetarists claim. The theory we discuss now is radically different.

Keynes's *General Theory of Employment, Interest and Money* is a great book in its originality, depth of insight, and sweep. Such books often contain elements that point in different directions and therefore can be interpreted in several ways. Chapters 15 through 18 presented the standard interpretation of Keynesian economics, summarized in the IS-LM model, in which two more or less stable and predictable curves intersect to determine GDP. This analysis is faithful to one aspect of Keynes's thought. But there is another component of Keynes's work that stresses uncertainty, unpredictability, and instability. These ideas have been taken up by some economists, who, while having divergent views on many issues, are grouped together as **post-Keynesians.**

Uncertainty and Its Implications

Keynes stressed the great uncertainty inherent in economic decisions (see the box on page 393). This aspect of Keynes's thought does not translate well into an IS-LM diagram, but is preserved and extended by the post-Keynesians. Keynes himself pointed to the erratic behavior of the stock market as showing that asset prices are not just the result of calm, rational deliberations, but also depend on fears and hopes, on waves of optimism and pessimism. To post-Keynesians expectations are far from rational.

They argue that the high degree of uncertainty under which economic decisions are made has important implications for monetary theory. By holding money, we ameliorate the burden of not knowing what the future will

Keynes on Uncertainty

In an article published in 1937, after many years of the Great Depression, Lord Keynes wrote the following about uncertainty:

> We have as a rule, only the vaguest idea of any but the most direct consequences of our acts. . . . How do we manage in such circumstances to behave in a manner which saves our faces as rational economic men? We have devised for the purpose a variety of techniques, of which much the most important are the three following: (1) We assume that the present is a much more serviceable guide to the future than a candid examination of past experience would show it to have been hitherto. . . . (2) We assume that the *existing* state of opinion as expressed in prices [including asset prices] and the character of existing output is based on a *correct* summing up of future prospects. . . . (3) Knowing that our individual judgment is worthless, we endeavor to fall back on the judgment of the rest of the world. . . . Now a practical theory of the future based on these three principles has certain marked characteristics. In particular, being based on so flimsy a foundation it is subject to sudden and violent changes. The practice of calmness and immobility, of certainty and security, suddenly breaks down. New fears and hopes will, without warning, take charge of human conduct. The forces of disillusion may suddenly impose a new conventional basis of valuation. All these, petty polite techniques, made for a well-panelled board room and a nicely regulated market, are liable to collapse. At all times, the vague panic fears and equally vague and unreasonable hopes are not really lulled, and lie but a little way below the surface.*

*The Collected Writings of John Maynard Keynes, Vol. 14 (London: Macmillan & Co., 1973), pp. 113–15.

bring, because money allows us to delay decisions until we know better what will happen. If you have saved some of your income and are worried that prices of stocks, bonds, and other assets will fall, you can avoid this risk by holding your savings in the form of money until you get a better idea about future stock and bond prices. Hence, one would expect the demand for money to depend on the extent of uncertainty and thus not be a stable and predictable function of income, interest rates, or other measurable variables.

Another implication that post-Keynesians draw from the existence of pervasive uncertainty is that investment decisions are driven as much, or more, by hopes and fears as by rational calculations, by what Keynes himself referred to as "animal spirits."[7] Hence, investment, too, is unstable. Post-Keynesians therefore believe that the private sector is not only much more unstable than monetarists think, but also more unstable than mainstream Keynesians think.

---

[7] Keynes did not mean to derogate entrepreneurs when he used the phrase "animal spirits." Unfortunately, some of his followers seem to use it in a derogatory way.

Money or Bank Credit?

Another aspect of post-Keynesian theory is its claim that what happens on the assets side of a bank's balance sheet is more important than what happens on the liabilities side. When a bank creates a deposit, it does so either by making a loan or by buying a security, so that on the assets side of the bank's balance sheet either loans or securities go up when deposits go up. Most economists think it makes little difference which of these it is. But post-Keynesians argue that the deposits created when a bank makes a loan generate in most situations a greater rise in GDP than do the deposits that a bank creates when it buys securities from the public. Someone receiving a loan quickly spends the proceeds, and aggregate expenditures rise. In contrast, someone who sells a security to a bank is less likely to spend the proceeds on buying goods and services. She may have sold the security in the expectation that interest rates will rise, so that she can buy such securities back again at a lower price. Or she may have sold the security to buy some other security, and the seller of that security will then hold money at least for some time. Therefore, post-Keynesians argue, bank loans are a more reliable guide to what will happen to aggregate expenditures than the quantity of bank deposits and hence the quantity of money are. Some of the money supply is held in speculative balances in anticipation of a decline in security prices and thus does not affect aggregate expenditures. This is not the case with bank loans.

Post-Keynesians are not the only ones who believe that money created by bank loans has more effect on aggregate expenditures than does money created by a bank's security purchases. But the majority of economists believe that in most situations the difference, if any, is too small to matter. Besides, with borrowers holding compensatory balances against loans, it is not obvious that loan dollars are spent more.

The Treatment of Time

Standard economic theory uses equilibrium analysis. It shows how the equilibrium position of the economy changes in response to a change in some variable, say, an increase in the marginal propensity to consume. In doing so, it assumes that all other variables are constant, and often describes the move to the new equilibrium through a series of steps in hypothetical periods. It might say, for example, that in Period I a rise in consumption reduces inventories, in Period II sellers restore their inventories and production rises, and in period III the accelerator induces a rise in investment. Post-Keynesians often work in a different way, by looking at changes in several variables at the same time. More important, they think it unhelpful to talk in terms of theoretical time, such as Period I or Period II. Instead, they look at actual time and say that a rise in consumption in January 1997 will have certain effects in June 1998, and so on. They do this because the same stimulus may call forth a different response at different times. In part this is because the economy learns from past experience. For example, a rise in oil prices will induce procedures to conserve oil, so that if oil prices fall back to their previous level, oil demand will now be less than it was before. Demand curves should not be treated as time-less.

The Aggregate Supply Curve and Stabilization Policy

In post-Keynesian theory changes in aggregate expenditures play little role in short-run price determination. Instead, firms set prices by adding a fixed markup to labor costs. These labor costs are not determined by a stable Phillips curve relating wage increases to the unemployment rate. Instead, wage increases depend largely on sociological and political factors, such as the attitude of labor unions and the dissatisfaction of workers with the prevailing distribution of income. Reducing aggregate expenditures is therefore not an effective way to curb inflation. It generates much misery by increasing unemployment and usually does not bring the inflation rate down significantly. Instead, post-Keynesians want to curb inflation by an incomes policy. They believe that such a policy can be effective, particularly if it is part of a social compact that reduces the inequality of the income distribution.

The Role of Monetary Policy

Thus, in post-Keynesian theory there is little good that countercyclical monetary policy can do. Prices depend on the attitude of unions, and output depends in large part on the hopes and fears that determine the perceived marginal efficiency of capital. Thus, instead of driving up interest rates during an inflation, the central bank should keep interest low at all times. This would help to reduce unemployment and also make the income distribution less unequal.[8]

Instead of the growth rate of money driving aggregate expenditures, it is aggregate expenditures that drive the growth rate of money. This is so because, as discussed in Chapter 13, the money supply is partly endogenous and expands as the demand for money rises. Suppose wages start to rise at a faster rate. If the resulting increase in the demand for money does not generate a sufficient rise in the money multiplier, the central bank will simply increase bank reserves. It *need* not do so. But it knows that if it does not, it may permit a recession as interest rates rise. And it also knows that holding reserves stable and letting higher interest rates generate a recession will not curb inflation. So it might as well increase reserves.

Moreover, the financial structure is often weak, with a number of financial institutions and large nonfinancial firms being close to bankruptcy. The central bank is therefore afraid that if interest rates rise, the decline in security prices, and hence in the value of the portfolios of financial institutions, could generate a financial crisis. The same is true for the rising interest payments that debtor corporations have to make. So the central bank has to act as a lender of last resort to ensure that a financial crisis will not occur. But according to some post-Keynesians, by always being ready to act as a lender of last

---

[8] More traditional economists would question whether the central bank could succeed in keeping real interest rates low for a long time, given the Fisher effect.

resort, the central bank is also financing inflation. It is therefore caught in a bind, a bind that reflects the instability of the capitalist system.

A Post-Keynesian Cycle Theory

We will now describe one of the ways in which post-Keynesian ideas can be used to explain business cycles, the way used by Hyman Minsky of Washington University, St. Louis. Toward the end of a recession pessimism fades and firms undertake more investment. The resulting rise in income generates further optimism and hence more investment—so far so good. But now something dangerous happens—the financial structure becomes more precarious. Minsky distinguishes among three types of finance: **hedge finance, speculative finance, and Ponzi finance.**[9] *Hedge finance* is a situation in which borrowers expect to be able to service their debt out of income receipts, as does a family taking out a mortgage or a firm building a new plant that will lower manufacturing costs. In *speculative finance* the borrower expects to have to sell assets to service the debt, a frequent occurrence in leveraged buyouts. Speculative finance is riskier than hedge finance because if asset prices fall, the borrower may not be able to obtain the funds needed to service the debt. *Ponzi finance* is even worse. It is a situation in which the borrower can service the debt only by additional borrowing. This is the riskiest type of finance because ultimately you cannot keep on borrowing to pay off previously incurred debts; that way lies sure bankruptcy.

As the expansion proceeds and optimism increases, more and more firms shift from hedge finance to speculative finance or from either of these to Ponzi finance. The further this process goes, the more fragile the financial structure becomes. Sooner or later it reaches the stage when even a small fall in incomes, such as occurs during a mild recession, is sufficient to make many firms incapable of repaying their debts or even of just paying the interest on them. As a result, dramatic bankruptcies occur. Creditors become frightened and insist on the repayments of loans that they otherwise would have renewed. The recession becomes unusually severe with massive unemployment.

Minsky then distinguishes between the situation before World War II and the current situation. In the prewar world, from time to time a financial collapse occurred, and occasionally resulted in massive bank failures. As firms were forced to raise cash to pay off the loans that creditors would no longer extend, they had to sell assets at distress prices. The fall in the prices of these assets hurt not only the firms that sold them, but also other holders of such assets, whose capital might be wiped out by the fall in the prices of their assets. Many of these firms would then fail as well.

Such a process is no longer likely because the Federal Reserve will not allow it. It steps in and lowers interest rates, and also puts pressure on banks to lend to large firms that would otherwise fail. But this policy, while preventing a severe recession, has two major disadvantages. First, in the past, financial

---

[9] Ponzi finance is named after a swindler who collected funds after World War I by promising a high rate of interest. He paid this interest not out of what he earned by investing these funds, but from new funds that came in. Eventually, the day of reckoning arrived, and he ended up in jail.

panics served a valuable function: they restored financial discipline. For some years afterward firms would be reluctant to take the risks of speculative or Ponzi finance. Now this curb on excessive risk taking no longer exists, or at least is not as strong as it used to be. Second, when the Fed acts as a lender of last resort in an incipient financial panic by increasing bank reserves, it lays the foundation for higher inflation.

SUMMARY

1   New classical economists accuse both Keynesian and monetarist theories of lacking rigorously explicated foundations in rational behavior. Much of this debate centers on the new classicals' assumption of price flexibility.

2   In new classical theory a change in aggregate expenditure that is correctly perceived has no impact on employment and output, but only on prices. Since both firms and employees have difficulty in distinguishing between a shift in aggregate expenditures and a shift in relative demand, some transitional unemployment results.

3   Traditional macroeconomics implies that when real GDP departs from its trend value, it starts to move back toward it again. Real business cycle theorists claim that this is not what the data show.

4   In real business cycle theory, changes in technology drive real GDP. Changes in employment reflect the amount of work that employees want to do at different real wages.

5   New Keynesians have provided a number of reasons why wages and prices may not move enough to clear markets. Among them are overlapping contracts, implicit contracts, and uncertainty about the effects of price cuts.

6   Post-Keynesian economists believe that our economy is inherently unstable, that waves of optimism and pessimism change the perceived marginal efficiency of investment, and hence GDP.

7   In post-Keynesian theory the supply of money does not play a causal role: instead, the money supply is usually endogenous. Bank loans are a better indicator than the money supply. In Minsky's model, as expansions continue, the balance sheets of firms deteriorate as speculative finance and Ponzi finance replace hedge finance. Ultimately this leads either to a major recession or to a bailout by the Fed with inflationary consequences.

KEY TERMS

new classical theory
sticky wages and prices
Lucas supply function
real business cycles

new Keynesian theory
post-Keynesian theory
hedge finance
speculative finance
Ponzi finance

QUESTIONS AND EXERCISES

*1   New classical economists claim that rational behavior suggests that wages and prices must be flexible. Can you think of some conditions consistent with rational behavior under which wages and prices would not be flexible?

2   Describe in your own words the Lucas supply function.

*3 Suppose that real GDP moves by discontinuous shifts rather than tending toward a trend value. Why is this hard to reconcile with theories that attribute changes in real GDP to variations in aggregate expenditures?

4 How do real business cycle theorists explain changes in employment?

*5 Post-Keynesian economists admit that changes in GDP and in the monetary growth rate are correlated. Why, then, do they reject the quantity theory?

6 Describe Minsky's theory of increasing financial fragility. Do you think it applies to recent conditions?

FURTHER READING

For excellent discussions of new classical economics see:

HALL, ROBERT, and JOHN TAYLOR. *Macroeconomics.* 4th ed. New York: Norton, 1993.

HOOVER, KEVIN. *The New Classical Macroeconomics: A Skeptical View.* Oxford: Blackwell, 1988.

KLAMER, ARDJO. *Conversations with Economists.* Totowa, N.J.: Rowman and Allanheld, 1984.

Good sources on real business cycle theory are the articles by Rodolfo Manuelli, Edward Prescott, and Lawrence Summers in Federal Reserve Bank of Minneapolis, *Quarterly Review* 10, (Fall 1986), 3–32. See also:

CHAN HU, and BHARAT TREHAN. "Real Business Cycles: A Selective Survey," Federal Reserve Bank of San Francisco, *Economic Review* (Spring 1991), 3–14.

MCCALLUM, BENNETT. "Unit Roots in Macroeconomic Time Series: Some Critical Issues," Federal Reserve Bank of Richmond, *Economic Quarterly,* 79 (Spring 1993), 13–44.

A good source on new Keynesian theory is the symposium "Keynesian Economics Today," in *Journal of Economic Perspectives,* 7 (Winter 1993), 3–82.

For authoritative statements of post-Keynesian theory see:

DAVIDSON, PAUL. *Money and the Real World.* New York: Wiley, 1972.

MINSKY, HYMAN. *Stabilizing an Unstable Economy.* New Haven, Conn.: Yale University Press, 1986.

MOORE, BASIL. *Verticalists and Horizontalists.* Oxford: Blackwell, 1988.

ROUSSEAS, STEPHEN. *Post-Keynesian Monetary Economics.* Armonk, N.Y.: E. S. Sharp, 1986.

FOUR

MONETARY
POLICY

The Goals of Monetary Policy

After you have read this chapter, you will be able to:

- List the various goals of the Fed.
- Understand why some of these goals conflict in the short run.
- Appreciate the constraints the Fed faces in aiming at these goals.
- Discuss the relative importance of these goals.
- Analyze the question of whether the Fed should have only a price-stability goal.
- Assess the pros and cons of giving the Fed the single goal of controlling inflation.

Monetary policy, like fiscal policy, has four goals: high employment, price stability, an appropriate exchange rate, and a high rate of economic growth. In aiming at these goals the Fed takes account of three constraints: it needs to prevent financial panics, to avoid "excessive" interest-rate instability, and to retain the confidence of foreign investors. This chapter starts with a discussion of each of the goals individually and then looks at the three constraints. After that it considers whether the Fed's goals are consistent with each other and concludes with a brief discussion of the interrelation of monetary and fiscal policies.

THE GOALS

High Employment

High employment is an obvious goal of any macroeconomic policy. Everyone wants to avoid massive unemployment, regardless of whether he focuses on the human misery that such unemployment creates or on the wasteful loss of output that it implies. But as soon as one tries to be more specific a problem arises, one already discussed in Chapter 19. This is the difficulty of estimating the NAIRU. If the Fed underestimates the NAIRU and aims at too low an unemployment rate, inflation will accelerate. This means that it is sometimes difficult to decide whether unemployment is too high or too low. Obviously, this is not always the case. In the 1930s, when at times over a quarter of the nonfarm labor force was unemployed, there was little doubt the unemployment rate exceeded its desirable level. But this is much less clear if the unemployment rate is, say, 6 percent.

Price Stability

The next goal, price stability, may *seem* an obvious one, but it is far from obvious. Consider an economy in which prices have been rising at a rate of, say, 100 percent per year for the last fifty years, and everyone knows with certainty that the inflation rate will continue to be 100 percent. What damage does this inflation do? It does not redistribute income because all wages and all contracts, as well as tax laws and accounting procedures, are adjusted for it. For example, if productivity is growing at a 2 percent rate, wages rise at a 102 percent rate each year, and the interest rate is, say, 103 percent instead of 3 percent. Such a fully anticipated inflation imposes only three types of losses. First, there is the bother and inconvenience of having to change price tags and catalog prices frequently. Second, since prices cannot be changed continually, they will be out of equilibrium for the presumably short periods between price changes. Third, inflation creates an incentive to hold too little currency because currency holdings lose their real value without having the compensation of the higher nominal interest rate that other assets have. Hence, people are put to the inconvenience of continual trips to banks or ATMs to get currency. This is called the **shoe-leather cost.**

But the inflations we actually experience are *not* fully anticipated, and our economy is *not* fully indexed. Thus, nominal rather than real interest income is taxed. For example, if the interest rate is 12 percent and the inflation rate is 10 percent, a taxpayer in the one-third marginal tax bracket receives an after-tax real rate of return of −2 percent ($12 \times 2/3 - 10$). At the same time, borrowers are allowed to deduct too much as interest payments from taxable income. In addition, the depreciation charges that firms are allowed to deduct against taxable income are too low because they are based on original cost rather than on replacement cost. This raises their tax liability. Perhaps largely for this reason, perhaps for others, inflation probably lowers stock prices.

Since inflation affects the tax burdens faced by corporations to varying degrees, it also leads to a socially inefficient allocation of investment funds, because after-tax profits become a less reliable guide to the true productivity of capital in various industries.

Another effect of unanticipated inflation is its impact on the distribution of income and wealth. Obviously, it hurts creditors, and hence the retired, and benefits debtors. In addition, it may help or hurt wage earners depending on whether wages lag behind prices. All in all, the evidence suggests that in the

1960s and 1970s the high inflation rate of those years helped the poor, and thus made the distribution of income less unequal. But this is not likely to be so for all inflations.

Regardless of what inflation does to the distribution of income among different income classes, it generates a substantial income redistribution *within* each income class, since some households are net borrowers and others net lenders. This type of redistribution is surely deplorable. It is no more equitable than would be a tax on everyone who was born on an even-numbered day. To anyone genuinely concerned with equity, this redistribution must be a major loss from inflation. In addition, as already discussed in Chapter 11, inflation redistributes income from the public to the government.

Another loss from inflation is that it creates uncertainty and insecurity. Households can no longer plan confidently for the distant future since they do not know what their fixed-dollar assets and liabilities will then be worth in real terms. More generally, people have been taught the virtue of saving for a rainy day. But such prudent behavior is punished, rather than rewarded, by unanticipated inflation. This is likely to cause people to lose faith in the government and in the equity and reasonableness of social conditions in general. While this effect of inflation cannot be quantified, it may well be a major, perhaps even *the* major, disadvantage of inflation. Thus President Carter wrote:

> The corrosive effects of inflation eat away at the ties that bind us together as a people. One of the major tasks of a democratic government is to maintain conditions in which its citizens have a sense of command over their own destiny. During an inflation individuals watch in frustration as the value of last week's pay increase or last month's larger social security check is steadily eroded over the remainder of the year by a process that is beyond their individual control. All of us have to plan for the future. . . . The future is uncertain enough in any event, and the outcome of our plans is never fully within our own control. When the value of the measuring rod with which we do our planning—the purchasing power of the dollar—is subject to large and unpredictable shrinkage, one more element of command over our own future slips away. It is small wonder that trust in government and in social institutions is simultaneously eroded.[1]

An Appropriate Foreign-Exchange Rate

Between 1982 and 1985 the dollar rose sharply relative to other currencies. This made U.S. tourists happy and, more important, the decline in the dollar prices of imported goods lowered the inflation rate in the United States. But it seriously hurt many industries that relied on exports or competed with imports. It was a major contributor to the economic problems of certain midwestern and eastern states that relied on steel-related production. Previously, in the second half of the 1970s, the dollar had fallen, and this had exacerbated inflation.

We defer discussion of the specifics of exchange-rate policy until Part Five, but it should be clear that neither situation is desirable. All the same, an

---

[1] Executive Office of the President, *Economic Report of the President* (Washington, D.C.: 1979), p. 7.

appropriate exchange rate has at most times not been a major goal of Fed policy because foreign trade accounts for about 12 percent of GDP in the United States, though occasionally it does become an important goal.[2] In countries in which foreign trade accounts for, say, 50 percent of GDP, exchange-rate equilibrium is usually a much more important goal.

Economic Growth

There is now much concern that our current rate of growth is too low. This is often stated rather misleadingly as a problem of U.S. competitiveness. But economics is not a football game, where one team wins and the other loses. Suppose our growth rate were to fall from 2 to 1 percent, while the Japanese growth rate fell from 5 to 0 percent. Would that make us better-off?

Our rate of economic growth depends on many factors, most of which are beyond the reach of macroeconomic policy, but this policy can influence one important determinant of the economic growth rate: investment. A higher rate of investment not only means more capital per worker, but is also an important way in which technological progress comes about, since innovations are often embodied in new equipment. The invention of a new machine does not increase productivity until firms invest by installing it.

One way of raising investment is to keep the real interest rate fairly low. But this is inherently expansionary, and to prevent inflation, such a policy would have to be accompanied by a restrictive fiscal policy, that is, by a large government surplus or, more realistically, by keeping the deficit small. This depends, of course, on Congress and the administration and thus is beyond the Fed's control.

THE CONSTRAINTS

The Fed faces a number of constraints in trying to attain its goals. We single out three here.

Prevention of Financial Panics

A financial panic, and the deep recession that is likely to ensue from it, would result in high unemployment. Hence the avoidance of financial panics could logically be treated as part of the high-employment goal. But the prevention of financial panics is such a basic concern of the Fed that it deserves separate treatment.

Prior to World War II financial panics were an infrequent, but important, event in U.S. economic history. At times, usually after fervent speculation had driven stock prices and perhaps basic commodity prices way up, these prices would collapse. Those who had bought such assets on credit now had to

---

[2] Thus, the "Record of Policy Actions" for the October 3, 1989, FOMC meeting stated: "While the dollar was an important factor influencing the course of the U.S. economy and prices, monetary policy should not be used, in the judgment of the Committee, to attain particular levels for the foreign exchange value of the dollar that could conflict with domestic policy objectives." *Federal Reserve Bulletin,* 76 (January 1990), 20.

sell them to pay off their creditors, who were unwilling to extend their credits now that the value of the collateral was shrinking. This reduced the prices of these assets further, and thus reduced the collateral and hence the creditworthiness of other borrowers. As some of the borrowers failed and were unable to repay their loans, some of their creditors might also fail. Among these creditors were banks, so that massive bank failures occurred during some financial panics. At other times bank failures, rather than a collapse of security prices, might start off a financial panic.

The main reason for the founding of the Federal Reserve was the hope that it would prevent financial panics. But during the early 1930s this hope proved ill-founded; there were massive bank failures in 1930, 1931, and 1933. Since then the Fed has treated the avoidance of financial panics as its primary function. It is not a continuous, everyday goal, like high employment or price stability, since it is only rarely that a financial panic threatens. But when it does, then it is the primary duty of the Fed to prevent it from happening. Thus, the Fed will reverse a restrictive policy when there is a more or less plausible threat of a financial panic. It will sharply reverse course and make reserves readily available through open-market operations. It is also likely to announce that it will readily lend to banks through the discount mechanism. More than that—it may also informally pressure banks to extend loans they have made, and thus prevent the exacerbation of a financial panic.

Interest-Rate Stability

Keeping interest rates relatively stable is traditional Fed policy. Indeed, apart from preventing financial panics, a major reason the Fed was established was to prevent sharp peaks in interest rates. There are several reasons why the Fed wants to avoid sharply fluctuating interest rates. One is that financial markets operate more efficiently if interest rates are stable. Many dealers in financial instruments—for example, government security dealers—hold inventories of securities that are extremely large relative to their capital. Hence, if interest rates rise sharply, the resulting fall in the value of their portfolios can inflict severe losses on them, losses amounting to a significant part of their capital. To be sure, if interest rates fall sharply, they have big gains. But equal probabilities of big gains and big losses do not cancel out, in part because people are risk averse and in part because a loss that is big enough to bankrupt a firm imposes secondary losses on it.

In addition, as we discussed in Part One, sharply rising interest rates can create serious problems for depository institutions that hold many long-term loans they made at lower interest rates. Moreover, unstable interest rates induce fluctuations in foreign-exchange rates. If interest rates rise in the United States, foreigners want to buy dollars to acquire U.S. securities, while Americans demand fewer foreign securities and hence supply fewer dollars. As a result of a greater demand for, and a smaller supply of dollars, the dollar rises on the foreign-exchange market. As we will explain shortly, such inappropriate exchange-rate movements create problems for the U.S. economy as well as for foreign economies, whose central banks then complain to the Fed.

Furthermore, the public objects to large fluctuations, or more precisely to large increases, in interest rates. Debtor interests are much more vocal than creditor interests, so Congress turns against the Fed when interest rates rise rapidly.

None of this means that stabilizing interest rates is necessarily a correct policy. The interest rate is a price set in a free market and must be at a level that equates the supply of and demand for money. Hence, if the Fed wants to keep interest rates stable, it has to change the supply of money when the demand for money changes. But since the demand for money rises at a faster rate during expansions than during recessions, a policy of stabilizing interest rates means that the Fed may let the money supply grow faster in expansions than in recessions and may thus exacerbate business fluctuations. This need not necessarily happen. In principle, the Fed could prevent sharp fluctuations in interest rates, while allowing interest rates to rise at a slower and steadier rate during expansions. But many economists doubt that the Fed can make such fine distinctions.

Maintaining the Confidence of Foreign Investors

Another constraint on Fed policy is the result of the large volume of foreign investment in the United States that has occurred in recent years. In the years 1991 to 1994 capital inflow equaled almost a third of personal savings. As a result the Fed now has to be concerned about how foreign investors would respond to changes in its policy and to other events.

This problem is sometimes overstated as follows: if foreign investors become afraid of a decline in the value of their U.S. assets, they will withdraw their capital. This is wrong. There is no way investors as a whole can withdraw their net capital from the United States. Any *individual* foreign investor can, of course, sell her U.S. assets for dollars and then sell the dollars on the foreign-exchange market for her own, that is foreign, currency. But when she exchanges the dollars for her own currency, someone else ends up holding these dollars. Since it is primarily foreigners who hold foreign currencies, it is likely to be another foreigner who sold her the foreign currency and is now holding the dollars, so that net foreign holdings of U.S. dollar assets is unchanged.[3]

However, although foreign investors jointly cannot sell their dollar assets, there is another problem. Suppose that foreign investors suddenly become convinced that the dollar will decline on the foreign-exchange market. As a result they sell their U.S. stocks and bonds and use the proceeds from these sales to try to buy their own currencies. Two things happen: the prices of stocks and bonds fall, and so does the exchange rate of the dollar as more dollars are offered on the foreign-exchange market. The first of these reduces wealth and raises the cost of financing, and may therefore throw the economy into a reces-

---

[3] What happens if she sells the dollars to a U.S. resident? Wouldn't net foreign holdings of dollars fall then? No, they would not, because the only way a U.S. resident can buy the dollars from her is to pay her in her own currency. In doing so, he reduces U.S. holdings of foreign currency, and this decline in U.S. holdings of foreign currency just balances the fall in foreign holdings of U.S. currency, so the *net* U.S. holdings of foreign currency are unchanged.

sion. At the same time the depreciation of the dollar raises import prices and hence the inflation rate.

To avoid such undesirable effects, the Fed may have to adopt policies that reassure foreign investors, policies that it would otherwise not adopt. It may, for example, have to adopt a more restrictive policy to reassure foreigners that it will prevent an increase in the inflation rate, an increase that would cause the dollar to fall on the foreign-exchange market.

Thus the Fed's freedom of action is constrained by its need to worry about financial panics, its wish to avoid excessive interest-rate fluctuations, and its need to retain the confidence of foreign investors. However, these constraints are not the only problem the Fed faces in pursuing its goals. Another serious problem is that in some ways its goals conflict; they are inconsistent with each other.

RELATIONS AMONG GOALS

The Fed has many different goals. Some of them may conflict, so that the Fed has to choose among them. Let us consider each in turn.

Since the long-run Phillips curve is vertical, there is no significant long-run trade-off between unemployment and inflation. But the short-run Phillips curve does provide such a trade-off temporarily, unless the public knows what the Fed is up to *and* if prices and wages are highly flexible.

The temptation to focus on the short run and to trade price stability, or more realistically a lower inflation rate, for lower unemployment in the short run is likely to take the following form. The FOMC makes its decisions under great uncertainty. It has to guess whether, at the time when its policy will become effective, aggregate expenditures will be too high or too low. If it is eager to lower unemployment, it will tend to err on the side of assuming that aggregate expenditures will be deficient and will therefore adopt an expansionary policy. Some of the time expenditures will actually be insufficient, and such a policy will be the appropriate one. But frequently aggregate expenditures will exceed the downward-biased forecast and the additional expenditure generated by the expansionary policy will be inflationary.

A second way the employment goal conflicts with the price-stability goal is through the Fed's response to supply shocks. Suppose that when a supply shock raises prices, the Fed creates additional money to keep real balances from falling. This will prevent much of the unemployment that would otherwise result. But the price level will be higher. A third way the unemployment and price-stability goals conflict operates through the exchange rate. By lowering the exchange rate of the dollar, the Fed can stimulate export industries and import-competing industries. However, such a policy is inflationary.

The next goal, an appropriate exchange rate, conflicts in the short run with high employment and price stability: a lower exchange rate of the dollar increases employment, while a higher exchange rate lowers the inflation rate. Hence if the Fed and the Treasury want to lower unemployment, they have an incentive to depress the exchange rate of the dollar below its appropriate level, and if they want to reduce inflation, they have an incentive to raise the exchange rate above the appropriate level. But suppose the Fed merely wants the exchange rate to exacerbate neither unemployment nor inflation. Then the maintenance of an appropriate exchange rate—that is, an exchange rate that fairly reflects the relative purchasing power of the dollar and of foreign currencies—does not conflict with the two other goals.

The goals of high employment and of economic growth are complementary in two ways. If firms are operating at capacity, as they tend to be in periods of economic growth, they are more willing to invest in new facilities than if they have much excess capacity. In periods of high employment and labor shortages, firms try to upgrade the skills of their labor force, and that stimulates economic growth. However, there is another side to the story. In periods of high employment and prosperity, firms tend to become slack about controlling their costs. Recessions tend to stimulate downsizing and other painful steps that raise productivity.

Economic growth and price stability have a more complex relationship. They conflict in the short run: policies that are too expansionary, and hence too inflationary, can achieve higher economic growth at first (1) by ensuring that more firms are short of capacity and thus eager to invest, (2) by temporarily reducing unemployment, and (3) perhaps by expanding the labor force as firms try to expand their work forces by more strenuous recruiting and training of labor. But inflation also lowers efficiency and probably lowers investment in the long run. Hence over the long run rapid economic growth and low inflation are likely to be complementary rather than conflicting.

WHAT SHOULD THE FED DO?

In the long run there are no conflicts among the Fed's goals, and it can pursue all at the same time. But in the short run there are some conflicts. An expansionary policy that reduces unemployment temporarily also raises the inflation rate. Inflation enhances economic growth in the short run. Raising the exchange rate of the dollar helps temporarily to lower the inflation rate, while lowering it temporarily reduces unemployment.

It is easy to say that the Fed should be farsighted and try to improve economic conditions over the long run rather than the short run. Yes, it is easy to say that in the abstract, but what would you actually do if you chaired the Board of Governors? Suppose the economy were in a recession with an 8 percent unemployment rate. Wouldn't you feel tempted to say, "Let's deal with today's problem today"? Perhaps you might say to yourself, "Yes, I know that an expansionary policy will reduce unemployment only temporarily, while probably raising the inflation rate over the long run. But we don't really know what will happen in the future, so why not do what we can to reduce the misery created by unemployment here and now?" Even if you would not think that way, but would steadfastly focus on the long run, neither the President nor Congress is likely to take such a long-run view and would pressure you to focus on the short run. This does not mean that politicians are stupid or venal, merely that they respond to the public's wishes. And the public may be insufficiently aware of the inflationary danger that an expansionary policy poses. During a

The Bundesbank's Dilemma

When the Berlin Wall collapsed in 1989 and Germany was reunified, the German central bank, the Bundesbank, faced a dilemma. Despite strong urgings by the Bundesbank, the German government decided to help East Germans by raising their wages and by converting their currency to the West German currency at a very favorable exchange rate. This resulted in a large budget deficit, an increase in the growth rate of the money supply, and a higher inflation rate.

The Bundesbank had built a superb reputation for curbing inflation over many years. Obviously, it did not want to lose this reputation by permitting higher inflation, particularly since its charter instructs it to place primary emphasis on price stability. But raising interest rates to curb money growth and inflation was an unappealing choice. Not only would it increase the already high unemployment rate in Germany, but it would also endanger the European Monetary System (EMS). (The EMS is an arrangement that very narrowly limits exchange-rate fluctuations among the participating countries and is intended to lead, within a few years, to a unified currency with a single central bank.) Higher German interest rates endangered the EMS because they attracted foreign funds into Germany. The resulting increased demand for the German currency, *deutsche marks* (DM), then put upward pressure on the exchange rate of the DM. To be sure, in principle, such pressure could be avoided if other countries raised their interest rates too. But many of them also had very high unemployment rates and were therefore unwilling to do so.

Financial markets expected that some European countries, rather than raise their interest rates, would let their currencies fall relative to the DM. Speculators therefore sold these currencies short and bought DM on a massive scale. And they were right: several countries had to let their exchange rates drop relative to the DM, and European monetary unification was severely set back. This is not to say that high German interest rates were necessarily the main cause of the EMS crisis, but it does show that when forced to decide on a specific policy, even Germany, a country in which foreign trade accounts for almost a quarter of GDP, put domestic considerations ahead of stable exchange rates.

recession the public treats unemployment as *the* problem and wants the government to do something about it right away. Then during the resulting expansion, when the inflation rate rises, inflation becomes *the* problem and the public wants the government to do something about that right away. This tendency to demand policies that ameliorate current problems, even though they subsequently have bad effects, puts pressure on the Fed to act inappropriately.

SINGLE OR MULTIPLE GOALS FOR THE FED?

A number of economists believe that to prevent such myopic policy making, Congress should direct the Fed to focus on a single goal, such as price stability or low inflation. If the Fed were constrained to focus on price stability, as, for example, the German Bundesbank more or less is, the economy would experience a lower inflation rate than it would in the absence of such a constraint. But other problems might become worse. We will look first at the case for such a constraint and then at the case against it.

The Case for a Single Goal

As previously discussed, in the long run the unemployment rate settles at the NAIRU and is therefore beyond the Fed's control. Hence, some argue that instead of having an employment target, the Fed should concentrate on the one goal that it can control, the inflation rate.[4] At present it cannot do that, because Congress has given it a mandate to worry about unemployment as well as about inflation. This means that the Fed is driven to adopt policies that reduce the unemployment rate only temporarily, and may indeed increase it over the long run, while raising the inflation rate.[5] By trying to do what it cannot do, the Fed loses the opportunity to do the one thing that it can do—control inflation.

Suppose the Fed were given a single inflation-related goal, such as keeping the inflation rate at its present level or bringing it down to zero, or keeping the price level constant.[6] To be sure, the Fed could not dictate the inflation rate precisely, but over the long run its positive and negative errors would cancel out, so that the public would know what long-run inflation rate to expect and would be able to make a reasonable guess about what the price level would be, say, ten years from now. At present, future price levels are one of the world's great unknowns; this makes it more difficult for businesses and households to plan efficiently.

If the public thus had firm expectations about the future inflation rate, it would be easier to stabilize the economy. Suppose the price level is expected to be stable. If prices rise, people know that prices will fall again. So they will hold off buying, and thus reduce aggregate expenditures and, hence, the inflation rate. Similarly, if prices fall, people know that they can now buy at unusually low prices. At present, when prices rise more (or less) than anticipated, people may well expect the same to occur next year and thus make decisions about purchasing in a way that destabilizes the economy.

Another advantage of giving the Fed a mandate to focus on price stability or, say, 2 percent inflation is that this would force it to pay attention to the long-run effects of its policies. With a goal of reducing unemployment the Fed has to focus on current conditions: excess demand for labor next year does nothing to help those who are unemployed this year. In contrast, focusing on the inflation rate or the price level is a longer-run goal; if the inflation rate is

---

[4] The Fed could also concentrate on stabilizing the exchange rate, but that is generally not considered an important enough goal.

[5] There is some, though hardly conclusive, evidence that over the long run a higher or more variable inflation rate raises unemployment.

[6] A policy of keeping the price level stable differs from a policy of holding down the inflation rate. Suppose the Fed aims at price stability, but all the same the price level rises in some years by, say, 2 percent. To keep the price level stable, the Fed would then have to engineer a 2 percent price decline in subsequent years. In contrast, if it aims at keeping the inflation rate stable, it would not have to offset any misses that had occurred in previous years.

above average this year and below average next year, creditors who will be repaid at the end of next year are not much worse off than if the inflation rate had been average in both years.

Many of the Fed's critics argue that the Fed pays too little attention to the long-run effects of its policies. They attribute this shortsightedness to its goal of keeping unemployment low, as well as to its attempts to do too many things. Thus Lawrence Roos, a former president of the St. Louis Federal Reserve Bank, wrote:

> Never once in my participation in meetings of the Federal Open Market Committee (FOMC) do I recall any discussion of long-range goals of economic growth or desired price levels. It was like trying to construct a house without agreeing upon an architectural design. Instead of seeking a few achievable goals, the Federal Reserve is supposed to solve all sorts of problems, including inflation, unemployment, lagging real output growth, high interest rates, balance of payments disequilibrium, volatile exchange rates, depressed stock prices, a sagging housing industry, and a world debt crisis. Such diverse goals represent a "wish list" designed for achieving utopian objectives; those who would have the Fed seek them pay no attention either to their consistency or to what monetary policy is capable of achieving. . . . This kind of thinking hampers the workings of the FOMC. . . . I recall no consensus on long-range goals, nor do I recall serious efforts to set policy on other than the shortest time horizons.[7]

If the Fed had a single goal, it would be more feasible than it is now to evaluate the Fed by seeing how closely it attains this goal. Congress could then punish it if it performed badly. At present, when it is trying to do a large number of different things, some of which may not be consistent with others, there is no bottom line, and neither Congress, the public, nor for that matter the Fed itself can readily tell how well it is functioning.

The Case against a Single Goal

Those who oppose giving the Fed the price level or the inflation rate as a single goal can marshal several arguments. One is that the Fed is not as powerless against the scourge of unemployment as those who just want a price-level goal claim. To be sure, the Fed cannot force the unemployment rate to be below the NAIRU for long, but it can counter temporary increases in the unemployment rate. Suppose that during a recession the unemployment rate rises to, say, 9 percent while the NAIRU is only 6 percent. If the Fed adopts an expansionary policy that brings the unemployment rate down to the NAIRU, this will not set off an ever-accelerating inflation. To be sure, those who oppose such a policy can argue that the NAIRU is an average rate over several years, so that a high unemployment rate this year helps to curb wage demands next year, as well as this year. Hence, if the Fed lowers unemployment this year, it will have to accept a higher unemployment rate next year. But the relationship need not be, and probably is not, linear; an additional 1 percent of unemployment in a recession year is not likely to curb wage demands as much as an

---

[7] Lawrence Roos, "Inherent Conflicts of U.S. Monetary Policymaking," *Cato Journal,* 5 (Winter 1986), 772–73.

unemployment rate 1 percent higher during a boom year. This suggests that to achieve the lowest unemployment rate compatible with curbing inflation, the Fed should keep unemployment at a stable level by putting more expansionary policies into effect at times when unemployment becomes unusually high. It would also reduce the previously discussed danger (see page 348) that high unemployment in one year will raise the NAIRU in subsequent years.

Moreover, if the Fed targets just the price level or the inflation rate, then, should a major supply shock occur, it will have to adopt a highly restrictive policy. Congress will have required it to create enough unemployment that the price increases in the industries subject to the supply shock are balanced by price decreases in other industries. That might require widespread nominal wage cuts and that, in turn, would require substantial unemployment.

Furthermore, if the Fed were to focus only on the inflation rate or the price level, it would have to relinquish not just its goal of keeping unemployment down, but other desirable goals as well. It would not pay enough attention to counteracting disequilibrium in the foreign-exchange market or to various special problems that arise from time to time. As a concrete example, consider the situation in the early 1980s. Wasn't the Fed justified in paying attention to the effect of its policies on interest rates and hence on the burden of LDC debt? Should it have ignored completely the possibility that sharply rising interest rates would induce some LDC debtors to default formally, and thus cause some of our major banks to fail?

More generally, one might argue that since conditions change from time to time in unanticipated ways, the Fed needs flexibility to do what is required in specific, unforeseeable circumstances and, therefore, should not have its hands tied by focusing exclusively on inflation. Given our limited ability to anticipate what will happen, it is both presumptuous and unwise to tie the Fed down to a particular policy that may look correct now, but may prove highly inappropriate in a few years.

Clearly, reasonable cases can be made on both sides of the issue. Whether one favors or opposes tying the Fed down to a single goal depends in large part on whether one believes that the Fed can be trusted to act correctly. This is an issue we will discuss in Chapter 26.

WHAT DOES THE FED DO?

What does the Fed actually do? How much importance does it attach to each of its goals? Unfortunately, this is difficult to determine. The Fed does not issue statements revealing the trade-offs it makes between various goals, nor does it tell us which goal it considers the most important.[8] Instead, it tends to deemphasize the short-run conflict between its goals and sometimes suggests that the achievement of any one goal is necessary in order to attain another. Such an unwillingness to reveal the hard choices it makes is not surprising. If

[8] Some economists have tried to explain the Fed's behavior by a regression equation in which the dependent variable is some measure of the Fed's actions, such as the growth rate of the base, and the independent variables are factors like the unemployment rate, the inflation rate, and the balance of payments. But many of the results thus obtained are sensitive to some more or less arbitrary details of the procedures that were used and hence are not compelling.

the Fed were to say that it is relinquishing one goal for the sake of the others, the proponents of the first goal would react angrily and might join a coalition that would trim the Fed's independence. But the reluctance to face conflict among goals is probably more than just a matter of political expedience. A governor who voted to adopt a restrictive policy, knowing that it would create substantial unemployment and, hence, much misery, would probably feel very uncomfortable about this decision. It is less disturbing for the governor to think that the restrictive policy is needed both to curb inflation and to prevent greater unemployment in the future.

The Fed's reluctance to spell out its goals also helps the Fed to maintain a good reputation. If accused of failing to attain one goal, the Fed can frequently point to another goal that, perhaps for reasons having little to do with monetary policy, has been attained.

The problem of determining the Fed's trade-offs between goals is complicated not only by its reluctance to reveal them, but also by the fact that its trade-offs probably vary from time to time. Given the great power and influence of the chairman of the Board of Governors, goals may change when a new chairman takes over. In addition, the Fed tends to accept the President's goals, and in general it is influenced by changing political attitudes. In the late 1970s, for instance, the occurrence of double-digit inflation eventually generated a strong constituency for curbing inflation. This caused—or permitted— the Fed to take a more restrictive stance. On the whole it *seems* that in the 1950s the Fed was relatively more concerned with price stability and that in the early and middle 1970s it placed more emphasis on unemployment. In the 1980s it focused again on curbing inflation, but less so than it had done in the 1950s.

In the early 1990s, the Fed said that it was aiming at price stability as a long-term goal, defining this as an inflation rate so low that in formulating their plans people would not pay much attention to inflation. More specifically, it defined its goal as an annual increase in the consumer price index of no more than ½ to 1½ percent. This goal should be interpreted cautiously. It does not mean that the Fed was willing to accept the substantial increase in unemployment required to bring the inflation rate down to 1½ percent or less in the near future. The Fed was clearly not willing to do that. At the same time, the announced policy was probably not just sanctimonious verbiage. It is best interpreted as an intention of constraining aggregate expenditures sufficiently over the *long run* to bring the inflation rate down eventually to the planned level. For the next few years the Fed is probably willing to settle for an inflation rate of perhaps 2 ½ or 3 percent.

Coordination of Monetary and Fiscal Policies

The goals of monetary and fiscal policies overlap since both are macroeconomic stabilization tools. This raises the question of whether (assuming that Ricardian equivalence does not hold) one can use fiscal policy in conjunction with monetary policy or whether, on the contrary, fiscal policy interferes with monetary policy.

An obvious way in which fiscal policy can support monetary policy is by taking over part of the general stabilization task, so that monetary policy can be used in a more moderate manner. If taxes are raised or expenditures are cut when aggregate expenditures are excessive, then the severity of the restrictive monetary policy required to prevent unacceptable inflation is reduced.

Can monetary and fiscal policies be made to share the burden in a way that uses the comparative advantages of each? One idea is to make use of a possible difference in their timing. Unless there is widespread agreement in Congress, changing taxes and government expenditures takes a long time. On the other hand, the Fed can change monetary policy rapidly. However, what matters is not just how long it takes to change policy, but also how long it takes for the change in policy to have its main effect on income. When one takes account of this lag, it is not obvious that monetary policy takes effect more quickly than fiscal policy.

But, on the whole, the idea of employing fiscal and monetary policies together founders on the fact that government policies of taxation and expenditure are usually not employed as countercyclical tools. Rather, government expenditures go up when there is a perceived need for additional government services. Taxes are raised primarily because government expenditures are going up or are cut because the public is fed up with high taxes. Countercyclical considerations play only a very limited role in fiscal policy.

The Government Budget Constraint

Fiscal and monetary policies are inevitably related. The government, like everyone else, has budgetary constraints. The Treasury must finance its expenditures either from its revenues or by borrowing from someone. But the government, unlike other sectors of the economy, has an apparent "out." It can borrow from itself, that is, from the Fed. As the Treasury sells securities to the public, the Fed can at the same time buy securities from the public, so that the public's holdings of government securities do not increase. In effect, the Fed lends to the Treasury. But this out has a nasty side to it. As the Fed buys government securities, it provides banks with additional reserves, so that the money stock increases. This process is called **monetizing the debt** and is, of course, inflationary.

Does the Fed monetize increases in the federal debt? It does so in an indirect way by stabilizing interest rates. As the Treasury sells more securities, interest rates tend to rise, and if the Fed tries to stabilize interest rates, it undertakes open-market purchases of government securities. This increases the money supply. There is also some (inconclusive) evidence that, apart from this indirect way via interest-rate stabilization, the Fed has also monetized part of the Treasury's security sales by increasing its open-market purchases when the Treasury has run a larger deficit.

But, regardless of whether the Fed does monetize deficits, it is obvious that, at least at those times when inflation is a serious problem, large deficits complicate the Fed's task. It is therefore not surprising that Federal Reserve chairmen like to lecture both Congress and the administration on the need for fiscal prudence. These lectures also have the advantage of giving the impression that the Fed is a staunch foe of inflation, even if it should, at the same time, be allowing the money stock to grow too fast.

SUMMARY

1 The Fed has several goals—high employment, price stability, economic growth, and exchange-rate stability. It is constrained by the need to avoid financial panics, a wish for interest-rate stability, and concern about the confidence of foreign investors.
2 Unemployment creates an obvious loss. Inflation creates relatively few problems *if* it is fully anticipated. But if it is not fully anticipated, then it distorts investment, has arbitrary effects on the distribution of income, and creates uncertainty and a feeling of loss of control.
3 In the short run there is potential conflict among goals, but the Fed tends to downplay this conflict and does not spell out its priorities.
4 Some economists have proposed that the Fed be given only a single goal—price stability. There are cogent arguments on both sides of this issue.
5 Fiscal policy and monetary policy share the same goals, but there are serious problems in coordinating them. Government deficits can be monetized, but the avoidance of large deficits would make the Fed's task easier.

KEY TERMS

goals of monetary policy
constraints on monetary policy

conflicts among goals
coordination of monetary and fiscal policies

QUESTIONS AND EXERCISES

*1 What are the goals of Federal Reserve policy? Either argue that one of them should not be treated as a serious goal, or argue that there is an additional goal that should be included.
2 Why does the Fed try to stabilize interest rates?
*3 Discuss: "In the long run there are no conflicts among the Fed's goals."
4 Describe the problems an inadequate fiscal policy can create for the Fed. Do you think fiscal policy is currently helping or hindering monetary policy?
5 Read through the current *Economic Report of the President* and prepare a statement of the trade-offs between various goals that are either explicit or implicit in it. Do you agree with these trade-offs?

FURTHER READING

AIYAGARI, S. RAO. "Deflating the Case for Zero Inflation," Federal Reserve Bank of Minneapolis, *Quarterly Review*, 14 (Summer 1990), 2–11. A good presentation of the case against a zero inflation goal.

BLACK, ROBERT. "The Fed's Mandate: Help or Hindrance?" Federal Reserve Bank of Richmond, *Economic Review*, 70 (July–August 1984), 3–7. A thoughtful discussion of the multiple-goals problem by a Fed Bank president.

BLINDER, ALAN. "Issues in the Coordination of Monetary and Fiscal Policies," Federal Reserve Bank of Kansas City, *Monetary Policy Issues in the 1980s* (1983), 3–34. An excellent response to much idle rhetoric.

BURNS, ARTHUR. *The Anguish of Central Banking.* Washington, D.C.: American Enterprise Institute, 1980. An excellent short discussion by a former Fed chairman.

FISHER, STANLEY. "The Benefits of Price Stability," Federal Reserve Bank of Kansas City, *Price Stability and Public Policy* (1984), 33–50. A good brief survey.

MAISEL, SHERMAN. *Managing the Dollar.* New York: Norton, 1973. Provides an excellent "feel" for the pressures under which the Fed operates.

RICHARDS, DANIEL. "What Inflation Policy Do American Voters Want and Do They Get It?" Federal Reserve Bank of Boston, *New England Economic Review* (September–October 1993), 33–44. An interesting discussion of the trade-offs between inflation and unemployment, including an analysis of how the public's trade-offs differ from the policy makers' trade-offs.

The Tools of Monetary Policy

After you have read this chapter, you will be able to:

- Discuss how the Fed generates changes in the money supply and in interest rates.
- Explain how the Fed undertakes open-market operations.
- Appreciate why open-market operations are the Fed's dominant tool for monetary policy.
- Understand the effect of changes in the discount rate and in reserve requirements.

The Fed does not issue edicts compelling firms and households to raise or lower aggregate expenditures. Instead, it changes bank reserves and interest rates, in an attempt to induce the public to change its expenditures. In this chapter we take up the first step in this process, the tools that the Fed uses to change bank reserves, the money supply, and interest rates.

OPEN-MARKET OPERATIONS

Open-market operations are by far the most important tool of monetary policy. The Fed's organization for open-market operations has already been discussed in Chapter 11. The FOMC sends a Directive to the account manager (or "Desk") at the New York Federal Reserve Bank who directs the actual purchases and sales of securities. He or she deals not with the general public, but with a small number of security dealers; some of them banks, and others, specialized wholesalers of government securities. The Desk is in continual contact with them, asking them for bids or offers on securities. It therefore knows the prices and interest rates on these securities at all times and has good information on conditions in the money market, what the Fed calls "the feel of the market." The Fed does not force anyone to buy or sell securities; it buys or sells at the prices the dealers quote to it. Some open-market operations are carried out not with securities dealers, but with foreign governments that keep deposits at the Fed.

The Fed is legally authorized to conduct open-market operations in U.S. Treasury securities, securities of government agencies such as GNMA (Ginnie Mae), certain state and local government securities, banker's acceptances, and so on. But in practice the great bulk of open-market operations is in short-term Treasury securities.

Most open-market operations are not really sales or purchases in the usual sense of those words. The great bulk of "purchases" are done under repurchase agreements (**repos**), that is, under agreements by which the sellers agree to buy the securities back again at fixed prices at certain dates. Similarly, most of the Fed's security sales are done under so-called **reverse repos**, more formally known as *matched sale-purchase transactions,* in which the Fed pledges to buy these securities back at fixed prices at particular times. The Fed uses such repos and reverse repos in part because most open-market purchases or sales are intended to affect reserves for only a very short time. By using repos and reverse repos, the Fed lowers transactions costs because it undertakes only one transaction instead of two, such as first a purchase and then a sale.

Most open-market operations are *defensive* rather than *dynamic.* Dynamic operations are those in which the Fed wants to change the volume of reserves. In contrast, the Fed undertakes defensive operations when it wants to keep reserves constant. To do this, it has to undertake open-market operations to offset the impact on reserves of the market factors (discussed in Chapter 14), such as changes in float or currency holdings.

Fluctuations in these market factors generate very large—but temporary—changes in reserves. To stabilize the money market and the supply of money, the Fed tries to offset these changes, except insofar as they happen to go in the direction and in the amount the Fed wants. To do this, the Fed expends considerable effort predicting the probable behavior of various market factors. The behavior of the federal-funds rate is an important indicator for the Fed: when reserves are in short supply, the funds rate rises. Hence, something that frequently triggers open-market operations is changes in the federal-funds rate as market factors supply or withdraw reserves. Such defensive operations account for the great bulk of open-market operations.

The effect of open-market operations on bank reserves has already been demonstrated in Chapter 14 by means of T accounts (see pages 249–50). In addition, open-market operations also affect the Treasury-bill rate and other interest rates. When the Fed buys Treasury bills, the price of Treasury bills goes up, so that the Treasury-bill rate falls. Then interest rates fall further, as banks or other security dealers use the reserves they received from the Fed in exchange for the Treasury bills to buy securities from others. The Fed can therefore use open-market operations to set the Treasury-bill rate at the level it wants; it simply buys or sells Treasury bills until the price of Treasury bills, and hence the Treasury-bill rate, is right. Changes in the yield of Treasury bills, in turn, affect other interest rates, particularly short-term rates.

How Open-Market Operations Are Used

Suppose the Fed wants to achieve a certain level of reserves. Staff economists at the Board of Governors and at the New York Fed make forecasts of the changes in reserves that market factors will generate on their own. They then take the difference between this predicted level and the desired level as their target for open-market operations and buy or sell securities accordingly. But usually the Fed focuses on the federal-funds rate: it stands ready to buy securities whenever the funds rate rises above the target range and to sell securities whenever it falls below the target range. For that the Fed does not have to forecast how market factors will change reserves; all it has to do is to call dealers to find out what the funds rate is.

THE DISCOUNT MECHANISM

The second tool of monetary policy comes from the **discount mechanism.** This mechanism is a device by which institutions that are required to keep reserves with the Fed can borrow from it.[1] It serves several functions. It is one way in which the Fed fulfills its lender-of-last-resort function, since any bank that is short of reserves can borrow from the Fed. If many depository institutions are short of liquidity, then the discount mechanism has to be supplemented by extensive open-market purchases, but even then the discount mechanism is useful in channeling funds to those institutions that are particularly vulnerable. If it should become necessary during a financial crisis, the Fed could make loans to securities firms to prevent a collapse of security prices, too.

Borrowing can take the form of *adjustment credit* or *extended credit*. The former, which accounts for the bulk of the borrowing, can be done fairly automatically, often over the telephone. It is intended to tide depository institutions over until they can get other funds when they face a sudden liquidity drain, due, for example, to a large deposit loss or a rapid upsurge in loan demand. It is short-term credit only—in fact the largest banks are supposed to repay the next business day. However, small banks that have a substantial seasonal pattern in their deposits or lending activities, such as banks in ski resort areas can borrow longer term for these seasonal needs.

Extended credit is available under two circumstances. One is if a depository institution faces special difficulties, for example, an extended deposit drain. The other situation is one in which a large group of depository institutions experiences liquidity strains. Institutions obtaining extended credit have to explain the need in some detail and submit an acceptable plan for restoring their liquidity.

Since, as Figure 23.1 shows, depository institutions can usually borrow from the Fed at less than prevailing market rates, it is necessary to limit their borrowing. They are not supposed to borrow for the sake of reinvesting the funds they have borrowed at a profit, but should borrow only in case of need.

---

[1] Banks normally borrow from the Fed by discounting their own promissory notes (using government securities as collateral), but they can, under certain conditions, instead discount a second time certain promissory notes they have discounted for their customers.

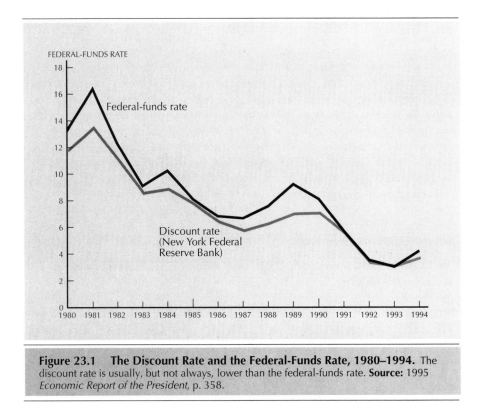

Figure 23.1   The Discount Rate and the Federal-Funds Rate, 1980–1994. The discount rate is usually, but not always, lower than the federal-funds rate. **Source:** 1995 *Economic Report of the President,* p. 358.

The Fed tries to enforce this provision by scrutinizing the activities of borrowing institutions. But the prohibition against borrowing for profit is vague and hard to enforce.

This does not mean, however, that all banks try to take advantage of the federal-funds rate–discount rate gap. Some may hold off borrowing because they know that if they borrow now, the Fed may make it more difficult for them to borrow at a later time, a time when their need to borrow may be greater or the federal-funds rate higher than it is now. Moreover, the Fed puts pressure on banks that borrow too often or too much, such as demanding an explanation from the bank's board of directors.

When banks do borrow they are under pressure to repay. The Fed believes that when a borrowing bank obtains additional funds its first priority should be to repay its loan from the Fed and not to buy securities or make more loans. Whether banks actually behave this way is disputed. It may depend on how much—and for how long—they have borrowed.

Moreover, one should distinguish between the behavior of individual banks and that of the whole banking system. Banks that have made extensive use of the discount privilege in the past may be under strong pressure to repay. But as they do so and borrow on the federal-funds market instead, the funds rate rises, which then sends other banks that have not borrowed much in the past to the Fed's discount window. Hence, even if the Fed effectively controls borrowing by individual banks, it may exercise less effective control over the total volume of borrowing.

THE DISCOUNT RATE

The Fed can vary the interest rate it charges borrowing institutions.[2] Thus it can induce banks and thrift institutions to increase or to reduce their borrowing and can change reserves in this way. But the volume of reserves involved is usually small compared to the change that results from open-market operations. All the same, the discount mechanism, or more specifically the discount rate, provides the Fed not just with a way of easing a financial crisis, but also with a way of changing reserves at other, more normal times.

In relating the discount rate to the level of borrowing, there is a serious complication. The inducement to borrow can, and does, vary even if the Fed keeps the discount rate unchanged. If the federal-funds rate rises, say, from 8¼ percent to 8½ percent and the discount rate stays put at 8 percent, then banks and thrift institutions have a greater incentive to borrow. Thus discount rate policy can become more expansionary without the discount rate itself changing. To keep its discount policy constant, the Fed would have to change the discount rate frequently. But this would create a problem. Many people interpret a rise in the discount rate as a restrictive policy, even if it is merely a response to rising interest rates on the open market. They argue that if the Fed raises the discount rate, it validates the prior rise in interest rates, by indicating that it expects interest rates to stay high. And a restrictive monetary policy has many critics. Hence, the Fed is sometimes under considerable political pressure not to raise the discount rate. There have been occasions when a President has criticized the Fed for raising the discount rate and Congress has held hearings on the matter.

Reductions in the discount rate have less political fallout, though the market may interpret a cut in the discount rate as an indication of a general decline in interest rates. Since interest rates are falling in the United States relative to interest rates in other countries, investors have an incentive to shift out of U.S. securities into foreign securities. To do so, they sell dollars on the foreign-exchange market and buy foreign currencies. As a result the value of the dollar relative to other currencies falls. This helps export industries whose goods are now cheaper for foreign buyers. It also helps U.S. industries that compete with imports by making imports more expensive to buy. But by raising the prices of imports, it also raises the inflation rate. Beyond this, the Fed is reluctant to lower the discount rate because it knows the criticism that will follow if it has to raise it again later on. Thus, the Fed has in actuality only limited freedom to change the discount rate.

If the discount rate is so low relative to the federal-funds rate that borrowing increases, the Fed can offset the resulting increase in reserves by additional open-market sales. Hence, the main effect of a discount rate that is too

---

[2] Although we always speak of *the* discount rate, there are actually several rates depending on the collateral and the maturity and size of the loan offered. In addition, the Fed charges a higher rate for unusually long-term loans or for unusually large loans due to special circumstances, such as a computer breakdown.

low relative to the federal-funds rate is that depository institutions make a profit at the Fed's expense by borrowing from it and lending at a higher rate.

The Announcement Effect

In addition to its effect on reserves, and hence on the money stock and interest rates, a change in the discount rate also affects people's expectations. Not only the financial community, but also the general public read about it in the newspapers. Here is an example: in November 1978, when President Carter wanted to stop the fall of the dollar on the foreign-exchange market by indicating to the world that the United States was ready to adopt a firm anti-inflation policy, one of the steps he took was to announce that he had asked the Fed to raise the discount rate.

When the Fed raises the discount rate, the public *may* interpret this as a sign that the Fed is acting to curb excessive expansion and feel that there is now less reason to fear inflation. It may therefore reduce inflationary activities, such as buying ahead to beat price increases or demanding higher wages to offset expected inflation. In contrast, when the Fed cuts the discount rate, people may read this as a sign that the Fed is now taking action to moderate a downturn. However, the public *may* also react in just the opposite way and treat a rise in the discount rate as a sign that the Fed shares its belief that inflation is becoming a more serious problem.

What is also troublesome for the Fed is that the public may take the change in the discount rate as an indication of the Fed's predictions and policy stance, even in those cases where the Fed changes the discount rate only because market rates have changed and it wants to keep the incentives to borrow constant. It is far from clear that, on the whole, the announcement effect of a change in the discount rate is helpful. It may well do more harm than good. Hence, some economists believe that the Fed should tie the discount rate to some open-market rate—say, ¼ percent more than last week's federal-funds rate. This would eliminate the announcement effect of discount rate changes entirely.

The change in the discount rate is not the only tool of monetary policy that has an announcement effect. Changes in reserve requirements are also reported in newspapers. Moreover, the financial and business specialists who make the important investment decisions are sophisticated enough to know how to interpret open-market operations and changes in the federal-funds rate. Large financial institutions employ economists—many of them former Fed economists—to predict what the Fed will do before the Fed does it or announces it. "Fed watching" has become an important industry.

RESERVE-REQUIREMENT CHANGES

Congress has given the Fed the power to vary reserve requirements within broad limits. For transactions accounts it can set them anywhere within a range of 8 to 18 percent, and for nonpersonal time deposits (that is, time deposits not held by households) it can set them anywhere between 0 and 13 percent.[3] Raising the reserve requirements affects the money stock in two ways. First, previously excess reserves are now transformed into required reserves and are therefore no longer available for deposit expansion. Second, the reserve ratio is one of the components of the denominator in the money multiplier. Hence, a rise in the reserve ratio lowers the money multiplier and thus lowers the deposit expansion that banks can undertake on the basis of their remaining excess reserves. Given the wide range within which the Fed can change reserve requirements, it has a *potentially* powerful tool here. But, despite its strength, the Fed does not use this tool often, since open-market operations are so much more efficient.

The Reserve Requirement and Monetary Policy

An older view of the reserve requirement treated it as the fulcrum of monetary policy. Suppose the Fed sells securities. Bank reserves then fall below the required level. At that point the reserve requirement forces the banking system (a term we will use here to include other depository institutions with checkable deposits) to sell securities, call in loans, or borrow from the Fed. If it were not for reserve requirements, this would not happen. Banks would simply run down the reserves they hold, and the open-market sales would be ineffective.

That view is naive. Even without a legally required reserve ratio, banks would hold a certain ratio of reserves to deposits to take care of their day-to-day needs for currency and for clearing balances, and they would be reluctant to let their reserves fall below (or rise much above) that level. Hence, banks would contract when open-market operations reduced their reserves, even if there were no legal reserve requirement.

A somewhat more sophisticated argument for having a reserve requirement is that if the banks could decide on their own what reserves to hold, the Fed would not know precisely the reserve ratio that banks will want to hold, and hence could not know how much open-market operation to undertake to change the money supply by a given amount. But although that argument may have had some validity at one time, it is no longer persuasive for three reasons. First, many banks are not constrained by the reserve requirement since their optimal holdings of currency and clearing balances exceed the reserve requirement. For these banks the reserve requirement is irrelevant and has essentially no effect on their reserve holdings. Therefore, the reserve requirement does not help the Fed a lot in deciding by how much the money supply will increase per dollar of additional reserves. Second, the main measure of the money supply that the Fed now looks at is *M-2,* and less than a quarter of *M-2* consists of the transactions accounts that currently have a reserve requirement. Third, nowadays the Fed pays more attention to interest rates than to the money sup-

---

[3] But the affirmative vote of no fewer than five of the seven governors is required to raise the reserve requirement above 14 percent for transactions accounts and above 9 percent for time deposits. In exceptional circumstances the Fed may set reserve requirements outside the above ranges for 180 days.

ply. And when it undertakes open-market operations to change the federal-funds rate, it can tell how much to buy or sell simply by looking at the funds rate prevailing in the market. It does not have to estimate the money multiplier, and therefore does not have to know what reserve ratio the banks will keep.

So, what function does the reserve requirement fulfill? One function is to serve as a tax on those banks that would keep lower deposits with the Fed, were it not for the reserve requirement. By forcing them to keep higher deposits, which earn no interest, the Fed forces them, in effect, to make an interest-free loan to the government. Second, it provides the Fed with an additional tool, albeit a clumsy and rarely used one.

The Relative Importance of These Tools

Open-market operations are by far a better tool than are changes in the discount rate. First, the Fed can buy or sell government securities to any extent it wants. Both the Fed and the public hold vast quantities of these securities, so that there is no practical limit to the magnitude of open-market operations. In contrast, it might not be feasible to vary the discount rate enough to change borrowing as much as the Fed would like. Open-market operations can also be carried out in very small steps, although in principle so could changes in the discount rate. But the problem is that when it changes the discount rate, particularly when the change is small, the Fed cannot know how much borrowing will change. In contrast, it can decide exactly how big a volume of open-market operations to undertake to make precise changes in reserves. Similarly, when it uses open-market operations, it knows exactly when the change in reserves will occur; with discount rate changes, it does not know precisely when the banks will change their borrowing. Moreover, banks might take some time to increase their borrowing, while open-market operations have an immediate effect on reserves.

If open-market operations have strong advantages over discount rate changes, they have even stronger advantages over reserve requirement changes. Banks would object vehemently if the Fed were to change reserve requirements continuously, because that would force them to continuously adjust their portfolios accordingly. If the reserve requirement were raised, banks without excess reserves would have to buy them on the federal-funds market at a time when many other banks were doing the same thing, while if the reserve requirement were cut, banks would have to scurry to find uses for their excess reserves. Moreover, as discussed in Chapter 7, for some banks the reserve requirement is not binding, because the currency they hold to take care of their business is more than they need to satisfy the reserve requirement. Such banks will not respond at all to changes in the reserve requirement.

For these reasons one can think of open-market operations as *the* tool of monetary policy, and of discount rate changes and reserve requirement changes as relatively minor, supplementary tools. Not very much would be lost if these two tools were abolished.

SELECTIVE CONTROLS

The tools discussed so far operate on aggregate expenditures by changing reserves and interest rates, and so affect the whole economy. In contrast, *selective controls* have their initial impact on specific markets that some economists think are relatively insulated from the effects of overall monetary policy, so that they have to be controlled by tools that focus specifically on them.

Stock Market Credit

The Fed controls the use of credit to purchase stocks listed on stock markets, as well as certain unlisted stocks. It has set down payments, or *margins,* for stock purchases; that is, it limits the percentage of the purchase price that may be borrowed. The Fed can raise the margin requirement to 100 percent to control a speculative stock market boom. The reason the Fed was given this power in 1934 can be seen by looking at the situation in the years 1927 through 1929. Then the price level was stable or falling gently, but there was a speculative boom on the stock market. The Fed was in a quandary. It had no power to affect the stock market directly. By raising the discount rate or by open-market operations, it could have made credit generally less available and, hence, could have limited the purchase of stocks on credit. But with stock prices rising rapidly, it would probably have taken a very substantial boost in interest rates to have a significant effect on stock market borrowing. This would have been too restrictive for the rest of the economy. If the Fed had had margin regulations available at that time, it could have limited stock market credit without such a restrictive effect on the rest of the economy.

Whether margin requirements actually reduce the volatility of stock prices in more normal situations is a disputed issue. In any case, margin requirements have not been used as an important policy tool. This is because in recent years we have not been confronted with a wild stock market boom driven by excessive speculation. The last time the margin requirement was changed was in 1974, when it was set at 50 percent. In any case, in recent years the efficacy of margin controls has been undermined by the development of futures markets that allow speculators to operate with very small down payments regardless of the margin that the Fed sets.

MORAL SUASION

Another tool is **moral suasion.** This simply means that the Fed *uses its power of persuasion to get banks, or the financial community in general, to behave differently.* Since the interests of the Fed frequently coincide with the long-run self-interest of financial institutions, this form of control may *in certain cases* be more effective than appears at first. To be sure, sometimes banks may feel that the stress is more on the "suasion" than on the "moral." For example, in 1965 when the Fed laid down guidelines to limit foreign lending, some banks, at least according to some reports, were afraid that if they ignored the guidelines, they might find it more difficult to borrow from the Fed. Admittedly, these fears may have been groundless; for an outsider that is hard to say. But in 1966 the Fed openly informed banks that discounting would be easier for banks that curbed their business loans and made more mortgage loans. The Fed's control over bank holding company activities and its power to prohibit proposed mergers have given it another potential threat over recalcitrant banks.[4] Some people think that moral suasion gives the Fed a powerful weapon, despite its questionable legal status.

The Fed exercises moral suasion not just over banks, but also over other financial institutions. It interprets its regulatory task not just as seeing that banks do not take too many risks, but also as preventing massive financial failures that could threaten to engulf banks or create a financial panic. Moral suasion is the only tool that the Fed can use for this task because Congress has not given it any more-substantive power.

Let us look at two examples. On May 17, 1982, a relatively small government securities dealer, Drysdale Government Securities Inc., failed. It had borrowed massively, both directly from banks and indirectly through loans arranged by Chase Manhattan Bank, one of the country's largest banks. When Drysdale failed, financial markets became scared. Those who had lent to it, through Chase Manhattan, argued that Chase should assume the losses; in fact, many of them had thought that they were lending to Chase itself, not to Drysdale directly. At first Chase had other ideas. But then Chairman Volcker had a heart-to-heart talk with Chase Manhattan, and it changed its mind and assumed $160 million of the losses. In addition, to prevent technical problems about deliveries of securities, the New York Fed lent several billion of its own securities to security dealers and let the banks know it would treat requests for discounts sympathetically. A potential panic was avoided.

In 1979 the Hunt brothers, a group of wealthy Texas oilmen, had tried to corner the silver market, borrowing massively from banks in the process. Their attempt failed, and in March 1980 silver prices collapsed dramatically. One of the largest brokerage firms, Bache, had lent more than $200 million to the Hunts and now it, too, faced bankruptcy. There was fear that the losses on loans to the Hunts could also sink some large banks. Additional bank loans would keep the situation from unraveling. But, as we will discuss in Chapter 27, the Fed had just imposed rules limiting bank loans, and loans to bail out the Hunts would have been counter to these rules. Chairman Volcker, who kept in close touch with the negotiations between the Hunts and their creditors, granted an exception.

Are these things that a central bank should do, or do they represent excessive interference with market processes? Where should one draw the line? Economists with different political views tend to answer this question differently.

---

[4] See Edward Kane, "The Central Bank as Big Brother," *Journal of Money, Credit and Banking,* 5 (November 1973), 979–81.

PUBLICITY AND ADVICE

The Fed has many ways of making its opinions known to the general public. The chairman of the Board of Governors frequently testifies before congressional committees, and journalists pay attention to press releases by the Fed and to the chairman's speeches. The directors and the presidents of the Federal Reserve Banks have many business contacts. Given the high regard in which the business community and its journalists hold the Fed, it has no difficulty in getting its views across to the general public. In these ways it can affect business expectations and, hence, actions. In addition, as discussed in Chapter 11, the Fed also acts as an informal economic adviser to the administration and Congress, so that its influence is not just confined to monetary policy.

SUMMARY

1 Open-market operations are the dominant tool of monetary policy. This is a strong tool that can, however, also be used in very small increments, frequently, and with predictable effects on reserves. The great bulk of open-market operations are defensive rather than dynamic.
2 Depository institutions that are required to keep reserves with the Fed can borrow from it. Borrowing is supposed to be for need rather than profit. But this rule is difficult to enforce.
3 The Fed can vary the discount rate to influence the volume of borrowing. Borrowing responds to the gap between the federal-funds rate and the discount rate; this means that, to keep borrowing stable, the Fed would have to change the discount rate frequently. But this creates political problems. Discount rate changes, as well as the use of other tools of monetary policy, have an announcement effect.
4 The ability to change reserve requirements gives the Fed an additional tool. However, the Fed does not normally use this tool.
5 The Fed also has selective controls over stock market credit.
6 Moral suasion, publicity, and advice round out the tools the Fed has available.

KEY TERMS

open-market operations	extended credit
repos	discount rate
reverse repos	announcement effect
adjustment credit	selective controls
discount mechanism	

QUESTIONS AND EXERCISES

1 Write an essay describing the use the Federal Reserve has made of its various tools in the last three years. (Information on this is available in the Federal Reserve's *Annual Reports*.)
*2 Why are open-market operations the most important tool of Fed policy?
*3 Borrowing from the Fed is supposed to be for need rather than for profit. How is it, then, that the volume of borrowing is correlated with the gap between the federal-funds rate and the discount rate?
4 Describe the Fed's selective controls.

FURTHER READING

FEDERAL RESERVE BANK OF NEW YORK (Paul Meek). *Open Market Operations.* New York, 1969. A lively and authoritative description.

FRIEDMAN, MILTON. *A Program for Monetary Stability.* New York: Fordham University Press, 1960. Chapter 2 is a stimulating discussion of reforms.

MEEK, PAUL. *U.S. Monetary Policy and Financial Markets.* New York: Federal Reserve Bank of New York, 1982. A highly informative and authoritative statement by a senior Fed official.

MELTON, WILLIAM. *Inside the Fed.* Homewood, Ill.: Dow Jones-Irwin, 1985. Chapters 7 and 8 give an excellent detailed discussion of open-market operations.

MEULENDYKE, ANN MARIE. *U.S. Monetary Policy and Financial Markets.* New York: Federal Reserve Bank of New York, n.d. Chapter 7 offers an authoritative and detailed description of open-market operations.

ROTH, HOWARD, and DIANE SEIBERT. "The Effects of Alternative Discount Rate Mechanisms on Monetary Control," Federal Reserve Bank of Kansas City, *Economic Review,* (March 1983), 16–29. An excellent discussion of the floating discount rate.

WEINER, STUART. "The Changing Role of Reserve Requirements in Monetary Policy," Federal Reserve Bank of Kansas City, *Economic Review,* 77 (Fourth Quarter 1992), 45–64. An excellent survey.

Targets and Instruments

After you have read this chapter, you will be able to:

- **Know what it means to say that the Fed is targeting GDP.**
- **Understand the debate about whether the Fed should use intermediate targets.**
- **Illustrate the relative advantages of money and interest rates as target variables.**
- **List the instruments the Fed can use to attain its targets and discuss the pros and cons of each.**

If you read Appendix A, you will be able to:

- **Understand more deeply the choice between the money stock and interest rates as a target for the Fed.**

BETWEEN TOOLS AND GOALS: TARGETS AND INSTRUMENTS

Chapter 22 presented the goals of monetary policy: high employment, low inflation, economic growth, and exchange-rate stability. The growth rate of nominal GDP, being the combination of the growth rates of real GDP and of inflation, encompasses the first three of these goals. (Given the Phillips curve, the growth rate of nominal GDP determines both the inflation rate and the growth rate of real income.) Moreover, the growth rate of nominal GDP has an important effect on the exchange rate. Hence, although strictly speaking the growth rate of nominal GDP is not itself directly one of the Fed's goals, we can, for convenience, think of the Fed as trying to attain a certain growth rate of nominal GDP, and treat it as if it were the Fed's goal.

Suppose now that the FOMC decides that the growth rate of GDP is too low. What should it do? The seemingly obvious answer—instruct the New York Fed to purchase securities—will not do. The New York Fed will want to know exactly how much to purchase or at what level to set the federal-funds rate. And that question raises a host of difficult issues, because the road from the Fed's tools to GDP is long and difficult to follow.

There would be no problem if (1) open-market operations had all their effects on GDP immediately and (2) the FOMC had completely accurate data on current GDP. In that case the Fed could just experiment. It could buy, say, $200 million of Treasury bills. If GDP rose too little, it could immediately buy more, and if it rose too much, it could sell some of the Treasury bills it had purchased. No harm done. Alternatively, suppose that open-market operations affect GDP only with a long lag but that the Fed can predict with complete accuracy both (1) the future course of GDP if it does not undertake any open-market operations and (2) the effect that each million dollars of open-market operations has on GDP. In that case, too, once the Fed has decided on the appropriate level of GDP, policy making would be a simple task requiring only a knowledge of elementary arithmetic.

But, alas, neither of these two sets of conditions holds. Open-market operations do take a long time to have their main effect, and the Fed can predict with great accuracy neither future GDP nor the effect of open-market operations on it. If the Fed's open-market operations are inappropriate either in their direction or in their magnitude, it can take the Fed a long time to discover this. In the meantime they may destabilize GDP.

How can this problem be resolved? Two approaches have been recommended. One is the **targets and instruments** approach developed by Karl Brunner and Allan Meltzer, and the other is so-called **GDP targeting**.

TARGETS AND INSTRUMENTS

In this approach the Fed interposes some **target variables** between its tools and its GDP goal. Such target variables are (or should be) closely connected to nominal GDP, so that by setting them at the appropriate levels, the Fed obtains its desired level of nominal GDP. This is analogous to setting a thermostat. Your goal is to have the furnace deliver heat in certain quantities. In principle you could manipulate the furnace directly. But it is much more convenient to set the thermostat. Take another example: suppose (indeed let us hope) that you decide to get an A in this course. You therefore plan to study for it a certain number of hours each week. The target you set yourself each week is to do that much studying, not because you value time spent studying as such, but because you figure that if you attain your studying target, you will achieve your goal of getting an A.

Now the connection between the setting of the thermostat and the temperature of the house need not be perfect: the thermostat may be inaccurate or may be situated in a draft. And, for better or for worse, the correlation between the time you spend studying and your grade is not perfect either. But still, the target helps you to attain your goal.

The FOMC's problem is more complicated for two reasons. First, there is not just a single potential target variable, such as the thermostat's setting, but several competing ones among which it can choose. Thus, Chapters 15 and 20 discussed the quantity theory, which claims that there is a close connection between the money supply and GDP, and so implies that the FOMC should target the money supply. But Chapters 15 to 18 also took up the income-expenditure approach, which asserts that the money supply is just one of several variables that one has to consider in predicting nominal GDP and that the interest rate is more closely connected to GDP than is the money supply. This implies that the interest rate and not the money supply is the appropriate target. Chapter 21 briefly discussed the theory that bank credit has a close relation to GDP. That brings us up to three variables competing for the honor of being the FOMC's target.

The second problem is that while you can set a thermostat precisely and can study a precise number of hours, the FOMC cannot attain its target variables precisely. Suppose, for example, that to achieve the GDP growth rate it wants, the FOMC needs to change the growth rate of *M-2*. The Fed's major tools comprise open-market operations, discount-rate changes, and changes in reserve requirements, not changes in *M-2*. It is the depository institutions, and not the Fed, that create the bulk of *M-2*. Hence, the FOMC has to use its tool of open-market operations, say, to set some variable, such as the base or the federal-funds rate, at a level that it thinks will induce the banks to supply a certain volume of deposits and the public to demand that volume of deposits. This amounts to using a second set of targets, such as the federal-funds rate, to attain the targets that are linked to the GDP goal.

Since it would be confusing to use the word *targets* both for the variables that are directly related to GDP and for those variables that are used to attain these targets, economists use the term **instruments** or **operating targets** for the secondary targets and keep the word *targets* for the variables that are directly related to GDP. We therefore have the following relation between the Fed's tools and its goals:

Tools → instruments → target variables → goals.

Here the arrows indicate only direction of influence and not complete control. Figure 24.1 shows the uncertain relation between the Fed's tools and GDP for one instrument (unborrowed reserves) and one target variable *(M-2)*. What makes it an uncertain relationship is that what ultimately happens to GDP depends on the market factors changing reserves, the factors changing the money multiplier, and the factors changing velocity. To be sure, the Fed can try to offset the effect of changes in these three factors, but it lacks the knowledge required to offset them completely. Thus, as we pointed out in Chapter 17, in the early 1980s when *M-1* velocity changed drastically, the FOMC was caught by surprise.

Criteria for Target Variables

There are four criteria a target variable should meet: **measurability, controllability, relatedness to GDP,** and **administrative and political feasibility.**

The measurability criterion raises two problems. First, accurate data must be available quickly. Unless the Fed can tell where it is relative to the target, it does not know what it has to do to attain this target. Suppose it wants *M-2* to grow at a 5 percent rate. If it does not know whether it is currently growing at a 3 percent rate or a 7 percent rate, it does not know what it should do. Sec-

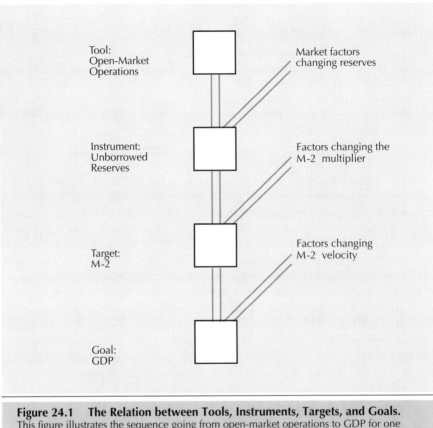

Figure 24.1   The Relation between Tools, Instruments, Targets, and Goals.
This figure illustrates the sequence going from open-market operations to GDP for one
particular combination of instruments and targets. As the factors listed on the right side of
the figure show, open-market operations are only one of many factors determining
unborrowed reserves, the money supply, and nominal income. Similar diagrams could be
drawn for other instruments, such as the federal-funds rate, and other targets, such as *M-1*
or the long-term interest rate.

ond, the Fed should know which specific measure of the target variable it
should use. Suppose it wants to target the money supply. Should it look at *M-1,
M-2,* or *M-3?*

The second criterion for choosing a target variable is controllability.
Unless the Fed has a reasonable chance of achieving, or at least approximating, its target, having the target does not do much good. For example, suppose that the Fed would use as its target changing business expectations. This
target is certainly related to its GDP goal, but there is not enough that the Fed
can do to affect expectations. Hence, the state of expectations is not a useful
target. Choosing unrealistic targets is not just unhelpful; it also makes for
sloppy policy; if a target is not achievable, there seems to be little purpose in
even trying very hard to reach it.

The third criterion, relatedness, is what using a target variable is all
about. The reason the Fed uses a target is precisely because it believes that

achieving the proper value for this target variable will result in attaining, or at least coming close to, its GDP goal. For example, suppose that the money stock had no effect on nominal income; why then should the Fed care whether it is growing at a 2 percent or a 20 percent rate?

The final criterion, administrative and political feasibility, relates to the extent to which the Fed can carry out its policy. We will discuss that later.

Let us now see how well the potential target variables meet the criteria. We will first discuss the choice between the money stock and the interest rate.

Applying the Criteria to Money and Interest Rates

Measurability. Both money and interest rates present serious measurement problems. As we pointed out in Chapter 12, the early estimates of the monetary growth rate contain significant errors. Interest rates have another problem. The nominal interest rates on certain instruments such as Treasury bills or AAA bonds (bonds issued by companies that are prime credit risks) are measured correctly, but some interest rates are not a good measure of the cost of borrowing, since they do not take into account the restrictions that banks impose when lending to firms. Credit rationing, too, is not something we can measure well, and that may blur the meaning of our interest-rate data. Suppose, for example, that the interest rate on bank loans is constant, but some previous borrowers are denied loans. In some sense, for these borrowers the interest rate on bank loans has become infinite. Last but not least, the key factor in a decision to invest is not the recorded nominal rate of interest, but the expected real after-tax rate.

Controllability. The Fed does not control *M-2* well, because most of *M-2* does not have reserve requirements against it (only the transactions-deposit component does) and *M-2* does not respond well to changes in the federal-funds rate, which the Fed can use in trying to control it. The Fed can set short-term interest rates but, as discussed in Chapter 5, that does not give it anything like precise control over the more important long-term rates. And even its control over short-term rates is constrained. One constraint is that if it sets short-term rates too low, the inflation rate accelerates, and hence it is eventually forced to raise the interest rate. Another limitation is that in setting the interest rate, it has to take into account that it will also affect international capital flows and hence the exchange rate of the dollar.

Relatedness. The third criterion for a target variable is its relatedness to the Fed's GDP goal. What is important here is not whether a change in the target variable has a large or only a small effect on GDP. If it has only a small effect, then in many cases the Fed can simply change the target variable by a larger amount than it otherwise would, and so get the effect on GDP that it wants. What is more important is how accurately the Fed can predict by how much GDP will change in response to a given change in the target variable, so that it knows by how much it should change that variable.

Does the money stock or the interest rate have a more predictable effect on GDP? This is a tough question, and an important one. It is important because if the money stock has a more predictable effect on nominal GDP than the interest rate does, then manipulating the money stock is, other things being equal, more efficient than setting a target for the interest rate. That is straightforward, but there is also a more subtle aspect to the question of whether the Fed should use an interest-rate or money-stock target.

Consider a situation the Fed is likely to face from time to time. Initially GDP and the interest rate are at levels the Fed considers appropriate, but then the interest rate rises unexpectedly. What should the Fed do? If it believes that the interest rate–GDP relation is more stable than the money-GDP relation (velocity), it should bring the interest rate back to its previous level by increasing the money supply. In contrast, if it believes that velocity is more stable, then it should keep the money supply constant (since it does not want GDP to change) and let the interest rate rise.

Which of these is the correct response depends on why the interest rate has risen. Suppose it has risen because velocity has changed: in terms of the Cambridge equation of Chapter 15, $M = kYP$, k (the public's desired ratio of its money holdings to its income) has increased. To prevent a decline in YP (nominal GDP), M has to rise correspondingly. If the Fed uses an interest-rate target, that will occur automatically since the Fed then supplies as much additional money as is needed to keep the interest rate stable at its previous level. (The interest rate will only be stable if the supply of money rises by as much as the demand for money.)

Now suppose that the rise in the interest rate is due to a rise in aggregate expenditures (YP). If the Fed uses a money-stock target, it keeps the money stock constant and lets the interest rate rise. This rise in the interest rate chokes off some of the rise in aggregate expenditures, and therefore keeps nominal GDP closer to the Fed's desired level. In contrast, if the Fed uses an interest-rate target and therefore prevents the interest rate from rising, it eliminates this automatic stabilizing effect of a rise in the interest rate, and nominal GDP rises further above the level that the Fed wants than it would have had the Fed used a money-stock target.

We therefore have the following rule: *If the unexpected change in the interest rate is due to a change in the Cambridge k, the Fed should use an interest-rate target. If it is due to a change in aggregate expenditures, it should use a money-stock target.* Appendix A at the end of this chapter develops this idea more thoroughly, using an IS-LM diagram.

This rule brings us face-to-face with a nasty problem. *When the interest rate changes, the Fed cannot be certain whether this is due to a change in the Cambridge k or to a change in aggregate expenditures.* All it observes is that the interest rate is, say, rising, and it has to decide whether to prevent this rise by increasing the money stock. Whatever decision it makes, under *one* set of circumstances it will be the wrong decision and will have destabilized the economy.

This is a horrible situation. It would not be so bad if the Fed could know whether unexpected changes in the interest rate are *usually* due to a change in the Cambridge k or to a change in expenditure incentives. It could then do that which would *usually* yield the right result. But the Fed does not really know which is the usual case and which is the unusual one.

Administrative and Political Problems. Before leaving the issue of targets, there is one more important, practical consideration. We have talked about the Fed choosing an interest-rate target consistent with its desired income level. But, as we discussed in Chapter 22, the Fed is also concerned with keeping interest rates stable. It is therefore continually tempted to keep the level of the interest rate unchanged, even though income is changing in an undesired way. On the other hand, with a money-stock target the Fed would quite clearly be required to let interest rates change. Hence, a money-stock target is less subject to abuse; it does not lend itself to the temptation of overemphasizing a day-to-day concern (interest-rate stability) at the expense of the longer-range, but much more important, task (stabilizing income). As the New York Federal Reserve Bank has put it:

> For the long run the function of monetary policy . . . is to stabilize the value of money. . . . In the short run it has powerful effects . . . on real growth and employment. Monetary policy neither can . . . nor should entirely ignore these important short-run concerns. But it does remain true that pressure to focus on short-run concerns at the expense of long-run goals tends to be a constant problem in monetary policymaking. *A basic function of the monetary targeting approach* [that is, the use of the monetary growth rate as a target] . . . *has been to keep the attention of the policymakers focused on the essential long-run price stability role of monetary policy—to put a little distance between monetary policy and the constant pressures to tinker for the sake of short-run objectives.*[1]

Moreover, the public opposes rising interest rates, but often favors the accompanying lower monetary growth rate because that seems to promise a lower inflation rate. Hence, the Fed can "sell" a restrictive policy much more easily to the public if it formulates it in terms of a certain monetary growth rate rather than a certain interest rate. To those who believe that a restrictive policy is needed, this appears as a substantial advantage of a money-stock target, though some may object on principle to such an attempt to manipulate the public.

All in all, the selection of a target variable involves controversies on three levels. First, there are narrow technical disagreements about the measurability of the variables and the extent to which they can be controlled. Second, there is a dispute about basic macroeconomic theory. Does the interest rate or the money stock have a more stable relation to GDP? Third, there is a dispute about what might almost be called the "sociology of central banking." If the Fed uses an interest-rate target, will it be able to resist the temptation to keep the interest rate stable rather than move it to the proper level?

Credit or Debt as Targets

Money and interest rates are not the only potential target variables. Another is the volume of outstanding credit. Put in the simplest terms, the reason for targeting money is that people use money to buy goods and services, so that their stock of money affects how much they buy. But, although ultimately we have to

---

[1] Federal Reserve Bank of New York, *1983 Annual Report,* p. 11, italics added.

pay by handing over money, we can also buy on credit. Hence credit, or its mirror image, debt, might predict income as well or even better than money does.

Other Possible Targets

Another potential target is the foreign-exchange rate. Suppose that the dollar falls on the foreign-exchange market. That the dollar is now worth fewer units of foreign currency means that the supply of dollars has risen relative to the demand for dollars. There may be several reasons why the supply of dollars outstripped the demand at the previous exchange rate. One plausible reason is that the Fed allowed the U.S. money supply to grow too much. Both Americans and foreigners would then expect the inflation rate to rise relatively faster in the United States than in foreign countries, so they would want to hold foreign currencies. Hence, the Fed can use the decline of the dollar on the foreign-exchange market as a signal that it should reduce the growth rate of the money supply until the exchange rate returns to its previous level.

The exchange rate has several advantages as a target. There is no measurement problem; reliable data are immediately available. And by changing the supply of dollars and short-term interest rates the Fed can affect the exchange rate.

However, so far we have assumed that the exchange rate has fallen because the supply of dollars has risen too much. In this case the exchange rate is sending the right signal. But the exchange rate may instead have fallen for some other reason. Suppose, for example, that yields on investments rise in other countries or fall in the United States. Investors then buy foreign currencies and sell dollars so that they can buy foreign securities. Hence, the dollar falls. Or suppose that Americans want to buy more imported goods. This too will reduce the exchange rate of the dollar. Similarly, changes in income in foreign countries can affect the exchange rate. So the exchange rate, like other targets, can send the wrong signal. However, an exchange-rate target has another advantage, unrelated to targeting monetary policy. By keeping exchange rates stable, the Fed would, as will be discussed in Part Five, facilitate international trade.

Another target that has been suggested is a commodity price index. Since the Fed is concerned with controlling inflation, a price index seems an obvious target. The problem is that by the time the CPI or the Producers Price Index starts to rise at a faster rate, demand has already been excessive for some time. However, the prices of commodities traded on organized exchanges, such as wheat, corn, rubber, or oil, react rapidly to inflationary pressures. Some economists, including Wayne Angell, a former Fed governor, have therefore argued that the Fed should try to stabilize an index of these commodity prices. The problem is that commodity prices are only a small proportion of all prices and are subject to special influences, such as a good wheat harvest or a change in OPEC policy. Hence, movements in a commodity price index can be unreliable indicators of how the CPI will behave.

An alternative target that former Governor Angell advocated is the slope of the yield curve. As explained in Chapter 16, when expectations of inflation rise, interest rates rise too. Hence, a rise in long-term interest rates relative to short-term rates may be due to the fact that the market expects a rise in inflation. Since economists believe that the market is usually right, one can argue that a steepening of the yield curve indicates that the inflation rate will increase. Well, it may indicate that, but it need not. The yield curve may steepen or flatten for other reasons too; the expected real rate of interest need not be constant. Hence, one can well argue that although sharp changes in the slope of the yield curve provide a signal that the Fed should take seriously, day-to-day changes in the yield curve are too noisy a signal of inflation expectations to serve as a target variable.

AN ALTERNATIVE APPROACH: MULTIPLE TARGETS

All the target variables we have looked at have serious drawbacks, so that relying on any single one of them is risky. Perhaps, rather than putting all its eggs in one basket, the Fed should target two or more variables at the same time. The chance that two target variables will both err in the same direction—say, both suggesting an inappropriate shift to an expansionary policy—is less, perhaps a good deal less, than the chance that any single target variable will do so. At least to some extent, the errors from two or more target variables will cancel out.

Some Mechanics of Using Two or More Target Variables

Given the fact that different target variables seem to require the Fed to act in different and mutually inconsistent ways, can the Fed actually target, in any meaningful sense, more than one variable at a time? The answer to this is yes and no. It can target two or more variables if it is willing to settle for a target range, perhaps quite a broad range, rather than for a precise target.

Suppose, for example, that the Fed sets a particular target for the money supply, say $900 billion. To make the public willing to hold exactly this amount of money requires a particular interest rate. If the Fed would prefer a different interest rate, that is unfortunate, but nothing can be done about it. To be sure, the Fed can bring about a different interest rate, but only by relinquishing its money-stock target and giving the public the money stock it wants to hold at the new interest rate. In the short run (until income—and hence the demand-for-money curve—has changed) the public's existing demand curve for money tells us the interest rate that corresponds to each particular quantity of money demanded. The Fed must settle for a combination of money stocks and interest rates that lies on this demand curve. A similar thing applies to bank credit. If the Fed selects a particular interest rate, the quantity of bank credit outstanding at that interest rate depends on the public's demand for bank credit and not on the Federal Reserve's wishes. A credit target also implies a specific money stock, and vice versa.

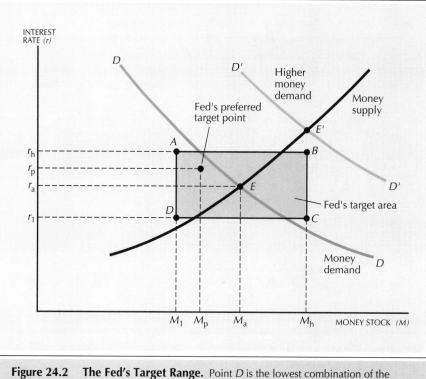

Figure 24.2 The Fed's Target Range. Point D is the lowest combination of the money stock (M_l) and the interest rate (r_l) acceptable to the Fed. Point B is the highest combination (M_h, r_h) acceptable to the Fed. The actual money stock is M_a, and the actual interest rate is r_a, an equilibrium point E. The Fed prefers a money stock of M_p and an interest rate of r_p, not quite the true equilibrium but still in the target area. If money demand were higher, equilibrium would be E', meaning that the Fed would have to either abandon its preferred money stock and interest rate or widen the target area.

Hence, the Fed must either use a single target variable or straddle by using a broad enough range for its targets, that within this range two or more targets are consistent. This is illustrated in Figure 24.2, where the ranges set for the interest-rate target and the money-stock target (shown by the rectangle *ABCD*) are broad enough so that, given the money-demand curve, r_p and M_p are consistent. As illustrated by the higher money-demand curve DD', at times even a broad range around the target points may not suffice to make two target ranges consistent. In such cases the Fed has to either make a choice or broaden the range.

INFORMATION VARIABLES

The FOMC uses several variables not as "targets" in the strict sense of the term, but as "information variables." An information variable is a variable that tells the FOMC how income is likely to change or how its policy is affecting income.

What Should the FOMC Have Done?

In late 1991, M-2 was growing at a low rate, a rate that put it near the lower limit of the FOMC's target range. With the economy in recession, the FOMC was worried about this. Other things being equal, the slow growth of M-2 suggested that a more expansionary policy was in order.

But other things are seldom equal. There was a shift among the components of M-2. While the more liquid M-1 component was increasing at a rapid pace, its growth was more than offset by the slow growth rate of the time deposits and money-market mutual funds components of M-2. To be sure, the FOMC had not set a target for M-1 because the velocity of M-1 had become unstable. But all the same, should it have ignored M-1 entirely and just looked at M-2?

One could make a case that M-2 was growing slowly only because of a special factor and therefore had little to tell us about how much income would rise. This factor was that with interest rates on deposits falling sharply, many people were shifting their time deposits into mutual bond funds and other assets, whose yields were falling much less sharply. Presumably the funds they were moving out of time deposits were funds they were not intending to spend soon; otherwise they would not have taken the trouble to shift them into mutual bond funds. If that was what was slowing the M-2 growth rate, then this slow growth bore little information about future expenditures or appropriate policy.

This suggests that the FOMC should have looked at M-1 instead, and with M-1 growing rapidly, there was little reason to adopt a more expansionary policy. But the FOMC had to worry that M-1, just like M-2, was giving a misleading signal. With yields on time deposits falling sharply, people had less of an incentive to move the funds they were not planning to spend soon out of transactions deposits into time deposits. With more idle funds accumulating in M-1, one would expect M-1 velocity to fall. Hence, the rise in M-1 was not a good reason for postponing a shift to a more expansionary policy. So what should the FOMC have done? A simple answer, as we can see, is hard to give. What the Fed did do was to let M-1 continue to grow at a fast rate and M-2 at a slow rate. In hindsight, that was a reasonable policy.

Unlike a target variable, an information variable need not be something that the FOMC can control in a meaningful way. For example, consumer optimism is a useful information variable if it helps to predict sales, and hence GDP, even though the FOMC can hardly decide to set the index of consumer confidence at, say, 89 percent.

However, to provide useful information on how monetary policy is operating, an information variable must, of course, be one that monetary policy does affect, that is, a step in the chain from open-market operations to GDP. For example, the FOMC might use the long-term interest rate as an information variable to see if the rise in the funds rate that it brought about is being carried forward to the long rate, which affects most investment. In contrast, the spread between the Treasury bill rate and the commercial paper rate, which is a useful information variable for GDP, does not tell the FOMC whether its policy is having its predicted effect.

The distinction between a target variable and an information variable is somewhat vague. It is not a distinction based on any inherent characteristics of the variables themselves, but on how the FOMC uses them, and that is often a matter of degree. Suppose, for example, that the FOMC expected M-2 to grow at a 5 percent rate, but is now told that it is growing only at a 2 percent rate. If the FOMC is using M-2 as its target variable, it will decide to adopt a more expansionary policy. But if it is using M-2 only as an information variable, the slow growth of M-2 will be just one bit of information it uses in deciding whether to change its policy, and hence it may do nothing.

TARGETING GDP

The use of many information variables can be thought of as targeting not any variable that is supposed to predict or determine the course of GDP, but many variables that jointly do so. This is called **GDP targeting,** because it focuses on the variables that determine GDP. In effect, it amounts to abandoning the simple goals-targets-instruments framework and using the GDP goal itself as a target. Since many variables determine GDP, the FOMC, so the argument runs, should look at many variables and should not ignore the information provided by any of the relevant variables. Suppose, for example, that the growth rate of M-2 rises sharply, while growth rates of M-1 and M-3 are falling. Credit is expanding rapidly, but interest rates are rising. Since all of these variables affect GDP, the Fed should pay attention to all of them. It should not claim, as it would if it were targeting, say, M-2, that M-2 is rising too fast, so a more restrictive policy must be adopted. Instead, it *may* decide that the fast growth rate of M-2 is outweighed by the slower growth rates of M-1 and M-3, and the rise in the interest rate, and hence it may opt for a more expansionary policy.

In this approach, the FOMC need not look at a particular set of variables all the time. It may at certain times pay attention to some variables that at other times it considers unimportant. Although in principle GDP targeting could be based on an econometric model, it is usually an intuitive approach to policy making. And it is this intuitive approach that the Fed is currently following much more than the targets-and-instruments approach. There is no doubt that there are benefits to looking at numerous variables, as GDP targeting does. Targeting just a single variable, say interest rates, ignores the information provided by all the other variables.

But it also has some disadvantages. First, using many target variables requires much more information than using just a single one, so that the FOMC has to process a great deal of information. Many people believe that the more information one has and uses, the better one's decisions will be. But this is not necessarily the case. The human mind is not a computer with an infinite amount of memory; it can absorb and use *effectively* only a limited amount of information. If given too much information, everything becomes a blur, and important news is buried in a plethora of inconsequential material.

At briefings, its staff provides the FOMC with a vast amount of information. When given such a massive dose of "this went up and that went down," one can easily lose sight of the variables that really matter.

A second disadvantage of using many target variables is that it eliminates the discipline that the use of a single target imposes on the Fed. If it has just one target variable, say *M-2,* then there is no question about what it must do when *M-2* diverges from its target. In contrast, if it has several target variables, it may say that at this particular time there are good reasons for paying less attention to *M-2* and paying more attention to the other target variables and so do nothing to bring *M-2* back to its target. The Fed *may* be right in deemphasizing *M-2* in this instance, but it may also be wrong, because it is under pressure to pay too much attention to current conditions. As we will discuss in Chapter 26, the substantial lag in the effect of monetary policy means that the Fed should often shift to a more restrictive policy at a time when unemployment is still high. The FOMC is reluctant to do this both because of its own concern about the plight of the unemployed and because of public and congressional opposition to such a seemingly hardhearted policy. If the Fed has several target variables, some pointing in one direction and some in another, it is harder for it to undertake what—in the long run—is the right policy. Compare this situation with one in which the FOMC has firmly committed itself to maintaining a certain monetary growth rate. If money grows faster than intended, that is all the FOMC needs to know to shift to a more restrictive policy.

A third problem with using many target variables instead of a single one is that it does not allow Congress, the White House, the public—or, for that matter, the Fed itself—to evaluate the Fed's efficiency. Suppose that the FOMC sets a 5 percent target for *M-2* growth. Then if *M-2* grows instead at an 8 percent rate, the Fed knows that it has made a mistake, and so does everyone else. Simple targets make for good discipline.

Finally, using a single target variable allows the Fed to make midcourse corrections, something that GDP targeting does not. Suppose, for example, that the Fed uses a long-term interest rate as its target, and lowers the federal-funds rate from 5 to 4 percent to reduce the ten-year government-bond rate from, say, 7 percent to the 6¾ percent that it thinks is required for its GDP goal. But the ten-year rate declines only to 6⅞ percent instead of to 6¾ percent. The FOMC now knows that it should cut the federal-funds rate even further. If it had used many variables instead of a single variable, it would have had difficulty determining that a midcourse correction was needed since some variables would probably have pointed in one direction and some in another.

The main issue in deciding whether to use a single target variable or GDP targeting is whether there is some variable that does have a close enough connection to GDP and that also can be measured and controlled with sufficient accuracy. In the 1960s and 1970s many economists believed that this was the case, and some advocated targeting interest rates, while others advocated targeting the money supply. But when velocity became much more variable in the 1980s and when it became apparent that interest rates had been a bad target in the 1970s, the weight of professional opinion, rightly or wrongly, swung toward GDP targeting. Perhaps the velocity of *M-2* will again become stable. If so, there is likely to be a swing back to targeting the money stock.

A Real GDP Target

If the Fed targets GDP, is it nominal GDP or real GDP that it should target? If the Fed estimates the inflation rate without error, then it does not matter which one it uses because each level of real GDP corresponds to a particular level of nominal GDP so that a real GDP target and a nominal GDP target are the same. But there is a difference between the two targets in the more realistic case in which the Fed does not know the inflation rate exactly. Suppose its inflation forecast is wrong because a supply shock occurs or the Phillips curve is steeper than the Fed thought. Prices now rise more than the Fed anticipated and so does nominal GDP. If the Fed has a real GDP target and stays with it, it will do nothing to offset the higher inflation rate. In contrast, if it has a nominal GDP target, its policy will lower both the inflation rate and real GDP. With some exaggeration one might say that with a nominal GDP target the Fed is, in effect, telling the public, "If you raise prices, you will also get a rise in unemployment," whereas with a real GDP target it is saying, "I will ensure a certain level of employment regardless of what you do to prices." Admittedly, this is something of an exaggeration because the Fed is likely to change both a nominal and a real GDP target as the inflation rate changes.

INSTRUMENTS

The FOMC does not set the money stock, long-term interest rates, or the volume of outstanding credit. Instead, it uses some instruments that change these target variables.One set of these instruments (or operating targets) consists of the various measures of reserves and the base discussed in Chapter 14. The federal-funds rate is another instrument. The Fed can use it to influence the long-term interest rate through the term-structure relation discussed in Chapter 4. It can also use the funds rate to influence the money supply, because by changing the interest rate the Fed can change the amount of money the public wants to hold. As the demand for money changes, the Fed adjusts the reserves of depository institutions accordingly.

A related instrument that the Fed uses is the volume of unborrowed reserves. If the Fed reduces unborrowed reserves, depository institutions will find themselves short of reserves, bid up the funds rate, and also reduce their loans and security purchases. The Fed prefers unborrowed reserves to total reserves as a target because it thinks that a total-reserves target would be too restrictive. If the demand for reserves rises, perhaps because the money multiplier has fallen, the banks cannot obtain any of the additional reserves that they need, and the reserves shortage could cause the funds rate to rise sharply. With an unborrowed-reserves target the banks have an "out"; they can borrow from the Fed, and hence the funds rate does not change that much. But since banks are reluctant to borrow from the Fed and prefer to borrow on the funds market, a shortage of unborrowed reserves raises the funds rate, which then reduces the demand for money and the demand for reserves to some extent.

Accommodating versus Nonaccommodating Policy

The discussion of open-market operations in the previous chapter drew a distinction between dynamic and defensive operations. A similar distinction is useful here. From time to time the Fed wants to change reserves, interest rates, and the money stock. At other times it wants them to be constant. But market factors are continually adding to or subtracting from reserves, changes in the supply of or demand for funds are changing interest rates, and variations in the money multiplier are changing the supply of money. The Fed watches for such changes, and often tries to offset them. But it sometimes lacks sufficiently reliable information. It therefore wants to have in place a mechanism that automatically supplies more reserves when they are needed and withdraws them when they are not needed. Using unborrowed reserves instead of total reserves as its operating target is one way in which the Fed automatically accommodates such changes in the demand for reserves. Another way is by using the federal-funds rate as its operating target. If depository institutions need more reserves, the funds rate starts to rise, and the Fed treats that as a signal to supply more reserves.

But such accommodation is not always the correct policy. Suppose that exports increase so that nominal income rises. This rise in income may be excessive. If the Fed accommodates the increased demand for reserves that accompanies the increase in income by holding down the federal-funds rate and by providing more reserves, it is destabilizing the economy. Conversely, in a recession the demand for money and reserves falls, and so does the federal-funds rate. If the Fed now withdraws reserves to keep the funds rate stable, it exacerbates the recession. In these cases, accommodation makes monetary policy procyclical. This should not be surprising. It is essentially the same point we made in discussing the interest rate versus the money stock as a target: if the shock is a rise in *YP*, then accommodating the increased demand for money and reserves is bad policy.

Another Look at the Discount Rate

Now that we have explained the pros and cons of accommodation, we can take up a topic postponed in the previous chapter: the desirability of hooking the discount rate to the federal-funds rate. Under the current system discounting works in a way that accommodates changes in the demand for reserves. As the demand for reserves increases, the federal-funds rate rises, and thus there is a greater incentive to borrow from the Fed at the fixed discount rate. Hence, those who believe that accommodation is undesirable tend to advocate making the discount rate vary automatically with the federal-funds rate, while those who favor accommodation prefer the present system.

Although academic economists may well argue that attaining the income goal is nearly always much more important than avoiding interest-rate fluctuations, it is likely that the Fed does not think so. The Fed has some responsibility for the smooth functioning of financial markets. Besides, remember it is the Fed, and not academic economists, that has to bear the brunt of criticism from the financial community and from Congress. This does not mean that the Fed's preference for accommodation is right; merely that it is understandable.

Accommodation as Fed Policy

Regardless of whether the Fed should accommodate changes in the demand for money, it has usually done so. *In the postwar period the* M-1 *growth rate has generally been higher in business cycle expansions than in recessions.* This cannot be justified by saying that the Fed was offsetting changes in velocity because velocity, too, grows faster in expansions than in recessions. This procyclical behavior of the monetary growth rate *suggests* that the Fed may well have been destabilizing rather than stabilizing.[2] At the very least it calls into question the Fed's claim that it has, in its own classic phrase, been "leaning against the wind."

Why has the Fed been so accommodative? The main reason is probably that it has tried to moderate changes in interest rates. The way the choice of accommodating or not accommodating arises in practice biases the Fed toward giving priority to interest-rate stability. The damage from sharply fluctuating interest rates, such as gyrations of security prices and thus greater uncertainty, is immediate and obvious. By contrast, the Fed can never be sure that the income level it is aiming at is really the right one; perhaps it will result in more inflation (or unemployment) than the Fed expects. In addition, the Fed can never be certain that its target level of reserves or the federal-funds rate will generate the desired level of income. For example, it may increase reserves because it thinks that the money stock is growing too slowly and next month the revised data might tell it that the money stock was growing at an appropriate rate. When the losses from a policy are certain and immediate, while the gains are uncertain and remote, it is always tempting to procrastinate in adopting this policy even if its expected payoff exceeds the expected losses in an objective calculation.

[2] In the period July 1953 to November 1982 the monetary growth rate was higher in every expansion than in the following recession. Going the other way round and starting with recessions, there is only one exception to the procyclical behavior of the monetary growth rate. This is not *necessarily* bad. It is *not* true that to stabilize the economy, one should raise income in the recession and lower it in the expansion. During the first part of the recession income is still above its normal level, and during the first part of the expansion it is still below its normal level. Hence, to stabilize income around its trend, monetary policy *should* lower income during the early stages of the recession. Thus, instead of seeing whether the money growth rate behaves pro- or anticyclically, one should compare it with some indicator, such as the unemployment rate, that tells us whether aggregate expenditure is insufficient or excessive. And if one compares changes in the growth rate of either *M-1* or *M-2* with cyclical changes in unemployment, then the monetary growth rate is seen to respond fairly well to unemployment. Does this mean that the Federal Reserve is actually stabilizing the economy? Not necessarily, because changes in the monetary growth rate affect aggregate expenditure with a lag, so that monetary policy could easily be destabilizing after all. But whether it is destabilizing cannot be determined unless one knows the lag in the effect of monetary policy. In addition, there is a problem with how one reads the data. While monetary growth rates were negatively correlated with unemployment in the 1950s, for the 1960s it depended on whether one started with recessions or expansions.

THE FED'S USE OF TARGETS AND INSTRUMENTS

We now look at the different operating procedures the Fed has used since the early 1950s.

The 1950s and 1960s

In these benighted years the Fed did not have much of an idea about targets and instruments; indeed, Karl Brunner and Allan Meltzer invented this framework only in 1964. Neither did it have a clear idea about targeting GDP. Instead, it looked on the stability of interest rates and the control of bank credit as central to its task. It focused on the money market and judged the appropriateness of its policy by the behavior of the Treasury bill rate, free reserves, and "money-market conditions," an impressionistic amalgam of variables dominated by free reserves. These variables seriously misled the Fed. Thus, during recessions, as firms borrowed less, interest rates fell. The Fed interpreted the lower interest rates as evidence that it was being expansionary, perhaps too expansionary, and tended to become more restrictive during recessions. In its concentration on what happened in the money market, the Fed seemed to lose sight of GDP.

The 1970s

During the 1970s the Fed came to place more and more emphasis on the growth rate of money, so that by the late 1970s it may have *seemed* that the Fed had two targets—the monetary growth rate and the federal-funds rate. In part, but only in part, this greater emphasis on money was in response to congressional pressure. In 1975 a congressional resolution required the Fed chairman to appear before House and Senate committees to reveal and justify the Fed's targets for monetary growth. This put *some* pressure on the Fed to keep monetary growth within its targeted range. However, this pressure was greatly diluted by three factors. First, the growth-rate target encompassed a broad range, say, 4 to 7 percent, even though a 4 percent growth rate may be consistent with, say, a 3 percent inflation rate, and a 7 percent growth rate with, say, a 6 percent inflation rate. Second, there was *base drift;* that is, the Fed could use as the base from which the growth rate is measured the money stock at the start of that period, even if this was outside the previously set range. Hence, if the money stock was too high, the old percentage growth rate would yield a larger money stock. (Under current rules, the Fed can let the base drift like this only once a year, not every quarter as before.) Third, the Fed set target ranges not just for *M-1,* but also for the broader money measures. Hence, when the Fed missed its target for one of its three money measures, it might claim that it had to miss that target to attain one of the other two. With three fairly broad target ranges, the Fed could frequently hit one of them, even if only by accident. As Figure 24.3 shows, *M-1,* which then was the most prominent measure of money, was frequently outside its target range.

    The fact that the Fed again and again missed its monetary targets is not surprising. Although in a formal sense the Fed was targeting money, it actu-

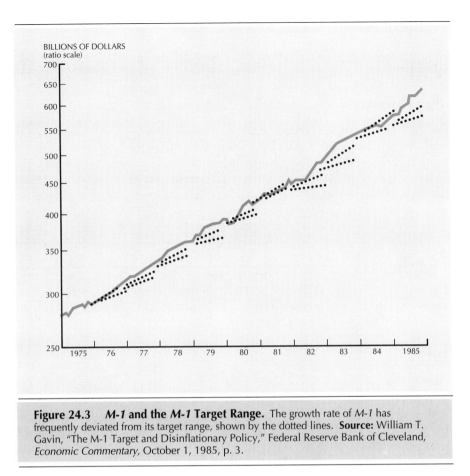

BILLIONS OF DOLLARS
(ratio scale)

Figure 24.3   *M-1* and the *M-1* Target Range. The growth rate of *M-1* has
frequently deviated from its target range, shown by the dotted lines. **Source:** William T.
Gavin, "The M-1 Target and Disinflationary Policy," Federal Reserve Bank of Cleveland,
Economic Commentary, October 1, 1985, p. 3.

ally did not give this target priority. In addition to the monetary targets the
FOMC also set a range for the federal-funds rate. Since the range for the federal-funds rate was fairly narrow, the Fed often could not both meet its monetary target and stay within its range for the federal-funds rate. The Fed had to
make a choice, and generally it chose to sacrifice its monetary target.

October 1979 to August 1982

In October 1979 the Fed changed its operating procedures substantially. This
was part of the so-called **monetarist experiment,** which we will discuss in Chapter 27. The Fed essentially adopted the targets and instruments framework
favored by the monetarists and used the money stock as its target. The federal-
funds rate, which previously had been allowed to vary only by 1¼ percent or so,
was now allowed to vary within a 5 percent range. At times it moved outside
even this broad range if the Fed thought that this was necessary for controlling the money supply. The instrument used to achieve the monetary target
was unborrowed reserves.

The results were unsatisfactory. We will discuss them in some detail in Chapter 27. In summary, as one would expect, interest rates fluctuated much more, but most surprisingly, so did the monetary growth rate. Many Keynesians blamed this on the inherent problems of targeting money, while monetarists blamed the Fed's procedures, such as its use of unborrowed reserves instead of total reserves as its instrument. But what actually accounted for much of the fluctuation of money was that the money multiplier had become much more unstable because, for some reason, the currency ratio behaved erratically.

September 1982 to the Present

For reasons that will be explained in Chapter 27, the Fed terminated the so-called monetarist experiment in the second half of 1982. It is not quite clear what the Fed's present targets are. FOMC officials, as is typical of policy makers, are eclectic and try to minimize the risk of making a wrong decision by combining parts of various theories rather than relying on any one theory. And, as is also typical of policy makers, their statements are often not very informative. Perhaps the safest thing to say is that insofar as the FOMC has a target at all, it is primarily targeting nominal GDP. The reason that is a safe statement is largely because the phrase *nominal GDP targeting* is so vague because it does not specify what variables are being considered. As a Fed official put it:

> As the 1990s open, . . . policymakers are reacting to information from a wide variety of sources, making frequent adjustments of the stance of policy in reserve markets when the evidence suggests that the existing posture is inconsistent with their long-run objectives. No one indicator, nor any one small set of indicators, dominates this policy-adjustment process. Indeed the whole intermediate indicator/target paradigm may not be very useful.[3]

The role of *M-2* seems to be, in large part, to act as a warning signal. The FOMC worries when *M-2* rises too fast or too slowly for a substantial period, and that provides useful discipline. The day-to-day pressures to keep interest rates low and to foster high employment present the FOMC with a pervasive temptation to resolve cases of doubt in the direction of monetary ease. Paying some attention to the growth rate of *M-2* is one way of counteracting the resulting temptation to say, "Yes, we must certainly be careful to avoid inflation, but right now let us be less restrictive." All the same, due to the instability of *M-2* velocity, the *M-2* target now has very little influence on monetary policy. That would probably change if *M-2* velocity were to become stable again, but that is a big "if."

It is not quite clear exactly what the Fed's main instrumental variable is. It frequently uses what it calls "reserve pressures." This vague term might mean the level of borrowed reserves, the federal funds rate, or a mixture of the two. But it is likely to mean primarily the federal-funds rate.

[3] Donald Kohn, "Policy Targets and Operating Procedures in the 1990s," *Federal Reserve Bulletin,* 76 (January 1990), 6.

The Fed's current procedures bear some resemblance to those it used in the 1960s and 1970s, when it lost control over the monetary growth rate and hence the inflation rate, because it is again deemphasizing monetary targets. But the Fed has learned from its prior experience. For example, in the 1960s and 1970s it waited to tighten monetary policy until the inflation rate rose. Now it tightens well ahead of that, as soon as real GDP seems to be approaching its ceiling.

THE DIRECTIVE

At the end of its meetings, the FOMC issues a Directive to the Desk at the Federal Reserve Bank of New York, telling it what policies to follow.[4] Money-market specialists scrutinize these Directives carefully for clues about Fed policy. Interpreting the Directive is an arcane art. Small changes in phrasing can carry important messages. For example, if in the previous Directive the FOMC said "a slight tightening of reserve pressures might be acceptable," and in the new Directive the word "might" is replaced by "would," or "acceptable" is replaced by "appropriate," this indicates some tightening of monetary policy. (Perhaps would-be Fed watchers should major in English, not economics!)

Appendix B provides excerpts from the Fed's summary of the discussion at an FOMC meeting.

SUMMARY

1   The Fed can use either a GDP target or certain intermediate targets that stand between its tools and its GDP goal.
2   What the appropriate target variables are is a debated issue. The relevant criteria are measurability, controllability, relatedness to the GDP goal, and administrative and political feasibility. Two main rivals are the monetary growth rate and interest rates, but the total debt of nonfinancial borrowers, the foreign exchange rate, commodity prices, and slope of the yield curve have also been suggested as targets.
3   If it is unpredicted changes in the Cambridge k that account for economic fluctuations, then the interest rate is a better target than the money stock. If it is instead unexpected changes in expenditure incentives, such as a rise in consumption, then the money stock is a better target. The Fed can use either a single target variable or a combination of target variables.
4   Using many variables at the same time as indicators of how GDP will change is called "GDP targeting." This is essentially what the Fed does now. It has the advantage of providing the Fed with much relevant information. It also has four disadvantages: it limits midcourse corrections, creates a potential for information flooding, reduces Fed discipline, and makes it harder to evaluate the Fed's policy. If the Fed uses real rather than nominal GDP as its target, it accommodates changes in prices.
5   The criteria for the instruments are similar to those for the target variables. The potential instruments are the federal-funds rate and a measure of reserves. Total reserves

[4] The FOMC usually meets eight times a year and sometimes also holds telephone meetings as the need arises. The so-called Minutes of the previous meeting that it issues at the end of the meeting are not actually "minutes" but summaries of discussion. Transcripts of actual discussions are issued only with a five-year lag. At the end of each meeting the FOMC issues a summary of the decisions made at that meeting.

are the least-accommodative measure, unborrowed reserves are in between, and borrowed reserves are the most accommodative.

6 The Fed tends to accommodate changes in the demand for reserves and money in part because it wants to keep interest rates stable.

7 In the 1950s and 1960s the Fed focused mainly on the Treasury bill rate. In the 1970s it started to pay more attention to the money supply, but paid most attention to the funds rate. It experimented briefly with monetary targets from October 1979 to August 1982.

8 The language of Fed Directives is closely examined by economists for clues about where Fed policy is headed.

KEY TERMS

tools
instruments, or operating targets
target variables
goals

GDP targeting
accommodative policy
information variables

QUESTIONS AND EXERCISES

**1 What are the advantages and disadvantages of targeting nominal GDP? Instead of real GDP?

2 Why would the Fed ever think of using a single target? What are the advantages and disadvantages?

3 What determines whether the money stock or interest rates is a better target?

*4 What are instruments? Why are they used?

5 Write an essay either criticizing or defending the Fed for accommodating changes in the demand for money.

6 Describe the evolution of the Fed's targeting procedures.

FURTHER READING

FACKLER, JAMES. "Should the Federal Reserve Continue to Monitor Credit?" Federal Reserve Bank of Kansas City, *Economic Review*, 13 (June 1988), 39–50. A strong argument for targeting credit along with money.

FEDERAL RESERVE BANK OF NEW YORK. *Intermediate Targets and Indicators for Monetary Policy.* New York, 1991. A comprehensive survey of the targeting and instrument issue.

FRIEDMAN, BENJAMIN. "The Value of Intermediate Targets in Implementing Monetary Policy," Federal Reserve Bank of Kansas City, *Price Stability and Public Policy* (1984), A stimulating critique of the targets and instruments approach.

GAMS, CARL. "Federal Reserve Intermediate Targets: Money or the Monetary Base," Federal Reserve Bank of Kansas City, *Review*, 65 (January 1980), 3–15. A provocative discussion of the issue of the base versus money as a target.

HEEBER, A. GILBERT. "Detecting Changes in Federal Reserve Policy," *Business Economics*, 26 (July 1991), 33–37. An excellent discussion of how to read between the lines of the "Record of Policy Actions."

KOHN, DONALD. "Policy Targets and Operating Procedures in the 1990s," *Federal Reserve Bulletin*, 76 (January 1990), 6.

MAYER, THOMAS. *Monetarism and Macroeconomic Policy*. Brookfield, Vt.: Edward Elgar, 1990. Chapter 9 provides a critique of GDP targeting.

MCNEES, STEPHEN. "Prospective Nominal GNP Targeting: An Alternative Framework for Monetary Policy," Federal Reserve Bank of Boston, *New England Economic Review,* (September–October 1987), 3–9. A good argument for targeting GNP.

MEEK, PAUL, ed. *Central Bank Views on Monetary Targeting.* New York: Federal Reserve Bank of New York, n.d. A collection of useful papers on monetary targeting procedures in various countries.

MEULENDYKE, ANN MARIE. *U.S. Monetary Policy and Financial Markets.* New York: Federal Reserve Bank of New York, n.d. Chapter 5 provides a detailed picture of FOMC policy making.

ROBERDS, WILLIAM. "What Has the Fed Wrought? Interest Rate Smoothing in Theory and Practice," Federal Reserve Bank of Atlanta, *Economic Review,* 77 (January–February 1992), 25–36.

Each year the *Review* of the Federal Reserve Bank of St. Louis and the *Review* of the Federal Reserve Bank of New York carry articles summarizing the FOMC's actions during the previous year.

Twice a year, the Fed chairman testifies on the Fed's monetary policy plans before Congress. This testimony, reprinted in the *Federal Reserve Bulletin* in March and August, is another useful source of information.

APPENDIX A:
MORE ON THE CHOICE BETWEEN AN INTEREST-RATE AND A MONEY-STOCK TARGET

In the text we discussed the choice between the money stock and the interest rate as a target for Fed actions in an informal way. A somewhat more formal way, developed by William Poole of Brown University, is to use an IS-LM model. In Figure 24.4A, the IS curve shifts around anywhere between IS_1 and IS_2. If the Fed uses a money-stock target, it generates a fixed supply of money and lets the interest rate increase as a rise in income raises the demand for money. Hence, the LM curve slopes upward in the usual way. As an increase, say, in the profitability of investment or in government expenditures shifts the IS curve from IS_1 to IS_2, income increases from Y_0 to Y_1. In contrast, assume that the Fed uses an interest-rate target. It then keeps the interest rate fixed at the desired level by meeting changes in the demand for money with corresponding changes in the supply, so that the LM curve becomes a horizontal line LM_2. As the IS curve shifts from IS_1 to IS_2, income rises from Y_2 to Y_3, that is, by more than it would have risen had the Fed used a money-stock target.

In Figure 24.4B, the IS curve is stable, but the demand for money fluctuates, so that the LM curve varies between LM_1 and LM_2. Suppose the Fed has a money-stock target that keeps the money supply constant (since it does not want income to change) and lets the interest rate fluctuate. Income then varies between Y_0 and Y_1. Now suppose instead that the Fed uses an interest-rate target and fixes the interest rate at r_2. This changes the LM curve to LM_3, so that income stays at Y_2.

Hence, if it is the LM curve that shifts, the Fed should use an interest-rate target. If it is instead the IS curve that shifts, the Fed should use the money stock as its target. What happens if both curves shift? Then the Fed should adopt an intermediate policy and let both the interest rate and the money

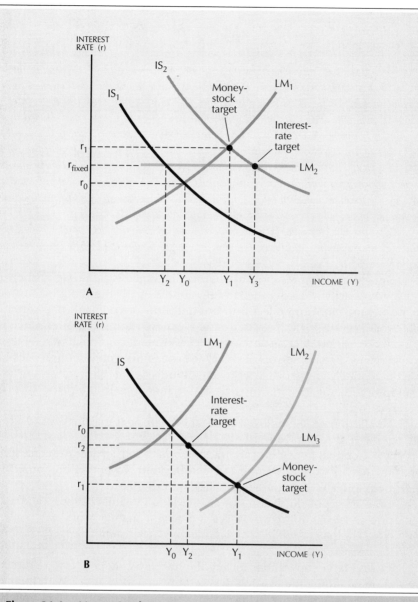

Figure 24.4   Money-Stock Target versus Interest-Rate Target. Whether a money-stock target or an interest-rate target contributes more to income stability depends on whether the shock to income is a shift in the IS curve, as in Part A, or a shift in the LM curve, as in Part B.

stock change to some extent. By how much it should allow each to change depends not only on the relative size of the shifts in the IS and LM curves, but also on the slope of these curves, since their slopes affect by how much income changes.

APPENDIX B:
EXCERPTS FROM THE MINUTES OF THE JANUARY 31–FEBRUARY 1, 1995
FOMC MEETING[1]

This meeting started with some housekeeping preliminaries, such as a listing of the persons present. It then surveyed economic conditions. Since it was the February meeting, the Committee then discussed its long-run ranges for the monetary and debt aggregates, in preparation for the Fed's presentation of these ranges to Congress, as required by the Humphrey-Hawkins Act. Next it turned to the appropriate policy for the period until the next meeting, and hence the Directive to be given to the Account Manager (also called the "Trading Desk") at the Federal Reserve Bank of New York. It then took up the ratification of swap agreements with foreign central banks, that is, in effect, the collateralized loans the Federal Reserve makes to other central banks, and concluded with another housekeeping issue, its policy on releasing information about FOMC meetings.

Here are some excerpts. (We have added some explanatory footnotes.) The first deals with current economic conditions and indicates what factors the FOMC considered particularly relevant.

The information reviewed at this meeting suggested a strong further rise in economic activity during the closing months of 1994. Although consumer spending appeared to be less buoyant and housing demand had softened somewhat, growth in business investment, exports, and inventories remained brisk. Industrial production and payroll employment continued to record substantial gains. Broad indexes of prices for consumer goods and services had risen moderately on average over recent months despite shrinking margins of unemployed resources and further sizable increases in the prices of many materials.

Nonfarm payroll employment advanced considerably further in December after a sharp rise in November. . . .

The nominal deficit on U.S. trade in goods and services widened somewhat further in November, and for October and November combined the deficit was well above its average rate in the third quarter. . . .

Consumer price inflation slowed a little in December despite a jump in food prices that was only partly offset by a decline in energy prices.

The discussion turned them to financial conditions, starting with a summary of policy since the last meeting.

Open Market operations during the intermeeting period were directed towards maintaining the existing degree of reserve pressures.[2] With the need for seasonal credit diminishing over the period, adjustment plus seasonal borrowing trended lower but averaged a little above anticipated levels. Near year-end, the Trading Desk accommodated heavy demands for reserves through System repurchase agreements (RPs). The federal funds rate averaged close to 5½ percent during the intermeeting period.

Most other market interest rates declined slightly on balance over the period after the December 20 meeting. Very short term interest rates fell after

---

[1] Taken from the *Federal Reserve Bulletin,* 81 (May 1995), 438–47.

[2] "Reserve pressure" is a Fed term meaning the levels of the federal funds rate and of borrowed reserves.

the first of the year, reflecting the disappearance of year-end premiums. More broadly, favorable news on inflation and indications of some unexpected slowing in the growth of final demand apparently led market participants to conclude that further tightening of monetary policy, though still expected to be substantial, would be less than previously thought and would be spread over a longer period. Yields on tax-exempt instruments declined considerably as concerns about the implications of Orange County's problems for the financial condition of other municipal governments abated. Strong earnings reports for the fourth quarter boosted major indexes of equity prices. In the foreign exchange markets, the trade-weighted value of the dollar in terms of the other G-10 currencies declined somewhat in the intermeeting period.[3]

The committee then took up the growth rates of M-2 and M-3 (M-1 is no longer considered) and its forecast of economic activity.

Growth of M2 and M3 strengthened in December, and data for the first half of January suggested a further acceleration in that month. Much of the pickup in M2 in December was due to rapid expansion in overnight RPs and overnight Eurodollars, which outweighed a further contraction of liquid accounts associated in part with depositor efforts to obtain higher returns by shifting funds into market instruments. The faster growth of M3 reflected, in addition to the acceleration of its M2 component, bank use of large CDs and nondeposit sources of funds to finance relatively robust demands for credit. From the fourth quarter of 1993 to the fourth quarter of 1994, M2 grew at the lower end of the Committee's range for 1994 and M3 in the lower half of its range. Total domestic nonfinancial debt had continued to expand at a moderate rate in recent months, and for 1994 it was in the lower half of its monitoring range.

The staff forecast prepared for this meeting suggested that growth of economic activity would slow substantially over the next several quarters and for some period thereafter would average less than the rate of increase in the economy's potential output. . . .

In the Committee's discussion of current and prospective economic developments, the members agreed that growth in economic activity could be expected to moderate considerably over the course of 1995, although inflation was likely to be higher than in 1994. They acknowledged that their current projections were subject to substantial risks. The expansion continued to display appreciable momentum and signs of slower growth were still quite limited and tentative. Even so, the members remained persuaded that the lagged effects of the policy tightening implemented over the course of 1994 would become increasingly evident in interest-sensitive sectors of the economy as the year progressed. The projected moderation in the growth of final demands, which probably would be concentrated at least initially in the housing and consumer durables sectors, would undoubtedly reinforce an expected cutback in inventory investment from its unsustainable pace in recent quarters. A key uncertainty in the outlook was whether the slowing in overall economic growth

---

[3] The trade-weighted exchange rate is the average exchange rate of the dollar against a basket of foreign currencies, with each of the currencies given a weight equal to U.S. trade with that country. The G-10 group of countries are the major industrialized market economies.

would be sufficient to relieve the current pressures on labor and other producer resources, which many members saw as portending higher inflation, or, indeed, whether such pressures would intensify further. Opinions differed to some degree with regard to both the likely extent of the prospective slowing in economic growth and the outlook for inflation. However, most of the members concluded that some rise in inflation appeared probable over coming quarters, and they were concerned that this upturn would not be reversed and could be extended in the absence of further monetary restraint.

Subsequently, the Committee turned to the task of setting policy for the period until the next meeting.

In the Committee's discussion of policy for the intermeeting period ahead, all the members indicated that they could support some firming in reserve conditions, though a few preferred to delay such an action pending the receipt within the next few weeks of significant new information that could help the Committee to evaluate whether and to what extent the economic expansion might be slowing. Most of the members were convinced, however, that current monetary policy should be adjusted promptly to a more clearly restrictive stance. In their view, prompt action was needed to counter inflationary pressures and inflationary expectations in an economy that already seemed to be operating at, and perhaps beyond, sustainable capacity levels and to be continuing to expand at a pace above its long-run potential. In these circumstances, a delay in tightening policy would incur an unacceptable risk of allowing further inflationary momentum to develop in the economy and would require more tightening over time than might otherwise be needed to achieve the Committee's objectives. Part of the risk involved a potential further decline in the dollar at a time when there already was considerable concern about rising pressures on prices. Some tightening of policy at this meeting was generally anticipated in markets, and a failure to take action now was likely in the view of a number of members to raise questions about the credibility of the System's anti-inflation resolve and to generate some unsettlement in financial markets, notably in the foreign exchange market where the dollar already appeared to be vulnerable to further weakness. In terms of balancing the policy risks that were involved, a prompt move would provide some insurance against what these members viewed as the principal risk in current circumstances—that of rising inflation. The risks of excessive tightening, while not completely absent, were believed to be limited in light of the apparent strength and momentum of the expansion, which many forecasters had underestimated over the past year. One member expressed the view that while monetary growth had been damped, continuing restraint on the growth of the narrow monetary aggregates was desirable to offset a previous buildup in liquidity and to help ensure that inflationary pressures would be contained.

Members who saw an advantage in postponing a decision to tighten policy commented that, in light of some scattered signs of a moderating expansion, it would be helpful to wait for certain key statistics that would become available within the next few weeks to judge the extent of any moderation. Data on retail sales in January might provide particular insights as to whether the softening in such sales in November and December was persisting. The favorable news on inflation in the fourth quarter had lessened concerns about an immediate inflation threat, and if the incoming information confirmed the need for further tightening, the short delay in implementing it would have only a minimal cost. In addition, an increase in monetary restraint would be likely to exacerbate the problems of Mexico and perhaps to some extent those of Canada and would have potentially adverse implications for U.S. trade with both of these key trading partners.[4] Because the probability that incoming information would counsel against any further policy tightening was certainly less than 50 percent so that only a matter of timing was likely to be involved, these members indicated that they would join with the other members in voting to tighten policy at this meeting.

Concerning the possible need to adjust policy during the intermeeting period, the members were unanimously in favor of adopting a symmetric directive. . . .[5]

At the conclusion of the Committee's discussion, all the members indicated that they could support a directive that called for increasing somewhat the degree of pressure on reserve positions. In the implementation of this policy, account would be taken of a possible increase of ½ percentage point in the discount rate that was under consideration by the Board of Governors. The members also agreed that the directive should not include any presumption about possible adjustments to policy during the intermeeting period. Accordingly, in the context of the Committee's long-run objectives for price stability and sustainable economic growth, and giving careful consideration to economic, financial, and monetary developments, the Committee decided that somewhat greater or somewhat lesser reserve restraint would be acceptable during the intermeeting period. According to a staff analysis, the reserve conditions contemplated at this meeting would be consistent with moderate growth in M2 and M3 over coming months.

At the conclusion of the meeting, the Federal Reserve Bank of New York was authorized and directed, until instructed otherwise by the Committee, to execute transactions in the System Account in accordance with the following domestic policy directive:

> The information reviewed at this meeting suggests a strong further rise in economic activity during the closing months of 1994. Nonfarm payroll employment was up considerably further in December after a sharp increase in November, and the civilian unemployment rate declined to 5.4 percent. Industrial production registered another large advance in December and capacity utilization continued to move up from already high levels. Current estimates indicate little change in retail sales over November and December, while housing starts posted sizable gains on balance over the two months. Orders for nondefense capital goods point to a continued strong expansion in spending on business equip-

---

[4] As discussed in the box on page 554, Mexico had experienced a major outflow of funds. Higher interest rates in the United States would attract additional funds from Mexico.

[5] A symmetric directive is one that attaches equal importance to deviations from the target in positive and negative directions. In contrast, an asymmetric directive might say that if M-2 and M-3 are growing at rates close to the tops of their ranges, a tightening of reserve pressures *would* be appropriate, while if they are growing near the bottoms of their ranges, an easing of reserve pressure *might* be appropriate.

ment; permits for nonresidential construction have been trending appreciably higher. The nominal deficit on U.S. trade in goods and services widened somewhat in October–November from its average rate in the third quarter. Prices of many materials have continued to move up rapidly, but broad indexes of prices for consumer goods and services have increased moderately on average over recent months.

Most market interest rates have declined slightly on balance since the Committee meeting on December 20, 1994. In foreign exchange markets, the trade-weighted value of the dollar in terms of the other G-10 currencies has declined somewhat over the intermeeting period. The Mexican peso has depreciated sharply against the dollar.

Growth of M2 and M3 strengthened in December and January. From the fourth quarter of 1993 to the fourth quarter of 1994, M2 grew at a rate at the bottom of the Committee's range for 1994 and M3 at a rate in the lower half of its range for the year. Total domestic nonfinancial debt has continued to expand at a moderate rate in recent months, and for the year 1994 it grew at a rate in the lower half of its monitoring range.

The Federal Open Market Committee seeks monetary and financial conditions that will foster price stability and promote sustainable growth in output. In furtherance of these objectives, the Committee at this meeting established ranges for growth of M2 and M3 of 1 to 5 percent and 0 to 4 percent respectively, measured from the fourth quarter of 1994 to the fourth quarter of 1995. The Committee anticipated that money growth within these ranges would be consistent with its broad policy objectives. The monitoring range for growth of total domestic nonfinancial debt was lowered to 3 to 7 percent for the year. The behavior of the monetary aggregates will continue to be evaluated in the light of progress toward price level stability, movements in their velocities, and developments in the economy and financial markets.

In the implementation of policy for the immediate future, the Committee seeks to increase somewhat the existing degree of pressure on reserve positions, taking account of a possible increase in the discount rate. In the context of the Committee's long-run objectives for price stability and sustainable economic growth, and giving careful consideration to economic, financial, and monetary developments, somewhat greater reserve restraint or somewhat lesser reserve restraint would be acceptable in the intermeeting period. The contemplated reserve conditions are expected to be consistent with moderate growth in M2 and M3 over coming months.

The Impact of Monetary Policy

After you have read this chapter, you will be able to:

- List the channels by which monetary policy affects GDP.
- Discuss how expectations can influence the effect of changes in monetary policy.
- Describe the effect of monetary policy in econometric models.

THE TRANSMISSION PROCESS

As pointed out in Chapter 20, a major difference between the monetarist and income-expenditure analyses of *how* money affects the economy is that monetarists do not spell out this transmission process in detail, while income-expenditure theorists do. Hence, before turning to the detailed income-expenditure story, here is a brief discussion of a portfolio process that summarizes the monetarist version of the transmission process, but is also entirely acceptable to income-expenditure theorists. We will deal first with domestic effects and will pick up the foreign-trade effect later in this chapter.

Portfolio Equilibrium

The basic story of the transmission process begins with each individual and his or her portfolio. Everyone has a portfolio of assets and liabilities and tries to keep the (monetary plus imputed) yields of all the assets equal at the margin.[1]

---

[1] Assets provide a yield, not only in monetary terms, such as, say, a 5 percent rate of interest, but also in nonmonetary terms, such as enhanced liquidity. If one of your assets provides you—at the margin—with a lower combined monetary and nonmonetary yield than another asset, you can increase your utility by selling some of that asset and buying other assets instead. The nonmonetary yield (and sometimes the monetary yield) of an asset typically declines as you hold more of it. As you sell some of your first asset, its marginal yield rises, while as you buy more of other assets, their marginal yields fall. Eventually, you get to the point where a dollar invested in any asset yields you the same utility, and that is your equilibrium position.

Now suppose that the quantity of money increases, so that at least some port-folios now include more money. Given, for the usual reasons, declining mar-ginal utility, the imputed yield on money falls. Hence, portfolio holders exchange money for other assets. What assets they buy depends on the cross-elasticities of demand, which, in turn, depend on the similarity between assets. For example, money and Treasury bills, being similar, are close substitutes (have a high cross-elasticity of demand). Not only are they both extremely safe assets in nominal terms, but the type of risk to which they are subject are also alike. They are both subject to inflation risk, but not to default risk. Similarly, there is no significant fall in their values if interest rates rise. Hence, those who initially hold excess money balances use them to buy mainly securities like Treasury bills, and interest rates on such securities fall. As the sellers of Trea-sury bills receive these excess money balances, they buy mainly assets that are not too dissimilar to Treasury bills, for example, commercial paper and three-year government securities. The sellers of these items, in turn, then buy other assets, and eventually the increased demand for assets spreads to all assets in the economy, until in the new equilibrium the (monetary plus imputed) yields on all assets are again equal. Among the assets whose prices are raised in this way are common stocks, and thus the value of corporations. As explained by Tobin's q theory of investment (discussed in Chapter 15), investment now rises. Moreover, as the yield on various assets such as money and bonds declines, the imputed yield on consumer durables starts to exceed these other yields, so that households buy more durables. Similarly, nondurable con-sumption may rise as saving declines.

The Income-Expenditure Interpretation

The income-expenditure story of the transmission process does not contradict the portfolio-equilibrium story just told, but describes the process in more detail and in terms of interest rates. Suppose the money supply increases and the interest rate falls (as just described). Since borrowing costs are lower, firms have an incentive to borrow and invest more. As discussed in Chapter 14, it is long-term investment that is particularly responsive to changes in the interest rate. So much is obvious. But there are also three less obvious channels by which lower interest rates encourage firms to invest.

One of these channels is an expectations effect. When firms see that the Fed is becoming more expansionary, they expect to see their sales rise. Hence, they are willing to invest more. Similarly, when monetary policy becomes highly restrictive, some firms may expect a recession.

A second channel is the result of capital rationing. As previously dis-cussed, the capital market is imperfect. Thus banks do not auction off their loanable funds, making loans to anyone who is willing to pay a high enough interest rate. Instead, they ration credit. When they obtain more reserves, they respond not just by lowering interest rates, but also by relaxing their credit standards, making loans to some customers they otherwise would have turned down. Other customers, who previously were given loans smaller than they had requested, now receive larger loans.

The third channel operates through stock prices. One component of a firm's cost of capital is the price of its stock. And if firms can sell new stock at a higher price than before, they are more likely to sell stock and use the proceeds to undertake physical investment, so that aggregate expenditures increase. But does a more expansionary policy actually raise stock prices, and if so, how?

Monetary Policy and Stock Prices

To see how changes in monetary policy affect stock prices, we deal first with a situation in which there is no fear of inflation. Assume that the Fed adopts an expansionary policy and the growth rate of money rises. The way stock prices are affected can be explained in three alternative ways. The first is to say that the public now holds more money in its portfolio, and since its monetary holdings were previously in equilibrium, it now holds excessive money and tries to exchange some of it for corporate stock. The second way of putting this is to look at relative yields and to notice that as people get more money, the implicit yield on money falls at the margin, so that it is now less than the expected yield (adjusted for risk) on stock. As they buy stock, they bid stock prices up until at the new price the expected (risk-adjusted) yield on a dollar invested in stock is no greater than the marginal yield on a dollar held as money. A third way is to say that the present value of a stock, and hence its price, are equal to an expected stream of future yields discounted at the interest rate. An increase in the quantity of money temporarily lowers the interest rate and so increases the present value of the expected future earnings on the stock and, thus, its price.

Knowing this, can you go out and make money on the stock market? No—sorry about that! Other people have this information too. So when you rush to your broker, you find that there are already many people there who want to buy stock too, and potential sellers are demanding a higher price. Remember efficient-markets theory from Chapter 3. Information that everyone else has is of no use to you in the stock market. Only if you know something (something right, that is) that others don't, can you cash in on it. Suppose, for example, you discover that the Fed raises the monetary growth rate in every month in which there is a full moon on a Thursday. Then, until others discover this too, you can predict stock prices in time to buy stocks before they go up.

Just to complicate things, there is the problem of inflation. If people believe that the higher monetary growth rate is inflationary, then *real* stock prices will probably not rise. Since, in fact, inflation raises the tax burden on corporations (as discussed in Chapter 19), it may well reduce real stock prices.

Consumption

A lower interest rate affects consumption as well as investment. At least over a period of a year or so, monetary policy might well change aggregate expenditures more through the consumption channels than through the investment channels. This is not surprising because consumption accounts for about two-thirds of GDP, while net investment accounts for only about one-eighth. The ways in which interest rates affect consumption have already been explained in Chapter 15. First, there is an effect (in an uncertain direction) of households changing the proportion of their incomes that they want to save rather than consume, because they now earn more on their savings. Second, households, in their capacity as investors in durables, react to lower interest rates as firms do. Third, a wealth effect raises consumption, as lower interest rates raise the value of stocks and bonds. Fourth, there is a liquidity effect as these increases in wealth raise the liquidity of households.

INTERNATIONAL TRADE EFFECTS OF MONETARY POLICY

At one time monetary policy was thought to have nearly all its impact on aggregate expenditures through its effects on domestic consumption and investment. But the U.S. economy has become much more open, so foreign-trade effects can no longer be treated as though they were a trivial complication. They now may well be the main channel by which monetary policy affects aggregate expenditures. To see how monetary policy affects imports and exports, keep in mind that a country's *total* transactions with the rest of the world must balance out at zero.

If a country imports more goods and services than it exports, it must transfer securities or money to other countries. This is widely understood. What is not so widely understood is the mirror image of this point, that if a country buys more claims (securities and money holdings) from the rest of the world than it sells to the rest of the world, then it must necessarily export more than it imports. Since goods and services plus claims, by definition, comprise all items of value that can be transferred, the more claims you give to others, the more goods and services you must get in exchange.

Monetary policy changes net exports in this indirect way by affecting net foreign claims on U.S. assets. Suppose that interest rates rise in the United States. Foreigners will want to hold more U.S. securities, while U.S. residents who previously would have bought and held foreign securities now want to hold U.S. securities instead. When net sales of U.S. securities to foreigners rise, net imports of foreign goods and services have to rise by a corresponding amount.[2] The mechanism that brings this about has previously been described: foreigners need dollars to buy U.S. securities, so the dollar rises on the foreign-exchange market; as a result, U.S. goods become more expensive relative to foreign goods, and exports decline while imports rise.

---

[2] In principle, foreigners' purchases of securities could exceed, or fall short of, their net sales of goods and services in the United States; the difference shows up as a change in their monetary holdings. But if money is defined as *M-1* or *M-2* (and large CDs are defined as securities, which is reasonable), their money holdings are very small because they could earn more by holding Treasury bills or large CDs.

There is, however, another international finance effect of monetary policy that tends to weaken it. This is that, as the interest rate rises in the United States, the increased purchases of U.S. securities by foreigners (and by those Americans who would otherwise have bought foreign securities) work to moderate the rise in the interest rate. This, in turn, reduces the impact of the Fed's restrictive policy on investment and consumption. However, in a system of flexible exchange rates this offset is limited. Since exchange rates fluctuate, foreigners take a risk in buying securities denominated in dollars rather than in their own currencies, and this limits capital inflows. This will be discussed further in Part Five.

The Credit Channel

The channels discussed so far are the traditional channels of monetary policy. While there is some disagreement about the details of how they function, there is general agreement about their existence and relevance. But in recent years a number of economists have focused attention on another channel that is more controversial—the credit channel.

This channel has two sources. One is a market imperfection: for many borrowers, such as small firms that cannot issue commercial paper, bank credit does not have close substitutes. Hence, if the Fed reduces bank reserves and banks therefore cut back their lending, some firms will no longer obtain the funds they need to carry out their investment programs, either because banks ration credit or because banks now charge such a high interest rate that they no longer want to borrow. In many ways this version of the credit channel is similar to the interest-rate channel we already discussed. It differs by focusing on bank loans and by arguing that it is the small firms unable to issue commercial paper that are forced to cut back investment. Large firms are much less affected because the interest rate on commercial paper does not rise as much as the interest rate on bank loans.

The other source of the credit channel focuses on the effect of a restrictive monetary policy on the creditworthiness of potential borrowers. As interest rates rise, the balance sheets of many firms deteriorate. They have to pay more interest on their outstanding floating rate loans, just at a time when the restrictive monetary policy is about to reduce the market for their products. Moreover, as asset prices decline, the value of the collateral that they can offer the lender also declines. Monetary policy therefore raises the interest rate that many firms have to pay in two ways: the pure rate of interest rises and the risk premiums that many firms, particularly small firms, have to pay rise. In addition, since firms are now riskier borrowers, banks may ration credit to them. Their investment therefore falls.

There is considerable disagreement about the importance of the credit channel. Critics ask whether banks are really forced to cut back loans all that much when open-market operations reduce their reserves. Why can't they sell large CDs (against which there is no reserve requirement) and restore their reserves that way?[3] Proponents of the credit view respond that for some banks, particularly for lesser-known banks, selling additional large (and hence not fully insured) CDs would be costly.

RATIONAL EXPECTATIONS

So far, the description of the way monetary policy affects the economy has been too mechanistic. It is high time to allow for the fact that people do not just react to events that have already occurred, but also respond to what they expect to happen—in other words, to take account of the new classical theory discussed in Chapter 21.

Assume now that prices are fully flexible and expectations are rational. Suppose that the Fed substantially increases the base. Not only will this initially reduce interest rates, and hence stimulate expenditures, but people, particularly well-informed decision makers, will realize what is going on. They will expect aggregate expenditures to increase. More specifically, they will expect wages and prices to rise. But if prices are expected to rise, it's rational for people to try to protect themselves against this by buying ahead now, by withholding goods from the market to sell them in the future, and by raising wages and prices right away. Hence, an increase in the growth rate of the base can lead to an immediate increase in prices. This is, of course, much more likely to happen at a time when high and variable inflation rates have conditioned people to watch the growth rate of the base than at a time when people have had little or no experience with inflation.

At the cost of being somewhat unrealistic, one can carry this example to an interesting conclusion. Assume that everyone knows that the increase in the base is inflationary, that all contracts have escalator clauses, and that laws and regulations do not inhibit a rapid adaption to inflation. If so, an increase in the growth rate of the base will result immediately in a *rise* in nominal interest rates as the higher rate of inflation is embodied in the inflation premium that is included in the nominal interest rate, so that the real interest rate remains constant. Hence, neither investment nor output rises, but the inflation rate responds instantly and fully to the higher growth rate of the base.

Admittedly the assumptions that people can accurately predict the impact of the higher growth rate of the base on prices, that prices are fully flexible, and that long-term contracts, tax laws, and so on are all fully indexed are extreme. But this example does warn us to watch for the way in which monetary policy affects expectations. Suppose, for example, that Congress were suddenly to direct the Fed to aim at keeping unemployment to 3 percent or to bring the Treasury bill rate down to ½ percent. This would bring about an almost immediate and very substantial increase in the inflation rate. Conversely, if Congress were to order the Fed to make price stability its only goal, the inflation rate could start to decline even before the Fed took any action.

---

[3] To be sure, in the first instance, as Bank A sells a large CD to a customer of Bank B, that bank loses reserves. But as banks sell more CDs, the buyers of these CDs reduce their transactions accounts, and hence the banking system's need for reserves falls.

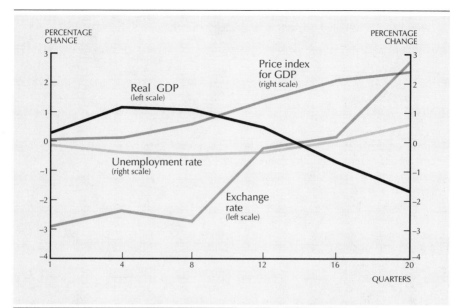

PERCENTAGE
CHANGE

PERCENTAGE
CHANGE

Price index
for GDP
(right scale)

Real GDP
(left scale)

Unemployment rate
(right scale)

Exchange
rate
(left scale)

QUARTERS

Figure 25.1   Predicted Effects of a Permanent 1 Percent Increase in *M-1* in the MPS Model. Initially real GDP rises, while unemployment falls. But these effects then fade away, while the price index for the GDP rises. (The source shows only 7 data points for the 20 quarters shown in this figure. The data points for the other quarters are interpolations.) **Source:** Flint Brayton and Eileen Mauskopf, "Structure and Uses of the MPS Quarterly Econometric Model of the United States," *Federal Reserve Bulletin,* 73 (February 1987), 105.

AN ECONOMETRIC MODEL

Thus monetary policy affects aggregate expenditures through numerous channels. One method of combining these channels in a way that takes account of their interaction is to use an **econometric model,** that is, a theoretical model of the economy whose coefficients have been estimated.

Figure 25.1 shows the estimated direct plus indirect effects of a permanent 1 percent increase in *M-1* according to the **MPS model.** This is the econometric model developed for, and used by, the Board of Governors.[4] In this model the effect of the increase in *M-1* on real GDP and other real variables eventually disappears; all the effect is absorbed by higher prices. But as Figure 25.1 shows, the shorter-run effects on real variables are substantial and have not disappeared even after five years.

A warning is in order. Figure 25.1 shows the estimates of just one of many econometric models. Table 25.1 shows the effects on real GDP and on the consumer price index of a 4 percent rise in the money supply according to 12 other models. Their predictions are highly diverse. Since, at best, only one of

[4] This model was developed especially to focus on the effect of monetary policy. It is called the MPS model because it was developed (under the direction of Franco Modigliani) at MIT and the University of Pennsylvania with financial support from the Social Science Research Council.

Table 25.1   Predicted Impact of Monetary Policy According to 12 Models

Model	Estimated Effect in the 2nd Year of a 4% Rise in the Money Supply On:*	
	Real GDP	CPI
Federal Reserve's multicountry model	1.5	.4
European Economic Community compact model	1.0	.8
Japanese Economic Planning Agency model	1.2	1.0
Project Link	1.0	-.4
Liverpool model	.1	3.7
McKibbon-Sachs model	.3	1.5
Haas-Masson smaller approximation of multicountry model	1.0	.8
Sims-Litterman vector autoregression model	3.0	.4
OECD interlink model	1.6	.7
Taylor's model	.6	1.2
Wharton model	.7	0
Data Resources Inc. (DRI) model	1.8	.4
Mean	1.2	.9
Standard deviation†	.8	1.0
Coefficient of variation‡	.7	1.1

*A 4 percent increase phased in over four quarters. Although some of the models are of foreign origin, they are simulated here for the United States.
†The standard deviation is a measure of the variation in a series. It is the square root of the mean squared deviations of each observation from the mean of the series.
‡The coefficient of variation is the standard deviation divided by the mean.
Source: Jeffrey Frankel and Katharine Rockett, "International Macroeconomic Policy Coordination When Policymakers Do Not Agree on the True Model," *American Economic Review*, 78 (June 1988), 324.

them can be right, the results from simulating the effect of macro policies with econometric models should be treated with great caution: the results depend strongly on the particular model used, and we do not know which is the best model.

SUMMARY

1   One can describe the transmission process in terms of portfolio balance. As firms and households receive more money, they bring their portfolios back into equilibrium by trading this newly acquired money for other goods and assets instead.

2   In the income-expenditure transmission story an increase in the monetary stock lowers interest rates; this raises investment via a lower cost of borrowing and perhaps higher stock prices.

3   Changes in interest rates affect the exchange rate of the dollar, so that, as interest rates fall, exports increase and imports decline; this reinforces expansionary domestic effects.

Was Monetary Policy Impotent in the 1990–91 Recession?

During the 1990–91 recession many people doubted that easing monetary policy would do much good. Thus the *New York Times* told its readers that Chairman Greenspan was pessimistic about the Fed's ability to spur the economy.* One reason was the heavy overhang of debt that had been incurred in the 1980s. This debt made both businesses and households very cautious and reluctant to borrow more. Greenspan believed that not only the size of the debt burden, but also the eagerness to reduce it, were unprecedented in the post-World War II period. In such a situation statistical indicators based on past experience provide little guidance. Moreover, as we discuss on page 372, many people believed that a credit crunch made banks reluctant to lend and that this would reduce the efficacy of monetary policy.

Such arguments are hard to evaluate, even by hindsight. Suppose that recovery does follow an easing of monetary policy. Those who believe that monetary policy was almost impotent can argue that the recovery was due to other factors. Similarly, if the economy does not recover, those who believe that the easier monetary policy was effective can claim that without it the economy would have been even worse off.

All the same, it is far from obvious that a debt overhang makes an expansionary monetary policy ineffective. To be sure, such an overhang reduces the willingness to spend; that is, it shifts the aggregate demand curve. But why should it reduce the interest elasticity of this curve? If it leaves this elasticity unchanged, then a cut of a given percentage in the interest rate will increase expenditures by the same percent as before. Of course, since expenditures are lower, this percent increase represents a smaller dollar increase than it would have, had expenditures not been held down by the debt overhang. But even so, monetary policy is far from impotent. Moreover, with so many bank loans having floating rates, an expansionary monetary policy significantly lowers the cost of servicing debts and hence saves some firms from bankruptcy.

*"Greenspan Pessimistic on Recovery," *New York Times,* (December 17, 1991), pp. A1, C2.

4   Monetary policy affects consumption by changing the reward for saving, by influencing the household's investment in durables, and through wealth and liquidity effects.

5   Some economists argue that monetary policy also works through the credit channel; small firms cannot borrow except from banks, and if banks were to cut back on lending in response to a reduction in their reserves, investment would fall.

6   Monetary policy also works through expectations; wages and prices could rise before the increase in the monetary stock actually takes place.

KEY TERMS

portfolio equilibrium   econometric model
net exports   MPS model
credit channel

QUESTIONS AND EXERCISES

1 Do you think monetary policy has had much influence on the behavior of income over the last ten years? To answer this question look at data presented in the *Economic Report of the President.* Document your conclusion by references to these or other data.

*2 Compare and contrast the monetarist and the income-expenditure approaches to the impact of monetary policy on income. Explain why this impact seems stronger in the monetarist than in the income-expenditure approach.

3 Describe the ways in which an expansionary monetary policy increases consumption.

*4 What does the credit view add to the discussion of the effects of a restrictive monetary policy?

FURTHER READING

BRAYTON, FLINT, and EILEEN MAUSKOPF. "Structure and Uses of the MPS Quarterly Econometric Model of the United States," *Federal Reserve Bulletin,* 73 (February 1987), 93–109. An explanation of the Fed's econometric model.

GERTLER, MARK, and SIMON GILCHRIST. "The Role of Credit Market Imperfections in the Monetary Transmission Mechanism: Arguments and Evidence," *Scandinavian Journal of Economics,* 95 (1993), 43–64. A good exposition of the credit channel.

MISHKIN, FREDERICK. "Monetary Policy and Liquidity: Simulation Results," *Economic Inquiry,* 16 (January 1978), 16–36. An interesting analysis of the importance of changes in household liquidity.

WOJNILOWER, ALBERT. "The Central Role of Credit Crunches in Recent Financial History," *Brookings Papers on Economic Activity,* 2 (1980), 277–326. A fascinating piece of "analytic description" arguing that monetary policy can curb a boom only by plunging the economy into a recession. It is brilliantly written—a pleasure to read.

Can Countercyclical Monetary Policy Succeed?

After you have read this chapter, you will be able to:

- Evaluate the problem that lags in the impact of the Fed's actions create for monetary policy.
- Explain why new classical economists reject discretionary monetary policy.
- Be aware of the Lucas critique.
- Appreciate the political and administrative problems of monetary policy.

In this chapter we look at some of the ways in which monetary policy can go wrong. You will learn why some economists think that the Fed should not try to counter economic fluctuations, but should follow a hands-off policy instead. Some of the problems we discuss are the result of politics rather than strictly of economics, but, as has already been suggested, politics plays an important role in economic policy.

The old-fashioned, traditional functions of monetary policy were to maintain the gold (or silver) standard and to prevent financial panics. In the early 1920s Keynes made the then radical suggestion of using monetary policy to stabilize the domestic economy on a continuous basis. Countercyclical monetary policy became conventional wisdom after 1929. More recently, this conventional wisdom has been challenged by a number of economists who have argued that it is a vain hope, that in attempting to stabilize the economy, monetary policy is likely to generate further instability and inflation. In this chapter we take up the reasons why they think so. This means dealing with three sets of problems: those created by the lag in the effect of monetary policy, by rational expectations, and by political and administrative difficulties.

THE PROBLEM OF LAGS

To stabilize GDP, it is not sufficient that the Fed's actions have a sufficiently strong effect on GDP. It is also necessary that this effect occurs at the right time—that it raises nominal GDP when it is too low and reduces nominal GDP when it threatens to be too high. This creates a problem for the Fed because its actions affect GDP only with a lag. Hence, if it undertakes open-market purchases during a recession by the time this raises GDP, the economy might be in an expansion with GDP already too high. If it then undertakes open-market sales, this restrictive policy may have its effects mainly during the next recession. We may therefore get the stabilizer's nightmare shown in Figure 26.1 in which monetary policy *increases* the amplitude of the business cycle. This possibility has to be taken seriously because in the postwar period business cycles have been short. In the years 1945 to 1991, the median length of a recession was only 10 months, and the median length of an expansion was 37 months.

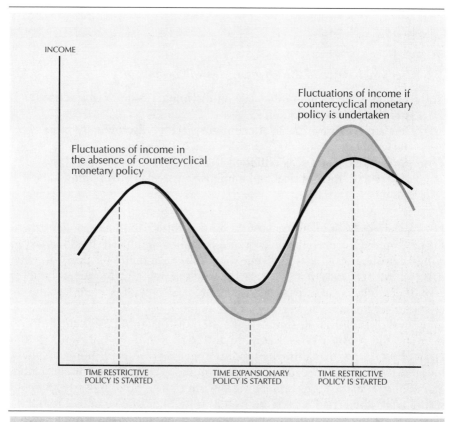

Figure 26.1   Effects of Badly Timed Stabilization Policy. A badly timed stabilization policy can be destabilizing.

A Formal Model

Milton Friedman has developed a model that highlights the importance of the proper timing of countercyclical monetary and fiscal policies. Assume that the trend of aggregate expenditures is just right and that we want to minimize fluctuations around this trend. A convenient way of measuring fluctuations is a statistical measure called the **variance.** (To obtain the variance take the difference between each observation and the mean and square it. Then take the average of these squared differences.) Since the variance involves the *squared* deviations from the mean, treating the minimization of the variance as the goal of stabilization policy means trying to minimize not the differences of aggregate expenditures from the desired level, but the *squares* of these differences. In turn, this implies that we are more than proportionally concerned about a few large differences than about more frequent small ones.[1] An implicit value judgment is also involved in the treatment of a dollar of excessive income as being exactly as undesirable as a dollar of shortfall in income.

All the same, let us assume that we *do* want to minimize the variance of nominal income. Changes in investment, and so on, cause income to vary. We designate the variance of income that is due to these private-sector fluctuations and is independent of policy by σ_x^2. Stabilization policy then consists of using monetary or fiscal policies to generate changes in income that offset these private-sector fluctuations. Since we are concerned only with reducing the fluctuation of income around its mean, and not with changing the level of income on the average, these policy-induced changes are sometimes positive and sometimes negative, but have a mean of zero. Their variance around this mean of zero we will call σ_y^2. The total variance of income, designated by σ_z^2, is the result both of the original fluctuations in income and of the policy-induced fluctuations. A theorem in statistics tells us that

$$\sigma_z^2 = \sigma_x^2 + \sigma_y^2 + 2R\sigma_x\sigma_y,$$

where σ_z^2 is the variance of income after the application of policy, σ_x^2 is the original variance of income, σ_y^2 is the variance directly induced by the stabilization policy, and R is the coefficient of correlation between them.[2]

[1] For example, compare two policies. Policy A generates the following series of deviations from the mean: 0, 4, 0; Policy B results in deviations 2, 2, 1. If the criterion is to minimize the absolute deviations, Policy A is superior. But if we are trying to minimize the square of the deviations, Policy B (with a sum of 9) is better. Specifically, we are using what is called a quadratic utility function, such as $U = f(P^2, U^2)$ where P is the excess of the actual inflation rate over the desired inflation rate and U is the excess of the actual unemployment rate over the full-employment rate. (Since both inflation and unemployment lower utility, f denotes a negative function.) This use of a quadratic utility function involves a value judgment, which not everyone may wish to accept.

[2] The correlation coefficient can best be explained by considering the regression equation $y = a + bx + u$ in which a is a constant, b measures the effect of x on y, and u is a randomly distributed variable. The computer is then kindly requested to select those values of a and b that allow x to explain most of the squared variation in y, that is, to minimize the square of u. If u is zero, then x and y are perfectly correlated; that is, since we know the constants, $a + b$, once given x we know what y has to be. In this case the correlation coefficient is unity (or minus unity if b is negative). Now suppose that there is no relation at all between x and y: assume, for example, that x is your age and y the last digit of your driver's license. In this case knowledge of x would not allow you to predict y at all; the correlation coefficient is zero. The square of the correlation coefficient tells you the proportion of y "explained" by x.

This equation shows the great importance of the correlation between the original variations in income and the variations induced by policy—that is, the timing of policy. If a policy is badly timed—R positive—so that it raises nominal income when nominal income is already above its mean and lowers it when it is below its mean, then we have the stabilizer's nightmare of $\sigma_z > \sigma_x$.

If this obvious point were all that the above equation shows, we would not have bothered to introduce it. But it also shows two other, not so obvious things. One is that it does not suffice for the policy to be *neutral* in its timing, that is, to be right half the time. If it is and $R = 0$, the last term in the equation drops out and the variance of income is equal to $\sigma_x^2 + \sigma_y^2$, which is, of course, greater than σ_x^2. Hence, if the Fed's timing is half-right, it is *de*stabilizing income. This suggests that stabilization policy may actually be destabilizing. As Table 26.1 shows, forecast errors are by no means trivial. Second, by algebraic manipulation one can obtain the maximum effective size of the stabilization policy's impact on income for each R. This is $\sigma_y^2 = -R\sigma_x^2$. Any policy that *tries* to stabilize more than this will actually stabilize less. For example, assume that the Fed adopts a policy powerful enough to offset all the fluctuation in income; that is, it sets $\sigma_y = \sigma_x$. If the correlation coefficient is −.5, such a policy will not succeed in reducing the net fluctuation of income at all.[3] And if the correlation coefficient is, say, −.4 it would actually *in*crease income fluctuations.[4] Too much can be even worse than nothing at all.

This way of looking at policy has much to teach. It shows the great importance of the timing of the impact of the policy, since this determines R. It warns us (1) that it does not take great errors in timing to be destabilizing and (2) that one must beware of adopting a policy that is too strong. Hence, the Fed must try to estimate accurately (1) future nominal income, (2) the impact of its policy on nominal income, and (3) the timing of this impact. Remember, however, that all of this applies only to what is strictly a *stabilization* policy, that is, to a policy that tries to even out fluctuations in nominal income. Policy may also be concerned with changing the average level of income. For example, a policy that causes the unemployment rate to fluctuate between, say, 5 and 7 percent is surely better than one that causes the unemployment rate to be absolutely stable at 12 percent.

Problems Created by the Lag

If monetary policy would have most of its effect on income almost immediately, the prediction of future income would not create a serious problem for the Fed. Since income changes very little over a short span of time, such as a month, the Fed could use the current level of income, with a small adjustment for the growth trend, as its estimate of income at the time its policy becomes effective. But this does not work if monetary policy takes a long time to affect

[3] If $\sigma_x^2 = \sigma_y^2$ and $R = -.5$, then the expression $\sigma_x^2 + \sigma_y^2 + 2R\sigma_x\sigma_y$ reduces to σ_x^2, which is the original fluctuation of income in the absence of stabilization policy. If the correlation coefficient is −.5, the maximum by which a policy of optimal size could reduce the variance of income is 25 percent; any policy more powerful than that would be less effective.

[4] In this case the variance of income would be $2\sigma_x^2 - .8\sigma_x^2 = 1.2\sigma_x^2$ compared to σ_x^2 in the absence of policy.

Table 26.1   Mean Forecast Errors for Nominal GDP

| | Time Forecast Is Made:* | | |
	Start of Quarter	Middle of Quarter	End of Quarter
Number of Forecasters in Sample	4	3	2
Forecast Is For Quarters Ahead	Mean Absolute Error (percent of GDP)†		
1	1.8%	1.5%	1.3%
2	1.5	1.4	1.3
3	1.4	1.7	1.4
4	1.4	1.3	1.2
5	1.4	1.3	1.3
6	1.3	1.3	1.4
7	1.2	1.2	1.2
8	1.2	1.1	1.2

*Forecasts made at different times during a quarter for the next quarter predict for different times ahead. For example, a forecast made on January 1 for the second quarter of the year predicts two quarters ahead; a forecast made on March 31 predicts only one quarter ahead.

†The mean absolute error is the mean of the unsigned errors. For example, the absolute mean of 1, 2, and −3 is 2. The period covered is 1986.1 to 1991.1.

Source: Based on Stephen McNees, "How Large Are Economic Forecast Errors?" Federal Reserve Bank of Boston, *New England Economic Review*, July–August 1992, p. 38.

income. Assume that most of the effect only occurs after two years. In two years the economy is likely to be in a different stage of the business cycle. Hence, if the Fed selects its policy on the basis of what income is currently, the correlation between the original income fluctuations (σ_x^2) and the income fluctuations caused by policy (σ_y^2) could be close to zero, or positive, so that monetary policy destabilizes the economy. If monetary policy has a long lag—as much of the empirical evidence suggests—then the Fed should use a forecast of income. Since obviously the Fed's forecasts are not without errors, this provides a limitation of the effectiveness of stabilization policy.

A second way in which the length of the lag is important is the leeway the Fed has to offset errors it has made. Suppose that it expected income to decline and therefore adopted an expansionary policy; income then turns out to be much higher than expected. If the lag is short, the Fed can quickly reverse itself and offset the effect of its previous action, but it cannot do so if the lag is long.[5]

---

[5] In principle, the Fed could avoid this problem by adopting a corrective policy that is much stronger than the initial policy it is trying to offset. For example, assume that only 20 percent of the impact on income occurs in the first quarter and that after one year monetary policy has 80 percent of its full effect. The Fed could then fully offset within a quarter a policy action that it took a year ago, *if* it were willing to adopt an offsetting policy that is four times as strong as the original policy. But such large policy changes have costs; in particular, they lead to violent swings in interest rates. There is also the *possibility* that a continual policy of quick offsets via stronger off-

There is still a third problem. To use stabilization policy effectively, the Fed must be able to predict the timing of the impact of its policy. That is no easy task because various methods of estimating the lag provide widely varying answers. Simulations of monetary policy with econometric models usually provide a longer estimate of the lag than do some other methods. And, as Table 26.2 shows, there is little agreement about the length of the lag even among econometric models.

What makes the problem even worse is that the lags may not be stable, but may vary substantially from time to time. Suppose that the Fed's staff were to tell the FOMC that the lag is, *on the average,* one year, but that, in one-third of the cases, it is only 6 months, and in another third it is 18 months. In deciding whether to adopt an expansionary or a restrictive policy, the FOMC would then not know whether to orient its policy toward the income level it expects to prevail in 6 months, in a year, or in 18 months. What the FOMC must consider is not the average lag, but the lag for the particular action it is contemplating. Hence, knowledge of the average lag is sufficient only if the lags cluster closely around this average. Thus, if the Fed were to use the average lag from its econometric model, this *could* make its policy destabilizing in the majority of cases, even if the model estimates the average lag correctly. However, this is not so if the Fed avoids all explicit forecasting and simply bases its actions on the current level of income.[6] A similar thing applies to the strength of its policy. The Fed must know not just the effect that a, say, $1 billion open-market operation has on GDP on the average, but also the effect in each par-

---

Table 26.2   The Effect on Real GDP of a 1 Percent Increase in Short-Term Interest Rates

Model	1st Year	2nd Year	3rd Year
MPS*	-.20	-.70	-1.10
DRI†	-.47	-.53	- .13
Fair‡	-.24	-.25	.03
FRBSF§	-.55	-.19	.04
Average	-.37	-.42	- .29

*The MPS model is the Board of Governors' econometric model.
†The DRI model is a large commercially available model.
‡The Fair model is a model developed by Ray Fair of Yale University.
§ The FRBSF model is a model developed by the Federal Reserve Bank of San Francisco.
Source: Glenn Rudenbusch, "What are the Lags in Monetary Policy?" FRBSF Weekly Letter Number 95-05, February 3, 1995.

---

setting policies would cause an explosive increase in the magnitude of policy moves. However, this does not appear likely.

[6] If the Fed bases its policy entirely on current income, then, surprisingly, the variability of the lag does no harm. In fact, the more variable it is, the greater is the probability that policy is stabilizing. We know of no intuitive explanation of this strange result that emerges from a mathematical analysis. See Haskell Benishay, "A Framework for the Evaluation of Short-Term Fiscal and Monetary Policy," *Journal of Money, Credit and Banking,* 4 (November 1972), 779–810.

ticular situation in which it takes action. Perhaps these effects are quite similar in most cases, perhaps not. We do not know.

Thus the existence of a significant lag in the effect of monetary policy creates three problems for the Fed. It must forecast income, even if only by saying that income will not change; it cannot offset past errors easily and quickly; and it must estimate the effect of its policies in each period.

Empirical Estimates of the Lag

It is convenient to divide the lag into two parts. There is first the **inside lag,** that is, *the lag from the time the need for action arises until the Fed takes action.* This is a distributed lag since the Fed is unlikely to undertake all its actions at one time. (A distributed lag is a lag in which the effects occur not all at one point but over several periods.) Usually it will undertake its new open-market policy in a series of steps spread out over several months because it is uncertain whether the new policy is the appropriate one and therefore wants to move slowly.

This inside lag can, but need not, be very short. It depends both on the extent to which the Fed is willing to take action on a forecast as opposed to waiting until conditions have actually changed and on how long it waits to make sure that a change has actually occurred. It also depends on whether the Fed changes policy in large steps taken quickly or in many small steps spread out over time. Thus if it is willing to undertake much of its open-market purchases before a business downturn actually occurs, the inside lag will be negative. The inside lag therefore depends on the Fed itself and on who is chairman of the Board of Governors.

Then there is the **outside lag.** This is *the distributed lag from the time of the Fed's action until income changes.* Before investment takes place, firms have to make a decision to invest: they have to draw up plans, place orders, and so on. For consumption, it may take some time until interest rates on consumer credit decline and until households respond to the rise in their money holdings and to the increase in security prices that results from lower interest rates.

The outside lag is more objective and much less subject to Fed control than the inside lag. Many economists have tried to estimate it. Some have used econometric models, while others have regressed income on money or have measured the lag between turning points in the monetary growth rate and business cycle turning points. Several economists have measured how long it takes firms to invest, while still others have (following the analysis described in Chapter 16) looked at the length of time it takes interest rates to return to their previous levels after changes in the monetary growth rate. Unfortunately, little agreement has been reached, though most, but not all, of these studies show that it takes *at least* two quarters for monetary policy to reach half its ultimate effect.[7] Beyond this limited agreement, the range of estimates is large;

---

[7] Journalistic accounts usually forget the qualifying "at least," and say that monetary policy has a six-month lag. A complication is that it is quite possible that the effect of monetary policy does not build up smoothly to a peak, but rises to a certain level and then declines to a lower level or cycles around some level.

How Does the Fed Forecast?

The Federal Reserve does not rely on any single forecasting method, but uses several. The Board of Governors' staff uses the MPS model, which it developed, and also employs economists who forecast conditions in various sectors of the economy. These two types of forecasts are combined in the "Green Book" (nonfinancial forecasts) and the "Blue Book" (financial forecasts), which the staff prepares prior to each FOMC meeting. In addition, for every FOMC meeting, each Federal Reserve Bank prepares a survey of conditions in its own District. These surveys are combined in a "Beige Book," which is made available to the public and is reported on by some newspapers. The staffs of the Federal Reserve Banks also make forecasts, which their presidents can present in the FOMC discussions. And, of course, the Fed has available various private forecasts, as well as forecasts by other government agencies.

How accurate are these forecasts? The evidence for prior years suggests that they are about as accurate as those of the major forecasting firms. So, the data in Table 26.1 are a fairly good guide to how well the Fed can predict GDP.

The FOMC has to predict not only the course of GDP but also how large a change in the funds rate or reserves is needed to bring GDP to its appropriate path. It can use its econometric model to do that, or it can rely on intuitive, seat-of-the-pants judgment. Neither we nor the FOMC have any data on how reliable these estimates are, but since the predictions of the impact of monetary policy made by various econometric models vary widely, as Table 25.1 shows, the FOMC's predictions may be subject to significant error.

the big econometric models, including the Fed's own MPS model, usually show long lags. A major reason why these models show such long lags is that most of them use a term-structure equation that shows a very slow adaptation of long-term interest rates to the changes that the Fed brings about in short-term rates.

All these methods are subject to some criticism, and the substantial disagreement among their results suggests that we should not be confident about our knowledge of the lag in considering the impact of monetary policy. Moreover, although little empirical work has been done on the extent to which the lag of monetary policy varies from case to case, the very limited amount of information that is available suggests that the lag is highly variable. If correct, this is most disturbing.

Policy Tools: A Further Consideration

We are now in a position to return to the discussion of the tools of monetary policy and to take up a sophisticated problem that we could not discuss before. Suppose several policy tools are available, such as open-market operations, discount rate changes, and reserve requirement changes, or, alternatively, fiscal policy and monetary policy, all of which are strong enough to change income by the required amount. Which one should be used? One possible answer is to use the strongest. But a moment's reflection will show that, unless there is a cost from using a tool too much or too often, there is no reason for choosing the strongest. Instead of looking at the strength, one should use the tool that has the most *predictable* impact. Moreover, it is generally better to use several tools at the same time. This is so because if their effects are not perfectly correlated, then an averaging-out process ensures that the variance of the impact is less for several tools used jointly than it is for any single tool. The exact mixture in which the tools should be used depends on their relative variances and on the correlation of their variances.

RATIONAL EXPECTATIONS AND MARKET CLEARING

As we discussed in Chapter 21, new classical economists believe that, with rational expectations and highly flexible wages and prices, changes in aggregate expenditures do not generate the variations in real income that we call business cycles. If aggregate expenditures fall, prices, not employment, adjust.[8]

If the rational-expectations theorists are correct and if wages and prices adjust quickly, an expansionary policy during recessions not only does no good, it does harm because it is inflationary. To see why, consider first an economy with rational expectations, completely flexible prices, and high employment. The government decides to undertake a long-run expansionary policy. The traditional story is that firms react to an increased demand at first by raising their output and only with a lag by raising their prices. This is so primarily because firms do not know whether this increase in demand is permanent or just temporary, and they want to avoid frequent price changes. But, say the new classical economists, this story is wrong. Entrepreneurs read newspapers, and hence, in this case when demand increases, they realize that it is due to an expansionary policy and that the higher demand will persist. So they raise prices right away instead of raising output.

In this example the government initiates a policy to raise aggregate expenditures during a period of high employment; this is hardly an example of a good stabilization policy under new classical, income-expenditure, or monetarist theory. So now assume instead that it raises aggregate expenditures whenever unemployment reaches 7 percent. If so, then whenever it becomes apparent that unemployment is approaching 7 percent, firms know that the government will raise aggregate expenditures and hence they raise their prices. Or, more realistically, they refrain from doing what they otherwise would have done during the recession—cut prices and wages.

Carrying this approach a bit further, rational-expectations theorists have argued that an *expected* increase in the monetary growth rate raises only prices and does not raise output even temporarily. Output rises temporarily only in response to an *unexpected* increase in the monetary growth rate. Hence, the only way the Fed could raise output and employment would be if it could

---

[8] On a very strict interpretation of new classical theory recessions do not occur. But if it takes some limited time to adjust wages and prices downward when expenditures fall, a temporary recession could occur.

adopt expansionary policies that are unexpected. But sooner or later the public will figure out any consistent Federal Reserve policy. The theory that only unexpected changes in the money supply affect output is highly controversial. While the empirical evidence was initially favorable to it, in subsequent empirical tests its performance has, on the whole, not been good.

Although new classical theory, if correct, destroys the justification for most stabilization policy, it implies that one policy would be highly effective, that is, a policy to terminate an inflation cold turkey, by drastically cutting aggregate expenditures. The usual story is that if a restrictive monetary or fiscal policy cuts aggregate expenditures, the initial result is a much greater fall in output than in the inflation rate. Firms and employees do not realize that the government is serious about ending inflation. They continue to expect inflation and therefore raise their wages and prices. Only after some time of high unemployment will the inflation rate decline substantially. Rational-expectations theory suggests such a painful recession is not necessary. Firms and labor will know that the government is adopting a policy that will end inflation, so that if they raise their wages and prices, their relative wages and prices will be too high. Hence, they will refrain from doing so, and the inflation will end. Many economists are skeptical, particularly since the experience of the early 1980s in both the United States and Britain seems inconsistent with such an optimistic view. Both Chairman Paul Volcker at the Fed and Margaret Thatcher, the then British prime minister, made it clear that they would cut aggregate expenditures to bring the inflation rate down. Even so, in both countries, it took a great deal of unemployment to do so. New classical economists can, of course, reply that the public did not believe what it was told, but could have been convinced by more drastic policy measures, such as a constitutional amendment requiring the Fed to make price stability its dominant goal. Such a hypothesis is hard to test.

Whether or not one accepts it in its stark form, new classical theory still offers an important lesson: the public should be told if the Fed adopts a restrictive policy and intends to stick with it. In general, one does not have to accept new classical theory completely to conclude that expectations do matter and that monetary policies will have different effects depending on what expectations they generate. For example, some of the variation in the lag with which changes in the money stock affect income *may* be due to differences in the extent to which the public realizes what is happening.

The Lucas Critique

Stabilization policy requires that the government be able to predict the effects of its new policy reasonably well. But, as Robert Lucas has pointed out, the theory of rational expectations implies that with the currently available tools of analysis this may—in principle—be an impossible task. Obviously, the only data that the government's economists have available are data gathered in the period before the proposed policy has been put into effect. These data therefore reflect only how the public has acted in the absence of the proposed policy and so may be a misleading guide to how the public would act under the new policy. Consider, for example, a new policy that from now on would cut personal income taxes during a recession and raise them again during the following expansion. To find out how big a tax cut is needed, economists calculate the marginal propensity to consume from past data on consumption and disposable income or they look at how consumption changed every time taxes were cut previously. But they may be in for a disappointment. The past data may show a high propensity to consume and a strong response to a tax cut. But now when taxes are cut as a countercyclical policy, the public *may* raise its consumption very little. It knows that, unlike in the past, taxes will now be raised again when the economy expands. And since the public sets its consumption on the basis of its long-run disposable income, it now reacts very differently to a tax cut than it did before.

The response of economists to this **Lucas critique,** as it is called, has varied. Robert Lucas himself, along with many other rational-expectations theorists, has argued that it invalidates the use of econometric models and other forecasting devices for predicting the effect of policy changes: for the time being, economists should simply admit their ignorance. Instead of trying to predict the effects of macroeconomic policies, they should do more work on microeconomics, specifically on learning how the public changes its behavior in response to changes in policy.

Other economists, particularly builders of large models, are more optimistic. They admit that, *in principle,* Lucas is right and that using their models to predict the effect of a new policy is not logical. But, they argue, the error that results from the failure to take the public's response to the new policy into account is usually small, so that their analyses still provide a useful first approximation. After all, nobody claims that econometric models or other forecasting techniques give perfect results. And the empirical evidence, in general, suggests that the Lucas critique is not of great substantive importance.

POLITICAL AND ADMINISTRATIVE PROBLEMS

Opponents of countercyclical monetary policy do not just point out the difficulties created by lags in the effect of monetary policy or argue that the private sector can handle changes in aggregate expenditures on its own. They also believe that the Fed's policy making is flawed, that the Fed could not be trusted to carry out countercyclical policy even if the lags were shorter. Milton Friedman, the leading opponent of countercyclical policy, has stated that the case against such a policy is "at least as much political as it is economic."[9] The argument that the Fed cannot be trusted to undertake correct policies has four components: that the Fed is subservient to its political masters, that the Fed maximizes its own welfare rather than the public's, that the Fed's policy making is inefficient, and that the Fed's policy is not consistent over time. We already discussed the first two of these in Chapter 11.

[9] Franco Modigliani and Milton Friedman, "The Monetarist Controversy: A Seminar Discussion," Federal Reserve Bank of San Francisco, *Economic Review* Supplement, Spring 1977, p. 18.

Inefficient Policy Making

Most economists assume that firms and households maximize utility and profits rationally and efficiently. Some buttress this assumption with the argument that firms that do not do so are sooner or later forced out of business or taken over. But there is no such Darwinian mechanism that ensures that the Fed operates efficiently.

One can therefore question whether the Fed's decision making is good enough for countercyclical policy to be nearly as effective as the lag in the effect of monetary policy would permit it to be. One can doubt this on three grounds. First, one can recognize the limitations on the assumption of rational behavior and make some allowance for the widespread and pervasive errors in decision making that psychologists have discovered. For example, there is much experimental evidence that even highly educated people err in estimating the probabilities of compound events, such as the probability that Event C will occur if the occurrence of Event C requires that both Events A and B occur.

Second, one can introduce some considerations of self-interest and argue that FOMC members (like other people) unconsciously do certain things that make them better-off as individuals, but make Fed policy less efficient. For example, it is painful to admit to oneself that one has made an error. Hence, people are tempted to insist that their current policies are correct, even if there is much evidence to the contrary. This is particularly likely to occur in a committee, because the various members reassure one another that they are right. Psychologists call this **group-think.**

Third, the Fed may unwittingly adopt inefficient procedures because they benefit the Fed as an institution or because they make life easier for individual policy makers. Thus Robert Hetzel, an economist at the Richmond Federal Reserve Bank, has suggested a way in which the Fed's attempt to preserve its autonomy interacts with political pressures on the Fed to degrade seriously the quality of its economic analysis and hence of its policy.[10] His hypothesis explains a puzzling observation: although most FOMC members are good economists, FOMC discussions are largely seat-of-the-pants, lack analytic edge, and are surprisingly vague. Hetzel's explanation is that the Fed is afraid that if it carries out policies that are highly unpopular, Congress will take away its independence. Hence it bends with the wind. If one uses a well-developed analytic framework (for example, income-expenditure theory or the quantity theory), then bending with the wind creates a nasty problem—your analysis tells you to do one thing, but you may want to do something else. This is unpleasant. Hetzel argues that to avoid this dilemma, the Fed eschews any well-developed analytic framework and instead uses vague reasoning that can be made to seem consistent with anything it wants to do. This, unfortunately, degrades the quality of thought that goes into policy making. Not much work has been done on these problems of inefficient policy making because they fall in between economics and psychology. But they may be important.

[10] Robert Hetzel, "The Political Economy of Monetary Policy," in *The Political Economy of American Monetary Policy,* ed. Thomas Mayer (New York: Cambridge University Press, 1990), pp. 99–114.

Time-Inconsistent Monetary Policies

A subtle difficulty in communication between the Fed and the public could result in a higher inflation rate. The problem arises because the Fed, if it is rational, should want output to be higher than it usually is. This is obvious if unemployment exceeds the NAIRU. But even at full employment, output is below its socially optimal level because taxes drive a wedge between the rewards that a person receives from working and the value of that person's output, so that people work fewer than the socially optimal number of hours.[11] In other words, income taxes act as an excise tax on work and, like other excise taxes, discourage the taxed activity. By generating a higher-than-expected inflation rate, the Fed can induce people to overestimate their real wages and hence to work more. This tempts the Fed to raise the inflation rate.

But people know that the Fed has an incentive to generate inflation, so they expect the inflation rate to be high. Thus, their hours worked, and their output, are no greater at the high inflation rate than before. We therefore have the bad effects of higher inflation, without the good effects of higher output. The policy that seemed beneficial before it was put into effect, and before people adjusted their expectations, is now harmful. (Hence, the name **time inconsistency.**)

So why should the Fed play this game? One answer is that it cannot help it. Since people think that it is rational for the Fed to raise the inflation rate, and since they expect the Fed to act rationally, they raise their wages and prices in anticipation.

That is one possibility. Another is that people know that the Fed knows inflationary policies will not raise output and employment, and so they expect that the Fed will not be tempted to adopt inflationary policies. This type of "I know that you know that I know that you know" story can get very complex, and economists have used game theory to analyze this problem. Unfortunately, the results they obtain depend on the specific assumptions made, and the realism of these specific assumptions is hard to determine. Moreover, it may be possible for the Fed to signal to the public that it will not play this time-inconsistency game. For example, one possibility is to appoint as Fed chairman someone who is known to be vehemently opposed to inflation. But the Fed has an incentive to send wrong signals, so here we go again. However, one may also ask whether the Fed is really rational enough to take into account that people want to work too few hours.

A SUMMING UP

Where does all this leave us? This is a legitimate question, but one that is hard to answer. Surely nobody would deny that lags, political pressures, self-interest, and inefficient policy making reduce the efficacy of countercyclical monetary policy. This much is settled. What is not settled is the answer to the next

[11] Although the proposition that people work too few hours is widely accepted by economists, it is open to challenge on the grounds that we use some of our income to compete with others in "conspicuous consumptions." Hence if someone works harder and increases her income, she is better-off, but her peers are worse off.

question: "By how much?" More specifically, do these factors prevent any, or most, countercyclical policy from actually stabilizing GDP? There is great disagreement here. A substantial majority of economists would answer no. They would readily agree that lags, political pressures, and perhaps the Fed's self-interest and time inconsistency reduce the efficacy of monetary policy. But they believe that, even so, the Fed can reduce economic fluctuations, at least to some extent, and should try to do so. However, other economists, led by Milton Friedman, the late Karl Brunner, and Allan Meltzer, disagree. They believe that attempts to stabilize GDP with monetary policy are likely to destabilize it.

SUMMARY

1 Monetary policy affects income with a distributed lag. Hence, it might be badly timed and therefore destabilizing. This depends on the correlation between the policy and the original fluctuation in income and on the strength of the policy.
2 The existence of the lag creates several problems. The Fed must forecast income, and it must predict the strength of its policy and its distributed lag. Moreover, the lag prevents the Fed from quickly offsetting any errors it has made.
3 The Fed should use not necessarily the strongest tools, but those with the most predictable effects. Usually it is best to employ several.
4 Rational expectations create another potential problem for the Fed. Under rational expectations, stabilization policy can be effective only if the government has better information than the public or if its policy affects the economy before the public can act.
5 Rational-expectations theory also argues that if the Fed reacts to a recession by a predictable expansionary policy, this policy will have its effects only on prices and not on output. However, this is much disputed. Rational-expectations theory also implies that, if the government changes its policy, then the economy will change too, so that the policy, which is based on past data, may no longer be valid.
6 There are some potential inefficiencies in the way the FOMC makes policy.

KEY TERMS

distributed lags
inside lag
outside lag

variance of income
Lucas critique
time inconsistency

QUESTIONS AND EXERCISES

*1 "The problem with monetary policy is not, as was once thought, that it is too weak, but that it is too strong." How could one make a case for this statement?
2 Explain why monetary policy is destabilizing if the correlation coefficient between σ_x^2 and σ_y^2 is zero or positive.
*3 Discuss the problem that the lag in the effect of monetary policy creates for the Federal Reserve.
*4 Why does a variable lag create a more serious problem than a stable one? What factors could account for its being variable?
5 Explain in your own words the rational-expectations criticism of stabilization policy.
6 Discuss: "Effective countercyclical policy is infeasible because the Fed is a political animal."

FURTHER READING

FRIEDMAN, MILTON. "The Effects of a Full Employment Policy on Economic Stability: A Formal Analysis," in his *Essays in Positive Economics*. Chicago: University of Chicago Press, 1953. This is a classic.

———. "Monetary Policy: Theory and Practice," *Journal of Money, Credit and Banking* 14 (February 1982), 98–118. A powerful indictment of the Fed.

HAVRILSEKY, THOMAS. *The Pressures on American Monetary Policy*. Boston: Kluwer Academic Publishers, 1933. A view of the Fed as dominated by the White House.

LOMBRA, RAYMOND, and MICHAEL MORAN. "Policy Advice and Policymaking at the Federal Reserve," *Carnegie-Rochester Conference Series on Public Policy* 12 (Autumn 1980), 9–68. A fascinating critique of how the FOMC makes decisions.

MAYER, THOMAS, ed. *The Political Economy of American Monetary Policy*. New York: Cambridge University Press, 1990. A collection of papers on the political and administrative aspects of Fed policy making, such as political business cycles.

MAYER, THOMAS. *Monetarism and Macroeconomic Policy*. Brookfield, Vt.: Edward Elgar, 1990. Chapter 6 contains a discussion of administrative problems that may degrade the making of monetary policy.

ROOSE, LAWRENCE. "Inherent Conflict in U.S. Monetary Policymaking," *Cato Journal* 5 (Winter 1986), 771–76. A sharp criticism of the way the FOMC makes policy by a former FOMC member.

SHEFFRIN, STEVEN. *Rational Expectations*. New York: Cambridge University Press, 1983. An excellent survey.

TAYLOR, HERB. "Time Inconsistency," Federal Reserve Bank of Philadelphia, *Business Review* (March–April 1985), 3–12. A clear exposition.

TOMA, EUGENIA, and MARK TOMA. *Central Bankers, Bureaucratic Incentives and Monetary Policy*. Boston: Kluwer Academic Publishers, 1987. Contains most of the leading articles on the public-choice theory of the Fed.

WILLETT, THOMAS. *The Political Business Cycle*. Durham, N.C.: Duke University Press, 1988. A collection of interesting papers on the political aspects of stabilization policy.

The Record of Monetary Policy

After you have read this chapter, you will be able to:

- Understand the Fed's initial conceptions of monetary policy.
- Appreciate the debate about monetary policy during the Great Depression.
- Explain the Fed's role in the high inflation of the 1960s and 1970s and in its termination in the 1980s.

Having looked at the principles governing monetary policy, the time has come to see how the Fed has actually conducted monetary policy. Instead of discussing monetary policy in a seemingly balanced way by giving equal emphasis to all periods, we focus on particular episodes to see how the Fed has dealt with certain major problems. The focus is on evaluating the efficacy of the Fed's monetary policy and on seeing what the Fed has learned from its experience, rather than on isolated facts.

THE EARLY YEARS

When the Federal Reserve System was inaugurated in 1913 one of its major goals, perhaps *the* major goal, was the maintenance of the gold standard, which at the time was generally considered the foundation of sound money. We will discuss the gold standard in Part Five. Here it suffices to note that under the gold standard "rules of the game," the Fed was supposed to let the quantity of money be determined by the country's gold stock. A gold inflow should have increased the quantity of money, and a gold outflow, decreased it.

Although the quantity theory of money played *some* role in its thinking, the second guiding idea of the Fed was the **real-bills doctrine.** According to this now-discarded theory, what matters is the *quality* rather than the *quantity* of money; as long as deposits are created as a result of short-term self-liquidating loans that finance real (as opposed to financial) activities, deposit creation cannot be inflationary.[1] Member banks could borrow from the Fed only by rediscounting **eligible paper,** that is, those *promissory notes they had discounted for their customers that met the requirements of the real-bills doctrine,* or by discounting their own promissory notes backed by government securities.[2] The theory was that this would provide an "elastic" currency that would allow the money supply to expand when the demand for money for real transactions increased. At such a time banks would discount more eligible promissory notes for their customers and could then rediscount this eligible paper with the Fed. This is an extreme example of the accommodative policy the Fed has followed so frequently.

Another guiding idea—the main reason the Fed was established—was the need to avoid financial panics. It was widely believed that recessions were often the result of financial panics that were, in turn, caused by excessive speculation. Hence, one of the tasks of the Fed was to limit speculation. The provision of an elastic currency, too, would help to prevent financial panics, since it would prevent banks from running out of currency. Bank failures, and the resulting panics, would also be reduced by the Fed's supervision of member banks and the centralization of member bank reserves in the Federal Reserve Banks. The law of large numbers makes centralized reserves a more effective barrier against failure than reserves that are kept individually by each bank.

A further goal of the Fed was to eliminate, or at least reduce, the pronounced seasonal swings in interest rates that occurred before 1914 and to avoid the sharp interest-rate increases that accompanied periods of financial stringency and panics.

All in all, the initial goals of the Fed were those that seemed reasonable to a small-town merchant in 1913, rather than those that an economist would now set for a central bank. Full employment had not yet been "invented"— the government did not even gather unemployment statistics. Although in the 1920s there were attempts in Congress to add a price-stabilization goal to the Federal Reserve Act, these attempts failed.

While we now set other goals for the Fed, these 1913 goals have not completely disappeared. We no longer have the gold standard, but the Fed has as one of its goals an appropriate exchange rate of the dollar. The Fed is still opposed to excessive speculation. The Fed is also still concerned about interest-rate fluctuations.

---

[1] The argument was that a loan to finance short-term productive activity would increase the value of output by as much as it increased demand. And with supply and demand increasing equally, prices would remain constant. This argument is invalid because part of the increase in the *value* of output may be due to higher prices. Under the real-bills doctrine the Fed could be financing ever-increasing inflation.

[2] In other words, a bank would take a promissory note for, say, $1 million from a customer and pay him $970,000 for it, and then take that note to its Federal Reserve Bank and receive $980,000 for it.

THE GREAT DEPRESSION

Understanding the Great Depression is important, not only for evaluating the Fed's record, but also for understanding how the economy reacts to monetary policy. At the time many economists argued that, at least during a major depression, monetary policy is ineffective. It was the experience of the Great Depression, as well as the publication of Keynes's masterpiece in 1936, that swung economists away from the quantity theory toward the income-expenditure approach. On the other hand, monetarists point to the Great Depression as showing exactly the opposite: the immense damage a perverse monetary policy can do and hence the great importance of money. And this view of the depression is not confined to monetarists, but is also held by many other economists.

Before turning to the rival explanations, here are some facts about the Depression. The upper turning point was reached in August 1929, that is, a few months prior to the stock market crash. The recession continued until March 1933 when an expansion started. This expansion reached a submerged peak, a peak that still had very substantial unemployment, in May 1937. The subsequent recession reached its trough in June 1938. The ensuing expansion carried into and through World War II. In the period 1929 to 1933, net national product fell by more than one-half when measured in current prices; real net national product fell by more than one-third, as did the wholesale price index. Table 27.1 shows the appalling unemployment rates as well as the GNP deflator. Surprisingly, despite very high unemployment, prices rose after 1933.

Turning to the monetary data, from August 1929 to March 1933 nominal *M-1* fell by one-quarter. This decline in the stock of money was the accompaniment of widespread bank failures, which occurred in three waves: October 1930, October 1931, and the final one in March 1933. The last of these led the government to close all banks for a few days, in a so-called bank holiday.

Why did the money stock fall so drastically? It was not due to a fall in the monetary base (the total of reserves and currency). Instead, it resulted from a sharp drop in two ratios: the ratio of deposits to currency and the ratio of deposits to reserves. The deposit-currency ratio fell because as some banks failed, depositors became scared (there was no federal deposit insurance then) and withdrew deposits from other banks. The banks then tried to protect themselves against such runs by holding more reserves per dollar of deposits, so that the deposit-reserve ratio fell. As a result, the deposit multiplier, and hence deposits, declined.

The discount rate fell radically in this period: from 5 to 6 percent at various Federal Reserve Banks in the fall of 1929 to 1½ to 3 percent in September 1931. Figure 27.1 shows that other short-term rates declined sharply, too. However, the rate on long-term government securities did not fall nearly as much, and the rate on Baa corporate bonds, that is, bonds of "lower medium grade" quality, actually rose substantially in the early part of the period before falling again. By 1939 the Baa rate was not far from its 1928 level. Moreover, the price declines that occurred in the early 1930s meant that for these years the real

Table 27.1   Unemployment, Prices, and Money, 1929–1941

Year	Unemployment as Percentage of Civilian Labor Force		GNP Deflator (1958 = 100)	Per Capita Nominal Money Stock as Percentage of 1929‡
	A*	B†		
1929	3.2	3.2	50.6	100.0%
1930	8.7	8.7	49.3	95.6
1931	15.9	15.3	44.8	89.5
1932	23.6	22.5	40.2	76.2
1933	24.9	20.6	39.3	71.2
1934	21.7	16.0	42.2	77.5
1935	20.1	14.2	42.6	92.1
1936	16.9	9.9	42.7	107.5
1937	14.3	9.1	44.5	110.4
1938	19.0	12.5	43.9	104.5
1939	17.2	11.3	43.2	115.8
1940	14.6	9.5	43.9	136.4
1941	9.9	6.0	47.2	158.1

*Counts those employed on work relief programs by the Works Progress Administration (WPA) as unemployed. The WPA was a governmental public works program for the unemployed.
†Counts those employed on work relief programs by the Works Progress Administration (WPA) as employed.
‡Money stock data are for June of each year.
Sources: U.S. Bureau of the Census, *Historical Statistics of the United States* (1976 ed.), pp. 135, 224; Michael Darby, "Three-and-a-Half Million U.S. Employees Have Been Mislaid," *Journal of Political Economy*, 84 (February 1976), 8; Milton Friedman and Anna Schwartz, *A Monetary History of the United States* (Princeton, N.J.: Princeton University Press, 1963), pp. 712–16.

rate of interest was substantially greater than the nominal rate shown in Figure 27.1. For subsequent years the real rate of interest was less than the nominal rate. But since the price level was lower in 1939 than in 1929, for the decade as a whole, the real rate exceeded the nominal rate of interest.

FEDERAL RESERVE POLICY

Where was the Fed while all of this was going on? For many years it was widely believed that, on the whole, it behaved well. Those who take this position tell the following story. Right after the stock market crash the Fed cut the discount rate and kept it low except in late 1931 when there was a gold outflow as fears developed that the United States would follow Britain off the gold standard. In a wrongheaded attempt to calm these fears, and to make people think that the United States would stay on the gold standard, even if it meant higher interest rates, the Fed raised the discount rate. But it soon lowered the discount rate again. The Fed did make a serious mistake in raising reserve requirements in 1936 and 1937, but it certainly cannot be blamed for the Great Depression. It

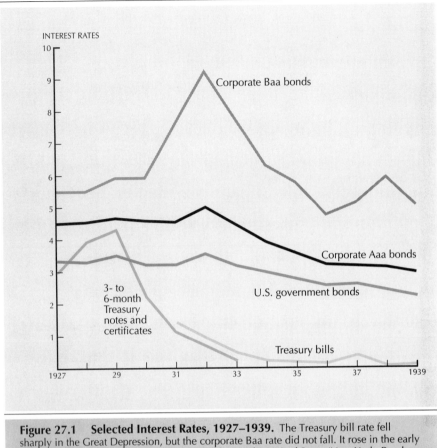

INTEREST RATES

Corporate Baa bonds

Corporate Aaa bonds

3- to
6-month
Treasury
notes and
certificates

U.S. government bonds

Treasury bills

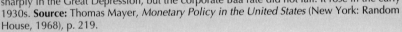

Figure 27.1   Selected Interest Rates, 1927–1939. The Treasury bill rate fell
sharply in the Great Depression, but the corporate Baa rate did not fall. It rose in the early
1930s. **Source:** Thomas Mayer, *Monetary Policy in the United States* (New York: Random
House, 1968), p. 219.

resulted from a massive collapse in the marginal efficiency of investment, the
stock market crash, and perhaps a decline in the marginal propensity to consume. Monetary policy is almost powerless in such a situation. The Fed kept
the discount rate and other short-term rates low, but business had little incentive to borrow. The Fed made reserves available, but banks simply held them as
excess reserves because of an absence of sound borrowers and an interest-rate
level so low that banks had little incentive to buy securities. You cannot push
on a piece of string.

Although some economists had challenged this view of monetary policy
earlier, it was the prevailing orthodoxy until the 1960s, when it was powerfully
challenged by Friedman and Schwartz and by Elmus Wicker of Indiana University. Many economists who are not monetarists now accept the Friedman-
Schwartz interpretation of the depression, at least in broad outline.

Given their monetarist outlook, Friedman and Schwartz placed much
more emphasis on reserves and the quantity of money than on interest rates.

Not All Holidays Are Carefree

The following holiday for banks was proclaimed on March 5, 1933:

BY THE PRESIDENT OF THE UNITED STATES OF AMERICA
"A PROCLAMATION

Whereas there have been heavy and unwarranted withdrawals of gold and currency from our banking institutions for the purpose of hoarding; and

Whereas continuous and increasingly extensive speculative activity abroad in foreign exchange has resulted in severe drains on the Nation's stocks of gold; and

Whereas these conditions have created a national emergency; and

Whereas it is in the best interests of all bank depositors that a period of respite be provided with a view to preventing further hoarding of coin, bullion or currency or speculation in foreign exchange and permitting the application of appropriate measures to protect the interests of our people; and . . . [There followed a listing of the laws that authorized the President's actions.]

Now, therefore, I, Franklin D. Roosevelt, President of the United States of America, in view of such national emergency and by virtue of the authority vested in me by said Act and in order to prevent the export, hoarding, or earmarking of gold or silver coin or bullion or currency, do hereby proclaim, order, direct and declare that from Monday, the sixth day of March, to Thursday, the ninth day of March, Nineteen Hundred and Thirty Three, both dates inclusive, there shall be maintained and observed by all banking institutions and all branches thereof located in the United States of America, including the territories and insular possessions, a bank holiday, and that during said period all banking transactions shall be suspended. During such holiday, excepting as hereinafter provided, no such banking institution or branch shall pay out, export, earmark, or permit the withdrawal or transfer in any manner or by any device whatsoever, of any gold or silver coin or bullion or currency or take any other action which might facilitate the hoarding thereof; nor shall any such banking institution or branch pay out deposits, make loans or discounts, deal in foreign exchange, transfer credits from the United States to any place abroad, or transact any other banking business whatsoever.

In witness whereof, I have hereunto set my hand and caused the seal of the United States to be affixed. . . . [There followed a provision for the Secretary of the Treasury to authorize exceptions and a list of definitions of terms used in the proclamation.]

Done in the City of Washington this sixth day of March—1 A.M. in the year of our Lord One Thousand Nine Hundred and Thirty-three, and of the Independence of the United States the One Hundred and Fifty-seventh.

[SEAL]

By the President: Franklin D. Roosevelt

Cordell Hull
Secretary of State

But they did point out that, while the discount rate and the commercial paper rate were low during most of the depression, this was not true for the interest rates that are more important for business borrowers, for instance, the Baa bond rate. The public, fearing further financial crises, bid up the prices of highly liquid securities such as commercial paper, and thus created an unusually large gap between interest rates on extremely liquid and safe securities and interest rates on other securities. Moreover, the discount rate, while low by historical standards, was not low relative to open-market rates, and thus provided banks with little incentive to borrow from the Fed. In addition, the low discount rate may not have had much significance because, as the late Clark Warburton pointed out earlier, it was accompanied by a very restrictive policy of discount-window administration that generally prevented banks from borrowing.

However, Friedman and Schwartz focus not on interest rates but on the Fed's open-market operations, or rather the lack thereof. The Fed did not undertake large-scale open-market purchases until 1932. In fact, until then it was offsetting the expansionary impact on the base that would have occurred naturally from the inflow of gold that took place at that time. Friedman and Schwartz therefore describe the Fed's policy as restrictive. In 1932 the Fed finally undertook open-market purchases for a short period—a fact that Friedman and Schwartz attribute to a wish to mollify Congress, which was then considering a fiscal policy the Fed thought too expansionary.

Why was the Fed so restrictive? One reason Friedman and Schwartz suggest is that it did not realize that its policy was so restrictive. Instead of looking at the decline in the quantity of money, the Fed looked at the discount rate and excess reserves. Friedman and Schwartz argue that the Fed misinterpreted what was happening to excess reserves. It did not realize that the great increase in the excess reserve ratio (from 0.2 percent in 1929–31 to 6.8 percent in 1935, and to 12.0 percent in 1940) was due to banks wanting excess reserves to protect themselves from potential runs. Instead, it believed that the high excess reserves signaled a lack of demand for bank loans.

However, Gerald Epstein of the New School for Social Research and Thomas Ferguson of the University of Texas, who studied the Fed's records in great detail, concluded that other factors were responsible for the Fed's unwillingness to be more expansionary. One was a concern about a potential gold outflow and about some Federal Reserve Banks' running short of the gold needed to back their notes and deposits. Another was a concern that if interest rates fell, many banks would have insufficient earnings to stay alive. An additional reason was a belief that a depression was needed to eliminate inefficient firms.[3]

---

[3] Gerald Epstein and Thomas Ferguson, "Monetary Policy, Loan Liquidation and Industrial Conflict: The Federal Reserve and Open Market Operations in 1932," *Journal of Economic History*, 44 (December 1984), 957–84. Concern about Federal Reserve Banks' running short of gold sounds strange now, but, at the time, the Federal Reserve Banks were required to back their currency notes and deposits with gold. Not just the whole Federal Reserve System, but each Federal Reserve Bank individually had to meet this requirement. The argument that a depression purges the economic system of inefficiency also sounds strange now, but was popular prior to and during the early years of the Great Depression.

But whatever the reason for the Fed's actions, or lack of actions, the Fed does not deserve any plaudits. As Wicker put it, by 1932 "it was becoming increasingly clear that [Fed] officials did not recognize any strong obligation to maintain the solvency of the banking system."[4]

Perhaps two things should be said in defense of this dismal record. First, the advice the Fed obtained from the writings of academic economists was not good either, and, second, by no means did all Fed officials agree with the prevailing policy. The New York Federal Reserve Bank in particular advocated much more expansionary policies, but it did not prevail.

Effects of Federal Reserve Policy

How much difference would it have made had the Fed aggressively undertaken substantial open-market operations that would have provided banks with the reserves they needed to meet deposit withdrawals and, thus, would have prevented so many bank failures? There already was an unusually severe recession in 1930 before there were any large-scale bank failures. This part of the Depression is not explained well by the Friedman-Schwartz analysis. But the economy had suffered such recessions in 1908, 1914–15, and 1921, and each time had recovered within a reasonable time. What was unique about the Great Depression was not only its depth, but also the tardiness of the recovery. Can these characteristics be attributed to the three waves of bank failures, and could the Federal Reserve have prevented these failures?

The answer to the first of these questions depends in large part on the importance of the quantity of money. It also depends on whether there were other factors at work that caused this depression to be so severe and prolonged. The answer to the second question, whether the Fed could have prevented the bank failures, depends on whether banks were only illiquid, but basically sound or whether they held too many bad assets.

Regarding the first issue, the importance of money, we have little to add to our previous discussion. But one does not have to be an out-and-out monetarist to accept a monetary interpretation of the 1930s given the great drop in the money stock. Income-expenditure theorists, too, consider such a decline to be a disaster. To be sure, the fall in the money supply was not the only thing that happened. Velocity also fell, but Friedman and Schwartz argue that this decline was not an independent factor causing the depression, but was induced by the fall in income. Hence, they say that the fall in velocity was ultimately the result of permitting banks to fail. Income-expenditure theorists, on the other hand, usually do not accept Friedman's theory of velocity that underlies the calculation that velocity dropped just because of the decline in income; they stress instead the effect of low interest rates on velocity. But even if it turns out that there were many other factors at work that could have caused a depression, it seems plausible to attribute much of its persistence and severity to the great fall in the money stock.

[4] Elmus Wicker, *Federal Reserve Monetary Policy, 1917–1933* (New York: Random House, 1966), p. 173.

Critics of the monetary explanation frequently argue that the drop in the money stock was only an intermediate cause and not the real or interesting cause. In their view, the bank failures resulted mainly from banks holding too many unsound assets, and hence they could not have been prevented by expansionary Fed policy. Friedman and Schwartz, on the other hand, argue that the massive bank failures would not have occurred if the Fed had undertaken large-scale open-market purchases. In their view, any deterioration in the quality of bank assets that occurred in the 1920s was minor.

They not only blame the Federal Reserve for dereliction of duty, but also suggest that most of the bank failures would not have occurred had the Fed not existed. Prior to 1913, when massive bank failures threatened, banks would all agree to suspend currency payments for a time, while still clearing checks among themselves. Depositors could then still make payments from one account to another. Banks that were temporarily short of currency and other liquid assets did not fail. But the existence of the Fed with its discount mechanism reduced the incentive that strong banks had to initiate, as they had previously done, a suspension of currency payments.

One does not have to be a monetarist to blame the severity of the Great Depression on bank failures. Bank failures not only reduce the quantity of money; they also reduce the supply of bank loans and disrupt the process of financial intermediation. A firm whose bank has failed has to find another bank that will lend to it. Even if it is an eminently sound firm, that may take some time, because another bank now has to familiarize itself with the firm's financial status.

Peter Temin's Challenge to the Friedman-Schwartz Interpretation

In the years since Friedman and Schwartz first presented their revisionist interpretation of the Great Depression it appears to have gained much support. But it is not without challenges. The most systematic of these challenges was made by Peter Temin of MIT, who raised many important issues.[5]

One of these is whether the observed decline in the money stock was the result of a shift in the supply curve of money, as Friedman and Schwartz claim, or the result of a shift in the demand curve for money. Suppose that the Depression was actually caused by an exogenous drop in consumption. As income declined, the demand for money declined too and so interest rates fell. Declining interest rates then reduced the money supply by inducing banks to hold more excess reserves and to borrow less from the Fed, and perhaps also by raising the currency-deposit ratio. Someone might then observe a reduction in the money supply along with the fall in income and conclude that the decline in the money supply caused income to fall, whereas actually the story is just the other way around. Temin argued that Friedman and Schwartz failed to show that the decline in the money stock was the cause rather than the effect.

In Temin's view there is no evidence that money was tight, at least in the earlier part of the Depression. The *real* money stock was slightly higher in 1931

[5] Peter Temin, *Did Monetary Forces Cause the Great Depression?* (New York: Norton, 1976).

than in 1929, though it did fall after that. Hence he argues that, since into 1931 prices fell enough to offset the decline in the nominal money stock, it was the decline in velocity, rather than a decline in the nominal money stock, that was responsible for falling output. What is going on here is the following: money, velocity, prices, and output all fell. Temin allocates the fall in prices to the fall in the money stock and thus attributes the drop in output to the decline in velocity. Friedman and Schwartz might well reply that this is totally arbitrary, that in response to joint changes in money and velocity (that is, in aggregate expenditures) prices and output change jointly, and the aggregate supply curve determines by how much each of them changes.

In addition, Temin points out that interest rates on liquid securities were low, which again suggests that there was no shortage of money. (We already discussed Friedman and Schwartz's response to this argument.) Moreover, Temin criticizes Friedman and Schwartz for not explaining the causes of bank failures sufficiently. Temin argues that part of the decline in the stock of money should be attributed to falling prices of farm products and to the agricultural distress that caused rural banks to fail. Many bank failures, Temin argues, were ultimately due to a real factor, the relative decline of agricultural prices, rather than to a monetary factor, such as Federal Reserve policy.

In addition to the rural banks, a large New York bank, the Bank of United States, failed. Temin argues that, contrary to the Friedman-Schwartz view, this failure was due to fraud and illegal activities by the bank's management, so that the Fed could not have prevented this failure. All these bank failures then frightened depositors into runs on other banks. When these banks tried to meet deposit withdrawals by selling bonds, bond prices fell. This then forced other banks to write down the prices at which they carried these bonds on their books; this in turn impaired the capital position of many of these other banks and forced them to close. Some other economists who have analyzed in detail the failures of certain large banks have supported Temin by pointing out that these failures were due to fraud and bad banking practices rather than to the Fed's policy.

Beyond the question of what caused bank failures, Temin accuses Friedman and Schwartz of overemphasizing the responsibility of the Fed and underplaying the responsibility of the private sector for the Great Depression. In his view the changes in the money stock that occurred were not *caused* by the Fed merely because the Fed could have prevented them.

An important issue arises here. Friedman and Schwartz blame the Fed for the Depression because it was passive and did not move aggressively with open-market operations to provide banks with the reserves they needed. They take some bank failures as a given and focus on the behavior of the Fed that allowed these failures to spread to other banks. In contrast, Temin takes the inaction of the Fed as his given and treats those factors that initially caused some banks to fail as the cause of the decline in the money stock. Hence, to a considerable extent the protagonists in this debate are talking past each other. Friedman and Schwartz ask whether the recession in 1929 would have turned into such a catastrophic depression if the Fed had done its duty, and answer with a no. Temin asks whether there were forces at work, other than Fed policy, that caused aggregate expenditures to fall, and answers with a yes. Both answers could be right. Temin's work does not vindicate the Fed.

An Alternative Interpretation: Credit, Debt, and Liquidity

The Friedman-Schwartz interpretation of the Great Depression has been challenged both on details and on basic issues. One challenge to a basic issue comes from adherents of the credit view, such as Ben Bernanke of Princeton University and Charles Calomiris of the University of Illinois. They do not dispute the importance that Friedman and Schwartz attribute to bank failures. But instead of stressing the liabilities side of banks' balance sheets and hence the reduction in deposits and money, they stress the assets side and thus the reduction of bank loans.

As banks failed, borrowing relations were disrupted. Firms that had borrowed from them now had to apply for loans at other banks, where they had to deal with loan officers who did not know them. Building a relation of trust, particularly during as stressful a time as the Great Depression, is not accomplished overnight. So the bank failures pulled down many firms that would have been sound if their banks had not failed, and reduced the borrowing and hence the expenditures of others. How many firms were destroyed by the failure of their banks is hard to say, and the aggregate effects are even harder to measure. On one hand, if a firm fails, that leaves more business for its competitors. On the other hand, the failed firm's owners and workers are now unemployed and will cut their consumption.

Some households, too, were caught in a liquidity bind, particularly those that, prior to the stock-market collapse, had bought stock on credit. And even households that were not in debt were reluctant to reduce their liquidity by buying durables at a time when unemployment was so high.

This story does not absolve the Fed from blame. But it does imply that large-scale open-market purchases by the Fed in, say, 1934 would not have been sufficient to bring the economy back to full employment.

Debt Deflation

Another explanation of the severity of the Great Depression focuses on the increase in the real value of debts as prices fell. Between 1929 and 1933 prices (as measured by the GNP deflator) fell by 22 percent. Since the nominal interest payments on their long-term debts remained fixed while the prices at which they sold their output were falling, many companies were no longer able to meet their interest payments and therefore went bankrupt. One way of looking at this problem is in terms of interest rates. Suppose that in 1929 a company that expected prices to be stable took out a loan at 6 percent, because it believed that it could earn, say, 10 percent on these funds. But because prices fell by 9 percent between 1930 and 1931, it was paying not a 6 percent, but a 15 percent real interest rate, much above what it was earning on these borrowed funds.

Moreover, falling prices reduced the market value of the company's assets. If it was highly leveraged, the value of its liabilities might exceed the value of its assets. This not only meant that it could not obtain additional loans, but it might also have violated its loan covenants, so that it would now be asked to repay loans when it was in no position to do so.

Households that had borrowed heavily to purchase homes or consumer durables faced similar problems.

A critical issue for the debt deflation theory is whether borrowers anticipated the fall in prices. If they did, then what caused them to come to grief was not falling prices, but their willingness to pay such a high real interest rate.

A Summing Up

The general question "What went wrong in the 1930s?" can be conveniently broken down into three component questions: (1) What started the depression? (2) Why was it so severe? (3) Why did it last so long? On the first question, there is considerable agreement with Friedman and Schwartz that monetary tightness was the initiating factor. The leading candidate to explain its severity is debt deflation. The credit view then explains well why the collapse of much of our depository and credit system caused the depression to last so long.

WAR FINANCE AND INTEREST-RATE PEGGING

During the Great Depression the problem was insufficient aggregate expenditures. During World War II it was the opposite. With a large proportion of output devoted to the war effort, aggregate expenditures were excessive. The government tried to limit the resulting inflation by raising taxes, by imposing wage and price controls, and by rationing. Monetary policy was in a strange situation. Normally when demand is excessive, the Fed would fight inflation by raising interest rates and limiting the growth rate of money. But during the war the overriding task of the Fed was to ensure that the government could borrow all it needed to finance the war at a low interest rate. In part this reflected the prevailing belief of the 1930s and 1940s that interest rates and the growth rate of money are not important determinants of aggregate expenditures, so that a restrictive monetary policy would not help much in curbing inflation. It also reflected a dissatisfaction with the way World War I had been financed. In that war, interest rates had risen sharply, and thus raised the Treasury's interest payments. In addition, there was a widespread belief that after World War II, the economy would return to the depression it had been in before the war. If interest rates were allowed to rise during the war, this might generate expectations of high rates that would make it difficult after the war to reduce long-term rates to the low levels appropriate to a depressed economy. For all these reasons the government decided not to rely on rising interest rates to curb inflation. Instead of being allowed to rise, interest rates were held down at the prevailing depression level by a policy of *pegging*.

Pegged Rates

Pegging meant that the Fed stood ready to buy all government securities offered to it at least at par, that is, at 100 percent of their face value. As a result the Fed potentially lost control over open-market operations and the supply of money. It was the public that decided how many securities the Fed had to buy in its open-market operations. Fed policy was totally accommodative.

The level at which interest rates were pegged was the then-prevailing level of the Great Depression, 2½ percent on long-term Treasury bonds and ⅜ percent on Treasury bills.[6] It should have been obvious, but was ignored, that pegging short-term rates much lower than long-term rates would generate trouble. If the Fed stands ready to buy long-term bonds at par, long-term bonds are in effect as liquid as short-term securities. Hence, everyone had an incentive to sell ⅜ percent Treasury bills to the Fed and hold 2½ percent bonds instead. Eventually, the Fed did end up holding nearly all the Treasury bills in existence.

During the war there was little dispute about monetary policy, and even in the early postwar years the Fed accepted interest-rate pegging with few complaints. One reason for this was the tardiness with which the persistence of the postwar inflation was recognized. Almost everyone expected a depression after the war, and it took some time for people to realize that the problem was excessive, rather than insufficient, aggregate expenditures. Another reason, already mentioned, was the low repute of monetary policy. Third, while pegging interest rates provided the *potential* for an explosive rise in the money stock, the explosion did not occur. Just the opposite: in 1949 the money stock was slightly lower than in 1947. It seems that for much of the period the equilibrium interest rate was below the pegged 2½ percent bond rate, so that the Fed was not called on to protect the peg by increasing bank reserves and the money stock. As velocity was rising rapidly, the demand for money did not grow.

All the same, as time went by, the Fed became more and more uneasy about its lack of control. With the outbreak of the Korean War in 1950, the Federal Reserve's restiveness turned into open opposition. As long as pegging was taking place, it was the Treasury, and not the Fed, that was, in effect, conducting monetary policy, since the Fed was bound to support the Treasury's decisions about interest rates on government securities. Now with renewed war, accompanied by inflation (the consumer price index rose by 11 percent between June 1950 and December 1951), the Fed wanted to reclaim monetary policy. The Treasury, on the other hand, wanted the pegging policy maintained.

In its dispute with the Treasury the Fed had substantial support among academic economists and, what is much more important, also in Congress. It therefore felt powerful enough to challenge the Treasury. In August 1950 it allowed some short-term government securities to fall slightly below par. A major row occurred, but was resolved in March 1951 by an agreement known

---

[6] After the war the bill rate was allowed to rise to 1 percent, still much too low a rate relative to the 2½ percent long-term rate.

as the **Accord** under which short-term interest rates were allowed to rise moderately and long-term rates to rise very slightly. The Fed was relieved of the burden of complete pegging, but, in effect, agreed to prevent government securities from falling much below par. This Accord lasted only until after the 1952 election, when the incoming Eisenhower administration restored the Fed's freedom.

THE GREAT INFLATION

As the endpaper shows, the inflation rate started to accelerate in the mid-1960s. What was unusual about this inflation was not only its magnitude but also its persistence. What was even worse was that each time the inflation rate rose, it would rise to a higher peak than before, and each time it fell during a recession, it would bottom out at a higher point than in the previous recession. In other words, it was not just that prices were rising, but also that the rate at which they rose was itself rising over time. By 1979 the consumer price index had risen by 130 percent over its 1965 level.

This inflation had several causes. The most obvious one was a series of supply shocks. In 1973–74 oil prices quadrupled and then doubled again in 1979–80. Food prices rose rapidly in 1972–73 as a result of bad harvests around the world. *In principle* such events need not have caused inflation. They could merely have raised prices in the year they occurred without generating inflation. (Remember, inflation is a *continuous* rise in prices.) But, not surprisingly, higher prices worked their way into higher wages, which then further raised prices, so that the inflation rate rose. Again, *in principle,* if wages and prices had been flexible enough and if the Fed had not allowed the money supply to rise, then higher oil and food prices would have been offset by lower prices of other goods and services. But wages and prices were not that flexible.

A second factor, probably a less important one, was the rise in government expenditures resulting from the Vietnam War and the War on Poverty. But the most important cause of the acceleration of the inflation rate was an overly expansionary monetary policy. Why was monetary policy so expansionary? One can tell three stories. One is that the Fed yielded to political pressures. Rising nominal interest rates were highly unpopular both in Washington and in the country as a whole, but a move to a less expansionary monetary policy would have raised nominal rates temporarily. The second story is that the intellectual clime of the time disposed the Fed, and others, to deemphasize the danger of inflation. The memory of the Great Depression had not yet faded, while all prior U.S. history suggested that the possibility of a major peacetime inflation was not something one needed to worry about. In addition, it seemed feasible to keep unemployment at a level that we now know would lead to accelerating inflation. A third story is that the Fed's targeting procedures were at fault, that by targeting interest rates, it unwittingly accommodated inflation. Each of the three explanations has *some* validity, but their relative contributions are hard to disentangle.

The second explanation has much validity in our view, though others might well dispute this. A sophisticated version of the political explanation also has much to contribute.[7] Imagine that an administration dedicated to price stability had been in office throughout the period. The President would then have pressured the Fed to be more restrictive and would also have nominated governors who were more concerned about inflation. As a result, the Fed would have been less willing to take the risk of operating the economy at too low a rate of unemployment.

Lowering the Inflation Rate

The high inflation rate caused many complaints. But what ultimately ended it was not just the opposition of retired people and others who lost by inflation, but also two crises in international finance. The first of these crises occurred in late 1978, when, in response to a rapid rise in the growth rate of money, there was a loss of confidence in the dollar, and it fell rapidly on the foreign-exchange market. There was a danger that foreign central banks (that had large holdings of dollars), as well as private holders, would dump their dollars on the market, and thus accelerate the dollar's fall. In response, on November 1, 1978, President Carter followed up an earlier call for "voluntary" wage and price controls with a series of emergency measures. The United States would borrow $30 billion of foreign currencies it could use to support the dollar in the foreign-exchange market. More fundamentally, Carter asked the Fed to adopt a restrictive policy. For a President, particularly a Democratic President, publicly to ask the Fed to raise interest rates was an extraordinary step with great symbolic significance.

However, what matters are not dramatic gestures, but the consistency with which they are followed up. The initial follow-up was strong, but transient; the monetary growth rate fell sharply, but not for long. In the second quarter of 1979 it rose again and stayed high for the rest of the year. It seemed as though the Fed had lost control over it. This by itself might not have caused a radical change in policy, but two other obviously connected events occurred.

The first was that the inflation rate accelerated sharply. The other was that a second exchange-rate crisis occurred, as foreigners lost confidence in the dollar, so that it fell sharply on the foreign-exchange market. The seemingly strong policy changes of the previous November had bought less than a year's respite. And this second crisis in the fall of 1979 seemed even scarier than the 1978 crisis.

One can make a reasonable case that the Fed faced disaster. It seemed unable to control the money stock. A rapid rise in the prices of gold (by $100 an ounce between late August and early October 1979) and of certain raw materials suggested that the high inflation rate made people think that the safe thing to do was to dump dollars and buy commodities. In addition, there was a danger that the dollar would again plummet on the foreign-exchange market as foreigners saw that the Fed's action of November 1978 had failed.

---

[7] The hypothesis that targeting interest rates was the main cause of the inflation is unconvincing because the inflation could have been curbed by the Fed's raising its interest-rate target sufficiently. (To say that this was politically impossible is to invoke the political explanation.) The Bank of Japan uses instruments and targets that are similar to those the Fed used in the 1970s, yet Japan has a low inflation rate. Where there is a will, there is a way.

Former governor Phillip Coldwell said about this episode: "We're on the verge of going into hyperinflation."[8] This statement may well have been an exaggeration, but the situation was scary. Something had to be done. Hence, on October 6, 1979, in an unusual and dramatic Saturday meeting, the Board of Governors adopted a new policy, which became known as the "Saturday night special." Despite the fact that it was widely (though wrongly) believed that the economy had already entered a recession, the Fed adopted a highly restrictive policy. It raised the discount rate by another percentage point to 12 percent, and it imposed an 8 percent reserve requirement on increases in certain managed liabilities of banks. In a more important step it announced that it would try to get a much better grip on the money stock by allowing the federal-funds rate to fluctuate more. As already discussed in Chapter 25, the previous range on the federal-funds rate had been insufficient to allow the Fed to control the money stock. Now the range was set at 5 percent, and even that broad range was not always treated as a binding constraint. Moreover, the Fed became less accommodative in supplying reserves.

The October 1979 policy initiative succeeded in stopping the threatened collapse of the dollar on the foreign-exchange market. In addition, the Fed succeeded in bringing the monetary growth rate down, though subsequently it was still high relative to the midpoint of the Fed's target ranges. Nominal interest rates rose sharply.

Although successful in the foreign-exchange market, domestically the October 1979 program seemed to have failed, at least at first. Financial markets did not believe that the Fed would control inflation. Had they anticipated that the Fed would succeed, long-term interest rates would have fallen along with the anticipated inflation premium that is contained in interest rates. But, instead, they rose!

The market was right. In three months, from December 1979 to February 1980, the consumer price index spurted at an annual rate of 17 percent. Credit markets became demoralized by the fear that the inflation rate, and hence interest rates, would zoom. How could market participants determine what interest rates to set on new bonds that they issued? They couldn't. As a result the long-term bond market as well as the mortgage market in large part suspended operations for a time, and even short-term markets, such as the commercial-paper market, ceased to function properly. Some major banks were reported to have difficulties in selling large CDs.

By March 1980 the October 1979 policy was in a shambles. Strange as it may seem, many people were actually hoping for a recession that would reduce both the inflation rate and interest rates. It is reported that when Federal Reserve Chairman Paul Volcker was asked whether monetary and fiscal tightening would result in a recession, he replied, "Yes, and the sooner the better."[9]

It was clear that, once again, something more had to be done, and in March 1980 President Carter announced a multifaceted program to break inflationary expectations. As part of this plan he revised the budget he had just sent to Congress to eliminate the projected deficit (though, as it turned

[8] Cited in William Greider, *Secrets of the Temple* (New York: Simon & Schuster, 1987), p. 104.
[9] Clyde Farnsworth, "Washington Watch," *New York Times,* March 17, 1980, p. D2.

out, not the deficit that actually occurred). The Fed's role in the program was twofold. One part was to tighten conventional monetary policy by raising reserve requirements on certain managed liabilities and to impose a special 3 percent surcharge on the discount rate paid by large banks that borrow frequently.

The second part was to impose credit allocation, that is, a system that rations credit by regulation, rather than by just letting the price of credit rise. Banks were told to let their loans expand by no more than 9 percent; with banks that were growing slowly in any case or had low capital and liquidity ratios staying well below this ceiling. This part of the program was voluntary, but there is an old saying: "You don't have to, but you'll be sorry if you don't." Since large- and medium-size banks frequently come to the Fed for permission to undertake mergers or to start holding-company affiliates, the Fed is not exactly powerless. To cut consumer spending, which was growing rapidly, the Fed also imposed a 15 percent reserve requirement on unsecured consumer loans, such as credit card and charge-account borrowing. This reserve requirement applied not only to banks, but also to other financial institutions, as well as to retailers. Finally, a 15 percent reserve requirement was also imposed on increases in the assets of money-market funds.

This credit control program was effective—much more effective than had been intended. The public seemed to respond to the President's wish that consumer credit be cut out of a mixture of patriotism and fear of worsening economic conditions. Outstanding consumer credit stopped growing and indeed fell. This response would have been most gratifying had it not been for one little fact—just two months earlier the economy had entered a recession! That recession could well have been the result of the October 1979 tightening of monetary policy.

RECESSIONS IN THE EARLY 1980s

The 1980 recession was shortlived, but so was the ensuing expansion. In mid-1981, before the recovery was complete, another recession occurred and carried unemployment to 10.8 percent, the highest level since the 1930s. As a result of the recession as well as of favorable supply-side developments, the inflation rate fell; the GDP deflator rose by only 4.1 percent in 1983 compared to 10.0 percent in 1981. But this sharp contrast is deceptive since the high inflation rate of 1980 had been in part due to the second OPEC oil shock.

During the 1981–82 recession there was concern about the danger of a financial collapse. The failure of some government securities dealers, as well as of a medium-size bank, Penn Square, combined with the threatened failures of some large firms and the inability of some countries (for example, Mexico) to repay their loans, all generated such fears. Many thrift institutions failed or had to be merged. Interest rates declined, but not by as much as the inflation rate did, so that real rates were unusually high. While some blamed this on the large current and prospective federal deficits, others blamed the Fed for not raising the monetary growth rate sufficiently.

The Fed was in a quandary. On the one hand it wanted to continue with its disinflationary policy, but on the other hand it wanted to ameliorate the recession. Five factors complicated its task. First, raising the monetary growth rate could generate fears that the inflation rate would rise again. This would result not only in more inflationary wage and price setting but would also raise the inflation premium that is included in the nominal interest rate. Second, there was much pressure on the Fed to lower interest rates, and bills to curb the Fed's independence gathered extraordinarily strong support in Congress. Third, with deregulation fostering new types of accounts, the problem of measuring money became much more severe. Fourth, as Figure 27.2 shows, expected nominal interest rates did not decline as much as the inflation rate, so that the real interest rate rose substantially. This was hardly a desirable development during a deep recession. It also worsened the problem of LDC debts, since these loans had been made at variable interest rates. Finally, there was a sharp fall in *M-1* velocity. After rising at a trend rate of about 3 percent per year during the 1960s and 1970s, *M-1* velocity suddenly *fell* by 4 percent between 1981 and 1982, the first significant drop in about thirty years. *M-2*

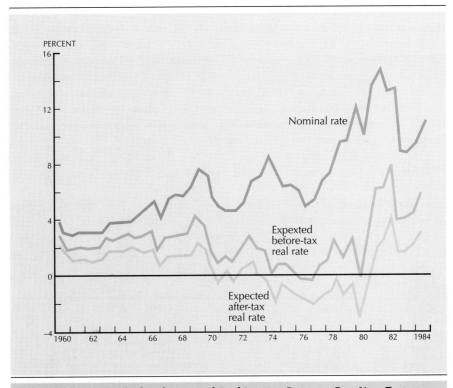

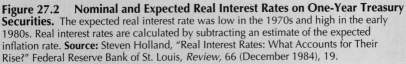

Figure 27.2   Nominal and Expected Real Interest Rates on One-Year Treasury Securities. The expected real interest rate was low in the 1970s and high in the early 1980s. Real interest rates are calculated by subtracting an estimate of the expected inflation rate. **Source:** Steven Holland, "Real Interest Rates: What Accounts for Their Rise?" Federal Reserve Bank of St. Louis, *Review,* 66 (December 1984), 19.

velocity also fell. In setting its monetary growth targets the Fed had expected *M-1* velocity to continue to rise. Hence, the fall in velocity meant that monetary conditions were much tighter than the Fed had intended.

The Fed responded by easing policy. The *M-1* growth rate accelerated rapidly in the second half of 1982.

Lessons from the Monetarist (?) Experiment

The policy adopted on October 6, 1979, was widely, but not necessarily correctly, interpreted as a radical shift toward monetarism. It was certainly monetarist in one important way: the Fed now put control over inflation ahead of maintaining high employment. In addition, the Fed tried harder than before to attain its monetary growth targets, and so allowed interest rates to fluctuate much more.

What were the results? As already mentioned, the inflation rate fell substantially, though with a lag, while unemployment rose sharply. Interest rates became much more variable. Much, but by no means all, of this increased variability of interest rates was only temporary, being due to the imposition, and subsequent elimination, of credit controls. That interest rates became much more variable once the Fed took its narrow bands off the federal-funds rate is hardly surprising. What is much harder to explain is that the monetary growth rate also became much more variable. Since the Fed was no longer constrained by a narrow range for the federal-funds rate, one would expect that it could control the growth rate of money much more accurately and keep it much more stable. Prior to October 1979, monetarists had argued that the Fed should allow more interest-rate variability to reduce the variability of the monetary growth rate. Instead we got the worst of both worlds.

Was the new policy a failure, and, if so, should this be treated as a practical refutation of monetarism? This is a much-debated question that obviously cannot be resolved here. All we can do is to outline the major issues.

One issue relates to the sharp drop in the inflation rate that started in 1981. Was it worth the accompanying rise in the unemployment rate? Suppose the Fed had been less adamant in fighting inflation and had tried to bring the inflation rate down more slowly. Could it have done so at a much smaller cost in unemployment, or was it necessary to adopt a drastic policy to break inflationary expectations?

Second, there is the sharp decline in velocity. Had the Fed been using an interest-rate target rather than a money-stock target it would have—as it should have done—accommodated this shift in the LM curve. Ironically, while a money-stock target would, we believe, have been a preferable target in the 1970s when the Fed was using mainly an interest-rate target, in the October 1979 through 1982 period, when the Fed was making more use of a money-stock target, an interest-rate target would have been better. Was this just a matter of bad luck, or is it a reflection of Goodhart's law (named after Charles Goodhart, of the London School of Economics) that a variable that has previously been stable will become unstable as soon as one relies on its stability in making policy?

Third, how much damage did the greater variability of interest rates inflict on the economy? Fourth, to what extent was this greater variance of interest rates the *inevitable* result of a policy that eliminated the previously tight constraints on movements in the federal-funds rate? Much of it may have been due to the greater variability of the monetary growth rate, which, in turn, *may* have been, in part, the result of faulty Fed procedures. If the money supply is less stable, one expects short-term interest rates, which measure the cost of holding money for a short period, to fluctuate more, too.

This brings us to a central issue. Does the high variability of the monetary growth rate indicate that monetarist policy must fail because the Fed simply cannot control the growth rate of money? On the surface this appears plausible. The Fed tried harder than before to control the monetary growth rate, yet the money stock grew at a more variable rate.

Monetarists respond that the Fed did not try hard enough. They argue that the Fed's attempt was doomed to failure because it used an inappropriate instrument, borrowed reserves, instead of using total reserves. Moreover, it did not make certain institutional changes that would have given it much better control over money. Actually, it is very hard to draw any lessons about the controllability of money from the 1979 to 1982 experience for two reasons. One is that it is *M-1* that the Fed tried to control. But at present, it is *M-2*, not *M-1*, that the Fed would try to control. Moreover, much of the greater variability of *M-1* during the monetarist (?) experiment was due to the erratic behavior of the deposit-currency ratio. This behavior could have been due to extraneous factors that would not recur if the Fed tries again to control the growth rate of money.

The End of the Monetarist (?) Experiment

In the second half of 1982 the Fed shifted away from monetarism. One reason was the danger of widespread bankruptcies, and even of a financial collapse, if interest rates rose any further. A second reason was that the high interest rates were imposing a great burden on LDC debtors, and the Fed feared that some of them would default, and cause some large banks to fail. Third, Congress threatened the Fed with dire retribution unless interest rates fell. Last, but not least, the decline in *M-1* velocity, and the resulting difficulty of predicting future movements of velocity, had undermined the case for monetary targeting. Now the LM curve seemed to shift much more than the IS curve, so that money was no longer a good target.

The Expansion during the 1980s and the 1990 Recession

The deep 1981–82 recession ended in November 1982 and was followed by the longest peacetime expansion on record. It is likely that what kept the expansion going for so long was its moderation. Since the unemployment rate was falling only slowly and foreign competition was still threatening U.S. jobs, the inflation rate did not rise until late in the expansion. Indeed, in the fourth year of the expansion, 1986, the consumer price index rose at the lowest rate,

1.1 percent, since 1964. Thus, although the Fed was not following a monetarist policy, it did hold down the growth rate of money sufficiently to reduce the inflation rate substantially. But after that low in 1986, the inflation rate (as measured by the consumer price index) rose again.

A recession in July 1990 terminated this extraordinarily long expansion. This recession is seemingly unconnected with the Gulf War, since it preceded Iraq's invasion of Kuwait. But it is possible that had that event not occurred, GDP would have risen enough in the third quarter for July 1990 not to have been a turning point. We will never know. This recession was mild, but long. A seeming recovery in the spring of 1991 soon stalled, and recovery did not come until the spring of 1992. The debt overhang and extensive consumer pessimism may well have been major reasons for the extraordinary weakness of this recovery.

The Credit Crumble

In 1991 an unusual problem arose. The commercial and industrial loans of banks essentially ceased to grow as they normally do. There seem to have been three reasons why banks were reluctant to make such loans. One was that with the phasing-in of the newly strengthened capital requirements, banks would have had to increase their capital if they made more loans. Given the prevailing low prices of bank stock, that was an expensive option. Second, it was said that banks, shocked by the recent rise in bank failures, were all of a sudden becoming much too cautious and much too ready to turn down loan requests. Third, bankers complained that the examiners were overreacting to charges of laxity in the past and were now being too strict, so that banks were forced to forgo making some sound loans. There were complaints that in this recession the Fed's expansionary policy would not succeed. For the Fed to lower interest rates does firms little good if they are unable to borrow. Hence, the White House tried to pressure bank examiners to be less restrictive. It is not clear to what extent such a response to the credit crumble was justified. The growth rate of bank loans typically falls in recessions as fewer sound firms want to borrow. That accounts for part of the credit crumble. To be sure, there is considerable evidence that it does not account for all of it, that banks have actually become more conservative. But this may not be all bad, given the high rate of bank failures in previous years.

A Soft Landing?

As it had done in some previous expansions, in 1994 and early 1995 the Fed tried to engineer a "soft landing," that is, to reduce aggregate expenditures by just enough to avoid the danger of inflation, without becoming so restrictive that a recession occurs. The Fed therefore raised the federal-funds rate no less than seven times, so that between early February 1994 and early February 1995 it had risen by 3 percentage points overall. At the same time, in four successive steps the Fed raised the discount rate by 2¼ points. Longer-term rates rose too, driven not only by the rise in short-term rates, but also by the increased demand for funds as the expansion accelerated.

Will the Fed this time achieve that shining goal of monetary policy, a soft landing? At the time of writing, it is too early to tell. Has it ever done so in the past? That too is hard to say. To be sure, one can point to cases where the landing was far from soft. But there may have been soft landings that went unnoticed, that is, cases in which were it not for Fed policy, the economy would have been more unstable than it was. While the failures of monetary policy show up as recessions or excessive inflation, potential recessions and potential inflationary spurts that do not occur leave few signs. The Fed's failures are much more visible than its successes.

Monetary Policy since 1982

How successful has monetary policy been since the Federal Reserve's decision to break the ever-rising rate of inflation? As we already discussed, on a tactical level the so-called monetarist experiment was not a success; even though it allowed great fluctuations in interest rates, the Fed did not succeed in stabilizing the growth rate of money. But on a strategic level the policy did succeed; the inflation rate came down from 12.3 percent in 1979 to 2.7 percent in 1993. To be sure, the Fed's policy carried a high price—the unemployment rate for all civilian workers was 9.7 percent in 1982 and 9.6 percent in 1983. But the job had to be done, and the Fed did it. *Perhaps* it could have been done at a lower cost in unemployment; that is hard to say.

What is *not* difficult to say is that monetary policy since 1982 has been extraordinarily successful. The Fed succeeded in keeping the inflation rate low; so far (mid-1995), there has been only one recession, and that was an unusually mild one. By historical standards this is a remarkably good performance. Will the Fed continue to be so successful? We can only hope.

SUMMARY

1 The Fed's original ideas were the great importance of maintaining the gold standard, the need to avoid financial panics, a wish to stabilize interest rates, and adherence to the real-bills doctrine.
2 In the Great Depression the money stock fell substantially. Friedman and Schwartz blame the Fed for not undertaking massive open-market purchases. But Temin argues that the fall in the money stock was due to a decline in the demand for money.
3 During and for some years after World War II the Fed pegged interest rates at the depression level. The policy was modified in 1951 by the Accord and was finally dropped in 1953.
4 In late 1978 the dollar fell sharply on the foreign-exchange market and a flight from the dollar was a real danger. The Fed responded with a temporarily restrictive policy that was insufficient, and in October 1979 the Fed had to adopt a stronger policy and to change its operating procedures by letting interest rates fluctuate much more. By early 1980 it was clear that even this policy was insufficient. In March, policy was tightened again and credit controls were imposed. Then 1981–82 saw the most severe postwar recession with fears about a financial collapse.

5 In October 1979 the Fed moved in a monetarist direction. It brought the inflation rate down, though at the cost of great unemployment. Interest rates rose sharply and fluctuated very much. In 1982 the Fed shifted away from monetarism.

6 An extraordinarily long expansion ensued, lasting through the second quarter of 1990. During the following recession there were complaints that stricter bank supervision and tougher capital requirements, as well as increased caution by bankers, was generating a credit crumble.

KEY TERMS

war finance
real-bills doctrine
interest-rate pegging

monetarist experiment
the Accord

QUESTIONS AND EXERCISES

1 Use the descriptions of monetary policy in recent issues of the *Economic Report of the President* and the Federal Reserve *Annual Report* to bring the discussion of this chapter up to date.

*2 Discuss: "In the Great Depression the Federal Reserve did all it could reasonably have been expected to do."

3 Discuss: "There has been little real improvement in the conduct of monetary policy. What looks like improvement is merely that the Fed, instead of being too soft on inflation, as it used to be, is now too soft on unemployment."

4 What do you think has been the Fed's biggest mistake in the postwar period?

5 For what action does the Fed deserve the most credit in the postwar period?

6 Take one issue in the dispute between the rival interpretations of the Great Depression given by Friedman and Schwartz and by Temin and write an essay on it.

7 What do you think is the most effective argument used by (a) Friedman and Schwartz and (b) Temin in their discussions of the Great Depression?

8 How would you try to decide whether the Fed was too restrictive during the 1990 recession?

FURTHER READING

BERNANKE, BEN. "Nonmonetary Effects of the Financial Crisis in the Propagation of the Great Depression," *American Economic Review* 73 (June 1983), 257–76. An interesting hypothesis that bank failures had their main impact by disrupting financial channels.

BRUNNER, KARL, ed. *Contemporary Views of the Great Depression*. The Hague: Nijhoff, 1981. A series of important articles on the Great Depression.

EICHENGREEN, BARRY. "Did International Economic Forces Cause the Great Depression?" *Contemporary Policy Issues* 6 (April 1988), 90–114. An interesting discussion of some international aspects of the Great Depression.

EXECUTIVE OFFICE OF THE PRESIDENT. *Economic Report of the President.* Washington, D.C. Each issue carries a history of monetary policy in the previous year.

FRIEDMAN, MILTON, and ANNA SCHWARTZ. *A Monetary History of the United States.* Princeton, N.J.: Princeton University Press, 1963. A classic. The chapter on the Great Depression has been published separately as *The Great Contraction*.

GREIDER, WILLIAM. *Secrets of the Temple.* New York: Simon & Schuster, 1987. A spirited argument that the Fed has been too concerned about inflation and has kept interest rates too high.

KETTLE, DONALD. *Leadership at the Fed.* New Haven, Conn.: Yale University Press, 1986. An interesting discussion of Fed chairmen by a political scientist.

MAISEL, SHERMAN. *Managing the Dollar.* New York: Norton, 1973. An important source for the history of the Fed in the 1960s.

MELTON, WILLIAM. *Inside the Fed.* Homewood, Ill.: Dow Jones–Irwin, 1985. Chapters 4 and 10 offer an excellent discussion of Fed policy since 1979.

PIERCE, JAMES. "The Political Economy of Arthur Burns," *Journal of Finance* 24 (May 1979), 485–96. A very good survey of monetary policy in the 1970s.

POOLE, WILLIAM. "Burnsian Monetary Policy: Eight Years of Progress?" *Journal of Finance* 24 (May 1979), 473–84. Another very good survey of monetary policy in the 1970s.

TEMIN, PETER. *Did Monetary Forces Cause the Great Depression?* New York: Norton, 1976. A major response to Friedman and Schwartz by a leading economic historian.

TIMBERLAKE, RICHARD. *Monetary Policy in the United States.* Chicago: University of Chicago Press, 1993. A comprehensive and critical account.

TOBIN, JAMES. "The Monetary Interpretation of History," *American Economic Review* 55 (June 1965), 464–85. A response to Friedman and Schwartz by a leading monetary theorist.

WHEELOCK, DAVID. "Monetary Policy in the Great Depression: What the Fed Did and Why," Federal Reserve Bank of St. Louis, *Review* 74 (March–April 1993), 3–29. A good discussion of Fed motives.

WICKER, ELMUS. *Federal Reserve Monetary Policy 1917–1933.* New York: Random House, 1966. A very thorough piece of historical research.

The Spring 1993 issue of the *Journal of Economic Perspectives* has several good articles on the Great Depression.

Alternative Monetary Standards

After you have read this chapter, you will be able to:

- Appreciate what a monetary standard is.
- Understand the pros and cons of several alternative standards.

The Fed operates within a framework called a **monetary standard,** which is a system of rules, traditions, and attitudes that govern the supply of money. Taken as a whole, the monetary standard represents the framework for day-to-day monetary policy. Such monetary standards often prevail for long periods of time. They become firmly established in people's thinking about what the world should be like, and are therefore not easily tampered with. Nevertheless, our current monetary standard—the subject of much of this book so far—is not the only one worth considering. So we now look at some other standards.

One is a gold-coin standard, in which the supply of money can change only as the supply of gold to the mint changes. In England, the classic gold-standard country, this rule became firmly rooted in people's expectations and traditions, and was not to be changed easily (see the box on page 507). Another example is today's U. S. monetary standard, which consists of a fiat currency and a central bank that manipulates reserves and short-term interest rates in an attempt to achieve the goals discussed in Chapter 22. Such a standard may seem obvious and natural to us now, but the gold standard, too, looked obvious and natural not so long ago. Indeed our current standard, with its fiat money, is rather a novelty. It just *might* turn out to be a relatively short interlude that future historians will point to as an example of arrogant folly.

Monetarists question the appropriateness of this standard. Because of the problems created by the lag of monetary policy, the danger of what they

---

If You Have a Standard, Stick to It

A monetary standard, in the full sense of the phrase, is not just a temporary arrangement defining the monetary unit, but is a principle that is adhered to through thick and thin. Here are two illustrations from Britain, the country that until 1931 was the temple of the gold standard.

During World War I, Britain, like most belligerents, left the gold standard. It returned to the gold standard in 1925 at the prewar price of gold in terms of pounds. It did that even though many people contended that British prices had risen more than U.S. prices, so that British prices would be forced to fall, and that would require a recession. This prewar price of gold in terms of pounds had been set by Sir Isaac Newton, the physicist who also served as director of the mint, in 1717. The decision to return to this prewar price of gold, costly in the short run, showed its importance in the eyes of the British.

The second example dates to 1931, when Britain faced a financial crisis. Foreigners, losing faith in the stability of the British pound, were withdrawing the funds they had invested in Britain. Two policies were possible. One was to devalue the pound, and thus break with the gold-standard rule of keeping currency stable in terms of gold. The other was to cut the large unemployment benefits that Britain was paying at the time.

The Labour Party, a party pledged to socialism, was in power. One might, therefore, have expected that the choice was obvious: leave the gold standard. But this monetary standard had such a hold on people that the Labour Party could not bring itself to do that. It split on this issue and one wing of the Labour Party formed a coalition government with the Conservative Party.

The new Conservative-Labour government then went off the gold standard. When one of the former Labour cabinet members heard about this, he is said to have exclaimed: "They never told us we could do that."*

*Cited in D. D. Moggridge, *The Return to Gold, 1925* (London: Cambridge University Press, 1969), p. 9.

---

see as inept Fed policy and its inflationary bias, they want to reduce the scope of Fed discretion and have the money supply grow at a stable rate (which could be zero). Hard-line monetarists, such as Milton Friedman, want to eliminate all central bank discretion and have an unchanging monetary base, or else have the base or the money supply grow a fixed rate, say, 4 percent per year. Moderate monetarists urge that the money supply should grow at a substantially more stable rate than at present, but not at a fixed rate. In following this policy, the Fed would be forced to give up many, though not all, of its attempts at countercyclical policy. Monetarists urge this not because they think that it is purely the Fed's fault that we have unemployment or that unemployment does not matter, but because they believe that the Fed is making a bad situation worse.

The money standard that monetarists advocate consists of more than the principle of more stable money growth. It also stresses the importance of price stability and of avoiding unpredictable inflation more than our prevailing standard does. It is therefore incompatible with seeking a temporary reduction in unemployment by exploiting the upward slope of the short-run Phillips curve.

In the 1960s and 1970s when Federal Reserve policy generated, or at least permitted, accelerating inflation and when the velocity of money was stable, the monetarists' policy recommendations gathered support among economists, though only a distinct minority of economists advocated a fixed monetary growth rate rule. But in the 1980s monetarism lost much of its support as the Fed showed that it was willing to bring the inflation rate down substantially and, what was more important, as the velocity of money became unstable. With a highly unstable velocity of *M-2*, a stable growth rate of *M-2* would result in a highly unstable *YP*. But while these changes have greatly reduced the attraction of monetarism, they have not by themselves negated the basic monetarist criticisms of our current standard: that the long and variable lags of monetary policy make effective countercyclical policy infeasible and that the central bank cannot be trusted. Whether the monetarists are right on these points is an empirical issue on which hard evidence is not easily obtained.

Feedback Rules

Some monetarists, such as Allan Meltzer, therefore advocate a monetary standard that makes some allowance for unpredictable variations in velocity, and yet does not give the Fed any discretion. This standard relies on a feedback rule that, in effect, allows the growth rate of money to vary in response to changes in velocity and in the growth rate of potential output. But since it sets out what the responses to velocity changes and changes in potential output should be, the Fed has no discretion.

The adjustment to changes in velocity and potential output that such a rule allows is slower than that which a fully informed central bank would make, but Meltzer argues that, due to our limited ability to forecast GDP and changes in velocity, such a mechanical and slow adjustment would provide results superior to those of a discretionary policy. He argues that such a feedback rule would not only improve day-to-day monetary policy but, what is more important, would also prevent such major blunders as the Fed's restrictive policy in the 1930s and its highly inflationary policy of the late 1960s and 1970s.

The simple rule that Meltzer proposed is designed to achieve zero inflation by setting the growth rate of the monetary base equal to the 12-quarter moving average of real GDP minus the 12-quarter moving average of base velocity.[1]

Bennet McCallum of Carnegie Mellon University has advocated a somewhat different feedback rule in which the base grows at an annual 3 percent rate minus the average growth rate of base velocity over the last four years plus the percentage rate by which last quarter's nominal GDP growth fell short of the target rate of growth of GDP. The Meltzer and the McCallum rules are just

---

[1] A moving average is an average that "moves" by adding additional observations and dropping prior ones. For example, a three-term moving average of the numbers 1, 2, 3, and 6 is 2 (the sum of the first three terms divided by 3) and 3.7 (the sum of 2, 3, and 6 divided by 3). Base velocity is GDP divided by the base. Students familiar with log notation will see that, when using logs to denote growth rates, $m + v = y + p$. So if m is equal to $y - v$, p is zero.

two examples of the feedback rules that can be developed. Another rule, suggested by John Judd and Brian Motley of the San Francisco Federal Reserve Bank, is

$$\Delta b_t = \Delta z^* - \Delta \overline{v}_t + \lambda(z^*_{t-1} - z_{t-1}),$$

where Δb_t is the growth rate of the base, Δz^* is the target growth rate of nominal GDP, $\Delta \overline{v}$ is the growth rate of base velocity over the prior four years, λ is the proportion of the miss in attaining the GDP target that the Fed wants to offset each quarter, and Δz is the actual GDP growth rate.

Two problems arise in determining whether a particular feedback rule would perform better than our current standard. One is the Lucas critique discussed in Chapter 26: the adoption of a feedback rule would change the way firms and households act, so that one might question whether tests of the rule that have been undertaken, using past data provide any relevant results. A second is that to test how well the rule works, one has to make some assumptions about the structure of the economy, and these assumptions may be wrong.

Imposing a Low-Inflation Goal on the Central Bank

Requiring the Fed to follow a mechanical feedback rule would be a radical departure from current policy, and something the Fed would fight vehemently. A more moderate reform would be to address the problem of time inconsistency, as well as the confusion and inflationary bias that multiple goals for monetary policy cause by giving the Fed a single overriding goal and constraint, price stability, or, perhaps more realistically, a low inflation rate. New Zealand passed legislation requiring the central bank governor to submit his or her resignation if inflation exceeds a predetermined rate. The Canadian central bank, the Bank of Canada, was recently given a somewhat similar constraint. The German Bundesbank has all along had an injunction to give price stability priority. It is likely that if and when the European central bank is established it, too, will be given a price-stability directive. The Federal Reserve endorsed a bill (which died in Congress) requiring it to lower the inflation rate and keep it low. Such legislation would meet one objection to current discretionary policy, though it would do nothing about other problems, like the lag in monetary policy and our limited ability to predict GDP and the effects of monetary policy.

The Gold Standard

A stable monetary growth rate rule, and a price-stability rule are not the only ways of depriving the government of discretionary control over the money supply. Another way is by returning to the gold standard. We will discuss the gold standard in some detail in the next chapter. Here we just discuss how it would limit the government's control over the money supply. For this it is not necessary that money actually consist of gold coins. A full gold standard exists if: (1) various types of money are convertible into gold; (2) the government buys and sells gold at a fixed price; (3) it does not inhibit the free import or export of gold; and (4) it does not offset the automatic effect of a gold inflow or out-flow on the money supply by, for example, open-market operations.

Suppose that these conditions are met and that the Fed increases the base. The money supply expands and, as discussed in Chapter 25, the dollar falls on the foreign-exchange market. Now that the dollar is worth fewer British pounds, French francs, and so on, someone will go to the U.S. Treasury, buy gold at its fixed dollar price, and sell this gold abroad for foreign currency. This will be profitable since the foreign currency is now worth more dollars. As the U.S. Treasury receives dollars for the gold that it sells to the public, the public's money stock falls. Moreover, the fall in the U.S. gold stock may induce the Fed to adopt a restrictive policy. Thus, any attempt by the Fed to increase the money supply unduly does not succeed.

Conversely, suppose the Fed is too restrictive. As interest rates rise and output and prices fall, the dollar rises on the foreign-exchange market. This provides an incentive to buy gold abroad at its fixed price in foreign currency

Currency Boards

An alternative to a conventional central bank is a currency board. Hong Kong provides an example. Its currency, the Hong Kong dollar, has a fixed exchange rate with the U.S. dollar. Its currency board can issue additional Hong Kong dollars and reserves for Hong Kong banks only in proportion to the increase in its holdings of U.S. dollars and other dollar-convertible currencies and assets. Such currency boards also exist in Argentina and Estonia, and may spread to other countries. Some economists have advocated that Russia and Mexico institute currency boards, as a way of preventing high inflation and restoring confidence in the ruble and the Mexican peso.

The important difference between a currency board and a central bank is that the currency board cannot follow a discretionary policy; its creation of money depends solely on the inflow and outflow of foreign currency, so that it is immune to political pressures. Moreover, the inflation rate in a country with a currency board has to be approximately equal to that of the country to which its currency is tied. Suppose its inflation rate is greater. As its prices rise at a higher rate than the prices of foreign goods, its exports fall and its imports rise. This increases the demand for foreign currency relative to its supply and thus tends to raise the price of foreign currency on the foreign-exchange market. As a result, the public buys foreign currency at the fixed rate from the currency board instead. The currency board then has to respond to the decline in its foreign currency holdings by reducing the money supply, and that reduces the inflation rate. Since the money supply is thus responding mechanically to changes in foreign-exchange holdings, the government cannot raise the money supply at a rate that is highly inflationary.

A currency board provides some insurance against a country's inflating at a much higher rate than the country whose currency it is using as reserves. But it is not complete insurance; the law that established the currency board can be repealed. Moreover, the greater protection against inflation that a currency board provides comes at a cost; the country can no longer follow an independent monetary policy. Indeed, its central bank cannot even act as a lender of last resort.

(that is, at its lower dollar price) and sell it to the U.S. Treasury. Since the Treasury is paying out dollars for this gold, the U.S. money supply expands again, and thus counteracts the Fed's restrictive policy.

Does this mean that the gold standard is desirable because it limits the Fed's powers? Not in the opinion of most economists. Obviously, those who believe that the Fed's actions have, on the average, a favorable impact on the economy oppose the gold standard. Those who want to eliminate the Fed's discretionary control over the money supply often reject the gold standard in favor of some other rule, such as a feedback rule. One reason is that the gold standard does not necessarily prevent the Fed from increasing the money stock at an inflationary rate *if other countries do the same.* In this case the dollar does not fall on the foreign-exchange market, so that the U.S. money stock is not reduced by gold exports.

Another problem with the gold standard is that it fixes the value of the dollar relative to gold, but not necessarily in terms of other goods. Suppose that there are large-scale gold discoveries. With an increased supply of gold, the price of gold must fall relative to the prices of goods and services. If the value of money is fixed in terms of gold, the value of money in terms of goods and services must fall; that is, we have inflation.

Conversely, suppose that over the years little additional gold comes on the market. Suppose further that velocity falls or at least does not grow as fast as output. Prices would then have to fall, and that might require the spur of substantial unemployment for some time.

Moreover, one may question whether those who support the gold standard in principle would really allow it to operate in practice. Suppose a gold outflow would require a substantial deflation in the United States, or a gold inflow a substantial inflation. Would the supporters of the gold standard still be there? Given the recent great swings in foreign-exchange rates and in gold prices, which under the gold standard would induce large swings in U.S. prices, this is a question worth asking. In addition, the gold standard requires countries to hold an asset, gold, that does not earn interest.

Private Money

Some economists, led by the late Friederich von Hayek of Freiburg University, Germany, want to introduce competition into the monetary system as a way of exercising discipline over the central bank. They would allow banks to issue their own money, money that would be distinct for each bank. People could then write contracts denominated either in government monies, such as the dollar or the pound, or in privately issued monies. Both types of money would circulate. The public would tend to hold that money whose value is least eroded by inflation. This would give each bank—*and the government*—an incentive to preserve the value of its money by limiting its quantity.

This is an ingenious scheme, but it too has some problems. First, given the public's conservatism on monetary matters, private money issuers might find it impossible to compete against the well-established government money. Second, there is the danger that a money issuer would initially pursue a conservative policy, build up a good reputation so that many people would become willing to acquire this money, and then, all of a sudden, flood the market with money, go out of business, and live happily ever after. Third a private money producer might become a monopolist since economies of scale would allow one producer to drive out the others. Economies of scale exist because the more one type of money is used, the more readily it is accepted, and hence the more convenient it is to holders.

A more radical approach would abolish government money altogether. It would also cut the link between the medium of exchange and the standard of value. The standard of value would consist of a commodity bundle containing a fixed amount of many different commodities. Since the price of such a bundle would move more or less in line with the general price level, anyone who made a contract to pay a certain number of such monetary units would neither gain nor lose significantly from inflation. Hence, it would be an excellent standard of value. The medium of exchange would be a check or currency note from a money-market fund denominated in commodity bundles. In such a system inflation would be no problem because the standard of value, the commodity bundle, would have a stable value in terms of all goods and services. Decreases in aggregate expenditures would also not create a problem. If people decide to buy fewer goods and to hold more money instead, they would simply increase their accounts with the money-market funds, which would then buy more of these commodity bundles. In such an economy that has no serious macroeconomic disturbances, the Fed could be abolished. Whether such a system would actually work needs much more investigation. But, in any case, it is too radical an idea to have a serious chance of adoption in the foreseeable future.

A Populist Standard

All the standards discussed so far would greatly reduce or eliminate the Fed's role. Another standard would give the Fed a very active role in maintaining full employment. The Fed would have one predominant goal, full employment, and a secondary goal, keeping interest rates low and stable. Hence, it would accommodate just about all increases in the demand for money.

How about the longer-run vertical Phillips curve and the danger that such an expansionary policy would generate accelerating inflation? Supporters of this standard reject the Phillips curve as a basis for policy. They consider it immoral to use unemployment to curb inflation. Instead, they would rely mainly on incomes policy. Moreover, they maintain that if we had a more equal income distribution, then unions would moderate their wage demands, and the slope of the Phillips curve would be less steep. A social compact, embodied in a widely accepted incomes policy rather than unemployment, they believe, is the appropriate way to curb inflation. Monetary restriction, and the resulting higher interest rates, only make inflation worse rather than better, because rising interest rates induce firms to raise prices to recover their higher interest costs. This position is accepted by only a small minority of economists, many of them post-Keynesians. Most U.S. economists are skeptical about the efficacy of social contracts and incomes policies.

SUMMARY

1 Monetary policy proceeds within a set of rules, traditions, and attitudes determining the behavior of the money supply. Such a monetary standard is often resistant to change.
2 Monetarists advocate a more stable monetary growth rate; some of them advocate a fixed growth rate for money or the base. They also strongly oppose inflation.
3 Some economists are in favor of a feedback rule according to which the growth rate of money or the base varies with economic conditions, but does so in a predetermined way.
4 Others want to impose a price-stability or low-inflation goal on the central bank. This has been done in some countries.
5 Another proposal for curbing the Fed's discretion is a return to the gold standard. However, this would not prevent inflation if other countries inflate too or if the world's gold supply increases.
6 Some economists advocate the institution of private money either alongside government money or as a replacement for it.
7 Other economists advocate a consistently expansionary monetary policy accompanied by an incomes policy.

KEY TERMS

stable monetary growth rate rule	gold standard
feedback rule	private money
currency board	

QUESTIONS AND EXERCISES

*1 Using what you have learned in previous chapters, what is a feedback rule?
*2 Give an argument for, and an argument against, a fixed monetary growth rate rule.
*3 Describe the arguments for and against a gold standard.
 4 Develop your own idea of a good monetary standard.

FURTHER READING

BRUNNER, KARL. "The Case Against Monetary Activism," *Lloyds Bank Review*, 139 (January 1981), 20–30. A sweeping attack on discretionary policy.

FRIEDMAN, BENJAMIN. "The Role of Judgment and Discretion in the Conduct of Monetary Policy," In *Managing Capital Markets*. Kansas City: Federal Reserve Bank of Kansas City, 1993, pp. 151–96. An excellent statement of the case for discretionary policy.

FRIEDMAN, MILTON. *A Program for Monetary Stability*. New York: Fordham University Press, 1959. A classic statement of the rules position.

———. "Monetary Policy: Theory and Practice," *Journal of Money, Credit, and Banking* 14 (February 1982), 98–118. A powerful indictment of the Fed's procedures.

GLASSNER, DAVID. *Free Banking and Monetary Reform*. New York: Cambridge University Press, 1989. A good presentation of the case for private money.

GREENFIELD, ROBERT, and LELAND YEAGER. "A Laissez-Faire Approach to Monetary Stability," *Journal of Money, Credit and Banking* 15 (August 1983), 302–15. A fascinating discussion of private money.

JUDD, JOHN, and BRIAN MOTLEY. "Nominal Feedback Rules for Monetary Policy," Federal Reserve Bank of San Francisco, *Economic Review* (Summer 1991), 3–17. An interesting test of feedback rules.

MCCALLUM, BENNETT. "Robustness Properties of a Rule for Monetary Policy," *Carnegie-Rochester Conference Series on Public Policy* 29 (Autumn 1988), 105–28. (See also the comments by Benjamin Friedman and McCallum's reply on pp. 205–15.) A classic statement of the case for feedback rules.

MELTZER, ALLAN. "Credibility and Monetary Policy," In *Price Stability and Public Policy*. Kansas City: Federal Reserve Bank of Kansas City, 1984, pp. 105–28. A clear presentation of the case for feedback rules.

MODIGLIANI, FRANCO. "The Monetarist Controversy; or, Should We Forsake Stabilization Policy?" *American Economic Review* 67 (March 1977), 1–19. An excellent criticism of monetarist policy prescriptions.

MODIGLIANI, FRANCO, and MILTON FRIEDMAN. "The Monetarist Controversy." Federal Reserve Bank of San Francisco, *Economic Review* (Spring 1977) supplement. An extremely stimulating debate.

SELGIN, GEORGE, and LAWRENCE WHITE. "How Would the Invisible Hand Handle Money?" *Journal of Economic Literature* 32 (December 1994), 1718–49. A stimulating discussion of privately issued money.

TOBIN, JAMES. "The Monetarist Counter-Revolution Today—An Appraisal," *Economic Journal* 91 (March 1981), 29–42. A powerful criticism of monetarism.

———. "Monetary Policy: Rules, Targets and Shocks," *Journal of Money, Credit and Banking* 15 (November 1983), 506–18. A strong defense of discretionary policy.

Finally, here is a book (available free from the Boston Federal Reserve Bank) that provides some excellent insights on many important questions on monetary policy: Federal Reserve Bank of Boston, *Goals, Guidelines, and Constraints Facing Monetary Policymakers*.

FIVE

THE INTERNATIONAL MONETARY SYSTEM

The Evolution of the International Monetary System

After you have read this chapter, you will be able to:

- Understand the major differences among different types of international monetary arrangements.
- Appreciate why international monetary arrangements change over time.

International monetary arrangements enable residents of one country to make payments to residents of other countries. Such payments are necessary because importers in one country must pay exporters in other countries; either the importers must first acquire the currencies of the countries in which the exporters live, or the exporters must, after being paid in the importer's currency, exchange it for their own currency. The **exchange rate,** which is the price of a foreign money in terms of domestic money, is determined in the foreign-exchange market. Changes in the exchange rate occur to restore or maintain balance between payments to foreign countries and receipts from these countries.

The needs of both industry and trade are enhanced by arrangements that minimize the additional costs, inconvenience, and risks of international transactions relative to domestic transactions. These costs, while generally small, vary with the type of international monetary arrangements and especially with the way the foreign exchange market is organized. Over the last century, international monetary arrangements have evolved from reliance on gold as the basis for international payments to reliance on national monies—and especially the U.S. dollar—as the basis for international payments. These changes in international payments arrangements are not random, but instead are responses both to monetary and structural economic disturbances and to changes in the relative economic size of individual countries and the ability of each of the large countries to achieve price level stability.

An international monetary system can be identified by three key features: the way the foreign-exchange market is organized, the types of assets used for financing or settling payments imbalances among countries, and the mechanisms of adjustment to payments deficits and to payments surpluses. The name given to the international monetary system has changed as the institutional basis for organizing the foreign-exchange market and for producing international reserve assets has changed. Before World War I, the term *gold standard* was applied to international financial arrangements; after World War I the phrase *gold-exchange standard* was used to describe the arrangement. The term *standard,* when used in the context of the gold standard, suggests a measure or unit of account, like a yard or a liter. The dominant feature of the monetary system in the nineteenth century was that national monies had values that were stated in terms of gold; thus the U.S. dollar was equal to 1.672 grams of gold of .900 fineness or pureness. After World War II the term **Bretton Woods System,** which was established by international treaty during World War II and functioned until the early 1970s, was applied. And since the early 1970s, the system has been without its own proper name, so it is usually referred to as the **post-Bretton Woods System.**

This chapter first describes each of the three international monetary systems that have prevailed for the last hundred years. Then attention is given to the economic and political factors that explain the evolution of international financial arrangements, especially the rise of the United States as a dominant economic power.

THE GOLD STANDARD

The nineteenth century is frequently described as the gold-standard era, although more detailed analysis suggests that for most countries the term is more appropriately applied to the period 1880 to 1913. A country "joined" the gold standard when its national legislature stipulated that its banks and financial institutions redeem or repurchase their notes and deposit liabilities on demand at a fixed price, the *mint parity,* in terms of a specified amount of gold. Thus at the beginning of January 1879, the United States went back on the gold standard, having left it in 1863; U.S. commercial banks once again were obliged to convert their monetary liabilities into gold on demand. The Act of Parliament of 1816 obliged the Bank of England to buy gold of 0.916⅔ fineness at 3 pounds, 17 shillings, 9 pence per ounce and to sell gold of the same fineness at the price of 3 pounds, 17 shillings, 10½ pence per ounce. Some countries pegged their currencies to silver as well as to gold, and so they were on a bimetallic standard; the monetary institutions in these countries were obliged to buy and sell both gold and silver on demand at the respective parity for each commodity money. The mint parities of major countries in the later part of the nineteenth century are shown in Table 29.1, together with the prices of major foreign currencies in terms of the U.S. dollar.

Table 29.1   Parities of Major Currencies under the Gold Standard

Country	Unit	Weight*	Fineness†	Value of 1 Ounce of Gold	U.S. Dollar Parity
United States (1879)‡	1 dollar	1.672	.900	US 20.67	—
Great Britain (1816)	1 pound	7.988	.917	BP 3/17/10 1/2	$4.86
France (1878)	1 franc	.322	.900	FF 107.1	$ .193
Germany (1871)	1 mark	.398	.900	DM 86.8	$ .238
Italy (1878)	1 lira	.3226	.900	IL 107.1	$ .193
Netherlands (1875)	1 florin	.672	.900	DF 51.7	$ .402

*Weight of standard coin in grams.
†The fineness of a standard coin is its proportion of pure gold.
‡The dates in brackets indicate the most recent date each national currency was pegged to gold.
Source: M. L. Muhleman, *Monetary Systems of the World* (New York: Charles H. Nicoll, 1894).

Managing a bimetallic system proved difficult because of the need to maintain a fixed-price relationship between the mint parity for gold and the mint parity for silver. From time to time, when there were large new discoveries of silver or gold, changes in one of the mint parities were necessary; there were several changes in the relationship between the U.S. dollar price of gold and the U.S. dollar price of silver in the nineteenth century before silver was formally demonetized.

A major by-product of commitments of individual countries to link their currencies to gold was a system of **pegged exchange rates;** the values of the British pound and other currencies were fixed in terms of the U.S. dollar. This arrangement contrasts sharply with the system of **floating exchange rates** that has prevailed since the early 1970s. Since under the gold standard the Bank of England was committed to buying and selling one ounce of gold at 77 shillings and 10½ pence and the U.S. Treasury was committed to buying and selling one ounce of gold at the parity of $20.67, the U.S. dollar price of one pound sterling could be calculated as $4.865 (once an adjustment was made for the somewhat greater pureness of the standard British gold coin).[1]

Some central banks bought and sold gold at their mint parities. Most central banks, however, bought gold at prices fractionally below their mint parities and sold it at prices fractionally above their mint parities. These small differences between the mint parities and the gold buying and selling prices were called **handling charges** and were intended to compensate the national cen-

[1] Thus, if an ounce of gold equals both 77 shillings 10½ pence times 0.917/.900 (the adjustment for differences in the proportion of pure gold in the several coins) and $20.67, then 20 shillings, or one pound, equals $4.865.

tral banks for the costs incurred in buying and selling gold. In addition, some central banks varied their gold selling prices modestly, increasing these prices when the demand for gold was strong; these countries were said to be on the "limping gold standard."

Gold and International Reserves

A key aspect of the gold standard was that central banks held a large part of their assets in the form of gold. Virtually all the assets of the Bank of England were gold. Other central banks held a large proportion of their assets in gold and the rest in government securities denominated in the British pound, the French franc, and their own currencies. Differences among central banks in the proportion of their assets held as gold reflected differences in their business needs. One reason that central banks outside Great Britain held such a large proportion of their assets in British pound–denominated securities was that their residents had sold or issued bonds denominated in the British pound: London was then the world's principal financial center. Similarly, borrowers resident outside France received French francs after issuing bonds in Paris. Moreover, these borrowers were obliged to acquire the British pound and the French franc to repay debts denominated in these currencies. And since Britain and France were economic powerhouses, holding funds denominated in pounds and francs made sense.

A second feature of the gold standard was that gold would be exported from the countries with payments deficits—broadly, those countries whose imports of goods, services, and securities exceeded their exports of goods, services, and securities—and imported by the countries with payments surpluses. Some of these payments imbalances were financed by *gold flows*. However, one of the paradoxes of the gold standard period was that gold transactions between the countries with payments deficits and the countries with the payments surpluses were modest. Shipments of gold between New York and London incurred costs of freight and insurance as well as the forgone interest on the wealth invested in gold between the date the payer acquired the gold in one country and the date the payee received the gold in the second country. Consequently, traders and investors preferred to make international payments by methods that were less costly than shipping gold.

To reduce costs of international payments, importers and exporters began to trade **bills of exchange,** which effectively were postdated checks. These bills were issued by importers or buyers and were IOUs indicating that payment for the purchase would be made in 30 or 90 days. Thus, a U.S. exporter of wheat to Great Britain would receive a bill of exchange denominated in the British pound and due in 30 or 90 days; the current market price of this bill would be below its face value on the maturity date, since the bill would have to be sold at a discount at the prevailing interest rate. The U.S. wheat exporter wanted U.S. dollars, not British pounds; he could sell this British pound bill of exchange in London and then buy gold in London to ship to the United States, which he would sell to obtain U.S. dollars. Or he could sell the bill of exchange in New York to a U.S. importer, who would ship the bill to London to make a payment there and avoid the costs and inconvenience of the gold shipment. The U.S. importer would pay for the British pound bill in U.S. dollars, so the U.S. wheat exporter would receive U.S. dollars. The U.S. wheat exporter would earn interest on the bill of exchange as it traveled from London to New York, while the U.S. importer would earn interest as the bill traveled back to London.

Because the costs of shipping the bill to London were below the costs of shipping gold to London, the U.S. importer would pay a higher U.S. dollar price for the bill than for the amount of gold that would generate the same amount of British pounds. But the ability to make the payment in London by shipping gold set an upper limit to the U.S. dollar price of these British pound bills of exchange in New York. Similarly, the ability to make a payment from London to New York by shipping gold set a lower limit to the U.S. dollar price that the U.S. exporter would accept for his British pound bills of exchange; if the U.S. dollar price of these bills was lower, the U.S. exporter would ship gold from London to New York instead.

"Rules of the Game"

The third feature of the gold standard was the mechanism for returning to stability or equilibrium in response to shocks. This system had built-in **"rules of the game"**: the countries with balance-of-payments surpluses would be forced to follow expansive monetary policies because the gold inflows would lead to an increase in the gold holdings of their central banks and hence to an increase in the domestic money supply. Conversely, the countries with balance-of-payments deficits and gold outflows would be forced to follow contractive monetary policies: the monetary liabilities of their central banks would decline as their central banks sold gold. Consumer price levels would rise in the countries where the money supplies were increasing; conversely consumer price levels would decline in the countries where the money supplies were declining. As the consumer price levels increased in one group of countries, their imports would rise in value and their exports would fall; in contrast, the imports of the countries with the declining price levels would fall in value and their exports would rise in value. This change in the relationship among national price levels would continue until balance-of-payments equilibrium was achieved—until gold flows had abated. Because international payments imbalances would automatically self-correct, the national central banks would not find it necessary to adopt discretionary measures to restore a payments balance. One important aspect of the operation of the rules of the game was that maintaining the fixed price of the national money in terms of gold required that national price levels vary.

This adjustment process appeared to be automatic, guided by an invisible hand. Most countries maintained their gold parities for an extended period. But whether countries actually followed the rules of the game has been debated extensively.

Gold and the Consumer Price Level

The fourth feature of the gold standard was the promise that the consumer price level would be stable in the long run. If monetary gold holdings were increasing rapidly worldwide, either because of new gold discoveries or because of new, cheaper techniques for refining gold ore, then central banks in many countries might be buying gold simultaneously, and so the money supplies in these countries would rise at the same time. At the new and higher consumer price levels, gold mining would be more costly, gold production would decline, and a damper or brake would be placed on further increases in the commodity price levels. Conversely, if the demand for gold for non-monetary uses increased, the consumer price levels would fall, because less gold would be available for monetary purposes. At the lower consumer price levels, more gold would be mined, national money supplies would increase more rapidly, and eventually the decline in the consumer price levels would be checked. So just as national price levels changed to restore balance-of-payments equilibrium, so changes in the world price level would prove self-limiting. Thus, stability in consumer price levels would be achieved over a period of several decades if not on a year-to-year basis.

The U.S. and British wholesale price levels for 1800 to 1950 are shown in Figure 29.1: the price levels at the outbreak of World War I are not much higher than those a century earlier. The average annual increase in the price levels was small, less than 1 percent. And there are very few years, except those during major wars, in which the annual change in the price level exceeded 3 percent.

The gold standard proved attractive to observers and monetary officials because of its anonymous, automatic, self-correcting properties and its promise of long-run price-level stability. And the rapid economic growth in the United States and many other countries during the half-century before World War I contributed to the view that the gold standard was the ideal monetary arrangement.

At the beginning of World War I most foreign countries ceased pegging their currencies to gold; they were concerned that otherwise there would be a surge in the individual demand for gold. During the war, price levels increased sharply because of a surge in military expenditures. After the war some countries, primarily those that had been neutral in the war, again pegged their currencies to gold at their prewar parities. Great Britain finally returned to the gold standard at its prewar parity in 1925, and so the prewar exchange rate between the U.S. dollar and the British pound was reestablished. But by then the British pound was overvalued, for the British price level had risen more rapidly than the U.S. price level. France, Belgium, and Italy eventually went back on the gold standard too, but only after a substantial increase in the price of gold in terms of their currencies. In retrospect, it appears that it would have been less costly to reestablish the gold standard if more countries had also been willing to increase the price of gold in terms of their currencies to match the increase in their commodity price levels that had occurred during World War I.

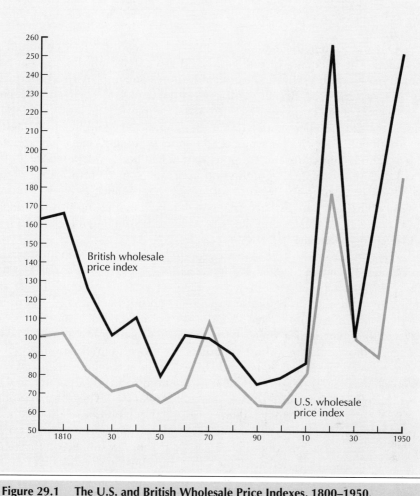

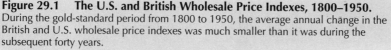

Figure 29.1   The U.S. and British Wholesale Price Indexes, 1800–1950.
During the gold-standard period from 1800 to 1950, the average annual change in the British and U.S. wholesale price indexes was much smaller than it was during the subsequent forty years.

THE GOLD-EXCHANGE STANDARD

The gold-exchange standard developed in the early 1920s in response to an anticipated shortage of gold due both to a reduction in the supply and an increase in the demand. The anticipated reduction in the supply of gold resulted from the increase in national price levels and the concomitant increase in costs of gold production. The anticipated increase in the demand for gold resulted both from the disintegration of the Austro-Hungarian Empire, which would lead to more countries with more central banks and therefore a greater need for gold reserves, and from the increase in national price levels during and after World War I. Because of the higher commodity price levels, gold was cheaper in terms of silver and other precious metals, but only as long as central bank parities in the 1920s were similar to those before the war.

One way to stem the demand for gold was to stop using it as a medium of exchange. The adequacy of monetary gold was extensively discussed at two conferences sponsored by the League of Nations, one in Brussels in 1920 and one in Genoa in 1922. Because national central banks were reluctant to raise the price of gold in terms of their currencies, the participants at these conferences recommended economizing on the demand for gold by discouraging the use of gold for private payments and concentrating monetary gold holdings in central banks. Moreover, a practice that had been evident before World War I received formal recognition and approval: some central banks would hold their reserves in the form of foreign exchange, such as bank deposits, Treasury bills, and bankers' acceptances, denominated in the British pound, the U.S. dollar, or some other currency. The shift from a gold standard to a **gold-exchange standard** had begun.

The shift from the gold standard to the gold-exchange standard meant, primarily, a change in the composition of international reserve assets. Central banks were still supposed to follow the rules of the game for the adjustment of their money supplies in response to inflows and outflows of gold and other international reserve assets, just as under the gold standard. Countries would still maintain parities for their currencies in terms of gold. Yet there was a change: if those countries whose securities were used as international reserve assets, namely the United States and Great Britain at the time, incurred payments deficits and foreign central banks acquired securities denominated in the U.S. dollar or the British pound, the United States and Great Britain would not follow the rules of the game and reduce the liabilities of their central banks. The money supplies in the countries with the payments surpluses would increase without a corresponding decrease in the money supplies in the countries with the payments deficits. The automatic adjustment tendencies of the gold standard were maintained, but in a more asymmetric fashion.

The gold-exchange standard was supposed to provide a framework in which national currencies would again exchange at their mint parities, and the world price level was supposed to remain stable. Yet exchange rates were not pegged during most of the period between World War I and World War II. In September 1931, six years after pegging the pound to gold at its 1913 parity, Great Britain decided that the level of interest rates necessary to maintain its parity for gold led to unemployment levels that were unacceptably high. So the British authorities stopped pegging the pound and allowed it to float. Changes in parities in the 1930s followed in a dominolike pattern: the U.S. dollar was devalued in 1933, and the French franc, the Belgian franc, and the Dutch guilder in 1936. The alignment of the exchange rates at the end of the 1930s was not very different from that at the end of the 1920s, however. Yet after this sequence of currency devaluations, the monetary price of gold was 75 percent higher in terms of most national currencies.

The growth of international reserves denominated in the British pound, the U.S. dollar, and other major currencies during the 1930s was modest. At the end of the 1920s, holdings of securities denominated in national currencies accounted for 20 percent of international reserves. At the end of the 1930s this ratio was lower, because the value of monetary gold holdings had increased sharply as a result of the effective worldwide increase in the price of gold, and this acted as a stimulus to gold production.

The monetary instability in the interwar period was reflected in the combination of sharp movements in exchange rates, high levels of unemployment, and especially the growth of ad hoc restrictions on international trade and payments. This instability is sometimes associated with the tension between Great Britain, whose economic power was declining, and the United States, whose economic position was on the rise. One aspect of this tension was that the interest rates the United States felt appropriate for its domestic economy induced investors to shift funds from London to New York. The Bank of England felt compelled to counter by raising interest rates to levels deemed high given the unemployment in Great Britain. In the early 1930s, there was also a conflict about the appropriate value for the U.S. dollar–British pound exchange rate; the value preferred by the U.S. authorities would have increased the competitiveness of U.S. goods more than the British authorities found acceptable.

This shift in economic power from Great Britain to the United States was inevitable given the increase in the size of the U.S. economy relative to the British economy. Whether this shift could have been accommodated with less instability is conjectural. Major policy errors contributed both to the variability of exchange rates and the high levels of unemployment. One error already noted was the unwillingness of countries to adjust exchange parities—the price of gold in terms of each national currency—to reflect the increase in post-World War I price levels. A second error was the unwillingness of some countries to raise their monetary gold prices to correspond with the increase in their national price levels relative to the increase in the U.S. price level.

THE BRETTON WOODS SYSTEM

During World II, the United States and Great Britain took the initiative to develop a set of economic institutions to deal with anticipated problems of the postwar period, and to avoid a repetition of the monetary and trade disturbances of the previous twenty years. The International Trade Organization (ITO) was envisaged as an organization for reducing tariffs, for establishing commodity arrangements to limit variations in prices of basic raw materials, and for coordinating national antitrust policies. Although the ITO never came into existence, the first article in its charter led to the **General Agreement on Tariffs and Trade** (GATT), which has been the dominant institution in promoting the reduction of tariffs and other trade barriers. The **International Bank for Reconstruction and Development** (the IBRD or the **World Bank**) was established in 1944 to finance the postwar recovery in Western Europe; once this task was completed at the end of the 1940s, the bank focused on various types of loans and technical assistance to developing countries. The third institution, the **International Monetary Fund** (IMF), was also established in 1944. It was founded to enhance stability in international payments both by providing rules for changes in exchange parities and for exchange controls on international payments and by managing a pool of national currencies that individual countries might borrow from to finance their payments deficits. The World Bank and the IMF are known as the **Bretton Woods institutions,** for the treaties establishing both institutions were signed at Bretton Woods.

The International Monetary Fund and the Bretton Woods System

The IMF was the institutional embodiment of what came to be known as the *Bretton Woods System.* This system differed sharply from both the gold standard and the gold-exchange standard in its legal aspects, as the earlier systems had had no international legal basis. Moreover, the Bretton Woods System was managed by international civil servants, responsible to the Board of Governors selected by the member countries (usually their secretaries of the treasury or ministers of finance) and a full-time board of executive directors, essentially ambassadors from its member countries.

Each member country of the IMF was required to state a parity for its currency in terms of gold or in terms of the U.S. dollar. Subsequent changes of the exchange parities required consultation with or approval by the Fund.

When the Fund was established, its capital was projected to be the equivalent of $10 billion. Countries joining the IMF were required to contribute to its capital, with the amount of each country's capital subscription or quota based on a formula that included the country's share of world imports and the size of its gold holdings. One-quarter of each country's capital subscription was payable in gold and the remaining three-quarters in its own currency, in the form of a non-interest-bearing demand note. By 1994 the capital of the Fund was the equivalent of $145 billion, which resulted partly from an increase in the number of member countries and largely from a series of increases in the size of each member's quota.

Whenever a member country had a payments deficit, it could borrow from the pool of national currencies held by the Fund, with the amount it might borrow geared to the size of its quota. About one-quarter of its quota was automatically available, and the rest was available on a discretionary basis. For example, in 1956, at the time of the Suez crisis in the Middle East, Great Britain borrowed nearly $2 billion from the Fund. In the Fund's terminology, Great Britain *drew* or bought U.S. dollars from the Fund with British pounds, with the consequence that the Fund's holdings of U.S. dollars declined, while its holdings of British pounds increased. The Fund obtained the dollars by cashing part of the U.S. dollar–denominated demand note received as part of the U.S. capital subscription. Great Britain paid interest to the Fund, with the interest rate based on the size of the loan in relation to Great Britain's quota and the length of the period that the loan was outstanding. When Great Britain repaid the loan, it purchased British pounds with U.S. dollars or some other currency acceptable to the Fund.

The Fund's rules sought to eliminate the use of exchange controls on payments for goods and services like shipping and tourism, although member countries were allowed to retain such restrictions during the postwar reconstruction period. Member countries were allowed to maintain restrictions on transactions in securities, such as stocks and bonds, for an indefinite period.

The Fund's Articles of Agreement provided that the ability of a member to borrow would not be conditional on its approval of the member's economic and social policies. Over the years, however, the Fund's management developed the view that credit should be extended only so long as there was a reasonable prospect that the member country could resolve its balance-of-payments problem.

Two important institutional innovations, one in the early 1960s and the second in the late 1960s, complemented periodic increases in IMF quotas as a way to increase the funds available to the IMF and the supply of international reserves. In 1963, to alleviate a possible shortage of currencies in the Fund, the Articles of Agreement were amended by the **General Arrangements to Borrow,** which formalized the terms on which the Fund could borrow the currencies of member countries. The major modification of the late 1960s involved the establishment of **Special Drawing Rights** (SDRs), a new international reserve asset. The motivation for introducing the SDRs was the belief that there would be a shortage of gold and of other international reserve assets and that most countries could not satisfy their demand for reserve assets without forcing the United States to incur payments deficits. The presumption was that the demand for international reserve assets might increase at a rate more or less commensurate with the growth in world trade or world income—basically an international variant of the quantity theory of money presented in Chapter 15. This approach led to estimates that the demand for international reserve assets might increase at a rate of $2 billion to $3 billion a year, at a time when monetary gold holdings were increasing at a rate of less than $1 billion a year.

Ten billion dollars of SDRs were produced in the 1968 to 1971 period, through a form of international open-market operation; each member country received newly produced SDRs in proportion to its share of total IMF quotas. Each member country could use SDRs to buy foreign currencies from other members or from the Fund. For example, if Great Britain had a payments deficit, it might sell some SDRs to the Fund to get U.S. dollars or some other national currency that it would use to support the British pound in the foreign-exchange market. In addition, SDRs began to develop some characteristics of a unit of account, and some countries began to state the parities for their currencies in terms of SDRs, just as, at earlier dates, they had stated their parities in terms of gold or the U.S. dollar.

During the 1950s and 1960s, international trade and payments grew rapidly, and exchange controls on international payments that had been adopted by countries in Western Europe in the 1940s were reduced. For the major industrial countries, the increase in national incomes was large and a sharp contrast to changes in national incomes in the immediate post-World War I era. One interpretation was that this boom in national incomes and international trade was attributable to the Fund and especially to the orderly arrangements for changes in exchange rates and the reduction in exchange controls. Indeed, one of the surprising features of the 1950 to 1970 period was that changes in exchange parities of major currencies were infrequent. Thus, the British pound was devalued once and the French franc was devalued twice, while the German mark was revalued twice and the Dutch guilder once. Parities for the Japanese yen, the Swiss franc, the Italian lira, and the Belgian franc were not changed.

An alternative explanation for the remarkable growth in the world economy was that the United States provided a stable framework for the growth of national incomes in other industrial countries by maintaining a relatively stable price level and open, accessible markets for foreign goods. U.S. imports were increasing at a rapid rate, with the result that many foreign countries realized balance-of-payments surpluses, so their holdings of international reserve assets were increasing. And these countries adjusted to their payments surpluses by relaxing their exchange controls on foreign payments.

The irony of the IMF system was that changes in parities proved to be quite infrequent. Payments imbalances were extended because there were no longer any rules of the game for the balance-of-payments adjustment. Countries were committed to their domestic full-employment policies, which often conflicted with adjustments necessary to achieve a satisfactory payments balance. Moreover, there was no agreement about whether the countries with the payments deficits or those with the payments surpluses should take the initiative in adjusting to payments imbalances. Finally, the reluctance to change parities reflected the belief in the countries with the payments deficits that devaluations would be viewed as evidence of the failure of their economic policies, while the countries with the payments surpluses believed that persistent imbalances reflected the inflationary policies of the countries with payments deficits.

The Fund's successes and failures were closely linked to the successes and failures of U.S. economic policy. When the Bretton Woods System was established, the U.S. international economic position was supreme. There was a strong belief that there would be a perpetual dollar shortage—that Europe's desire to spend dollars would persistently exceed its ability to earn dollars at any exchange rate. Even though the devaluations of the currencies of these countries in 1949 led immediately to a European payments surplus and a corresponding deficit in the U.S. payments balance, the concern about a dollar shortage remained for a decade.

The story of the U.S. payments balance after 1950 can be segmented into three stages. In the first, which ran from 1950 to the mid-1960s, the annual U.S. payments deficits were small and largely reflected the desire of other countries to add to their holdings of gold and U.S. dollar securities; their demand for international reserve assets was the cause of the U.S. payments deficit. In the late 1960s, the U.S. payments deficits began to increase above the level that could readily be explained by the foreign demand for gold and U.S. dollar assets. In a three-year period, 1969 to 1971, the cumulative U.S. payments deficit reached $40 billion, partly as a consequence of the decline in competitiveness of U.S. manufactured products and partly in response to speculation about a devaluation of the U.S. dollar. In the fall of 1969, the German mark was revalued; in the spring of 1970, the Canadian authorities ceased pegging their currency, and the Canadian dollar immediately appreciated by

How Long Do Monetary Constitutions Last?

The Bretton Woods System, centered around the International Monetary Fund and the International Bank for Reconstruction and Development (World Bank), takes its name from the village of Bretton Woods, New Hampshire. It was there that delegates from the United States and about forty other countries met at the Mt. Washington Hotel for three weeks in July 1944 to negotiate the treaty that led to the establishment of both of these international monetary institutions.

More than four decades later the Mt. Washington Hotel, built in 1902, went bankrupt. Like so many grand resort hotels built in the early 1900s, the Mt. Washington Hotel had probably been in bankruptcy before. Resort hotels often go bankrupt when there is a major slowdown in the economy or when travel patterns change sharply. But these resort hotels also usually emerge from bankruptcy, with the mortgage lenders holding an auction to get the highest possible price for the property and, in many cases, also providing a mortgage to the winning bidder.

None of these lenders would extend credit to the buyers of these hotels if they thought these buyers were likely to go bankrupt, yet the lenders certainly know how often these hotels have gone bankrupt in the past. Nor do the buyers of these bankrupt properties see foreclosure in their own futures, despite the knowledge of their predecessors' failures. Yet the economic environment changes in unanticipated ways, and these resort properties become bankrupt again and again.

The fate of these grand resort hotels, with their cycles of founding, foundering, failure, and resuscitation under new management, make a good metaphor for international monetary constitutions. These monetary constitutions usually work for as long as they "fit" the economic environment for which they were designed. But when the environment changes sharply in unanticipated ways, the constitution is abandoned, just as the resort hotels go bankrupt when the economic environment changes sharply. As the resort hotels change themselves to fit new economic realities, so too do the parties to international monetary arrangements adjust to meet the new economic era, believing that this time their arrangements will outlast any economic vicissitudes. Looking at international monetary arrangements in this light, wouldn't it be fitting for the new incarnation of the Mt. Washington Hotel to be the site of the next international monetary negotiations?

---

nearly 10 percent. For the next 15 months, the pressures for a revaluation of the currencies of other countries or a devaluation of the U.S. dollar became more intense.

When the U.S. inflation rate was low, the Bretton Woods System worked. As U.S. economic policies became less successful—as the U.S. inflation rate increased in the late 1960s—the U.S. payments deficit became larger than could readily be explained by the demand of other countries for payments surpluses and for increases in their holdings of international reserve assets. The Fund was powerless to effect a change in the alignment of exchange rates of the major countries. The United States could finance a payment deficit as long as the countries with the payments surpluses were willing to add to their holdings of U.S. dollar securities. As long as international payments imbalances were those of smaller industrial countries, the Fund had been useful in inducing the return to payments equilibrium. But when the imbalances involved the largest industrial countries, the Fund mechanism proved ineffective.

With the increase in the inflation rates in the 1970s, countries could no longer successfully maintain their parities, and the move away from parities meant that a system of floating exchange rates was inevitable. The Fund rules on exchange parities became obsolete. And with the explosion in the growth of international reserve assets in the 1970s, the Fund mechanism seemed irrelevant to meeting the need for international reserves.

The Breakdown of Bretton Woods

In August 1971 the U.S. Treasury formally suspended gold sales to foreign official institutions. (Sales to others had been ended earlier.) The U.S. government also adopted a tariff surcharge of 10 percent on dutiable imports and adopted a set of price and wage ceilings to forestall further increases in the U.S. price level. The rationale for the tariff surcharge was that such a surcharge would induce other industrial countries to revalue their currencies; the premise was that the surcharge would be dropped once these countries had revalued their currencies. Negotiations with the Europeans and the Japanese formalized this bargain; at the beginning of 1972, in the context of the **Smithsonian Agreement,** the U.S. dollar price of gold was increased to $38 per ounce (so the U.S. dollar was effectively devalued by about 12 percent) and the tariff surcharge was withdrawn. A new set of currency parities was established; however, these parities were retained for little more than a year. As U.S. payments deficits continued, speculation against the U.S. dollar increased. Because of the inability of national monetary authorities to adopt policies that would have made the new system of pegged exchange rates viable, floating rates again became inevitable, as they had been in the years immediately after World War I.

The move to floating rates in the early 1970s occurred because there was no viable alternative mechanism to accommodate the sharp changes in the relationship among national price levels. One impetus to these changing relationships was the increase in inflation in the United States to levels higher than those in some of its major trading partners, as the price and wage controls adopted in August 1971 were relaxed. Whereas the U.S. record for price stability had stimulated the foreign demand for dollar securities in the 1950s and early 1960s, the failure of the United States to maintain a low inflation rate in the early 1970s led to a reduction in the foreign demand for dollar securities. Finally, the surge in the world price of petroleum and the large payments surpluses of OPEC nations led to sharp changes in the pattern of money flows; movements in exchange rates were believed necessary to accommodate these changes in national payment surpluses and deficits.

Comparisons were drawn between the decline of U.S. economic power in the 1970s, the breakup of Bretton Woods, and the weakness of the U.S. dollar with the decline of British economic power in the 1920s, the breakdown of the gold standard, and the weakness of the British pound. One factor common to both experiences was the reluctance to increase the monetary price of gold to compensate for the worldwide inflation during and after both world wars. But the comparison has its shortcomings: the dominant U.S. economic position in the 1940s and 1950s was bound to be temporary, lasting only as long as Germany and Japan were still recovering from the economic decline associated with the war. Hence, the decline in the U.S. share of world income was inevitable. In this sense, the ability of the United States to provide a framework for global monetary stability was bound to diminish. But the surge in the U.S. inflation rate was not inevitable.

In the early 1970s, the Fund charter was modified to accommodate the adoption of floating exchange rates by the major industrial countries—these practices were, in fact, in violation of treaty commitments. New rules were developed so that countries might permit their currencies to float.

One surprise has been the vast range of prices for the U.S. dollar in terms of various foreign currencies. In the first half of the 1980s, the foreign-exchange value of the U.S. dollar increased by more than 50 percent; in the mid-1980s, the U.S. dollar depreciated even more rapidly. More importantly, the United States developed a large trade deficit during the early 1980s and at the same time the U.S. dollar became increasingly overvalued. The deficit persisted at the rate of 1 to 2 percent of U.S. national income through the late 1980s, the recessionary early 1990s, and later into an economic recovery. Over the same time period the dollar became undervalued; this suggests that there exists a severe shortcoming in the operation of the floating exchange rate system.

The European Community has recognized the costs and risks of large movements in exchange rates. In the mid-1970s member countries of the European Community began to develop arrangements to limit the movement in the price of the currencies of each member in terms of the currencies of other members. A system of pegged exchange rates was developed; changes in parities became less frequent. Inflation rates of the European countries began to converge. And in December 1991 the member countries committed themselves to move toward a common European currency, the **ECU (European Currency Unit),** by the end of the 1990s.

SUMMARY

1 An international monetary system is identified by three key features: the organization of the foreign-exchange market, the assets used to finance payments imbalances, and the mechanism for adjustment to payments imbalances.

2 The gold standard involved a set of mint parities for each national currency in terms of gold, transactions in gold to finance payments imbalances, and changes in national money supplies induced by gold inflows and outflows as a means to facilitate balance-of-payments adjustment.

3 Stability in U.S. and British price levels was greater during 1800 to 1920 than in subsequent decades.

4 The gold-exchange standard was developed in the 1920s to provide a new source of international reserve assets in the form of assets denominated in the British pound, the U.S. dollar, and other national currencies.

5 The International Monetary Fund was established in the 1940s to ensure that changes

in exchange rates would be orderly. The Fund was endowed with a pool of national currencies that might be lent to countries with balance-of-payments deficits.

6 Special Drawing Rights (SDRs) were a new reserve asset established in the late 1960s within the framework of the IMF.

7 One notable feature of the 1950s and the early 1960s was that the currency parities of the industrial countries were changed infrequently.

8 The move from pegged exchange rates to floating exchange rates in the early 1970s occurred at a time of significant differences in rates of inflation among the major industrial countries.

KEY TERMS

gold standard
gold-exchange standard
Bretton Woods System
international reserves
rules of the game
pegged exchange rates
International Monetary Fund (IMF)
World Bank

General Agreement on Tariffs and
  Trade (GATT)
Special Drawing Rights (SDRs)
General Arrangements to Borrow
European Community
ECU
post-Bretton Woods System

QUESTIONS AND EXERCISES

*1 Describe the major differences between the gold standard and the Bretton Woods System of adjustable parities.

*2 List the major alternatives by which a country might achieve equilibrium in its payments balance when a disturbance has led to a payments deficit or a payments surplus.

*3 Why did the gold standard break down at the beginning of World War I? Why did the Bretton Woods System of adjustable parities break down in the early 1970s?

4 How well has the system of floating exchange rates operated?

FURTHER READING

ALIBER, ROBERT Z. *The International Money Game,* 5th ed. New York: Basic Books, 1987. A romp through the major issues in international finance.

COOMBS, CHARLES. *The Arena of International Finance.* New York: Wiley, 1976. A central banker's brief for pegged exchange rates.

MAYER, MARTIN. *The Fate of the Dollar.* New York: Times Books, 1980. A journalist's view of international monetary developments.

SOLOMON, ROBERT. *The International Monetary System, 1945–1976.* New York: Harper & Row, 1977. A comprehensive blow-by-blow account of negotiations.

TEW, BRIAN. *The Evolution of the International Monetary System, 1947–77.* London: Hutchison, 1977. A succinct analysis of the Bretton Woods System and its breakdown.

TRIFFIN, ROBERT. *Gold and the Dollar Crisis.* New Haven, Conn.: Yale University Press, 1961. A classic on the U.S. international financial dilemma.

YEAGER, LELAND B. *International Monetary Relations.* New York: Harper & Row, 1966. An excellent text with comprehensive historical treatment.

30

Exchange Rates and the Balance of Payments

After you have read this chapter, you will be able to:

- Understand why the U.S. dollar price of the German mark and of the Japanese yen have varied so extensively.
- Explain the distinction between spot exchange rates and forward exchange rates.
- Distinguish between the balance of payments and the payments balance.
- Understand the implications of changes in the foreign-exchange value of the U.S. dollar on the U.S. trade balance.

As we mentioned in the previous chapter, one of the big surprises of the 1970s and the 1980s was the magnitude of the changes in the foreign-exchange value of the U.S. dollar. In the late 1970s, the U.S. dollar began to appreciate; by the end of 1984, the price of the U.S. dollar was 60 percent higher in terms of the German mark and the Japanese yen than it had been five years earlier. In the spring of 1985, foreign currencies began to appreciate; by the end of the 1980s exchange rates were more or less at the levels of the late 1970s. Changes in the price of the U.S. dollar in terms of the German mark and the Japanese yen have been much larger than the changes in the relationship between the U.S. inflation rate and the inflation rates in Germany and Japan.

This chapter focuses on both the organization of the foreign-exchange market and the factors that explain the large movements in the foreign-exchange value of the U.S. dollar.

The two most important features of any international monetary system for our purposes are the exchange rate and the payments balance. As we have seen, the exchange rate is the price of a foreign money in terms of domestic money. It is determined in the foreign-exchange market. Changes in the exchange rate occur to restore or maintain balance between payments to foreign countries and receipts from these countries. The **payments balance,** which is frequently viewed as a measure of how well a country is doing, is one entry in the **balance of payments,** which is the accounting record of all payments as well as all receipts between domestic residents and foreign residents. The payments balance is the value of the transactions of the central bank or monetary authority in official reserve assets, such as gold, U.S. Treasury bills, bank deposits, and claims on the International Monetary Fund.

If imports of goods, services, and securities exceed exports of goods, services, and securities during any period, the country has a *payments deficit,* which must be financed with the funds obtained from selling securities or borrowing abroad. If exports of goods, services, and securities exceeds imports of goods, services, and securities, the country has a *payments surplus.*

At any moment, the U.S. dollar prices of U.S. goods, services, and securities can be compared with German prices of comparable goods, services, and securities available in Germany through use of the exchange rate. Merchants in each country seek to take advantage of any significant difference between the prices of domestic goods and comparable foreign goods; the exchange rates permit them to compare the prices of Chevrolets, say, with the prices of Volkswagons. Similarly, producers in each country seek to determine whether they have a competitive advantage in foreign markets because their selling prices are below those of foreign firms. Large investors do not use the foreign-exchange market because they want to hold foreign monies; rather they buy foreign exchange—essentially a foreign money—as a necessary intermediate step before they can buy a foreign good or a foreign security.

The terms on which national currencies trade with each other determine the significance of the segmentation of the world into separate **national currency areas** like the U.S. dollar area, the Japanese yen area, the German mark area, and other national currency areas. If exchange rates were fixed and known with certainty, then the differences among national monies would be a trivial matter (except for differences in political risk, which involve the likelihood that exchange controls will be applied to international payments), of little more significance than the difference between two $50 bills and one $100 bill or between the currency notes issued by the Federal Reserve Bank of San Francisco and those issued by the Federal Reserve Bank of New York. Individuals and investors would be indifferent about the currency denomination of their securities and their liabilities. Changes in the consumer price level in one country would correspond to the changes in the consumer price levels in other countries, at least to the extent that the goods in each national market basket are similar in amount. National money supplies would be readily summed into a world money supply, as under the gold standard.

If exchange rates moved freely, but at the same time were known with certainty for all future dates, individuals and investors would still be indifferent about the currency denomination of their securities and their liabilities. In such a world, the differences in interest rates on similar securities denominated in different currencies would fully reflect anticipated changes in exchange rates, and by definition these anticipated changes would be realized. These differences in interest rates would compensate investors for losses incurred from holding securities denominated in a currency that would depreciate.

Substantial uncertainty about future exchange rates characterizes the international money and capital markets for the last twenty years. Even if countries pledge to maintain fixed or pegged exchange rates (for instance, when £1 was equal to $2.80 in the 1950s and 1960s), investors recognize that on occasion parities may be altered. Because of this uncertainty about exchange rates, traders and investors are concerned about the currencies in which they denominate their securities and their liabilities. Hence, they must ask what factors segment the U.S. dollar currency area from the currency areas for the German mark, the Japanese yen, and other national currencies and how significant each of these factors is.

FOREIGN-EXCHANGE TRADING

Although the financial center in each of the major countries is sometimes said to have its own foreign-exchange market, the markets for foreign exchange in London, New York, Frankfurt, and Tokyo actually are geographic components of one worldwide market. The major banks in each financial center are linked by telephone and telex to the major banks in other financial centers as well as to those in their own centers. The units traded in this market are demand deposits; the basic unit in U.S. dollar–British pound trades is a deposit of £100,000, and the basic unit in U.S. dollar–German mark trades is DM200,000. At any moment, the prices or exchange rates for one currency in terms of another are virtually the same in every financial center; the differences in prices quoted for comparable large transactions are significantly smaller than $\frac{1}{10}$ percent and frequently no more than several $\frac{1}{100}$ percents.

The foreign-exchange market is the largest market in the world in terms of the volume of transactions; on some days the volume of trading may reach $300 billion. The volume of foreign-exchange trading each day or each month is many times larger than the volume of international trade and investment in the comparable period; indeed individuals and firms involved in international trade and investment participate in less than 10 percent of the foreign-exchange transactions. Most foreign-exchange transactions involve a bank as a buyer and a bank as a seller.

The foreign-exchange market is extremely competitive; there are many participants, none of whom is large relative to the market. Prices—exchange rates—change continuously, and the change frequently is as small as $\frac{1}{100}$—or 20 German marks on a U.S. dollar–German mark trade that involves 200,000 German marks. If the demand for the U.S. dollar in terms of the German mark increases, the German mark price of the U.S. dollar will increase, say from 1.800 marks per dollar to 1.801 marks per dollar. The major international commercial banks act both as dealers for their own account and as brokers for the accounts of importers and exporters and international investors. In their role as dealers, banks maintain a net long or short position in a currency and seek to profit from changes in the exchange rate. (A long position means their holdings of deposits denominated in one currency exceed their liabilities denominated in this same currency; a short position is the opposite situation.) In their role as brokers, banks deal in foreign exchange with their commercial customers, such as international oil companies, so that they can profit from the spread between the rates at which they buy from some customers and sell to others. Banks also engage in the foreign-exchange business because it helps them to obtain customers for their other banking services. If a U.S. firm wishes to buy 150 million German marks to make a payment in Frankfurt, the bank that offers German marks at the lowest price in terms of the U.S. dollar is most likely to get the business; almost immediately, the bank will seek to buy an equivalent amount of German marks to minimize its risk of loss from any subsequent appreciation of the mark, unless the bank believes the mark will depreciate.

In their transactions with their customers, banks quote both the price at which they will buy and the price at which they will sell, usually in the form of 1.8380–90 marks per dollar, for a standard number of German marks; the small difference of 0.0010 marks between the price at which the banks offer to sell and the price at which they offer to buy compensates the banks for the costs incurred in their foreign-exchange transactions. If a multinational oil company wants to buy U.S. dollars, the bank will buy its German marks at the rate of 1.8390. If instead this company wants to buy German marks, the bank will buy its U.S. dollars at the rate of 1.8380. The difference of 0.0010 per mark is known as the **bid-ask spread** and amounts to 200 marks on a purchase of DM200,000, or about $120, which is $\frac{12}{100}$ percent of the U.S. dollar value of the transaction. The size of the bid-ask spread differs by currency and by the bank providing the quotation. The major international banks quote smaller bid-ask spreads than banks in provincial centers, where competition may be less extensive. The rates quoted also indicate whether the bank wants to increase or reduce its position in a currency; if a bank owns more German marks than it thinks optimal, it will set its quotes low enough to discourage sellers of marks and encourage buyers of marks.

Foreign-exchange brokers are used in many financial centers to bring buyers and sellers together in an anonymous fashion; the brokers relay the exchange rates quoted by particular banks to various customers. Most commercial customers do not use brokers; instead they may "shop" the banks for the most attractive rates. Commercial banks frequently deal with each other through brokers, and central banks deal with commercial banks through brokers.

ORGANIZATION OF THE FOREIGN-EXCHANGE MARKET

The pattern of the organization of the foreign-exchange market parallels the pattern of trade financing. More international trade transactions are denominated or invoiced in the U.S. dollar than in any other currency. Thus, in U.S.-Canadian trade, Canadian exporters to the United States quote a price in U.S.

dollars and receive payment in U.S. dollars. Similarly, Canadian importers pay U.S. dollars for their purchases of U.S. goods. The Canadian importers and exporters prefer to undertake their foreign-exchange transactions close to home—in Canada rather than the United States—with the result that a larger share of U.S.-Canadian dollar transactions occur in Toronto than in New York. They prefer to undertake foreign-exchange transactions with banks close to their home offices rather than with banks in distant foreign centers both for convenience and to reduce indirect transactions costs.

Paradoxically, because such a large volume of international trade and financial transactions are denominated in the U.S. dollar, most foreign-exchange transactions involving the U.S. dollar occur outside the United States.[1] The principal center for German mark–U.S. dollar transactions is Frankfurt; New York is the secondary center. Similarly, Tokyo is the principal center for Japanese yen–U.S. dollar transactions and London for British pound–U.S. dollar transactions. Banks in each center specialize in trading the domestic currency against the U.S. dollar. New York is a secondary center for all foreign currencies.

Within most major financial centers—London, Frankfurt, New York—a large number of banks participate actively in the foreign-exchange market. A few banks are dealers in the currencies in which they specialize; these banks hold large inventories of foreign exchange. When banks are not dealers, they participate as brokers, buying and selling foreign currencies on the basis of exchange-rate quotations from dealers.

One consequence of organizing the market along the lines of a series of currency pairs, each involving the U.S. dollar, is that the financial counterpart to many international trade transactions involves two foreign-exchange transactions. Assume, for example, that a German distributor of automobile parts buys Japanese-produced components. The banks in Frankfurt quote a Japanese yen–German mark rate based on their rates for the U.S. dollar in terms of both the German mark and the Japanese yen. The banks in Frankfurt are not likely to hold a significant amount of Japanese yen in their inventories, so the bank that sells the yen to the Frankfurt importer undertakes two transactions: it first buys U.S. dollars with German marks, and then it buys Japanese yen with U.S. dollars. Since the Japanese yen–U.S. dollar market is primarily in Tokyo, the bank may act as a dealer in the first transaction and as a broker in the second.

Once the rates for both the German mark and the Japanese yen are known in terms of the U.S. dollar, the price of the German mark in terms of the Japanese yen—or the cross rate—can be inferred. For example, on December 14, 1994, the yen-dollar rate was 100.260 Japanese yen per dollar, and the mark-dollar rate was 1.5691 German marks per dollar, so the cross rate was 156.5 Japanese yen per German mark.

Trading in foreign exchange occurs on an almost continuous basis, since the markets in various cities are located in different time zones. A bank in Los

---

[1] Prior to World War I much more U.S. trade was denominated in foreign currencies, so relatively more of the foreign-exchange transactions associated with U.S. exports and imports occurred in New York.

Angeles can trade with banks in London from late evening through mid-morning Los Angeles time, with banks in New York from early morning to early afternoon, and with banks in Tokyo from late evening to early morning.

THE RELATION BETWEEN THE SPOT EXCHANGE RATE AND THE FORWARD EXCHANGE RATE

Traders and investors who want to alter the currency denomination of their assets or liabilities can readily do so by increasing their loans denominated in the U.S. dollar and using these U.S. dollar funds to reduce their loans denominated in another currency, say the German mark. Or they can reduce their holdings of securities denominated in the U.S. dollar and use these funds to increase their holdings of securities denominated in the German mark.

Spot transactions in foreign-exchange *involve an exchange of deposits two days after the date of the contract.* Forward transactions in foreign exchange *involve an exchange of deposits at specified future dates,* 30, 90, or 180 days in the future. Traders and investors frequently prefer forward exchange contracts because these transactions do not tie up scarce working capital. And swap contracts in foreign exchange combine a spot exchange contract with a forward exchange contract; Alpha Bank transfers a U.S. dollar–denominated demand deposit today to Beta Bank in exchange for a German mark–denominated demand deposit, while Beta Bank agrees to transfer a U.S. dollar–denominated demand deposit to Alpha Bank in 30 days in exchange for a German–mark denominated demand deposit; the difference between the two exchange rates is an implied interest rate.

Forward exchange contracts are generally available on maturities up to a year or longer in the major currencies. That some forward contracts have standard maturities—three months, six months, and one year—reflects the fact that the terms of payment on commercial trade transactions are standardized. Banks also offer maturities to match the particular needs of individual traders; a bank can supply a 39-day forward contract or a 78-day forward contract. (Forward contracts in foreign exchange, which are bought and sold by the major banks, should be distinguished from futures contracts in foreign exchange, which are traded on financial exchanges in Chicago, London, and Singapore; these futures contracts have standardized maturity dates and amounts.) Transactions costs associated with forward exchange contracts are modestly higher than those on spot exchange contracts. Moreover, these costs are higher on the more volatile currencies. The spot exchange rates and forward exchange rates for major currencies relative to the dollar are shown in Table 30.1

If a currency is less expensive in the forward market than in the spot market, the currency is at a *forward discount.* And if the currency is more expensive in the forward market, then the currency is at a *forward premium.*

Banks act as intermediaries between buyers and sellers in the forward exchange market, just as they do in the spot exchange market. A bank may combine a long spot position with a short forward position in a particular currency to limit its exposure in the currency; if the currency appreciates, the value of the long spot position increases and so does the value of the short forward position. If the currency depreciates, the opposite holds true.

Table 30.1 Foreign-Exchange Rates

| | | Closing Market Rates on December 20, 1994 (foreign currency units per U.S. dollar) | | |
| | | Forward Rate | | |
	Spot Rate	30 Days	90 Days	180 Days
Canadian dollar	1.3935	1.3929	1.3927	1.3934
British pound*	1.5600	1.5604	1.5601	1.5601
French franc	5.4125	5.4089	5.4020	5.3851
German mark	1.5700	1.5689	1.5661	1.5590
Swiss franc	1.3275	1.3251	1.3203	1.3121
Japanese yen	100.14	99.80	99.16	97.99

*U.S. dollars per British pound.
Source: *Wall Street Journal*, December 21, 1994.

One of the basic propositions in international finance is that the difference between a forward exchange rate and a spot exchange rate, when expressed in annualized percentage terms, equals the difference between interest rates on domestic securities and interest rates on comparable foreign securities whose maturities are identical with that on the forward contract. For example, on January 4, 1995 the 90-day forward exchange rate was 1.5542 German marks per U.S. dollar and the spot exchange rate was 1.5590. The difference between these two exchange rates is 1.23 percent, which is calculated as $4(F\text{-}S)/S$, where F represents the value of the forward exchange rate and S represents the value of the spot exchange rate; the term in the brackets is multiplied by four to convert the percentage in the brackets into an annual percentage rate. Those investors who seek to profit from anticipated changes in exchange rates continually evaluate whether it will be more profitable to alter their position in foreign exchange by spot exchange transactions or by forward exchange transactions. Some investors prefer to buy the foreign currency in the forward market if the currency is cheaper there than in the spot market, adjusted for the difference between the domestic interest rates and foreign interest rates. Other investors buy a currency in the financial center in which it is cheap and sell the same currency in the center in which it is expensive, after adjustment for any difference between the spot and forward exchange rates and the interest-rate differential. The first group are called **speculators;** *they seek to profit from anticipated changes in exchange rates.* The second group are known as **arbitragers;** they seek to profit from deviations between the interest-rate differential and the interest equivalent of the spread between the forward exchange rate and spot exchange rate. Arbitragers avoid exchange risk, while speculators seek to profit from carrying this risk.

That the observed forward exchange rate reflects the value predicted from the interest-rate differential results from the transactions of both arbitragers and of firms involved in international trade. Assume a U.S. firm bought some machine tools in Germany and has agreed to pay 10 million German marks in three months. The U.S. firm might buy German marks in the spot exchange market today and invest the marks in Frankfurt, either in a money-market security or in a bank deposit, at the prevailing interest rate; at the maturity of the investment, the importer will pay the German seller of the machinery. If the importer can invest funds in Frankfurt at 8 percent, the importer would buy DM9,804,000; with accumulated interest, the importer would have DM10,000,000 in three months. If the spot exchange rate is 2 German marks per U.S. dollar, the investor would need $4,902,000 to acquire the DM9,804,000. The cost of this transaction is the interest rate of 10 percent that the importer might earn on a comparable U.S. dollar security for 90 days. This type of transaction is sometimes called "leading and lagging"—the investor advances or "leads" the date of acquisition of the German marks.

Alternatively, the importer might buy the German mark in the forward exchange market and so would need to pay for the marks in 90 days, when the forward contract matures. If the mark is at a forward premium of 2 percent, the importer would owe $5,025,000 for DM10,000,000. In the interim, the U.S. importer would continue to own a money-market security in U.S. dollars, earning an interest rate of 10 percent on this investment over the 90 days. An investment of $4,902,000 in the U.S. money market for 90 days at a 10 percent annual interest rate would yield the necessary $5,025,000.

So the costs to the U.S. importer of buying the German mark in the spot market and of buying the German mark in the forward market tend to be comparable; the premium on the German mark in the forward exchange market approximates the excess of the interest rate on the U.S. dollar security over the interest rate on the German mark security. If there were a marked advantage to buying German marks on the forward exchange market rather than the spot exchange, savvy investors would take advantage of it, and the price of the German mark in the forward exchange market would increase.

Some U.S. importers may decide to acquire German marks immediately prior to the date when payment is due, because in the interval between the date when they enter into the commitment to pay German marks and the date when they buy the German marks, they have a foreign-exchange exposure.

For both groups of importers, the choice of the financing pattern depends on the relationship between the interest rate on German mark securities and the interest rate on comparable U.S. dollar securities on the one hand and the spot exchange rate and the forward exchange rate on the other. The relationship between the money-market interest-rate differential and the difference between the spot and forward exchange rates is known as the **interest-rate parity theorem.** The formal expression is

$$a \frac{(F-S)}{S} = \frac{1+r_d}{1+r_f},$$

where a is the factor by which the percentage difference in the two exchange rates can be converted into an annualized rate of return (for example, a is 4 if the forward exchange rate quotation is for a 90-day forward contract), F is the forward exchange rate, S is the spot exchange rate, r_d is the domestic interest rate, and r_f is the foreign interest rate.

Empirical studies indicate that the differences between the forward exchange rates inferred from the interest-rate differential and the observed forward rates are almost always less than 1 percent and frequently only several tenths of 1 percent. That there is any measurable deviation from interest-rate parity reflects either that investors encounter costs and incur risks in undertaking transactions to take advantage of the apparently riskless arbitrage profit opportunity or that investors do not consider the securities available in the domestic and foreign money market perfect substitutes for each other.

Traders and investors prefer forward transactions to leading and lagging as a way to alter their foreign-exchange exposure because of the greater convenience. But traders and investors lead and lag if the costs of acquiring the foreign exchange in the forward market exceed the costs in the spot market, that is, if the forward discount is significantly larger than the discount "predicted" by the interest-rate differential.

FORWARD EXCHANGE RATES AS FORECASTS OF FUTURE SPOT EXCHANGE RATES

Whether U.S. importers with payments to make in Germany in 90 days will hedge their foreign-exchange exposure by buying German marks in the forward exchange market or instead wait until the payment must be made and then buy the German marks in the spot exchange market partly depends on their views about how closely the spot exchange rate on the day the forward exchange contract matures will approximate the exchange rate in the forward contract. The empirical question involves the relationship between the value of the exchange rate in the forward exchange contract and the value for the spot exchange rate on the dates when these forward contracts mature. If traders and investors who buy and sell foreign exchange consider some currencies riskier than others, they may demand a risk premium. So there may be a systematic difference between forward exchange rates and spot exchange rates on the dates the forward exchange contracts mature. The size of this risk premium and whether it is excessively large relative to the risk itself need to be determined.

Forward contracts of varying maturities are not likely to predict accurately the spot exchange rate on the various dates when the forward contracts mature, because of the large number of unforeseen disturbances or shocks that can occur between the dates when traders and investors buy the forward contracts and the dates when these contracts mature. Those who suggest that the forward exchange rates are likely to be biased predictors of future spot exchange rates—that investors demand a risk premium for buying foreign exchange in the forward market—rely on the analogy of payment for risk bearing in other markets. They assert that if investors are risk averse, then the *average* of the exchange rates on a set of forward mark contracts would be below the *average* of the spot exchange rates on the dates when these forward exchange contracts mature, so that the sellers of forward marks would incur, on average, a loss. Moreover, investors cannot avoid this loss by leading and lagging, for the difference between the interest rates on German mark securities and the interest rates on U.S. dollar assets of comparable maturities would also incorporate a comparable risk premium.

The response to this risk-premium argument is that while some traders and investors are sellers of German marks in the forward exchange market, others are buyers of German marks in the forward market. If those in the first group pay risk premiums, then those in the second group, who are also hedging their foreign-exchange positions, will receive profits, which are mirror images of the premiums paid by those in the first group. And if both the importers of German goods and the exporters of German goods seek to hedge their exposures in the German mark in the forward exchange market, neither may actually pay significant risk premiums even though both would be willing to pay.

Several empirical studies support the idea that there is a significant risk premium, but most do not; either the marginal investors are not risk averse or the willingness of each group of importers and the willingness of each group of exporters to pay a risk premium have proven to be more or less offsetting. However, forward exchange rates appear to be somewhat biased forecasts of the spot exchange rates on the dates the forward exchange contracts mature. These two statements can be reconciled if the average of the forecast error between the forward rate and the spot rate at the maturity of the forward contracts is modest relative to the premium deemed appropriate for carrying the foreign-exchange risk.

THE LEVEL OF THE EXCHANGE RATE

The foreign-exchange market is one component of the international money market, which includes the various national markets in bank deposits and money-market securities, such as Treasury bills, bankers' acceptances, and commercial paper. Unlike the other markets in international money, however, the foreign-exchange market involves the trading of securities—domestic demand deposits and foreign demand deposits—that are not unique to that market, in the sense that gold is unique to the gold market and wheat to the wheat market. Instead, the demand deposits denominated in different currencies are acquired to facilitate payments in a foreign currency. Thus, German importers and investors buy U.S. dollars so they can then acquire commodities and securities available in the United States—or so they can profit from the anticipated appreciation of the U.S. dollar.

Since all foreign-exchange transactions are intermediate to some other economic transaction, the question is how the exchange rate is determined and why exchange rates vary so extensively within a year or even a few months, as Figure 30.1 makes evident. One response is that the exchange rate, which is the price of one national money in terms of another national money, moves to the level where prices of similar goods and securities available in the several countries are more or less equal, or at least differ by no more than transaction and transportation costs. If, at the prevailing exchange rate, the prices of similar goods available in the several countries differ significantly, traders would buy the goods in the countries in which they are cheap, ship them to the coun-

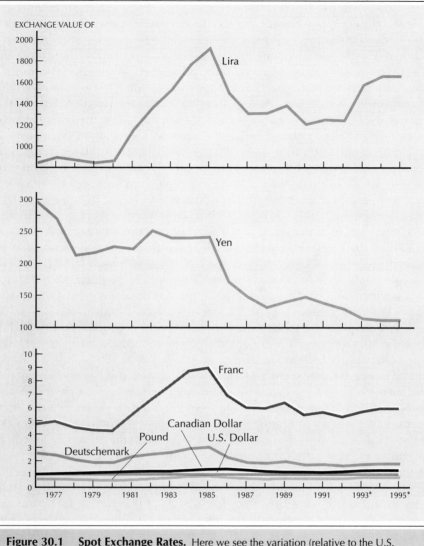

EXCHANGE VALUE OF

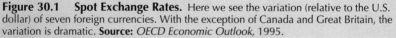

Figure 30.1   Spot Exchange Rates. Here we see the variation (relative to the U.S. dollar) of seven foreign currencies. With the exception of Canada and Great Britain, the variation is dramatic. **Source:** *OECD Economic Outlook,* 1995.

tries in which they are dear, and profit from the price differential. The prices of these goods would rise in the first country and fall in the second, and, at the same time, the value of the first country's currency in the foreign-exchange market would increase. Arbitrage in commodities would continue until the difference in the prices of similar goods at the new exchange rate would no longer exceed transactions and transportation costs. In this case, then, the exchange rates move to reduce the differences in the prices of comparable goods available in different countries.

This relationship between the prices of tradable goods in different countries and the exchange rate is known as the **purchasing-power parity (PPP) theory.** At times the prices of similar goods available in the several countries are compared at the exchange rate in the *absolute version* of this relationship. Usually, however, *changes* in the commodity price levels in the several countries are compared with *changes* in the exchange rate in the relative version of PPP; the expression is $\Delta FC/\$ = \Delta P_F / \Delta P_{US}$ where $\Delta FC/\$$ is the rate of change of the price of the U.S. dollar in terms of foreign currency, ΔP_F is the rate of change in the foreign price level, and ΔP_{US} is the rate of change in the U.S. price level.

The proposition that the exchange rate moves to reflect changes in national price levels, while strongly held, is not consistent with much recent data—certainly not data for year-to-year comparisons and perhaps not even data over periods shorter than three or four years.

During the 1970s and the 1980s, as in the 1920s, changes in the exchange rates in a quarter or a year were several times larger than the contemporary change in relative national price levels. For example, from 1979 to 1985, the foreign-exchange value of the U.S. dollar increased by 60 percent in terms of the German mark and the Japanese yen, even though the U.S. price level was increasing slightly more rapidly than the price levels in Germany and Japan. From 1985 through 1990, the foreign-exchange value of the U.S. dollar declined sharply, even though the U.S. inflation rate was only slightly higher than the inflation rates in Germany and Japan. From 1990 through 1993, the U.S. dollar appreciated modestly.

Transactions in securities explain the large, sudden movements in exchange rates. Investors shift funds among comparable securities denominated in different currencies to profit from the differences between the interest-rate differentials and anticipated changes in exchange rates. From the investor's point of view, the level of the spot exchange rate is "just right" when, given the interest rates on domestic securities and the anticipated rate of change of the exchange rate, the interest rates on comparable foreign securities are at levels such that no significant profit can be made from shifting funds between these two securities. Thus $r_\$ = r_f + (\Delta E/E)^*$, where $r_\$$ is the interest rate on U.S. dollar securities, r_f is the interest rate on comparable foreign securities of the same maturity, and $(\Delta E/E)^*$ is the anticipated rate of change of the price of the U.S. dollar in terms of the foreign currency rate during the interval until the maturity of the two securities. This statement is known as the **Fisher proposition,** after Irving Fisher who formulated it in the 1920s.[2]

As new information about each country's imports and exports, inflation rate, money-supply growth rate, and election campaign leads investors to conclude that securities denominated in the German mark will prove a less attractive investment than U.S. dollar–denominated securities, they will sell German mark securities and buy U.S. dollar securities, and the German mark will depreciate until the anticipated return on the German mark securities,

---

[2] Analysts frequently confuse the interest-rate parity theorem with the Fisher proposition: the former involves the efficiency of arbitrage in circumstances in which all values are known, while the latter involves investment decisions in an uncertain environment.

adjusted for the anticipated change in the German mark price of the U.S. dollar, is equivalent to the return on U.S. dollar securities.

The anticipated rate of change of the exchange rate $(\Delta E/E)^*$ depends both on investors' estimates of where the spot exchange rate will be at various future dates and on the level of the current spot exchange rate. In equilibrium, the anticipated rate of change of the spot exchange rate equals the money-market interest differential. If investors believe that $r_\$ \neq r_f + (\Delta E/E)^*$, then in the move to equilibrium, the adjustment may occur in both the foreign and the domestic money-market interest rates, as investors shift funds from the securities of one money market to the securities of another money market; however, the volume of funds shifted may be small relative to the volume of funds in the two money markets. Consequently, much of the adjustment in the move to equilibrium after a shock occurs in the current spot exchange rate and the current forward exchange rate, with the consequence that the changes in these exchange rates may be much greater than those inferred from the contemporary changes in the several national price levels.

ANALYZING EXCHANGE-RATE DISTURBANCES

Changes in exchange rates reflect both monetary and nonmonetary, or structural, disturbances; the key difference is that monetary disturbances are associated with changes in interest rates. Assume investors become bearish on German mark securities at a time when interest rates on these securities and comparable dollar securities are identical. Increased bearishness will be reflected in both the increase in interest rates on German mark securities and the depreciation of the German mark in the spot foreign-exchange market. If interest rates on German mark securities do not increase, then the value of the mark for the spot exchange rate will move to the value for the anticipated spot exchange rate, perhaps abruptly.

Alternatively, assume that the German Bundesbank adopts a more contractive monetary policy, and interest rates on German mark securities increase. At the same time, the anticipated spot exchange rate remains unchanged, perhaps because investors believe that the move to a more contractive monetary policy eventually will be reversed. Then investors would acquire German mark–denominated securities because of the higher interest rate, and the German mark would appreciate. As long as interest rates on German mark securities remain higher than those on U.S. dollar securities, the only factor that can equalize the return to investors from holding U.S. dollar securities and German mark securities is the depreciation of the German mark. Paradoxically, in response to the increase in interest rates on German mark securities, there will be a sudden unanticipated appreciation of the German mark, followed by a slow depreciation of the mark, with the anticipated annual rate of depreciation equal to the excess of interest rates on German mark securities over those on U.S. dollar securities.

Price movements in other asset markets, such as the markets for stocks, bonds, wheat, and soybeans, are also large and comparable to those in the for-

Why Has the Foreign-Exchange Value of the U.S. Dollar Been So Variable?

Ask someone what determines the exchange rate of a country's currency and you're likely to hear: "The price of goods produced in that country relative to the price of comparable goods produced in other countries." Ask why the exchange rate changes and you're likely to hear that "the inflation rate in one country is higher than in its trading partners'." Common sense—but such common sense doesn't always tell the whole story.

The big surprise in the 1970s, 1980s, and early 1990s has been that the movement in the foreign-exchange value of the U.S. dollar in terms of the German mark and the Japanese yen has been much larger than virtually anyone had anticipated, four to five times larger than the changes that would have been consistent with the difference between the U.S. price level and the price levels in Germany and Japan.

One general rule about the behavior of exchange rates is that when the U.S. inflation rate increases, the U.S. dollar depreciates more than could be inferred on the basis of an increase in the U.S. price level relative to price levels in Germany and Japan. Similarly, when the U.S. inflation rate declines, the U.S. dollar appreciates by more than could be inferred based on the change in the relationship between national price levels. A second general rule is that the forward exchange rate almost always underpredicts the change in the spot exchange rate in those periods when the change in the spot exchange rate has been large; the depreciation of the U.S. dollar in the late 1970s was much greater than the forward exchange rate suggested, and in the early 1980s the U.S. dollar appreciated even though an inference based on the forward exchange rate would have had the U.S. dollar depreciating.

The spot exchange rate at any moment is the anticipated spot exchange rate for various future dates, discounted to the present by the interest rate, or more precisely, by the difference between the domestic and foreign interest rates. When the U.S. inflation rate rises, investors estimate the impact this increase will have on the anticipated spot exchange rate and then discount this anticipated value to the present. When the U.S. inflation rate falls, investors revise their estimates of the future spot exchange rate and then discount this value to the present.

Thus, the principal reason that the foreign-exchange value of the U.S. dollar has varied so extensively is that there have been sharp changes in the anticipated U.S. inflation rate. The implication is that changes in the foreign-exchange value of the U.S. dollar will become modest only when changes in the U.S. inflation rate relative to the inflation rates in Germany and Japan are modest.

eign-exchange market. At any moment, the spot prices in these markets in equilibrium are the anticipated spot prices discounted to the present by the interest rate. In the foreign-exchange market, the discount factor is the difference between the money-market interest rates on similar securities denominated in different currencies. For example, if interest rates on U.S. dollar Treasury bills are 10 percent and interest rates on German mark Treasury bills are

8 percent, then the discount factor is 2 percent a year. If the anticipated values remain unchanged, then during each week and each month the German-mark price of the U.S. dollar should increase at the rate of 2 percent a year, or 0.166 percent a month, 0.038 percent a week, or 0.0055 percent a day. Even a weak currency—one that might depreciate at a rate of 20 percent a year—would depreciate at an average daily rate of 0.0624 percent, or by much less than the changes in exchange rates that are observed on most days. That the changes in exchange rates on a daily and weekly basis are frequently many times larger than these values reflects sharp movements in anticipated spot exchange rates.

Many factors affect anticipations of the value of the spot exchange rate in the future, including investor estimates of inflation rates, as well as current and prospective money-supply growth rates. Thus, traders and investors may extrapolate from recent changes in domestic and foreign price levels to project estimates of future national price levels and the values of anticipated spot exchange rates for various future dates. Similarly, changes in money-supply growth rates may lead to changes in estimates of the national inflation rates, which in turn lead to changes in the estimates of the value of spot exchange rates for various future dates.

Some analysts believe that the German mark appreciates when U.S. monetary policy becomes more expansive or German monetary policy becomes more contractive, because investors associate a move to a more expansive monetary policy with a higher inflation rate. Changes in inflation rates appear to provide the basis for estimates of the value of future spot exchange rates. And today's spot exchange rate is linked to the value of future spot exchange rates by national differences in interest rates. Thus, if U.S. monetary policy becomes more expansive, investors may believe that the U.S. dollar may depreciate because of the expected increase in the U.S. inflation rate. And if interest rates on U.S. dollar securities decline, the U.S. dollar may immediately depreciate.

CENTRAL BANK INTERVENTION IN THE FOREIGN-EXCHANGE MARKET

For a long time the currencies of the major countries were pegged to each other, initially because each currency had a mint parity in terms of gold. After World War II, many foreign countries stated the parities for their currencies in terms of the U.S. dollar. Under the Bretton Woods System of pegged exchange rates, each central bank committed itself to limiting the range of movement in the price of its currency around its parity, initially at 0.25 percent either side of parity, subsequently at 1 percent, and later at 2.4 percent. Within these limits, currencies were free to float, although many monetary authorities intervened within these limits to smooth the hour-to-hour and day-to-day changes in the foreign-exchange value of their currencies.

Most central banks have intervened in the foreign-exchange market by buying and selling U.S. dollar demand deposits. A central bank was obliged to prevent its currency from depreciating below its lower support limit and appreciating above its upper support limit. In the former case, central bank would buy its own currency from commercial banks operating in the exchange market and sell U.S. dollar–denominated demand deposits to these banks. These transactions were effectively open-market purchases and sales using U.S. dollar–denominated demand deposits rather than domestic bonds. Such transactions reduced the reserves of banks.

The ability of the central bank to prevent its currency from depreciating below its lower support limit depended on its holdings of U.S. dollars and the amount of U.S. dollars that it could borrow. Even if a national monetary authority had the foreign exchange necessary for intervention, its need to support its currency in the exchange market might be inconsistent with its efforts to undertake a more expansive monetary policy to achieve its domestic employment objectives.

If a country's currency tended to appreciate, its central bank was obliged to sell more of its currency to limit its appreciation in the exchange market. In effect, this central bank undertook an open-market purchase of U.S. dollars, with the purchase financed by increasing the reserves of banks. Such open-market purchases of U.S. dollars might confound its desire to limit the expansion of its money supply. Thus Germany, with a strong currency in the 1960s and early 1970s, faced the choice between maintaining the established exchange parity for the German mark, with the consequence of a more rapid than desired increase in the German money supply, or limiting the growth in the reserves of the banking system in Germany at the cost of either revaluing the mark periodically or permitting the mark to float. While the Bundesbank might have undertaken open-market sales of mark-denominated securities to counter or neutralize its open-market purchases of dollar securities, such transactions were not costless, for interest rates on German mark securities increased to levels higher than those deemed desirable for domestic objectives. Moreover, as interest rates on German mark securities increased, investors would have shifted out of U.S. dollar–denominated securities into German mark–denominated securities, and so intensified the problem for the Bundesbank.

The Bundesbank's transactions in the foreign-exchange market are shown in Figure 30.2. The price of the U.S. dollar in terms of the German mark is measured on the vertical axis, and the volume of U.S. dollars demanded and supplied is measured on the horizontal axis. As the German mark price of the U.S. dollar increases, the amount of U.S. dollars demanded declines. As the mark price of the dollar increases, the amount of U.S. dollars supplied increases. At *OP* the demand and supply of U.S. dollars are equal; *OP* is the price or exchange rate that clears the exchange market without official intervention. If the Bundesbank had pegged the mark at *OP′*, the demand for U.S. dollars would have exceeded the supply, and the Bundesbank would have sold U.S. dollars equal to *AB* during each period; Germany would have had a payments deficit. If, instead, the Bundesbank had pegged the mark at *OP″*, the Bundesbank would have bought U.S. dollars equal to *A′B′*, and Germany would have had a payments surplus.

In the late 1960s and the early 1970s, the maintenance of parity for the German mark conflicted with the achievement of Germany's domestic eco-

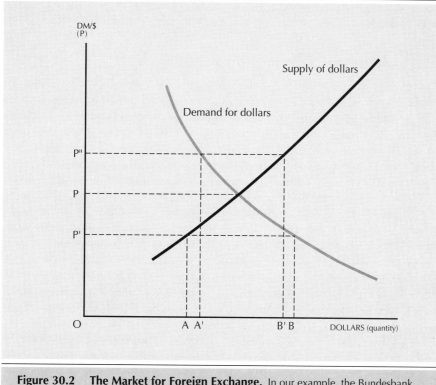

Figure 30.2 **The Market for Foreign Exchange.** In our example, the Bundesbank faces the market for dollars as shown. If it pegs the mark at P'', Germany would have a payments surplus; at P', Germany would have a payments deficit. At P, the market clears without official intervention.

nomic objectives. No such conflict was supposed to occur with floating exchange-rate systems, since the German mark price of the U.S. dollar would change to neutralize any tendency to a payments surplus or deficit. Monetary policy was supposed to be directed solely to the attainment of domestic economic objectives; changes in the foreign-exchange value for the German mark were continuously to ensure that Germany's receipts would be equal to its payments. Hence, the Bundesbank should not have had to undertake open-market operations in foreign exchange that might offset either partially or fully its open-market operations in domestic securities.

The paradox is that central bank intervention in the foreign-exchange market has been much more extensive in the floating exchange-rate period, at least as judged by changes in their holdings of international reserve assets. Some central banks have intervened to limit or smooth the day-to-day and week-to-week movements in the foreign-exchange values of their currencies. Some have intervened because they wanted to add to their holdings of international reserve assets; in some of these countries the growth in the holdings of international reserve assets provides the basis for the growth in their domestic money supplies. Some have intervened because changes in the exchange rates complicated the attainment of their domestic economic objectives.

THE SEGMENTATION OF NATIONAL MONEY MARKETS

One of the key policy issues in international finance, known as the **optimum currency area issue,** involves whether there are any economic gains from maintaining independent national central banks, each with its own currency. Does the Bank of Canada have the capacity to cause interest rates in Canada to deviate significantly from U.S. interest rates? If the Bank of Canada attempts to follow a more expansive monetary policy and buys bonds denominated in the Canadian dollar, is it possible that the sellers of Canadian bonds will then buy U.S. bonds, so that the interest rates on Canadian bonds will remain virtually unchanged? If the Canadian dollar is pegged to the U.S. dollar, is it possible for interest rates on Canadian dollar securities to differ significantly from interest rates on U.S. dollar securities? And if the Canadian dollar is not pegged, can changes in Canadian monetary policy affect any real variables, such as the level of employment, or will the impact of these changes be limited to altering nominal values, such as the Canadian price level and the exchange rate?

The scope for national monetary independence depends on how fully investors believe that securities that are alike in all attributes except for currency of denomination are close, near, or good substitutes for each other. If investors believe that these securities are close substitutes for each other, then national money markets are integrated. If, on the other hand, investors feel that they are distant substitutes for each other, then national money markets are segmented.

Transactions costs might deter investors from shifting funds among securities denominated in different currencies; exchange controls might deter these shifts as well. Such shifts might also be deterred by exchange risk, in the form of uncertainty about future exchange rates, or political risk, in the form of uncertainty about changes in exchange controls. Investors are likely to shift funds to profit from differences in interest rates only if they are compensated for these costs and for the associated risks. At most, the differential in interest rates on similar securities denominated in different currencies adjusted for any anticipated changes in exchange rates cannot exceed the sum of these costs and the payments demanded by investors for incurring the risks associated with the movements of funds across the borders between currency areas. Transactions costs in the foreign-exchange market are small or even trivial, especially for large international firms; transactions costs are smaller still for the major international banks. Transactions costs have two components—one involves those external to the firm, the actual costs incurred in buying and selling foreign exchange, and the other involves those internal to the firm, the costs incurred in managing its foreign-exchange or international monetary investments. Transactions costs to the commercial customers are measured by the bid-ask spread: the difference between the prices at which traders and investors could buy and sell a relatively large amount—$3 to $5 million—of a particular currency at any moment. The costs encountered by commercial customers in using the foreign-exchange market are substantially smaller than those they would incur with transactions of equivalent value in most other markets, such as the government-securities market or the stock market. Depending on the currency, the time, and the maturity of the forward contracts, the cost of a foreign-exchange transaction of $1 milion would be a mere $100 to $500, or from $\frac{1}{100}$ to $\frac{1}{20}$ percent. Transactions costs are smaller the less volatile the currency; thus, bid-ask spreads in the Canadian dollar generally have been lower than bid-ask spreads in the British pound, the German mark, other European currencies, and the Japanese yen. Transactions costs on the spot transactions are smaller than those on forward transactions. Transactions costs on forward contracts with relatively near maturities—those shorter than six months—are smaller than those on longer maturities. That transactions costs are so small reflects the technical efficiency of payments, the virtually riskless character of the transactions, and the large size of the transactions.

Transactions costs on interbank transactions in the foreign-exchange market are smaller than those on the transactions between banks and customers—much less risk is associated with interbank transactions. That the transactions costs encountered by banks are so much lower than those incurred by their commercial customers means that the banks have an advantage in responding to any opportunities to make a profit in this arena.

Measuring the payments demanded by investors for carrying exchange risk and political risk is more difficult. First, one must ask whether firms are risk averse and require payment for bearing these risks. It is sometimes argued that firms are (or should be) risk neutral and seek to maximize profits; if so, they would require no special payments for carrying these risks; in this case the costs they would incur in hedging their exposure to foreign exchange is trivial in the long run if not in the short run. Yet firms may nevertheless be deterred from moving funds internationally by the uncertainty about this cost.

National financial markets appear segmented to a greater extent than can readily be explained by transactions costs. Segmentation provides some opportunity for national monetary independence under pegged exchange rates. If, over time, traders and investors become more knowledgeable about the returns, the risks, and the costs of altering the currency mix of their assets and liabilities, so that the segmentation of national money markets declines, changes in monetary policy will be less effective in altering real variables.

THE BALANCE-OF-PAYMENTS ACCOUNTS

As we mentioned at the outset, the data on the international transactions of a country are presented in its balance-of-payments account, a record of payments and receipts, organized by major type of transactions, between residents and nonresidents during a particular period such as a quarter of a year. Table 30.2 summarizes U.S. international transactions for 1992 to 1993.

The development of the balance-of-payments accounts is based on the system of double-entry bookkeeping. All transactions represent exchanges of equal value; for every import of a good, service, or security, there must be a corresponding export of a good, service, or security, so the balance-of-pay-

Table 30.2 U.S. International Transactions Summary (millions of dollars; quarterly data seasonally adjusted, except as noted*)

	Item Credits or Debits	1991	1992	1993
1	Balance on current account	-6,952	-67,886	-103,896
2	Not seasonally adjusted	-74,068	-96,097	-132,575
3	Merchandise trade balance†	416,913	440,361	456,866
4	Merchandise exports	-490,981	-536,458	-589,441
5	Merchandise imports	-5,485	-3,034	-763
6	Military transactions, net	51,082	58,747	57,613
7	Investment income, net	14,833	4,540	3,946
8	Other service transactions, net	23,959	-15,010	-14,620
9	Remittances, pensions, and other transfers	-3,461	-3,735	-3,785
10	U.S. government grants (excluding military)	-13,811	-13,297	-13,712
11	Change in U.S. government assets other than official reserve assets, net (increase, −)	2,900	-1,652	-306
12	Change in U.S. official reserve assets (increase, −)	5,763	3,901	-1,379
13	Gold	0	0	0
14	Special drawing rights (SDRs)	-177	2,316	-537
15	Reserve position in International Monetary Fund	-367	-2,692	-44
16	Foreign currencies	6,307	4,277	-797
17	Change in U.S. private assets abroad (increase, −)	-60,175	-63,759	-146,213
18	Bank-reported claims‡	4,753	22,314	32,238
19	Non-bank-reported claims	11,097	45	-598
20	U.S. purchases of foreign securities, net	-44,740	-45,114	-119,983
21	U.S. direct investments abroad, net	-31,295	-41,004	-57,870
22	Change in foreign official assets in United States (increase, +)	17,199	40,858	71,681
23	U.S. Treasury securities	14,846	18,454	48,702
24	Other U.S. government obligations§	1,301	3,949	4,062
25	Other U.S. government liabilities§	1,177	2,572	1,666
26	Other U.S. liabilities reported by U.S. banks‡	-1,484	16,571	14,666
27	Other foreign official assets‖	1,359	-688	2,585
28	Change in foreign private assets in United States (increase, +)	80,935	105,646	159,017
29	U.S. bank-reported liabilities‡	3,994	15,461	18,452
30	U.S. non-bank-reported liabilities	-3,115	13,573	14,282
31	Foreign private purchases of U.S. Treasury securities, net	18,826	36,857	24,849
32	Foreign purchases of other U.S. securities, net	35,144	29,867	80,068
33	Foreign direct investments in United States, net	26,086	9,888	21,366
34	Allocation of special drawing rights	0	0	0
35	Discrepancy	-39,670	-17,108	21,096
36	Due to seasonal adjustments	. . .	. . .	. . .
37	Statistical discrepancy in recorded data before seasonal adjustment	-39,670	-17,108	21,096
	Memo			
	Changes in official assets			
38	U.S. official reserve assets (increase, −)	5,763	3,901	-1,379
39	Foreign official assets in United States excluding line 25 (increase, +)	16,022	38,286	70,015
40	Change in Organization of Petroleum Exporting Countries official assets in United States (part of line 22)	-4,882	5,942	-3,847

*Seasonal factors not calculated for lines 6, 10, 12–16, 18–20, 22–34, and 38–40.
†Data are on an international accounts (IA) basis. The data differ from the census basis data, shown in Table 3.11, for reasons of coverage and timing. Military exports are excluded from merchandise trade data and are included in line 6.
‡Reporting banks include all kinds of depository institutions besides commercial banks, as well as some brokers and dealers.
§Associated primarily with military sales contracts and other transactions arranged with or through foreign official agencies.
‖Consists of investments in U.S. corporate stocks and in debt securities of private corporations and state and local governments.
Source: *Federal Reserve Bulletin*, various issues.

ments account must necessarily balance. When a U.S. firm imports Scotch whisky, it exports U.S. dollars, usually in the form of demand deposits, in payment. The U.S. balance-of-payments account shows an increase in U.S. exports of demand deposits and an increase in U.S. commodity imports. The British payments account, in contrast, shows an increase in British commodity exports and an increase in the British imports of U.S. demand deposits.

The data for the entries in the balance-of-payments account are obtained in various ways. Data on commodity imports and exports are obtained from U.S. tariff collection authorities. Data on tourist expenditures are estimated by sampling returning travelers. Data on exports of securities are obtained from reports filed by banks and brokerage firms. Because the sum of all recorded receipts and the sum of all recorded payments in a calendar quarter or a calendar year are unlikely to be equal, a statistical discrepancy results, which is recorded in line 35. The value for this entry is the residual between recorded payments and recorded receipts (the difference between receipts and payments is added to the smaller figure so that the two values are equal to each other).

The millions of international transactions are summed into three major categories. The merchandise trade balance (line 3) is the difference between the values of commodity exports and commodity imports, usually with imports valued at their landed price, so the value of imports exceeds that reported by the exporting countries by the amount of cargo insurance and freight (CIF) costs. A country has a trade surplus if the value of its commodity exports exceeds the value of its commodity imports. The current account balance (line 1) includes all transactions in commodities, together with all transactions in services such as transportation, tourism, royalties and license fees, film rentals, investment income, private remittances such as Social Security payments, and various gifts such as religious charities, UNICEF, and foreign aid.

The characteristic of all international transactions not included in the current-account balance is that they involve transactions in assets or securities with nonresidents, ranging from equities and direct investment to non-interest-bearing demand deposits; transactions in monetary gold, government securities, and bonds are included in the capital-account balance. Lines 11 through 33 summarize various capital-account transactions.

The most important conceptual relationship in the balance-of-payments account is the relationship between the current-account balance and the capital-account balance; all international transactions are included in the calculation of one of these balances, and no transaction is included in both. (Although purchases of foreign investments are in the capital-account balance and the dividends and interest on these investments are in the current account, these are separate transactions, even in time.) Because of the double-entry character, a surplus on the current account means that there is a deficit of the same arithmetic value on the capital account. Thus, if the United States has a current-account deficit (U.S. imports of goods and services exceed U.S. exports of goods and services), the United States must necessarily—by definition—have a capital-account surplus, so U.S. exports of securities must exceed U.S. imports of securities. The size of the United States' net international debtor position is increasing.

The last major group is the payments balance, at one time thought to be a measure of how well a country was doing internationally; this balance is the sum of lines 38 and 39. Payment surpluses were considered indicative of a successful economic performance, and payments deficits of a less successful performance, perhaps because of the association of payments deficits and domestic inflation. Initially payments surpluses were associated with gold inflows and payments deficits with gold outflows. Subsequently transactions in other types

The Collapse of the Mexican Peso

Mexico prospered in the early and middle 1990s when foreign investment poured in, attracted by low labor costs and the prospect of a North American free trade area. Mexico seemed ready to emerge from third-world poverty. The large current-account deficit that mirrored the capital-account surplus was driven by rising imports rather than by falling exports, and more and more Mexicans enjoyed the good life.

Then, in late 1994 the ceiling fell in. Foreign investors became fearful. Would Mexico be able to continue financing such a large import surplus (8 percent of GDP by the end of 1994), and would the Mexican government be able to make payments on the great volume of dollar-denominated securities it had issued? Two spectacular assassinations and a local rebellion also raised doubt about Mexico's political stability.

The resulting decline in foreign investment and the resulting pressures on the balance of payments should have led the government to adopt restrictive policies or to devalue, or both. But since there was an election coming up, the government did not want to do either. (This is hardly surprising. Prior to the two previous elections in 1982 and 1988, it had also followed policies that led to balance-of-payment deficits and U.S. emergency loans, though on a much smaller scale than in 1994.) Finally (after its hard-fought election was over), Mexico did devalue, but not by nearly enough. Speculators, foreign investors, and Mexicans trying to protect the values of their assets sold pesos massively, so that in the first four months of 1995 the peso declined by more than 50 percent relative to the dollar.

The results were devastating. Import prices rose sharply, and so did the cost of living. The government tried to restore confidence and maintain foreign investment by raising interest rates to extreme levels. Bankruptcies and unemployment soared. There was a danger that Mexico's plight might frighten foreign investors in some other Latin American countries and plunge these countries into the same disaster.

Not surprisingly, other countries tried to help Mexico out of its crisis in the belief that the Mexican economy was fundamentally sound and merely had to weather a temporary lack of liquidity. President Clinton offered Mexico $20 billion of standby credits and loan guarantees secured by a lien on Mexico's oil exports. International institutions pledged another $17.8 billion, while other nations pledged $12 billion in short-term credits. Will this $49.8 billion suffice, and will Mexico be able to repay its drawings on these credits? The answers to both questions should be "yes," but it is too early to tell whether what "should be" is also what "will be."

of assets, including liquid assets denominated in the major currencies and claims on the International Monetary Fund, were included in the calculation of the payments balance.

At times, the entry "payments balance" has been thought of as the sum of "financing transactions," with all international transactions segmented into either an autonomous category or an induced category and those items in the induced category considered to be the payments balance. Because of the reliance on the concept of double-entry bookkeeping, the value for the entry on the autonomous payments necessarily equals the value for the entry for the induced payments, but with an opposite sign. So if U.S. exports of goods, services, and long-term securities exceed U.S. imports of goods, services, and long-term securities so that there is a surplus on the U.S. autonomous account, there must be a deficit on the induced account; U.S. imports of monetary gold and foreign-exchange reserves exceed U.S. exports of monetary gold and foreign-exchange reserves.

In an alternative approach the monetary authorities consider the payments balance to be the sum of transactions in money—liquid assets including gold. A country with a payments surplus imports monetary assets: in effect it has a deficit in the money account; its imports of money exceed its exports of money. The shorthand approach is to measure a country's payments surplus or deficit by the change in its central bank's holdings of international money.

Over the last twenty years, various agencies in the U.S. government have debated which transactions are to be included in the measurement of the U.S. payments balance. Prior to 1964, changes in the foreign holdings of liquid dollar securities of foreign commercial banks and foreign private parties, as well as of foreign central banks, were included in the measurement of the U.S. payments balance. By the late 1960s, the U.S. authorities took the view that only the transactions of monetary authorities should be included. The decision to exclude changes in liquid dollar holdings of foreign commercial banks and foreign private parties at a time when they were adding to their holdings of liquid dollar securities led to a reduction in the measured U.S. payments deficit. The United States was exporting money because these foreign groups wanted to add to their holdings of U.S. dollar securities year after year after year. With the move to the floating exchange-rate system, the U.S. authorities downplayed the significance of the payments balance.

SUMMARY

1 A foreign-exchange market is necessary in a multiple-currency world. The assets traded in this market are demand deposits denominated in different currencies. The price is the exchange rate.

2 London is the principal center in the world for trading in foreign currency; New York is the next-busiest center.

3 Most foreign-exchange transactions are either forward contracts, which provide that deposits will be exchanged at specified future days, or swaps, which involve an exchange of a demand deposit in one currency today for a demand deposit in a foreign currency at a specified future date.

4 Forward exchange contracts are available from banks and should be distinguished

from currency futures contracts, which are traded on financial exchanges in Chicago, New York, and London.

5 The interest-rate parity theorem stipulates that the percentage difference between the spot and forward exchange rates will be equal to the difference between interest rates on domestic and foreign securities with maturities equal to that of the forward exchange contract.

6 Some evidence suggests that forward exchange rates may be thought of as the market's best estimate of what the spot exchange rates will be on the dates when the forward exchange contracts mature.

7 The purchasing-power parity theory states that changes in exchange rates should reflect the differences between changes in the prices of comparable market baskets of goods available in different countries.

8 The Fisher proposition is that domestic interest rates should equal world interest rates plus the anticipated rate of change of the exchange rate.

9 Central-bank intervention in the foreign-exchange market has been much larger in the period when currencies have been floating than in prior decades when exchange rates were pegged.

10 The balance-of-payments account is the accounting record of transactions in goods, services, and securities between domestic residents and foreign residents.

11 The payments balance measures the purchases and sales of reserve assets by the national monetary authorities.

KEY TERMS

payments balance	interest-rate parity theorem
balance of payments	purchasing-power parity theory
currency areas	Fisher proposition
spot foreign exchange	forward discount
forward foreign exchange	forward premium

QUESTIONS AND EXERCISES

*1 Discuss why the costs and risks associated with transactions in the foreign-exchange market are important for the effective operation of monetary policy in an open economy.

2 Why is the volume of dollar-mark foreign-exchange transactions in Frankfurt larger than the volume in New York?

3 Describe how the values of exchange rates for forward exchange contracts on various maturities are related to the spot exchange rate. What are the consequences of an increase in the interest-rate differential on the relationship between the spot exchange rate and the forward exchange rates?

*4 Describe the determinants of the level of the spot exchange rate. If interest rates on mark-denominated assets fall, why might the price of the dollar in terms of marks increase? Why might the mark price of the dollar increase even if the interest-rate differential remains unchanged?

FURTHER READING

ALIBER, ROBERT Z. *Exchange Risk and Corporate International Finance.* New York: Halsted Press, 1979. A systematic guide for analysis of exchange-rate movements.

FEDERAL RESERVE BANK OF BOSTON. *Managed Exchange Rate Flexibility: The Recent Experience.*

Boston: Federal Reserve Bank, 1978. A conference volume with numerous essays analyzing the movement of exchange rates in the 1970s.

FRIEDMAN, MILTON. "The Case for Fluctuating Exchange Rates," in *Essays in Positive Economics*. Chicago: University of Chicago Press, 1953, pp. 157–203. A classic statement of the case for floating exchange rates.

INTERNATIONAL MONETARY FUND. *Annual Report*. Washington, D.C.: yearly. This report discusses annual developments in the foreign-exchange markets.

KUBARYCH, ROGER. *The New York Foreign Exchange Market*. New York: Federal Reserve Bank, 1979. A comprehensive description of the institutional aspects of the foreign-exchange markets in the United States.

Future Directions for the International Monetary System

After you have read this chapter, you will be able to:

- Understand the concept known as the optimal currency area.
- Compare the arguments used by proponents of pegged exchange rates to those used by the proponents of floating exchange rates.
- Explain why gold may continue to have an international monetary role.

One insight from the survey of international monetary arrangements over the last one hundred years is that they rarely remain fixed for more than twenty or thirty years. Periods when the United States and other large industrial countries have pegged their currencies are followed by periods when they stop pegging their currencies, usually because the costs of doing so become too high in terms of achieving some domestic economic objective. And these periods of floating exchange rates almost always are characterized by significant differences in national inflation rates and substantial and frequently abrupt movements in exchange rates. The initiatives that lead to pegged exchange rates almost always reflect a desire to reduce the costs and the risks that traders and investors associate with movement in exchange rates.

The implication is that once again there will be a move back toward a system of pegged exchange rates for most industrial countries, as we are already seeing among the members of the European Community. But such a move raises many questions, especially concerning the institutional context for such a move. How likely is a return to the gold standard? How likely is a return to pegged exchange rates within the context of the International Monetary

Fund? Or will either the economic preconditions or the political preconditions for a return to pegged exchange rates remain unsatisfied, and thus leave us to rely on our current system of floating exchange rates?

Getting from a system of floating exchange rates characterized by sharp movements in rates to a system of pegged exchange rates will only occur within the context of changes in the financial position of the United States and other industrial countries. One big change in the 1980s was in the pattern of international investment: the United States moved from being the largest international creditor at the beginning of the 1980s to being the largest international debtor at the beginning of the 1990s. A second big change was the external debt crisis of Mexico, Brazil, and other developing countries; these countries had greatly increased their external indebtedness in the 1970s and then in the 1980s were unable or unwilling to pay interest according to schedule. A third big change was the development of a mechanism to limit movements in the exchange rates by the member countries of the European Community. Reviewing these developments is useful before considering how the arrangements might change.

INTERNATIONAL MONETARY DEVELOPMENTS IN THE 1970s AND 1980s

Change in international monetary arrangements in the 1970s and the 1980s was more extensive than in any previous period. The market price of gold, which had been $35 at the end of the 1960s, reached $970 in January 1980. And through most of the 1980s, the gold price moved within a range of $350 to $500; in the early 1990s, the range was $350 to $400. The foreign-exchange value of the U.S. dollar in the 1980s moved through a wide range: from the late 1970s to the spring of 1985 the U.S. dollar appreciated by more than 60 percent in terms of most foreign currencies. And then, within two years, the U.S. dollar depreciated rapidly.

The system of floating exchange rates did not conform to the textbook model; the range of movement in the exchange rate was much greater than the differences between the increase in the U.S. price level and the increases in the price levels in Germany, Japan, and other large industrial countries. The national monetary authorities intervened extensively to dampen the amplitude of the movement in exchange rates. Indeed, by the measure of purchases and sales of international reserve assets, central-bank intervention in the foreign-exchange market was more extensive during the floating exchange-rate period than in the previous decades with pegged exchange rates; in the absence of intervention, the range of movements in the foreign-exchange value of the U.S. dollar would have been even larger.

When the U.S. dollar was depreciating in the late 1970s, the monetary authorities in many foreign countries sought to diversify the currency composition of their international reserve assets; they acquired more securities denominated in currencies other than the U.S. dollar, especially the German mark, the Swiss franc, and the Japanese yen. In the 1960s, one of the major concerns had been the shortage of international reserves, which culminated in the establishment of the SDR arrangement and the production of 10 billion

SDRs. In the 1970s, total reserves minus gold increased sevenfold, from $40 billion at the end of 1969 to $275 billion at the end of 1979; if monetary gold is included and valued (conservatively) at $300 an ounce, total reserves increased from $80 billion to $600 billion. From 1980 to 1994, total reserves increased further so that by 1994 if gold is valued at $350 an ounce, international reserves stood at $1,467 billion.

The changes in international financial relationships reflect the surge in the world inflation rate in the 1970s and the sharp decline in the inflation rate in the 1980s. Inflation rates were at their highest levels at the end of the 1970s. While the inflation rate was intensified by the succession of increases in the price of crude petroleum promoted by OPEC in 1973–74 and then again in 1978–79, the world inflation rate was already at double-digit levels before the fourfold increase in the price of crude petroleum by 1973–74. Nevertheless, these sharp increases in the price of oil in 1974 and again in 1979 caused the annual world inflation rate to rise more rapidly, perhaps by as much as 2 to 3 percentage points during this period. In some countries the impact was greater, because the price increase of oil triggered increases in the prices of other commodities and expectations of future price increases.

In periods of accelerating inflation, the private demand for gold increased because investors believed that gold was a hedge against inflation. Gold was undervalued at the end of the 1960s; its price had remained constant since 1934 while the world commodity price level had increased by a factor of four. The rapid increase in the gold price in the late 1970s suggested expectations of continued and accelerating inflation.

From time to time, the rules concerning official transactions in gold have been changed. In the mid-1970s the national monetary authorities agreed not to deal in gold except at the official price. Then the official price was abandoned and a few monetary authorities raised the valuation attached to their holdings of gold. Many monetary authorities consider gold an important component of their international reserves, and few have sold significant amounts of gold.

The gold price fell sharply, as did the prices of many other real assets such as real estate, when anticipations of continuing inflation were shattered. Investors shifted funds back into U.S. dollar securities in response both to higher interest rates on U.S. dollar securities and to the downward revision in the anticipated U.S. inflation rate.

OPTIMAL CURRENCY AREAS AND MONETARY UNIONS

One of the central issues in international finance involves the area over which particular currencies are in use. Should each country have its own currency, as virtually all now do, or should countries merge their currencies, as the member countries of the European Community plan to do? Would it be worthwhile for certain large countries, say China or Brazil, to develop two or more currencies for distinct regional areas within each country?

One feature of the last several decades has been an increase in the number of countries and the number of currencies. Initially, this was due in large measure to the breakup of the British, French, Portuguese, and Dutch empires. But, with the breakup of the Soviet Union and other Eastern bloc nations, many more countries and currencies emerged. In the past emerging countries have often tied their currency at first to that of the power that had held sway; these currencies are now, however, often allowed to float.

On a more abstract level, the issues about unification of national currencies involve the attributes of countries whose currencies might be merged so as to maximize their economic welfare. The gains from currency unification involve the more efficient allocation of resources and capital and the reduction in costs associated with the use of the foreign-exchange market. If there were only one currency in the world, these costs would disappear. The United States, comprising fifty states, is a unified currency area. Financial capital flows smoothly and efficiently from high-saving, slow-growth regions to low-saving, high-growth regions; one indication of the almost frictionless movement is that interest rates on comparable securities are virtually the same in capital rich and capital poor regions. Payments can be made on a virtually costless basis from Maine to California—and to Hawaii and Alaska—by check. Internationally, the segmentation of Western Europe into more than 15 national currency areas incurs costs that will be avoided if the national currencies are merged as planned.

The costs of currency mergers are those associated with the loss of a central bank in all but one of the areas or countries, and thus with the decline in the ability to manage monetary policy to enhance employment and price-level objectives in the area, country, or region. If the Federal Reserve Bank of Chicago were independent of the other regional Federal Reserve Banks, it might pursue a more expansive monetary policy whenever the unemployment rate in the Midwest increased significantly. This has proved to be a very potent issue in EC negotiations. The value of having a separate currency area centers on the advantage attached to being able to alter the rate of growth of the money supply. The significance of the costs (and benefits) of unification of national currencies varies with the choice of countries involved and with the similarity of their economic structures.

One logical proposition relevant to optimizing the number of currency areas is that there should be no more central banks than there are **labor markets.** A labor market is an area in which excess demand for labor and excess supply of labor of the same type cannot exist at the same time. If labor is perfectly mobile among several labor markets, then they are effectively one larger labor market: wage levels cannot differ significantly in the several geographic regions because unemployed workers would move to the firms with excess demand for labor; also, competition among workers would maintain reasonably uniform wages, since no firm would pay a higher wage to attract labor than the prevailing market wage. More than one central bank would be redundant (as 11 of the regional Federal Reserve Banks are with respect to exchange rates) in that the unemployment rates in these labor markets would always be identical with those in other labor markets.

Hence, in order for separate national central banks to make sense, there must be a segmented labor market and labor must not be perfectly mobile among these markets. Then, economic welfare might be enhanced if the central banks in the areas with high unemployment followed an expansive monetary policy while the central banks in the areas with inflation followed a more contractive monetary policy. Still, despite segmented labor markets, independent central banks would be redundant if financial capital were perfectly mobile between currency areas, for one central bank could not, by changes in its monetary policy, induce a change in its interest rates on securities relative to world interest rates. So, in order for separate central banks to make sense, not only must labor markets be segmented, national capital markets must also be partially segmented from each other.

Even if both labor markets and capital markets are partially segmented so that independent monetary policies are both needed and feasible, the costs of maintaining separate national currencies may exceed the benefits. If the gains from the enhanced flow of goods and securities and the elimination of the costs of operating the foreign-exchange market are larger than the costs of higher unemployment because of a reduction in the number of central banks, then maintaining separate currencies will not make sense.

The patterns of currency-area unification follow this logic. Thus, mergers of national currencies tend to occur among countries or areas that are in close enough geographic proximity so that a large volume of trade takes place among these countries or areas. The business cycles in these areas also tend to be similar in timing and amplitude. Small countries have much to gain in terms of the increased flow of goods and financial capital from merging their currencies with each other or with the currency of a large country. Large countries like the United States have already realized these gains; both Canada and Mexico might also gain from merging their currencies with the U.S. dollar because both would have access to the U.S. financial markets on more favorable terms. Such mergers might develop now that the North American Free Trade Agreement has been ratified. However, before Mexico can merge its currency with the U.S. dollar, it must reduce its inflation rate to the level of the U.S. inflation rate. And at some distant stage, the development of closer relations among the central banks in the United States, Canada, and Mexico might follow from the development of free trade.

The insights generated by the analysis of the costs and benefits of currency unification are applicable to two other questions. The first is whether the interests of an individual country are better served by pegging its currency in the foreign-exchange market or by permitting its currency to float. The second is whether, if a country decides to peg its currency, its interests are advanced by pegging the currency to the U.S. dollar, the German mark, the Japanese yen, or some other currency.

The European Community and Currency Unification

History suggests that currencies are merged to secure political objectives; currency unification is seen as an important step toward political unification. This was the case in the late nineteenth century when currency unification was extensive within Germany, Japan, and Italy—in each case as part of a program of political unification. The most ambitious effort to merge national monies in recent years has been that of the European Community. This effort followed the Treaty of Rome (1957), which led to the elimination of tariffs on internal trade among members of the community, to the development of a common external tariff and a common agricultural policy, and to the harmonization of social security, welfare policy, and business taxes in the member countries. So it might seem natural for the member countries to harmonize or coordinate monetary policies and to move toward a common communitywide money, a change that would eventually require mergers of their central banks.

One motive for currency unification in Western Europe is that political unification is viewed as a desirable objective. A merger of national currencies would be a meaningful step toward this objective. Some note the growth of intra-European trade: an increasing share of the trade of individual European countries is with other EC members. Payments from one country in Europe to another would be facilitated by a single currency, as would trade within Western Europe. The move to a European currency would provide a modest amount of trade protection for European firms in competition with firms producing in the United States and in other non-European countries. The development of a European currency area might also provide monetary stability and better enable the European countries to insulate their economies from monetary shocks produced in the United States.

Once a decision to merge currencies has been reached, the authorities must decide how to realize this objective. One approach is to harmonize monetary policies and then, if inflation rates are similar, to peg each currency to a common unit of account. An alternative approach involves pegging these currencies in the foreign-exchange market and then harmonizing monetary policies so as to reduce the likelihood of extended payments imbalances at the established parities. The Europeans have been following the second approach.

The likelihood that any large countries outside Western Europe will merge their currencies in the near future is low. Moreover, there may be substantial setbacks in efforts toward currency unification in Western Europe. One setback has been the unification of the two Germanies, which has resulted in a surge in interest rates on German mark securities and significant increases in interest rates in nearby countries.

FLOATING OR PEGGED EXCHANGE RATES?

Perhaps the most enduring issue facing us today is whether to continue with floating exchange rates or to return to a system of pegged exchange rates. Once again, this is largely a debate between those who want greater flexibility for domestic policy makers, and hence floating exchange rates, and those who prefer the easier movements of goods and capital, and hence a system of pegged exchange rates.

Prior to World War I, the U.S. dollar and other major currencies were pegged to gold. Basically, central banks were able to maintain their parities because they followed the "rules of the game" for adjustment to payment imbalances; their money supplies declined (or increased less rapidly) when they were in payments deficit and increased when they were in payments surplus.

The period from 1919 to 1926 was the first extensive period when many countries permitted their currencies to float. At the outbreak of World War I, the central banks in most European countries stopped pegging their currencies to gold at their mint parities; they embargoed gold exports and supported their currencies at levels 5 to 15 percent below their prewar parities. Inflation was extensive in these countries but inflation rates differed. At the end of the war, the dominant objective was to return to the 1913 gold parities. But attaining this objective was not immediately feasible because of the large and differential increases in national price levels that had occurred during the war. So currencies continued to float.

Some countries attempted to deflate their economies and their price levels so that pegging their currencies to gold at their 1913 parities would again be possible. A few countries—Great Britain and several countries that had been neutral during the war including Switzerland, the Netherlands, and the Scandinavian countries—succeeded in again pegging their currencies at their 1913 parities. The other Allies—France, Belgium, and Italy—eventually pegged their currencies in the late 1920s, after continued inflation and extended depreciation of their currencies; at these new parities, the price of the U.S. dollar was five to ten times higher than it had been before the war. The defeated belligerents—Germany, Austria, Hungary, and Russia—also pegged their currencies to gold, but only after hyperinflations and subsequent currency reforms.

The exchange-rate experience in the 1930s was substantially different from that of the 1920s. Great Britain permitted the pound to float in September 1931; a few countries—Ireland, Denmark, Sweden, and some members of the British Commonwealth—pegged their currencies to the British pound, with the result that a sterling currency area was formed; all the currencies in this area floated together in terms of the U.S. dollar and the other currencies that were still pegged to gold. When President Roosevelt took office in early March 1933, he closed all U.S. banks, nationalized private U.S. gold holdings, and prohibited the U.S. Treasury from buying and selling gold. For the next ten months, the U.S. dollar price of gold increased; the U.S. dollar was depreciating in terms of gold and most foreign currencies. At the end of January 1934, the U.S. dollar price of gold was again fixed, this time at $35 an ounce, so the effective increase in the U.S. dollar price of gold was 75 percent. Then speculative pressures developed against currencies that were still pegged to gold and, in mid-1936, the French franc, the Belgian franc, and the Dutch guilder were devalued.

One conclusion to be drawn from the operation of floating exchange rates during the interwar period was that international trade and investment would be deterred or increasingly disrupted because of uncertainty about exchange rates in the future. A second conclusion was that speculation in the foreign-exchange market would be destabilizing, that the amplitude of exchange-rate movements would be larger, and that speculators would cause the trend value of the exchange rate to follow a path different from the path it would have followed in their absence. Thus, if speculators sold a weak currency, the price of foreign monies in terms of this currency would increase, and the price of imports and the general price level in the country with the weak currency would increase more rapidly. In contrast, the domestic price level would increase less rapidly in those countries whose currencies were acquired by speculators. So speculation would be self-justifying. At a later stage, this behavior led to what has been called "vicious and virtuous cycles"—speculators buying currencies with low inflation rates and selling the currencies of countries with the high inflation rates, so that the currencies of the first group of countries would appreciate, while the currencies of the second group of countries would depreciate.

The Controversy between Proponents of Pegged and Floating Exchange Rates

The proponents of floating exchange rates criticized these conclusions, but only after asserting that the primary advantage of a floating exchange-rate system was that countries would be able to achieve greater monetary independence. They claimed that countries would be able to follow monetary policies free of an external constraint, because any tendency toward a payments deficit would automatically lead to a depreciation of their currencies. For example, if a country with a floating exchange rate followed an expansive monetary policy, one that would be associated with a larger payments deficit than the country could readily finance with a pegged exchange-rate system, its currency would depreciate. Similarly, no country would be obliged to purchase large amounts of foreign exchange, and hence increase its own money supply, to maintain the parity for its currency; instead, its currency would appreciate and the monetary base would not be affected by currency flows.

The pro-floaters also argued that international trade and investment would not be deterred by uncertainty about exchange rates, because traders and investors would hedge their foreign-exchange commitments through forward contracts. Hence, countries would have greater freedom to follow policies leading to price levels that would differ from those in other countries; countries would have greater freedom to pursue employment objectives that differed from their neighbors' as well. The pro-floaters argued, too, that speculation would not be destabilizing, because anyone who speculated against long-run trends would soon go bankrupt.

The critics of floating exchange rates responded by arguing that there were inadequate forward exchange market facilities for most currencies and that hedging foreign-exchange exposure was not costless. They also asserted that monetary independence was a chimera and that countries would have less control over their own price and income targets than the proponents of floating exchange rates promised. Moreover, the critics noted that the removal of the exchange parities would eliminate one of the last barriers to domestic inflation, that countries would use—and abuse—their increased monetary independence, with the consequence that the inflation rates would rise.

Uncertainty and Independence under a Floating-Rate System

The resolution of the issue between the proponents and the critics of floating rates partly involves the nature and consequences of uncertainty under the floating-rate system. Greater monetary independence can be achieved under a system of floating exchange rates only if the increased uncertainty about

President Kemp and the Gold Standard

Jack Kemp, one-time quarterback of the Buffalo Bills, former Secretary of Housing and Urban Development, and occasional candidate for the U.S. presidency, has advocated a return of the U.S. dollar to the gold standard. Kemp has observed that when the U.S. dollar was pegged to gold, the U.S. inflation rate averaged less than 1 percent a year. In contrast, the U.S. inflation rate averaged over 7 percent a year in the 1970s and over 5 percent a year in the 1980s: the 1970s and 1980s were the longest single period in which the U.S. dollar was not pegged to gold.

The first act of the first U.S. Congress in 1792 was to fix the gold content of the then-standard U.S. coin, the double eagle, which had a value of $20. For most of the subsequent two hundred years, the price of the U.S. dollar was fixed in terms of the British pound and of other major currencies, as long as these currencies had fixed values in terms of gold. The United States first stopped pegging the U.S. dollar to gold during the Civil War, because it was impossible to maintain the U.S. parity for gold when the government's financial policies were inflationary. The break in the fixed U.S. dollar price of gold of $35 per ounce in August 1971 was a result of high inflation: the U.S. price level in 1971 was 29 percent higher than the U.S. price level had been in 1965.

One insight this look at history provides is that a return to a pegged exchange rate involving the U.S. dollar is not likely to be possible until the inflation rates in the United States and in other large industrial countries, especially Japan and Germany, are similar. The first step will be for one country to take the initiative and peg its currency to some asset.

The most likely scenario is that the United States, the countries of the European Community led by Germany, and Japan will agree to peg their currencies to Special Drawing Rights (SDRs) at more or less the same time, after their inflation rates become similar. The country most likely to take the initiative in this move back toward a system of pegged exchange rates is the one that feels it has the most to lose from a continued reliance on a system of floating exchange rates, presumably because its trading partners gain too much of a competitive advantage when their currencies are not pegged.

Throughout the first half of the 1990s, the U.S. dollar has been significantly undervalued, so U.S. goods have had a price advantage in world markets in this period. Until these circumstances change, the U.S. government probably won't be the one to take the initiative in the move back toward some type of pegged exchange rate unless someone as committed to the idea as Jack Kemp makes it into the White House. Even then, such a move remains doubtful.

exchange rates leads to more extensive segmentation of national money markets. In the absence of increased segmentation, the scope for monetary independence would not increase. The increase in uncertainty necessary for greater monetary independence also deters trade and investment. True, the uncertainty of traders and investors about exchange rates in the future can be hedged through the purchase of forward exchange contracts, and hedging may be costless to the extent that forward exchange rates are unbiased predictors—on average—of future spot exchange rates. Yet hedging is not risk-less, because forward rates individually are not very good predictors of the spot exchange rates on the dates when the forward exchange contracts mature. The benefits of greater monetary independence with floating exchange rates cannot be attained without increased uncertainty, and the cost of this increased uncertainty is a reduced level of trade and investment or, in an increasingly integrated world economy, a reduction in the rate of growth of trade and investment. The economic significance of this cost and its value relative to the value of greater monetary independence remain important and unresolved empirical issues.

The critics of floating rates base their assertion that speculation would be destabilizing on the observation that changes in exchange rates have been much larger in amplitude than the difference in contemporaneous changes in national price levels. The proponents of floating rates respond that the period-to-period movement in the exchange rates follows a random walk, that there is no systematic or predictable movement in exchange rates, and hence that the exchange market is efficient.[1] They continue that there are no *runs* in the time-series of exchange-rate movements—periods when the direction of changes in exchange rates can be accurately predicted from past changes in the exchange rates. But if the exchange-rate movement follows a trend, the economic forces that drive the exchange rate also may follow a trend. Alternatively, the monetary authorities may have been leaning against the wind when intervening in the foreign-exchange market—and retreating. In the last several years, some analysts have concluded that the foreign-exchange market is not efficient, that for brief episodes day-to-day changes in exchange rates have been serially correlated, particularly when the amplitude of movements in exchange rates is large because of a significant change in the difference in national inflation rates.

The efforts of national monetary authorities to follow independent monetary policies appears likely to lead to large movements in the spot exchange rate since the current spot rate primarily reflects anticipated spot exchange rates. Changes in monetary policy affect the current spot exchange rate because of the impact these changes have on anticipated inflation rates. And changes in anticipated inflation rates affect anticipations of the values of market exchange rates at various future dates and the interest rates at which these anticipated market exchange rates are discounted to the present. Thus, a move toward a more expansive monetary policy would be associated with an anticipation of a more rapid increase in the domestic price level and a decline in the domestic interest rate; each of these factors would cause domestic currency to depreciate. Conversely, a move toward a more contractive monetary policy would be associated with the appreciation of domestic currency, both because of the reduction in the anticipated domestic inflation rate and the increase in the interest rate on domestic securities. The large apparent swings in exchange rates reflect the fact that changes in monetary policy have been offsetting,

---

[1] A financial market is said to be efficient when market prices of assets adjust immediately and fully to any new information. If good news and bad news occur randomly, then the changes in the price of the asset should follow a random walk.

either because a contractive domestic policy is followed by an expansive domestic policy or because it is followed by contractive policies abroad.

If these changes in exchange rates induced by changes in monetary policy are substantial, then the authorities may be obliged to intervene in the exchange market to limit the induced movement in the exchange rates. Assume, for example, that the U.S. authorities follow a more expansive monetary policy. If the U.S. dollar tends to depreciate in the foreign-exchange market, then foreign monetary authorities may buy U.S. dollars to limit the appreciation of their own currencies. The purchase of dollars leads to an increase in their money supplies. Unless these sales are offset by a tendency for the U.S. dollar to appreciate, there is upward bias in the growth of national money supplies. The authorities may have less control over their money supplies in the floating-rate period than in the pegged-rate period, because the private capital flows are so much larger.

Problems of Managing an Exchange-Rate System

The proponents of floating exchange rates frequently point to the difficulties of managing a pegged-rate system. Changes in parities almost always occur after too long a delay because the authorities hope that divine providence will intervene so that an almost certain change in a parity will not be necessary. But the move to floating exchange rates in the early 1970s did not occur because the proponents of floating exchange rates won the arguments; rather, in a period of increasing inflation and greater divergence among countries in their inflation rates, the authorities were unwilling to incur the domestic political costs associated with the policies necessary to maintain the pegged-rate system. This system might have been maintained if the foreign monetary authorities, especially those in Germany, had been willing to accept the U.S. inflation rate, but the Germans preferred a lower inflation rate.

The evidence of the last one hundred years suggests that the monetary system has a tendency to gravitate toward pegged rates—so long as such a system is feasible. If inflation rates among major countries are similar and low, a return to pegged rates seems likely. Many countries will peg their currencies to that of a nearby and larger metropole. The members of the European Community are now committed to a common currency. Hence, the number of major countries with floating rates will decline, currency blocs will develop, and eventually pegging will reduce the exchange-rate movements among the major currency blocs.

A **crawling-peg exchange system** has been proposed as an arrangement that combines the advantages of both a pegged- and a floating-rate system. Under this system, on frequent occasions, perhaps as often as once or twice a month, the authorities would change their parities, usually by no more than 2 or 3 percent. Because the changes in parities are frequent, no political trauma is supposed to be associated with these changes. Because the amount of the change is so small, few traders and investors would deem it worthwhile to attempt to predict the timing of these changes and profit from them. Between the changes in the parity, the monetary authorities would peg the currency;

however, because of the frequency of changes in the parity, the domestic monetary implications of pegging the rate would be slight.

THE SUPPLY OF RESERVE ASSETS

In the 1960s monetary authorities in many countries were concerned that the supply of international reserve assets was increasing at too slow a rate. In the 1970s there was an unplanned and unanticipated surge in the level of reserve assets, which contributed to the increase in the inflation rates in many countries as the monetary base of many countries expanded. One of the major concerns to result from this experience was the need to manage the growth of reserves in order to limit the impact of inflation. A related problem involves the components of reserves, whether gold and liquid securities denominated in the U.S. dollar, the German mark, and other currencies will continue, along with SDRs, to serve as reserve assets.

The surprise in the 1970s and the 1980s was the growth in the volume of reserve assets, despite the fact that currencies had been floating. Foreign central banks acquired U.S. dollar assets to limit the appreciation of their currencies when private parties, both American and non-American, unloaded their dollar holdings. At the end of 1965, international reserves totaled $67 billion; when floating began in 1973, reserves totaled $150 billion. Determining the value at the end of 1991 is complicated by the need to place a value on monetary gold holdings. But if monetary gold is valued at $350 per ounce, reserves exceed $900 billion. Even after an adjustment for the increase in commodity price levels, the increase in the real value of international reserve assets has been substantial. If gold remains in monetary limbo, countries in deficit will be able to sell gold at or near its market price (or else borrow from other countries using their gold as collateral) to obtain currencies to finance their payments deficits.

Another concern that arose in the 1960s was that the international monetary system could not produce international reserves without forcing the United States to incur payments deficits. As we discussed in Chapter 29, the United States was the major supplier of reserves, both in the form of gold and liquid dollar assets. During the 15-year period from 1950 to 1965, U.S. gold sales to foreign official institutions were almost as large as new gold production. As foreign central banks added to their holdings of liquid dollar securities and as U.S. gold holdings declined, the ability of the United States to maintain its $35 gold parity for the indefinite future appeared increasingly questionable. The conundrum was that to the extent the United States was successful in reducing its payments deficit, most other countries would no longer be able to increase their holdings of gold and other reserve assets. But unless the United States could reduce its payments deficit, the $35 parity could not be maintained.

Yet another problem was the asymmetry between the apparent ease with which the United States financed its payments deficits and the difficulties other countries encountered in financing their payments deficits. Other countries spent reserves they owned and reserves they borrowed from international institutions; either they had to acquire reserves to finance payments deficits, or they had to borrow from foreign official institutions to finance these deficits and subsequently repay these loans. In contrast, since other countries were willing to acquire U.S. dollar–denominated assets, that part of the U.S. deficit not financed by gold sales could be financed automatically, through this kind of "passive borrowing." Such automatic financing led to the concern that the growth of international reserves might be uncontrolled.

Gold as International Money

Gold is no longer used as a domestic money, nor do any countries peg their currencies to gold. Whether gold will again have a role as an international reserve asset depends on the outcome of two forces. One is a continuation of the pressures for economic efficiency that led to the progressive decline in gold's monetary role in the last century. The U.S. authorities have sought to reduce the international monetary role of gold—to remove it from the center of the monetary system. And they have succeeded, for in the years since the price of gold has been variable, central banks have rarely traded gold with each other. Rather, they have hoarded their gold, because its market price has been so much higher than its official price.

Still, gold was an important monetary asset for centuries; investors and monetary institutions acquired gold because it held its value better than most other monetary assets; the cliché was that gold was a good inflation hedge. Moreover, partly because of its underlying commodity value, gold maintained its value over a wider geographic area than any other monetary asset, for gold had credibility as a monetary asset that other assets lacked. More importantly, there was relative price-level stability in the century of the gold standard, if not on a year-to-year basis, at least over several decades. Whether price-level stability was a consequence of the commitment to maintaining national currencies pegged to gold is debatable. But the period since gold has been shifted from the center of the system has been one of much more rapid inflation than experienced during the previous century. Some U.S. politicians have concluded that a persuasive case for the return to the gold standard, or at least for pegging national currencies to gold, can be made.

On the other side, those who argue for reducing the monetary role of gold still further contend that gold is not readily manageable as a reserve asset. Once a generation the monetary price of gold would have to be increased to avoid a cumulative shortage of gold. And investors would continually speculate about the timing and amount of these increases. Proponents of the monetary role of gold reply that such increases are likely to be necessary only if inflation continues; with a stable price level, there is no evidence that the monetary price of gold would have to be raised.

The case for maintaining gold as a reserve asset has several elements. First, gold already is an important monetary asset; second, it has a large constituency among central banks (otherwise they wouldn't continue to hold gold); and third, considering gold as an acceptable reserve asset would restore balance to central-bank portfolios, now overloaded with assets denominated in the U.S. dollar. The United States would certainly benefit, since the U.S. gold holdings are approximately equal to the combined holdings of the three other largest holders.

The importance attached to gold suggests that once again a monetary role will develop for it: clearly, the value of gold in international reserve assets is so great that no substitute can readily be found. Several scenarios for enhancing the monetary role of gold are feasible. For example, if central banks make arrangements so that countries with payments deficits will be able to sell gold to other central banks to obtain the foreign-exchange necessary to support their currencies in the foreign-exchange market, then the monetary role of gold may again become viable. Alternatively, if the United States and other countries agree to a new monetary price for gold in terms of their currencies as part of a complex negotiation involving the roles of gold and other reserve assets, then the monetary role of gold may also be renewed.

The U.S. Dollar and Other Fiat Assets

A major concern in the evolution of the international financial system is the role of the U.S. dollar as a reserve asset. While holdings of dollar assets are increasing, holdings of assets denominated in the German mark, the Swiss franc, and the Japanese yen are also likely to increase. International institutions are likely to continue producing reserve assets as well. Nevertheless, it seems highly unlikely that the U.S. dollar will be phased out as an international reserve asset or even that its role will decline significantly. Reserves denominated in various national currencies grow as foreign central banks acquire the currencies of the countries with which they have major trade and financial relations, provided these countries have a reasonable record for commodity price-level stability. Inevitably, only the currencies of a very few countries are acquired as reserve assets.

Over the long run, the growth of reserve assets denominated in different currencies is usually determined by demand; the countries acquiring these assets first decide on the volumes of reserves they wish to acquire and then decide on the currency denominations of these reserve assets. On several occasions, however, changes in the volume of reserve assets have represented excess production, as with the British pound during World War II and with the U.S. dollar between 1969 and 1971. Excess production of reserve assets occurs because countries with payments surpluses are reluctant to revalue their currencies.

Initially the U.S. dollar became a reserve asset because foreign monetary authorities found it to their advantage to acquire U.S. dollar securities, not because U.S. authorities planned such a role for the dollar. A key policy issue is whether U.S. interests are served by having the U.S. dollar used as an international reserve asset. The United States gains several advantages from being an international banker. One, the seigniorage gain, involves the profits from the production of money—the difference between the cost of producing money and its purchasing power in terms of other goods and services. In a competitive banking system, such gains would be competed away in the form of higher interest rates on dollar deposits. But U.S. interest rates are likely to be lower, not higher, because of the foreign demand for dollar assets.

A second advantage for the United States is greater flexibility in financing its payments deficits, an advantage that became apparent in the late 1960s. Because foreign central banks bought U.S. dollar securities, the U.S. payments deficit could be financed more easily than the payments deficits of other countries at the prevailing exchange rate.

Despite these advantages, in the 1960s some analysts concluded that the use of the dollar as a reserve-asset currency was *not* in the U.S. national interest. First, they argued that using the dollar as a reserve asset meant that the United States had less control over its monetary policy because changes in U.S. interest rates would be constrained as the Federal Reserve worried that shifts of funds to foreign financial centers by private investors would be larger because of the volume of U.S. dollar assets owned by foreign central banks. To the extent that foreign official institutions were *buyers* of dollar assets rather than of gold, these shifts of private funds presented no problem; the constraint became apparent only if foreign official institutions might *sell* dollars and buy gold as interest rates on U.S. dollar assets fell. Second, they argued that the United States had less control over the foreign-exchange value of the U.S. dollar than other countries had over the foreign-exchange value of their currencies, since the Fed had to worry that a U.S. devaluation would be followed by comparable devaluations of other currencies. Finally, critics argued that increases in the export of U.S. securities led to smaller exports of U.S. commodities, which was a cost to the producers of commodities if not to the U.S. economy as a whole.

Now that foreign holdings of dollar securities exceed $300 billion, the question becomes whether changes in the demand for these assets can have a significant impact on the U.S. economy. If foreign holders of dollar securities decide to shift to reserve assets denominated in a foreign currency, the U.S. dollar would depreciate in the foreign-exchange market. When the U.S. dollar has been weak in the exchange market, there have been proposals for new arrangements to manage foreign dollar holdings. One proposal is that the United States extend exchange guarantees on foreign dollar holdings, so that if the dollar depreciates by more than a specified amount, the U.S. authorities make a direct payment to some or all foreign official holders of dollars to compensate them for their exchange losses. Another proposal would have some or all foreign central-bank holdings of dollar assets transferred to the International Monetary Fund, which would then hold these claims on the United States. The U.S. authorities could extend a maintenance-of-value guarantee on the dollar holdings of the Fund, and the Fund in turn could extend a similar guarantee on its liabilities to foreign official institutions. A third proposal is that the U.S. authorities begin to support the dollar in the foreign-exchange market to limit the variations in the dollar's foreign-exchange value. U.S. authorities might draw on U.S. reserves and borrow foreign currencies from the International Monetary Fund and from foreign central banks to do so.

The common feature of all these proposals is that the U.S. authorities incur the exchange risk on some or all U.S. dollar securities held by foreign official institutions. The presumption is that U.S. willingness to acquire the foreign-exchange exposure would limit variations in the foreign-exchange value of the dollar. As a result, foreign central banks would be less reluctant to intervene in response to sharp movements in exchange rates that seem out of line with general underlying economic trends.

In 1991 the members of the European Community committed themselves to the development of their own international currency—the ECU (European Currency Unit). The ECU will be both a unit of account for central banks and private parties and a store of value. And to the extent that the demand for ECUs as an international reserve asset increases, the demand for U.S. dollars as an international reserve asset will decline. The Japanese yen may also develop as an international reserve asset in response to the growth in the Japanese share of world trade and the large capital exports from Japan; foreign countries with Japanese yen liabilities will acquire Japanese yen securities to reduce their foreign-exchange exposure. And to the extent that the foreign demand for the ECU and the Japanese yen as international reserve assets increases, the demand for U.S. dollar assets will increase less rapidly.

THE ROLE OF MULTINATIONAL MONETARY INSTITUTIONS

One proposal to resolve the problems resulting from the use of assets denominated in major national currencies as reserve assets is to establish an international institution to produce reserve assets. Member countries would hold reserves in the form of deposits in this institution; when a member country had a payments deficit, it would transfer part of its deposits to the accounts of countries with payments surpluses. This type of arrangement has a number of advantages. First, reserves could be produced without the need for any particular national currency to become overvalued. Second, the seigniorage attached to the production of international money could be distributed to all countries. Third, the rate of growth of international reserves could be managed, and the overproduction of reserves could be limited.

The International Monetary Fund is a reserve-producing institution in embryo. But the development of this role for the IMF has been slow for several reasons. One problem has been a fear that decisions about the rate of growth of reserves will be dominated by inflation-prone countries, which would favor a more rapid rate of growth of reserves. This would mean that countries with the strongest commitments to price stability would realize larger-than-desired payments surpluses from acquiring the liabilities of the international institution and so would face the choice of either accepting a higher-than-desired inflation rate or continually revaluing their currencies. If, as seems not unlikely, reserves were produced at too rapid a rate, the countries with surpluses would be reluctant to acquire deposits in the new institution.

Individual countries will be concerned about whether attaining national objectives will be easier if an international institution produces reserve assets. U.S. authorities would necessarily be concerned about the implications for the management of domestic monetary policy raised by U.S. participation in such an institution. If the United States were to have a payments deficit under this system, financing it might prove more difficult than under the current arrangement, because foreign official institutions would no longer acquire dollar assets, and so U.S. monetary policy might have to be directed toward reducing the deficit. If the United States were to have a payments surplus under this system, it would be obliged to extend credit to countries with payments deficits.

National attitudes regarding the idea of a central reserve-producing institution generally reflect whether a country is more likely to incur payments deficits or payments surpluses. Those countries with a tendency toward higher inflation and payments deficits generally favor the development of such an institution, since they believe financing their deficits in the future would be easier. Countries with a tendency toward payments surpluses are more skeptical, since they would be obliged to extend credit to countries with the payments deficits.

Over the next several decades, U.S. monetary authorities and their counterparts in Western Europe and Japan are likely to consider various proposals for changes in international financial arrangements. Many will seek methods to reduce the range of movement in exchange rates. Some will seek to make arrangements that would lead to a reduction in the frequency and severity of the disturbances that countries import from their trading partners. Some will seek to develop arrangements that will enhance the effectiveness of monetary policy without infringing on freer international trade and payments.

TOWARD A NEW INTERNATIONAL MONETARY SYSTEM

Since the breakdown of the Bretton Woods System of pegged exchange rates, the arrangements for organizing the foreign-exchange market and producing international money seem too haphazard to qualify as an international monetary system. As we discussed in Chapter 29, an international monetary system must be orderly and based on an international treaty. Some proposals to achieve greater monetary order seek to improve the operation of the floating exchange rates, while others favor a return to pegged exchange rates, either on a global or a regional basis. Some proposals seek to alter the assets used as international reserves. One issue is whether gold should continue to be phased out as an international reserve asset or whether it should be reinstated in this role; another issue is whether the roles of U.S. dollar assets and assets denominated in other currencies should be modified.

A key issue is how the changes in these institutional frameworks would affect the management of monetary policy—both the need or demand for monetary independence in the major countries and the ability of the U.S. monetary authorities and those in other countries to follow the policies they believe appropriate to achieve their domestic objectives. The demand for monetary independence arises because the phases of the business cycle are not perfectly correlated across countries; even if they were, countries differ in the importance they attach to full employment and to price stability as objectives of national policy. But individual countries may encounter significant external constraints should they decide to pursue greater monetary independence:

changes in a country's monetary policy may have a significant impact on the flows of capital or on the foreign-exchange value of its currency. The goal in developing a new set of international monetary arrangements is to allow countries to pursue their domestic objectives without forgoing the advantages of openness and specialization possible in the international economy or to arrive at the most satisfactory compromise between independence and the free and unrestrained movement of goods and of capital.

Some of the proposals are ambitious in that the arrangements for the organization of the foreign-exchange market and for supplying international reserve assets would be modified extensively. A new system implies a set of rules—perhaps based on an international treaty like the Bretton Woods Agreement—that would require the participating countries to commit themselves to following particular practices about exchange-market intervention and international reserve holdings and to refrain from other measures. Adhering to some of these commitments is likely to have *no* significant cost; even without a treaty, most countries would behave much as if they were following the commitments. To the extent that adherence to the commitments would have a cost, in that several of the participating countries would be obliged to pursue measures they would not have pursued in the absence of the treaty, the key question is how long they will abide by these commitments at the expense of their own national interests. Treaties that are too far in front of the consensus, treaties that are expensive to domestic interests, may, like the Smithsonian Agreement or the French Constitution, soon be ignored.

So a major issue involves the impact of changes in international monetary arrangements on national economic policies. The relevant question is how long efforts of central banks to peg or manage the foreign-exchange value of their currencies can cause the exchange rate to differ significantly from the values they otherwise would have. Intervention can have a greater impact on the exchange rate in the short-run—a few months or even a year—than over a more extended period. In the long run, exchange rates are determined by relative prices and incomes and by anticipations of changes in relative price levels.

Success in devising an international monetary arrangement that will remain viable for an extended period—twenty or thirty years—depends on the relationship between the implied commitments and the prevailing set of monetary and even political relationships. The adoption of a system of pegged exchange rates during an inflationary period is likely to prove difficult; one characteristic of inflation is that the rates of price-level increases differ sharply across countries and vary significantly from one year to the next, so countries are likely to find the domestic costs of adhering to their parities for an extended period too high.

If the proposed international monetary arrangements are to be viable, they must be consistent with the distribution of political and economic power among nations. The gold standard succeeded during a period when Great Britain was the dominant economic power and when British policies led to a stable world price level. The Bretton Woods System flourished during a period when U.S. economic and political power was dominant and U.S. economic policies led to a stable price level. As the U.S. economic position declined with the resurgence of the German and Japanese economies, the fragility of the Bretton Woods System became apparent. The system did not break down, however, until the U.S. price level began to increase at a rate higher than 5 percent a year. Any new set of arrangements must be consistent with a dispersion of economic power among at least three major economic centers—the United States, the European Community, and Japan. Proposals that require extensive centralization of authority are not likely to be viable as long as nationalist pressures remain strong.

Changes in international arrangements involve a complicated interplay of interests of various countries. Few central bankers and treasury officials attempt to optimize a universal interest. Rather, in developing positions on these issues, each deals with a national variant on the familiar theme, "What's in it for me?" Each country's policy makers make an implicit cost-benefit analysis of the adoption of each proposal on the well-being of their constituents and on the ability of their own governments to realize their objectives. Relatively few national monetary authorities would agree to proposals that might advance the universal interest if the cost to their own constituents was high.

International monetary problems become acute when national interests diverge sharply. Differences in the relative importance of various economic objectives across countries are more extensive than differences within countries. Moreover, within countries there are usually established legal procedures, frequently based on a written constitution, for determining the public interest or at least for resolving problems, whereas the procedures for determining the general interest of a group of countries are still vague. Developing solutions for the problems might be easier if national interests were more malleable. A frequent proposal is that the national authorities coordinate their policies. But such proposals often ignore the divergence of national interests. Because such interests change only slowly, we face the problem of devising a set of international arrangements that will best accommodate the interests of many different countries.

SUMMARY

1 The source of international monetary problems is that national interests diverge.
2 The Bretton Woods System of pegged exchange rates broke down because of the surge in the world inflation rate and the efforts of several countries to realize inflation rates lower than those in the United States.
3 If countries were to join a currency or monetary union, they would benefit from the elimination of the various costs of using the foreign-exchange market in their transactions with each other; however, their economic welfare might be adversely affected unless their business cycles are similar.
4 For most of this century, the major industrial countries have pegged their currencies with the exception of two periods—the first half of the 1920s and from 1973 on.
5 The movements in exchange rates in the 1970s have not conformed to the claims previously advanced by their proponents. Thus, the range of movements in exchange rates has been wide, and countries have had smaller monetary independence than they would have preferred.

6 In the 1960s, there was almost uniform belief that there would be a shortage of international reserve assets; in contrast, in the 1970s, international reserve assets increased at a very rapid rate.

7 The increase in the market price of gold has had a major impact on the value of central-bank holdings of monetary gold. The self-interest of many central banks will be advanced if arrangements develop so they can once again use gold to finance payments deficits.

8 Holdings of dollar-denominated assets are the next largest component of international reserve assets after monetary gold holdings. The United States has almost certainly benefited from the foreign demand for dollar assets.

KEY TERMS

crawling-peg exchange rates
optimal currency area
European Monetary System

reserve currency
monetary gold
labor market

QUESTIONS AND EXERCISES

1 Discuss the costs and the benefits of maintaining separate national currencies. Why might the major countries in Western Europe now think the time appropriate to merge their currencies?

*2 Discuss the basic argument for floating exchange rates and the arguments for a system of pegged, adjustable parities. What conditions must be satisfied if the major countries are again to peg their currencies?

*3 During the 1960s financial officials in the major countries were concerned with the shortage of international reserves. Discuss the conditions that might lead to the conclusion that the volume of international reserves is too small or too large.

4 Why has the relationship between the demand for reserves and the supply of reserves changed in the last decade?

FURTHER READING

FRANKEL, JEFFREY A. *The Obstacles to Macroeconomic Policy Coordination in the 1990s and an Analysis of International Nominal Targeting.* University of California, Berkeley, 1991.

KRUGMAN, PAUL. *Peddling Prosperity: Economic Sense and Nonsense in an Age of Diminishing Expectations.* New York: Norton, 1994.

SCHMIDT, WILSON E. *The U.S. Balance of Payments and the Sinking Dollar.* New York: New York University Press, 1979. The title tells the story.

Glossary

A PRIORI DEFINITION OF MONEY: A way of defining money that focuses on the inherent characteristics of money.

ABSOLUTE LIQUIDITY PREFERENCE: A hypothetical situation in which interest rates are so low that any additional funds will be held as money rather than as securities.

ACCELERATOR: The relation between a change in demand and the investment undertaken by firms to meet this demand.

ACCOMMODATIVE POLICY: A monetary policy that accommodates the money supply to the demand for money.

ACCORD, THE: The resolution of a dispute between the Federal Reserve and the Treasury in March 1951 that gave the Fed somewhat greater leeway to raise interest rates.

ADJUSTED BASE: The monetary base adjusted for changes in reserve requirements.

ADJUSTMENT CREDIT: Short-term loan by the Federal Reserve to a depository institution to allow it to adjust to a temporary loss of reserves or an increased need for reserves.

AGGREGATE DEMAND CURVE: A curve in the price–real income plane relating the total demand for goods and services to the price level.

AGGREGATE SUPPLY CURVE: A curve in the price–real income plane relating the total supply of goods and services to the price level.

ANNOUNCEMENT EFFECT: That part of the effect of a discount rate change that operates by changing people's expectations.

APC: The average propensity to consume.

ASYMMETRIC INFORMATION: Unequal information between the parties to a contract or deal.

BALANCE OF PAYMENTS: An accounting system recording the flows of international payments. It includes imports, exports, and foreign investment, as well as the holding of foreign assets by central banks.

BALANCE OF TRADE: The value of goods exported minus the value of imports.

BANK CAPITAL: That part of a bank's total assets that represents what its stockholders own; its net worth.

BANK FOR COOPERATIVES: A government agency that borrows in the private market and provides funds to agriculture.

BANK INSURANCE FUND: A fund administered by the FDIC to insure bank deposits.

BANKER'S ACCEPTANCES: An order to pay drawn on a bank's customers that the bank has agreed to pay on the customers' behalf.

BASE: Reserves of depository institutions plus currency held by the public.

BETA COEFFICIENT: A measure of the undiversifiable risk of a stock. It measures the sensitivity of a stock's price to the overall movement of stock prices.

BID-ASK SPREAD: The difference between the prices at which someone offers to buy or to sell the identical item.

BILLS OF EXCHANGE: A method by which importers and exporters settled debts denominated in foreign currencies. A bill of exchange was effectively a postdated check.

BIMETALLIC SYSTEM: A system in which currency is denominated in two metals (traditionally gold and silver) and redeemable in them at a fixed rate.

BOARD OF GOVERNORS: A seven-member board in charge of certain central functions of the Federal Reserve System. It sets reserve requirements and the discount rate and has a majority vote in the Federal Open Market Committee's decisions on open-market operations.

BRETTON WOODS SYSTEM: A system adopted after World War II that established the International Monetary Fund and the World Bank and provided for the occasional adjustment of exchange rates.

BROAD MONEY: See *M-2* and *M-3*.

BUNDESBANK: The German central bank.

CALL OPTION (or CALL): The right to buy a security at a previously specified price.

CALL PROTECTION: The protection that the holder of a bond has against its being redeemed before maturity; often it is the right to receive a special payment if the bond is redeemed before maturity.

CAMBRIDGE EQUATION: $M = kY$, where M is money, k is the proportion of income held as money, and Y is income.

CAMBRIDGE *k*: The proportion of income held as money.

CAMEL: An acronym for a set of criteria used in bank examination: capital adequacy, quality of management, earnings, and liquidity.

CAPITAL: The net worth of a firm; that is the value of its owners' stake in it or the value of its assets minus its debts. It is an entry on the liabilities side of the balance sheet.

CAPITAL-ACCOUNT BALANCE: The balance on all transactions in assets with nonresidents including items such as equities, direct investment, and bonds.

CAPITAL ASSETS PRICING MODEL (CAPM): A model of asset pricing that has the price of an asset depend on its expected return and its undiversifiable risk.

CASH ITEMS IN THE PROCESS OF COLLECTION: Checks that a bank has sent for clearing to the bank on which they are drawn, but that have not yet cleared.

CASUALTY COMPANIES: Firms that insure against certain losses, other than loss of life, such as fire, theft, and floods.

CENTRAL BANKS: Governmental institutions charged with preventing financial panics, the management of monetary policy, and certain other functions, such as supervising banks. The Federal Reserve, the Bank of England, and the Bundesbank are examples.

CERTIFICATES OF DEPOSIT: Time deposits evidenced by a certificate. They do not allow checking, but pay interest.

CHICAGO SCHOOL: In macroeconomics, a group of economists led by Milton Friedman, who adhere to monetarism.

CHIPS: Clearing House Interbank Payments System, a system for clearing wire transfers of funds (particularly international transfers).

CLEARING BALANCES: Balances maintained by banks at a Federal Reserve Bank to clear checks and electronic transfers.

COLA: Cost of living adjustment.

COLLATERAL: An asset that is used as security for a loan.

COMMERCIAL BANKS: Banks that take deposits and are less restricted in making business loans than are savings and loans and mutual savings banks.

COMMODITY MONEY: Full-bodied commodity money consists of coins, say, silver, whose value as a commodity is equal to their value as a coin.

COMMON STOCK: A financial instrument denoting ownership of a corporation.

COMMUNITY REINVESTMENT ACT: A law requiring banks to serve the reasonable credit needs of the communities in which they are located.

COMPENSATING BALANCES: Deposits that banks require a borrower to maintain with the bank.

CONSUMPTION FUNCTION: The relation between consumption and the variables, such as income, wealth, and interest rates, that determine it.

CONTINGENT CLAIMS: Claims that become effective only if a certain event occurs. Fire insurance is an example.

CONVERTIBLE BOND: A bond that can be converted at a fixed date into common stock at a fixed price.

CORRESPONDENT BANKS: Banks that have entered into a cooperative arrangement, typically a large city bank and several smaller banks. The large city bank provides certain services to its country correspondent banks, who keep deposits with it.

COST-PUSH INFLATION: An inflation generated by an upward shift of the supply curve, due to such factors as higher import prices, poor harvests, or union militancy.

COUPON: The interest payable (usually semiannually) on a security.

CPI: The consumer price index, a measure of prices paid by consumers.

CRAWLING-PEG EXCHANGE SYSTEM: A system that allows central banks to change their parities at will and assumes that monetary authorities will then peg the currency. These changes are assumed to happen so frequently and for such small amounts that effectively the pegging would continually lag the change in parities.

CREDIT CHANNEL: The way monetary policy changes aggregate demand by affecting the availability of credit from various lenders.

CREDIT CRUMBLE: The reluctance of banks in the early 1990s to make loans.

CREDIT MONEY: Money that does not have a commodity value equal to its monetary value and cannot be redeemed in such money.

CREDIT RATIONING: The refusal to lend to everyone who is willing to pay the prevailing interest rate.

CREDIT RISK: Default risk.

CREDIT UNIONS: Depository institutions that make mainly consumer loans and some mortgage loans to their members.

CREDIT VIEW: An approach that stresses not the quantity of money, but the quantity and availability of various types of credit.

CROWDING IN: A rise in private expenditures as government expenditures raise private-sector wealth.

CROWDING OUT: Generally the negative effect of an increase in one type of expenditures on other expenditures. Often used more specifically to denote the negative effect of government deficits on private expenditures.

CURRENCY BOARD: A governmental agency, existing in some countries, that allows the currency supply to change only in one-to-one accord with changes in the country's holdings of foreign currency reserves.

CURRENT-ACCOUNT BALANCE: The balance on all international transactions in commodities and services, such as tourism, license fees, investment income, private remittances, and gifts.

CUSTOMER RELATIONSHIP: The tendency of banks to establish a long-term relationship with firms that borrow from them.

DEFAULT RISK: The risk that a borrower will not repay a loan or make the required interest payments.

DEMAND DEPOSITS: Checking deposits that pay no interest.

DEMAND-PULL INFLATION: An inflation generated by excess demand.

DEPOSIT ASSUMPTION: The FDIC's taking on itself the liability for paying off the insured deposits of a failed bank.

DEPOSIT MULTIPLIER: The coefficient relating money to a reserves variable. There are separate deposit multipliers for *M-1, M-2,* and *M-3* and for the base, total reserves, and unborrowed reserves.

DERIVATIVES: Strictly speaking, securities whose values are derived from the values of other securities that collateralize them. The term is sometimes used more broadly to denote exotic and risky financial instruments.

DESK: The unit at the New York Federal Reserve Bank that carries out open-market operations.

DIRECTIVE: The instructions about open-market operations that the FOMC sends to the New York Federal Reserve Bank at the end of its meetings.

DISCOUNT RATE (in monetary policy):   The rate at which the Federal Reserve lends to depository institutions.

DISCOUNTING: Making a loan and subtracting the interest payment from the amount lent. For example, if the interest payment on a $1,000 loan is $100, the borrower receives only $900, not $1,000.

DISTRIBUTED LAGS: If *X* affects *Y*, not just in one period, but in several periods, the lag in its effect is called a distributed lag.

DOUBLE COINCIDENCE OF WANTS: A situation in which A's demand for good X happens to coincide with B's willingness to supply X and B's demand for good Y happens to coincide with A's willingness to supply Y.

DURATION: A measure of the time over which the purchase of a security ties up the buyer's funds, taking into account interest received during the life of the security.

EARNING ASSETS: The assets of depository institutions on which they earn a direct yield, for example, securities, but not reserves.

EFFICIENT-MARKETS THEORY: The theory that markets make efficient use of all the available information, so that asset prices are set at their equilibrium values.

ELECTRONIC PURSES: Prepaid cards that can be used to make payments that are electrically deducted from the balance on the card.

ELIGIBLE PAPER: Promissory notes discounted by banks that the bank can, in turn, discount again at the Federal Reserve.

EMPIRICAL DEFINITION OF MONEY: A way of defining money that focuses on which measure of money is most useful in predicting and controlling changes in income.

ENDOGENOUS-MONEY VIEW: The view that the supply of money is determined in large part by the demand for money.

EURODOLLAR DEPOSITS: Deposits denominated in U.S. dollars in banks outside the United States.

EUROMARK DEPOSITS: Deposits denominated in Deutschmarks (the Germany currency unit) in banks outside Germany.

EUROPEAN COMMUNITY (EC):   A group of Western European nations establishing a common market by eliminating barriers to trade and investment.

EUROPEAN CURRENCY UNIT (ECU):   A currency unit universally accepted within the European Community. It has yet to be fully established.

EUROPEAN MONETARY SYSTEM: A system by which the currencies of its member nations are fixed within fairly narrow bands.

EXCESS RESERVES: Total reserves minus required reserves.

EXCHANGE RATE: The price of foreign money in terms of domestic money.

EXPECTATIONS-AUGMENTED PHILLIPS CURVE: A Phillips curve that relates wage or price increases to the expected inflation rate, as well as to the unemployment rate.

EXPECTATIONS EFFECT (on interest rates):   The effect on interest rates or expectations about the inflation rate.

EXTENDED CREDIT: Longer-term loans by the Federal Reserve to a depository institution that faces a reserve shortage that is not amenable to quick adjustment.

FACE VALUE: The amount for which a bond or other fixed-income security is to be redeemed at maturity.

FDIC: Federal Deposit Insurance Corporation, a federal agency that insures deposits up to a certain limit, currently $100,000.

FEDERAL FUNDS: Deposits at the Federal Reserve that can be transferred by wire. They consist mainly of the reserves of depository institutions.

FEDERAL FUNDS RATE: The interest rate on federal funds.

FEDERAL HOME LOAN BANK BOARD: A now defunct federal agency that supervised savings and loan associations.

FEDERAL HOME LOAN BANKS: Federal agencies that supervise savings and loan associations and provide loans to them.

FEDERAL HOME LOAN MORTGAGE CORPORATION (FREDDIE MACK): A government corporation that obtains funds in the private market and makes them available to savings and loan associations.

FEDERAL INTERMEDIATE CREDIT BANKS: Government agencies that borrow in the private market and provide intermediate-term loans to agriculture.

FEDERAL NATIONAL MORTGAGE ASSOCIATION (FANNY MAE): Formerly a government agency, now a private corporation, that channels funds into the home mortgage market by selling its own securities and making the funds available to mortgage lenders.

FEDERAL OPEN MARKET COMMITTEE (FOMC): The main policy-making part of the Federal Reserve System. It determines open-market operations.

FEDERAL RESERVE BANKS: The 12 regional organs of the Federal Reserve System.

FEDERAL RESERVE BOARD: An older name for what is now the Board of Governors of the Federal Reserve System.

FEDERAL SAVINGS AND LOAN INSURANCE CORPORATION (FSLIC): A now defunct federal agency that insured savings and loan associations and mutual savings banks.

FEDWIRE: The Federal Reserve's wire system for transferring funds.

FEEDBACK RULES (for monetary policy): Proposed rules for the growth rate of an aggregates variable, such as the base. The rule sets out the response of the aggregates variable to such factors as the gap between potential and actual GDP.

FIAT STANDARD: A monetary standard under which money does not consist of full-bodied commodity money and is not convertible into full-bodied commodity money.

FINANCIAL INTERMEDIARIES: Institutions that issue claims on themselves and hold claims on others.

FIRREA: Financial Institutions Reform, Recovery and Enforcement Act, the law that dealt with the savings and loan debacle.

FISHER EFFECT: The tendency for nominal interest rates to incorporate an adjustment for the expected inflation rate.

FISHER PROPOSITION: The proposition that interest-rate differentials between countries are offset by expected changes in their exchange rates, so that domestic and foreign securities appear to be equally good investments.

FLOAT: The float (specifically "bank float") is the value of the checks for which the Federal Reserve has credited the depositing banks, but not yet debited the banks on which they are drawn.

FLOATERS: Securities with interest rates that vary directly with variations in other interest rates or asset prices.

FLOATING EXCHANGE RATES: Foreign-exchange rates that are free to vary depending on supply and demand.

FORWARD DISCOUNT: A situation when a currency is less expensive in the forward market than in the spot market.

FORWARD PREMIUM: A situation when a currency is more expensive in the forward market than in the spot market.

FORWARD TRANSACTIONS (specifically in foreign-exchange markets): Transactions with deferred payments, usually 30, 60, 90, or 180 days after the date of the contract.

FREE BANKING: A system that imposes very few restrictions on opening and operating a bank.

FREE RESERVES: Excess reserves minus borrowed reserves (other than seasonal or extended borrowings).

FRICTIONAL UNEMPLOYMENT: Unemployment due not to a shortage in available jobs, but to a mismatch between available workers and available jobs or to a lack of information about available jobs.

FULL-BODIED MONEY: A monetary unit that has a value as a commodity equal to its face value.

GDP TARGETING: The policy of using GDP as the target variable for monetary policy.

GIRO: A payments system used by many countries in which the payments process is initiated by the recipient.

GOLD BULLION STANDARD: A system by which relative values of different currencies are determined using gold as the measure. It requires ready convertibility of money into gold and free import and export of gold.

GOLD COIN STANDARD: A system under which gold coins form the standard money and have a value as gold equal to their value as coins.

GOLD-EXCHANGE STANDARD: A system under which domestic currency is convertible not directly into gold, but into another currency that is convertible into gold.

GOLD STANDARD: A monetary standard under which the monetary unit is either gold or is convertible into gold, together with unrestricted importation and exportation of gold.

GOVERNMENT NATIONAL MORTGAGE ASSOCIATION (GINNE MAE): A government agency that supports the mortgage market by such activities as guaranteeing a package of mortgages, so that they can be securitized.

HEDGE FINANCE: A situation in which borrowers expect to be able to repay debts out of their incomes.

HEDGING: Combining assets (or assets and debts) that respond in opposite ways to certain risks, so that the combination is less risky than each of the assets individually.

HIGH-POWERED MONEY: Reserves of depository institutions plus currency held by the public.

HUMAN CAPITAL: The discounted value of a person's future earnings.

HYPERINFLATION: A very severe inflation; a common definition is an inflation rate of over 50 percent per month.

IMF: International Monetary Fund.

IMPLICIT CONTRACTS: Informal agreements or mutual expectations, such as employees not shirking even when they know they will not be caught and, in return, not being replaced whenever unemployed workers can be hired at a lower wage.

INCOME AND PRICE EFFECTS (on interest rates): The rise in the interest rate subsequent to an increase in the money supply, as the higher money supply raises incomes and prices.

INCOME-EXPENDITURE THEORY: A theory that explains changes in nominal income by focusing on the motives for expenditures.

INCOME VELOCITY: The number of times per year that the average dollar of money becomes income.

INCOMES POLICY: A policy of trying to curb inflation by devices ranging from appeals for wage and price restraint to laws prohibiting wage and price increases.

INDEXING: Provisions for automatic increases in wages, prices, and so on, tied to the behavior of a price index.

INDIRECT BARTER: A situation in which someone barters a good for another good he or she does not intend to consume, but to use for further barter.

INDUCED ACCOUNT OR CATEGORY: The net total of all imports or exports of monetary gold and foreign-exchange reserves.

INFLATION: A significant and sustained rise in the general price level.

INFLATION PREMIUM: That component of the nominal interest rate that is intended to offset the decline in the real value of the principal.

INSIDE LAG: The lag from the time that the need for a different policy arises until this policy is adopted.

INSIDE MONEY: Money that is a debt of a member of the private sector, such as a bank deposit.

INSTRUMENTS: Variables that the Fed uses as intermediate steps in its attempt to attain its target variables.

INTEREST-RATE PARITY THEOREM: A theorem relating the money-market interest-rate differential to the difference between the spot and forward exchange rates.

INTEREST-RATE PEGGING: The policy of not allowing interest rates on government securities to exceed a specified level.

INTEREST-RATE RISK: The risk that the value of a security will change due to a change in interest rates.

INTEREST-RATE SWAPS: An arrangement under which borrowers swap their loan liabilities. For example, a firm may swap its liability under a fixed-rate loan for another firm's liability under a variable-rate loan.

INTERNATIONAL BANK FOR RECONSTRUCTION AND DEVELOPMENT (IBRD): The official name of the World Bank.

INTERNATIONAL MONETARY FUND (IMF): An international institution that manages a pool of currencies that individual countries might borrow. It also advises on and evaluates stabilization programs and exchange rates.

INTERNATIONAL RESERVES: Gold, Special Drawing Rights, and securities held by central banks denominated in currencies other than their own.

INTERNATIONAL TRADE ORGANIZATION (ITO): An organization set up to regulate the rules of international trade, such as tariff levels.

INVERSE FLOATERS: Securities with interest rates that vary inversely with variations in other interest rates.

INVESTMENT: As used in macroeconomics, this term refers to increases in the stock of capital.

INVESTMENT BANKS: Financial institutions (not to be confused with "banks" in the ordinary sense of the term) that help firms to issue securities and provide other services, such as arranging mergers and acquisitions.

IS CURVE: A curve in the income–interest rate plane that relates each interest rate to the level of income that corresponds to it.

IS-LM DIAGRAM: A diagram relating interest rates and income to show the combination of interest rates and income levels that equilibrate the markets for goods, money, and (implicitly) securities.

KEYNESIAN CROSS: A diagram relating aggregate expenditure and its components to income.

LDC: Less-developed countries, sometimes called "third-world countries."

LEGAL TENDER: Something that must be accepted in settlement of a debt unless some other form of settlement has been specified.

LENDER OF LAST RESORT: A lender (usually the central bank) that makes loans to banks and perhaps other financial institutions as a means of preventing financial crises.

LETTER OF CREDIT: A document stating that a bank will accept drafts drawn on it on behalf of a customer.

LIABILITY MANAGEMENT: Depository institutions determining the inflow of funds by such means as changing the interest rate they pay on large certificates of deposit, or purchasing federal funds.

LIBOR: The London Interbank Offering Rate, the rate at which very large banks lend to each other. It is used as a base rate in setting interest rates on some large loans.

LIFE-CYCLE HYPOTHESIS: A theory relating consumption to a household's total wealth, including its human wealth.

LINE OF CREDIT: An arrangement by which a borrower can borrow up to a certain amount more or less automatically.

LIQUIDITY: An attribute of an asset relating to the ability to get money for it. It depends on (1) how fast the asset can be sold at a normal price, (2) the transactions costs of selling it, and (3) the stability and predictability of its price.

LIQUIDITY EFFECT (on interest rates): The initial effect of changes in the money supply that move interest rates in the opposite direction.

LIQUIDITY PREMIUM: The payment needed to compensate the holder of an asset for giving up liquidity.

LIQUIDITY TRAP: A hypothetical situation in which interest rates are so low that any additional funds will be held as money rather than as securities.

LM CURVE: A curve in the income–interest rate plane that equates supply and demand in the money market.

LUCAS CRITIQUE: The proposition that since a change in policy changes people's behavior, one should not use their past behavior to predict the effect of the new policy.

LUCAS SUPPLY FUNCTION: An aggregate supply function that slopes upward only because suppliers are not able to distinguish quickly between changes in the aggregate demand and changes in the relative demand for their goods.

M-1: A narrow definition of money based on immediate spendability. It includes currency, traveler's checks, and checking deposits.

M-2: A broad definition of money that adds small savings and time deposits and certain money-market funds, overnight repurchase agreements, and Eurodollars to *M-1*.

M-3: A broad definition of money that adds to *M-2* large time deposits and those money-market funds, repurchase agreements, and Eurodollars that are not included in *M-2*.

MARGINAL EFFICIENCY OF INVESTMENT: The increase in the value of output resulting from a small amount of investment.

MARGINAL PRODUCTIVITY OF CAPITAL: The change in the value of output resulting from a small change in capital stock.

MARKET EQUILIBRIUM CURVE: A curve tracing out the combination of points on the axes at which the market is in equilibrium.

MARKET RISK: The risk that the value of an asset will change because of a change in interest rates.

MARKING TO MARKET: Carrying securities on the books at their actual market values rather than at their acquisition values.

MATCHED SALE-PURCHASE TRANSACTIONS: The purchase of securities under an agreement to resell them at a fixed date at a fixed price. Also called "reverse repos."

McFADDEN ACT: A federal law that from 1927 until 1997 required national banks to observe the same branching restrictions as state banks. It effectively prevented the establishment of interstate branches of banks.

MEDIUM OF EXCHANGE: Any item that is generally accepted as payment in a broad enough range of transactions.

MEMBER BANKS: Banks that are members of the Federal Reserve System.

MERCHANDISE TRADE BALANCE: The value of all goods exported minus the value of imports.

MINT PARITY: Exchange rates that correspond to the relative gold values of currencies.

MODIGLIANI-MILLER THEOREM: The theorem that under certain conditions the costs of funds to a corporation is the same from borrowing as from selling stock.

MONETARIST EXPERIMENT: A policy of the Fed from October 1979 to the fall of 1982 that attempted to control the money supply more accurately by allowing much greater variations in interest rates. Whether this policy was really "monetarist" is disputed.

MONETARY AGGREGATES: These are the following targets and instruments: measures of the money supply, credit, and reserves.

MONETARY BASE: Also called the "base," consists of the reserves of depository institutions and currency held by the public.

MONETARY STANDARD: The system of laws, customs, and expectations that regulates monetary policy.

MONETIZATION OF FEDERAL DEBT: A process by which the Federal Reserve buys government securities held by the public, and thus reduces the government debt held by the public, but increases the base, and hence the money supply.

MONEY: Something that functions as a medium of exchange or a standard of value. (See also medium of exchange, standard of value, *M-1, M-2,* and *M-3.*)

MONEY DEMAND FUNCTION: The relation between the demand for money and the variables, such as income and interest rates, that determine it.

MONEY-MARKET MUTUAL FUNDS: Firms that invest the funds they receive from their stockholders in very safe, short-term securities, such as Treasury bills and commercial paper.

MONEY SUBSTITUTES: Highly liquid assets, such as Treasury bills, that are held instead of money because they pay a higher interest rate.

MONEY SUPPLY THEORY: The theory relating the money multiplier to its determinants.

MORAL HAZARD: The hazard resulting from a contract changing the behavior of one of the parties to it. For example, insuring one's car against theft reduces one's incentive to lock the car.

MPC: Marginal propensity to consume, the change in consumption resulting from a small change in income.

MULTIPLIER: The relation between a change in investment (or other exogenous expenditures, such as government expenditures and exports) and changes in income.

MUTUAL FUNDS: Funds that hold securities and sell their own securities to the public.

NAIRU: The lowest rate of unemployment that is compatible with the inflation rate not accelerating.

NARROW BANK: A proposed type of bank that holds only highly liquid and safe assets, such as Treasury bills, and does not make loans.

NARROW MONEY: *M-1,* currency, traveler's checks, and checkable deposits.

NATIONAL BANKS: Banks chartered by the federal government.

NATURAL RATE OF UNEMPLOYMENT: The lowest rate of unemployment that does not generate accelerating inflation.

NEAR-MONEY: An asset that is highly liquid but not as liquid as money. An example is a Treasury bill. The exact definition of near-money depends on whether one defines money as *M-1, M-2,* or *M-3.*

NEW CLASSICAL THEORY: A theory based on the propositions that expectations are rational and that markets clear quickly.

NOMINAL INCOME: Income in current dollars, that is, income not adjusted for inflation

NOMINAL INTEREST RATE: The interest rate as stated without an adjustment for changes in the purchasing power of the principal or the interest payments.

OFF-BALANCE-SHEET FINANCING: A bank's financing of its customers in ways that do not show up on its balance sheet.

OFFICE OF THRIFT SUPERVISION: The federal agency that supervises savings and loan associations.

OFFSHORE BANKING MARKET: A group of banks that take deposits and make loans in a currency other than the currency of the country in which they are located.

OPEN-MARKET OPERATIONS: The purchase or sale of securities by the Federal Reserve System.

OPTIMUM CURRENCY AREA: The optimum size of the region in which there should be a single currency and hence a single monetary policy.

OTHER CHECKABLE DEPOSITS: Deposits with unlimited check writing that pay interest.

OUTSIDE LAG: The lag from the time a new policy is adopted until it has its effect.

OUTSIDE MONEY: Money that is the debt of the government, such as currency and bank reserves, or the debt of foreigners.

P*:   The equilibrium price level given the supply of money.

PEGGED EXCHANGE RATES: Exchange rates that are kept fixed.

PERMANENT INCOME: The discounted value of the lifetime income stream. The term is often used loosely to denote long-run average income.

PERMANENT-INCOME THEORY: A theory relating consumption primarily to long-run (permanent) income rather than to the income received during a short period, such as a year.

PHILLIPS CURVE: A curve relating the rate of wage or price increases to the unemployment rate.

POLITICAL BUSINESS CYCLES: A policy of adopting expansionary policies before elections and offsetting restrictive policies after elections.

PONZI FINANCE: A situation in which borrowers expect to be able to service a debt only by renewed borrowing.

PORTFOLIO: All the assets a person owns. The term can also be used in a broader sense to include debts owed.

PORTFOLIO MANAGEMENT: Administering a portfolio to maximize the utility of its combination of yield and risk.

PORTFOLIO RISK: The risk of the entire portfolio, as distinct from the risk of any particular asset in it.

POST-BRETTON WOODS SYSTEM: The current exchange-rate system which allows currencies to float against other currencies and where rates are determined by demand and supply.

POST-KEYNESIAN THEORY: A version of Keynesian theory that stresses uncertainty, the role of money as a protection against uncertainty, instability, and the path dependence of macroeconomic events.

PRECAUTIONARY DEMAND: The demand for money to safeguard against unexpected needs for money or to take advantage of bargains.

PREFERRED STOCK: Stock on which a minimum dividend has to be paid before any dividend can be paid on common stock.

PRIMARY CAPITAL: The capital that represents the equity of a bank's owners. It consists mainly of outstanding stock and surplus and retained earnings.

PRIMARY MARKETS: Markets in which securities are sold for the first time.

PRIMARY RESERVES: Vault cash, deposits with the Federal Reserve, and deposits with other banks.

PRIME RATE: The interest rate charged business borrowers that meet certain fairly high standards.

PRIVATE MONEY: Money issued by banks with very little government supervision or regulation.

PUBLIC-CHOICE THEORY: The theory that government officials pursue policies that are in their self-interest.

PUBLIC-INTEREST THEORY: The theory that government officials pursue the public interest.

PURCHASING-POWER PARITY (PPP): The relation between the prices of tradable goods in different countries and the exchange rates of their currencies. Purchasing-power parity is achieved when exchange rates exactly reflect the relative purchasing powers of currencies.

PURCHASING-POWER RISK: The risk that inflation will reduce the real value of a debt by more than was expected.

PUT: The right to sell a security at a previously fixed price.

Q **THEORY OF INVESTMENT:** A theory that explains the volume of investment by comparing the cost of constructing new capital assets with the prices at which such capital assets can be bought in the security markets.

QUANTITY THEORY: A theory that attributes changes in nominal income primarily to changes in the supply of money.

RANDOM WALK: A variable, say stock prices, is said to be a random walk if its future behavior cannot be predicted from its past behavior.

RATIONAL-EXPECTATIONS THEORY: The theory that in forming their expectations people make effective use of all the available information.

REAL BALANCE EFFECT: The effect on aggregate demand and hence on prices of a disequilibrium in the supply and demand of real balances. Whether these balances include government securities and inside money or just outside money is controversial.

REAL-BILLS DOCTRINE: The belief that monetary policy should concern itself not with the quantity of money and credit, but with the quality of the loans made by banks and should accommodate changes in the demand for reserves arising from the changes in the demand for credit for productive uses.

REAL BUSINESS CYCLES: Fluctuations in GDP due to changes in supply, such as faster productivity growth, lower real wages, and higher supply of labor at the prevailing real wage.

REAL INCOME: Income stated in dollars of constant purchasing power.

REAL INTEREST RATE: The nominal interest rate adjusted for inflation by subtracting the inflation rate from the nominal interest rate.

REDLINING: Refusal to make mortgage loans or offer insurance in certain areas because of the low incomes or minority status of their residents.

REGULATION Q: A regulation that imposed ceilings on the interest rates that depository institutions could pay their time and savings depositors. It was phased out in the early 1980s.

REPOS: Repurchase agreements.

REPRESENTATIVE FULL-BODIED MONEY: A monetary unit that has a value as a commodity that is less than its face value, but can be exchanged for another type of money (full-bodied money) that does have a commodity value equal to its face value.

REPURCHASE AGREEMENTS (REPOS): Agreements in which people who sell securities agree to buy them back at fixed prices at certain dates. Essentially collateralized loans.

REVERSE REPOS: Agreements to buy securities and resell them at certain dates at fixed prices. More formally called "matched sale-purchase transactions."

RICARDIAN EQUIVALENCE: The theory that government deficit spending does not raise income because the public, realizing that this implies higher taxes in the future, cuts back correspondingly on its consumption.

RISK: As used in economics, the risk of an asset refers to the probability of a change—in either direction—of the asset's value.

RULES OF THE GAME: Under the gold standard, countries with balance-of-payments surpluses were expected to follow expansionary monetary policies, and countries with deficits were to follow restrictive policies.

SACRIFICE RATIO: The percentage increase in unemployment required to lower the inflation rate by 1 percentage point.

SAVINGS AND LOAN ASSOCIATIONS: Depository institutions making mainly mortgage loans.

SAVINGS ASSOCIATION INSURANCE FUND: A fund administered by the FDIC to insure deposits in savings and loans and some mutual savings banks.

SAVINGS BANKS: Depository institutions that make mainly mortgage loans, but have a greater freedom of asset choices than savings and loans have.

SECONDARY CAPITAL: Certain long-term borrowing by a bank that it can count as part of its capital.

SECONDARY MARKETS: Markets in which previously issued securities are bought a second time.

SECONDARY RESERVES: Assets that are highly liquid, but not as liquid as primary reserves.

SECURITIZATION: The issuance of homogeneous, and hence more marketable, securities backed by a pool of heterogeneous loans, such as mortgages.

SEIGNIORAGE: The profit the government earns on the creation of money.

SELECTIVE CONTROLS: Federal Reserve control over specific channels of credit. The only current selective control is control over margin purchases of securities.

SHOE-LEATHER COSTS: The costs and inconveniences that result from holding only a limited proportion of one's total assets as currency.

SMITHSONIAN AGREEMENT: An arrangement entered into in 1972 that set exchange rates accompanying the devaluation of the U.S. dollar. These new exchange rates held for only about a year.

SPECIAL DRAWING RIGHTS: A payments medium created by the International Monetary Fund for its members.

SPECULATIVE FINANCE: A situation in which borrowers expect to be able to repay debts only by selling some of their assets.

SPOT TRANSACTIONS (specifically in foreign-exchange markets): Transactions requiring payment within two days.

STANDARD OF DEFERRED PAYMENT: The units in which debts are expressed.

STANDARD OF VALUE: The measuring rod of economic values, for example, the dollar in the United States and the yen in Japan.

STANDBY LETTER OF CREDIT: A bank's agreement to guarantee a customer's liability, such as the repayment of a loan from a third party.

STATE BANKS: Banks chartered by a state government.

STICKY WAGES AND PRICES: Wages and prices that are slow to adjust to changes in supply and demand.

STRIPPING: Dividing the ownership rights of a security into parts (such as the right to obtain interest or dividends and the right to obtain any capital gains) that can be sold separately.

TARGET VARIABLES (TARGETS): Variables that the Fed uses as intermediate steps in its attempt to influence real income and inflation.

TERM LOANS: Loans with a maturity of five years or more.

THRIFTS: Savings and loans, mutual savings banks, and credit unions.

TIME INCONSISTENCY: A policy is time inconsistent if it is the preferred policy at one time but not at other times without the preferred outcomes having changed.

TRANSACTIONS DEMAND: The demand for money arising from transactions.

TRANSACTIONS DEPOSITS: Deposits on which an unlimited number of checks can be written.

TRANSACTIONS VELOCITY: The number of times per year that the average dollar of money becomes a receipt to someone.

TREASURY CURRENCY Currency issued by the U.S. Treasury as distinct from the Federal Reserve. It consists essentially of coins and one dollar bills.

TREATY OF ROME: An agreement in 1957 that led to the elimination of tariffs on internal trade among members of the European Community and to the development of a common external tariff and agricultural policy.

UNBORROWED RESERVES: Total reserves minus borrowings from the Federal Reserve.

UNDERWRITING (of securities): The purchase by investment banks of securities issued by a corporation to be resold to the public.

UNIVERSAL BANKS: Banks that provide a wide variety of financial services and have close connections with nonfinancial firms. They do not exist in the United States.

USER COST OF CAPITAL: A measure of the cost of using capital, consisting of depreciation and obsolescence, and the firm's cost of funds, including opportunity costs.

VARIANCE: The sum of the squared deviations from the mean divided by the number of observations. It is equal to the square of the standard deviation.

VAULT CASH: The currency held in the premises and automatic teller machines of a depository institution.

WORLD BANK: An international institution that makes loans to developing countries.

YIELD CURVE: A curve relating the yields of securities to their maturities.

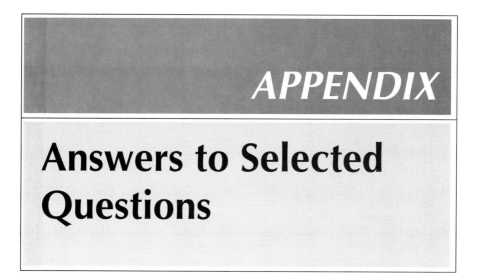

APPENDIX

Answers to Selected Questions

Note: Many of the questions are intended to elicit thinking rather than rote replies. Hence, they do not have a single "correct" answer. Even for factual questions, different, equally good answers may bring in different facts by selecting different details from among those given in the book.

CHAPTER 1

2. This is a meaningless question since it does not specify the period over which income is measured. Money holdings usually exceed hourly but not yearly income.

5. Money is more liquid than other assets. One does not have to exchange it for anything else to spend it. Its value in terms of the standard of value and debts is fixed.

7. Credit money has value because other people are willing to accept it in exchange for their goods and services.

10. We do not generally give money for Christmas gifts because it is a standard of value and we do not want the recipient to know exactly how much the gift cost.

CHAPTER 2

1. Such a memo might point out that, since finance provides control over resources, an underdeveloped, and thus inefficient, financial industry would cause an economy's resources to be misallocated. It might also mention that an inefficient financial system would provide too low a reward to savers and charge borrowers too much, so that saving and investment would be too low.

3. Suppose interest rates on newly issued bonds go up, say from 6 to 7 percent. Holders of the old 6 percent bonds who want to sell them have to lower the price to induce someone to buy a 6 percent bond when they can buy a 7 percent bond of the same maturity and degree of risk. Conversely, if interest rates fall, buyers compete for the old, higher-yielding bonds and drive up their price. But bond prices do not change in

strict proportion to the interest rate because the bond will ultimately be redeemed at its face value. Suppose, for example, that the interest rate falls from 8 to 4 percent. Anyone who looks just at the annual interest received would then be tempted to pay up to $2,000 for an 8 percent $1,000 bond because, regardless of whether he buys one old bond for $2,000 or two new bonds for $1,000 each, he would receive $80 of interest. But if he pays as much as $2,000 for the old bond he would be sorely disappointed when the bond matures and he gets back only $1,000 instead of the $2,000 he paid for the bond. Hence, rational investors will only pay less than $2,000 for the old 8 percent bond.

CHAPTER 3

2. One reason is moral hazard. If you are insured against being fired, you have less incentive to work hard enough to keep your job, and are therefore more likely to be fired. (*Note:* The government's unemployment insurance system is only a partial insurance system since it replaces only a part of your lost wages. It also has a provision about being fired "for cause.") Another reason is adverse selection. Employees often know better than an insurance company could whether they are about to be fired. Those who know that the probability is high are much more likely to buy insurance than those who think it is low.

5. Any variety of examples might be appropriate, for example, being less careful about locking your door because you have burglary insurance as an example of moral hazard, purchasing more life insurance because you believe you have a weak heart or having your firm repurchase its stock because you have reason to think that its profits will be higher than the market expects as examples of asymmetric information, and offering a money-back guarantee as an example of signaling.

CHAPTER 4

1. One basic distinction is that between wholesale and retail markets. Another is the distinction between auction markets and over-the-counter markets.

3. Purchasing derivatives can increase *or* reduce risk. It depends on the correlation of the risk of the derivative with the risk of the rest of the buyer's portfolio. For example, buying some derivatives that fall in price when interest rates rise reduces the risk of a portfolio if the other assets in the portfolio are ones whose prices rise when interest rates rise.

5. Checkable deposits are traded in foreign-exchange markets. A forward exchange contract differs from a spot exchange contract in that the settlement date is more distant.

7. A call option is the right to *buy* a specific amount of a particular security at a specific price from the seller of the call option. A put option is the right to *sell* a specified amount of a security at a specific price to the seller of the put option.

CHAPTER 5

2. The slope of the yield curve depends on expected changes in interest rates and on the liquidity premium.

4. The extreme market segmentation theory implies that investors cannot be bribed to move out of their preferred maturates by differences in the yields of long- and short-term securities. There is no reason why they should act that way.

6. It suggests that the market probably expects short-term interest rates to rise. Since the

market has much information, one can take this as an indication that interest rates will rise. However, one should be cautious. The rise in long-term rates could also be due to an increase in the liquidity premium, or the market could be wrong.

CHAPTER 6

2. Banks are regulated by the requirements set for a bank charter and by bank examinations that see whether the bank is sound and is obeying the various regulations issued by its supervisory authorities. For national banks these are the Office of the Comptroller of the Currency; for state banks, the state banking authority; for member banks (and hence all national banks), the Federal Reserve; and for virtually all banks, the FDIC.

4. a. This is wrong because the FDIC, and to some extent large depositors, share some of the risk that banks take. Moreover, bank failures have unfavorable indirect effects, such as a possible reduction in the money supply and disruptions of the payments mechanism.

   b. Such a proposal would greatly reduce bank failures, but would also raise bank costs and, hence, result in a shrinkage of the banking industry. One can also argue that this would put banks at a competitive disadvantage relative to other financial firms.

7. a. Large banks usually have several smaller correspondent banks, often located outside the main financial centers. These correspondent banks keep demand deposits with the city correspondent bank, which, in turn, provides them with certain services, such as foreign-exchange transactions.

   b. Savings banks are thrift institutions that rely mainly on savings deposits and make mainly loans to households, though they also make some business loans and hold a more diversified set of assets than savings and loans.

   c. Credit unions are the smallest of the three types of thrift institutions, though growing rapidly. They take deposits and make mainly consumer loans.

CHAPTER 7

2. CDs are certificates of deposit, that is, evidence of the ownership of a deposit. Negotiable ones can be sold in the money market; nonnegotiable ones cannot.

4. Credit rationing is the unwillingness of lenders to make a loan to everyone who is willing to pay the prevailing interest rate or the unwillingness to make a loan as large as the borrower wants. The reason banks ration credit is that they cannot be sure that the lender will repay the loan. A risky lender might be willing to pay a very high rate of interest, but may not be around when the time comes to repay the principal.

7. The bank, as the original lender, and often as "Johnny on the spot," is better able to evaluate the riskiness of the loan than the purchaser of the loan is. On the principle that she who has a comparative advantage in doing the job should be the one to do it, it makes sense for the selling bank to bear the risk of the loan.

9. This is nonsense. Banks do not lock up some of their assets as "capital." They can lend out the funds they obtained as capital (say, by retaining earnings) just as much as they can lend out deposits. Capital is an entry on the liability side of the balance sheet and not an entry on the assets side that competes with loans.

CHAPTER 8

1. The rationale for an external currency market is differential national regulation.
2. Most offshore banks—and virtually all the large offshore banks—are branches of domestic banks. These offshore branches cannot close or fail while the head office remains open. And it is unlikely that one of these banks would fail. Thus, it is likely that such a collapse would have little effect on the domestic banking system.

CHAPTER 9

1. This statement is wrong. Banks gain all the rewards for taking risk, but, if the risky investment turns sour, part of the cost is borne by the FDIC. It is a game of "Heads I win; tails you lose (or at least bear some of the loss)."
3. Answers will differ here. On one side of the issue it can be argued that removing deposit ceilings allowed those institutions most willing to take risks—and therefore holding the highest-yielding assets—to bid deposits away from sounder institutions. Moreover, institutions that were failing in any case had an incentive to go for broke, and expanded asset choices allowed them to do so. On the other side it can be argued that the removal of deposit ceilings was necessary because of the threat of disintermediation and that it reduced the riskiness of savings and loans by reducing their concentration on fixed-rate mortgages which have such high interest-rate risk. Moreover, it might be argued that those institutions willing to take excessive risk could have taken such risks by choosing risky assets from among those traditionally available to them.

CHAPTER 10

3. Charging banks extra for taking greater risk seems sensible, and indeed, to a quite limited extent the FDIC now does that. It not only gives banks an incentive to avoid excessive risk taking, but is also fairer to those banks that take fewer risks. On the other hand, there is a question whether the FDIC can determine accurately enough just how much risk a bank is taking.
4. A higher capital requirement not only gives banks an incentive to take less risk, since they are staking more of their funds, but also provides a bigger cushion to absorb losses, and hence makes it less likely that a bank will fail.

CHAPTER 11

1. This statement is essentially correct; central banks do not concern themselves with earning a profit, but with national goals, such as high employment. They generally make loans only to banks—for very different motives than commercial banks—and have as their main functions controlling the money stock and interest rates and preventing massive bank failures. The Fed is totally unconcerned with making a profit; it is run by government officials (except for the vestigial boards of directors).
3. A lender of last resort is an institution that stands ready to make loans to other financial institutions during a time of crisis when other lenders are not able to do so. To be a lender of last resort, it limits the amount it lends at other times.
5. a. The major policy function of the Federal Reserve Banks is that their presidents serve on the FOMC. Their power over the discount rate is minor since the Board of Governors can decide whether to accept their request for a change or can make them change it.

b. The Board of Governors controls reserve requirements and the discount rate and has a majority vote on the FOMC and, hence, on open-market operations. In addition, it controls other tools of monetary policy such as publicity and advising the President and Congress.

c. The FOMC controls open-market operations.

7. There are many examples of this. The member banks "elect" a majority of the directors, but the chairman of the board of directors is a class C director. Large, medium, and small banks vote separately for directors to prevent any group from dominating. Class B directors must be borrower types to balance the class A directors. The bank presidents serve on the FOMC to provide some regional counterweight to the Washington-based Board of Governors. The President nominates Board members with the advice and consent of the Senate and, once they are confirmed, cannot remove them—they have 14-year terms. But the chairman, *qua* chairman, is appointed by the President to a 4-year term.

CHAPTER 12

2. One example would be a regulation that requires banks to enforce a 30-day waiting period for withdrawals of passbook deposits. Given this regulation, passbook accounts should probably not be in *M-2*.

4. There is no clear answer. On the one hand, one can point to food stamps being a highly liquid medium of exchange, so that they should be in *M-1*. On the other hand, they can be used only for certain specific purchases. And if they are to be included in money, how about subway tokens, merchandise coupons, and so on?

CHAPTER 13

1. BANK D

Assets		Liabilities	
reserves with F.R.	$729.00	demand deposits	$7,290.00
loans + securities	$6,561.00		

BANK E

Assets		Liabilities	
reserves with F.R.	$656.10	demand deposits	$6,561.00
loans + securities	$5,904.90		

BANK F

Assets		Liabilities	
reserves with F.R.	$590.49	demand deposits	$5,904.90
loans + securities	$5,314.41		

BANK G

Assets		Liabilities	
reserves with F.R.	$531.44	demand deposits	$5,315.41
loans + securities	$4,783.97		

3. BANK A

Assets		Liabilities	
reserves with F.R.	$5,000	demand deposits	$10,000
loans + securities	$5,000		

BANK B

Assets		Liabilities	
reserves with F.R.	$2,500	demand deposits	$5,000
loans + securities	$2,500		

BANK C

Assets		Liabilities	
reserves with F.R.	$1,250	demand deposits	$2,500
loans + securities	$1,250		

BANK D

Assets		Liabilities	
reserves with F.R.	$625	demand deposits	$1,250
loans + securities	$625		

4. BANK A

Assets		Liabilities	
reserves with F.R.	−$1,500	demand deposits	−$10,000
loans + securities	−$8,500		

BANK B

Assets		Liabilities	
reserves with F.R.	−$1,275	demand deposits	−$8,500
loans + securities	−$7,225		

BANK C

Assets		Liabilities	
reserves with F.R.	−$1,083.75	demand deposits	−$7,225
loans + securities	−$6,141.25		

BANK D

Assets		Liabilities	
reserves with F.R.	−$921.19	demand deposits	−$6,141.25
loans + securities	−$5,220.06		

BANK E

Assets		Liabilities	
reserves with F.R.	−$783.00	demand deposits	−$5,220.06
loans + securities	−$4,437.06		

BANK F

Assets		Liabilities	
reserves with F.R.	−$665.56	demand deposits	−$4,437.05
loans + securities	−$3,771.49		

6. BANK D

Assets		Liabilities	
required reserves with F.R.	−$1,054.75	demand deposits	−$4,219
loans + securities	−$3,164.25		

BANK E

Assets		Liabilities	
required reserves with F.R.	−$791.06	demand deposits	−$3,164.25
loans + securities	−$2,373.19		

BANK F

Assets		Liabilities	
required reserves with F.R.	−$593.29	demand deposits	−$2,373.19

No reduction in loans + securities is required since the bank has sufficient excess reserves.

Deposits destroyed: $10,000 + $7,500 + $5,625 + $4,219 + $3,164.25 + $2,373.19 = $32,881.44

truncated multiplier = $3.29

CHAPTER 14

1. *Sales to a bank:*

Federal Reserve

Assets		Liabilities	
securities held	−	deposits of banks	−

Bank

Assets		Liabilities
reserves with the Federal Reserve	−	
securities held	+	

Sales to the public:
Federal Reserve T account as before

Bank

reserves with Federal Reserve (after check clears)	−	deposits

3. In the long run, unlike in the short run, the Fed can offset unexpected changes in reserves and in the money multiplier. (Another answer would be that if the Fed makes mistakes in estimating the interest rate required to induce the public to demand a certain quantity of money, it can correct that mistake in the long run.)

4. Base includes currency held by the public. Total reserves include required reserves and borrowed reserves.

Answers to Questions from the Appendix

1. Bank reserves increase by the sum of items 1, 2, 4, 5, 6, 9, and 11, minus items 3, 7, 8, 10, 12, and 13, that is, by 29 − 10 = 19.

4. All these statements are false.

   a. The fact that the country has more gold (assuming it was bought from foreigners) does not mean that the money stock has increased. If the country has obtained this gold because its jewelers bought more gold to make into rings, for example, then the money stock would not have increased. More generally, since gold held in the Treasury, or other gold for that matter, is not money, the mere fact that the Treasury has more gold does not *directly* increase the money stock.

   b. The fact that some people are receiving more checks does not increase the money stock because these checks are drawn on the accounts of others. Instead, an increase in float increases bank reserves (not money) because the Fed has given credit for these checks to depositing banks while not yet debiting the accounts of the banks on which they are drawn.

   c. The fact that some of this currency may be deposited later on will raise reserves then, but what happens now is that the amount of currency in circulation has increased, not fallen. More currency in circulation, with total currency constant, means that less currency is held by banks so that reserves have decreased.

   d. Bank borrowing from the Fed increases, instead of decreasing, the banks' reserves with the Fed. Reserves consist of vault cash plus deposits with the Fed, not *net* assets with the Fed. (And even if it did, borrowing would not reduce net assets.)

CHAPTER 15

2. Income velocity is the number of times a dollar of money becomes income; that is, $V = Y/M$. You could write $M = kPY$ where Y is the output of consumer goods, P the price level of consumer goods, and k the proportion of their total expenditures on consumer goods that people hold in the form of money.

4. According to the quantity theory, an increase in the marginal efficiency of investment will cause the interest rate to rise as firms borrow more to take advantage of the opportunities to earn a higher profit. Such a rise in the interest rate, will, in turn, cause velocity to rise. And a rise in velocity will mean a rise in income.

5. 6.7 percent. Under the conditions cited, each 1 percent rise in nominal income involves a $\frac{1}{2}$ percent rise in real income that raises the demand for money by 1 percent. It also implies a $\frac{1}{2}$ percent rise in prices that raises the demand for money by $\frac{1}{2}$ percent, since we can assume that the public wants to hold the same real money stock as before so that the elasticity of demand for money with respect to the price level is unity. Since a 1 percent rise in nominal income is raising the demand for money by $1\frac{1}{2}$ percent, nominal income has to rise by 6.7 percent (10/1.5) for the supply and demand for money to remain in equilibrium.

9. One factor is the dependence of consumption on long-run income, rather than just on income in the current period. Another factor is that investment responds only slowly to changes in sales for several reasons. Firms do not want to invest if sales increase only temporarily. A high rate of investment distracts a firm's efforts from other activities. Moreover a rapid rise in investment, and hence in borrowing, may raise a firm's cost of funds. More generally, if many firms try to invest more at the same time, the rate of interest rises. And it does so also if consumption rises. Such increases in interest rates constrain aggregate demand.

CHAPTER 16

1. Interest is much more important than its share of GDP indicates because the interest rate has important effects on expenditures.

3. The initial effect of a higher monetary growth rate is to lower the interest rate. But this initial effect is soon overcome by another effect. In a price-flexible economy we start out from full employment. Hence, the increase in demand that occurs when the growth rate of money increases drives up the inflation rate. The rise in the inflation rate, in turn, raises the nominal interest rate.

5. If expectations are adaptive, they will never catch up with a continually rising (or falling) inflation rate. Hence, the Fisher effect does not imply that the real interest rate is constant. Rational expectations catch up with the actual inflation rate. Moreover, rational expectations are more accurate than adaptive expectations, so that with rational expectations one would expect the Fisher effect to be more accurate and, hence, real rates more stable than with adaptive expectations.

CHAPTER 17

1. For most people it is not worthwhile to invest income that will be spent during the pay period. However, it is worthwhile to invest savings when they accumulate to a certain sum. This sum is determined by the net interest rate (that is, the interest rate on securities minus the interest rate on money) and the cost and trouble of investing in securities. When the potential yield on investment begins to exceed the cost and trouble of investing, then money balances should be invested. With a high income it

might be worthwhile to invest funds that will be used during the pay period, and also, since savings pile up faster, it becomes worthwhile to invest these savings sooner.

3 There is something to that. It should be obvious without much discussion that the demand for money depends on the interest rate. But it is useful to discuss this topic to see the specific ways in which the demand for money depends on the interest rate.

5. No; other possibilities are net domestic product (a more specific measure of welfare than GDP), personal income (a better measure of the income received by households than GDP or NDP), or disposable personal income (a better measure of the income actually paid out to households than personal income). Still another possibility is final domestic sales, which include imports but exclude exports and inventory investment.

CHAPTER 18

2. Two monotonic curves can intersect at only one point. The answer to the previous question implies that both curves are indeed monotonic.

4. An infinitely interest-elastic supply of money.

6. Government deficit expenditures can crowd out private expenditures in two ways. One is by raising the interest rate. The second, portfolio crowding out, occurs if the public's increased holdings of government securities raises the public's demand for money, so that the LM curve shifts downward. On the other hand, if the public treats government securities as substitutes for money holdings, the LM curve can shift downward by enough to lower interest rates and thereby crowd in public expenditures.

CHAPTER 19

2. No, it does not because the short-run Phillips curve depends on price expectations and the long-run Phillips curve is vertical. If the government selects a menu that involves inflation, it will get less and less of a reduction in unemployment along with the inflation.

4. The aggregate demand curve slopes downward because the higher prices are, the lower real balances (for a given stock of nominal balances) are and, hence, the lower real aggregate expenditures are. The aggregate supply curve slope can be explained along rational expectations lines due to misperceptions of prices. However, the text also gives a more Keynesian and simpler explanation.

5. Since inflation is a *continuous* rise in the price level, supply shocks could *directly* cause inflation only if there were a whole series of negative supply shocks; this is unlikely. However, if monetary policy is accommodative, the efforts of various groups to protect their real incomes by getting higher nominal incomes to offset the rise in prices could result in a single supply shock setting off an inflation. But should that inflation be attributed to the initial supply shock or to the increase in the growth rate of money as the Fed accommodates the supply shock?

CHAPTER 20

1. Friedman describes the transmission process in terms of changes in the supply of money, and not in terms of changes in interest rates. A more important difference is that Friedman does not trace the effect of monetary policy on GDP by looking at the

specific types of expenditures that compose GDP. He believes that we do not know enough to do that correctly, so he looks directly at the historical relation between changes in the money supply and GDP without specifying the particular types of expenditures that are affected by monetary policy.

2. One possible approach is to compare growth rates of money and nominal income or to analyze the behavior of velocity. Another is to make a cross-country comparison. A sophisticated answer might discuss the problem of causality and might propose, for example, seeing whether changes in the monetary growth rates were due to the Fed's decision to change aggregate expenditures, or to a wish to accommodate changes in demand.

3. No; in the quantity theory a change in the money supply is the dominant cause of changes in nominal income, while in the income-expenditure theory it is only one of several factors that change nominal income.

CHAPTER 21

1. Different students may come up with different answers. A general answer is that with the high transactions costs of changing prices and recontracting, wages and prices would not be flexible, though behavior would still be rational. For example, oligopolists may find it hard to obtain implicit agreement on a new price. Or a price may have been extensively advertised and, hence, expensive to change. Moreover, once a wage agreement is reached, it may be costly for both management and unions to renegotiate it and for the union to sell it to its members. Informal contracts, too, are hard, perhaps even harder, to change because of the potentially serious effect on morale of imposing a wage cut that is perceived as unfair.

3. It is difficult to reconcile because, if aggregate expenditure falls, then, as the economy recovers from the recession, one would expect it to move back toward equilibrium. If expenditure stays at the lower (trend-adjusted) level, then we have a situation that differs from the cyclical movements usually ascribed to changes in expenditure, that is, to recessions coming to an end and being succeeded by expansions.

5. They reject the quantity theory because they believe that changes in the money supply are caused by changes in GDP, rather than the reverse.

CHAPTER 22

1. The goals are price stability (or more realistically a low inflation rate), high employment, economic growth, and international equilibrium in the sense of a stable and reasonable exchange rate of the dollar, and a high rate of economic growth.

3. In the long run there is no trade-off between unemployment and inflation; the Phillips curve is vertical. Similarly, in the long run inflation does not raise the rate of economic growth. Nor in the long run do either inflation or high unemployment generate international equilibrium.

CHAPTER 23

2. The advantages of open-market operations are that this is a tool that can be used to achieve small changes in reserves but also very large ones and that it works quickly. In addition, the resulting change in reserves can be predicted precisely, and open-market operations are readily reversible. The discount rate has the (occasional) advantage that it influences expectations in the desired direction via its announce-

ment effect. However, it has several disadvantages. One is that the announcement effect is sometimes undesired. In addition, the Fed cannot predict precisely how reserves will change. Moreover, discount-rate changes can be used to bring about neither very small nor very large changes in reserves, and they cannot be (or at least have not been) undertaken on a continual basis. Changes in reserve requirements also have an announcement effect (which may sometimes be desirable and at other times undesirable), cannot be (or more precisely, for some reason that is not clear, have not been) undertaken in small steps, and cannot be undertaken frequently. Moreover, banks must be given time to adjust to changing reserve requirements. However, unlike discount-rate changes, changes in reserve requirements can have a very strong effect on excess reserves.

3. One possible answer is that depository institutions borrow for profit as well as need, despite the fact that they are not supposed to. Another is that, when interest rates rise, some banks lose deposits to other banks and, thus, then borrow for "need."

CHAPTER 24

1. Suppose that the FOMC knows exactly what the inflation rate will be. In that case it does not matter whether it targets nominal or real GDP since each nominal GDP target is translatable into a specific real GDP target. But the FOMC cannot predict the inflation rate without error, and that is why it does matter whether it uses a nominal or real GDP target. Assume, for example, that it predicts 3 percent inflation and expects real GDP to grow by 2 percent. It will then aim for a 5 percent growth rate of nominal GDP. Suppose its estimate of inflation is wrong and the inflation rate is actually 4 percent instead of 3 percent. A 5 percent growth rate of nominal GDP then means that real GDP rises by only 1 percent. This slower growth rate of real GDP and the resulting increase in unemployment then put downward pressure on the inflation rate.

   In contrast, if the Fed had used a real GDP target, it would have raised nominal GDP as the inflation rate rose. Real GDP would then have continued to grow at the planned 2 percent rate, and there would have been no downward pressure on the inflation rate. In other words, the Fed would have accommodated the higher inflation.

4. Instruments might be described as lower-level targets. They are variables, such as short-term interest rates or unborrowed reserves, that the Fed sets to attain targets such as the long-term interest rate or the money stock.

CHAPTER 25

2. The monetarist approach uses a stable demand function for money, so that a change in the supply of money brings about a predictable change in income. Changes in income, according to this approach, are due primarily to changes in the money stock, rather than to any instability in the private sector. In the Keynesian approach, on the other hand, changes in income are frequently due to such factors as changes in the marginal efficiency of investment. In this approach, moreover, the demand function for money is not so stable, so that the effect of a change in the supply of money could readily be offset or exacerbated by a shift in the demand function. Monetary policy is just one of many factors changing income. Moreover, the effect of a rise in the money stock is partially offset by a movement down the demand curve for money as the interest rate falls. Part of the reason why the impact seems stronger in the monetarist

model is that in this model a rise in the money stock does not lower the interest rate for long. Another reason is that frequently monetarists think that the demand curve for money is less interest elastic and the IS curve more interest elastic than Keynesians believe. In addition, monetarists stress that money affects income through many more channels than just "investment." (An alternative way of answering this question is along the lines that in income-expenditure theory a change in the money stock affects the interest rate and that the interest rate then affects investment, which, together with the multiplier, changes income. There are many slips along this complex chain. In the monetarist approach money affects income directly.

4. The credit market is an imperfect market; many borrowers cannot switch readily between various lenders. A restrictive monetary policy puts pressure in the first instance on banks. Hence, those borrowers, such as small businesses, who are dependent on bank credit are unusually strongly affected by a restrictive monetary policy. Even if a restrictive policy has little overall effect on the total volume of credit outstanding, it can still reduce investment by making it harder for small firms to obtain the bank loans they need to invest. In addition, as interest rates rise, the market value of the assets held by some firms falls. And with this fall in the value of the collateral that they can offer, they become less creditworthy, and therefore obtain fewer funds for investment.

CHAPTER 26

1. The optimal size of stabilization policy depends on the coefficient of correlation between the policy and the original fluctuations in income. A policy stronger than the optimal level will be a less effective stabilizer. And it can easily be so strong that it will actually destabilize income. For example, suppose that the correlation coefficient is zero. Any policy will then increase total fluctuations, and so will a strong policy if the correlation coefficient is negative, but small.

3. There are actually three problems. The Fed must forecast income, it must predict the effect of its policies on income, and it cannot reverse these policies quickly.

4. With a stable lag the Fed could just use an estimate of an average lag. With a variable lag the Fed would have to know the lag for each specific case in which it is considering policy. Econometric models, or for that matter other econometric techniques, may not be much help here. One factor that could account for a variable lag is that at different times different types of investment are affected differently. If heavy construction is affected more significantly, the lag will be longer than if inventory investment is affected more significantly. Another factor is expectation. At times firms may hesitate to respond to an expansionary policy, fearing that it will be reversed soon. At other times they may respond right away. Environmental laws may also slow the effect of monetary policy by lengthening construction periods.

CHAPTER 27

2. This used to be a widely accepted view. The supporters can cite the low discount rate and the low short-term rates in general, as well as the large volume of excess reserves. Opponents, on the other hand, can cite the catastrophic fall in the money stock and can argue that the Fed could have prevented bank failures by pumping in reserves, but did not do so.

CHAPTER 28

1. A monetary feedback rule sets the policy that the central bank has to follow by specifying its reaction to prior changes in the economy. For example, a simple rule might specify that the money supply is to increase each year by 2 percent plus an additional ½ percentage point for each 1 percent change in velocity in the previous year.
2. One argument for such a rule is that governments tend to be inherently inflationary because debtors have more political influence than creditors and because inflation reduces unemployment in the short run. Since governments therefore pressure central banks to be inflationary, a central bank should be able to tell its government: "Sorry we are not allowed to do what you want us to do because we are legally obligated to follow a fixed rule." Another argument is that such a rule would reduce expectations of inflation, and thus make it less costly to bring the inflation rate down. On the other hand one can argue that such a rule would force a central bank to be unduly restrictive if there is a major supply shock or some other event, such as a threat of massive bank failures, that demands a flexible response by the central bank.
3. One advantage of a gold standard is that it constrains the government's tampering with the money supply. If the government adopts a more inflationary policy than other countries, it will lose gold and thus be forced to bring the inflation rate under control. Another advantage is that if several countries adhere to the gold standard, the exchange rates of their currencies are fixed relative to each other, and this reduces the risk of international trade and investment. The main disadvantage of the gold standard is that it prevents a country from carrying out an independent monetary policy.

CHAPTER 29

1. The gold standard did not provide for changes in gold (and hence currency) parities, while the Bretton Woods System provided a mechanism for orderly changes in the parity for a country's currency. Under the gold standard a country's monetary policy was supposed to be responsive to gold purchases and gold sales by its central bank, while the Bretton Woods System provided that the country's monetary policy would be independent of gold flows. Under the gold standard increases and decreases in a country's price level were the mechanism for balance-of-payments adjustment, whereas the Bretton Woods System accepted price-level stability as an objective of national policy.
2. A country might achieve equilibrium in its balance of payments by changes in its price level, by changes in the foreign-exchange value of its currency, and by changes in the severity and scope of exchange controls on international payments. Changes in tariffs and export subsidies might also be used.
3. The gold standard broke down at the beginning of World War I partly because countries wanted to hoard gold, but primarily because of the large differentials in national inflation rates. The Bretton Woods System of pegged exchange rates broke down because of significant differences in national inflation rates.

CHAPTER 30

1. Most international trade transactions between the United States and Germany are denominated in U.S. dollars. German importers contract to pay in U.S. dollars; German exporters contract to receive U.S. dollars. Since both importers and exporters

undertake their foreign-exchange transactions near their home offices in Germany, the volume of dollar-mark transactions is larger in Frankfurt than in New York.

4. The current level of the spot exchange rate is the anticipated value discounted to the present by the money-market interest-rate differential. If interest rates on mark-denominated assets decline, investors would shift funds from mark-denominated assets into U.S. dollar assets, and the price of the U.S. dollar in terms of the mark would increase. The mark price of the U.S. dollar might increase even if the interest rate differential remains unchanged because of a structural disturbance, such as an increase in the price of German imports or a decline in the price of German exports.

CHAPTER 31

2. The greatest benefit of floating exchange rates is monetary independence—the rate of growth of the money supply in an individual country will not be affected by changes in its payments balance. Thus, the rate of growth of the money supply will not be constrained by the concern that the country would then have a payments deficit; instead, the country's currency would depreciate. Similarly, a payments surplus would not lead to a rapid increase in the money supply; instead the country's currency would appreciate. The basic argument for a system of pegged exchange rates is that the uncertainty about exchange rates would be reduced; this in turn would lead to higher levels of trade and investment. The major conditions that must be satisfied if the major countries are again to peg their currencies is that their inflation rates must be low and similar, and their interest rates must be similar.

3. One basis for determining whether the volume of international reserves is too small or too large is whether countries as a group are competing to acquire reserves or whether, instead, many countries are acquiring more international reserves than they would like. A too-rapid growth in the supply of international reserves would be associated with significant rates of inflation.

INDEX